No ....   Class ....

Author ....

Title ....

D0351628

BRISTOL CITY COUNCIL .... VICE
PLEASE RETURN SOON BY LATENA .....D

BRITAIN

1558–1689

Derrick Murphy
Irene Carrier
Elizabeth Sparey

BRISTOL CITY COUNCIL	
Askews	08-Apr-2003
941.055	£19.99
FW	

(((Collins

AN 2677102 0

Published by Collins Educational
An imprint of HarperCollins *Publishers* Ltd
77–85 Fulham Palace Road
Hammersmith
London W6 8JB

© HarperCollins*Publishers* Ltd 2002
First published 2002

ISBN 0 00 713850 4

Derrick Murphy, Irene Carrier and Elizabeth Sparey
assert the moral right to be identified as the authors of
this work.

All rights reserved. No part of this publication may be
reproduced, stored in a retrieval system, or transmitted
in any form or by any means, electronic, mechanical,
photocopying, recording or otherwise, without either
the prior permission of the Publisher or a licence
permitting restricted copying in the United Kingdom
issued by the Copyright Licensing Agency Ltd,
90 Tottenham Court Road, London W1P 9HE.

British Library Cataloguing in Publication Data
A catalogue record for this book is available from the
British Library.

Edited by Steve Attmore
Design by Derek Lee
Cover design by Derek Lee
Map artwork by Tony Richardson
Picture research by Celia Dearing
Production by Jack Murphy
Printed and bound by Martins the Printers, Berwick

ACKNOWLEDGEMENTS
Every effort has been made to contact the holders of
copyright material, but if any have been inadvertently
overlooked the publishers will be pleased to make the
necessary arrangements at the first opportunity.

The publishers would like to thank the following for
permission to reproduce pictures on these pages.
(*T = Top, C= Centre, B = Bottom, L = Left, R = Right*)

By permission of the British Library 202, 322; Crown
copyright: Historic Royal Palaces 196; Fotomas Index
31, 32, 33, 52R, 63, 65, 94, 97, 101, 109, 113, 115, 124,
128, 185, 239, 240T, 244, 248, 259, 262, 272, 274, 277,
307, 312, 314, 316, 331, 333, 365BL, BC, BR; Getty
Images/Hulton Archive 304, 309, 318, 352, 373; A F
Kersting 127T; Mary Evans Picture Library 290; © The
Trustees of the National Museums of Scotland 133BR,
143; © National Museums and Galleries of Wales 27; By
courtesy of the National Portrait Gallery, London 52L,
158, 160, 162, 175, 184, 189, 198, 199, 200L, 211, 217,
240B, 281, 300, 360, 365T; Scottish National Portrait
Gallery 133T, 133BL, 200R; Shakespeare Centre Library,
The Shakespeare Birthplace Trust 126; Wigan Heritage
Service 127B.

Cover picture: *The Battle of Marston Moor in 1644*, painted
in 1819 by Abraham Cooper. Harris Museum and Art
Gallery, Preston, Lancashire/Bridgeman Art Library.

The text extracts from *James VI and I* by Irene Carrier
(1998) by permission of Cambridge University Press. Text
extracts from the following titles are reprinted by
permission of Oxford University Press: *Tudor England* by
John Guy (1988); *The Later Tudors: England 1547–1603* by
Penry Williams (1995); *The Causes of the English Civil
War: The Ford Lectures Delivered in the University of Oxford
1987–1988* by Conrad Russell (1990); *The Restoration:
A Political and Religious History of England and Wales,
1658–1667* by Ronald Hutton (1985); *Reluctant
Revolutionaries: Englishmen and the Revolution of 1688* by
W.A. Speck (1988). Pearson Education for text extracts
from the following: *Elizabeth I* by Christopher Haigh
(Profiles in Power series, 1988); *England and Europe 1485
to 1603* by Susan Doran (Seminar Studies, 1986); *The
Emergence of the Nation State* by Alan Smith (1984); *The
Age of Elizabeth: England under the Later Tudors 1547–1603*
by D.M. Palliser (1st edition, 1973); *The Stuart Age* by
Barry Coward (1980); *Politics under the Later Stuarts,
Party Conflict in a Divided Society, 1660–1714* by
Tim Harris (1993). Extract from *The Interregnum*, edited
by G.E. Aylmer (Macmillan, 1972) by permission of
Palgrave.

Contents

Study and examination skills

- Differences between GCSE and Sixth Form history
- Extended writing: the structured question and the essay
- How to handle sources in Sixth Form History
- Historical interpretation
- Progression in Sixth Form History
- Examination techniques

This chapter of the book is designed to aid Sixth Form students in their preparation for public examinations in History.

Differences between GCSE and Sixth Form History

- **The amount of factual knowledge required for answers to Sixth Form History** questions is more detailed than at GCSE. Factual knowledge in the Sixth Form is used as supporting evidence to help answer historical questions. Knowing the facts is important but not as important as knowing that factual knowledge supports historical analysis.

- **Extended writing is more important in Sixth Form History.** Students will be expected to answer either structured questions or essays.

Structured questions require students to answer more than one question on a given topic. For example:

1. In what ways did the Interrregnum of 1649 to 1660 bring religious change to England?

2. To what extent was there a revolution in political and religious affairs between 1649 and 1660?

Each part of the structured question demands a different approach.

Essay questions require students to produce one answer to a given question. For example:

To what extent did James I's foreign policy have consistent aims and objectives?

Similarities with GCSE

- **Source analysis and evaluation**

The skills in handling historical sources, which were acquired at GCSE, are developed in Sixth Form History. In the Sixth Form sources have to be analysed in their historical context, so a good factual knowledge of the subject is important.

● Historical interpretations

Skills in historical interpretation at GCSE are also developed in Sixth Form History. The ability to put forward different historical interpretations is important. Students will also be expected to explain why different historical interpretations have occurred.

Extended writing: the structured question and the essay

When faced with extended writing in Sixth Form History, students can improve their performance by following a simple routine that attempts to ensure they achieve their best performance.

Answering the question

What are the command instructions?

Different questions require different types of response. For instance, 'In what ways' requires students to point out the various ways something took place in History; 'Why' questions expect students to deal with the causes or consequences of a historical question.

Are there key words or phrases that require definition or explanation?

It is important for students to show that they understand the meaning of the question. To do this, certain historical terms or words require explanation. For instance, if a question asked 'how far' a king or politician was an 'innovator', an explanation of the word 'innovator' would be required.

Does the question have specific dates or issues that require coverage?

If a question mentions specific dates, these must be adhered to. For instance, if you are asked to answer a question on Early Stuart Parliaments it may state clear date limits such as 1610 to 1629. Also, questions may mention a specific aspect such as 'domestic', 'religious', 'economic' or 'foreign policy'.

Planning your answer

Once you have decided on what the question requires, write a brief plan. For structured questions this may be brief. This is a useful procedure to make sure that you have ordered the information you require for your answer in the most effective way. For instance, in a balanced, analytical answer this may take the form of jotting down the main points for and against a historical issue raised in the question.

Writing the answer

Communication skills

The quality of written English is important in Sixth Form History. The way you present your ideas on paper can affect the quality of your answer. The Government 'watchdog' on quality and standards in public examinations, QCA, has placed emphasis on the quality of written English in the Sixth Form. Therefore, punctuation, spelling and grammar, which were awarded marks at GCSE, require close attention. Use a dictionary if you are unsure of a word's meaning or spelling. Use the glossary of terms you will find in this book to help you. If you acquire a mark scheme published by your examination board it should make specific reference to the standard of written English.

The introduction

For structured questions you may wish to dispense with an introduction altogether and begin writing reasons to support an answer straight away. However, essay answers should begin with an introduction. These should be both concise and precise. Introductions help 'concentrate the mind' on the question you are about to answer. Remember, do not try to write a conclusion as your opening sentence. Instead, outline briefly the areas you intend to discuss in your answer.

Balancing analysis with factual evidence

It is important to remember that factual knowledge should be used to support analysis. Merely 'telling the story' of a historical event is not enough. A structured question or essay should contain separate paragraphs, each addressing an analytical point that helps to answer the question. If, for example, the question asks for reasons why the war with Spain began in 1585, each paragraph should provide a reason for the outbreak of war.

Seeing connections between reasons

In dealing with 'why'-type questions it is important to remember that the reasons for a historical event might be interconnected. Therefore, it is important to mention the connection between reasons. Also, it might be important to identify a hierarchy of reasons – that is, are some reasons more important than others in explaining a historical event?

Using quotations and statistical data

One aspect of supporting evidence that sustains analysis is the use of quotations. These can be either from a historian or from a contemporary. However, unless these quotations are linked with analysis and supporting evidence, they tend to be of little value.

It can also be useful to support analysis with statistical data. In questions that deal with social and economic change, precise statistics that support your argument can be very persuasive.

Source analysis

Source analysis forms an integral part of the study of History. In Sixth Form History source analysis is identified as an important skill in Assessment Objective 3.

In dealing with sources you should be aware that historical sources must be used 'in historical context' in Sixth Form History. Therefore, in this book sources are used with the factual information in each chapter. Also, a specific source analysis question is included.

Assessment Objectives

1 knowledge and understanding of history
2 evaluation and analysis skills
3 a) source analysis in historical context
   b) historical interpretation

How to handle sources in Sixth Form History

In dealing with sources a number of basic hints will allow you to deal effectively with source-based questions and to build on your knowledge and skill in using sources at GCSE.

Written sources

Attribution and date

It is important to identify who has written the source and when it was written. This information can be very important. If, for instance, a source was a private letter between Oliver Cromwell and Henry Ireton on the issue of Charles I's trial this information could be of considerable importance if you are asked about the usefulness (utility) or reliability of the source as evidence of Cromwell's views on the fate of the King.

It is important to note that just because a source is a primary source does not mean it is more useful or less reliable than a secondary source. Both primary and secondary sources need to be analysed to decide how useful and reliable they are. This can be determined by studying other issues.

Is the content factual or opinionated?

Once you have identified the author and date of the source it is important to study its content. The content may be factual, stating what has happened or what may happen. On the other hand, it may contain opinions that should be handled with caution. These may contain bias. Even if a source is mainly factual, there might be important and deliberate gaps in factual evidence that can make a source biased and unreliable. Usually, written sources contain elements of both opinion and factual evidence. It is important to judge the balance between these two parts.

Has the source been written for a particular audience?

To determine the reliability of a source it is important to identify to whom it is directed. For instance, a public speech may be made to achieve a particular purpose and may not contain the author's true beliefs or feelings. In contrast, a private diary entry may be much more reliable in this respect.

Corroborative evidence

To test whether or not a source is reliable, the use of other evidence to support or corroborate the information it contains is important. Cross-referencing with other sources is a way of achieving this; so is cross-referencing with historical information contained within a chapter.

Visual sources

Maps

Maps that appear in Sixth Form History are either contemporary or secondary sources. These are used to support factual coverage in the text by providing information in a different medium. Therefore, to assess whether or not information contained in maps is accurate or useful, reference should be made to other information. It is also important with written sources to check the attribution and date. These could be significant.

Statistical data and graphs

It is important when dealing with this type of source to check carefully the nature of the information contained in data or in a graph. It might state the information in old forms of measurement such as pre-decimal currency: pounds, shillings and pence. One pound equalled 20 shillings, or 240 pence. Be careful to check if the information is in *index numbers*. These are a statistical device where a base year is chosen and given the figure 100. All other figures are based on a percentage difference from that base year. For instance, if 1558 is taken as base year for wool exports it is given a figure of 100. If the index number for 1605 is 117 it means that wool exports have risen 17% since 1558.

An important point to remember when dealing with data and graphs over a period of time is to identify trends and patterns in the information. Merely describing the information in written form is not enough.

Historical interpretation

An important feature of both GCSE and Sixth Form History is the issue of historical interpretation. In Sixth Form History it is important for students to be able to explain why historians differ, or have differed, in their interpretations of the past.

Availability of evidence

An important reason is the availability of evidence on which to base historical judgements. As new evidence comes to light, historians today may have more information on which to base their judgements than historians in the past. For instance, sources for Stuart history include the Calendar of State Papers – correspondence between individuals and reports by foreign ambassadors to England. Occasionally, new evidence comes to light that may influence judgements about England in the Stuart period.

Also, archaeological evidence is important in History. The archaeological study of Civil War battlefields has produced considerable evidence of warfare and weapons in the mid 17th century.

'A philosophy of history?'

Many historians have a specific view of history that will affect the way they make their historical judgements. For instance, Marxist historians – who take their view from the writings of Karl Marx the founder of modern socialism – believe that society has been made up of competing economic and social classes. They also place considerable importance on economic reasons in human decision making.

The role of the individual

Some historians have seen the past as being moulded by the acts of specific individuals who have changed history. Elizabeth I, Charles I and Oliver Cromwell are seen as individuals whose personality and beliefs changed the course of 16th- and 17th-century history. Other historians have tended to 'downplay' the role of individuals; instead, they highlight the importance of more general social, economic and political change. Rather than seeing the above as individuals who changed the course of history, these historians tend to see them as representing the views of a broader group of individuals.

Placing different emphasis on the same historical evidence

Even if historians do not possess different philosophies of history or place different emphasis on the role of the individual, it is still possible for them to disagree because they place different emphases on aspects of the same factual evidence. As a result, Sixth Form History should be seen as a subject that encourages debate about the past based on historical evidence.

Progression in Sixth Form History

The ability to achieve high standards in Sixth Form History involves the acquisition of a number of skills:

● Good written communication skills

● Acquiring a sound factual knowledge

● Evaluating factual evidence and making historical conclusions based on that evidence

● Source analysis

● Understanding the nature of historical interpretation

● Understanding the causes and consequences of historical events

● Understanding the themes in history which will involve a study of a specific topic over a long period of time

● Understanding the ideas of change and continuity associated with themes.

Students should be aware that the acquisition of these skills will take place gradually over the time spent in the Sixth Form. At the beginning of the course the main emphasis may be on the acquisition of factual knowledge, particularly when the body of knowledge studied at GCSE was different.

When dealing with causation, students will have to build on their skills from GCSE. They will not only be expected to identify reasons for a historical event but also to provide a hierarchy of causes. They should identify the main causes and less important causes. They may also identify that causes may be interconnected and linked. Progression in Sixth Form History will come with answering the questions at the end of each sub-section in this book and practising the skills outlined through the use of the factual knowledge contained in the book.

Examination techniques

The ultimate challenge for any Sixth Form historian is the ability to produce quality work under examination conditions. Examinations will take place each January and June.

Here is some advice on how to improve your performance in an examination.

● **Read the whole examination paper thoroughly**

Make sure that the questions you choose are those for which you can produce a good answer. Don't rush – allow time to decide which questions to choose. It is probably too late to change your mind half way through answering a question.

● **Read the question very carefully**

Once you have made the decision to answer a specific question, read it very carefully. Make sure you understand the precise demands of the question. Think about what is required in your answer. It is much better to think about this before you start writing, rather than trying to steer your essay in a different direction half way through.

● **Make a brief plan**

Sketch out what you intend to include in your answer. Order the points you want to make. Examiners are not impressed with additional information included at the end of the essay, with indicators such as arrows or asterisks.

● **Pace yourself as you write**

Success in examinations has a lot to do with successful time management. If, for instance, you have to answer an essay question in approximately 45 minutes then you should be one-third of the way through after 15 minutes. With 30 minutes gone you should start writing the last third of your answer.

Where a question is divided into sub-questions make sure you look at the mark tariff for each question. If in a 20-mark question a sub-question is worth a maximum of 5 marks then you should spend approximately one-quarter of the time allocated for the whole question on this sub-question.

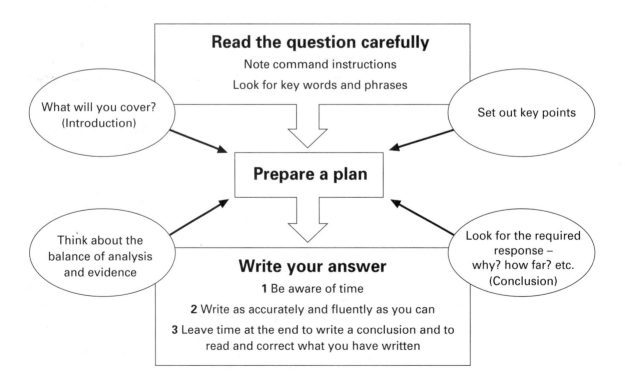

Read the question carefully

Note command instructions

Look for key words and phrases

What will you cover? (Introduction)

Set out key points

Prepare a plan

Think about the balance of analysis and evidence

Look for the required response – why? how far? etc. (Conclusion)

Write your answer

1 Be aware of time

2 Write as accurately and fluently as you can

3 Leave time at the end to write a conclusion and to read and correct what you have written

Britain 1558–1689: a synoptic assessment

1.1 In what ways did the economy develop in the years 1558–1689?

1.2 How did society change between 1558 and 1689?

1.3 How important was personality in the changing nature of monarchic power from 1558 to 1689?

1.4 How far could monarchs impose their power and authority in the years 1558–1689?

1.5 To what extent did the Church of England provide a solution to religious problems in England, 1558–1689?

Key Issues

● *How far did the economy and society change in the period 1558–1689?*

● *To what extent was monarchy and monarchic power increasingly limited between 1558 and 1689?*

● *To what extent did Britain become a more religiously tolerant country in the period 1558–1689?*

Overview

Aristocracy: Large-scale landowners who had the right to sit in the House of Lords. They possessed a variety of titles such as Earl, Marquis, Duke, Lord.

THE period 1558–1689 was one of considerable social, economic, political and religious change. British society went through major changes. Towns grew rapidly – London in particular. However, a major area of historical debate has surrounded the position of the leading landowning families. It has been claimed that the position of the **aristocracy** declined in this period. In addition, during the 17th century, the rise of an urban, commercial middle class has been regarded as a contributory factor in the political upheavals of the 1640s.

In economic terms, Britain also changed dramatically in the period 1558–1689. Although the economy remained based on agriculture, the period saw the diversification of domestic industrial production. It also marked the growth of British trade abroad. This led to the beginnings of a colonial empire. By 1689, English colonies had been established in north America, from the Carolinas to French Canada (see map on page 15).

Overseas trade with Europe, at the beginning of the period, was dominated by the export of wool and woollen cloth. In the 17th century, trade rivalry developed with the newly-created Dutch Republic. On three occasions from the 1650s onwards, this led to war. In general, economic factors were beginning to take priority over religious considerations in determining foreign policy.

Perhaps the most important developments of the period involved politics. In 1558, the British Isles comprised three kingdoms. Two of these – England and Ireland – were ruled by the Tudor family, although large areas of Ireland remained outside the effective control of the monarch until well into the 17th century. Scotland was a separate kingdom. A 'union of crowns' between England and Scotland occurred in 1603, when James VI of Scotland became James I of

Interregnum: The period
1649–1660 between the
execution of Charles I and
the restoration of
monarchy.

Arminianism: A religious
doctrine associated with
Protestantism. Named after
Arminius who, at the 1609
Synod of Dort, put forward
a view of Protestantism that
was more moderate than
the religious views of most
English Puritans. Arminians
were accused, by some
Puritans, as trying to make
Protestantism similar to
Catholicism. A leading
Arminian in England was
William Laud, who was
Archbishop of Canterbury
from 1633 to his death in
1645.

*What do you regard as
the most important
change to occur in
Britain between 1558
and 1689?*

*Give reasons for your
answer.*

England. While this created problems for his son, Charles I – the problem of the
three kingdoms contributed to civil war – the British state was now in formation.
Apart from a few years during the **Interregnum**, there was no political union until
the Act of Union of 1707, which created Great Britain from England and
Scotland.

1558–1689 was a period of constitutional change within England. This had an
important impact on monarchical power and authority. Lack of clarity over the
constitutional powers and privileges of Crown and Parliament led to civil war
and the execution of the King in the mid 17th century. For the one and only time
in English history, a republic was created, which lasted from 1649 to 1660. After
the restoration of monarchy, constitutional uncertainty still existed. In 1688 and
1689, there was further upheaval when the Stuart monarch James II was overthrown by political forces within England, Scotland and Ireland. After this, some
aspects of monarchical power were established in law. The English monarchy had
changed from one regarded as holding its power from God to a contractual one
whose power was vested in it by the people. The question remains as to whether
these revolutionary events came about as a result of the structural problems in
England's constitution or whether they were dependent on short-term causes and
clashes of personality.

Political upheaval was linked to religious change. In 1558, England was a
Catholic state. During Elizabeth's reign, the Church of England was created and
established along broadly Protestant lines. The Church of England faced
challenges, however. Catholics wished to win back England to the Catholic
Church. Extreme Protestants, known as Puritans, wished to reform the Church of
England along the lines of continental Protestant, especially Calvinist, churches.
Most, however, conformed to Anglican practice.

The rivalry between Anglican, Puritan and Catholic became more extreme in
the 17th century. The Church of England was increasingly dominated by a new
brand of Protestantism, known as **Arminianism**. This threatened to create a
narrower Church than Elizabeth's, and one from which Puritans were excluded.
The polarisation of England's Protestants was an important cause of the civil
wars. The republican Interregnum of 1649–1660 stands out as a more tolerant
period, although religious extremists frightened those in authority.
Between 1660 and 1689, the re-established Church of England struggled
to come to terms with the existence of nonconformity, which was only
really acknowledged in 1689 (see Chapter 10). Fear of Catholicism
remained an important factor in politics throughout the century;
Catholicism remained illegal.

Therefore, 1558–1689 was one of the most important periods for
political and religious change in the history of Britain. It is not surprising
that the historian Christopher Hill entitled his study of the 17th century
'The Century of Revolution' (published in 1961).

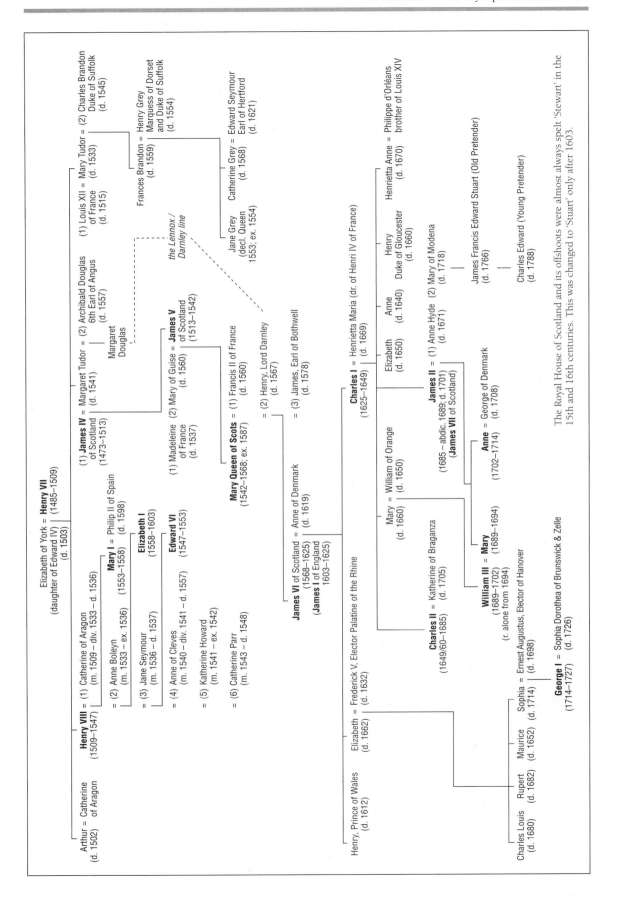

The Royal House of Scotland and its offshoots were almost always spelt 'Stewart' in the 15th and 16th centuries. This was changed to 'Stuart' only after 1603.

1.1 In what ways did the economy develop in the years 1558–1689?

Common land: Land held in common ownership where any agricultural labourer had the right to graze their livestock or collect wood. Wanstead Flats, in east London, is an example of what remains of common land – hence the existence of grazing cattle in the middle of London!

Enclosures: The practice where some landowners put hedges around large fields and created bigger and more productive units of farming.

Chartered companies: Donations from the monarch went to certain companies, granting them rights and privileges.

Throughout the period 1558–1689, Britain was an agricultural country. The wealth of the country was linked directly to events such as the size and quality of the harvest. Periods of harvest failure led inevitably to a rise in grain prices and, in some cases, starvation. The 1590s was one of the worst decades for harvest failure and starvation for the whole period.

Most men and women lived in villages and engaged in subsistence agriculture, producing just enough food to feed themselves. However, during the period, several enterprising landowners attempted to improve agriculture through enclosing **common land**. This practice helped to increase the productivity of agriculture by allowing stock rearing and grain growing to occur in larger units. **Enclosures** caused considerable resentment among ordinary farm labourers or tenant farmers. They saw common land as an important area for grazing their livestock. Protests against enclosure occurred across the period. Occasionally, as in the Midlands Revolt of 1607 and the enclosure riots of the early 1640s, violence accompanied protest.

Enclosures did provide some improvement. The need for crops to feed livestock and the development of new methods of farming after 1650 led to dramatic increases in, for instance, the sheep population of southern and eastern England. Sheep farming was an important agricultural activity which provided the raw material for England's main export, wool and woollen products such as cloth.

Most of England's wool exports reached Europe through the port of Antwerp in the Netherlands. However, this trade was severely disrupted during the Dutch Revolt and after the outbreak of war with Spain in 1585. Alternative outlets for English exports were sought at Emden and Hamburg. There were attempts to improve England's wealth from wool and cloth. In 1614, Sir William Cockayne persuaded James I to support a plan whereby English woollen goods would be finished and dyed in England rather than in the Low Countries. The Cockayne Project of 1614–16 (see Chapter 6) led to retaliation by the Netherlands, which banned the import of English cloth and sought alternative sources of unfinished cloth. It is estimated that total exports of English unfinished woollen cloth fell in value from £1.2 million in the early 17th century to £846,000 by 1640. The English woollen trade did not recover until the end of the 17th century. Another important factor affecting wool production was the Civil War period, but the wool trade was also adversely affected by the Thirty Years War in Europe (1618–1648).

Another feature of English trade was the development of **chartered companies**. Apart from taxation, this was the government's most important involvement in economic matters. The creation of these companies helped to broaden the base on which to finance the monarchy without going to Parliament. During Elizabeth I's reign, the Muscovy, Levant, Eastland and Barbary companies were all given exclusive trading rights with specific parts of Europe and the Mediterranean.

Perhaps the most important chartered company in the period was the East India Company. Formed at the end of Elizabeth's reign, it was established to exploit the trade with India and the East Indies. However, it came into direct competition with the Dutch East India Company. Trade rivalry with the Dutch was a recurrent feature of the 17th century. Dutch

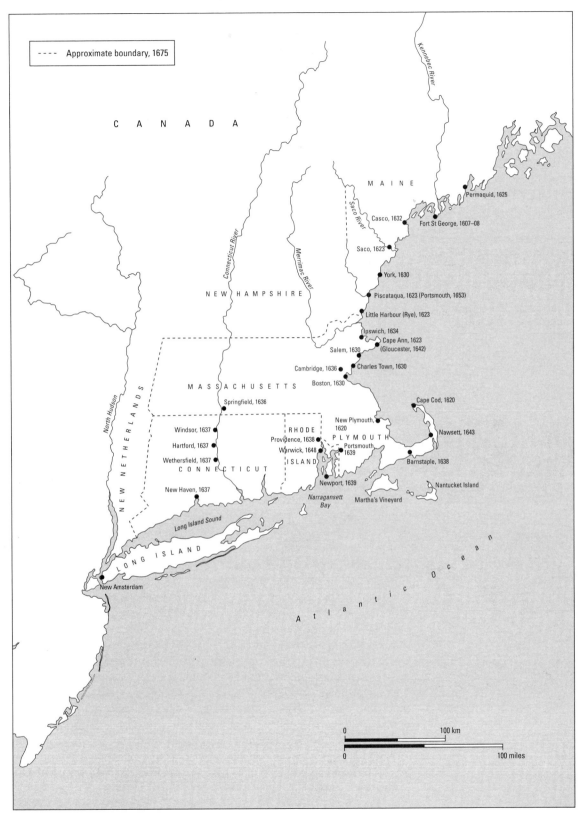

New England colonies: early settlement

Colonies: Countries controlled by a more powerful country, which uses the colony's resources in order to increase its own power or wealth.

1. Between which years was there the greatest increase in iron production?

2. What was the percentage increase in iron production between the 1550s and the 1650s?

Output of iron 1550–1660	
In tonnes per year	
1550s	5,000
1580s	15,000
1600s	17,500
1620s	19,000
1630s	20,000
1650s	24,000

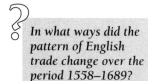

In what ways did the pattern of English trade change over the period 1558–1689?

exploitation of the North Sea herring fishery increased tension between the Dutch and the English. As a result, an important cause of the three Dutch Wars (1652–54, 1665–68 and 1672–74) was trade and commercial rivalry.

Although the English tended to miss out to the Dutch East India Company in the Far East, they were more successful in North America. By 1689, English **colonies** had been firmly established from Canada, down the Atlantic seaboard to South Carolina. Dutch rivalry had been removed during the Second Dutch War (1665–68) when New Amsterdam became New York. In the West Indies, during the English Republic, England acquired Jamaica in 1655. This formed the main English base for trade rivalry with other European trading states, such as Spain, France and the Dutch Republic. The West Indies were important for a variety of tropical products, most notably sugar cane and its by-products (rum and molasses).

Such increases in trade led to the growth of both the merchant navy and the royal navy. Between 1570 and 1640, the merchant fleet trebled in size from 50,000 tonnes to 150,000 tonnes. The Royal (and from 1649–1660 States) Navy also saw considerable growth. The foundation of naval success in the 18th century was laid by the Stuarts, from 1603, who greatly increased Elizabeth's fleet.

Although predominantly an agricultural country, England did possess some industry. Shipbuilding was firmly established in areas such as Deptford, near London. Iron production was located in areas with ample supplies of wood, which was used to make charcoal (the main fuel in iron smelting). The Weald area (Kent/Sussex border), the Forest of Dean in Gloucestershire, South Yorkshire and the West Midlands were the main areas of iron production. Lack of timber retarded the growth of the domestic industry, but from the early 17th century onwards imports of Swedish iron helped to offset this problem. Nevertheless, the development of the blast furnace at the end of the 16th century improved domestic production.

1.2 How did society change between 1558 and 1689?

Contemporary: Someone who lived at the time of the historical event.

In studying the structure of society, historians have been fortunate that three important **contemporary** studies exist, dating from the 1560s, 1570s and 1600. They give an insight into the way in which people at the time categorised themselves, and each other. William Harrison identified four social groups in 1600. These were gentlemen, citizens or burgesses, yeomen and artificers or labourers. While it is clear who was at the very top of the social hierarchy, it is more problematic to establish dividing lines between the classes lower down. Indeed, people at the time also found it difficult. A man's status was dependent on his standing in local society – his wife and daughters were categorised with him. Wealth did matter, but since those in the south and east were generally better off than those in the north and west, a southern yeoman might well be richer than a northern gentleman.

A key characteristic of English society was the freedom to move up and down the social hierarchy. This has led both contemporaries and historians into debate about changes that were taking place. The historian Lawrence

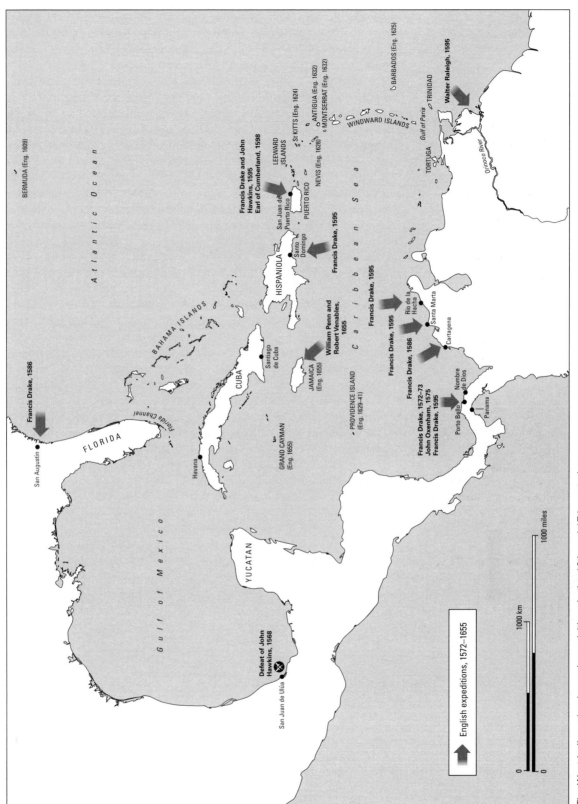

The West Indies: plunder and acquisitions in the 16th and 17th centuries

Marxist historians: A school of historians who highlight the importance of social and economic factors in historical development.

Gentry: The class, immediately below the aristocracy, which consisted of gentlemen of good breeding.

Stone identifies, in *The Causes of the English Revolution, 1529–1642* (1996), a crisis of the aristocracy, while **Marxist historians** have attributed the mid-17th century revolution to the rise of the **gentry**. While social mobility certainly existed, general patterns are harder to determine.

An important feature of the period was the growth in population. According to Lawrence Stone, 'the doubling of the population in the 120 years before the civil war is a critical variable of the period, an event the effects of which spread out into every aspect of society'. The inflation of the period – partly the result of population pressures on scarce resources – also had a destabilising effect.

Another of the results of population growth was the development of towns, in particular London. From the 1520s to 1700, London's population grew from about 50,000 to around 575,000, representing an ever-increasing proportion of the country's population. This growth far exceeded that of

Principal noble families in England, 1603

1. *In what ways did society between 1558 and 1689 differ from society at the beginning of the 21st century?*

2. *What do you regard as the most significant change in society between 1558 and 1689? Give reasons for your answer.*

European cities of the time. By 1700, the population of Naples was approximately 300,000, that of Amsterdam 150,000 and Rome's was 100,000. Only Constantinople (now Istanbul) was larger.

Within England, the size of London was even more startling. By 1650, Norwich, the next largest city, had a population of about 20,000, followed by Bristol with 18,000. Towns such as York, Plymouth, Colchester, Coventry, Ipswich and Newcastle upon Tyne had populations of between 5,000 and 10,000. Overall, in 1650, only 5% of the population lived in towns over 5,000 outside London.

London came to dominate trade and commerce. The City of London dominated finance. As the civil wars were to prove, whoever held London would eventually control the country politically.

1.3 How important was personality in the changing nature of monarchical power from 1558 to 1689?

Whig historians: Those in the tradition of famous 19th-century historians such as Lord Macaulay. They see English history as culminating in the triumph of parliamentary government and the 17th century as a period of constitutional struggle between Crown and Parliament.

In *The Whig Interpretation of History* (1931), the historian Sir Herbert Butterfield addressed one of the main themes of British domestic history. In simplified form, **Whig historians** suggested that, from the Middle Ages to the early 20th century, the major domestic development was the transition from a powerful monarchy to a parliamentary democracy with a constitutionally limited monarch.

Within this theme, the period 1558–1689 was central. As queen, Elizabeth I's power was termed 'absolute' by contemporaries. In 1559, she became Governor of the Church of England. Although her power, like that of any 16th-century monarch, was limited by the extent of government bureaucracy and her ability to collect tax, she ruled as well as reigned. In 1924, the American historian Wallace Notestein produced an article entitled 'The Winning of the Initiative by the House of Commons' (see Chapter 2). Notestein's thesis was that by the time of the early Stuart monarchs the King and his Privy Council were losing control over the House of Commons. This led to clashes between monarch and Parliament over finance and foreign policy in the reign of James I. When Charles I dispensed with Parliament, from 1629 to 1640, it was termed 'the Eleven Years Tyranny'.

Therefore, the two political 'revolutions' which affected Britain in the 17th century – in 1642–1660 and 1688–1689 – were seen as the inevitable clash between a monarch who wished to retain personal power and those who wished the King to rule with Parliament under the constraint of the law.

This interpretation has been subject to questioning for some time. It fails to take account of a number of factors: the extent of royal control over Parliament, particularly through the House of Lords which included the 26 most senior bishops appointed by the Crown; specific historical circumstances; and the personality of individual monarchs. Above all, it ascribes more sense of purpose to activities in the House of Commons than existed. Essentially, the MPs were local men representing local communities. They rarely addressed themselves to national issues.

In an era of personal monarchy, the characteristics of the individual king or queen were bound to have an impact on the workings of politics. As a woman in a man's world, Elizabeth learned to use her gender to good effect. She countered the problems of her questionable legitimacy, England's weak international standing and the need to re-establish a Protestant church in a Catholic land. By the end of her reign, national and Protestant loyalty were closely identified. Although Elizabeth had weakened the monarchy's financial position, infrequent meetings of Parliament and her ministers' careful management of that institution had averted most potential clashes. There is no evidence of concerted challenges to the Crown's prerogative powers or of determined attempts to increase parliamentary privilege.

Contemporaries eagerly anticipated the accession of James I, hoping that he would resolve the problems of Elizabeth's final decade. James, a foreigner, sometimes antagonised Parliament with talk of the Divine Right of Kings (see page 132). His religious policy was certainly a disappointment to many and his financial troubles also had an adverse effect on relations with Parliament. Members of Parliament (MPs) were increasingly aware of the significance of the English Parliament in a Europe where Catholicism was gaining ground and where Catholic kings were reluctant to call meetings of representative institutions. James compromised when necessary. There is no evidence that he held a grudge with parliaments, or, despite the small percentage of government finance that derived from parliamentary grants, that he avoided calling Parliament.

His son, Charles, was not as successful in creating a positive public image. His insecurity, illustrated by the stutter (speech impediment) which rendered him shy and hesitant to explain his actions, was a distinct disadvantage. As with many insecure people, compromise was viewed by Charles as a sign of weakness. He took criticism as a personal attack. Relations with Parliament deteriorated in the late 1620s as Charles assumed the MPs were challenging his power. Misinterpretation of Charles's unexplained actions was central to the breakdown of relations between King and Parliament in 1640–42. Individual circumstances are now considered to be a more important cause of the civil war than structural weaknesses in the constitution. The monarch was executed before the monarchy was abolished, suggesting that Charles rather than monarchy itself was the problem.

Britain's republican experiment lasted only 11 years. As Head of State, Oliver Cromwell found it, if anything, more difficult than Charles I had to work with Parliament. Issues of religion, finance and the balance of power were as unresolved during the republic as under the preceding and succeeding monarchy.

Charles II had many of the characteristics of James I. He was pleasure loving and willing to compromise most of his principles. Astutely, he left many troublesome issues to Parliament, and was disinterested in government. Charles did regard foreign policy as his domain. The association of Catholicism and absolute government was a recurrent concern of MPs, leading to worries about Charles's preference for a pro-French foreign policy. However, the only issue on which Charles took a stand was the threat to exclude his brother from the succession. During the Exclusion Crisis, Charles II displayed considerable political skill through the dissolution of successive parliaments, resulting in the defeat of his opponents. By this time, he was in a stronger financial position than either of his Stuart predecessors.

In contrast to his brother, James II is often considered to have more of the personality traits of his father, Charles I. His assumption that dispensing groups from the law would prove acceptable, and his naïve belief that once the Catholic religion was legalised the population would gradually revert to the true faith, were misplaced. James II's attempt to gain parliamentary support for his objectives came to an end with William of Orange's invasion in 1688. There is considerable evidence, however, to suggest that James II's downfall had more to do with ill-fortune than political inevitability. Nor can it be divorced from events in western Europe, in particular the conflict between William of Orange and Louis XIV of France.

After the 'Glorious Revolution' of 1688–89, it is open to question as to how much more limited the monarchy was than it had been beforehand. The historian Geoffrey Holmes, in *Britain after the Glorious Revolution, 1689–1714* (1969), described the revolution settlement as, 'one of the most misapplied and misleading terms which historians have ever had the misfortune to coin'. According to the historian Roger Lockyer:

> 'the most striking thing about the Revolution settlement (1688–89) was its moderation. It did not establish parliamentary government. The King was left free to choose and dismiss his own ministers and judges, and he could summon, dissolve, **prorogue** and adjourn Parliament as he thought fit. … The "glory" of the Revolution consisted in its conservatism: it kept the traditional constitution and made only minor adjustments to bring it back into balance.'

In 1690, John Locke published his 'Two Treatises on Government'. In this **retrospective** justification of the Glorious Revolution, Locke established the contractual theory of monarchy. James II had been deposed because he ignored the will of the people as represented in Parliament. No future English monarch could claim to rule by divine right. If not a revolution, this certainly represents a major change in perceptions of monarchical legitimacy.

Prorogue: To bring a session of Parliament to an end without dissolving it, thus keeping open the possibility of another session.

Retrospective: To look back over a past event.

1. Explain the meaning of the term 'personal monarchy'.

2. What do you regard as the most important political powers possessed by monarchs between 1558 and 1689? Give reasons for your answer.

1.4 How far could monarchs impose their power and authority in the years 1558–1689?

The idea that monarchs had considerable power and authority in the period is without question. They could call and dissolve parliament, sign international treaties and declare war. As governor of the established church, the monarch had spiritual, as well as political, authority over his/her subjects. Yet it is questionable how far the monarch's will, or indeed the laws of the land, could be imposed on the population.

Management of Parliament was a key to monarchical authority at the centre. This could be achieved by a number of methods. The most effective was the judicious use of Privy Councillors (see page 33) to steer debate within the two houses. It was also possible to influence election results – a process known as 'the packing of Parliament'.

A central part of the Whig interpretation of the period is that the House of Commons was deliberately trying to erode the monarch's prerogative power and to establish and extend its own privileges. Although this interpretation has been challenged, Parliament undeniably restricted the monarch's power. Parliamentary statute (an Act of Parliament) was the highest form of law, and any monarch who ignored

Parish: The smallest unit of administration of the Church of England. Associated with a church local to a village or an area of a town.

Justices of the Peace (JPs): Appointed for every shire (district) and served nominally for a year at a time. They first appeared in the late Middle Ages as the Crown tried to cut down on the powers of the sheriffs. Most of them were local gentry who were unpaid. Their chief task was to see that the laws of the country were obeyed in their area.

Lords Lieutenant: Appointed by the monarch. There was one appointed for each county by the end of Elizabeth I's reign. A Lord Lieutenant's main task was to organise the militia (see page 78).

1. *What factors prevented monarchic power from being 'absolute' in Britain between 1558 and 1689?*

2. *To what extent were the political problems faced by monarchs in 1558–1688 of their own making?*

this did so at his/her peril. Extraordinary taxation could only be levied with parliamentary assent. This restricted the monarch's foreign policy, as this money was necessary for war. MPs questioned the management of wars they had paid for, even if they were not actively seeking to control the foreign policy.

Relations between monarch and many MPs broke down in 1642 when the Civil War began. In the long term, however, this strengthened royal authority. After the Restoration, MPs were more cooperative and more suspicious of those who challenged the Crown too aggressively in Parliament. The benefits of monarchical government outweighed the drawbacks for the ruling élite.

To the vast majority of the population, government meant local government. **Parish** and county officials, drawn from the local gentry, were their point of contact with the central government at Westminster. The government relied heavily on the support and work of local landowners and unpaid **Justices of the Peace (JPs)**. The law was only enforced when the local officials were willing and able to apply it. The collection of tax was inefficient, with inbuilt corruption.

In a country without a standing army (with the exception of the Interregnum and the reign of James II) and with limited government financial resources, monarchical power was bound to be restricted. For internal law and order and military defence, monarchs had to rely on **Lords Lieutenant** to raise and equip county militias. When local aristocrats became disaffected, whole areas of the country could be lost from royal control. The Rebellion of the Northern Earls in 1569 is the last example of this feudal unrest. Nevertheless, during the First Civil War, the influence of the local aristocracy was significant in the taking of sides, and the country was split geographically.

However, monarchy itself was not challenged during this period, other than by a tiny minority. Popular unrest was endemic, but it was usually economic in cause, localised and directed towards the immediate causes of hardship. Enclosure and food riots were more common than major rebellion.

From the mid 17th century, a more professional civil service developed. Although it is difficult to judge the precise extent of its impact, this was certainly a contributory factor in the more efficient collection of taxes. After the Restoration, it is apparent that the gentry – alarmed by the challenges to the established conventions of society that had appeared during the Interregnum – were more inclined to work cooperatively with the monarch.

1.5 To what extent did the Church of England provide a solution to the religious problems in England, 1558–1689?

At the Peace of Augsburg, 1555, it was decided that within the Holy Roman Empire (present-day Germany, Austria and the Czech Republic) the religion of a state should be that of the state's ruler. This idea of religious uniformity within each European state became an aspiration of the majority of European states from the mid 16th century to the end of the 17th century. Toleration of different religious views, as in the Dutch Republic, became the exception rather than the rule.

In 1558, England was a Roman Catholic country. The monarch decided

England's religion, with the approval of Parliament, and it was a universal assumption that all must follow the religion chosen by the monarch. In 1689, this changed. Parliament dictated the monarch's religion and a measure of toleration was allowed to most Protestants to worship as they chose. The religious problems of the period concerned disagreements about what religion the people of England should follow. During the final 40 years, disagreement centred around coming to terms with religious diversity.

The accession of Elizabeth I was a turning point in the history of religion in England. Her predecessor, Mary I (1553–58), had re-established the Catholic religion. In an international climate of religious conflict across Europe, Elizabeth established the Church of England in the first five years of her reign. What is also significant is the fact that it was based on law passed by Parliament. The organisational structure was very similar to the Catholic Church with bishops and priests (the latter were usually termed vicars or pastors). However, in terms of religious belief the Church of England contained many Protestant ideas.

The priority in 1558 was to convince a predominantly Catholic country to become Protestant. At first this was done gently. From 1570, when Elizabeth I was excommunicated by the Pope, matters became more urgent. Despite the presence in the country of the Catholic claimant to the throne, Mary Queen of Scots, and various plots to place her on the throne, Catholics remained loyal. Protestant propaganda equated loyalty to the Crown with conformity to the Church of England. The Catholic missionaries could do little to prevent Catholics becoming Protestant. By the late 1580s, England was helping Dutch Protestant rebels and Mary Queen of Scots was dead. When Philip II of Spain sent his armadas (fleets of ships) against England, there was no chance of a Catholic uprising.

Puritans – those whom the historian Patrick Collinson terms 'the hotter sort of Protestants' – also challenged the established church. They wanted further reforms to the English Church, especially its structure. However, by the end of Elizabeth's reign, the Puritan clergy had been disciplined by Archbishop Whitgift of Canterbury, although many of the laity were still committed Puritans. A few extremists, who had attempted to set up separatist churches, had been eliminated. **Separatism** did not re-emerge until the 1630s (see Chapter 10).

Separatism: Complete separation from the Church of England. Separatist groups emerged in the reign of Elizabeth I, but had largely disappeared by 1640.

By the time of the death of Elizabeth in 1603, perhaps 5% of the people were still committed Catholics. They hoped that James, whose mother had been Catholic, would be more sympathetic towards them. They were proved wrong, and the Gunpowder Plot of 1605 gave the government the excuse to clamp down on Catholic **recusants**. Similarly the Puritans, aware that James was Scottish Calvinist, anticipated alterations to the Church. However, James was attracted to a church structure with bishops, as this enhanced his power. He made no concessions to the Puritans at the Hampton Court Conference. The more extreme ones subsequently left the country, first going to the Netherlands and then to America where they would be freer to worship as they pleased.

Recusants: Roman Catholics who refused to attend the services of the Church of England. When convicted, they could receive heavy fines and the loss of property. 'Recusant' comes from the Latin word for 'refuse'.

An additional concern during James's reign was the appearance of a competing branch of Protestantism. The Dutch theologian Arminius rejected some of the central Calvinist beliefs and held that worship should emphasise the ceremonial. In short, the new form of Protestantism looked Catholic. James's unusually modern approach, in accepting diversity, pleased no one. His creation of a balanced bench of bishops simply put off clashes until later. Restoration Anglicans recognised the weakness of tolerating such a range of practices in the church.

Charles I made no attempt to maintain the balance. His preference for the ceremonial of the Arminian church was clear when he appointed William Laud first Bishop of London then Archbishop of Canterbury (in 1633). Laud became a close adviser, and masterminded reforms in the church. These were resented as too narrow, verging on Catholicism. Criticism from educated Puritans earned them harsh punishments usually reserved for the poor. **Emigration** or separatism seemed, to many, the only options.

Emigration: When people leave their native country to go and live in another country.

When Parliament met in 1640, one of the issues which was hardest to solve was that of the form of the Church of England. This was established by law, yet Laud had contrived to alter it – at least that is how some MPs viewed his actions. During the Civil War, some religious radicals, known as independents, began to challenge the need for a national church. In 1648, those MPs who were responsible for the trial of the King tended to be independent in religion. Although it is notoriously difficult to categorise the religion of people in the 17th century, their religious views were the main distinguishing characteristic; the research done by David Underdown, for his book *Pride's Purge* (1985), shows this. Statistically, the preponderance of independents could not have occurred by chance.

During the Interregnum, army influence ensured that there was relative religious toleration. Although a state church existed, in the absence of church courts its ministers could not discipline their congregations. The main criterion for being accepted as an approved minister was godliness, not specific beliefs. **Sects** were everywhere, with only the most shocking being suppressed. Fear of religious radicalism grew among the ruling élite, as much because of outrageous behaviour and the challenge to the social hierarchy as because of religious beliefs. Their beliefs were often the basis for these challenges since sectarians failed to recognise earthly authority concerning beliefs. Nevertheless, during the Interregnum many were religiously conservative, still using the Book of Common Prayer.

Sects: Protestant religious groups who were not members of the Church of England. These groups took a variety of forms. They included Separatist churches which developed during the latter part of Elizabeth I's reign, through a variety of sects during the Civil War and Interregnum. After 1662, the term 'Protestant Nonconformist' or 'Dissenter' was used because it referred to those Protestants who refused to accept the Act of Uniformity.

The position, structure and authority of the Church of England changed considerably between 1642 and 1660. For instance, in February 1642 the Bishops' Exclusion Act forbade Anglican bishops to sit in the House of Lords. In the Ordinances of August 1643 the destruction of religious images, such as crosses and religious statues, was ordered. In 1646, the authority and position of bishops was abolished. In some ways these changes amounted to a second reformation. However, Parliament in the Civil War and Interregnum period did not alter the Elizabethan Acts of Supremacy or Uniformity.

Charles II wisely left the Restoration Church settlement to Parliament. In doing so, he moved the process on whereby Parliament became increasingly responsible for deciding religious matters. Although Charles tried to move England towards a more tolerant position, he withdrew his two Declarations of Indulgence on Parliament's insistence. The restored Church of England was narrow, more like Charles I's Arminian church. Vicious laws against the sects, especially Quakers, were enacted. However, they were not uniformly applied either geographically or throughout the reign. It has been suggested that society was becoming more secularised, with a separation of religion and politics, but religion could still be a

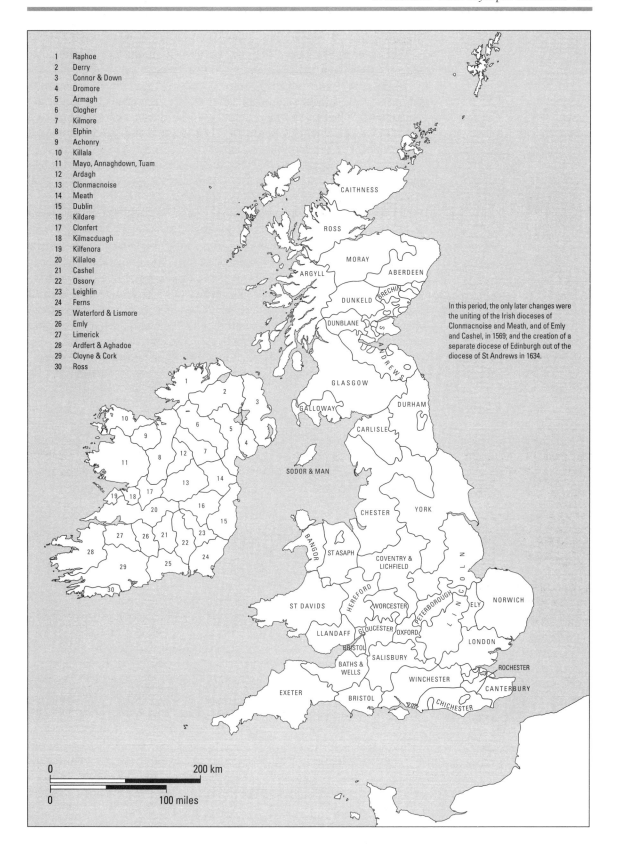

1 Raphoe
2 Derry
3 Connor & Down
4 Dromore
5 Armagh
6 Clogher
7 Kilmore
8 Elphin
9 Achonry
10 Killala
11 Mayo, Annaghdown, Tuam
12 Ardagh
13 Clonmacnoise
14 Meath
15 Dublin
16 Kildare
17 Clonfert
18 Kilmacduagh
19 Kilfenora
20 Killaloe
21 Cashel
22 Ossory
23 Leighlin
24 Ferns
25 Waterford & Lismore
26 Emly
27 Limerick
28 Ardfert & Aghadoe
29 Cloyne & Cork
30 Ross

In this period, the only later changes were the uniting of the Irish dioceses of Clonmacnoise and Meath, and of Emly and Cashel, in 1569; and the creation of a separate diocese of Edinburgh out of the diocese of St Andrews in 1634.

CAITHNESS
ROSS
MORAY
ABERDEEN
ARGYLL
DUNKELD
BRECHIN
DUNBLANE
ST ANDREWS
GLASGOW
GALLOWAY
DURHAM
CARLISLE
SODOR & MAN
CHESTER
YORK
BANGOR
ST ASAPH
COVENTRY & LICHFIELD
LINCOLN
NORWICH
HEREFORD
WORCESTER
PETERBOROUGH
ELY
ST DAVIDS
LLANDAFF
GLOUCESTER
OXFORD
LONDON
BRISTOL
SALISBURY
ROCHESTER
BATHS & WELLS
WINCHESTER
CANTERBURY
EXETER
BRISTOL
CHICHESTER

0 ————— 200 km
0 ————— 100 miles

The dioceses of the Churches of England, Scotland and Ireland, 1559–1560

Arbitrary government: Government by a monarch without consulting Parliament or leading members of the aristocracy. Associated with the growth of absolute monarchy or absolutism in late 17th- and 18th-century Europe.

1. In what ways did the position of the Church of England change from 1558 to 1689?

2. Was England a more religiously tolerant country during Elizabeth I's reign (1558–1603) than during the period 1603–1689? Give reasons for your answer.

highly political issue. The Exclusion Crisis demonstrated this. Catholicism became increasingly associated with **arbitrary government** – the very issue over which Charles I had lost his throne and his head.

During the reign of James II, fears concerning a Catholic monarch were realised. James dispensed groups from the law, thus undermining Parliament. When his wife produced a Catholic heir, matters came to a head. James fled abroad when his Protestant son-in-law, William of Orange, invaded the country.

The new monarchs accepted the Bill of Rights which stated that the monarch must be Protestant (William was Dutch Calvinist). The Toleration Act of 1689 allowed Protestant Nonconformists (Dissenters) to worship as they chose and to set up schools. In this sense, the Toleration Act was a milestone. By its passage, Parliament accepted that England was no longer exclusively Anglican in religion. Nevertheless, Parliament determined the religion of the monarch and decided on the laws concerning religious practices, rather than the monarch deciding the religion of the country. Religion remained on the political agenda. The 1701 Act of Settlement established that the monarch must be a member of the Church of England. Also, in Queen Anne's reign, Tory cries of 'the Church in danger' led to the Occasional Conformity and Schism Acts. Protestant Nonconformists were to be kept out of political office, and for a time no nonconformist schools were allowed.

1. Why was the power of the English monarchy periodically limited by Parliament between 1558 and 1689?

2. To what extent were the years 1558–1689 a period of increasing religious intolerance?

3. Which group provided the more serious challenge to the Church of England between 1558 and 1688, Catholics or Puritans and Protestant Nonconformists (Dissenters). Explain your answer.

English government under Elizabeth I, 1558–1603

Key Issues

- How effective was the conduct of central government in Elizabethan England?

- How effective was the conduct of local government in Elizabethan England?

- How convincing is the claim that the quality of English government declined significantly during the later stages of the reign of Elizabeth I?

Philip and Mary are accompanied by Mars, the god of war. Elizabeth is accompanied by symbols of peace and prosperity. What political messages does the painting convey? How effectively did it get its message across?

'The Family of Henry VIII: an Allegory of the Tudor Succession', which was painted in around 1572

Framework of Events

1558	November: Elizabeth succeeds to the throne and appoints William Cecil Secretary of State; Marquis of Winchester remains Lord Treasurer
1559	Acts of Supremacy and Uniformity
1560	Robert Dudley emerges as the Queen's favourite
	Recoinage begins
1562	Queen catches smallpox and almost dies
1563	Differences between Queen and Parliament over succession
1564	Robert Dudley is created Earl of Leicester
1566	Differences between Elizabeth and Parliament over marriage and succession
1568	Mary Stuart arrives in England, having abdicated from throne of Scotland; kept under 'house arrest' by Elizabeth
1569	Plot to marry Mary Stuart to the Duke of Norfolk
	October: Norfolk sent to Tower
	Rising in the north led by the Earls of Northumberland and Westmorland
1570	February: final defeat of northern rebels in Cumberland
	August: release of Duke of Norfolk
1571	April–May: difficulties between Elizabeth and Parliament over succession
	William Cecil is raised to peerage as Lord Burghley
	September: Duke of Norfolk is implicated in Ridolfi Plot against Elizabeth and re-arrested
	Treasons Act makes it high treason to deny the royal supremacy
1572	March: death of Lord Treasurer Winchester
	June: execution of Norfolk
	May–June: further difficulties between Elizabeth and Parliament over succession
	July: Burghley is appointed Lord Treasurer
	Reform of poor law, providing system for relief of deserving poor
1573	Sir Francis Walsingham is appointed Secretary of State
	Creation of 'trained bands'
1576	Peter Wentworth's parliamentary speech extolling freedom of speech; imprisoned in Tower of London by order of Parliament
	Poor Relief Act – stocks of raw materials to be provided throughout the country to give work to unemployed
1579	Privy Council advises Queen against proposed marriage to Duke of Alençon
1581	Parliament increases recusancy fines to £20 per month
1583	Throckmorton Plot
1584	Differences between Queen and Parliament over succession
1585	Act of Parliament against Jesuits and seminary priests
1586	January: Star Chamber decree tightens censorship of press
	Babington Plot
	November: both Houses of Parliament petition Queen for execution of Mary Stuart
1587	February: execution of Mary Stuart
	Cope's Bill and Book
	March: Wentworth makes another parliamentary speech in favour of freedom of speech
	April: Sir Christopher Hatton is appointed Lord Chancellor
1588	September: defeat of Spanish Armada
1590	Death of Walsingham
1591	Death of Hatton
1593	Wentworth is arrested for raising in the Commons issue of the succession
1596	Sir Robert Cecil is appointed Secretary of State
1597	Monopolies a key issue in parliamentary session
	More comprehensive Poor Law

1598	August: death of Burghley
1599	Lord Buckhurst is appointed Lord Treasurer; Robert Cecil appointed Master of the Court of Wards
1600	June: Earl of Essex is condemned to lose all of his offices and imprisoned at the Queen's pleasure (released in August)
1601	January: failure of Essex revolt
	February: execution of Earl of Essex
	Revised Poor Law enacted
	November: Elizabeth makes 'Golden Speech' to House of Commons
1602	Cecil begins secret correspondence with James VI of Scotland to prepare him for the succession to the English throne
1603	March: death of Elizabeth I.

Overview

THE reputation of Elizabeth I stands very high among English monarchs. Her virtues have not only been emphasised in scholarly and popular biographies but also in the cinema and on the television screen. The foundations of this reputation lie in the:

● glittering nature of the Elizabethan Court;

● explosion of English literary and musical culture;

● defeat of the Spanish Armada;

● successful re-creation of the Church of England;

● the skill of Elizabeth's image makers.

How much of this image survives a study of Elizabethan government and administration? On the one hand, there existed a government founded on the principles of economy, peace and caution. It was headed by an intelligent monarch who was advised by a group of perceptive and hard-working ministers. On the other hand, the Queen could be shrewish (wicked), and her desire for economy often lapsed into meanness. For example, she deliberately starved the Church of resources by refusing to make appointments to bishoprics (office of bishop). The conservatism of the administration ensured that few substantial changes were introduced in order to make government more efficient, thereby storing up trouble for Elizabeth I's successor.

On the whole, historians of Elizabethan England have tended to emphasise the former rather than the latter. Only Christopher Haigh has been prepared to emphasise the negative side of Elizabeth's reign. It is undeniable that for much of Elizabeth's reign England was provided with cheap but effective government, characterised by what the historian Penry Williams calls 'the informal cooperation and goodwill of the great men of the localities' (1995). Until the late 1580s, taxes remained low. Social stability was maintained through the development of a successful and long-lasting system of poor relief. Most importantly, peace was largely maintained at a time when much of western Europe was faced by turmoil and violence. Despite its faults, there was much to be admired in the Elizabethan system of government.

2.1 How important to Elizabethan government was the role of the Queen?

Though the image of Tudor monarchs was bolstered through propaganda, few English people in the 16th century seriously questioned the right of the monarch to rule. Elizabeth I was clearly aware of this from the start of her reign. The Spanish ambassador, the Count of Feria, noted as early as December 1558 that Elizabeth was 'incomparably more feared than her sister and gives her orders and has her way as absolutely as her father did'. Elizabeth herself was keen to reinforce the message that she was her father's daughter, telling Parliament in 1559 that 'we hope to rule, govern and keep this our realm in as good justice, peace and rest, in like wise as the king my father held you in'. Clearly, Elizabeth intended to govern in line with the popular image of her robust and ruthless father, Henry VIII.

This was no easy task. She had to overcome the prejudice against female rulers, which had been reinforced by the disasters of the later stages of Mary's reign. Also, she had to overcome the popular stereotype of women, which emphasised their physical, intellectual and emotional inferiority to men. Even as devoted a servant as William Cecil was occasionally annoyed by what he perceived to be her feminine weaknesses. He moaned in 1560, for example, that a diplomatic dispatch from Paris was 'too much for a woman's knowledge'.

The Queen, nevertheless, enjoyed much power. In particular, it was the right of the monarch to exercise the prerogative powers of the Crown:

Proroguing: The right of the monarch to suspend parliamentary sessions until further notice.

- calling, **proroguing** and dissolving Parliament;

- declaring war and making peace;

- appointing and dismissing ministers and judges;

- determining the monarch's own marriage and naming a successor.

Elizabeth defended these rights robustly. They remained key issues throughout the reign. She was first urged to name a successor during the 1559 Parliament. The lack of a named successor seemed particularly acute in 1562 when Elizabeth became dangerously ill from smallpox. In the early stages of her reign there were two possible successors. According to Henry VIII's will, which the Queen had the power to set aside, the succession should have passed to Lady Catherine Grey, younger sister of Jane Grey. Some of Elizabeth's ministers felt that Catherine had the advantage of being a Protestant. Unfortunately for Catherine, that was the only advantage she possessed. Elizabeth had little time for her relative, whom she imprisoned in the Tower in 1561 after her secret marriage to the Earl of Hertford.

The strongest claimant on dynastic grounds was Mary Queen of Scots – the granddaughter of Henry VIII's sister, Margaret. The possibility of Mary's succession alarmed many of Elizabeth's ministers, on account of her Catholicism and her close connections with the French Court. (See the discussion of Elizabethan foreign policy on pages 82–84.)

In the circumstances, therefore, it was understandable that the Privy Council should have urged marriage on the Queen. The Council's tactic was to petition Elizabeth to marry and, when that failed, to use Parliament as a means of raising public concern about the succession. In 1563, both Houses of Parliament petitioned the Queen to marry; the

Francis Bacon (1561–1626)
Politician, philosopher and essayist. He was nephew of Elizabeth I's adviser, William Cecil (Lord Burghley), but turned against him when Burghley failed to provide Bacon with **patronage**. Bacon studied law at Cambridge University from 1573, was part of the English embassy in France until 1579 and became MP in 1584. He helped to secure the execution of the Earl of Essex as a traitor in 1601. Bacon was knighted on the accession of James I in 1603, becoming the first Baron Verulam in 1618 and Viscount St Albans three years later. Soon after becoming **Lord Chancellor** in 1618, Bacon confessed to bribe-taking, was fined £40,000 (later remitted by the king), and spent four days in the Tower of London.

Francis Walsingham (1532–1590)
As Secretary of State (1568–90), Walsingham was primarily responsible for foreign affairs. Like the Earl of Leicester he was a firm supporter of a 'Protestant' foreign policy. Walsingham organised a large and effective secret service operation, which was responsible for uncovering many Catholic priests.

Patronage: The disposal of jobs and offices – which were the gift of the monarch or leading ministers. This was one way in which men and women could be bound to royal service and remain loyal to the King or Queen.

Lord Chancellor: The King's minister responsible for the running and supervision of the entire kingdom's law courts. He was senior judge. The Lord Chancellor also kept and looked after the Great Seal of England which was used to authorise important official state business.

Queen responded by saying that she had vowed to remain unmarried but would settle the succession at an appropriate time.

By 1566, when Elizabeth's refusal to name a successor was regarded by her subjects as irresponsible, the situation had become even more bad-tempered. The failure to name a successor, in the event of the Queen's premature death, would cause much innocent blood to be spilt. Elizabeth I's response to such criticism was to prohibit Parliament from further discussion of the issues. Nevertheless, marriage and succession were to remain areas of contention between Queen and Parliament for much of the reign, especially at the time of her on–off courtship with the Duke of Alençon in 1579. Even as late as 1601 she refused to confirm to Parliament the name of her successor.

Did Elizabeth trust her ministers?

In general, the Queen did trust her ministers and seldom interfered in day-to-day administrative matters. Occasionally, however, she involved herself directly in the decision-making processes: often frustrating her ministers by delaying key decisions as long as possible, especially in foreign affairs; or annoying them because of the scale of her interference. This was spectacularly so in 1593 when she rejected the pressure of both the Cecil and the Essex factions to appoint Nicholas Bacon as Solicitor General. One historian, Alan Smith, has suggested that royal interventions were beneficial; the Queen could 'keep the Crown's servants on their toes'.

William Cecil, Lord Burghley (1520–1598)
Cecil was knighted in 1553 and made Baron Burghley in 1571. Secretary to the Duke of Somerset, he was briefly imprisoned after the Lord Protector's fall from power in 1549. He was restored to favour in 1550 and served the Duke of Northumberland as Secretary of State (1550–53). It was Cecil who brought the news of Mary I's death to Elizabeth, whom he served as Secretary of State (1559–72) and as Lord Treasurer (1572–98). He was the most consistently influential of all Elizabeth I's advisers, managing Parliament, organising the Court of Wards, being the leading member of the Privy Council and offering policy advice on all issues. He was hard working. However, his political and institutional attitudes were deeply conservative. Thus, he was unable to contemplate any changes to administrative systems, which were becoming significantly less effective during his final years.

Naturally, this contrasted with the view of the Crown's servants who frequently complained to each other about Elizabeth I's methods. On one occasion, Francis Walsingham wrote to William Cecil (Lord Burghley) that 'I would to God her Majesty could be content to refer these things to them that can best judge of them as other princes do'. In 1575, Sir Thomas Smith complained that 'this irresolution doth weary and kill her ministers, destroy her actions and overcome all good designs and counsels'. Moreover, the Queen was good at blaming others if things went wrong. For example, in 1588 Lord Burghley wrote to Francis Walsingham that 'all irresolutions … are thrown upon us two in all her speeches to everybody'.

On the whole, relations between the Queen and her principal ministers were cordial and productive. As Alan Smith has pointed out, 'the Queen depended in some measure upon her councillors for advice, … (but) she alone made the final decisions'. He argues that 'in the last analysis credit for the triumphs of the period must therefore go to Elizabeth herself'. By the same criterion, she must also accept responsibility for the mistakes and for the flawed inheritance that she passed on to James I.

> 1. What do you regard as being the most important of the Queen's roles in government?
>
> 2. To what extent did Elizabeth I rely on her ministers to make key decisions?

2.2 How important to Elizabethan government was the Royal Court?

The Royal Household: a survey

> What impression of Queen Elizabeth and her courtiers is this intended to convey?

The Royal Household was divided into two parts. One part was purely functional: the Household proper supplied the physical needs of the Court, such as food, drink and transport. The other part, the Royal Court,

Painting entitled 'Eliza Triumphans, 1600'

Robert Dudley (1532–1588)
Created Earl of Leicester, Dudley was a **Privy Councillor** and favourite of the Queen. He strongly favoured a 'Protestant' foreign policy, which sometimes brought him into conflict with the more cautious Lord Burghley, with whom he was in competition for the distribution of patronage. Despite the closeness of his personal relationship with Queen Elizabeth, he rarely exercised the same influence over policy making as did Burghley. His conduct as commander of the English forces in the United Provinces in 1586–87 severely offended the Queen.

Privy Councillor: Member of the Privy Council, an inner ring of advisers to the monarch. There is evidence that a Privy Council appeared for a few months in 1536–37, and re-emerged in 1540 after the fall of Thomas Cromwell.

Christopher Hatton (1540–1592)
A courtier and favourite of the Queen, who was reportedly impressed by Hatton's shapely legs. Despite being a somewhat lightweight figure, Hatton was appointed Lord Chancellor. Allegedly pro-Catholic in his sympathies, he nevertheless took a key role in bringing Mary Queen of Scots to trial.

Queen's Champion: This post was based on the practice of medieval chivalry. It was invented by Sir Henry Lee who appointed himself the Queen's Champion. He represented the Queen's honour at **Accession Day Tilts** and other tournaments. The whole thing reinforced the 'Gloriana' myth.

Accession Day Tilts: These were jousting tournaments that were staged annually on the anniversary of the Queen's succession (17 November 1558). These tournaments were open to the public.

was as vital politically during Elizabeth I's reign as it had been during the reigns of her predecessors. The Royal Court existed wherever the Queen might be at a particular time, irrespective of whether she was resident in one of the royal palaces or in the great house of one of her wealthy subjects whilst undertaking a royal progress.

The Court had two main areas: the Presence Chamber and the Privy Chamber. Subjects with the right connections might gain access to the Presence Chamber relatively easily. This was where the monarch was seen occasionally. Admission to the Privy Chamber, the private rooms of the monarch, was strictly controlled.

The Lord Chamberlain controlled this whole area. Elizabeth I revived the practice of appointing only great nobles to the post. Her first two appointees were Charles, Lord Howard of Effingham, and the Earl of Sussex. Under Henry VIII and Edward VI, the monarch's principal attendants were the Gentlemen of the Privy Chamber. These courtiers had come to exercise considerable political influence, as the intimate body servants of the King. Under Mary I and Elizabeth I, the ladies of the bedchamber undertook these functions. As a result, the political significance of the Privy Chamber was much diminished. The ladies of the bedchamber could exercise little political influence in their own right, and so the role of the gentleman of the Privy Chamber became less significant. Even so, presence at Court could be crucial to political success. Thus, the Earl of Shrewsbury, who was not a regular courtier, lost a battle in the early 1590s for control in Nottinghamshire to the Stanhope family, who were strongly represented at Court. A few years later, Robert Cecil secured crucial promotions while his rival, the Earl of Essex (see page 241), was absent on foreign expeditions.

On the other hand, the ceremonial aspects of courtly life became even more important. According to historian Christopher Haigh, the rituals of court life were used as techniques of political control. Elizabeth deliberately politicised her Court by making courtiers – such as Robert Dudley (Earl of Leicester), Christopher Hatton and Robert Devereux (Earl of Essex) – into politicians. She also turned her politicians – such as Lord Burghley – into courtiers. In the process, politics became a full-time business in which personal relationships at Court were crucial. Ritual aspects were emphasised, especially from the 1570s when the **Queen's Champion**, Sir Henry Lee, devised the **Accession Day Tilts**. Not only did the tilts enable the Queen to be accessible to her subjects, it also meant that she could become the focus of the affection and flattery of her young courtiers.

The Queen was also the public focus of the Court during royal progresses, which took place in over half the summers of Elizabeth I's reign. Though geographically restricted to the South, south Midlands and

Gentry: The class, immediately below the aristocracy (see page 70), which consisted of gentlemen of good breeding.

Masques: Court productions involving music, dancing and acting.

Astraea: A virgin goddess who returned to Earth to proclaim a new golden age. It was easy for Elizabethan writers to draw parallels between Astraea and Queen Elizabeth.

Propaganda: Information, often exaggerated or false, which is spread by political parties, governments or pressure groups in order to influence others.

East Anglia, the progresses were, nevertheless, important. They enabled the Queen to be seen by ordinary subjects as well as the nobility and **gentry**. In Christopher Haigh's view they represented 'major public relations exercises', but there was more to them than that. According to the historian David Loades, the progresses showed that Elizabeth I had a 'genuine rapport with her people, which was demonstrated repeatedly in different circumstances'.

The Court was also the focus of more private rituals. Court **masques** were used to reinforce the Queen's 'Gloriana' image, originally derived from Edmund Spenser's poem 'The Faerie Queene'. The cult of the goddess **Astraea** was publicised. Such rituals bound Elizabeth's courtiers more closely to her through ties of loyalty and obedience. Some historians – for example, Frances Yates and Roy Strong – have argued that these images were an essential part of Elizabethan **propaganda**. However, the private and sophisticated nature of much of the ritual had little effect on the wider public.

How important was political patronage to Elizabethan Government?

Queen Elizabeth lacked a civil service, paid local officials and an army. It was therefore difficult for Elizabethan government to enforce its will. In the circumstances, the Crown was forced to depend on two features to secure its authority: the exploitation of the mystique of monarchy and the capacity of the Crown to reward the governing classes by the distribution of offices and wealth. It was this distribution of offices and wealth that formed the patronage system. No Tudor government could be effective without organising its patronage rationally. The governing classes which benefited from this distribution of patronage were small.

The historian Wallace MacCaffrey estimates that no more than about 2,500 men took a serious interest in political matters at any one time during Elizabeth I's reign. MacCaffrey believes that Elizabeth 'kept a firm and economical hand' on patronage. The value of honours was maintained by keeping grants of peerages and knighthoods to a minimum. More frequently awarded were grants of office. These were eagerly sought, not only because they often conferred honour and prestige on the recipient, but also because there were usually assets to be exploited. Fees from offices were almost always inadequate. Corruption, therefore, became an essential part of the system as officers sought to exploit their offices for maximum profit. MacCaffrey estimates that at least 1,000 'gentlemen-placemen' held office at any one time during Elizabeth I's reign; in other words, a considerable proportion of the political nation depended on royal patronage for some part of their livelihood.

Patrons: Those who could offer jobs, promotions or favours to other individuals.

This system, with its potential for profits and political advancement, led to intense competition for advancement. For much of Elizabeth I's reign, such competition was organised through competing **patrons**, with the Queen ensuring that there was more than one route to advancement. The main route for most of her reign was through Lord Burghley, though other potential patrons – such as Robert Dudley, Christopher Hatton and Francis Walsingham – also carried influence. Lord Burghley's importance rested on his political closeness to the Queen. It also depended on his control of offices, such as the Lord Treasurership and mastership of the Court of Wards, which gave him direct control over a large number of

Sir Francis Knollys (?1514–1596)

A gentleman-pensioner at the Court of Henry VIII, Knollys came to political prominence under the Protector Somerset. A strong Protestant who was exiled during Mary's reign, Knollys' career benefited from his marriage to Queen Elizabeth's cousin, Catherine Carey. Under Elizabeth he became Vice-Chamberlain of the Household. He spoke regularly in the House of Commons, where he took a strongly anti-Catholic line. He was also a known defender of Puritan preachers, as well as a critic of church courts.

Monopoly: Having total control and therefore no competition. In Elizabethan times the Earl of Essex, for example, had the monopoly on the import of sweet wines. In other instances, the granting of a monopoly was a way of rewarding merit. For example, the composers William Byrd and Thomas Tallis had the monopoly on sale of music paper.

1. What was the political importance of the Royal Court during Elizabeth I's reign?

2. How did the system of patronage work during Elizabeth I's reign?

3. Why, and with what political consequences, did the system break down during the 1590s?

appointments. However, he also had a wider role as confidant to a large number of the governing class. He smoothed over family quarrels. He assisted such fallen aristocrats (members of the ruling classes) as the Countess of Westmorland. He promoted the interests of colleagues such as the Earl of Huntingdon and Sir Francis Knollys. He secured appointments to bishoprics and other church offices, and appointed members to the regional councils. Much of this work was accomplished through the efforts of Burghley's own patronage secretary, Sir Michael Hickes, who was responsible for processing the many requests for advancement that Burghley received.

Despite his predominance, Lord Burghley did not seek to control patronage completely. In the final years of Elizabeth I's reign, however, the situation changed. This was partly a reflection of the fact that Burghley outlived all of his contemporaries and therefore became predominant in his final years. It also reflected the less subtle approach adopted by his son, Robert, to the distribution of patronage as his political importance rose during the 1590s. Most importantly it reflected, in the view of historian Alan Smith, the response of the ambitious Earl of Essex to being denied what he considered to be his rightful place as the controlling dispenser of patronage. In contrast, Christopher Haigh considers that the main responsibility for the situation lay with the Queen herself. She had presided over an ageing administration, which had concentrated power in too few hands. In the process, government had become 'the tool of a single and unscrupulous faction'. The charismatic Earl of Essex became the natural focus for the discontented and excluded.

By September 1599, however, when the Earl of Essex left his post in Ireland without the Queen's permission and burst unannounced into her bedchamber, any hopes placed in him were doomed. He was stripped of his offices, banished from Court and, in September 1600, he was financially ruined when Elizabeth refused to renew his **monopoly** on the import of sweet wines. In desperation, Devereux thought about launching a coup. The intent was to remove his enemies, rather than the deposition of the Queen. Unfortunately for the Earl of Essex, his plans were not sufficiently thought through. In any case, Robert Cecil had rumbled his purposes. Essex's disastrous rising on 8 February 1601 was prompted by a visit from four Privy Councillors, whom he took hostage. Then the Earl of Essex tried to raise the City of London in his cause. The attempt was doomed to failure and, within 12 hours, Essex and his supporters were forced to surrender. Within two weeks, the Earl of Essex was executed.

For much of Elizabeth I's reign the patronage system, however corrupt it might seem by modern standards, played its part in helping to ensure reasonably effective government. The collapse of the system in the 1590s heightened discontent among the governing classes, reduced the quality of government and forced the Earl of Essex's rebellion.

Source-based questions: Patronage and corruption in Elizabethan government

SOURCE A

Mr Hickes. Our very hearty commendations remembered. Understanding by the bringer hereof … your readiness and willingness in preferring and furthering such petitions and suits as the last [law] term he had cause for us in our names to prefer to the right honourable our very good lord the Lord High Treasurer of England [Lord Burghley], we have therefore thought it our part not only to yield unto you out hearty thanks for the same, but also earnestly to desire continuance of that your great courtesy and friendship, for which you shall be assured both to find us thankful and also ready to the uttermost of our powers to do any pleasure to you or any your friends as opportunity anyway may serve ….

Letter from the Mayor and Burgesses of Hull to Sir Michael Hickes, private secretary to Lord Burghley, 28 April 1590

SOURCE B

Right honourable,

Your Lordship having always been an especial patron to the see [bishop's office] of Durham, wherein it has now pleased God and Her Majesty to place me, though unworthy, and myself reaping the fruit of your Lordship's extraordinary furtherance in obtaining the same, and seeking by all good means, but contrary to my expectation, not finding any office or other particular presently void, either fit for me to offer your Lordship or sue for your Lordship to receive at my hand, I have presumed in lieu thereof to present your good Lordship with a hundred pounds in gold, which this bringer will deliver to you.

Letter from Dr Toby Matthew, Dean of Durham, to Lord Burghley, thanking him for his promotion to the bishopric of Durham, April 1595

SOURCE C

Viewed as a system of political patronage, Elizabethan government shows certain defects. It lacked adequate safeguards against a free-for-all scramble for spoils. In some measure Burghley's ceaseless supervision staved off the worst abuses, but this was a protection which waned with the ageing statesman's health and strength. The nature of the prizes encouraged a reckless competition … They were, first of all too small, … and the incumbent was driven to increase his income by any means open to him … Second, the terms of appointment were in many cases ill-defined … and this encouraged the office-holder to exploit his opportunities, often to the detriment of both Crown and subject. Third, the private exploitation of political advantage created a vast 'black market' in which political influence and favour were increasingly bought and sold. Like most black markets it raised prices; the heavy cost of political success made each participant more ruthless in the exploitation of whatever advantage he possessed. … Lastly, the poverty of the Crown drove it to make unwise concessions to suitors for favour or place. Grants of monopoly … were tempting to the Crown because they offered an increase in income for no outlay. But grants of this speculative type … [resulted in] angry resentment on the part of subjects …

Yet in judging the regime as a whole, high praise must be given for the transformation of English political habits which was accomplished during these years. By the end of the reign Englishmen were turning away from their bad old habits of conspiracy and treason … Under … Burghley and his royal mistress they had learned the peaceful, if sometimes corrupt, habits of a new political order.

From 'Place and Patronage in Elizabethan Politics' by Wallace MacCaffrey in Elizabethan Government and Society: Essays presented to Sir John Neale, *edited by S.T. Bindoff, J. Hurstfield and C.H. Williams, 1961*

SOURCE D

[Essex] desperately turned his mind to a coup in the autumn of 1600. When Elizabeth refused to renew his patent of sweet wines in September, his credit structure collapsed. She had effectively condemned him to a life of poverty, nor would she answer his appeal for an audience … Creditors were pressing for payment and starting to arrest his servants who had stood surety for him. Yet Essex's motivation went beyond this. A faction leader who was denied access to the monarch was in an untenable position: the earl saw himself as compelled to act because his court opponents had exploited their 'corrupt' monopoly of power.

From Tudor England *by John Guy, 1988*

1. Study Source C.

With reference to Source C and the information contained in this chapter, explain the meaning of the two terms highlighted in the context of the political system as it operated during the reign of Elizabeth I.

a) 'a system of political patronage'

b) 'grants of monopoly'.

2. Study Sources A and B.

What is revealed in Sources A and B about the nature and effectiveness of Lord Burghley's role as a political patron?

3. Study Sources C and D.

To what extent do Source D's comments about the Earl of Essex contradict the claim made in Source C that 'by the end of the reign Englishmen were turning away from their bad old habits of conspiracy and treason'.

4. Study all four sources and use information contained in this chapter.

To what extent might it be argued that the Elizabethan system of government was both corrupt and inefficient?

2.3 Was the Privy Council an effective instrument of government?

The Privy Council had emerged during Henry VIII's reign as the 'select ruling board' of the realm. It had several functions:

● It advised the monarch on policy, and carried out decisions.

● It had a broad responsibility for administration and public expenditure.

● It coordinated the work of agencies of government.

● It exercised some judicial (law-making) functions. Under the terms of his will, Henry VIII appointed 16 privy councillors to form a Council of Regency for his son Edward VI. This number had grown under Mary I. One of Elizabeth's first actions was to limit the size of the Privy Council to 19. In the process she removed many who had owed their position to their household service to Mary.

In political terms, Elizabeth had largely recreated the Privy Council that had existed earlier. She had rehabilitated those, like William Cecil, who had been out of favour under Mary. In cases such as Robert Dudley, she appointed the sons of those who had served in the previous 'Protestant' administration. Relatively few great nobles served on Elizabeth I's Privy Councils and she only ever appointed one clergyman, Archbishop Whitgift.

The Council was a professional and largely cooperative body, small enough to deal with business efficiently. In the words of Christopher Haigh, it was 'dangerously weak and narrow in its membership'. Regional **magnates** and the old nobility were largely ignored. This might have contributed to the outbreak of rebellion in 1569. Few councillors (Sir Christopher Hatton was an exception) exercised real influence unless they were committed Protestants.

The main functions of the Council were to discuss matters of state and to present advice to the Queen. It is not always easy to reconstruct these functions. The bulk of remaining evidence comprises formal decisions, often

Magnates: Rich people who have gained a lot of money, originally from inheritance and landowning. With this wealth comes power and possible authority. Since Tudor times, the term 'magnate' has become associated with money earned from a business or industry.

relating to fairly trivial matters. As a result, there are few indications of the political debates that were conducted within the Council. The main areas of disagreement within the Privy Council tended to concern foreign policy. Disputes occurred between the Earl of Leicester and Francis Walsingham, on one hand, and Lord Burghley, on the other. The Earl of Leicester wanted a foreign policy to support Protestant interests abroad; Lord Burghley, although a committed Protestant, placed English national interests first.

Reconstructing the Council's administrative functions is more straight-forward. The Council instructed a whole range of individuals and institutions, such as **Justices of the Peace**, Lords Lieutenant, sheriffs (see page 43), subsidy commissioners and borough councils. Often, their instructions concerned the enforcement of law and order, including laws against riot, **vagrancy** and illegal alehouses. The Council also attempted to enforce regulations regarding wages and prices. It could also enforce the spending of public money. However, among its most important administrative tasks were the continued enforcement of the 1559 religious settlement and oversight of arrangements for national defence.

Towards the end of Elizabeth I's reign, the Privy Council was often meeting six times a week. By the 1590s, the Privy Council had become a more organised body than it had been 50 years earlier, even though its functions had not changed. However, two important questions need to be asked about the Privy Council during the reign of Elizabeth I:

● How effectively did it fulfil its functions?

● How important was the Privy Council in deciding government policy?

How important was the Privy Council in deciding government policy?

Regarding the Council's effectiveness, the historian John Guy, in particular, takes an optimistic view. Tudor governments, of which the Privy Council was the most important part, 'got things done'. Regarding the latter question, it was sometimes possible for the Council to persuade the Queen to take a policy decision against her better judgement, but only at some risk. At the beginning of the reign, William Cecil, by threatening to resign, was able to force the Queen to follow the advice of most of the Council by inter-vening in Scotland. However, there were also instances when the Queen chose to ignore the advice of the Council. This happened in 1562 and 1566 when the Council urged marriage on the Queen. Moreover, it took ten months, following the assassination of William the Silent on 10 July 1584, for the majority of the Council to persuade the Queen that England should intervene directly in the Netherlands on the side of the Dutch rebels. The Privy Council, in the words of historian Penry Williams, 'could and did reach conclusions upon policy, but the final decision rested with the Queen, who seldom attended meetings and might easily ignore their conclusions'.

On the other hand, on one notable occasion the Council was able to act collectively in a way that it knew was against Elizabeth's wishes. It sent the warrant for the execution of Mary Queen of Scots without telling the Queen until they had confirmation that the execution had taken place. Elizabeth was furious, declined to see Lord Burghley for a month, refused normal relations with the Council for four months and had Secretary of State William Davison arrested. There was to be no repetition of such behaviour.

Justices of the Peace (JPs): Appointed for every shire (district) and served nominally for a year at a time. They first appeared in the late Middle Ages as the Crown tired to cut down on the powers of the sheriffs. Most of them were local gentry who were unpaid. Their chief task was to see that the laws of the country were obeyed in their area.

Vagrancy: The act of being a vagrant or vagabond. These were people who did not have a home. They roamed the countryside, usually begging.

1. How effective was the Privy Council in fulfilling its functions?

2. How important was the Privy Council in deciding government policy?

2.4 How important was Parliament to the functioning of Elizabethan government?
A CASE STUDY IN HISTORICAL INTERPRETATION

For a long time, there were two competing interpretations of the nature and significance of Elizabethan Parliaments. On the one hand, it was assumed that Parliament was subordinate within an autocratic state (i.e. control was in the hands of a single person). On the other hand, it was assumed that Parliament had evolved from being an under-developed institution in the later medieval period to maturity under Elizabeth I. Such views are particularly associated with A.F. Pollard and his distinguished student, John Neale. This historical interpretation suggests that an important theme in English history was the rise in political importance of Parliament, dating from the later Middle Ages, and the decline in the power of the monarch. In accepting this, Neale also followed the argument put forward in 1924 by the American historian Wallace Notestein that Parliament's political victory over the monarch can be traced back to the 1590s, when the House of Commons won the political initiative at the expense of a tired and increasingly incompetent government. Neale believed that Elizabeth I's reign helped to establish England as one of Europe's most important states. Another historian, Christopher Haigh, describes Neale as putting forward a 'romantic and nationalist' view of Elizabeth I's reign.

Neale argued that there was a new desire among the gentry to become members of the House of Commons, and that Members of Parliament were becoming better educated and were increasingly able and willing to challenge the control exercised on Parliament through privy councillors and the Speaker. In addition, many such members were Puritans who were using Parliament as a way to bring about radical change in the Church of England.

Neale's views reflected the 'Whig interpretation of history'. It placed parliamentary developments in Elizabeth I's reign in a historical framework which emphasised the importance to English history of the emergence of the House of Commons as the dominant political and constitutional force. Neale was writing at a time (the 1950s) not only when the House of Commons enjoyed more prestige than it does now, but also when Britain was still perceived in some quarters as a world power. It was not surprising that his views should have come under attack with the decline in the political importance of the House of Commons and Britain's decline as a major power.

The most serious attack on Neale came from Geoffrey Elton. Writing in 1984, Elton argues that Neale had both over-estimated the importance of the House of Commons and under-estimated the importance of the House of Lords. In making this last point, Elton was heavily influenced by the work of the American historian Norman Jones, in particular his *Faith by Statute* (published in 1982). This emphasised the degree of Catholic opposition to the 1559 Religious Settlement in the House of Lords. Furthermore, Geoffrey Elton challenged Neale's claims about the greater assertiveness and anti-government attitudes of the House of Commons and its 'puritan' members. One such member, Thomas Norton, was identified by historian M.A.R. Graves as being in reality a client and business organiser for Lord Burghley rather than an opponent of the Crown, as Neale had

Government of Elizabethan England

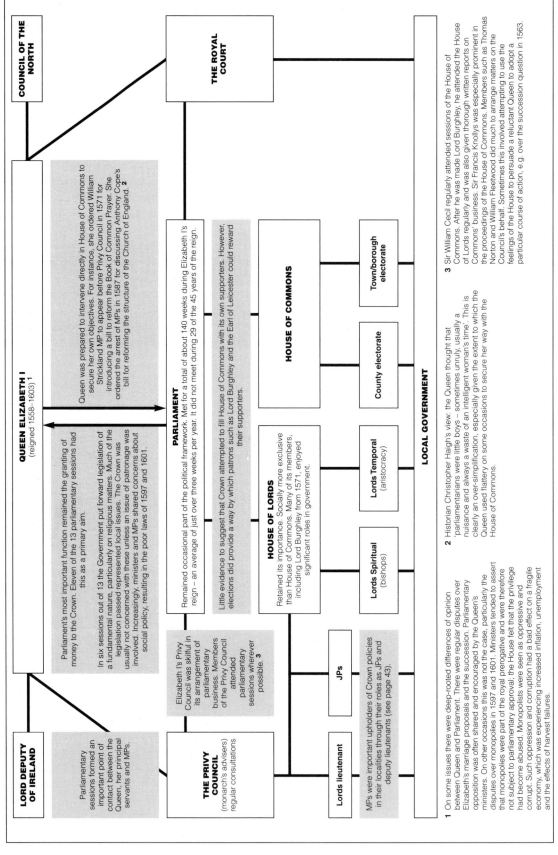

COUNCIL OF THE NORTH

THE ROYAL COURT

LORD DEPUTY OF IRELAND

Parliamentary sessions formed an important point of contact between the Queen, her principal servants and MPs.

QUEEN ELIZABETH I
(reigned 1558–1603) [1]

Parliament's most important function remained the granting of money to the Crown. Eleven of the 13 parliamentary sessions had this as a primary aim.

In six sessions out of 13 the Government put forward legislation of a fundamental nature, particularly on religious matters. Much of the legislation passed represented local issues. The Crown was usually not concerned with these unless an issue of patronage was involved. Increasingly, ministers and MPs shared concerns about social policy, resulting in the poor laws of 1597 and 1601.

Queen was prepared to intervene directly in House of Commons to secure her own objectives. For instance, she ordered William Strickland MP to appear before Privy Council in 1571 for introducing a bill to reform the Book of Common Prayer. She ordered the arrest of MPs in 1587 for discussing Anthony Cope's bill for reforming the structure of the Church of England. [2]

PARLIAMENT

Remained occasional part of the political framework. Met for a total of about 140 weeks during Elizabeth I's reign – an average of just over three weeks per year. It did not meet during 29 of the 45 years of the reign.

Little evidence to suggest that Crown attempted to fill House of Commons with its own supporters. However, elections did provide a way by which patrons such as Lord Burghley and the Earl of Leicester could reward their supporters.

HOUSE OF COMMONS

Town/borough electorate	County electorate

HOUSE OF LORDS

Retained its importance. Socially more exclusive than House of Commons. Many of its members, including Lord Burghley from 1571, enjoyed significant roles in government.

Lords Spiritual (bishops)	Lords Temporal (aristocracy)

THE PRIVY COUNCIL
(monarch's advisers) regular consultations

Elizabeth I's Privy Council was skilful in its arrangement of parliamentary business. Members of the Privy Council attended parliamentary sessions wherever possible. [3]

LOCAL GOVERNMENT

JPs	Lords lieutenant

MPs were important upholders of Crown policies in their localities through their roles as JPs and deputy lieutenants (see page 43).

1 On some issues there were deep-rooted differences of opinion between Queen and Parliament. There were regular disputes over Elizabeth's marriage proposals and the succession. Parliamentary opposition was often shared and encouraged by the Queen's ministers. On other occasions this was not the case, particularly over disputes over monopolies in 1597 and 1601. Ministers tended to assert that monopolies were part of the royal prerogative and were therefore not subject to parliamentary approval; the House felt that the privilege had become abused. Monopolists were seen as oppressive and corrupt. Such oppression and corruption had a bad effect on a fragile economy, which was experiencing increased inflation, unemployment and the effects of harvest failures.

2 Historian Christopher Haigh's view: the Queen thought that 'parliamentarians were little boys – sometimes unruly, usually a nuisance and always a waste of an intelligent woman's time'. This is clearly an over-simplification, especially given the extent to which the Queen used flattery on some occasions to secure her way with the House of Commons.

3 Sir William Cecil regularly attended sessions of the House of Commons. After he was made Lord Burghley, he attended the House of Lords regularly and was also given thorough written reports on Commons' business. Sir Francis Knollys was especially prominent in the proceedings of the House of Commons. Members such as Thomas Norton and William Fleetwood did much to arrange matters on the Council's behalf. Sometimes this involved attempting to use the feelings of the House to persuade a reluctant Queen to adopt a particular course of action, e.g. over the succession question in 1563.

claimed. The 40-strong 'Puritan Choir', which Neale had identified as being important in expressing anti-government attitudes, never existed. Elton claims that 'the members of that "choir" formed no party and few of them were Puritans'. More recently, the historian David Dean has claimed that the Puritans were 'an extremely active and well-organised lobby', though one which did not accept an anti-government position.

Given the nature of such arguments and counter-arguments, it is important to establish what can be accepted with confidence about parliaments in the Elizabethan era. The diagram (opposite) provides a pictorial representation of the points of contact in the English government under Elizabeth I. Study it closely before reading on.

Parliament, therefore, served many uses and performed many functions. It is important to recognise that the most eminent of recent Tudor historians, Geoffrey Elton, argues that politically it was 'only a secondary instrument to be used or ignored by agencies whose real power base and arena of activity lay elsewhere – at Court or in Council'. On the other hand, another 'revisionist' historian, M.A.R. Graves, has put forward the view that Parliament was an 'important but irregular part of Elizabethan government'. The relationship between Crown and Parliament was based on cooperation. Most parliamentary business took place without fuss. At other times, 'Queen, Council, Lord and Commons managed to work through political crises together'.

2.5 What were the main features of Elizabethan local government?

In a society where communications were as difficult to maintain as they were in Elizabethan England, it was essential for central government to maintain a range of networks by which the localities could be governed.

Regional government

A series of institutions was maintained to oversee government in key regions. This was particularly important at the English frontier with Scotland. Not only was Scotland a foreign power, the border area was also notorious as a centre of rustling (cattle stealing) and other forms of banditry. To minimise the scale of the problems that this might involve, the Crown had created three **marches**. By the time of Elizabeth I's reign, the government had abandoned the idea of giving control of these to the local nobility. There was too much danger of their becoming over-mighty subjects. Instead, the wardens were either reliable nobles with estates in other parts of the country or loyal gentry from the localities whose advancement depended on Crown favour. A similar system applied on the Welsh border. There, however, the situation was different. Since 1536, an English-style shire administration had been imposed upon Wales, which had, in effect, been incorporated into the English state.

In the case of both Wales and the North, the Councils provided a further tier of regional government. The Council in the Marches of Wales had some jurisdiction over Shropshire, Worcestershire, Herefordshire, Gloucestershire and, until 1569, Cheshire. However, its main function was as a regional law court. The Council in the North had a mixed history during the first few years of Elizabeth I's reign. It established considerable prestige and influence under the presidency of the Earl of Huntingdon

Marches: Border areas each under the control of a warden.

England in the 16th century

(1572–96), although even then the extent of its control outside Yorkshire remained rather sketchy.

Lords Lieutenant

It was the Duke of Northumberland who had originally established the idea that a lord lieutenant should be appointed in each county 'for the levying of men and to fight against the King's enemies'. After his fall from power, Lords Lieutenant were appointed only occasionally. From 1585, in the light of worsening relations with Spain, Lords Lieutenant were appointed in every shire. They were assisted in their work by **deputy lieutenants** and by **muster captains** and **muster masters** who offered professional assistance in the training of local militias. The other duties of the Lord Lieutenant included raising money, keeping watch over Roman Catholic **recusants** and generally supervising county affairs.

Assize judges

England was divided into six circuits, each of which was visited twice a year by professional judges who sat in the county towns to hear both civil and more serious criminal cases. The **Assize Courts** helped the central government maintain contact with the regions. Liaison between judges and Justices of the Peace could be developed through the Assizes.

Sheriffs

The sheriff held the oldest royal office in each county. Though the role was less significant than it had been during the Middle Ages, the sheriff still had some important functions. For example, he oversaw county elections, collected certain revenues and presided over executions. The responsibility that the sheriff traditionally exercised in respect of the maintenance of law and order was passing to the Justices of the Peace.

Justices of the Peace (magistrates)

By Elizabeth I's reign, Justices of the Peace (JPs) had become the central figures in local government. They had a dual role: they maintained law and order at a local level; and had also become the linchpins of administration at county level. Their wide-ranging duties included:

- presiding over the Quarter Sessions (courts of law dealing with offences committed within the county and meeting four times in the year);

- examining suspects;

- arresting rioters;

- dealing with the increasing number of administrative matters which were becoming their responsibility under new legislation;

- often being the recipients of orders and requests issued by the Privy Council.

Membership of the magistrates' bench became, during Elizabeth I's reign, one of the key means by which the social position of a gentleman could be assessed. This represented a considerable advantage to the Crown. It meant that there was never a shortage of volunteers for what was often a difficult task, which was largely unpaid. Certainly the task of JPs was considerably more complicated by the end of the 16th century. They were given administrative responsibilities under no fewer than 176 new Acts of

---

Deputy lieutenants: Normally drawn from amongst the leading gentry of a county, deputy lieutenants were appointed by Lords Lieutenant to assist them in their duties.

Muster captains/masters: Those responsible for bringing together for inspection men eligible for military service, together with their arms.

Recusants: Roman Catholics who refused to attend the services of the Church of England. When convicted, they could receive heavy fines and the loss of property. 'Recusant' comes from the Latin word for 'refuse'.

Assize Courts: These were courts that tried the most serious cases at a local level. The Assize judges visited each county twice a year to hear the cases.

Parliament. Most importantly, the Poor Laws recognised their very important position within local administration.

Church Courts

Operating under the authority of the bishop, these courts exercised a range of functions that are nowadays the responsibility of the secular (not concerned with religion or the Church) courts. Their areas of authority included matrimonial disputes, disputes over wills and sexual misconduct. These cases brought them frequently into contact with local populations and increased the extent to which the Church could function as an agent of social control.

Local officials

Local government in the Elizabethan era could not function effectively without the cooperation of local officials. Each division of a county had a high constable who acted as a link between the county administration and the parishes. Parish constables, elected annually by ratepayers, were the link between their village community and superior officials. They were responsible for such tasks as arresting vagrants (tramps or beggars), supervising alehouses, repairing the highway and maintaining the village stock of weapons and armour.

Corporate boroughs

Administrative systems in the towns differed from those that existed in the counties. Corporate boroughs were self-governing towns where control was vested in the aldermen and councillors. They could establish their own by-laws, administer the town's corporate property, and carry out the instructions of central government. In addition, the mayor and senior aldermen often sat as Justices of the Peace within the confines of the town.

1. Draw a diagram showing how Elizabethan local government was organised.

2. Which do you consider was the most important office in Elizabethan local government, and why?

2.6 How successful was Elizabethan government?

In addition to assessing the overall quality of Elizabethan government, it is necessary to examine the claim that Elizabethan government became less effective during the last third of the reign. The historian Christopher Haigh describes the Queen in the 1590s as 'politically bankrupt'.

For much of her reign Elizabeth I had clearly been successful, when judged by the standards of her time. Before 1585, she largely avoided wars. As a result, the revenue demands that her administration imposed were relatively modest – until the second half of the 1580s. The rebels of 1569 were not even able to use problems of taxation as an excuse for their actions.

Queen Elizabeth I was fortunate also in the quality of her ministers, such as Lord Burghley, Francis Walsingham and Walter Mildmay. (Sir Christopher Hatton was arguably less effective.) Lord Burghley, in particular, had a huge capacity for work, overseeing many aspects of government and handling royal patronage with skill. Mildmay, as the long-serving Chancellor of the Exchequer, was Burghley's chief assistant in financial matters. He handled his responsibilities with great skill and discretion. Walsingham, as Secretary of State, did have his differences with Lord Burghley over foreign policy. Along with the Earl of Leicester, he usually favoured a more openly 'protestant' (and expensive) foreign policy. Nevertheless, he worked effectively with Lord Burghley for much of his time in office.

Relations with Parliament were usually good. However, there were disputes over marriage and the succession – when parliamentary opinion was often closer to that of the Privy Council than the Privy Council's was to the Queen. These good relations were reinforced by the skill of parliamentary managers such as Mildmay, Norton and Fleetwood. It is also important to note that most MPs knew that there were certain boundaries that they could not cross in expressing their opinions. The nature of those boundaries was expressed by Mildmay, in 1576, when he commented:

> 'we must not forget to put a difference between liberty of speech and **licentious speech**, for by the one men deliver their opinions freely but with this caution, that all be spoken pertinently, modestly, reverently and discreetly. The other, contrariwise, uttereth all impertinently, rashly, arrogantly and irreverently, without respect of person, time or place.'

As Christopher Haigh points out, such limitations on the manner of debate caused far less trouble than the Queen's use of the **prerogative** to prevent debate on issues which she considered too sensitive, such as the role of the Church of England.

It is more difficult to estimate the effectiveness of local government. In contrast to Spain, for example, the Crown had no properly paid officials who could be relied upon to run the localities. Instead, there was a reliance on unpaid officers. This worked well up to a point. The office of Justice of the Peace gave its holder considerable local prestige. This meant that JPs usually worked hard to follow orders from the Privy Council or to enforce laws passed by Parliament. There is little evidence to suggest that JPs abused their position when conducting their office. They were often selective in the approach to their duties. In the words of Penry Williams, 'the main burden of county government was carried out by a few devoted and conscientious men: model officials or tiresome busybodies depending on one's point of view'. Nevertheless, there is evidence of selectivity of approach. In Lancashire, for example, there is little to suggest that the JPs ever did much to enforce legislation against Catholics. In largely Catholic Lancashire that might not have been too much of a shock. Yet a similar situation happened in Suffolk, which was much more strongly Protestant and where Catholic influence remained among the JPs until the late 1580s. At the more humble level of constable, there was much hard work and a genuine attempt to cope with the demands of the office.

There is evidence to suggest that, certainly in the first 30 years of the reign, government was conducted with effectiveness at both national and local level. This was certainly not the case during the latter stages of the reign, when a combination of factors placed immense strain on the Elizabethan system of government. The patronage system broke down in the hands of Robert Cecil. The ageing Queen was becoming, in the words of historian A.G.R. Smith, 'irascible [angry and bad-tempered] and embittered'. Many of her most trusted ministers – Lord Burghley, Sir Christopher Hatton and Sir Francis Knollys – died during the 1590s. The long-lasting war with Spain created immense financial pressures. At a local level, officials found it increasingly difficult to cope with the financial and administrative demands which government was making.

Licentious speech: In this context Mildmay was referring to those who were going too far in criticising the Queen.

Prerogative: The powers that the King or Queen used to govern the realm. Some of these came from the monarch's rights as feudal overlord of the kingdom and, on occasion, this allowed the monarch to act outside the law. But even then the King or Queen could not ignore the common law of England.

1. What evidence would you put forward (a) to support and (b) to disprove the claim that Elizabethan government up to 1588 was successful?

2. 'Thirty years of illusion, followed by 15 years of disillusion.' How far does the evidence which you have read in this chapter support this claim?

To make matters worse, these pressures coincided during the second half of the 1590s with a massive series of social strains. A series of harvest failures created food shortages that, in turn, increased the pressures of inflation. Moreover, many parts of the country were affected in 1597 with a severe outbreak of plague.

At the heart of many of these administrative problems lay the government's conservatism. There was no willingness, among Elizabeth and her ministers, to change methods of government in the light of changing political and financial circumstances. Historians whose views on the reign are as contrasting as those of A.G.R. Smith and Christopher Haigh share this view of the disastrous final years. To the former, Elizabethan government in the 1590s 'was bankrupt of new ideas in a changing world'; to the latter 'her reign had been 30 years of illusion, followed by 15 years of disillusion'. Admittedly, Elizabethan England had largely avoided the conflicts that had afflicted neighbouring France. Moreover, the Spanish threat had been safely overcome. By 1603, however, few people were prepared to give the Queen much credit for these successes. She had reigned too long, and the succession of King James was widely welcomed.

Religion in Elizabethan England

Key Issues

- *How radical was the Elizabethan Church Settlement of 1559 to 1563?*
- *How far were Catholics a threat to Elizabeth I?*
- *What impact did Puritanism have on Elizabethan England?*

Framework of Events

1558	November: Elizabeth I becomes Queen, at the age of 25
1559	15 January: Elizabeth displays her displeasure at the elevation of the host at communion in the Royal Chapel
	March–April: Conference between Catholic and Protestant theologians at Westminster
	May: Acts of Supremacy and Uniformity become law
	July: Royal Injunctions on religious beliefs
	Matthew Parker becomes Archbishop of Canterbury
1563	Convocation approves the Thirty Nine Articles (of faith)
1566	Vestiarian Controversy over the wearing of vestments by Elizabethan clergy
1568	William Allen founds the Catholic college at Douai (Netherlands) to train priests for the mission to England
	Mary Stuart arrives in England from Scotland
1569	Rebellion of the Northern Earls begins
1570	Rebellion ends in failure. Papal Bull of Excommunication against Elizabeth I
	Thomas Cartwright delivers spring lectures at the University of Cambridge on the organisation of the Church
1571	Ridolfi Plot by Catholics
1572	Duke of Norfolk executed for treason. Cartwright, Field and others begin a campaign to reform the Elizabethan Church along Genevan lines
1574	Seminary priests begin arriving in England from Douai
1575	17 May: Matthew Parker dies; replaced as Archbishop of Canterbury by Edmund Grindal
1576	December: Queen orders Archbishop Grindal to suppress Prophesying
	May: Grindal is suspended as Archbishop and placed under house arrest
	John Aylmer, Bishop of London, placed at head of Ecclesiastical Commission to suppress Prophesying
	November: execution of Cuthbert Mayne, seminary priest
1579	English College founded in Rome under the supervision of the Jesuits

1580	Edmund Campion and Robert Parsons (Jesuits) arrive in England
1581	Parliament passes legislation against Catholics, seminary priests and Jesuits
	Parsons and Campion implicated in Throckmorton Plot against Elizabeth
	Grindal dies and is replaced as Archbishop of Canterbury by John Whitgift
	Beginning of concerted attack on Presbyterianism
1584	Bill and Book proposals by Presbyterians in parliament
1585	Act against Jesuits and Seminary Priests
1586	Babington Plot against Elizabeth which implicates Mary Stuart
1587	Mary Stuart is executed
	Anthony Cope MP reintroduces Bill and Book proposal in Parliament
1588	Spanish Armada
	John Field and Earl of Leicester die
	Martin Marprelate Tracts published
1589	More Martin Marprelate Tracts
1590	Thomas Cartwright brought before Court of High Commission
1591	Royal Proclamation against Jesuits
	Hacket Affair
1593	Act against Seditious Sectaries
	Execution of Separatists: Barrow, Greenwood and Penry
1594	William Allen dies
1598	Height of Archpriest Controversy within English Catholicism
1602	Royal Proclamation against Jesuits
1603	Thirteen Seminary priests accept Elizabeth as head of state.

Overview

WHEN Elizabeth I became Queen in 1558, England had gone through over 25 years of religious change. The 'National Catholicism' of her father, Henry VIII, was followed by more radical religious reform under her half-brother, Edward VI. In the five years before the start of her reign, Mary I, her half-sister, had attempted to re-establish England as a Catholic country.

When Elizabeth I ascended the throne, it seemed clear to contemporaries that further religious change was inevitable. Catholic Europe regarded Elizabeth as illegitimate. Also, she had been educated by Protestants such as Roger Ascham. However, any change in England's religious position was affected by a number of factors.

Firstly, England was still an ally of Catholic Spain in its war with France. When Elizabeth became Queen, England had lost Calais – its last possession on the continent. The monarch also feared invasion from France's ally, Scotland. Any radical change in the religion of the country could have had a major impact on England's position in foreign affairs. Throughout the early years of Elizabeth I's reign, the issue of religion was linked closely to foreign affairs. This was most apparent in the issue of the succession to the throne. The strongest claimant, on the death of Elizabeth, was Mary Stuart (Mary Queen of Scots). Until her execution in 1587, Mary Stuart created major political and religious problems for Elizabeth I.

Secondly, although Elizabeth was unlikely to keep England a catholic country, it was unclear what type of Protestantism she would adopt. In mid-16th century

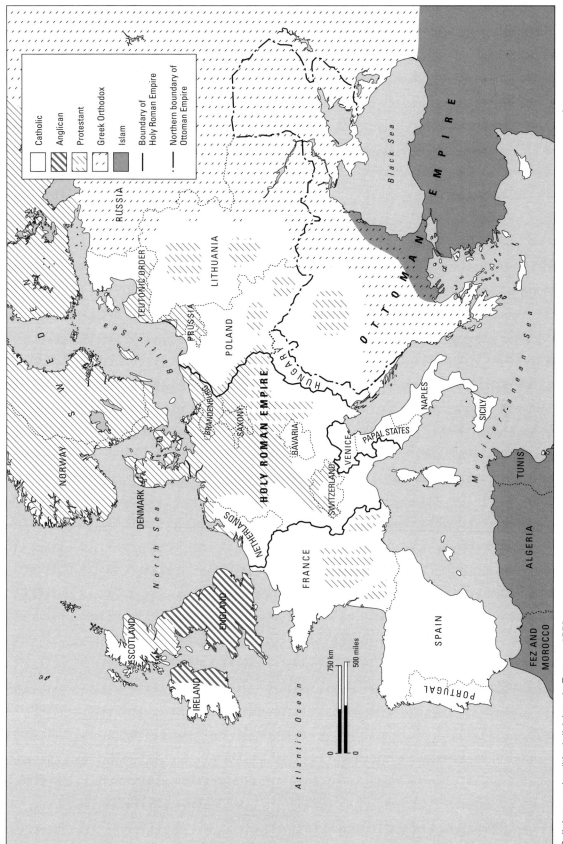

Religious and political divisions in Europe, 1559

Legend:

	Catholic
	Anglican
	Protestant
	Greek Orthodox
	Islam
	Boundary of Holy Roman Empire
	Northern boundary of Ottoman Empire

Map labels:

RUSSIA

SWEDEN

NORWAY

TEUTONIC ORDER

LITHUANIA

PRUSSIA

POLAND

BRANDENBURG

SAXONY

HOLY ROMAN EMPIRE

BAVARIA

HUNGARY

OTTOMAN EMPIRE

DENMARK

NETHERLANDS

SWITZERLAND

VENICE

PAPAL STATES

NAPLES

SICILY

FRANCE

SPAIN

PORTUGAL

ENGLAND

SCOTLAND

IRELAND

TUNIS

ALGERIA

FEZ AND MOROCCO

Black Sea

Baltic Sea

North Sea

Mediterranean Sea

Atlantic Ocean

750 km

500 miles

Europe, Protestantism took a variety of forms. In the German part of the Holy Roman Empire and in Scandinavia Lutheranism was dominant (see insert below). However, there were other forms of Protestantism. Originating in Switzerland was Zwinglianism (see insert). Also, centred on Switzerland, was Calvinism (known as Presbyterianism in Scotland) which adopted different beliefs and church organisation. When the Marian exiles returned from the Continent, they did not all have the same religious beliefs.

Religion and religious affairs were a dominant theme in Elizabethan England. Religious issues have involved controversy and debate among historians. Did the Religious Settlement of 1559 to 1563 reflect Elizabeth I's own religious views? Why did Catholicism survive in Elizabethan England? How extensive was support for Puritan ideas during the reign?

The differences between Catholicism, Lutheranism, Calvinism and Zwinglianism

Catholicism

In structure, the Catholic Church is a hierarchy with the Pope as Head of the Church. He ruled an area of central Italy known as the Papal States. The Pope is elected by the College of Cardinals for life. Once elected, the Pope has the power to appoint cardinals, archbishops and bishops throughout the Catholic Church. The Church is divided into provinces, under the control of an archbishop. Within a province, a diocese is administered by a bishop. The lowest level of administration is a parish, administered by a priest. In addition to the 'secular' clergy (bishops, priests etc.) are 'regular' clergy. These are monks and nuns who live in monasteries and convents, respectively. They perform a variety of tasks such as helping the poor and education.

Transubstantiation: This is the belief that the bread and wine actually change into the flesh and blood of Christ during the course of the Mass.

Catholics believe that, in authority, the Pope is a direct descendent of St Peter. The most important ceremony is Mass, which was said in Latin. All Catholics are expected to go to Mass on Sundays and some Holy Days. The central feature of Mass is communion. Catholics believe in the doctrine of **transubstantiation**.

Catholics also believe in venerating saints. In addition to Sunday worship, there are also Holy Days which commemorate the lives of saints (e.g. St Peter and St Paul) or important events such as Christmas and Good Friday. Catholic churches usually have statues of saints and Jesus. The altar, where the priest celebrates Mass, is adorned with candles and a cross (see picture on page 58).

Lutheranism

This Christian religion began in the Holy Roman Empire in the 1520s and spread to Scandinavia. In organisation, Lutheran Churches were **Erastian**. The Church was also episcopalian (i.e. it was administered by bishops who, in turn, appointed ministers). In religious belief, Lutherans place great emphasis on the study of the Bible. Therefore, Lutherans believe there are two sacraments – Baptism and Communion – because these are mentioned in the

Erastian: The Head of State was also the Head of the Church (i.e. both political and religious power belonged to the ruler).

Consubstantiation: This doctrine states that the bread and wine at communion do not become the body and blood of Jesus Christ. Instead there is a 'spiritual' presence of Christ.

New Testament. Catholics believe there are Seven Sacraments. Lutheran Church services contain Bible reading and communion. However, Lutherans believe in **consubstantiation**. Lutherans also believe clergymen should wear simple vestments (clerical clothes).

Zwinglianism

This is named after Huldrych Zwingli (1484–1531), the Swiss Protestant reformer. Zwingli believed that only Jesus Christ could be head of the Christian Church. Like Lutheranism, they placed great emphasis on the Bible as the source for religious belief. On the issue of communion, Zwinglians believed the service was merely a memorial service to commemorate the Last Supper. They also rejected other Catholic beliefs, such as masses for the dead and the use of religious statues and paintings in churches.

Calvinism

This is named after Jean Calvin (1509–1564), the French Protestant reformer. Although French-born, the centre of Calvinism was Geneva in Switzerland. Calvinists believed in a church structure that was very different from Catholicism and Lutheranism. In Calvinism, there were no bishops. Instead, the church was made up of independent groups (congregations) led by elders. The Elders chose the clergyman, known as a minister.

Predestination: The belief that God decided who should and who should not be 'saved' from the beginning – therefore such things as 'good works' were irrelevant to salvation.

Calvinists accepted Lutheran ideas such as the belief that you could get to heaven by faith (belief in God) alone. However, they also believed in **predestination**. This stated that God had already chosen those who would get to heaven. This denied the existence of free will which, in effect, gave a person the freedom to choose between good and evil – which Catholics believed. On the issue of communion, Calvinist belief was somewhere between the Lutheran and Zwinglian view. In Scotland and England, Calvinists were known as Presbyterians.

Like Lutherans and Zwinglians, they believed clergymen should wear simple vestments (clerical clothes).

3.1 What were Elizabeth I's personal religious beliefs?

On 5 February 1550, the Protestant bishop John Hooper wrote to the Swiss Protestant reformer Bullinger concerning the religious beliefs of the future Elizabeth I: 'She not only knows what the true religion is, but has acquired such proficiency in Greek and Latin that she is able to defend it.' This view of the personal religious beliefs of Elizabeth I has not always been accepted by historians. The historian A.F. Pollard, in his *History of England* (published in 1919), claimed that Queen Elizabeth I was 'indifferent to religion'. In the 1950s, Sir John Neale took the view that Elizabeth planned to return England to the religion of her father's day, a form of National Catholicism.

However, there is sufficient evidence to suggest that Elizabeth I was both religious and interested in Protestantism. The political faction that

These two illustrations of Queen Elizabeth I were made during her reign. The first (left) shows Elizabeth on her accession to the throne (unknown artist, c.1600). The contemporary engraving (right) was made later in her reign.

1. What image of Elizabeth I are these pictures trying to portray? Give reasons to support your answer.

2. How useful to a historian are these portrayals of Elizabeth I?

surrounded her mother during the early 1530s had Lutheran sympathies. Also her education, by Roger Ascham and in the households of Sir Anthony Denny and Queen Katherine Parr, was grounded in the 'new religion'.

It is now accepted that Elizabeth was a sincere and committed Protestant. As Christopher Haigh notes in his study of Elizabeth I, written in 1998: 'There should be little doubt of Elizabeth's personal Protestantism.' But what type of Protestantism did Elizabeth follow? The American historian Winthrop Hudson believes that she did not wish to re-establish the National Catholicism of her father or Lutheranism. In his view, Elizabeth favoured the Zwinglian model of 'pure' religion, which was indicated in the 1559 version of the Book of Common Prayer.

Yet there is evidence to suggest that Elizabeth was a political realist. She was aware that her religious beliefs differed from those of other rulers, both Catholic and Lutheran. She was also aware of the difficult position England faced in foreign affairs. The idea of a coalition of Catholic forces, under the leadership of Spain and France, against England was a concern throughout her reign.

England in 1558 was a country with a large proportion of its population still Catholic. It was also a country where there were many different types of Protestant ideas and beliefs. Therefore, Elizabeth adopted religious policies that were aimed not to drive Catholics into outright opposition to her regime. Throughout her reign, Elizabeth restrained Protestant preaching of a radical type. She did not persecute Catholics unless they offered a direct threat to her rule. She was reluctant to support Protestant rebels abroad.

Was this conservatism in religion merely a tactic to prevent threats to her rule at home and abroad? There is evidence to suggest that these views also reflected Elizabeth's own personal religious beliefs. For instance, throughout her reign she had a deep dislike of clerical marriage. She also insisted on the use of a cross and candlesticks on the altar of the Royal Chapel. According to the historian Patrick Collinson, in *Windows in a Woman's Soul: Questions about the Religion of Queen Elizabeth I*: 'It remains possible that the Elizabethan compromise of Protestantism was a concession not only to the conservative prejudices of Elizabeth's subjects but to her own feelings.'

This view is of considerable importance in any historical interpretation of the religious nature of the Elizabethan Settlement of 1559.

***

The organisation of the Church of England during the reign of Elizabeth I

The Head of the Church
At the top of the church structure was Queen Elizabeth I. Under the 1559 Act of Supremacy, Elizabeth was the Supreme Governor of the Church of England. The church organisation of Elizabethan England can be regarded as Erastian. Some contemporaries believed that the control of the Church by the State was shared between monarch and Parliament. This was based on the belief that the Church Settlement of 1559 was a joint act by Queen and Parliament. Queen Elizabeth I believed that the monarch alone had control. She merely used Parliament to introduce these changes. Throughout her reign, Elizabeth I consistently opposed any attempt by Parliament to debate the Church Settlement.

The province
England and Wales were divided into two provinces: Canterbury and York, each under the control of an archbishop. If you look at the map on page 54 you will see that Canterbury was much the larger. Because it covered the southern and central parts of England and Wales, it was richer and politically more important. The Archbishop of Canterbury had a residence in London, at Lambeth Palace, across the River Thames from Whitehall and parliament.

Convocation: Assembly of clergy who could discuss church matters.

Each province had a **convocation**. With strong Catholic influences at the beginning of her reign, it is not surprising that Elizabeth used Parliament rather than Convocation to pass the religious settlement.

The diocese
There were 27 dioceses in England and Wales. In charge of each diocese was a bishop who was appointed by the Queen. The bishop had several duties, including ordaining parsons (vicars and other

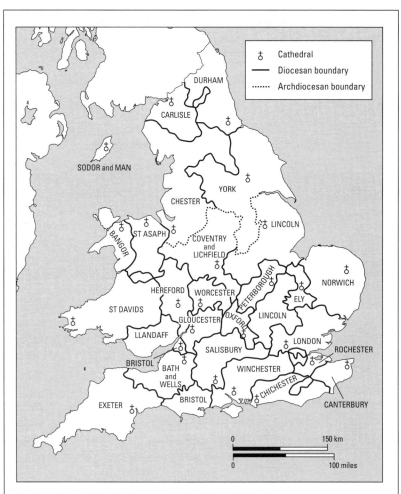

The English and Welsh dioceses during Elizabeth I's reign

members of the clergy without special rank) and consecrating churches. He was also responsible to the Queen for making sure the clergy followed the Act of Uniformity and Royal Injunctions of the Elizabethan Church Settlement.

The bishop's own church was a cathedral which was usually administered by a dean. Deans were also appointed by the Queen.

The parish

This was the smallest unit of church organisation. During Elizabeth I's reign, there were approximately 10,000 parishes in England. In each parish there was meant to be a clergyman – a parson. Other names for the clergy of a parish were vicar or rector. In the early part of Elizabeth's reign, there was a shortage of suitably qualified clergy. The parson was responsible for the spiritual welfare of his congregation. In return, he received an income partly from tithes (taxes, usually in the form of goods and produce) and partly from renting out land owned by the parish. To assist the parson were two churchwardens who were appointed by the parson and the parishioners for a term of one year. Their main task was the repair and upkeep of the church.

'Elizabeth's view of religion was based on political considerations.'

'Elizabeth was a committed Protestant.'

Using the information is this section, which view do you regard as the most accurate?

Give reasons to support your answer.

3.2 *The Elizabethan Church Settlement*
A CASE STUDY IN HISTORICAL INTERPRETATION

The Elizabethan Church Settlement, which formed the foundations of the Church of England, was established in the years 1559 to 1563. It was laid down mainly by the Parliament of 1559, which passed four Acts relating to religion:

● an Act of Supremacy, dealing with church organisation

● an Act of Uniformity which dealt with the form of worship

● and two acts dealing with church property:
  – the Act of Exchange allowed the Queen to use revenues from dioceses if there was a vacancy for a bishop;
  – the other Act restored to the monarch money which derived from the **First Fruits and Tenths** that Elizabeth's elder sister, Mary I, had restored to the Church during her reign (1553–58).

First Fruits and Tenths: A tax paid by clergymen to the monarch. They had to pay all of their first year's income and 10% of every other year's income.

In addition to these Acts, the Settlement also involved Royal Injunctions, introduced in July 1559, which filled in much of the detail of religious practice not covered in the Act of Uniformity. In 1563, Convocation, rather than Parliament, produced the Thirty Nine Articles. These contained the main statements of belief of the Church of England. Parliament approved the Articles in 1571 with the passage of the Subscription Act.

Since the establishment of the Church Settlement, historians have differed in their interpretation of the motives of Queen Elizabeth and the nature of the religious changes that were made.

Why have historians differed in their interpretations of the Church Settlement?

Contemporaries of Elizabeth I – like John Foxe who published *Acts and Monuments* in 1563 – believed that Elizabeth had pushed through Parliament a Protestant religious settlement in the face of Catholic opposition. This view is supported by evidence from her first months as queen that she was a committed Protestant. At the Christmas Mass of 1558, Queen Elizabeth I made a public display of walking out when Bishop Oglethorpe decided to raise the host (the bread used during the religious service). This action showed her disapproval of the Catholic church service.

On 27 and 28 December 1558, Elizabeth issued proclamations that religious books, such as the Bible, and prayers, such as the Lord's Prayer, should be in English rather than Latin. Early in the following year, she refused to follow the procession of monks participating in the Opening of Parliament. On 1 February 1559, the Privy Council ordered the English ambassador to Pope Paul IV to return to England. Finally, Elizabeth allowed William Bill, Queen's Almoner and a known Protestant, to make the first official sermon at St Paul's Cross, outside St Paul's Cathedral in London. When Bishop Christopherson, the Catholic bishop of Chichester, criticised William Bill's sermon on the following Sunday, he in turn was criticised by the Queen and placed under house arrest.

Together with her background and education, these actions strongly suggested that Queen Elizabeth I wished to have a Protestant religious settlement. The so-called compromise, or *via media* (middle way), nature of the changes of 1559–63 suggests that the Queen was prevented from achieving her aims by conservative catholic forces in Parliament and by Convocation. However, there was the hope felt by Protestants in England that, at last, they had a monarch who would introduce the 'new religion'. Therefore, the views of Foxe and other contemporaries, such as William Camden, were affected by this belief.

This view of the Settlement was challenged by Sir John Neale in a series of books published in the 1950s. In *Elizabeth I and her Parliaments, 1559–1581* (published in 1953), Neale argued that the Settlement was the result of a conservative Queen being forced into a more protestant Religious Settlement by a group of radical Protestants in the House of Commons – the so-called 'Puritan choir.'

Neale came to this view for several reasons. Firstly, he placed considerable weight on the international situation in 1558–59. When Elizabeth came to the throne in November 1558, England was still at war with France. The government did not possess the revenue to continue fighting. Therefore, Elizabeth had to follow a conservative religious policy in order not to upset Catholics at home or abroad. The Treaty of Cateau-Cambrésis, which ended the war with France, was not signed until 2 April 1559.

Secondly, Neale believed that a significant body of opinion in the House of Commons supported a radical religious settlement. This group was led by Sir Francis Knollys and Sir Anthony Cooke. Sir John Neale noted that approximately one-quarter of the 404 members of the House of Commons acted together to force a reluctant Queen towards Protestantism.

However, Sir John Neale's interpretation has been criticised by several historians. Geoffrey Elton, in an essay on Parliament published in 1984, believes Neale's methods of working out the religious views of MPs to be incorrect. According to Elton:

> With good grounds, leading members of the House [Commons] were identified as Puritans, so that what leading members did became Puritan activities, and when something happened that might be connected with reformist views in religion the notional Puritan group was alleged to be behind it. In fact, members of that "choir" formed no party and few of them were Puritans.

In addition, Neale's view can be criticised for giving the House of Commons more influence than it in fact possessed in 1559. Because the Commons became a dominant force in early Stuart England, its role in the Church Settlement of 1559 has been overstated. According to M.A.R. Graves, historian of Elizabethan parliaments, the actions Neale thought came from a group of radical Protestant MPs were actually the work of William Cecil and the Privy Council, following the wishes of the Queen.

The historian who, more than any other, led the criticism of Sir John Neale's view is Norman Jones. In *Faith by Statute: Parliament and the Settlement of Religion in 1559* (published in 1982), Jones argues that Elizabeth I and her advisers established a settlement which reflected their own religious views. Opposition to this settlement came from Catholics in the House of Lords, not radical Protestants in the House of Commons.

Jones believed that Elizabeth planned to re-establish Royal Supremacy over the Church and to reintroduce the Book of Common Prayer of 1552.

The main opposition to these proposals came from Catholic bishops in the House of Lords. As an example, on 21 February 1559 a religious Bill was presented to the House of Lords which, if enacted, would have made Elizabeth supreme head of the church with a Protestant form of religious worship. By the time the Bill had been debated, the Lords had decided that Elizabeth might become supreme head, if she wanted, but they would not accept the responsibility of giving the title to her. The Lords also amended radically the proposals for changing religious worship. As Jones notes in his essay 'Elizabeth's First Year', in Christopher Haigh's *The Reign of Elizabeth I* (1984): 'By 23 March the Queen and Cecil, having badly miscalculated the strength of resistance to religious change in the Lords, found themselves in a difficult position.'

Only after the recall of Parliament after Easter and the imprisonment of some Catholic bishops did a new Act of Uniformity pass the House of Lords, by three votes. It became law on 8 May 1559. All the Catholic bishops in the Lords voted against. Convocation also opposed the changes.

Although the Settlement of Religion passed by Parliament in 1559 contained elements of compromise, it was a compromise close to the Queen's original view. Throughout the rest of her reign, Elizabeth I was unwilling to allow Parliament to discuss the Religious Settlement. This suggests her general satisfaction with what was produced between 1559 and 1563.

What religious changes were made by the Elizabethan Church Settlement?

The Act of Supremacy, May 1559

In *The Royal Supremacy in the Elizabethan Church* (1969), historian Claire Cross states that 'one of the main functions of the First Parliament of Elizabeth was to re-establish formally the Queen's authority over the English Church'. Unlike her father, Elizabeth was not proclaimed 'supreme head'. Instead she became 'supreme governor'. This form of words was aimed at placating both Catholics and the more extreme Protestants who disliked the idea of a woman taking on such an important religious position.

The Act also required all the clergy to take an oath recognising the Royal Supremacy over the Church. This gave Elizabeth the opportunity to remove Catholic clergy who refused the oath. Apart from Bishop Kitchen of Llandaff and the Bishop of Sodor and Man, all the Catholic bishops refused. Together with existing vacancies, this enabled Elizabeth to appoint 25 bishops – although she seemed in no hurry to fill all the vacancies. However, she did appoint Matthew Parker as Archbishop of Canterbury, John Jewel for Salisbury, Edmund Grindal for London and Richard Cox for Ely.

When the oath was issued to the lower clergy, only 4% refused to take it – about 200 in all, in the period November 1559 to November 1564.

The Act also required a visitation (tour) of the Church nationwide. The first visitation began at the end of June 1559, to administer the Oath of Supremacy and to deliver the new Royal Injunctions on Religion. For this purpose, a commission of clergy and laymen was created – the Court of High Commission. The commission was used to locate and prosecute people with Catholic sympathies.

?

1. *Explain in what ways historians have differed in their interpretation of the reasons behind the Elizabethan Church Settlement?*

2. *What reasons can you give to explain why John Foxe, John Neale and Norman Jones have provided different historical interpretations of the Church Settlement?*

Matthew Parker (1504–1575)
Educated at the University of Cambridge and ordained a priest in 1527, Parker became chaplain to Ann Boleyn and a supporter of Lady Jane Grey. He lost his religious position under Queen Mary. Parker was regarded as a moderate Protestant.

1. *Using the information contained within the illustrations below, explain how a Catholic Church service differed from the Protestant service towards the end of Edward VI's reign.*

2. *Use the information from this chapter. The Elizabethan Church Settlement introduced a new form of church service. How far did it differ from the two church services shown below?*

1 Wall painting
2 Server
3 Surplice
4 Rood screen
5 Sanctuary lamps
6 Cross with statue of St John (left) and Virgin Mary (right)
7 Missal
8 Reredos
9 Hanging tabernacle
10 Chalice
11 Chasuble
12 Alb
13 Priest
14 Rushes strewn on floor
15 Altar
16 Stained-glass window

Catholic form of worship and vestments during the reign of Mary I (1553–58)

1 'Eagle' lectern for Bible
2 Surplice
3 Scarf of black silk
4 Priest
5 Wall tablets containing the Ten Commandments
6 Plain glass in window
7 Royal coat-of-arms
8 Pulpit for preaching
9 Book of Common Prayer at north end of table. The priest stands there at communion service
10 Ordinary bread
11 White linen cloth
12 Flagon of wine

Protestant form of worship and vestments towards the end of the reign of Edward VI (1547–53)

The Act of Uniformity, May 1559

This Act dealt with the form of worship. It made attendance at church on Sundays and Holy Days compulsory. There was a fine of 12d [5p] for non-attendance. This money was to be used to aid the poor.

The most controversial part of the Act centred on the new Book of Common Prayer. This book was based on the Edwardian Books of Common Prayer of 1549 and 1552, but there were significant differences. Most notable was the wording to be used during a communion service, which was a combination of words from the 1549 Book followed by words from the 1552 Book. When a parson gave the bread to a person taking communion, the parson was meant to say the words from the 1549 Book: 'The Body of Our Lord Jesus Christ, which was given for thee, preserve thy body and soul unto everlasting life.' This was to be followed by words from the 1552 Book: 'Take and eat this in remembrance that Christ died for thee, and feed on him thy heart by faith with thanksgiving.' This formula of words was a masterstroke of compromise because it contained the possibility of pleasing Catholics and Lutherans, who believed in the spiritual presence of Christ at communion, and the Zwinglians who regarded communion as merely a way to remember the Last Supper.

The Act of Uniformity also allowed crosses and candlesticks to be placed on the communion table and laid down regulations for the type of clothes worn by clergymen. The dress regulations led to the Vestiarian Controversy of 1566.

The Royal Injunctions, July 1559

These were drawn up by William Cecil. Numbering 57 in all, they filled in much of the detail about the day-to-day organisation of the Church not contained in the Act of Uniformity. In many ways they were similar to the Injunctions issued in 1538 by Thomas Cromwell and by Protector Somerset in the 1540s. Their aim was to ensure a uniformity of religious practice. For instance, preaching was to be licensed by a bishop. Once licensed, preachers had to preach once a month. Another injunction stated that all books and pamphlets had to be licensed by the Court of High Commission or a council of bishops. Every church was ordered to display a bible in English and every parson was expected to instruct young members of a parish to know the Lord's Prayer, the Catechism (a book containing the main religious beliefs) and the Ten Commandments.

Some aspects of the Royal Injunctions pleased Protestants – such as the injunction to close shrines and outlaw pilgrimages. However, other injunctions – such as the use of a wafer as a host at communion, like the Catholic Mass, instead of bread as laid down in the 1552 Book of Common Prayer – disappointed them. They were also disappointed by the removal of the Black Rubric of the 1552 Book, which forbade kneeling at communion. The act of kneeling, to Protestants, symbolised the 'real' presence of Christ at communion. What also disappointed radical Protestants were the injunctions concerning the wearing of vestments (clerical clothes) and the injunction preventing the further destruction of altars.

Although more extreme Protestants may have been displeased by several Royal Injunctions, it seems clear that these 'laws' represented the religious views of Elizabeth I. The one area which did not conform to this view was the injunction which allowed clerical marriage, something Elizabeth had always disliked. However, any future wife of a clergyman had to be interviewed first by a bishop and two JPs to ensure she was of a suitable moral standard.

The Thirty Nine Articles, 1563–1571

While the Royal Injunctions dealt with the day-to-day administration and organisation of the Elizabethan Church, it took until 1563 for the doctrine (religious beliefs) of the Church to be produced. Instead of using Parliament, Elizabeth allowed Convocation to deal with this matter.

The Thirty Nine Articles (of faith) owed much to previous pronouncements, such as the Forty Two Articles from the reign of Edward VI. Introduced by Convocation in 1563, they became law when Parliament passed the Subscription Act in 1571. Historian Susan Doran, in *Elizabeth I and Religion 1558–1603* (1994), states that the Thirty Nine Articles were 'something of a hybrid, containing features that were Lutheran, Zwinglian and Calvinist'. For instance, Article XVII stated that 'Predestination to Life is the ever-lasting purpose of God, whereby he hath constantly decreed by his counsel, secret to us, to deliver from curse and damnation those whom he hath chosen in Christ out of mankind'. The wording seemed to go against the views on predestination held by Calvinists and contained words and phrases that could be acceptable to both Lutherans and Zwinglians.

On the issue of Communion, Article XXVIII stated: 'The Body of Christ is given and taken in the Supper [communion] only after an heavenly and spiritual manner. And the mean whereby the Body of Christ is received and eaten [the wafer or host] in the Supper is Faith.' This formula of words denied the 'real' presence of Jesus Christ in the communion service, which was central to Catholic religious beliefs. Instead, it was similar to the Lutheran belief of consubstantiation (the spiritual, not bodily, presence of Christ).

Financial aspects of the Settlement

When Elizabeth I became Queen, the monarchy was in deep financial crisis. This was mainly as a result of the French War. Like her father, Elizabeth used her religious settlement to provide the Crown with much-needed revenue. One of her first actions was to take under royal control the church taxes of First Fruits and Tenths. Although Henry VIII had taken these taxes from the Church, Mary I had returned them. This 1559 Act allowed Elizabeth the revenue without increasing taxes on the laity (non-clerical population).

More controversial was the Act of Exchange, also passed in 1559. This Act involved the transfer of property. It was passed, after a lot of debate, giving Elizabeth the right to take over property once held by bishops. It also stopped bishops from making money from renting out land for more than 21 years, except to Elizabeth herself. The result of this Act of Exchange was to take considerable wealth away from the Church. It also allowed Elizabeth and her government to put pressure on bishops by threatening to use parts of the Act against them. This ensured that the bishops followed Elizabeth's wishes in religious affairs. It was not surprising that this Act passed with protests from the newly appointed Protestant Bishops.

Conclusion

According to Christopher Haigh, in his study of Elizabeth published in 1998:

The ecclesiastical decisions of 1559–1563 seemed to make no coherent sense, and the 'Elizabethan Settlement' had, apparently, settled nothing. But to the surprise of everyone except the Queen, the uneasy compromise was maintained and Elizabeth tried to freeze her Church in the form it had reached by 1563.

It is true that the religious beliefs contained in the settlement included elements of Lutheranism, Zwinglianism, Calvinism and Catholicism. However, the Thirty Nine Articles remain, to this day, the basis of doctrine for the Church of England. The organisation of the Church owed much to the Catholic model, with a hierarchical structure where power came from the top downwards from the Queen, through the bishops to the parish clergy.

On matters of administrative control and finance, the Church was firmly under the control of the monarchy. The Settlement could, therefore, be described as 'Erastian', with the State controlling both political and religious life. In this sense, it had more in common with the Lutheran churches in the Holy Roman Empire. However, not everyone accepted the precise nature of state control of the church. The historian Claire Cross, in her study of the Royal Supremacy and the Elizabethan Church, believes that the term 'Erastian' could be used in two ways. One body of thought saw the Church Settlement as a joint act by Queen and Parliament. Elizabeth viewed it differently. She saw the Church Settlement as created by her using Parliament.

The religious changes of 1559–63 were clearly Protestant but not enough to totally alienate Catholics at home and abroad. Both Philip II of Spain and the Pope hoped that England and Elizabeth would return to the Catholic fold. However, to many, the Settlement was not Protestant enough. Throughout the rest of Elizabeth's reign, and beyond, radical Protestants attempted to introduce more 'protestant' reforms, to make the Church of England a church of the 'godly' rather than a church born out of compromise.

1. What parts of the Elizabethan Church Settlement could be described as:

a) Catholic

b) Lutheran

c) Zwinglian

d) Calvinist?

Give reasons to support your answers.

2. The Elizabethan Church Settlement has been described as an 'Erastian' Church Settlement.

a) Explain the meaning of the term 'Erastian'.

b) Explain the ways in which the Church Settlement was 'Erastian'.

3.3 How far were Catholics a threat to Elizabeth I?

At the beginning of the reign, most people in England were still Catholic. In a study of wills at the beginning of Elizabeth I's reign, *The Stripping of the Altars* (1992), Eamon Duffy has shown that Catholic beliefs were held by large sections of the population. Therefore, Elizabeth and her Protestant supporters were faced with a difficult task in implementing the Religious Settlement.

Elizabeth also found herself facing a difficult situation in foreign affairs. In 1558, England was an ally of Catholic Spain against France and Scotland. Once it was seen that England had left the Catholic fold to become a Protestant country, Elizabeth expected opposition from across the Catholic world. Throughout her reign, there was a fear of foreign Catholic intervention in English affairs. The most serious threat came from Mary Stuart, who possessed the strongest claim to the English throne on the death of Elizabeth. As Queen of France, then Scotland, Mary acted as a potential leader of English Catholics against Elizabeth. This problem became serious following Mary's decision to leave Scotland to seek refuge in England in 1568 – and lasted until Mary's execution in 1587.

Popes during Elizabeth I's reign

1556–59	Paul IV
1559–65	Pius IV
1565–72	Pius V
1572–85	Gregory XIII
1586–90	Sixtus V
1590	Urban VIII
1590–91	Gregory XIV
1591	Innnocent IX
1592–1605	Clement VIII

What reasons can you give to explain the lack of opposition from Catholics to Elizabeth's religious changes, in the years 1558–68?

How strong was English Catholicism from 1558 to 1568?

At the beginning of the reign, the main opposition came from the Catholic bishops in the House of Lords. As the study of the Church Settlement illustrates, it was this group, rather than a band of radical Protestants in the House of Commons, who provided the main obstacle to the passage through Parliament of the Religious Settlement.

In the first decade of her reign, Elizabeth has been credited with adopting a moderate policy towards Catholics. This was due, in part, to the international situation where Elizabeth had to maintain English independence in a western European world dominated by France and Spain. It was also due to Elizabeth I's inability to enforce her religious settlement in all parts of the country. For instance, in Lancashire and Sussex the local gentry were Catholic, which protected Catholics from the effects of Elizabethan laws against them.

Although the period 1558–68 saw little persecution of Catholics, they, in turn, seemed to lack leadership and direction in dealing with the new religious situation. There was a lack of clear papal leadership. It was not until 1562 that Pope Pius IV made a statement prohibiting Catholics from attending Anglican services. However, this papal statement was not made known to English Catholics until 1566. This lack of action was partly due to Philip II's ability to persuade the Pope that England could be won back to Catholicism by peaceful means, through diplomacy. The Pope even had hopes that Elizabeth might attend the Council of Trent. It was only after the election of a new pope, Pius V, in 1566 that papal opposition to Elizabeth became more hostile.

To what extent was the Rebellion of the Northern Earls a Catholic revolt against Elizabeth's religious changes?

Mary Stuart arrived in England from Scotland in 1568. As the person with the strongest claim to the throne on Elizabeth's death, she was the focus of a series of plots and conspiracies against Elizabeth. The Rebellion of the Northern Earls could be regarded as one example of Catholic opposition to the Elizabethan Church Settlement. There is considerable evidence to support this view.

It has been claimed that the Northern Earls (Northumberland and Westmorland) planned to overthrow Elizabeth and replace her with Mary Stuart, who was to marry the Duke of Norfolk. The Rebellion began when both earls were ordered to go to London to face charges on this matter.

In *Tudor Rebellions*, Anthony Fletcher and Diarmaid MacCulloch identify strong Catholic influences in the people who launched the revolt. For instance, Richard Norton, sheriff of Yorkshire, had taken part in the Pilgrimage of Grace in 1536; while other agitators for rebellion, such as Thomas Markenfeld and Dr Nicholas Morton, had visited Europe and had become enthusiasts of the Catholic Counter-Reformation before returning home in 1568.

The proclamations made by the rebels also had a strong Catholic content and, during the rebellion, several actions by the rebels displayed their religious views. For instance, on entry into Durham on 14 November 1569 the rebels carried a banner displaying the Five Wounds of Christ. When the rebels arrived at Durham Cathedral, they celebrated the Catholic Mass and destroyed any evidence of Protestantism.

The area of the Northern Rebellions, 1569–70

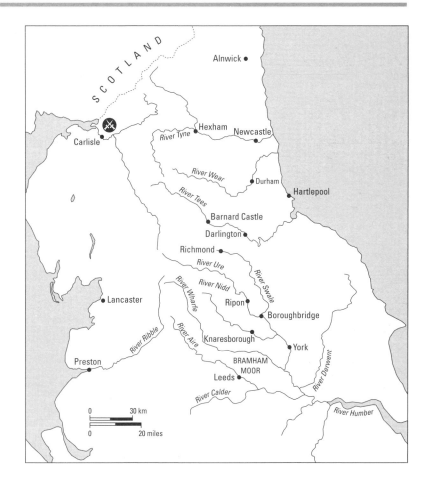

Papal bull: Decree issued by the Pope.

Finally, to coincide with the Rebellion, the Pope was to issue a **papal bull** declaring Elizabeth I excommunicated (totally cut off) from the Catholic Church. This was to encourage Catholics in England and Europe to take up arms against Elizabeth. Unfortunately, the papal bull, *Regnans*

The Pope excommunicates Queen Elizabeth I in 1570

1. What message is this illustration trying to make about the role of the Pope in the Rebellion of the Northern Earls?

2. How reliable is this contemporary illustration to a historian writing about the Rebellion of the Northern Earls?

in Excelsis, was issued on 22 February 1570 (see page 172) – after the Northern Rebellion had collapsed.

Overall, the Rebellion of the Northern Earls lacked organisation and direction. It began in early November 1569, but the main rebellion was over by Christmas. However, in January 1570, another rebellion took place. Lord Dacre raised 3,000 troops before he was defeated in the battle of Naworth, near Carlisle. Many rebels escaped to Scotland – such as the Earl of Northumberland who was later handed back to the English in 1572 to be executed at York. Although Elizabeth ordered the execution of 700 of the rebels, only 450 suffered that fate.

However, the Northern Rebellion cannot be seen as purely religious in origin. In the spring of 1569, the Earl of Leicester and the dukes of Norfolk and Arundel attacked Cecil's anti-Spanish foreign policy. Of greater importance was the opposition of the northern nobility to the increasingly central control exercised by Elizabeth's chief minister, William Cecil, over northern England. This was most apparent in Cecil's interference in the Council of the North (see Chapter 2). According to historian Lawrence Stone, in *The Crisis of Aristocracy* (1967), the rebellion was 'the last episode in 500 years of protest by the Highland zone [The North] against interference from London'.

1. What evidence is there to suggest that the Northern Rebellion was caused by opposition to Elizabeth's religious changes?

2. How far was the Northern Rebellion a Catholic revolt against Elizabeth?

3.4 How successful were Elizabeth's policies in dealing with the Catholic threat?

What policies did the Government introduce to deal with Catholics?

From the beginning of the reign, the government introduced a variety of policies to ensure that Catholics conformed to the new religious settlement. In the Act of Supremacy all clergy, and subsequently professionals such as schoolmasters, had to take the Oath of Supremacy recognising Elizabeth as Supreme Governor. Anyone who held that the Pope was still Head of the Church in England lost property for the first offence. For a second offence, the person lost all his property and was imprisoned. In the case of a third offence, the person concerned faced execution.

The Act of Uniformity placed a fine of 12d [5p] on anyone who failed to attend Church on Sundays and Holy Days. The Act also placed penalties on clergymen who failed to follow the 1559 Book of Common Prayer. Clergymen failing to follow the terms of the Act faced six months' imprisonment and the loss of one year's income for a first offence, one year's imprisonment for a second offence and life imprisonment for a third offence.

Although the penalties contained in the Elizabethan Church Settlement Acts of 1559 seem harsh by today's standards, they were not seen that way by contemporaries. In particular, the Acts did not provide the opportunity for the creation of martyrs who died for the Catholic cause.

However, the events of 1569–71 forced the Government into a harsher policy towards Catholics. The Rebellion of the Northern Earls was quickly followed by the papal bull of excommunication. In 1571, the Ridolfi Plot was uncovered. This planned a rising of English

A contemporary woodcut of the Ridolfi Plot against Elizabeth I. On the left, Catholic noblemen and a Catholic priest are plotting against the Queen. On the right, the Earl of Northumberland is being executed for treason.

1. What message is this woodcut trying to make about those who were involved in the Ridolfi Plot?

2. How far can this woodcut be regarded as a piece of government propaganda?

Treason: The crime of betraying your country, e.g. by helping its enemies or by trying to overthrow its king/queen. Historically, it is a crime punishable by death.

Jesuits: Catholic order of priests founded by St Ignatius Loyola in 1534 to fight against the Reformation. From 1540, the Jesuit Order came under the direction of the Pope. Jesuits were highly intelligent, well-educated priests. Their religious education lasted seven years. The Jesuit Mission to England aimed to convert all England back to Catholicism.

Catholics, supported by the Duke of Alva's Spanish troops based in the Netherlands. The plot aimed to depose Elizabeth I and place Mary Stuart on the English throne. It was uncovered by Francis Walsingham's secret service. The Duke of Norfolk was executed for **treason** in March 1572 and the Spanish ambassador was expelled.

The Parliament of 1571 not only approved the Thirty Nine Articles of 1563, it also passed three Acts aimed at English Catholics:

● The Treason Act re-enacted the terms of the 1534 Act, making it high treason for anyone to write that Elizabeth I was not the lawful queen.

● Another law made it a treasonable offence to bring papal bulls into England.

● A further Act made it an offence to leave England without permission for more than six months. Anyone found guilty was to lose all their lands.

However, these policies did not have the effect of ending either plots against Elizabeth or attempts to sustain and spread Catholicism. In 1574, seminary (college trained) priests from Douai in the Netherlands began arriving in England. From 1580, **Jesuits** began their mission to win England back to Catholicism. The Throckmorton, or Guise, Plot of 1581–84 involved planned invasions of England from Scotland and then the Netherlands in attempts to establish Mary Stuart on the throne. In 1585, the MP Dr Thomas Parry was convicted for planning to murder Elizabeth. In the following year, Anthony Babington of Derbyshire also planned to murder Elizabeth and release Mary Stuart from house arrest. Finally, in 1588, 'the Enterprise of England', the Spanish Armada, planned an invasion of England from the Netherlands.

The events of the 1570s and 1580s meant that policy towards Catholics was interlinked with policy towards Mary Stuart and foreign policy. These ultimately involved war with Spain from 1585. The parliaments of 1581 and 1585 wanted to take harsh measures against Catholics. Even though the Queen intervened to reduce the severity of proposals, two important laws were passed. The Act to Retain the Queen's Majesty's Subjects in their

True Obedience and the Act against Seditious Words and Rumours were aimed at priests arriving from the continent. Under these Acts, the Jesuit Edmund Campion and two missionary priests, Alexander Bryant and Ralph Sherwin, were executed in December 1581.

In 1585, in response to the influx of more catholic priests from the continent, Parliament passed an 'Act against Jesuits, seminary priests and such other disobedient Persons'. This made any Catholic priest guilty of treason. Of the 146 Catholics executed between 1586 and 1603, 123 were convicted using this Act.

Further legislation, passed in 1587 and 1593, increased fines for non-attendance at Anglican church services (recusancy) to the point where Catholic recusants were forced to stay within five miles of their homes. This prevented recusants moving to a different area to avoid paying fines. In addition, Royal Proclamations in 1592 and 1602 established commissioners to find Catholic priests, in particular Jesuits.

Government policy against Catholics, although initially mild, became increasingly harsh as Catholic issues became involved with foreign policy and the arrival of priests from the continent. In *English Catholicism 1558–1642* (1984), Alan Dures notes that 'by 1603 the rigours of Elizabethan government policy had eliminated Catholicism within the Elizabethan church, so that Catholicism was now a distinctive, separated religion'.

Given government opposition, why did Catholicism survive?

How important were seminary priests and Jesuits in the survival of Catholicism?

The English who remained Catholic after 1558 were many and varied. The most important were members of the gentry and their dependents, leading to what Alan Dures has termed 'seigneurial' Catholicism. This helps to explain why Catholicism was strong in certain parts of the country, such as Lancashire and Sussex. The Catholic gentry possessed the political power in a locality to hide priests and protect Catholics from paying recusancy fines.

Another group, identified by historian H.G. Alexander in *Religion in England 1558 to 1662* (1968), was composed of 'young men, many of whom were younger sons of traditional Catholic families; though unlike their fathers, they had left home to seek wealth either in London or military service'. Individuals such as Anthony Babington (**Babington Plot**) came from this group. There were also scholars who came to Catholicism from accepting its theology (religious beliefs). Jesuits like Edmund Campion and other Oxford-educated scholars come into this group.

Finally, there still existed in England 'peasant' Catholicism among the rural poor. Eamon Duffy in *The Stripping of the Altars* (1992) supports the view that the 'Old Religion' persisted amongst this group. The Jesuit Thomas Stanney noted the existence of this group in his tour of Hampshire, in about 1590.

During the first 15 years of Elizabeth's reign, the Catholic population was leaderless with little contact with Counter-Reformation Catholicism on the continent. However, from 1574, links were established. In 1568, William Allen founded a college (seminary) for training priests for missionary work in England. The first four seminary, or missionary, priests arrived in England in 1574. By 1580, the numbers had risen to approximately 100.

? 1. What events prompted the Elizabethan government to take actions against Catholics?

2. What do you regard as the main Catholic threat to Elizabeth? Give reasons to support your case.

Babington Plot (1586): This was a Catholic plot discovered by Sir Francis Walsingham. Anthony Babington and his accomplices planned to murder Elizabeth, free Mary Stuart and then make her Queen. This action was to be supported by Catholic troops from the continent. Mary Stuart's involvement in the Plot led to the decision to execute her in the following year.

Cardinal William Allen (1532–1594)
Educated at Oxford University; left England for ever in 1565. In 1568, he founded Douai College in the Netherlands to train seminary priests for the Catholic mission to England.

Edmund Campion (1540–1581)
One of the first Jesuits to reach England in 1580. Campion spent his time supporting Catholicism in Lancashire. He was arrested and executed for treason in 1581. Was made a saint in the 20th century.

In 1580, Robert Parsons and Edmund Campion were the first Jesuits to arrive in England. The Jesuits were highly educated and highly motivated catholic priests who aimed to win England back to Catholicism. These groups of priests worked closely with the Catholic gentry during their mission.

Much historical controversy has surrounded the role of seminary priests and Jesuits in the survival of English Catholicism. In a series of works, including *Elizabethan Catholicism* and *English Catholic Community, 1570 to 1850* (1976), John Bossy argues that the seminary priests and Jesuits were a major success in guaranteeing the survival of English Catholicism. Once the old Marian priests had either died or had been forced to submit to the new religious changes through government policy, it was the missionary priests who kept Catholic communities alive.

However, the role of these priests has been criticised more recently by Christopher Haigh in 'The Church of England, the Catholics and the People' (1984). He takes the view that the mission to England was not very effective. This was in part due to the geographical distribution of missionary priests. Most worked in the South East. For instance, in 1580 half the missionaries were in Essex, which had a relatively small Catholic community. Haigh contends that the priests should have operated in the North where most English Catholics lived. He also believes that too much emphasis was placed on looking after the Catholic gentry to the detriment of other sections of the Catholic community.

Although Haigh's views widened the historical debate on this issue, they seem unduly harsh. The missionaries arrived at ports close to the part of the continent where they had been trained – ports such as Dover (Kent) and Rye (Sussex). Many chose to operate close to London because the capital was an obvious focal point for activity.

Finally, the support of the Catholic gentry was of considerable importance to the survival of missionary priests. Without their support it would have been difficult for them to avoid capture by the Elizabethan authorities. Also, if Catholicism was ever to be restored as the religion of England, gentry support was vital.

How strong was English Catholicism by 1603?

By the time of Elizabeth I's death, Catholicism survived in England, in spite of government action. Between 1581 and 1603, 180 Catholics were executed for treason, 120 of them priests. Also, by 1603, the Catholic community was served by around 400 seminary priests and 12 Jesuits in England. Catholicism remained particularly strong in counties such as Lancashire, where it was supported by much of the county gentry.

It is difficult to know precisely the size of the Catholic community. One method of calculating the number of Catholics would be to find out how many were fined for being recusants. Recusancy increased during Elizabeth I's reign. For instance, in the East Riding of Yorkshire there were 40 adult recusants and 70 others who refused to take communion in the period 1570–78. This number had risen to approximately 200 recusants by 1590. However, this method is unreliable for several reasons. Firstly, the increased number of recusants might be due to an improvement in efficiency of the authorities, or their greater willingness to seek them out. Secondly, in areas of the country where Catholic gentry still possessed political power, the number of recusants may not have reflected the true

1. What actions did seminary priests and Jesuits take to win support for Catholicism?

2. How important were seminary priests and Jesuits to the survival of Catholicism during Elizabeth I's reign?

size of the Catholic community. This may have been due, in part, to a reluctance to convict recusants because of the heavy penalties facing them towards the end of Elizabeth I's reign.

Although Catholicism survived as a separate religion, it was not united. Beginning in 1594, a split became apparent between the seminary priests and the Jesuits. This was the so-called Archpriest Controversy. This was partly brought about by the uncertainty following the death of William Allen in October 1594. The issue came to a head in 1598 when George Blackwell was appointed Archpriest (chief priest) for England by Rome. Although not a Jesuit, Blackwell worked closely with them. The opponents of this development, known as Appellants, appealed to Rome against this appointment.

The issue highlighted a major difference of opinion about the nature of English Catholicism. The Appellants saw a direct link between the pre-Reformation English Church and the Catholic community of the 1590s. Their aim was to make Catholicism a tolerated religious minority. In contrast, the Jesuits wished to see a full restoration of Catholicism in line with the major developments in the Counter-Reformation in Europe.

In the final year of Elizabeth's reign, 13 Appellants had talks with the Government and were willing to sign a declaration recognising Elizabeth as Queen and refusing to support any Catholic invasion of England.

1. What problems did the English Catholic community face during the 1590s?

2. 'The threat posed by Catholics to the Elizabethan Church was grossly exaggerated.'

Using the evidence contained in this chapter, how far do you agree with this statement?

3.4 Why did Puritanism develop in Elizabethan England?

Who were the Puritans?

One of the biggest problems facing historians in their study of Protestantism in Elizabethan England is finding an acceptable definition of the term 'puritan'. At the time 'puritan' was used as a term of abuse for those Protestants who criticised the Church Settlement. Therefore, 'Puritans' included Protestants who possessed widely differing opinions. Some merely disliked certain aspects of the Royal Injunctions or the Thirty Nine Articles. Others were critical of the Church structure. Although they never formed a unified group there were organised groups which could be described as 'Puritan', such as **Presbyterians**. Patrick Collinson has quoted a 16th-century writer who described Puritans as 'a hotter type of Protestant'. In this sense a puritan could be described as a Protestant who did not regard the Church Settlement as the final reform of the Church. Although it is difficult to generalise, Puritans tended to come from the educated elements in society, such as lawyers, merchants and skilled workers. By the end of Elizabeth's reign, Puritanism was strongest in London, the South and the Midlands. It was weakest in the North and Wales. Puritans wanted a 'godly' or 'pure' church stripped of all unnecessary ceremonial. They placed great emphasis on studying the Bible and preaching. In religious belief they accepted the Calvinist views on predestination (see insert on page 51).

There has been some debate among historians about whether or not Puritans and puritan ideas helped to develop the capitalist economic system. At the beginning of this century, the German sociologist Max Weber, in *The Protestant Ethic and the Spirit of Capitalism* (1902), believed there was a direct link between radical Protestantism and **capitalism**.

Presbyterians: Those who believed that everyone should be forced to belong to a national church. The Presbyterian Church, unlike the traditional Church, had no bishops but a government of national and regional synods and local classes, run by deacons and elders.

Capitalism: Economic system based on the theory that possession of capital or money leads to the making of profits through the power of investment.

1. What reasons can you produce to explain why Puritanism developed during the reign of Elizabeth I?

2. Why have historians found it difficult to produce a precise definition for Puritanism during the reign of Elizabeth I?

1. Which parts of the Elizabethan Church Settlements did Puritans dislike?

2. What reasons can be given to support Puritan opposition to parts of the Elizabethan Church Settlement?

However, the historian M.M. Knappen, in *Tudor Puritanism* (1939), believed that Puritans were suspicious of capitalist methods and were very traditional in their views on economic matters.

When did Puritans begin to criticise the Church Settlement?

Although Puritans were unhappy about certain aspects of the Acts of Supremacy and Uniformity in 1559, the first major conflict with the government occurred in 1566 over the wearing of vestments – the Vestiarian Controversy. However, dissatisfaction among Puritans had already surfaced at Convocation in 1563, during the production of the Thirty Nine Articles. Puritans attempted to include in these Articles the reduction of Holy Days, the end of the use of the sign of the cross at baptism and a simplification of the vestments worn by a parson. These proposals were defeated by one vote.

In 1566, the Archbishop of Canterbury, Matthew Parker, issued his Book of Advertisements. These were designed to ensure conformity of practice within the Church of England. Although the Advertisements dealt with a variety of matters, such as preaching licences, the main issue was the vestments worn by the clergy. Parker insisted clergy wear a surplice and the cope (cloak). All Anglican clergy were asked to make a pledge to conform. However, 37 clergy in the diocese of London refused to obey. These were suspended from office and ultimately some were deprived of their positions.

The Puritans who opposed the wearing of Anglican vestments had influential supporters. Two heads of Oxford colleges – Laurence Humphrey of Magdalen and Thomas Sampson of Christ Church – supported by continental reformers Martin Bucer and Peter Martyr, regarded the Anglican vestments as too similar to Catholic vestments. However, the issue was not simply one of wearing vestments. It was also an issue of authority and obedience. Queen Elizabeth and Matthew Parker were determined to establish uniformity even though it created opposition from Puritans. Although the vast majority of Anglican clergy conformed in 1566, the issue remained throughout Elizabeth's reign. For instance, some of the London clergy who defied the Advertisements held services at the Plumbers' Hall, London until discovered by the sheriff's officers in June 1567.

3.5 What impact did Puritanism have on the Elizabethan Church?

Thomas Cartwright (1535–1603)
A Puritan who helped found the Presbyterianism movement in England. Spent time abroad, including being minister to the English congregation in Antwerp in the Netherlands. He was imprisoned by Elizabeth I for his extreme views on several occasions.

Why did Presbyterianism become a major issue in the 1570s?

On the continent Calvinism was spreading from Geneva to France, the Netherlands and the British Isles, in particular to Scotland. The British variant of Calvinism was termed Presbyterianism. This proved to be the first serious challenge to the Church Settlement from Protestants. The central issue was an attack on church organisation and involved considerable activity in the House of Commons. In the development of this movement, two individuals stand out: Thomas Cartwright and John Field.

The Presbyterian movement received national recognition in 1570 through Thomas Cartwright's Spring Lectures at the University of

---

John Field (1545–1588)
A leader of the Presbyterian movement. He was co-author with Thomas Wilcox of 'The Admonition to Parliament' of 1572, which put forward the demand for radical religious change. His death in 1588 was a major blow to the Presbyterian cause.

1. Why did Presbyterianism develop in England in the 1570s?

2. Why did Presbyterianism survive in spite of Elizabeth I's opposition?

Aristocracy: A Greek word meaning, literally, 'the government of a state by its best citizens'. The aristocracy consisted of titled families whose wealth passed down the generations by inheritance. About 200 or so families controlled most of the nation's wealth and dominated the social and political leadership.

Cambridge. He openly criticised the organisation of the Elizabethan Church into archbishops, bishops, parsons and deacons. In defence of his views, he used the example of the early Christian Church, which is described in the Acts of the Apostles (in the Bible). In its place Cartwright suggested the use of a Presbyterian form of church government which had been established in Geneva by John Calvin and by John Knox in Scotland. Instead of a hierarchy with the Queen as Supreme Governor, the Church would comprise separate congregations each led by lay elders who chose the minister.

Cartwright's views caused so much concern that he was removed from his professorship in December 1570 by John Whitgift, the University Vice-Chancellor. Cartwright's views found sympathy in the House of Commons, where William Strickland attempted to launch a parliamentary campaign in the 1571 Parliament in favour of Presbyterianism. Cartwright introduced a Bill that met several Puritan objections to the Church Settlement. He wished to reform the 1559 Book of Common Prayer making it more radical. He wanted to see the introduction of private baptism, a change in clerical vestments and an end to kneeling at communion. Puritans also attempted further reform in the 1572 Parliament. On both occasions, intervention by government prevented progress. In 1571, Strickland was imprisoned for his efforts. The next year, the Queen sent an instruction to Parliament preventing the introduction of religious bills not approved by the bishops.

Outside Parliament, a group of Presbyterians led by John Field and Thomas Wilcox kept up their campaign by producing a manifesto called 'The Admonition to Parliament', which called for changes in church government and religious practice towards a Calvinist model. For his efforts, Field received one year's imprisonment. In spite of the efforts of these individuals, Presbyterianism would not have developed without important political support. Presbyterians received sympathetic support from Ambrose Dudley (Earl of Warwick), Henry Hastings (Earl of Huntingdon) and Francis Russell (Earl of Bedford). The most important support came from Robert Dudley (Earl of Leicester) and Sir Francis Walsingham. To them, and other political sympathisers, the main threat to the Elizabethan Church Settlement came from the Catholic community and the development of the Counter-Reformation in Europe. The massacre of French Protestants, in Paris, on St Bartholemew's Day (24 August 1572) emphasised this fear.

What impact did Presbyterianism have in England in the 1570s and 1580s?

Even though Presbyterianism was supported by influential members of the **aristocracy**, its impact was limited by official opposition from Elizabeth and the government. Until his death in 1575, Archbishop Parker attempted to enforce the Church Settlement. Thomas Cartwright was forced into exile in 1573. Parker also used his power to interrogate clergy in London who were thought to be sympathetic to Presbyterianism. Several were subsequently imprisoned. Also, Presbyterianism had a narrow power base. It was centred on towns, many in the South East. With its emphasis on scripture reading, it was also limited to the educated classes.

Following Parker's death, Edmund Grindal was appointed Archbishop of Canterbury in 1576. It seemed that Presbyterian ideas would now receive more sympathy from the Elizabethan Church leadership. Grindal had a reputation for wishing to heal divisions within the Church and to introduce further reforms. Petitions were made to Parliament urging more radical Protestant reform.

Of greater significance was the development of **prophesying**. Elizabeth I saw these meetings of parsons as opportunities for Puritans to spread their views on the Church and wished to suppress them. This led to a clash between monarch and the Archbishop of Canterbury. Grindal was bold enough to write to the Queen stating: 'Bear with me … if I choose rather to offend your earthly majesty than to offend the heavenly majesty of God. Remember Madam, that you are a mortal [human] … Although ye are a mighty Prince, yet remember that he which dwelleth in heaven is mightier.'

Grindal's action led to his suspension as archbishop in 1577 and his forced confinement in his home. He remained suspended until his death in 1583. His duties as archbishop were performed by commissioners appointed by the Queen. Grindal was replaced by John Whitgift. Although he believed in Calvinism, Whitgift's elevation to the position of archbishop led to a concerted attack to enforce support for the Elizabethan Church Settlement. In October 1583, he ordered all clergy to subscribe to three articles:

● to recognise the Queen as Supreme Governor;

● to use the 1559 Book of Common Prayer, and no other;

● to conform to the Thirty Nine Articles of 1563–71.

This led to a backlash. Over 400 clergy refused to subscribe to the three articles. Influential lay supporters such as Lord Burghley (William Cecil) and the Earl of Leicester came to their aid. Following a petition to the Privy Council by 38 Kentish gentry concerning the lack of preaching in their county, Whitgift modified his second article. Clergy were now required to agree to use the 1559 Prayer Book. As a result, most of the 400 clergy agreed to subscribe. In early 1584, Whitgift introduced 24 articles to be answered under oath. The aim was to isolate and then prosecute the leaders.

In spite of Whitgift's efforts, Presbyterianism retained influence in the country. Under the leadership of John Field, Presbyterians began a concerted attempt to force through religious reform. H.G. Alexander, in *Religion in England 1558 to 1662*, describes the development as 'the first really effective pressure group in parliamentary history'.

In the parliament of 1584–85, Peter Turner attempted to introduce a 'Bill' and a 'Book'. The Bill aimed to introduce a new form of Church government based on ministers and lay elders. The Book aimed to introduce a set of religious beliefs based on the English edition of the Genevan Prayer Book. This parliamentary action was supported by extensive petitioning of Parliament on the issue from Presbyterians around England. These attempts failed. The failure reflects the power of the Queen and the Privy Council to control developments in Parliament.

The final parliamentary attempt to alter the Church Settlement came in 1587 by the MP Anthony Cope. His proposal was more radical than Turner's and coincided with the uncovering of the Catholic Babington Plot. The suggestion that the Elizabethan Church adopt the Genevan

---

Prophesying: Described by historian Patrick Collinson as 'universities of the poorer clergy', prophesying or exercises were meetings of lower clergy (parsons) to discuss religious topics. These meetings usually occurred with the approval of the local bishop.

Edmund Grindal (1519–1583)
Like Matthew Parker, Grindal was educated at Cambridge University. He was chaplain to Edward VI, but spent Queen Mary's reign in exile before becoming Archbishop of York in 1570 and Archbishop of Canterbury in 1576. Elizabeth I suspended Grindal from duty from 1577 over prophesying.

John Whitgift (1530–1604)
Like Parker and Grindal, Whitgift was educated at Cambridge University, where he became Master of Pembroke and Trinity colleges and Professor of Divinity. He served as Bishop of Worcester, before becoming Archbishop of Canterbury in 1583.

Star Chamber: Nickname given to members of the Royal Council who dealt with certain legal matters and some aspects of law enforcement.

1. **What actions did the Government take to limit the influence of Presbyterianism?**

2. **Why did Presbyterianism decline so rapidly after 1588?**

Separatists: An extreme group of Puritans who believed the creation of a truly reformed Protestantism could only take place outside the Church of England.

Prayer Book and abolish all the existing regulations and laws of the Church alienated moderate Puritans and ensured that Cope's attempt at reform through Parliament would fail. Cope and four other Puritans were arrested and imprisoned in the Tower of London for their criticism of the Church Settlement.

The impact of Presbyterianism should not be seen simply through its effect on the hierarchy of the Church or through parliamentary support. In the country at large the Classical Movement (from the Latin *classis* meaning group) developed in the 1580s. Beginning in the late 1570s, members of the clergy began to meet in groups or classes to discuss religious matters of common interest, such as the Book of Common Prayer. According to M.A.R. Graves and R.H. Silcock, in *Revolution, Reaction and Triumph of Conservatism* (1984), 'at their most developed they virtually set up local Presbyterian churches'. The example most quoted by historians was at Dedham, in north Essex, where they met on a monthly basis from 1582 to 1587.

The year 1588 can be regarded as the high-water mark of Elizabethan Presbyterianism. John Field, its most effective organiser, died. One of the group's most influential supporters at Court, the Earl of Leicester, also died in that year. Sir Francis Walsingham died in 1590. By the beginning of the 1590s, Whitgift faced little opposition from the Privy Council for his attacks on the Presbyterians. Also the threat from Catholic Europe seemed to be reduced following the execution of Mary Stuart in 1587 and the defeat of the Spanish Armada in the following year.

However, the decline of Presbyterianism was partly self-inflicted. The publication of the Martin Marprelate Tracts in 1588 and 1589 (seven in all) isolated the more radical Puritans from moderates. Published anonymously, these tracts (pamphlets) were an extreme attack on the structural organisation of the Elizabethan Church. Even Thomas Cartwright was shocked. They gave Whitgift and the government the opportunity to launch a concerted attack on the Puritan press. Government officials led by Richard Bancroft discovered secret printing presses. Using the Courts of High Commission and **Star Chamber**, Puritan leaders were arrested and interrogated.

Matters went from bad to worse with the Hacket Affair. Hacket, a Presbyterian leader, proclaimed himself the new Messiah (promised deliverer) in 1591. Although Hacket died in November 1591, the credibility of Presbyterianism was compromised. By 1593, the Presbyterian movement in England was effectively leaderless and clearly in decline. By 1603, the movement comprised around 300 clergy and some 75,000 lay members.

How did Puritanism develop in the 1590s? The problem of Separatism

The **Separatists**, also known as Brownists, were an extreme group of Puritans. In some ways the Separatists provide the link between Elizabethan Puritanism and the revolutionary Puritanism of the 1640s.

The first Separatist Church was founded by Robert Browne in Norwich, in 1581. Shortly afterwards, the congregation moved to Middelburg in the Netherlands.

As a movement, Separatism attracted only a small minority of Puritans. In 1593, Walter Raleigh believed that there were between 10,000 and

Although small in number, why did the government fear Separatism more than Presbyterianism?

1. By 1603, how strong was Puritanism in England?

2. Using the information from the section, explain how far Puritanism posed a threat to the Elizabethan Church Settlement either in the years 1558–80 or 1580–1603.

12,000 Separatists in England. However, its radicalism made it seem a major threat to the Elizabethan Church. As a result, the 1593 Act against Seditious Sectaries was aimed at groups such as the Separatists. In that year, Separatist leaders Henry Barrow, John Greenwood and John Penry were executed. Government action did not destroy Separatism, but it did force most of the remaining Separatists into exile in the Netherlands.

Conclusion

By the close of Elizabeth I's reign, Puritans had failed in their attempts to bring radical reform to the Elizabethan Church Settlement. However, the Church of England possessed a majority of clergy who supported the Calvinist idea of predestination but who rejected the Church organisation associated with Geneva. The Lambeth Articles of 1595, drafted by Cambridge academics, contained a strong Puritan theology. Although never officially adopted, they did reflect the religious beliefs of Whitgift. The issue of religious belief within the English Church would continue into the next century, with growing conflict between Puritans and those who adopted views of a more 'catholic' nature, the Arminians (see Chapter 6).

3.6 How strong was the Church of England in 1603?

By 1603, the Elizabethan Church seemed firmly established as the religion of the vast majority in England. Catholicism, which had been the religion of most of the population, was now reduced to a sect. In counties such as Lancashire, Catholicism was able to muster support across the population. In most of the rest of the country, it had become the religion of a small number of gentry.

The Elizabethan Church also survived the varied assaults of Puritans. What had seemed to many Protestants the first steps towards the creation of a 'godly' church at the beginning of the reign had an air of permanence by the end. Elizabeth I had consistently opposed discussion and reform of the Settlement in Parliament. MPs such as Strickland and Cope, who attempted to challenge this position, quickly found themselves under arrest.

In Elizabeth's drive to maintain the Settlement she had made John Whitgift Archbishop of Canterbury (1583–1604). This proved to be effective in enforcing uniformity. Whitgift was made a Privy Councillor in 1586. His use of the Courts of High Commission and Star Chamber effectively silenced the Presbyterian movement. However, the failure to allow further reform did create problems for Elizabeth's successors. Both James I and Charles I faced the increasingly militant demands of Puritans in the first half of the 17th century.

Elizabeth's impact on the Church went beyond enforcing the Acts of Supremacy and Uniformity. Using the financial aspects of the Settlement, such as the Act of Exchange, she was able to milk the Church of revenue, thereby undermining the authority of her bishops. According to Penry Williams, in *The Later Tudors, 1547–1603* (1995), 'by about 1580 the

1. What were the main strengths and weaknesses of the Elizabethan Church in 1603?

2. How successful was Elizabeth in dealing with the threats posed by Catholics and Puritans to the Church Settlement?

established Church had won control of the commanding heights of society'.

Did the Elizabethan Church provide the trained Protestant clergy to make the Settlement effective at parish level? In attempting to enforce uniformity, Elizabeth I had thwarted attempts to develop preaching, by her attacks on prophesying. Nevertheless, important development did take place. Patrick Collinson, in his study *The Elizabethan Puritan Movement* (1967), notes that two new Cambridge Colleges were established during the reign (Sidney Sussex and Emmanuel) to train clergy. By 1603, the Church had made moves towards providing an all-graduate clergy.

Source-based question: Catholics and Elizabeth I

SOURCE A

This very woman, having seized on the kingdom, and monstrously usurped [taken illegally] the place of supreme head of the church in all England, and the chief authority and jurisdiction thereof, hath again reduced the said kingdom into a miserable and ruinous condition, which was so lately reclaimed to the Catholic faith and a thriving condition. We seeing that wicked actions are multiplied one upon the other, as also the persecution of the faithful groweth every day heavier by the means of Elizabeth.

We do, out of the fullness of our apostolic power, declare Elizabeth as being a heretic and favourer of heretics. Moreover we do declare her to be deprived of her pretended title to the kingdom aforesaid [England].

We command all and every noblemen, subjects, people that they not obey her or her orders and laws.

From The Papal Bull of Excommunication [Regnans in Excelsis] *issued by Pope Pius V, 22 February 1570 against Elizabeth I*

SOURCE B

28 November 1574: The Queen has appointed commissioners who are examining the principal Catholics, bishops and others ... the substance of their examination being as follows:

If they recognise the Queen as head of the Church of England. To this they have all replied to the same effect, although examined separately, that they did not, and that the Supreme Pontiff [the Pope] is head of the Universal Church and the vicar of our Lord Jesus Christ. They were then

asked if they recognised the Queen as sovereign, to which they replied they did. They were then asked if the service in use in churches here, by order of the Queen was acceptable to God. They replied that it was not. It was performed outside the unity of the Church and [against] its sacred doctrine.

Each one had to sign his name to his confession for the information of the Queen and Council. People expect that severity will come of this.

From The Calender of State Papers *edited by M. Hume. Elizabeth I enforces support for her position as Supreme Governor of the Church of England, 1574*

SOURCE C

The government's first line of defence against Catholics at home lay in the ecclesiastical courts, whose proceedings reveal wide resistance to the settlement from an early date: there were many charges of recusancy and of refusal to take communion. However, the ... courts were inadequate to deal with the task of enforcing conformity. Many officials were sympathetic to the Catholic cause; the courts themselves were too heavily loaded with other business to deal with recusancy; and when they did act they were able to inflict only negligible punishments. The work of the ecclesiastical commissions established early on in London and York was more impressive: with spiritual and secular members, a brisk procedure, and the power to fine and imprison, they were able to bring effective pressure to bear.

From The Later Tudors *by Penry Williams, 1995*

Source-based question: Catholics and Elizabeth I

1. Study Source C.

Using the information contained in this chapter on Elizabethan Catholicism, explain the meaning of the two terms highlighted in Source C.

a) ecclesiastical courts

b) recusancy

2. Study Source A.

How, by its use of language and style, can you tell this is an official pronouncement by the Pope?

3. Study Sources A and B.

How far do these two sources agree on why Elizabeth I should be opposed by English Catholics?

4. Study Sources A, B and C and use information from the section on Elizabethan Catholicism.

'The Government faced major problems in trying to make English Catholics accept the Elizabethan Church Settlement.'

On the evidence of the three sources, and of information from this chapter, how far do you agree with this statement?

4 Elizabethan foreign policy

Key Issues

● *Did Elizabeth I follow a consistent foreign policy?*

● *How far did England's relationship with France and Spain change during Elizabeth's reign?*

● *What impact did Scotland and Ireland have on Elizabeth's foreign policy?*

4.1 What problems did Elizabeth face in foreign affairs at the beginning of her reign, 1558–1564?

4.2 How far did England's relations with France change in the years 1564–1603?

4.3 How did Scotland affect Elizabethan foreign policy?

4.4 Why did England go to war with Spain from 1585?

4.5 How important were voyages of discovery and colonisation during Elizabeth I's reign?

4.6 How did Ireland affect Elizabeth's foreign policy?

4.7 Historical interpretation: Who made Elizabethan foreign policy?

Framework of Events

1558	April: Calais surrenders to the French
1559	January: Philip II of Spain proposes marriage to Elizabeth
	April: Treaty of Cateau-Cambrésis with France
1560	February: Treaty of Berwick between Scottish Protestants and England
	July: Treaty of Edinburgh leads to English and French withdrawal from Scotland
1562	September: Treaty of Hampton Court with French Protestants
	November: Shane O'Neill Rebellion in Ireland
	December: John Hawkins leads slaving expedition to west Africa
1563	July: Treaty of Amboise leads to Warwick's surrender at Le Havre
1564	April: Treaty of Troyes with France: Calais stays French
1567	February: Lord Darnley, Mary Stuart's husband, is murdered
	May: Mary Stuart marries Earl of Bothwell, Darnley's murderer
	June: Battle of Carberry Hill, Scotland: Mary Stuart defeated
	July: Mary Stuart abdicates in favour of her son, now James VI of Scotland
1568	May: Mary Stuart defeated in Battle of Langside by Earl of Moray and flees to England
	September: clash between English and Spanish at San Juan de Ulloa (Ulua)
	November: Spanish bullion ships (the Genoese Loan) arrive in Plymouth and Southampton
1569	June: Irish rebellion in Munster
1570	February: Papal Bull of Excommunication against Elizabeth I
	Butler of Ormond Rebellion in Ireland
1572	March: Elizabeth refuses to allow Dutch 'sea beggars' to land in England
	April: Treaty of Blois with France
	August: St Bartholomew's Day massacre of Protestants in Paris
1574	May: Elizabeth renews Treaty of Blois
1579	July: Desmond Rebellion in Ireland begins (ends in 1580)
	Marriage negotiations between French Duke of Alençon and Elizabeth
1580	September: Francis Drake completes circumnavigation of the world. Union of Spain and Portugal under Philip II

1581	March: Irish rebellion in Munster (ends in 1583)
1583	February: failure of marriage negotiations with Duke of Alençon
1584	January: expulsion of Spanish ambassador
	June: assassination of William the Silent
	Treaty of Joinville between Philip II and French Catholic League
1585	May: English ships in the Atlantic seized by Spain
	English colony is established in North America
	August: Treaty of Nonsuch with Dutch rebels
1586	October: Mary Stuart is declared guilty of treason
1587	February: English troops surrender to Duke of Parma in Netherlands
	Execution of Mary Stuart
1588	July: Spanish Armada is defeated
1589	July: failure of Drake's armada against Spain
1591	August: Earl of Essex lands at Dieppe with English army to aid Henry IV
1592	January: Earl of Essex is recalled from France
1593	Henry IV of France converts to Catholicism
1595	January: beginning of Tyrone Rebellion in Ireland
	August: Drake and Hawkins lead expedition to the West Indies
1596	October: fears of Spanish invasion of England and Ireland
1598	August: Battle of Yellow Ford in Ulster: Tyrone defeats English
1599	September: truce in Ireland between Earl of Essex and Tyrone
1600	Founding of East India Company
1601	July: fear of Spanish invasion of England
	December: Battle of Kinsale: Tyrone is defeated by English army under Mountjoy
1603	March: Elizabeth I on her death bed announces James VI as her successor.

Overview

ELIZABETH I's reign of 45 years covered some of the most momentous events in English history. In the Oxford History of England volume *The Reign of Elizabeth* (first published in 1936), the historian J.B. Black stated: 'Few rulers have impressed themselves so forcibly on the memory and imagination of the English race as Queen Elizabeth I.'

The defeat of the Spanish Armada in 1588, the establishment of the first English colonies in North America and the extension of English influence over Scotland and Ireland, all laid the foundations for the rise of Britain as a major power by the early 18th century. How successful was Elizabeth's foreign policy?

The reign began with England at war with France. It ended with England at war with Spain. The reign also began with English military intervention in Scotland. It ended with English military intervention in Ireland. The war with France meant that Elizabeth began her reign with major financial problems. Lack of finance affected Elizabeth's foreign policy throughout the reign. In the final decade of her reign, with military involvement in Ireland and France and war with Spain, England again faced major financial and economic problems.

Elizabeth's reign coincided with the Catholic Counter-Reformation. Throughout her reign, Elizabeth feared a Catholic Crusade by France and Spain against England. Towards the end of the 17th century, England became a major European power. However, in the period 1558 to 1603 England was a second-rate power compared with both Spain and France. In the late 16th century, France had a population around four times larger than England. Spain controlled the Netherlands, Franche-Comté and extensive territories in both Italy and the

New World: The Americas (North and South) which had been discovered only a short while before (at the end of the 15th century).

New World (see map opposite). Fortunately for Elizabeth, France was affected by the Wars of Religion from 1562 to 1598, which limited the threat from there. Spain faced a major revolt in the Netherlands after 1566. The Spanish also had to face periodic threats from Ottoman Turkey, such as the siege of Malta in 1565. Both of these problems involved considerable expenditure by the Spanish.

The Netherlands, or Dutch, Revolt proved to be the issue that led to a war between England and Spain, 1585–1604. The Netherlands was an extremely important area for England for a number of reasons. Firstly, Antwerp was the centre for the sale of English wool and cloth, both of which were of great value to the English economy and the prosperity of Antwerp (see Chapter 5).

Secondly, the Netherlands occupied an important, strategic position from which an invasion of England could be launched. It was only 30 miles (48 km) from Dover and about 100 miles from the Thames estuary. For both reasons, Elizabeth I was determined that the area should not fall under the direct control of either France or Spain. It has been the subject of debate among historians whether or not Elizabeth followed a consistent foreign policy. On the issue of the Netherlands, Elizabeth supported the idea of its self-government throughout her reign.

An issue that also lasted throughout Elizabeth's reign was the succession to the throne. From the moment Elizabeth became queen, it was expected that she would marry and have children. However, Elizabeth never married. This had important consequences for foreign affairs. During the period 1559–87, the problem of Mary Stuart's claim to the throne raised major problems concerning religion and relations with both France and Scotland. Elizabeth also used the prospect of marriage as a diplomatic weapon to further English interests. At various times, she engaged in marriage negotiations. In the 1560s, the **Habsburg** Archduke Charles was a possible husband. In the 1570s, Elizabeth actively sought French suitors, for diplomatic reasons – in the form of the Duke of Anjou and the Duke of Alençon. By the end of the 1580s, Elizabeth was beyond 'marriageable and child-bearing' age.

Habsburg: Member of the Imperial family ruling Austria from 1282. The dynasty was officially the House of Habsburg-Lorraine after 1475.

Faced with warfare and military intervention on the continent, Scotland and Ireland, England's martial power changed considerably. The English army was improved through the creation of trained bands of soldiers. The lord lieutenant of each county was given the responsibility of raising the **militia** and providing military training. Although these forces were never seriously tested through invasion, Elizabeth I's reign witnessed this important development. Of greater importance was the development of the English navy into an ocean-going force. Although the number of ships over 100 tons only grew from 22 in 1558 to 29 in 1603, the improvement in the quality of English ships and gunnery was considerable. The war with Spain, after 1585, was fought not just in the Netherlands but across the Atlantic to the New World.

Militia: Part-time armed force raised in each county, usually when there was fear of invasion. The Lord Lieutenant had the responsibility of raising and organising the militia.

Duke of Anjou (1551–1589)
Henry, Duke of Anjou, was the second son of Henry II and Catherine de Medici. He was involved in marriage negotiations with Elizabeth I in 1569. Became Henry III of France in 1574. Assassinated in 1589.

Duke of Alençon (1554–1584)
Francis, Duke of Alençon, was the youngest son of Henry II and Catherine de Medici. When Henry III became King of France in 1574, Francis became the Duke of Anjou. He was involved in marriage negotiations with Elizabeth I from 1572–76 and from 1578–84. Anjou led French armies into the Netherlands in attempts to take Antwerp for the Dutch rebels. His last attempt, in 1583, ended in disaster.

North West Passage: Belief that it was possible to sail north of Canada in order to get to Asia. This was not possible due to ice fields.

Elizabeth I's reign also saw an increase in voyages of exploration. Although not as impressive as either Portuguese or Spanish expeditions, the search for the **North West Passage** and the establishment of settlements in Virginia (North America) laid the foundations for British control of North America by the mid-18th century.

Closer to home, Elizabethan policy towards Scotland and Ireland increased English control over the British Isles. Much discussion among historians has taken place in recent years about the aims of English policy in these two areas (see *Tudor Ireland* by Steven Ellis). However, what is clear is that the results of English involvement led to substantial change. Following Elizabeth's death, England and Scotland possessed the same monarch – James VI and I. Also, by 1603, the Gaelic Chieftains of Ireland had been defeated. In 1605, 'the Flight of the Earls' saw the leaders of Gaelic Ireland leave for the continent.

A number of important questions have been asked about foreign policy during Elizabeth I's reign. Did England follow a consistent policy? Who controlled or influenced English policy? Was it Elizabeth I? Or was it politicians such as William Cecil (Lord Burghley) or the earls of Leicester and Essex? What is clear is that foreign policy was conducted at a time when communications were very poor by modern standards. Letters to and from the continent could take weeks, if not months, to arrive. Knowledge of what was happening on the continent was also poor. Only a few ambassadors existed at the major courts in Europe by the late 16th century. Therefore, decision making was based on a limited amount of knowledge.

Europe in 1580

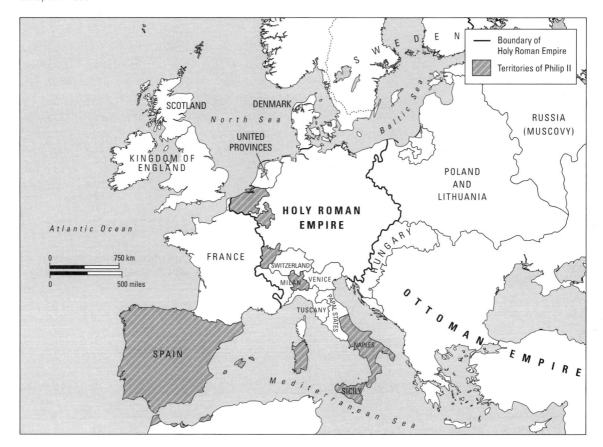

4.1   *What problems did Elizabeth face at the beginning of her reign, 1558–1564?*

When Elizabeth became Queen, England was at war. As part of an Anglo–Spanish alliance, England had gone to war with France in 1557. Although the war was brought to an end in 1559, because both France and Spain were financially incapable of continuing the struggle, the war will be remembered in England for the loss of Calais. As the last remnant of England's once-mighty possessions in France, the loss of Calais was more symbolic than material. The war also proved to be very expensive. As one contemporary, Sir John Mason, noted: 'our state can no longer bear these wars'.

Although Elizabeth was willing to delay the peace agreement until she had retrieved Calais, her ally, Philip II of Spain, wished to end the war. In April 1559, the Treaty of Cateau-Cambrésis ended the Habsburg–Valois wars. France retained Calais for a period of eight years. After that date, it had to be handed back to England.

Crown: A unit of currency. Worth about one-quarter of a pound (sterling).

If France failed to do this, they would have to pay England 500,000 **crowns**. Unfortunately for Elizabeth I her military intervention in France, during the First War of Religion (1562–64), broke the 1559 Treaty. Although English monarchs continued to call themselves kings of France until 1802, Calais was never recovered.

Elizabeth's problems were not limited to France. They also involved France's ally, Scotland. Britain's 'northern kingdom' had been allied with France against England, in the 'Auld Alliance', since the Middle Ages. The link between England's two opponents came closer in July 1559 with the death of the French King Henry II during a tournament to celebrate the Treaty of Cateau-Cambrésis. His successor was Francis II, aged 15, who was married to Mary Stuart, Queen of Scotland. Although Francis II was legally king, real political power in France was held by Francis, Duke of

Regent: Person who is given royal authority on behalf of another. It usually applies when the monarch is a minor (under age).

Guise, who was the brother of Mary of Guise, **Regent** of Scotland. The death of Henry II also coincided with the revolt of the Lords of the Congregation, which started the Protestant Reformation in Scotland.

In the years up to 1564, England intervened militarily in both France and Scotland. The intervention in France proved to be a failure, while military intervention in Scotland was successful. On 20 September 1562, England signed the Treaty at Hampton Court (sometimes termed the Treaty of Richmond) to assist **Huguenots** during the First War of Religion in France. This intervention may have been undertaken for religious reasons. The newly-crowned Queen was involved in re-establishing the Protestant faith in England. It might seem logical that she should aid fellow Protestants in France. However, throughout her reign, Elizabeth was reluctant to support rebels against legitimate monarchs. This was due, in part, to her own feeling of insecurity. She was regarded throughout Catholic Europe as the illegitimate child of Henry VIII and Anne Boleyn. One of Elizabeth's priorities in the early part of her reign was to establish her position as monarch.

Huguenots: French Protestants. Genevan Calvinists who settled in France were named after Victor Hugues and were known as Huguenots.

A more plausible reason for Elizabeth's military intervention was to exploit divisions in France between Catholic, and Protestant, in order to try to secure the return of Calais. The 1562 Treaty stated that England would give the Huguenot leader, Louis de Bourbon Condé, a large loan of 140,000 crowns and 3,000 English troops under the command of the Earl of

Garrison: To place soldiers in a town to protect it.

Warwick, brother of Robert Dudley, to **garrison** the port of Le Havre. The loan would be repaid once Calais was returned to England. Unfortunately, military intervention failed. The Earl of Warwick's troops suffered from plague while garrisoning Le Havre. English intervention also coincided with the end of the First War of Religion. A combined assault on Le Havre by French Catholics and Protestants captured the port on 26 July 1563. By the Treaty of Troyes (April 1564), England gave up all rights to Calais, which had been contained in the Treaty of Cateau-Cambrésis.

English defeat in France contrasted with success in Scotland. Scotland's alliance with France had always posed a major threat for England. For instance, while Henry VIII was at war with France, in 1513, the Scots attempted an invasion of northern England. Fortunately, an English army under Catherine of Aragon routed the Scots at Flodden. In 1559, French influence over Scotland was at its height. Mary of Guise was the Regent of Scotland. The French Queen was Mary Stuart. One thousand French troops were garrisoned in Leith, the seaport for Edinburgh, with a French expeditionary force of a further 9,500 ready to be sent to Scotland.

The politician most responsible for England's subsequent policy towards Scotland was William Cecil, the Secretary of State. Cecil feared a Catholic crusade against Protestant England, led by France. He was able to persuade fellow members of the Privy Council and the Queen to send financial aid to the Scottish Protestants. In 1559, England sent £5,000 in aid. The most important part of English policy was the decision taken on 16 December 1559 to send an English fleet, under Sir William Wynter, to the Firth of Forth to intercept the French expeditionary force. Fortunately for Wynter, the French fleet was severely damaged in a storm off the Netherlands.

In February 1560, the second part of English policy was completed with the signing of the Treaty of Berwick with the Scottish Protestants. Under the treaty, Elizabeth offered the Scottish Protestants her protection. The Treaty was followed by military intervention: 8,000 English troops under Lord Grey entered Scotland and marched on Leith. The subsequent Treaty of Edinburgh, signed in July 1560, was the crowning triumph of Cecil's policy. Both French and English troops were withdrawn from Scotland. Mary Stuart recognised Elizabeth as Queen of England and freedom of worship was allowed.

Elizabeth was not particularly happy with the Treaty of Edinburgh. She had hoped for the return of Calais. She was also concerned that she was being seen to assist rebels against a fellow monarch. However, the treaty protected England against attack from Scotland and helped to establish Protestantism there.

The military interventions during the early years of the reign illustrate important aspects of Elizabethan foreign policy. England did not possess the military power to recover Calais. The temporary religious divisions in France gave Elizabeth a 'window of opportunity'. Once this division was over, English military intervention was doomed. In Scotland, Cecil's swift actions and poor weather conditions in the North Sea brought French intervention in Scotland to an end. Through supporting Scottish Protestantism, Cecil had created a pro-English force which would lead eventually to the union of the two kingdoms on Elizabeth's death.

1. What were the reasons for English military intervention in both France and Scotland?

2. Why do you think England was successful in its policy towards Scotland and unsuccessful in its policy towards France?

4.2 How far did England's relations with France change in the years 1564–1603?

What factors affected Anglo–French relations?

France had been England's traditional enemy in Western Europe since the 14th century. In the early Tudor period, England had been at war with France on several occasions during the reign of Henry VIII and towards the end of Mary I's reign. The early years of Elizabeth I's reign can be seen as the end of one era of Anglo–French relations. The Treaty of Troyes of 1564 brought to an end English ambition to re-establish territorial claims in France.

English monarchs such as Henry VIII had sought to gain territory in France. English monarchs also feared attack from France or from France's traditional ally, Scotland. Fortunately for Elizabeth I, France was involved in a series of religious civil wars from 1562 to 1598 which limited its ability to exercise political influence outside its own territory. On one side of the conflict were Huguenots. On the other side, were Catholics who wished to eradicate Protestantism in France. This group was led by the Guise family. There was also a group of moderate Catholics who wished to rule France but were also willing to allow Protestants freedom to practise their religion. These were termed the 'politiques'. The most notable of these was Catherine de Medici, who ruled France as Regent during the 1560s and early 1570s. Anglo–French relations were affected greatly by this intermittent religious warfare.

France in the 16th century

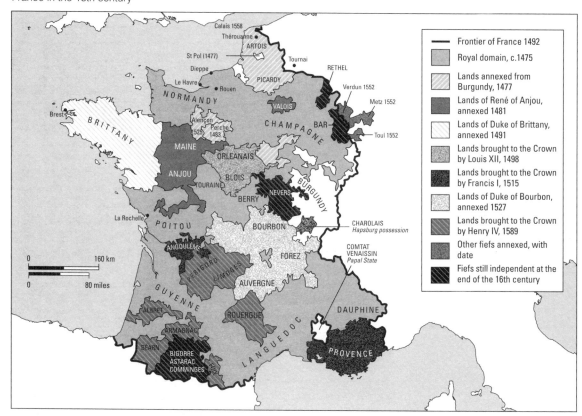

———	Frontier of France 1492
	Royal domain, c.1475
	Lands annexed from Burgundy, 1477
	Lands of René of Anjou, annexed 1481
	Lands of Duke of Brittany, annexed 1491
	Lands brought to the Crown by Louis XII, 1498
	Lands brought to the Crown by Francis I, 1515
	Lands of Duke of Bourbon, annexed 1527
	Lands brought to the Crown by Henry IV, 1589
	Other fiefs annexed, with date
	Fiefs still independent at the end of the 16th century

During Elizabeth I's reign, Anglo–French relations were also affected by events in the Netherlands. The English desire to keep the Netherlands independent from direct French or Spanish control was an important principle of English policy throughout the reign. The Netherlands was important to England both as a major export market for woollen goods and because it was regarded as a possible base for the invasion of England.

The issue of the Catholic Counter-Reformation was also important. A constant nightmare for Elizabeth I was the possibility of the creation of a Catholic Alliance of France and Spain against England. In this respect, the secret Treaty of Joinville of 1584 between the French Catholic League and Spain was a turning point in Elizabethan foreign policy. It was of considerable importance in forcing England into a war with Spain and hastening English military intervention in the Dutch Revolt.

Why did Anglo–French relations change in the years from 1564?

Following the Treaty of Troyes of 1564, Anglo–French relations remained relatively friendly. However, with the outbreak of the disturbances in the Netherlands in 1566 and the worsening of relations between England and Spain from 1568, Elizabeth attempted to improve relations with France. The major Elizabethan fear was the presence of a large Spanish army under the Duke of Alva in the Netherlands.

One ploy that was adopted effectively by Elizabeth for much of her reign was to use the prospect of marriage for diplomatic reasons. In 1569, Elizabeth began a series of marriage negotiations with Henry, Duke of Anjou (second son of Catherine de Medici). When it seemed that these negotiations were faltering, a second set was begun between Elizabeth and Catherine's youngest son, the Duke of Alençon. Although marriage never occurred, the two monarchies signed the Treaty of Blois in 1572. The Treaty committed the two countries to providing military and naval assistance if either were attacked by a third country (i.e. Spain). England and France also agreed to help bring peace to Scotland, which was experiencing civil disorder. It also gave England certain economic advantages concerning the export of English cloth.

The Treaty of Blois was almost stillborn. Firstly, the leading Huguenot, Admiral Coligny, persuaded King Charles IX to send a French army into the Netherlands to aid the Protestant rebels against Spain. This action raised major fears in England about French intentions in the Netherlands. Of greater significance was the Massacre of St Bartholomew's Eve on 24 August. In the following month, the Catholic Guise faction massacred 13,000 Huguenots. The incident plunged France into another war of religion, until 1577. Elizabeth I and her government were deeply alarmed by French Catholic aggression. It coincided with the Ridolfi Plot by Catholics against Elizabeth in England (see Chapter 3). Although Elizabeth was against formal intervention in France, she did allow English volunteers to assist the Huguenots in the defence of the port of La Rochelle, in 1573. In spite of these difficulties, the Treaty of Blois was renewed in 1574.

Anglo–French relations in the years to 1584 were affected mainly by the deterioration in England's relations with Spain, in particular the presence of a large Spanish army in the Netherlands. Given Elizabeth's reluctance to aid rebels against a ruling monarch and England's limited financial and military resources, English policy aimed at inducing France to intervene against Spain. After 1578, Elizabeth again used the diplomatic ploy of

Duke of Alva (1507–1582)
Born Fernando Alvarez de Toledo. He was a Spanish soldier and statesman (Governor of the Netherlands 1568–1573). He was sent at the head of large Spanish army to suppress revolt against Philip II's rule. He founded the Council of Troubles (known as Council of Blood) which condemned thousands to death without right of appeal. Replaced by the moderate Luis de Requesens in 1573 when Philip II wanted to adopt a more conciliatory policy.

Admiral Coligny (1519–1572)
Declared conversion to Protestantism in 1559. He was the leading Huguenot during the 1560s. In 1572, Catherine de Medici formed a plot with the extreme Catholic Duke of Guise to assassinate Coligny. The assassination attempt failed on 22 August 1572. This led to the Massacre of St Bartholomew's Eve when Coligny was murdered (24 August 1572).

marriage negotiations, this time with the Duke of Anjou's younger brother, the Duke of Alençon. Although Elizabeth was personally keen on marriage, the negotiations came to nothing.

Having failed to achieve French support through one plan, Elizabeth tried another. English aid was offered to the Duke of Anjou to launch an attack on the Netherlands. Anjou had attacked the Spanish in the southern Netherlands, in 1578, without success. In September 1580, in the Treaty of Plessis le Tours, the Dutch rebels offered Anjou **sovereignty** over the Netherlands. Although the English provided over £60,000 in aid to the Duke of Anjou, his lack of military ability led to defeat at Antwerp in 1583. His death the next year effectively ended English attempts to use French military intervention against the Spanish in the Netherlands.

Sovereignty: The legal claim over territory.

The turning point in Elizabethan relations with France came in 1584. The rise of the French Catholic League and its treaty with Spain at Joinville convinced Elizabeth that a Franco–Spanish Catholic Crusade against England was becoming a possibility. Elizabeth now accepted the idea of military intervention in the Netherlands through the Treaty of Nonsuch the following year. She also accepted the need to oppose the Catholic League in France by supporting Henry of Navarre, who became Henry IV in 1589. In that year, England sent 4,000 troops to aid Henry at Dieppe. In 1591, a further 3,000 troops were sent to Rouen. Finally, between 1591 and 1595, an English military force was maintained in Brittany at considerable expense. The aim of this policy was to help secure Henry IV's hold on the French throne. It was also used to deny the Spanish control of the French ports of St Malo, Brest and Dieppe.

Throughout the period 1564 to 1603, English policy towards France was dominated by concerns over national security. Either the French were to be used against the Spanish in the Netherlands or were to be supported to prevent the Spanish, or their French allies in the Catholic League, from controlling the Channel ports. However, the need to prevent France and Spain becoming allies against England in a Counter-Reformation Crusade was the main concern. The Treaty of Joinville of 1584 stands out as a significant factor in changing the course of English foreign policy not only towards France but also Spain and the Netherlands. By 1603, Anglo–French relations had changed considerably from the way they had been in 1558. France was no longer seen as the major threat to English national security. Both England and France, under Henry IV (1589–1610), had come to fear Spain.

4.3 How did Scotland affect Elizabethan foreign policy?

How important was the issue of national security?

Scotland affected Elizabethan policy in a number of ways. Firstly, since the Scottish war of independence in the early 14th century, Scotland and France had periodically formed the 'Auld Alliance' against England. In the 16th century, the two nations had been at war during the reigns of Henry VIII and Edward VI. So, by the start of Elizabeth I's reign, Scotland was an important factor in English national security. The issue of national security was made worse in 1558–1560 by the presence of Mary of Guise as Queen Regent of Scotland as well as by the presence of French troops in Scotland.

However, English military intervention ended when the Treaty of Edinburgh in 1560 brought French involvement in Scotland to an end.

How did the issue of religion affect Anglo–Scottish relations?

Another factor affecting Anglo–Scottish relations after 1558 was religion. Elizabeth I's accession to the throne coincided with the start of the Scottish Reformation. In 1557, the Band of the Lords of the Congregation was formed from leading noblemen sympathetic to Protestantism. It was formed under the leadership of Lord James Stuart (Mary Stuart's half-brother) and the Earl of Argyll. In 1559, John Knox, the Calvinist Protestant, returned to Scotland. These two developments led to the rise of Protestant opposition to the rule of the Catholic Mary of Guise. English military intervention, which led to the Treaty of Edinburgh, gave vital support to the establishment of Scottish Protestantism. The Treaty guaranteed freedom of religious worship. On 20 December, the first General Assembly of the Protestant Church of Scotland met in Edinburgh.

Elizabeth and her advisers realised that the success of the Protestant nobility helped to guarantee pro-English rule. However, as Susan Doran states in *England and Europe 1485–1603* (published in 1986):

> Elizabeth, after 1560, consistently demonstrated a marked reluctance to give financial and military aid to the Protestant pro-English party in Scotland. Only extreme pressure from her Council or men on the spot could induce her to give it limited support in 1570, 1571 and 1572. These were times when the threat of French intervention seemed to be greatest.

Esme Stuart (?1542–1583)
Created Earl of Lennox in 1581. He was responsible for the execution of the Earl of Morton for the latter's role in the murder of Lord Darnley. Esme Stuart was expelled from Scotland in 1582 for attempting to invade England to release Mary Stuart.

This policy of non-intervention was most apparent during the civil war (1565–68) between the supporters of Mary Stuart and her Protestant opponents. Also, Elizabeth did not intervene when the pro-English Earl of Morton was overthrown by Esme Stuart in the years 1579–81, even though Esme Stuart was regarded as a possible agent of the Guise faction in France. There is evidence that English money aided Protestant conspirators who kidnapped James VI of Scotland in the Ruthven Raid of August 1582. It is not clear whether Elizabeth was aware of this development.

However, Anglo–Scottish relations were improved greatly by the Treaty of Berwick, in July 1586, between Elizabeth I and James VI. Under the treaty, James VI was to receive an annual pension of £4,000 from England ensuring his political independence from France. Both signatories agreed to assist each other if either were attacked by a third power. Also, both parties agreed to maintain the religion followed in each state (i.e. Protestantism). Although the succession to the English throne was not mentioned, James VI's claim was not ruled out.

How did Mary Stuart affect Anglo–Scottish relations?

Mary Stuart, Queen of Scots, had a considerable impact on Elizabeth I's reign, both in foreign and domestic policy, from 1558 to her execution in 1587. In 1559, as the wife of the French king, Francis II, Mary was seen as a threat to national security as a possible agent of France. As a Catholic Queen of Scotland, in the 1560s, she posed a threat to the pro-English party of Scottish Protestants. However, Mary's main impact on Elizabethan history was her role in the question of the royal succession.

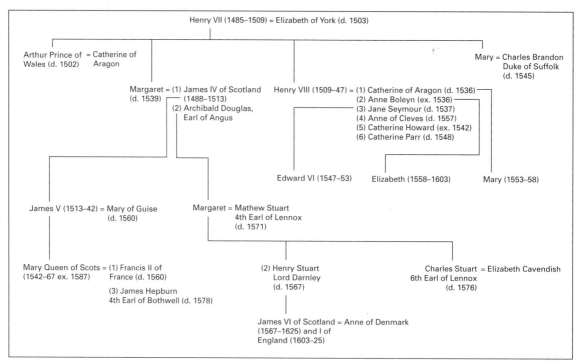

Henry VII (1485–1509) = Elizabeth of York (d. 1503)

Arthur Prince of = Catherine of
Wales (d. 1502)   Aragon

Mary = Charles Brandon
       Duke of Suffolk
       (d. 1545)

Margaret = (1) James IV of Scotland
(d. 1539)   (1488–1513)
            (2) Archibald Douglas,
                Earl of Angus

Henry VIII (1509–47) = (1) Catherine of Aragon (d. 1536)
                       (2) Anne Boleyn (ex. 1536)
                       (3) Jane Seymour (d. 1537)
                       (4) Anne of Cleves (d. 1557)
                       (5) Catherine Howard (ex. 1542)
                       (6) Catherine Parr (d. 1548)

Edward VI (1547–53)   Elizabeth (1558–1603)   Mary (1553–58)

James V (1513–42) = Mary of Guise
                    (d. 1560)

Margaret = Mathew Stuart
           4th Earl of Lennox
           (d. 1571)

Mary Queen of Scots = (1) Francis II of
(1542–67 ex. 1587)   France (d. 1560)

(3) James Hepburn
4th Earl of Bothwell (d. 1578)

(2) Henry Stuart
Lord Darnley
(d. 1567)

Charles Stuart = Elizabeth Cavendish
6th Earl of Lennox
(d. 1576)

James VI of Scotland = Anne of Denmark
(1567–1625) and I of
England (1603–25)

The relationship between Mary Stuart, Henry VIII and Elizabeth I

1. Using the family tree, explain the relationship between:

a) Mary Queen of Scots and Elizabeth I

b) Mary Queen of Scots and Lord Darnley, her second husband.

2. If you were a Catholic, why do you think Mary Queen of Scots had a stronger claim to the English throne than Elizabeth I? Give reasons to support your answer.

The issue of the royal succession was a dominant theme throughout Elizabeth I's reign. When she became Queen, in 1558, it was expected by nearly all of her contemporaries that she would marry. The issue of the succession became extremely important in 1562, when Elizabeth almost died from smallpox. In spite of its importance, Elizabeth I consistently refused to allow the issue to be discussed publicly or in Parliament.

Early in the reign, Elizabeth's infatuation with Robert Dudley (created Earl of Leicester in 1564) caused considerable disquiet among her advisers. This concern reached its height in 1560 when Dudley's wife, Amy Robsart, died in mysterious circumstances. Fortunately, Elizabeth did not marry Dudley. Instead, until the mid-1580s, Elizabeth used the prospect of marriage for diplomatic purposes.

In the 1560s, Archduke Charles Habsburg, the younger son of the Holy Roman Emperor, was considered. Differences over religion brought this potential match to an end. Also in the 1560s was the possibility of marriage to a Scot, James Hamilton. Son of the Earl of Arran, Hamilton was in line of succession to the Scottish throne. However, by 1566 he had become mentally unbalanced. The most important use of marriage negotiations involved during the period 1569–84 the sons of the French Regent, Catherine de Medici: the dukes of Anjou and Alençon (see section 4.2).

The main succession issue involved Mary Stuart. She had a very strong claim to the English throne (see family tree). From 1568, when she fled from Scotland to England after military defeat in a civil war, Mary became the centre of intrigue involving Spain and English Catholics. From 1568 to 1587, she was under 'house arrest' in England, mainly in Staffordshire. In 1569, the Rebellion of the Northern Earls aimed to re-establish Catholicism. Mary Stuart was to replace Elizabeth as Queen. In 1571, the Ridolfi Plot aimed to murder Elizabeth and replace her with Mary. In

1583, the Throckmorton (or Guise) Plot aimed to achieve the same result. The Babington Plot of 1586 showed a clear link between Mary and the conspirators in an attempt to replace Elizabeth with Mary, as the start to the return of England to Catholicism. In 1587, Elizabeth I finally gave her permission to issue an execution warrant against Mary.

A central question which has occupied historians is why Elizabeth showed a reluctance to take action against Mary Stuart, in the years 1568–87. Mary was clearly a major threat to Elizabeth. As long as Mary lived, she was to be the focus of plots by English Catholics and the Spanish against Elizabeth.

Most importantly, Elizabeth I was reluctant to take action against fellow monarchs. Many Catholic monarchs in Europe disputed Elizabeth's claim to the English throne. If Elizabeth had agreed to the execution of Mary Stuart she would undermine her own position. It would have given English Catholics more reasons for removing Elizabeth.

Linked to this first factor was the fear of French and Spanish reaction to the execution of Mary Stuart. The Catholic Crusade of France and Spain against England could have become reality as a result of Elizabeth's own actions. It was only after the 1584 Treaty of Joinville (see section 4.2) and the 1585 Treaty of Nonsuch that Elizabeth was finally persuaded to take action. In the Babington Plot, Sir Francis Walsingham had intercepted the correspondence between Antony Babington, an English Catholic, and Mary. Babington was acting as a go-between for the Spanish who planned to release Mary Stuart from house arrest through the use of a Spanish army. It was only after July 1586, when Mary had written expressing her approval of the plot, that Elizabeth allowed the trial of Mary to take place. In October 1586, at Fotheringay Castle in Nothamptonshire, Mary was tried for 'imagining and encompassing Her Majesty's death'. A court of 30 found her guilty. Even though Elizabeth I was petitioned by Parliament to execute Mary, she did not herself take action. Although Elizabeth signed the death warrant on 1 February, it was the Privy Council – in particular Burghley and Walsingham – who sent the death warrant to Fotheringay Castle, where Mary was executed on 8 February 1587.

Following the execution, Mary was given a royal funeral and Elizabeth talked of putting members of the Privy Council on trial for murder. She refused to see Burghley for weeks after the execution. The Secretary of State, William Davison, who took the death warrant to Fotheringay Castle, was imprisoned for a while in the Tower of London. The execution caused considerable disquiet in western Europe. It helped to cement the alliance between the French Catholic League and Philip II. However, England was already at war with Spain and Mary's death removed a major internal threat to Elizabeth. After 1587, English Catholics were reluctant to see Elizabeth replaced by a Spanish Queen.

1. In what ways did Scottish issues affect England during Elizabeth I's reign?

2. Explain why Mary Stuart was a major problem for Elizabeth I in the years 1558–87. In your answer consider the following issues:

a) national security

b) religion

c) relations with France and Spain.

(You may wish to consult Chapter 3 on religion in Elizabethan England.)

3. What do you regard as the most important issue affecting Anglo–Scottish relations during Elizabeth's reign? Give reasons for your answer.

4.4 Why did England go to war with Spain from 1585?

The dominant theme in Elizabethan foreign policy was Anglo–Spanish relations. From 1585 to 1604, England was at war with Spain. This war centred on the Spanish military presence in the Netherlands. However, the war also involved conflict at sea and in the West Indies.

Anglo–Spanish conflict played a part in the Tyrone rebellion in Ireland and military intervention in France, both during the 1590s.

For much of the early Tudor period, England and Spain had been on friendly terms. In 1489, Henry VII had signed the Treaty of Medina del Campo with Spain. The marriage of Catherine of Aragon to Henry VII's sons, Arthur and Henry, brought the Tudor and Habsburg dynasties closer together. In 1554, Mary Tudor married Philip II of Spain. This dynastic link involved England directly with a war against France between 1557 and 1559. Therefore, on the accession of Elizabeth I, England and Spain were military allies. The history of Elizabeth's early reign reflects the gradual deterioration of relations between England and Spain, to the point where by 1585 both nations believed war was unavoidable. Why did Anglo–Spanish relations deteriorate in the years 1558–85?

Why were the Netherlands an important issue in Anglo–Spanish relations?

When Charles V, the Holy Roman Emperor, abdicated in 1555 he divided his lands. Ferdinand became Holy Roman Emperor and ruler of the Habsburg lands of Austria and Bohemia. Philip II of Spain became ruler of the Habsburg lands in Italy, Franche-Comté and the Spanish lands in the Americas. He also became ruler of the Habsburg lands in the Netherlands.

The Netherlands was extremely important to England. On the issue of national security, the Netherlands was regarded as the natural invasion route from the continent to England. Using ports such as Antwerp, a continental army was only a day's sailing from the coasts of Essex and Kent. Throughout Elizabeth I's reign, England had followed a policy which attempted to prevent both France and Spain from gaining control of this area. Charles V, although ruler of the Netherlands, had allowed the area considerable self-government. Philip II attempted to gain more direct control of the area from the 1560s. Spain's military presence posed a direct threat to English national security. In many of the Catholic plots against Elizabeth – such as the Babington Plot of 1586 – Spanish military assistance from the Netherlands was seen as vital for their success.

The Netherlands were also important because of the outbreak of the Dutch Revolt in 1572. Anti-catholic disturbances had occurred in the southern Netherlands in 1566, a series of events known as the **Iconoclastic Fury**. However, after 1572, the Spanish faced open revolt from the provinces of the northern Netherlands. To Philip II and many Englishmen, the Dutch Revolt was an important aspect of the conflict between Catholic and Protestant. Within the English Court and Privy Council, influential members such as the Earl of Leicester and Francis Walsingham pressured Elizabeth to take action to assist the Protestant rebels.

Finally, the Netherlands was extremely important for English overseas trade. Antwerp was the European base for the **Merchant Adventurers**. This organisation had control over the export of English woollen cloth. In his study of economic and social history, *The Age of Elizabeth* (published in 1983), historian D.M. Palliser notes:

> The bulk of English exports consisted of wool and woollen cloth. For example, in the year ending Michaelmas [Autumn] 1565, for which figures survive, cloth accounted for 78% of all exports, and wool … and textiles of all kinds for over 90%.

Iconoclastic Fury (1566): Outbreak of anti-church riots in the southern Netherlands. It was characterised by the destruction of church statues and images.

Merchant Adventurers: A group of merchants who traded individually but were regulated (i.e. acted upon an agreed set of regulations). Together they shipped their cloth in fleets of ships, and displayed them at shows in Antwerp (before moving to Calais) on specific days. The Adventurers did not live up to their name: they pursued a safety-first policy of easy profits and they did not try to find new markets. However, they did control English cloth exports and operated a form of 'closed shop', stopping other wool merchants from trading.

It was because of the area's economic importance that successive English governments attempted to stay friendly with the Habsburg rulers of the Netherlands.

Embargo: Order preventing foreign ships entering or leaving ports.

When England's export trade in woollen goods to the Netherlands was interrupted, it caused economic hardship to both areas. In 1563–64, 1568–73 and 1586–87, an **embargo** was placed on English exports to Antwerp. This involved attempts to find alternative outlets. In 1564, the port of Emden, just outside the Netherlands, was chosen. In the late 1560s, cloth exports were redirected to Hamburg. However, the cloth embargoes came to show how important the Netherlands was to the English wool trade.

The Netherlands during the War of Independence

Why were the years 1568–1573 a turning point in Anglo–Spanish relations?

Excommunicate: To cut off totally from the Church in Rome; destined for eternal damnation.

During the first decade of Elizabeth I's reign, Anglo–Spanish relations were relatively friendly. Philip II hoped to keep England as an ally against Valois France. He helped to influence the Pope not to **excommunicate** Elizabeth I in 1558. To the Pope, she was the illegitimate child of an unauthorised marriage. In addition, when Philip II made the offer of marriage to Elizabeth in 1559, she declined. However, throughout the period up to 1568 Philip held out the hope that Elizabeth might return to Catholicism.

Elizabeth also wanted to maintain Anglo–Spanish friendship. In the early part of her reign, Elizabeth still regarded France as the main threat to national security. Also, as she established her regime, Elizabeth could not afford to become involved in conflict overseas. The lack of finance was to be an important constraint on an active foreign policy throughout her reign.

There were signs of future Anglo–Spanish hostility in the years 1562–64. The individual mainly responsible for this development was Cardinal Granvelle, Philip II's chief minister in the Netherlands alongside the Regent, Margaret of Parma. Granvelle believed Elizabeth I was involved in an international conspiracy in favour of Protestants. She supported the Lords of the Congregation in Scotland in 1560. She also signed the Treaty of Hampton Court of 1562 with French Protestants. In 1563, Elizabeth I allowed England to be a base for Protestant **privateers** to attack French Catholic shipping. In November 1563, Cardinal Granvelle placed an embargo on all English exports to Antwerp from London. He used the outbreak of plague in London to justify his actions. However, in December 1564, normal relations with the Netherlands were resumed following Granvelle's dismissal. This development was aided by de Silva, the Spanish ambassador to the English Court, from 1564–68.

Privateers: Pirates. Privateers sometimes received Letters of Marque which allowed them to fight for a country. Any ship they captured could be sold for profit.

There were a number of reasons why Anglo–Spanish relations deteriorated so rapidly after 1568. The most important reason was the appearance of a Spanish army of 10,000 in the Netherlands from August 1567, under the Duke of Alva. The army was increased later to 50,000. Philip II had sent the army into the Netherlands to quell the disturbances, which had begun in 1566. Such a large military force was seen as a threat to the national security of both England and France. The issue was made worse by Alva's 'Council of Blood', which executed leaders of the disturbances such as the counts of Egmont and Hoorn. To Elizabeth I and her advisers, if Alva was successful in defeating Protestantism in the Netherlands he might consider defeating '**heresy**' in England.

Heresy: The rejection of the doctrines and authority of the Roman Catholic Church.

Anglo–Spanish relations were also adversely affected by events within England. The arrival of Mary Stuart from Scotland, in 1568, provided English Catholics with a figurehead. The following year saw the outbreak of rebellion in northern England, which coincided with the Pope's decision to excommunicate Elizabeth in the Papal Bull '*Regnans in Excelsis*'. In 1571, the Ridolfi Plot was uncovered. All these events suggested that there was an international Catholic conspiracy against Elizabeth that involved the Spanish king.

Conflict over the West Indies and the New World also contributed to conflict. The main culprit was John Hawkins. In 1562–63, 1564–65 and 1567–68, Hawkins led three expeditions to west Africa to purchase slaves for sale in Spain's New World territories. These acts broke the Spanish control of trade with its own colonies. Hawkins' final voyage ended in a major Anglo–Spanish clash at San Juan de Ulloa (sometimes spelt Ulua) in September 1568, off Mexico. Most of the English fleet was captured or sunk. Many English sailors were captured. Both monarchs were determined not to allow Hawkins' expeditions to disrupt Anglo–Spanish relations. However, the issue of the Genoese Loan of 1568 did bring a rapid deterioration in relations. Historians have long debated who was responsible.

In November 1568, five unarmed Spanish ships, carrying silver bullion (400,000 florins, equivalent to £80,000) to pay Alva's army in the Netherlands, were forced by bad weather and fear of pirates to sail into Plymouth and Southampton. The Spanish ambassador to the English court, Don Guerau de Spes, obtained permission from William Cecil to transport the bullion overland to Dover, from where it was to be taken to the Netherlands. The bullion came from Genoese bankers who were lending the money to Philip II. Technically, the loan would not be made until the bullion arrived in Antwerp. In December 1568, Elizabeth took over the Genoese loan for herself. The event led to the seizure of English ships and goods in the Netherlands and the reintroduction of an embargo on English trade.

This issue had a major impact on Anglo–Spanish relations. According to historian Charles Wilson, in *Queen Elizabeth and the Revolt of the Netherlands* (1970), the actions of Elizabeth and Cecil were regarded as 'costly and senseless'. However, the blame for the incident may lie elsewhere. G.D. Ramsay, in *The Foreign Policy of Elizabeth I* (1984), claims that: 'In little more than three months de Spes, through sheer bungling, managed to wreck the ancient Tudor–Habsburg alliance.'

According to Ramsay, de Spes acted before Elizabeth took any steps to take over the loan. Cecil had met de Spes on 21 December 1568 to discuss who owned the loan. De Spes jumped to the 'wrong' conclusion that Elizabeth had already decided to seize the loan. He wrote to the Duke of Alva asking for permission to seize English ships and goods, which he did on 28 December. Elizabeth I retaliated by banning all Spanish trade with England. De Spes was dismissed from the English Court in December 1571. It also led England to seek a defensive alliance with France – the Treaty of Blois in 1572. Elizabeth I also began marriage negotiations with the Duke of Anjou, Catherine de Medici's son.

Attempts were made to mend Tudor–Habsburg relations. In 1573, the Convention of Nymegen reopened English trade with the Netherlands. The Convention of Bristol (1574) attempted to limit English raids on the West Indies. Elizabeth also expelled Dutch pirates (the 'Sea Beggars') from English ports, as part of the reconciliation process with Spain. However, the Sea Beggars attacked and captured the Dutch port of Brill (see map on page 89). This action led to the reopening of armed conflict in the Netherlands, which would eventually lead England into war with Spain.

The years 1568–74 are a turning point for several reasons. After 1574, England adopted a foreign policy position where it was independent from both Spain and France. Although in defensive alliance with France during the 1570s, England remained concerned about the action of what were seen as western European's two major military powers. From 1574, England's fear of Spain and concern over Spanish control of the Netherlands would lead a reluctant Queen towards war.

Alexander Farnese, Duke of Parma (1546–1592)
Italian, former ruler of state of Parma in Italy. Farnese was one of Philip II's most able military commanders. He became commander of the Spanish Army in the Netherlands in 1578, at the age of 32. He helped to recapture territory captured by the Dutch Rebels, the most notable being the port of Antwerp in 1585. The Spanish Armada of 1588 was meant to transport his army across the Channel to invade England. From 1590, the Duke of Parma fought in the French Wars of Religion on behalf of the Catholic League.

Mercenaries: Professional soldiers who sold their services to the highest bidder. They were therefore not motivated by any sense of loyalty to the cause for which they were fighting.

Why did England go to war with Spain in 1585?

Throughout the remainder of the late 1570s and early 1580s Elizabethan foreign policy was concerned primarily with developments in the Netherlands. The failure to pay the large Spanish army there led to the sack of Antwerp (The Spanish Fury) of 1576 which forced all 17 provinces of the Netherlands into open revolt.

Under the leadership of Don John and, from 1578, the Duke of Parma (Alexander Farnese), the Spanish began to win back territory in the southern Netherlands. Elizabeth I's main aim was to remove the Spanish army and return the Netherlands to self-government.

During this period, Elizabeth attempted to mediate between the two sides. This policy achieved temporary success with the Pacification of Ghent of October 1578. This called for the expulsion of all foreign troops. However, Philip II rejected the idea.

Elizabeth I also attempted to use foreign troops to aid the rebels. In 1578, she attempted to get John Casimir of the Palantine to lead an army of **mercenaries**. This did not happen. Finally, she hoped to use the Duke of Anjou to lead a French army against Spain. This also proved unsuccessful both in 1578 and 1581.

English policy was hampered by division in the Privy Council. The Earl of Leicester and Francis Walsingham were in favour of direct English intervention in support of the rebels. The Earl of Sussex was against forcing Spain into open warfare.

The decisive year in moving England towards direct intervention was 1584. The assassination of William the Silent in Delft removed the main leader of the Dutch rebels. In France the Duke of Anjou died, removing the chance of French military intervention. Then, in December 1584, the Treaty of Joinville was signed between Philip II and the French Catholic League. Not only did it seem that the Dutch rebels would now be defeated, it also raised the prospect of a Franco–Spanish Catholic Crusade against England.

These developments led directly to the Treaty of Nonsuch, in June 1585, between England and the Dutch rebels. Under the treaty, England would provide an army of 6,000 commanded by the Earl of Leicester. This treaty was a milestone in Elizabethan policy. Having tried to avoid war with a major power throughout her reign Elizabeth, at last, committed England to a war with Spain. The Treaty of Nonsuch is also significant because it was signed with a rebel force against a legitimate monarch. By siding with the Dutch, Elizabeth I had gone against a major principle which she had been following during her reign.

Why were the Spanish willing to go to war with England in 1585?

Elizabeth I was not the only monarch who wished to avoid war. Philip II also wanted to avoid open conflict with England. During his reign, Philip II had to face open revolt in the Netherlands. He also had to fight the Ottoman Turks in the Mediterranean. Both conflicts cost considerable amounts of money. Once Elizabeth had signed a treaty with the Dutch rebels, Philip had little choice but to go to war.

There were other reasons. Philip II also hoped that Catholicism could be restored in England. In this way he hoped to see Mary Stuart replace Elizabeth as Queen. On a number of occasions – such as the Rebellion of the Northern Earls 1569–70, the Ridolfi Plot and the Babington Plot – attempts were made to achieve this end. However, once Mary Stuart was executed in February 1587, this hope ended.

Philip was also concerned about the possibility of a new outbreak of conflict with France. For much of the period 1515–59, France and Spain had been at war. The French Wars of Religion, which began in 1562, weakened France militarily. Also, the rise of French Protestantism encouraged the Catholic Guise faction to seek allies in their fight against 'heresy'. The Treaty of Joinville of December 1584 provided Philip II with a French alliance.

Finally, with the death of the King of Portugal in 1580, Philip II became ruler of Spain and Portugal. It placed at his disposal a large ocean-going fleet, which would give him the means of fighting England.

How did the war between England and Spain develop, 1585–1604?

England's war with Spain involved armed conflict in the Netherlands, in the New World and Ireland. However, the most notable event of the conflict was the Spanish Armada of 1588.

The route of the Spanish Armada, June–September 1588

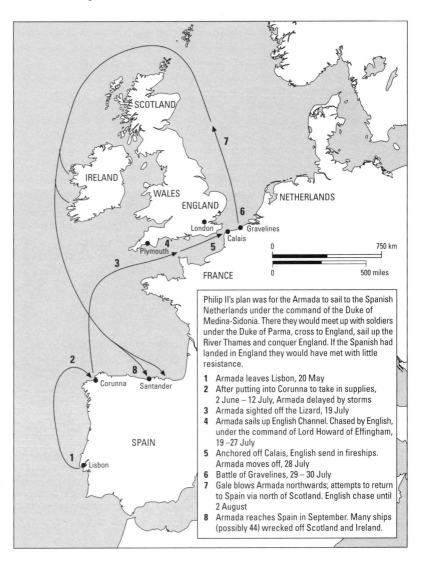

Philip II's plan was for the Armada to sail to the Spanish Netherlands under the command of the Duke of Medina-Sidonia. There they would meet up with soldiers under the Duke of Parma, cross to England, sail up the River Thames and conquer England. If the Spanish had landed in England they would have met with little resistance.

1 Armada leaves Lisbon, 20 May
2 After putting into Corunna to take in supplies, 2 June – 12 July, Armada delayed by storms
3 Armada sighted off the Lizard, 19 July
4 Armada sails up English Channel. Chased by English, under the command of Lord Howard of Effingham, 19 –27 July
5 Anchored off Calais, English send in fireships. Armada moves off, 28 July
6 Battle of Gravelines, 29 – 30 July
7 Gale blows Armada northwards; attempts to return to Spain via north of Scotland. English chase until 2 August
8 Armada reaches Spain in September. Many ships (possibly 44) wrecked off Scotland and Ireland.

Using the map and information contained in this chapter, why do you think the Spanish Armada of 1588 failed in its objective?

The Earl of Leicester's military intervention in the Netherlands created many problems for Elizabeth. In January 1586, Leicester accepted the title of Governor-General of the Netherlands. This suggested that the Dutch were independent from Spain. It also went against Elizabeth's aim of regaining self-government for the Netherlands under Philip II.

The Earl of Leicester proved to be inept as a military commander. The English army had no real experience of continental warfare. It also suffered major supply problems. Nevertheless, Leicester's intervention helped to prevent the Duke of Parma over-running the provinces of Holland and Zeeland. Although Leicester was recalled in November 1586, he returned in June 1587 with an army of 5,000 to prevent the Duke of Parma from taking the ports of Sluys and Flushing. The failure to capture a 'deep-water' port had important repercussions for the Spanish Armada.

The 'Enterprise of England', or Spanish Armada, has captured the imagination of generations. The 'defeat' of Europe's most powerful nation and the prevention of invasion are seen as one of Elizabeth I's greatest triumphs. However, in the conditions at the time, the success of such an expedition was unlikely. The initial plan was for the Armada to leave Lisbon and link up with Parma's army in the Netherlands. Then an invasion of England would take place, supported by English Catholics. Philip II hoped that the mere presence of such a large fleet would act as a deterrent to Elizabeth and force her to make peace with Spain. The choice of the Duke of Medina-Sidonia as commander is a case in point. He lacked experience for such a venture and asked Philip not to be appointed.

The geography and wind patterns of the English Channel also played their part. The English Channel is shaped like a funnel (see map on page 93). Once the Spanish fleet had entered the Channel, it became increasingly difficult for it to turn back if something went wrong. Also, the prevailing

1. What information about the nature of warfare in the reign of Elizabeth I does this woodcut reveal?

2. How useful is this woodcut to a historian writing about warfare at sea in the late 16th century? Explain your answer.

A contemporary woodcut of warfare at sea

Fireship: A ship laden with firewood. It was set alight and floated towards enemy shipping.

winds blow from the south west forcing the Spanish to the north east. In the naval fighting in the Channel the English Navy, with superior long-range gunnery, kept the Spanish from landing. The turning point came with a **fireship** attack on the Armada as it lay at anchor off Gravelines. Any attempt to land on the Netherlands coast was thwarted because of shallow seas and dangerous sandbanks. Once the Armada had passed the Straits of Dover, it had to go 'north about' the British Isles to return to Spain. Most Armada ships were lost in rough seas off Scotland and Ireland.

The Armada episode of 1588 was not the only attempt to launch a seaborne attack during the war. In 1596 and 1597, Philip II planned further armadas. This time the Spanish attempted to land in Cornwall and Ireland. However, rough seas prevented Spanish success. The Spanish did land an expeditionary force at Kinsale in Ireland, in 1601. This was forced to surrender after a siege by the English under Lord Mountjoy.

The English also undertook naval expeditions. In 1589, Francis Drake failed in an attempt to launch a naval attack on Spain. However, the English were more successful in sending expeditions to Dieppe and Brittany, in France, in the 1590s (see section 4.2).

Warfare was not confined to Europe. The English and Spanish fought an ocean-going naval war across the Atlantic and in the New World. The most notable success was Drake's attack on the Spanish naval base of Cadiz in 1587, which disrupted preparations for the Spanish Armada. Throughout the war, Drake, Richard Hawkins and other 'Elizabethan sea-dogs' attempted to disrupt the movement of Spanish colonial trade. By the time of Elizabeth I's death, England's involvement in the war must be seen as successful. The main foreign policy objective was national security. This was ensured. Although the Spanish had regained effective control of the southern Netherlands, they had not subdued the north. Secondly, the accession of Henry IV in France and the 1598 Edict of Nantes had brought to an end the possibility of a Franco–Spanish Catholic Crusade.

In organising national defence, major improvements had taken place in both the English army and navy. The creation of trained bands and the work of lords lieutenant had improved military defence greatly. In naval terms, the improvement in ship design and the administration of the Admiralty created a fleet that could operate across the Atlantic, as well as in the narrow seas around the British Isles.

According to historian Alan Smith, in *The Emergence of the Nation State* (published in 1984):

> There is no doubt that the Anglo–Spanish War of 1585–1604 was a decisive event in the struggle of Counter-Reformation Catholicism to suppress the Reformation. Elizabeth's intervention in the Netherlands and later in France made sure that neither Catholicism nor Spain would win a complete victory.

1. What were the main issues affecting relations between England and Spain in the years to 1585?

2. Why can the years 1568–74 be seen as turning point in Anglo–Spanish relations?

3. Who do regard as more responsible for the worsening of Anglo–Spanish relations in the years 1558–85: England or Spain? Give reasons for your answer.

4.5 *How important were voyages of discovery and colonisation during Elizabeth's reign?*

Colonisation: Taking over a new area to form a community politically connected with the country from which the settlers originated.

The 16th century was a period of exploration and **colonisation** by western European states. In the lead were the Portuguese and Spanish. Both states established vast new territories in the Americas. England, on the other hand, had become involved in exploration on a limited scale. In the reign of Henry VII, the Genoese explorers Sebastian and John Cabot had discovered Newfoundland. In the reign of Mary I, Sir Hugh Willoughby and Richard Chancellor had discovered a sea route north of Scandinavia to Muscovy. During Elizabeth I's reign, Francis Drake made a circumnavigation of the globe between 1577 and 1580. However, the main direction of English exploration involved attempts to discover a North West and a North East Passage to Asia. In 1580, Arthur Pett and Charles Jackman tried to build on the work of Willoughby and Chancellor in an attempt to go north round Europe to Asia. Trying to find a North West Passage, Martin Frobisher and John Davis attempted to discover a route west of Greenland and north of Canada. In 1576 and 1578, Frobisher made three voyages, without success. He was followed, in 1585 and 1587, by John Davis. Any study of a world map will show that both westward and eastward attempts to find sea routes to Asia were impracticable.

A dominant factor behind exploration was the development of trade. This became important with the disruption of overseas trade with the Netherlands. Following Willoughby and Chancellor's voyage, the Russia or Muscovy Company was created by royal charter in 1555. To exploit trade with Spain and its Empire, a Spanish Company was formed in 1577. In 1581, Elizabeth I allowed the formation of the Turkey Company to trade with the Muslim Ottoman Empire. This company was later merged with the Venice Company to form the Levant Company. In 1600, the East India Company was formed to exploit trade with the East Indies (modern-day Indonesia).

Even with these developments, by the time of Elizabeth I's death, English overseas trade was still dominated by woollen exports through Antwerp in the Netherlands. Over 70% of exports took this route, although English merchants were beginning to trade directly with Germany, Spain and the Baltic. The development of Baltic trade was increasing, with English trade usually in profit. The English did not make much impact on Mediterranean or New World trade, however.

Attempts at colonisation were associated with the war with Spain. The first English colonies on the continent of North America were established in 1585 and 1587. The individual most responsible was Sir Walter Raleigh. The two colonies were located in Virginia (America). Both failed due to food shortages. In the case of the second colony, no trace was ever found of the 150 original colonists. It was not until the establishment of Jamestown, Virginia, in 1607, that a permanent English colony was established.

To most Elizabethans, the idea of colonisation did not mean establishing settlements in North America. For the majority, colonisation involved establishing estates in Ireland. English involvement in Ireland was an important development during Elizabeth I's reign. The 1587 English colony in Virginia involved 150 colonists. By 1598, over 5,000 English settlers had begun to colonise the province of Munster in Ireland.

1. What changes took place in English overseas trade during Elizabeth I's reign?

2. Do you regard the search for new trading opportunities and colonisation as important developments during Elizabeth I's reign? Give reasons to support your answer.

4.6 How did Ireland affect Elizabethan foreign policy?

A survey of Ireland in 1558

English involvement in Ireland can be traced back to 1189 when the only English Pope, Adrian IV, granted Henry II the Lordship of Ireland. In 1541, the English link with Ireland was strengthened when Henry VIII was declared King of Ireland. However, by the accession of Elizabeth I English influence in Ireland was limited.

The area of greatest English influence was the **Pale**. This area was inhabited mainly by English-speaking people who regarded themselves as English. English law was in operation here. The area also had its own Parliament but, since the reign of Henry VII, Poynings Law had been in operation. This declared that the Irish parliament was subject to the English Parliament. The government of the Pale was under the control of a Lord Deputy, appointed by the English monarch.

In the north east of Ireland, in the county of Antrim, Scottish settlers had established a colony. The settlers were Presbyterian (Calvinist) Protestants (see Chapter 3). Most of the rest of Ireland was controlled by Anglo-Irish (The Old English) noble families. The Fitzgeralds were earls of Kildare and earls of Desmond. They controlled large areas of Leinster and Munster. The Butlers of Ormond also had large estates in Leinster and Munster. The O'Neill family dominated the province of Ulster. During the Yorkist (1461–85) and early Tudor period, these earls were used in order to control Ireland on behalf of England.

When English governments attempted to alter this arrangement, conflict usually arose. In 1533–34, the Kildare Rebellion affected much of eastern Ireland when Thomas Cromwell attempted to replace Lord Kildare as Lord Deputy with an Englishman, Sheehy Skeffington. Irish opposition to the introduction of Protestantism also caused the rebellion.

Pale: An area around Dublin (see map on page 98).

1. What evidence is there in this illustration to suggest that the Gaelic Irish were regarded as uncivilised by the Elizabethan English?

2. Compare this illustration with the engraving of the Earl of Essex (page 101). Which do you regard as more useful to a historian writing about Elizabethan England? Give reasons to support your answer.

A contemporary illustration of a Gaelic Irish chieftain eating a meal

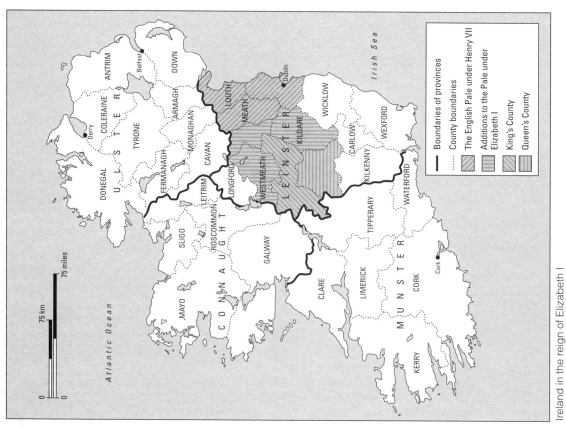

Ireland in the reign of Elizabeth I

Legend:
— Boundaries of provinces
⋯ County boundaries
The English Pale under Henry VII
Additions to the Pale under Elizabeth I
King's County
Queen's County

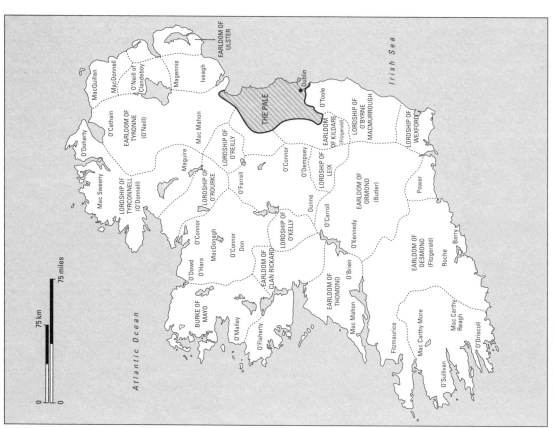

Ireland in about 1530

Brehon Law: The code of law that prevailed in Ireland before its occupation by the English. Brehon was an Irish judge.

In west Ireland, and within the area controlled by the Anglo-Irish families, lived Irish clans (families). Both the Anglo-Irish and the Irish clans spoke Gaelic Irish. In addition, the Irish clans possessed a different kind of land tenure that followed **Brehon Law**, not English law. Irish clans chose their chieftains and land was owned collectively by all the clan. Clans such as the McCarthy Mor and McCarthy Reagh lived in west Cork. Irish clans dominated the area beyond the river Shannon (Connacht and Clare).

In 1560, Elizabeth I was declared Supreme Governor of the Church of Ireland. However, Protestantism had made little impact in Ireland outside the Pale. The majority of the Irish remained Catholic. During Elizabeth I's reign, Ireland would be an area where conflict between Catholic and Protestant would take place. In 1579, troops financed by Pope Gregory XIII landed at Smerwick, in Kerry. In 1601, Spanish troops landed at Kinsale in Cork, to aid the Tyrone rebellion.

What policies did Elizabeth's predecessors follow to increase English control of Ireland?

Primogeniture: Land law in operation in England and Wales that allows the eldest son to inherit all land and property on the death of a father.

During the reign of Henry VIII, a new policy was used to increase English control. Under Lord Deputy Sir Warham St Leger and his 'right-hand' man, Thomas Cusack, the policy of 'surrender and regrant' was introduced in the 1540s. Under this policy, Gaelic chieftains would surrender their clan titles and then receive English titles. Land law for the clan would change from Brehon Law to the English law of **primogeniture**. For instance, in 1543 the O'Brien chieftain was given the title of Earl of Thomond while Burke became Earl of Clanrickard. However, this policy was abandoned in 1556 by Thomas Radcliffe (Earl of Sussex), who was Lord Deputy 1556–60 and Lord Lieutenant from 1560 to 1564.

The Earl of Sussex adopted a more aggressive policy, which sought to increase English control through colonisation. Two areas in central Ireland – termed King's and Queen's counties – were created from the Gaelic counties of Offlay and Leix. But it wasn't until 1563 that settlers began to arrive in this area. Unfortunately, the colonies did not prove popular. The Earl of Sussex also aimed to limit the power of the main Anglo-Irish chieftains such as Kildare and O'Neill.

What policies did Elizabeth follow towards Ireland in the years to 1567?

Guerrilla warfare: A style of campaign fought against a regular army by a small bands of armed men and women. Their tactics are generally to exploit their knowledge of the local area to undermine the enemy.

For the first 20 years of her reign, Elizabeth I's government followed the policy laid down by the Earl of Sussex and carried on by his successor, Sir Henry Sidney. This policy led to open rebellion by the Anglo-Irish and Irish. Unfortunately, the policy failed to take into consideration the finance and military support needed to make it a success.

The most immediate problem facing Elizabeth I was Shane O'Neill's rebellion in Ulster, which had begun in 1558 shortly before her accession to the throne. Shane had rebelled because the title of Earl of Tyrone had been given to his illegitimate half-brother, Matthew. The Earl of Sussex failed to defeat Shane O'Neill militarily. His army was insufficient for the task. Also, the Irish adopted a **guerrilla warfare**-style campaign. By 1563, a treaty was signed between Elizabeth and O'Neill giving the latter effective control over Ulster. However, Sir Henry Sidney was more successful. In 1566, he raided Ulster and captured several O'Neill strongholds.

Sidney's presence encouraged others to stand up to the O'Neill's. Shane became involved in a feud with a lesser Irish clan in Ulster, the O'Donnells of Tyrconnell (modern-day Donegal). Having suffered defeat at the battle of Farsetmore in 1567, Shane was killed by the MacDonalds (Scottish settlers in Antrim).

The removal of Shane O'Neill gave Elizabeth the opportunity to follow a policy that was a central feature of her Irish policy: colonisation.

How successful was the policy of colonisation in Ireland?

From 1569, English policy involved the encouragement of settlers (The New English) with grants of land. These plantations would provide the basis for future English control. Although the Dublin Parliament was generally against this policy, grants of land were made to Sir Peter Carew and Sir Warham St Leger in Munster. In 1571, Sir Thomas Smith was granted land in east Ulster (modern-day Down).

The immediate effect of this policy was to spark off rebellion in Munster by Butler and James Fitzmaurice Fitzgerald. Although the rebellions were put down by 1572, Fitzmaurice returned with foreign troops in the period 1579–82 to lead another rebellion with the support of the Earl of Desmond. Only after this rebellion was defeated did the 'plantation' of colonists in Munster begin to take place in any numbers, many to lands confiscated from the Earl of Desmond. Although 15,000 colonists were intended for Munster, by the end of the century only 4,000 had taken residence.

Tudor plantations in Ireland

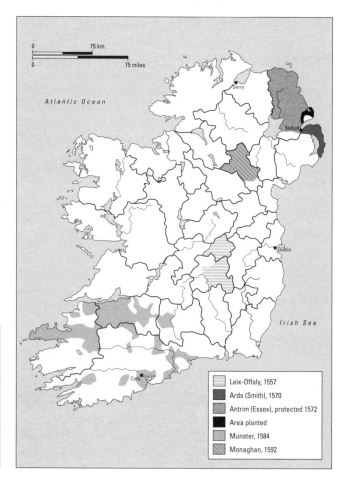

Use the information in this section. How far was there a connection between the plantation of English colonists in Ireland and Irish revolts against English rule?

How serious was the Tyrone Rebellion of 1595–1603?

In *Tudor Ireland* (1985), the historian Steven Ellis states that English policy towards Ireland can be seen as a failure. Indeed, Elizabeth I's Irish policies for much of her reign were not successful. Her government failed to provide the Lord Deputy and the English administration in Dublin with sufficient resources to make her policies a success. The plan to increase control through colonisation was of limited success in Munster and failed to develop in Ulster. This policy created resentment among the Anglo-Irish, which resulted in intermittent rebellion.

The most serious problem Elizabeth faced came during the latter part of her reign. The Tyrone Rebellion almost brought English rule in Ireland to an end. Its defeat, ironically, led to the Tudor conquest and control over the whole island. This was achieved at considerable financial expense and through major military involvement.

The rebellion came when Hugh O'Neill (Earl of Tyrone) was able to gain effective control over Ulster. He arranged a marriage alliance with his traditional enemies, the O'Donnells of Tyrconnell. Then, following the death of Turlough O'Neill, Hugh became undisputed leader of his clan. He also possessed considerable military might. According to historian Penry Williams, in *The Later Tudors* (1995), 'He [O'Neill] posed a greater threat to the English presence in Ireland than any Irish lord of the century.' O'Neill commanded an army of 1,000 cavalry and 5,000 infantry of which

Robert Devereux, 2nd Earl of Essex (1566–1601) from a contemporary engraving by Robert Boissard

1. What message is this engraving trying to give about the Earl of Essex as a military commander?

2. Use the information contained within this chapter. How far do you think the Earl of Essex was an effective military commander?

Hugh O'Neill, Earl of Tyrone (?1540–1616)

Second son of Matthew O'Neill. Created Earl of Tyrone in 1584. Became chief of the O'Neills in 1595. With Owen Roe O'Donnell, he led Irish opposition to English rule. Following defeat at Kinsale (1601–02), Hugh O'Neill fled Ireland. He died in Rome.

1. What were the main aspects of Elizabethan policy towards Ireland?

2. How did Elizabeth's policy towards Ireland differ from that of her predecessors?

3. Why do you think it took so long for the English to gain control of Ireland during Elizabeth I's reign?

4,000 were musketeers. He also sought military aid from Spain. Only bad weather in 1597 prevented a Spanish armada landing in Ireland.

O'Neill's Rebellion took place during the war with Spain and during a period of considerable economic hardship in England brought on by successive harvest failures in the mid-1590s (see Chapter 5).

O'Neill had several spectacular military successes over the English. In the battle of the Yellow Ford, in 1598, he defeated an English army of 4,000. The victory allowed O'Neill and his allies to occupy most of Connacht and Leinster. It also forced Elizabeth I to take more effective action. Her government raised an army of 17,000. Unfortunately, she chose the Earl of Essex to lead it. In 1599, his campaign against O'Neill ended in disaster. His army suffered military defeat and mass desertion, forcing the Earl of Essex to demand a truce from O'Neill. Essex's defeat and his loss of prestige at Court led to an attempted coup, which led to his execution in 1601.

Fortunately for Elizabeth, the appointment of Charles Blount (Lord Mountjoy) to the position of Lord Deputy, in 1600, proved a turning point in English fortunes. With an army of 13,000, he outnumbered and outmanoeuvred O'Neill. The decisive engagement came at Kinsale where Mountjoy defeated O'Neill and a Spanish expeditionary force in December 1601. The defeat brought to an end the resistance of Gaelic Ireland to English rule. O'Neill and other Gaelic chiefs left Ireland for Spain in 1605 (the 'Flight of the Earls').

The Tyrone Rebellion illustrated a major problem for English policy. Only with major financial and military resources could England gain effective control over Ireland.

4.7 Who made Elizabethan foreign policy?
A CASE STUDY IN HISTORICAL INTERPRETATION

Historians such as William Camden, J.E. Neale and A.L. Rowse tended to see the reign of Elizabeth I as an age of greatness, when England began to establish itself as a leading power in western Europe. However, when Elizabeth became Queen in 1558 she possessed little knowledge or understanding of foreign affairs. An important question posed by historians of the Tudor period is: who made Elizabethan foreign policy?

Part of the problem is the limited amount of primary evidence available to the historian. The main sources of information are:

● State Papers and correspondence between the Queen and her principal advisers. However, the coverage they give is limited.

● treaties and correspondence between England and foreign powers;

● reports by ambassadors, either English ambassadors abroad or foreign ambassadors at the English Court. However, there are questions of reliability concerning these reports.

Throughout her reign, Elizabeth found it difficult to find suitable individuals to act as ambassadors. John Man, the English representative at the Spanish Court until 1567, was a noted anti-Catholic who regarded the Pope as Antichrist. Also George Gilpin, who was once secretary to the Merchant Adventurers, was likely to issue reports which reflected his economic interests. Similarly, the quality of foreign representatives at the English Court was open to question. Don Guerau de Spes, the representative of Spain from 1568 to 1571, was unfamiliar with England. He reported to Philip II that the Principal Secretary, William Cecil, was a 'bare-faced' heretic. The most reliable foreign reports were those of the Venetian representative to the Doge (ruler) of Venice.

Foreign policy was traditionally controlled by the monarch. Throughout her reign, Elizabeth I played a full and active role in foreign affairs. Her employment of the prospect of marriage to a foreign prince is a case in point. However, the day-to-day running of foreign affairs was handled by her Principal Secretary. Until 1572, foreign affairs were handled by William Cecil. He played a major role in deciding policy towards Scotland in the years 1558–60. From 1573 to 1587, Sir Francis Walsingham filled this role, although Cecil still possessed influence in foreign affairs. During the latter part of Elizabeth I's reign, foreign affairs were again handled by William Cecil (now Lord Burghley). After his death, they were handled by his son, Robert Cecil.

The Principal Secretary received reports from English agents and representatives abroad. Apart from news from formal representatives at some of the leading European Courts, reports were received from English ships, trading companies such as the Muscovy Company and the Merchant Adventurers, and English agents such as the one placed at St Jean-de-Luz on the border between France and Spain. Problems of communication made a regular flow of quality information difficult.

Outside the formal structure dealing with foreign affairs there were other influences. For instance, throughout her reign Elizabeth faced the problem of differing factions at Court. Considerable debate took place on the issue of the Dutch Revolt between Cecil, who favoured a cautious approach, and the Earl of Leicester who wanted more intervention to support fellow Protestants. Similar splits over foreign affairs appeared in the 1590s between Robert Cecil and the Earl of Essex.

Occasionally, the full Privy Council was consulted about foreign affairs. In *The Making of Elizabethan Foreign Policy 1558–1603* (1990), the historian Richard Wernham notes that Elizabeth did this in December 1559 before intervening in Scotland. In June 1565, she also consulted the Privy Council about English policy towards the marriage of Mary Stuart to Lord Darnley and again over Dutch policy following the assassination of William the Silent in 1584.

Elizabethan Parliaments played a very limited role in foreign affairs. This was due, in part, to the short amount of time Parliament was in session during Elizabeth's reign. However, Parliament did discuss the issue of the succession in 1566 and of Mary Stuart in 1572.

Considerable debate has taken place between historians about the aims and objectives of Elizabethan foreign policy, in particular concerning policy towards the Netherlands. In *Tudor Foreign Policy* (1973), P.S. Crowson states that 'the 45 years of Elizabeth's reign was a time of pessimism, of insecurity and of agonising national danger under the overshadowing power first of France and then of Spain'.

Given England's limited financial and military resources, it would seem that Elizabeth would want to avoid conflict in foreign affairs. In *Queen Elizabeth and the Revolt in the Netherlands*, Charles Wilson believes that Elizabeth adopted a very reactive foreign policy. She merely reacted to events without having any overall aim or objective. For instance, Wilson believes that Elizabeth suffered from an irrational fear of France which did not take into account the disruption caused by the French Wars of Religion. The clearest example of Elizabeth's lack of policy was her handling of the Netherlands issue. Wilson regards her policy as a failure.

On the other hand, Richard Wernham, in *Before the Armada* (1966), believes Elizabeth had clear aims and objectives. On the issue of the Netherlands, Wernham identifies three aims:

● to remove the Spanish army;

● to prevent France gaining control of the Netherlands;

● to return the Netherlands to self-government which it had experienced under Charles V.

However, given its limited military and financial resources, England was restricted in what it could do in foreign affairs.

Perhaps Elizabeth I's foreign policy was not quite 'an age of greatness', as seen by William Camden in 1617 (when he subtitled his *Annales* 'The True and Royall History of the famous Empresse Elizabeth, Queene of England, France and Ireland … of Divine Renown and Happy Memory') and some later historians. However, Elizabeth I had to operate within the constraints of finance and resources permitted for a nation of three million in a western Europe dominated by France and Spain in the era of the Catholic Counter-Reformation. As the Richard Wernham notes in *The Making of Elizabethan Foreign Policy* (1980): 'National policy … was shaped quite as much by circumstances as by the will of the Queen or the persuasions of her privy councillors or the interests of commerce or the pressures of religion.'

If the main aim of foreign policy is to protect national security and to prevent invasion, then Elizabeth's foreign policy was a success.

1. Draw a chart showing all the factors that influenced Elizabethan foreign policy.

2. What problems have faced historians in their attempt to understand who made English foreign policy during the reign of Elizabeth I?

3. Why do you think historians have disagreed about Elizabeth I's policy towards the Netherlands?

Source-based questions: The trial and execution of Mary Stuart

SOURCE A

By the time that Anthony Babington's plot to assassinate Elizabeth was spawned, Walsingham's network was complete. He wrote to Leicester, 'If the matter be well handled, it will break the neck of all dangerous practices during her Majesty's reign.'

When Mary endorsed the planned murder in a dictated letter (17 July 1586), she was trapped. The Babington conspirators were tried and hanged, but Elizabeth agonised even more over Mary's execution than she had over Norfolk's after the Ridolfi Plot.

Since the Tower was considered insufficiently secure and too close to London, Mary was sent to Fotheringay Castle, where her trial formally began on 14 October 1586. Her judges were a committee of nobles, privy councillors, and leading judges appointed under the terms of the Act for the Queen's Safety. Although Mary objected that she was a queen and thus not subject to English common law, she was persuaded that she damaged her reputation by refusing to defend herself. She denied any complicity in attempted assassination, but by virtue of her letter to Babington she was plainly guilty.

From Tudor England *by John Guy, 1988*

Source-based questions: The trial and execution of Mary Stuart

SOURCE B

Her Majesty in not executing justice upon the Scottish Queen shall foster and nourish that only hope which the Catholics have to re-establish their religion within this realm. The Scottish Queen's life cannot stand with Her Majesty's safety and quiet estate of this realm, being as she is the only ground of all practices and attempts both at home and abroad.

Mercy and Pity is nothing else but cruel kindness; but in the Scottish Queen experience teaches that the more favour she receives the more mischief she attempts.

What dishonour were it, in sparing the life of so grievous an offender, to hazard the lives of so many thousands of true subjects, being left to so malicious a woman.

Argument, urging the execution of Mary Stuart, put forward by Sir Christopher Hatton, a Privy Councillor, during 1586–87

SOURCE C

Ambassadors from France and Scotland presented themselves at court with vigorous pleas and petitions for clemency, which could not be ignored. It was only too apparent that the affairs of Mary Stuart were inextricably bound up with the general European situation. To endanger the completed alliance with Scotland or the goodwill of France, at a time when the great duel with Spain was looming over the horizon, was a heavy price to pay for ridding England of the enemy within the gate. In January 1587 the intercession of France was largely nullified [cancelled out] by the discovery (or was it an invention?) of a fresh plot against the queen's life, emanating, it was said, from the French embassy in London. A 'great fear' swept over the country. It was reported that the Spaniards were at Milford, that Mary had escaped, that the northern counties were in revolt, that the capital was on fire. Elizabeth was heard to murmur the words 'Aut fer, aut fer; ne feriare, feri' ['suffer or strike; in order not to be struck']. On 1 February she signed the death-warrant.

From The Reign of Elizabeth by J.B. Black, 1936

SOURCE D

[Mary Stuart] was a free and absolute Princess and had no superiour but God alone. They said, she was Queen Elizabeth's very near Kinswoman, who made her a large Promise, on the Word of a Prince, of all Courtesie and kind Hospitality, as soon as she arrived in England, being thrown out of her Kingdom by her rebels. Yet on the contrary had kept her still in prison, and violated the sacred rights of hospitality; that she could not be otherways reputed than as a prisoner taken in war. She could not commit treason, because she was no subject, and Princes in equal degree have no power or sovereignty over one another. Moreover, that it was never heard of, that a Prince should be subjected to the Stroke of an Executioner.

From A History of the Most Renowned and Victorious Princess Elizabeth, late Queen of England by William Camden, 1615

1. With reference to Sources C and D, and to information contained within this chapter, explain the meaning of the two terms highlighted in the sources:

a) 'the completed alliance with Scotland' (Source C)

b) 'a free and absolute Princess and had no superiour but God alone' (Source D).

2. Study Sources A and B.

How far do these sources agree on the reasons why Mary Stuart should be tried and executed?

3. Study Sources B and D.

How useful are these sources to a historian writing about the issue raised by the trial and execution of Mary Stuart?

4. Study all four sources and use information contained within this chapter.

'The problems Mary Stuart created for Elizabeth I can only be understood if they are seen as part of England's relations with France and Spain.'

Assess the validity of this statement.

5 Social and economic history in the reign of Elizabeth I

Key Issues

- *In what ways did society change in Elizabeth's England?*

- *How successful was Elizabethan government in dealing with social and economic problems?*

- *How far did industry, trade and agriculture change during Elizabeth's reign?*

Framework of Events

1560	December: recoinage begins
1561	October: recoinage completed
1563	Statute of Artificers regulates conditions of employment
	Act for the Relief of the Poor (Beggars Act)
	Embargo on English woollen trade with the Netherlands (ends 1564)
1568	Resumption of embargo on English woollen trade with the Netherlands
1572	Act for the Punishment of Vagabonds and for the Relief of the Poor and Impotent
1576	Act for the Setting of the Poor to Work and for avoiding of Idleness
1587	Christopher Marlowe writes *Tamburlaine*
1588	William Shakespeare begins writing plays. The first plays include *Henry VI*, *Richard III* and *Love's Labours Lost*
1589	Edmund Spenser begins writing 'The Faerie Queene'
1593	Outbreak of plague
1594	Shakespeare begins writing *A Midsummer Night's Dream*
	First of four years of poor harvests
1596	Shakespeare begins writing *Merchant of Venice* and *Henry V*
1597	Shakespeare's play *Romeo and Juliet* is published
	Act for the Relief of the Poor; Act for the Punishment of Rogues, Vagabonds and Sturdy Beggars
1598	Outbreak of famine due to four years of poor harvests
	Act on Husbandry and Tillage to stop depopulation in the countryside
1599	Shakespeare begins writing *Julius Ceasar*
	Globe Theatre built
1600	Formation of East India Company
	Fortune Theatre opens in London
	Ben Johnson's *Every Man in his Humour* is published
1601	Poor Law of 1597 reissued in modified form
	Shakespeare's *Merry Wives of Windsor* is published.

Overview

THE reign of Elizabeth I was a period of change in social and economic history. During the last half of the 16th century, England experienced a rapid rise in population from three to four million. The rise placed considerable pressure on agriculture to produce enough food for this expanding population. By the time of Elizabeth's death in 1603, the food resources of the country were not sufficient to meet demand.

England was an overwhelmingly agricultural country. The vast majority of the population lived in villages. However, cities and towns did grow in size. The largest city by far was London. In fact, London contained two cities: the City of London was the commercial and business centre of the country; the City of Westminster contained the Parliament building and the Palace of Whitehall, making it the centre of government. Town growth occurred not only because of a rise in population but also because of migration from the countryside.

The aristocracy dominated the social structure of Elizabethan England. Over the past 50 years, historians have debated the importance of the aristocracy. Some have put forward the view that the importance of the aristocracy was in decline. It was faced with the rise in importance and size of the gentry.

Elizabeth I's reign was affected by a number of social and economic problems. The problem of rising prices (inflation) affected the early years of her reign and the 1590s. Elizabeth's government overcame the first period of inflation but not the second. In addition, both central and local governments had to deal with the issue of poverty and vagrancy. During the reign, many laws were passed at national and local level to deal with these problems. By 1603, the idea that central and local government had a responsibility for helping the poor was firmly established.

Agriculture did not experience great change in Elizabeth's reign. Sheep farming and the production of wool dominated this part of the economy. Wool and woollen cloth dominated overseas trade. These commodities were exported to Antwerp, in the Netherlands. However, this trade was disrupted on a number of occasions by the outbreak of conflict in the Netherlands against Spanish rule.

Cottage industry: Industry where manufacturing occurs in individual households. Also known as 'putting out'. Householders would acquire raw materials from a central location, manufacture in their own homes and then return the finished work.

Industry was also dominated by the woollen and textile industry. Most industry was on a small scale, with **cottage industry** predominating. During Elizabeth I's reign, this industry experienced change. The New Draperies were producing lighter, cheaper cloth for internal trade and export.

Perhaps the most enduring development in the social history of Elizabethan England was the development of drama and poetry. The reign has been described as the 'Age of Shakespeare'. Although the 'Bard of Avon' was the most notable literary figure, others, such as the playwright Ben Johnson and the poets Edmund Spenser and John Donne, played an important part in the development of English literature.

5.1 What changes took place in the size and structure of the population?

How much did the population increase?

During the reign of Elizabeth I the population of England increased considerably. In the 1550s, the population had reached approximately three million, rising to around four million by the time of Elizabeth's death in 1603. In this period, population growth was limited by two factors. Just before the start of Elizabeth's reign there was a major outbreak of influenza which had increased the death rate. In the mid-1590s, England suffered from four bad harvests in a row. By 1597, many parts of the country were facing an acute food shortage leading, in some cases, to famine.

The population was mainly centred on the South East and the Midlands. By far the largest city was London. By 1603, it had a population of 130,000–150,000. This made it as one of Europe's largest cities, along-side Paris and Naples. To illustrate the size of London in comparison with other English cities, the second largest city in Elizabethan England was Norwich – with a population of only 15,000. Other regional centres were Newcastle, Bristol, Exeter and York. Apart from London, there were only 18 towns with populations over 5,000. Around 90% of English men and women lived in villages.

Historians of Elizabethan England have found it difficult to find accurate information on population structure and growth. The most useful sources of information are parish registers. These contain information on baptisms, marriages and funerals. However, they do not contain information about child death shortly after birth as this was before a baptism was seen as necessary.

The main reasons for the increase in population during the Elizabethan period were a rise in fertility and a fall in the death rate. Between 1561 and 1600, the death rate averaged 25 per 1,000. The birth rate averaged 34.5 per 1,000 between 1561 and 1586, falling slightly to 32 per 1,000 by 1600. According to the historian Alan Smith in *The Emergence of a Nation State* (1984): 'The late Elizabethan era was "a golden period of low mortality" in which the expectation of life at birth exceeded 40 years, a figure not reached again until the 19th century.'

How was Elizabethan society structured?

In studying the structure of Elizabethan society, historians have been fortunate that three contemporary studies of quality exist. Sir Thomas Smith wrote *De Republica Anglorum* in the 1560s but it was not published until 1583. William Harrison wrote a *Description of England* in the 1570s. Finally, Thomas Wilson wrote *The State of England anno domini 1600*. Each of these studies provides the historian with an insight into the organisation of society at different times in Elizabeth I's reign.

According to William Harrison, English society could be divided into four groups: gentlemen, citizens or burgesses, yeomen and artificers or labourers. Those individuals in the group entitled 'gentlemen' occupied the top section of society. This group included the monarch, the aristocracy and the gentry. To Sir Thomas Smith, Queen Elizabeth was 'the head, and the authoritie of all thinges that be doone in the realm of England'.

Below the monarch came the major landowners of England, the aristocracy, who had the right to sit in the House of Lords. According to the historian D.M. Palliser, the aristocracy numbered 57 at the start of Elizabeth's reign, falling slightly to 55 by the time of her death. Families such as the Howards, Percys and Stanleys were members of the aristocracy.

The other group that formed Harrison's category of 'gentlemen' was the gentry. This term has caused problems for historians as it is open to a number of definitions. Suffice to say that the gentry were landowners who did *not* have the right to sit in the House of Lords. They comprised knights of the shires and individuals who could call themselves 'esquire'. The historian Lawrence Stone, in *The Crisis of the Aristocracy*, claims that there were 600 knights in Elizabethan England in 1558. This number fell to 550 by 1603. Esquires were described by Thomas Wilson as those 'gentlemen whose ancestors are or have been knights, or else are the heirs of their houses'. Wilson believed that the combined numbers of knights and esquires in England numbered 16,000 in 1601. This seems a rather high figure.

Elizabethan costume (from left to right): a wealthy merchant; a noble lady; a middle-class lady; a young squire

1. In what ways does the costume of the middle-class lady differ from the noble lady?

2. How do the costumes shown in the illustration help to emphasise the differences in wealth and social structure in Elizabethan society?

Opulentus mercator Londinensis in Anglia.   *Nobilis puella ornatus apud Londinenses.*   *Vulgarium foeminarum in Anglia institur. gentilis.*   *Plebeg adolescentis in Anglia habitus.*

Freehold: Ownership of land or property where the owner possesses complete control, including the right to decide who owns the property on their death.

Tenants-at-will: Control of land or property with no right of control. A tenant could be forced to hand back land or property without forewarning.

Typhus: A contagious disease associated with poor levels of hygiene and diet.

Elizabeth I's England was a predominantly rural society. Therefore, below the 'gentlemen' in order of social importance were yeoman farmers. This group was made up of those who held land by **freehold** to the value of 40 shillings [£2]. However, with inflation in the Tudor period, this definition lost its value. Yeomen were independent farmers who owned their land. Their farms varied in size according to the region and type of agriculture. Fifty acres [20 hectares] was an approximate size of a yeoman farm.

Below yeoman farmers came husbandmen. These were farmers who held small amounts of land by various methods of tenure. Some were freeholders. Others were merely **tenants-at-will**. However, the overwhelming majority of the rural population was made up of cottagers or day labourers. These individuals rented small cottages and worked for others. With low wages and poor diet, it was this class who were most vulnerable to diseases such as influenza and **typhus**. During the periods of poor harvests in the 1590s, many suffered badly. In some parts of the North West many suffered starvation and famine.

1. **What reasons can you give to explain the rise in population during Elizabeth I's reign?**

2. **William Harrison divided Elizabethan society into four groups: gentlemen, citizens or burgesses, yeomen and artificers. How accurate do you regard his description?**

Townspeople in Elizabethan England comprised only a small proportion of the population. Throughout the reign towns grew, mainly due to migration from the countryside. In towns at the top of the social ladder were burgesses and merchants. This group not only possessed the most wealth but also occupied the key positions in town government. During the last half of the 16th century, the legal and medical professions became more important in town life.

Beneath these groups came the artificers or skilled craftsmen. This group comprised craftspeople such as masons, tailors, butchers and carpenters. The Statute of Artificers of 1563 laid down that craftsmen had to complete a seven-year apprenticeship before qualifying. The Act also laid down the rates of pay to be received within each craft. At the bottom of the social scale came casual labourers. This group was usually made up of migrants from the countryside. It was also the group who, in hard economic times, provided the main source of vagrants and beggars.

5.2 *How far did society change during Elizabeth's reign?*
A CASE STUDY IN HISTORICAL INTERPRETATION

There has been considerable debate among historians about the nature and extent of change in Elizabethan society. Rising prices, a growing population and major changes in landownership brought about by religious upheaval resulted in social change. How great was this change? Which groups, in society, were most affected?

Was there a crisis among the aristocracy?

In 1941, in an article in *Proceedings of the British Academy*, the historian R.H. Tawney stated that the ownership of property had seen major changes in the century before the outbreak of the Civil War in 1642. He believed that the old-fashioned, large-scale landowners, the aristocracy, had begun to decline in importance. Increasingly, a new class of landowner, the gentry, was rising in both wealth and social importance.

In 1948, Lawrence Stone took up Tawney's views. In a historical article in the *Economic History Review* entitled 'The anatomy of the Elizabethan aristocracy', Stone accepted the view that the aristocracy had declined in importance. However, he believed this was due mainly to over-expenditure on their part. He stated that over 60% of the aristocracy were facing financial ruin by the time of Elizabeth I's death.

Then, in 1953, in an article in the *Economic History Review* entitled 'The gentry, 1540–1640', Hugh Trevor-Roper (later Lord Dacre) criticised Stone's view. He believed that Stone had wrongly interpreted historical evidence on the amount of money owed by the aristocracy. He also stated that instead of a rise in the importance of the gentry, there had been a 'massive decline' in what he called the 'mere' gentry. These were small-scale landowners. Trevor-Roper believed that these had suffered economic decline due to inflation. He did point out that some members of the gentry did rise in importance. These were usually courtiers or merchants who were involved in monopolies at the end of Elizabeth I's reign.

By 1959, Trevor-Roper's views were under attack from Perez Zagorin in an article entitled 'The social interpretations of the English Revolution' in the *Journal of Economic History*. Zagorin's main concern was the lack of

Copyholders: A form of land ownership where a person leases land but over a long period. The copyholder could pass on the lease to his/her children.

1. From the evidence contained in this section, do you think the aristocracy declined in power and influence during Elizabeth I's reign? Give reasons for your answer.

2. Why do you think historians have differed in their views on the aristocracy and gentry in Elizabeth's England?

1. Study the information contained in the table on the right.

In which decade did nominal wage rates rise the most for:

a) skilled workers

b) unskilled workers?

2. In which decade was the gap between nominal wages and real wages at its greatest for:

a) skilled workers

b) unskilled workers?

Can you give a reason why this gap existed?

3. During Elizabeth I's reign did the standard of living rise or fall for skilled workers and unskilled workers in London? Give reasons for your answer.

important links in Trevor-Roper's argument. He felt Trevor-Roper had made a rather dubious link between gentry who owned small farms and estates and the effects of rising prices. In 1961, J.R. Hexter in *Reappraisals in History* made an important observation on Trevor-Roper's views. Hexter pointed out that, in his attempt to explain the outbreak of civil war in the 17th century, Trevor-Roper had tried to prove that the gentry had risen in importance at the expense of the aristocracy, thereby providing a strong economic reason for that conflict.

In 1983, the economic historian D.M. Palliser, in *The Age of Elizabeth*, points out that the gentry did increase in wealth and number during the reign of Elizabeth I but not necessarily at the expense of the aristocracy. New lands had become available following the dissolution of the monasteries and chantries (small chapels). There was also a rise in population. Greater wealth could be earned from agriculture. Therefore, the proportion of landed wealth owned by the gentry increased. This trend was emphasised by Elizabeth I's reluctance to increase the number of lords.

In *The Later Tudors, 1547–1603* (1995), Penry Williams points out that the evidence available suggests that landowners did prosper, in particular after 1570. However, he states that not all landowners were successful:

> Revenues had to be raised to meet inflation and this might be difficult for landlords with estates largely held by **copyholders**. By and large the adjustment seems to have been hardest for the lesser (mere) gentry, who lacked the reserves to meet periods of crisis.

Did the standard of living fall for skilled and unskilled workers in London?

A STUDY IN STATISTICAL EVIDENCE

Nominal[†] and real wage[*] rates in London 1550–1599

Decade	Nominal rates of pay		Real rates of pay	
	Skilled [artificers]	Unskilled [artificers]	Skilled	Unskilled
1550–59	159	148	75	70
1560–69	200	173	90	78
1570–79	200	189	84	79
1580–89	200	200	78	78
1590–99	222	209	71	67

[†] 'Nominal wages' refers to the amount of money received.
[*] 'Real wages' refers to the amount of goods money will buy. Real wages fall in times of price rises (inflation).

The numbers in the table are index numbers based on the base decade of the 1460s.
Therefore, 1460s = 100.
Example: the nominal rate of pay for skilled workers in the 1550s is 148. This means that nominal wages were 48% higher than in the 1460s.

5.3 How successful was Elizabeth's government in dealing with the problem of inflation?

A general rise in prices, known to economists as inflation, affected Elizabeth I's reign at her accession and in the 1590s. The issue was seen as sufficiently important to be included on Elizabeth's tomb in Westminster Abbey, London. Her ability to end the inflation at the beginning of her reign was placed alongside other achievements, such as the re-establishment of the Church of England and the defeat of the Spanish Armada.

What caused inflation in Elizabethan England?

In 1549, 'A Discourse of the Common Weal of this Realm of England' was published. It is most probably the work of Sir Thomas Smith who later wrote a survey of Elizabethan England. In this pamphlet he laid the cause of inflation at the door of the **debasement of the coinage** during the last years of Henry VIII. The proportion of gold and silver in coins was secretly reduced in 1542–44. A public debasement followed in the year 1544–51.

Debasement of the coinage: Reducing the value of currency so it actually bought less. In the 16th century this meant reducing the amount of pure silver in a coin.

Clearly, the reduction of gold and silver in coins did lead to a rise in prices. This can be explained through the 'Quantity Theory of Money'. Irving Fisher, an economist, put forward this view in 1919. It stated that an increase in the supply of money into an economy can lead to a general rise in prices. The theory is explained through the use of a formula:

$$MV=PT$$

(M is the supply of money. V is the velocity [or speed] with which this money circulates within an economy. P is the price level. T is the number of transactions involving the use of money in an economy.) It is accepted by monetarist economists that V and T remain relatively constant. Therefore, any increase in M leads to an increase in P. This causes inflation.

The need to debase the coinage was due to the high cost of warfare during the last years of Henry VIII's reign and the rule of Protector Somerset. For instance, the approximate cost of Henry's wars of the 1540s was £3.6 million. Unfortunately, taxation produced only £1 million. Even the sale of monastic lands only brought in £1 million. Therefore, there was a shortfall of £1.6 million. This gap was to be closed by issuing more coins from the same limited amount of gold and silver available.

Although the Quantity Theory of Money helps to explain why inflation occurred at the start of Elizabeth I's reign, it does not explain why inflation returned in the 1590s. By the last decade of Elizabeth's reign, the rise in population meant that demand was outstripping food resources. This was combined with a series of poor harvests, beginning in 1594, which meant that demand greatly exceeded supply. The considerable rise in the price of a staple food such as corn helps to explain why inflation reappeared.

However, R.B. Outhwaite in *Inflation in Tudor and Early Stuart England* (1968) states that 'we must avoid making population pressure do all the work' in explaining the inflation of the 1590s. Inflation affected all of western Europe, not just England. One factor which helps to explain western European inflation is the importation of large amounts of silver from Spanish mines in the New World, such as Potosi in Peru. This increased the supply of money. There were also increased government costs resulting from war with Spain and rebellion in Ireland. These helped increase the demand for goods, thereby forcing up prices.

What actions did Elizabeth's government take to deal with inflation?

In December 1560, the government ordered that all debased money be returned. This was replaced by new coins containing more silver, thus returning the quality of coinage to the position it held before the debasement of 1542–44. The recoinage was completed by October 1561. This policy had the effect of limiting the money supply and re-establishing public confidence in the coinage. Fortunately for Elizabeth I, her stocks of silver were increased by the acquisition of the Genoese loan in 1568 (see Chapter 4).

The government also attempted to limit demand through controlling wages. The Statute of Artificers of 1563 set wage limits for skilled workers. Unfortunately, the reappearance of inflation in the 1590s meant that the standard of living of these workers fell as the cost of living rose.

> 1. What reasons can you give to explain why inflation occurred in Elizabeth I's England?
>
> 2. What steps did Elizabeth I's government take to control inflation?
>
> 3. How successful was Elizabeth I's government in dealing with inflation during her reign?

5.4 How did Elizabethans deal with the issues of poverty and vagrancy?

In an article in *The Reign of Elizabeth I* entitled 'Poverty and Social Regulation in Elizabethan England' Paul Slack stated: 'After the Anglican Church, the English poor law was the most long-lasting of Elizabethan achievements.'

During Elizabeth I's reign, Acts were passed to deal with poverty and vagrancy, in 1563, 1572, 1576 and 1597. In 1601, Parliament introduced laws that lasted, with minor alteration, until 1834. The twin issues of poverty and vagrancy did not only interest central government. Many towns dealt with these issues through local laws. Norwich, Ipswich and

> 1. What message is this woodcut trying to make about beggars in Elizabethan England?
>
> 2. Use the information in this section. How did Elizabethan government attempt to deal with the types of beggar shown in the woodcut?

A contemporary woodcut illustration of beggars. The title reads (from left to right): 'Beggers Bush', 'A Maundering [travelling] Begger' and 'A gallant Begger'. The two people under the 'begger's bush' are physically handicapped.

Cambridge were three East Anglian towns that introduced laws dealing with the poor. Policy at national and local level had to deal with two problems. First, how should the government punish and deter vagrants and beggars? Second, what should they do to help 'the deserving poor' such as orphans, the elderly or the infirm?

What were the causes of poverty in Elizabethan England?

In a study on poverty and vagrancy in Tudor England (published in 1994), the historian John Pound notes various reasons to explain the poverty. He states that the rise in population (43% between 1550 and 1600) helped to put pressure on limited food resources. This was most important during the 1590s. In addition, harvest failure created famine or near-famine conditions (dearth). The worst decade for these problems was the 1590s. However, there had been poor harvests earlier in the reign, such as 1556 and 1586. As a result, dearth existed across England in 1555–57, 1586–87 and 1596–97.

Another cause of poverty was the outbreak of illness and plague. The reign began with the effects of the influenza epidemic, which had affected the end of Mary's reign. There was also a smallpox epidemic in 1562 which almost took the life of the Queen. Throughout the reign, there were severe outbreaks of plague in towns. The plague outbreak in London in 1563 accounted for the deaths of over 20% of the city's population. There were also epidemics in 1583–86 and 1590–93.

Enclosure and engrossing: 'Enclosure' was a process where some landowners put hedges around large fields and created bigger and more productive units of farming. 'Engrossing' was the amalgamation of small farming units into a larger one, allowing the houses that went with the 'amalgamated' land to decay.

Husbandry and tillage: Husbandry refers to pastoral farming, tillage refers to arable farming.

The **enclosure and engrossing** of land in the past has been blamed for creating poverty in the countryside. However, by the start of Elizabeth I's reign, the enclosure of common land had passed its peak. It was only during the crisis of the 1590s that the issue of **husbandry and tillage** was again regarded as a major economic problem. In 1598, Parliament passed the Act on Husbandry and Tillage. This attempted to retain tillage, and with it employment, in the countryside.

Inflation also caused poverty through the rise in the cost of living. During Elizabeth I's reign, the Statute of Artificers had placed an upper limit on the wages of skilled workers. At the same time, the standard of living of most town workers fell as a result of rising prices. Unemployment in towns was also made worse by the embargoes on wool exports to the Netherlands in 1563–64, 1568–73 and in the 1580s.

Finally, the end of warfare placed large numbers of soldiers and sailors in poverty. For instance, after the cancellation of an attack on Portugal in 1589, large numbers of discharged soldiers and seamen roamed the southern counties of Kent and Sussex.

Who were the poor?

According to the historian A.L. Beier, about half the population of Tudor England was unable to support itself. This included those members of society who were incapable of work, such as the very young or very old. Also included were the infirm – such as the blind or physically handicapped – and widows, a social group who found it very difficult to find work. During periods of harvest failure and depression in the cloth trade, the numbers would be increased by the inclusion of families who merely fell 'on hard times'. These groups comprised 'the deserving poor'.

Poverty was at its greatest in towns. In a census in Norwich, made in

1570, the poor comprised approximately 25% of the population (500 men, 850 women and 1,000 children). Added to this list were the 'undeserving poor', who were seen as a threat to social order. They included rogues and villains who made a living from crime. There were also beggars. During wartime, the list of the 'poor' would also include former soldiers and sailors. These were feared, in particular, because they were usually armed. Finally, this group would also include migrants who had left their own area to look for work. Cities such as London and Norwich had large numbers of migrant workers.

Under the terms of the 1576 Poor Law Act, a third category of poor was created: the deserving, able-bodied unemployed. These were given the opportunity to work in return for some **poor relief**.

Poor relief: Giving assistance to the poor. This could be money, housing or work.

What actions were taken to deal with poverty and vagrancy?

The way in which the national government in Elizabethan England dealt with these issues stands as a major example of government intervention to maintain social control and order.

A major theme of government policy was to deter and punish the undeserving poor. The 1563 Act continued the policy begun earlier in the Tudor period of whipping able-bodied beggars. This was followed, in 1572, by an Act for the Punishment of Vagabonds and for the Relief of the Poor. This was the harshest law of Elizabeth I's reign. It was passed following the rebellion of the Northern Earls (1569–70). The government feared more outbreaks of disorder. This Act declared that all vagabonds above the age of 14 were to be whipped and burned through the right ear unless some honest person took them into **domestic service**. The Act also allowed for imprisonment for a second offence of vagabondage and the possibility of execution for persistent offenders. Any children of a convicted beggar were to be placed in domestic service. Ear-boring and execution were not removed until 1593.

Domestic service: Work in a household which usually involved cooking, cleaning etc.

A more enlightened approach was put forward in the 1576 Act for the setting of the poor on work, and for avoiding idleness. For the first time, towns were required to give the unemployed some work. This would

1. *Use the information in this section. Which Acts of Parliament encouraged the treatment of vagrants shown right?*

2. *Study the two illustrations on vagrancy and beggars (here and on page 113). Why do you think these two woodcuts were produced in Elizabethan England? You might consider the audience for each illustration.*

A vagrant being whipped through the streets of a town. In the distance (left) is the gallows – a reminder of what might happen to a vagrant.

involve setting up stockpiles of wool and other commodities for the poor to work on. If any member of the poor would not work then they were to be placed in a local prison. The prison would be financed from a local tax, the rates.

However, during the economic crisis of the 1590s Parliament was forced into passing harsher laws against the 'undeserving poor'. In 1597, the Act for the Punishment of Rogues, Vagabonds and Sturdy Beggars was passed. The Act demanded that all counties and cities should have local prisons to house these groups. In addition, anyone caught offending for the first time was to be whipped and then sent back to the parish of their birth. Those individuals who continued to re-offend were to be sent to the **galleys**, or could be executed.

Galleys: A type of warship with sails and oars. Large numbers of oarsmen were required. Once sent to the galleys, offenders were rarely freed.

In addition to deterring the undeserving poor, the Elizabethan government extended the power of central government on matters relating to helping the poor. The 1563 Act declared that anyone who refused to pay for the aid of the poor could face imprisonment. It also introduced fines from £2 to £20 for officials who failed to organise help for the poor. The 1572 Act established, for the first time, a national poor law rate (tax). This Act was a turning point in helping the poor. For the first time, towns were given the responsibility for providing work for the able-bodied unemployed.

Finally, the 1597 Act for the Relief of the Poor laid the foundations for the poor law for the next 250 years. It declared that each parish should appoint an 'overseer of the poor'. This official had the task of finding work for the young unemployed. He also had to hand out help to the 'deserving poor'. The Act also gave overseers the right to take away goods and property from anyone who refused to pay taxes to aid the poor.

Apart from Acts of Parliament, central government took other action to aid the poor. The Privy Council made efforts to increase the food supply during periods of food shortage. In 1576, it ordered the government of the City of London to buy corn. It also intervened to prevent the export of corn during the 1590s.

Town governments also played a major part in providing assistance for the poor. The historian D.M. Palliser notes that, by 1569, the East Anglian town of Ipswich had established a compulsory poor tax, a school for the young poor, a local house of correction and a hospital for the poor. Norwich, England's second city at the time, followed with a detailed town plan to deal with poverty and vagrancy in the 1570s. In London, five hospitals were established, including the Bethlehem hospital for the insane, the Bridewell for vagrants and Christ's for orphans.

An important source of aid for the poor came from private charity. The most important groups to provide aid were merchants and tradesmen. Aid was usually made in a will.

How successful were government actions?

The fact that the 1597 and 1601 Poor Law Acts remained in force for over 250 years is a measure of their success. By the time of Elizabeth I's death, central government had accepted the responsibility of providing a minimum level of subsistence for the poor. In addition, one of the main aims of the Poor Law was to prevent major disturbances and outbreaks of disorder by the poor. Even though Elizabeth's reign saw periods of great food shortages, there were no major disturbances. As historian Penry

1. What caused poverty and vagrancy in Elizabethan England?

2. What actions were taken to help the deserving poor and to deter vagrancy?

3. How successful were government policies to deal with poverty and vagrancy?

Williams states in *The Tudor Regime* (1981): 'Even the combination of war and harvest failure in the 1590s produced no serious eruption by the dispossessed.'

However, John Pound takes a more moderate view on the effect of government action in *Poverty and Vagrancy in Tudor England* (1971). He believes that contemporaries exaggerated the problem. He notes that 'both poverty and vagrancy were fairly well contained, and to say that either created a dangerous national situation would be to strain the evidence'.

Source-based questions: The Poor Law

SOURCE A

With us the poor is commonly divided into three sorts, so that some are poor by impotency [not through their own fault], as the fatherless child, the aged, blind, lame, and the diseased person that is judged to be incurable: the second are poor by casualty, as the wounded soldier, the decayed householder, and the sick person visited with grievous and painful disease; the third consisteth of thriftless poor, as the rioter that hath consumed all, the vagabond that will abide nowhere but runneth up and down from place to place, and finally the rogue and the strumpet [prostitute].

From A Description of England *by William Harrison, 1577*

SOURCE B

Names of the Poor to be Reviewed Weekly in St Peters of Southgate

Richard Rich of the age of 35 years, a husbandman which worketh with Mrs Cattrell and keepeth not with his wife and helpeth her little. And Margaret his wife of the age of 40 years she spins and Joan her daughter, of the age of 12 years, that spins also. Peter Browne a cobbler [shoemaker] of the age of 50 years and hath little work. And Agnes his wife of the age of 52 years that worketh not, but have lain sick since Christmas. She spins having three daughters, the one of the age of 18 years, the other of the age of 14 years, the which all spin when they can get it, but now they are without work.

From The Norwich Census of the Poor, *1570*

SOURCE C

And when the number of the said poor people forced to live upon alms [charity] be by that means truly known the said justices, mayors, sheriffs, bailiffs and other officers shall within like convenient time devise and appoint, within every their said divisions, meet and convenient places by their discretions to settle the same poor people for their habitations and abidings, if the parish within which they shall be found shall not or will not provide for them; and shall also within like convenient time number all the said poor people within their said several limits, and thereupon set down what portion the weekly charge towards poor relief and sustentation of the said poor people will amount unto within every their said several divisions and that done, they ...shall by their good discretion tax and assess all and every the inhabitants, dwelling in all and every city, borough, town, village, hamlet and place known within the said limits, to such weekly charge as they and every of them weekly contribute towards the relief of the said poor people.

From An Act for the Punishment of Vagabonds and for the Relief of the Poor and Impotent, 1572

Source-based questions: The Poor Law

1. Study Sources A and B.

In which 'sorts' of poor, mentioned by Harrison in Source A, would you place the people mentioned in Source B? Give reasons to support your answer.

2. Study Source B.

How useful is this source to a historian writing about the poor in Elizabethan England?

3. Study Source C.

How, by its use of language and style, is it possible to tell that this is an official document?

4. Study Sources A, B and C and use information from the chapter.

How were the poor (mentioned in Sources A and B) dealt with by central and local government during Elizabeth I's reign?

5.5 How far did trade and industry change during Elizabeth I's reign?

Were there any major changes in the pattern of trade?

A popular view of Elizabeth I's England is that trade went through considerable change. The foundation of the Muscovy, Levant and East India companies seems to support this view. However, the vast majority of trade during Elizabeth's reign was internal or coastal. Goods were transported within England either by road or navigable river. In addition, a coastal trade along the east coast brought bulky goods such as coal from Newcastle and the North East to London. Internal trade by road involved the extensive use of packhorses. Packhorse routes through the Lake District and across the Pennines linked Westmorland with Cumberland (both these counties are now in Cumbria) and Durham, and Lancashire with Yorkshire.

On the navigable rivers, small commercial craft brought cities such as York into contact with Hull and with trade with the continent. Merchants from York were able to transport woollen cloth and lead down the rivers Ouse and Humber to Hull. In return, they transported fish and coal back to York.

Staple: A place where a company or organisation, such as the Merchant Adventurers, had the exclusive right to buy and sell goods.

In external trade, the main commodities were woollen cloth and goods to the Merchant Adventurers' **staple** in Antwerp, in the Netherlands. (For a fuller coverage of the Netherlands trade see Chapter 4.) During Elizabeth I's reign, the Netherlands trade was interrupted by trade embargoes on English goods made in 1563–64, 1568–73 and 1586–88. These embargoes forced English merchants to seek new outlets for English woollen goods. Emden in East Friesland and Hamburg in north Germany were both chosen for short periods during these embargoes.

Although the trading companies to the Levant and the East Indies were to play an important role in English trade in the 17th century, they had little impact on Elizabethan trade.

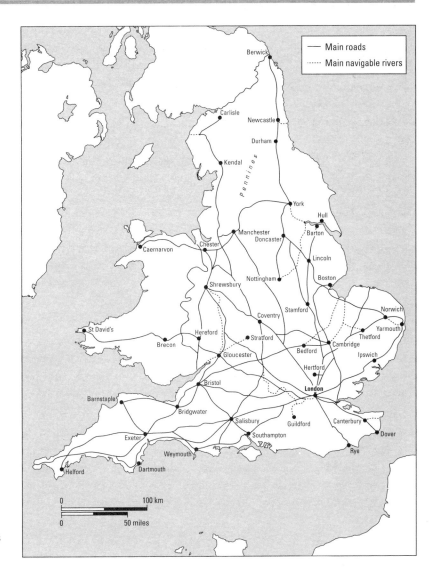

Main roads and navigable rivers
in England, 1600

What changes took place in industry?

Compared with areas such as the Netherlands, England was a backward, undeveloped country in industrial terms. The vast majority of industrial concerns were family businesses. A business was managed and operated by a craftsman (artificer) who was involved directly in the manufacturing process. Craftmen were organised into craft guilds. These guilds tried to set standards for the quality of work and wage rates. The 1563 Statute of Artificers contained detailed information about wage rates and the supply of labour in each craft. In any large town, a wide variety of crafts could be found, such as bakers, tailors, weavers, shoemakers and carpenters. In the countryside, an important craftsman was the blacksmith.

England produced a wide variety of goods and materials during Elizabeth I's reign. These included iron, coal and lead. However, the most important industry by far was the textile industry. This industry was

1. Describe the pattern of trade with the Baltic and Mediterranean areas as shown in the map.

2. How far was English trade with the Baltic different from English trade with the Mediterranean? Give reasons to support your answer.

located near the raw material (wool). It also required water power and a plentiful source of workers. Production was usually decentralised – work was 'put out' to workers who manufactured cloth in their own cottages. The industry was centred on East Anglia, the West Country and parts of west Yorkshire.

The main products of the English textile industry at the start of Elizabeth I's reign were broadcloths and kerseys. The latter were smaller and lighter fabrics. Usually the products were known from the place of manufacture such as 'Tauntons' or 'Bridgwaters.'

Trade in the Baltic and the Mediterranean in Elizabeth I's reign

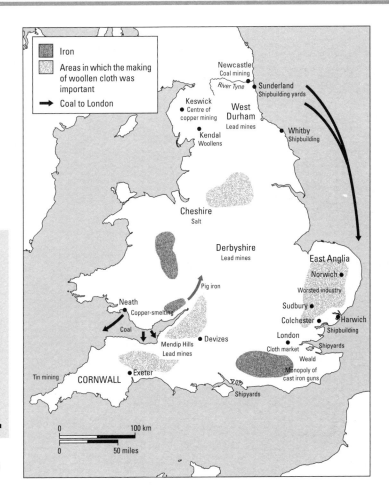

Industry in Elizabethan England

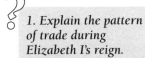

1. Describe the nature and location of industry shown in the map of industry in Elizabethan England.

2. Use the information in this chapter. Why was the woollen industry located in East Anglia, west Yorkshire and the West Country?

Long-stapled wool: Long wool that could be combed instead of carded before conversion into yarn. Carding was a more expensive process involving a wire brush or teazels.

1. Explain the pattern of trade during Elizabeth I's reign.

2. How far did trade and industry change during Elizabeth I's reign?

A major change took place in the textile industry from the 1560s onwards with the development of the 'New Draperies'. These were cheaper and lighter cloths. This new development was due, in part, to a scarcity of wool. The new fabrics were made from **long-stapled wool**. An example of this new cloth was a worsted, named after a village in north Norfolk.

Of greater significance was the arrival from western Europe of textile workers. The outbreak of disturbances in the Netherlands from the mid-1560s and the French Wars of Religion led to large numbers of Protestants seeking refuge in England. They brought with them their skills in textile manufacture. Eventually, English manufacturers began to copy these techniques.

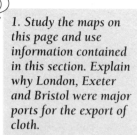

1. *Study the maps on this page and use information contained in this section. Explain why London, Exeter and Bristol were major ports for the export of cloth.*

2. *Explain the pattern of broadcloth exports in the graph.*

3. *Use information in this chapter and in Chapter 4. Why was there a major fall in the export of broadcloths in the 1560s and 1570s?*

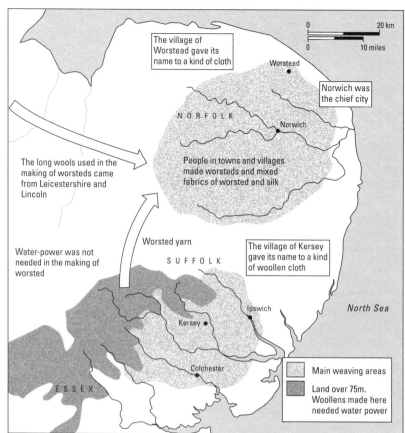

The village of Worstead gave its name to a kind of cloth

Worstead

Norwich was the chief city

NORFOLK

Norwich

The long wools used in the making of worsteds came from Leicestershire and Lincoln

People in towns and villages made worsteds and mixed fabrics of worsted and silk

Worsted yarn

SUFFOLK

The village of Kersey gave its name to a kind of woollen cloth

Water-power was not needed in the making of worsted

Ipswich

Kersey

North Sea

Colchester

ESSEX

| | Main weaving areas |
| | Land over 75m. Woollens made here needed water power |

The woollen industry in East Anglia

Export of broadcloths, 1485–1603

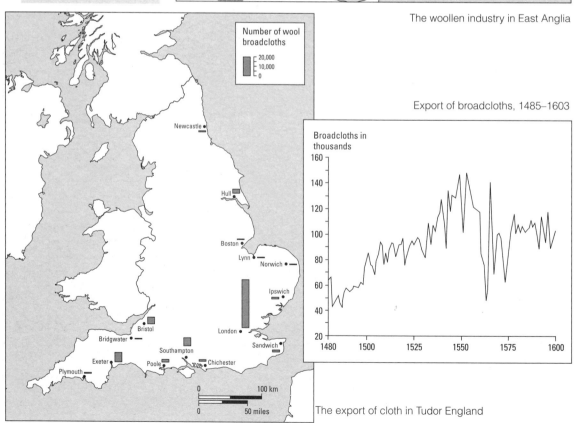

Number of wool broadcloths

20,000
10,000
0

Newcastle

Hull

Boston

Lynn

Norwich

Ipswich

Bristol

Bridgwater

London

Southampton

Sandwich

Exeter

Poole

Chichester

Plymouth

Broadcloths in thousands

160
140
120
100
80
60
40
20

1480   1500   1525   1550   1575   1600

The export of cloth in Tudor England

5.6 Were there any changes in the pattern and development of agriculture?

A survey of agriculture

Elizabethan England was an overwhelmingly agricultural economy. However, there was a wide variety of agricultural practices across the country. The type of farming depended mainly on geographical and climatic factors. For instance, wool production was dominant in the Fenland area of eastern England. This low-lying, former marshy area was ideal for sheep grazing. In north-west England, in the Cheshire Plain, the climate and terrain allowed the development of the Cheshire cheese industry.

In simple terms, farming could be divided into different categories. Arable farming involved the planting and harvesting of crops such as corn. Arable land was usually divided into three strips with one strip left fallow (with no crop) each year. Pastoral farming involved the grazing of livestock such as cattle and sheep. Mixed farming, as the term suggests, was a mixture of both. An important part of Elizabethan agriculture was woodland farming. This involved the grazing of pigs and cattle. It also involved the cutting of timber, which was the most important building material in Tudor England.

Enclosures in 16th-century England

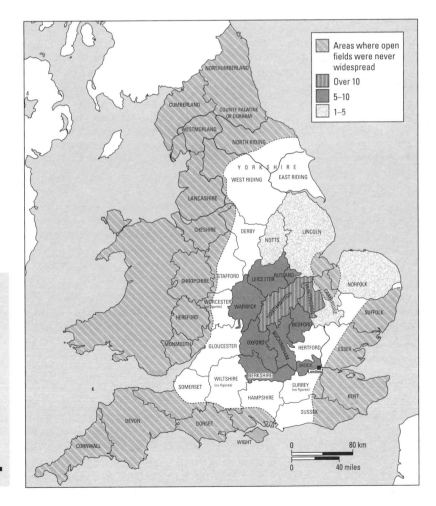

1. Describe the pattern of enclosures in Tudor England.

2. Study the two maps (right and on page 124). Which types of farming areas were most affected by enclosure? What reasons can you give to support this development?

A woodcut from Spenser's *The Shepherd's Calendar*, 1579

Farming regions in England, 1500–1640

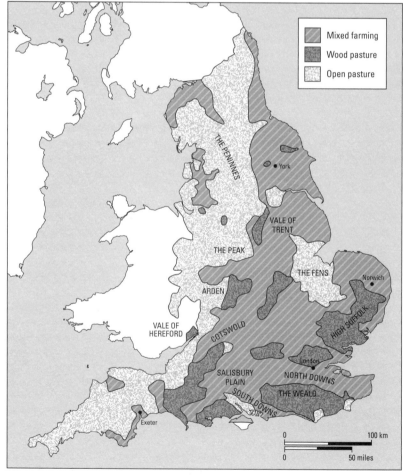

Were enclosures a problem in Elizabethan England?

During the early Tudor period, considerable concern was shown by contemporaries about the adverse effects of enclosure and engrossing. Both processes were associated with the expansion of sheep farming. They were seen as responsible for creating unemployment in the countryside. It took far fewer workers to tend sheep than to produce arable crops. For instance, Parliament passed laws against enclosure in 1489, 1533 and 1536. However, none of this legislation proved effective in slowing down the rate of enclosure.

By the time Elizabeth I became queen, enclosure was no longer a major issue. However, as Elizabeth's reign came to an end, the issue again became important. A succession of bad harvests affected England from 1594. Studies of Leicestershire and Staffordshire had shown an increase in enclosure and rural depopulation in the early 1590s. Parliament passed the Act on Husbandry and Tillage in 1598. This Act, which remained in force until 1624, banned any further conversion of arable land into pasture.

5.7 How important were developments in English culture during Elizabeth I's reign?

According to historian Penry Williams, in *The Later Tudors* (1995), culture can be defined as 'a network of shared values, together with the writings, pictures, performances, festivities, and so on in which they are embodied'. In Elizabethan England, it is possible to make a distinction between 'popular culture' and the culture of the educated upper classes, 'high culture'. Popular culture, as the name suggests, was culture enjoyed by most of the population below the educated upper classes. High culture was enjoyed by those who comprised William Harrison's group of 'gentlemen and citizens or burgesses'.

What factors affected the development of high culture?

Renaissance: Period of European history covering the 15th century to 17th century. It was associated with the re-discovery of Ancient Greek and Roman literature and the study of man. It was also associated with the spread of literacy to the lay (non-clerical) population.

The development of culture in Elizabethan England was affected directly by social developments earlier in the century. The European **Renaissance** (the 'New Learning') helped to increase the level of literacy. Increased interest in learning was aided by the development of printing. Printing, in turn, helped the development of education and private libraries. Around 5,000 books survive from the late 15th century to 1557. For the period 1580–1603 alone there are approximately 4,300 books still in existence.

In the century before the accession of Elizabeth I, many grammar schools were founded. For instance, Stockport Grammar School in Cheshire and Brentwood School in Essex. Edward VI's reign alone saw the creation of a large number of schools that still bear his name. In addition, there was an increase in university places. Cardinal Wolsey founded Cardinal, later Christ Church, College at Oxford in the 1520s. To gain a university-level education students could attend Oxford, Cambridge or the Inns of Court in London. The latter provided a legal training. As a result, the level of literacy improved considerably. By 1558, the group William Harrison termed 'gentlemen' were literate. By 1603, so were the majority of yeomen.

High culture was also supported by royal and aristocratic patronage. Both Henry VIII and Elizabeth I were noted patrons of the arts. Elizabeth's

Court became a centre of artistic activity. This was partly due to the 'Gloriana Cult', which was actively encouraged by Elizabeth's supporters. The portrayal of Elizabeth as the centre of national life helped to develop popular support for the regime.

How did 'high culture' develop during Elizabeth I's reign?

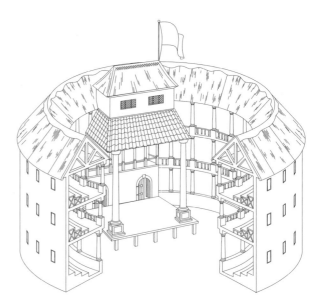

An Elizabethan stage

The two dominant art forms at this time were drama and poetry. To many, the 'Age of Elizabeth' is really the 'Age of Shakespeare'. William Shakespeare reached the height of his literary powers during the last years of Elizabeth I's reign. However, Elizabethan drama was not limited to Shakespeare alone. Ben Johnson, who wrote *Volpone the Wolf* and *Every Man in his Humour*, was also a playwright of repute.

The development of drama was aided not only by patronage but also by the development of theatres, particularly in London. The opening of the Globe Theatre in 1599 and the Fortune Theatre a year later attracted the audience for the plays by Shakespeare and other playwrights.

Poetry also went through a period of considerable creativity. Edmund Spenser's 'The Faerie Queene' stands out as an example of the quality of Elizabethan poetry. It is also an example of literature aiding the 'Gloriana Cult'. Towards the end of Elizabeth's reign, the development of Metaphysical poetry, most closely associated with John Donne, was established.

Unlike drama and poetry, there was little development in either painting or sculpture. In both cases, producing portraits of leading members of society was the main avenue for artists to develop these art forms.

In a broader context, there were important developments in English music and architecture. In music, Thomas Tallis, who received royal patronage, wrote in both English and Latin. In architecture, a distinctive English style was developed. Homes for the gentry, such as Gawsworth Hall in Cheshire, offer an example of this style.

Little Moreton Hall, Cheshire: an Elizabethan manor house

1. Study the two Elizabethan houses.

2. What do you regard as the main architectural features of Elizabethan houses?

3. How far are these houses similar in design and construction?

Crooke Hall, near Wigan

How did 'popular culture' develop?

Several medieval pastimes were still popular in Elizabethan England. In rural areas, hunting, fishing and archery were followed. Fairs and markets attracted both townspeople and rural dwellers alike. At these events, amateur plays and 'circus-style' acts would take place. There were also spectacles such as bear-baiting and cock-fighting. On a more gory level, public executions attracted large crowds throughout the period. Towards the end of Elizabeth's reign, open-air theatres began to attract craftsmen

Ballads: Form of song that told a story.

and town dwellers. On a literary level, **ballads** were popular. So were 'chap-books'. These were small, cheap books sold by pedlars.

A feature of 'popular culture' that also survived throughout the Elizabethan period was magic and witchcraft. Magic was most closely associated with popular medicine and healing. In a society where a large number of poorer people lacked education, the survival of such ideas is perhaps understandable. In periods of extreme economic hardship, such as the 1590s, the belief that witches were responsible for misfortune was not uncommon.

London from the South Bank in Elizabethan England. London Bridge, with its shops and array of traitors' heads, spans the river, leading to the City (left) and the Tower (right).

1. **What factors helped the development of high culture in Elizabeth I's England?**

2. **How did high culture differ from popular culture? Give reasons to support your answer.**

3. **To what extent was Elizabeth's reign 'A Golden Age' for English culture?**

6 James VI and I, 1603–1625

6.1 Succession and the union of Scotland and England

Key Issues

- Was 1603 a turning point in British history?

- Why was the Union of Crowns between England and Scotland so controversial?

- How successful was James VI and I in his attempts to 'unite' England and Scotland?

6.1.1 How strong was the claim of James VI of Scotland to the English throne in 1603?

6.1.2 What was the character of James VI and I as depicted by his contemporaries?

6.1.3 What was the attitude of James VI and I towards Union?

6.1.4 What were the problems facing James in achieving Union?

6.1.5 How far was constitutional union achieved?

6.1.6 How far was religious union achieved?

Framework of Events

1566	19 June: birth of James
1567	Murder of Lord Darnley, father of James
	Abdication of Mary Queen of Scots
	29 July: James becomes James VI of Scotland with Earl of Moray as Regent
1568	Flight of Mary Queen of Scots to England
1587	Execution of Mary Queen of Scots
1589	Marriage of James VI to Anne of Denmark
1594	Birth of Prince Henry
1595	Birth of Princess Elizabeth
1596	'Demonologie', a treatise on witchcraft, is written by James
1598	*Trew Law of Free Monarchies* – a book on government by James
1599	*Basilikon Doron* – a book on kingship written by James for his son
1600	Birth of Prince Charles
1603	Death of Elizabeth I and accession of James VI to the throne of England
1604	Debates on Union in the English and Scottish Parliaments
	Royal Proclamation on Union
1606	Union flag designed
1606–07	Second session of English Parliament dominated by debates on union
	In Scotland, James promotes bishops
1608	Colville's Case (Calvin's Case) raises issue of naturalisation of post-nati
1610	Courts of High Commission restored in Scotland
	Scots involved in the Plantation of Ulster
1611	Exile of Andrew Melville
1617	Visit of James to Scotland
1618	Five Articles of Perth.

Overview

T HE change of dynasty in England in 1603 was a very important event. The House of Tudor – during whose rule the union of England and Wales had taken place – ended with Elizabeth I. Relations between England and Scotland had been bad for centuries. Any chance of union was thought more likely to be by military conquest than by marriage. However, Margaret Tudor had married James IV of Scotland, and the Treaty of Greenwich between England and Scotland in 1543 had provided for the marriage of Mary Queen of Scots to the son of Henry VIII of England. That came to nothing when Mary was married to the **Dauphin** of France, Francis. By the late 16th century, the Tudor dynasty through the male line was about to expire (see family tree opposite). Therefore, the marriages of Margaret Tudor – the first to James IV and the second to the Earl of Angus – were to assume great importance in the English, as well as the Scottish, succession. In 1603, the Stuart dynasty of Scotland united the whole island in a peaceful manner, creating the Kingdom of Great Britain. With the exception of the **Interregnum** period (1649–60), the Stuart dynasty ruled Britain until 1714, presiding over some of the most important and turbulent events in British history.

Dauphin: Heir to the French throne. The 'auld alliance' was traditionally between Scotland and France.

Interregnum: Literally, 'between reigns' – the period in English history when England was a republic, 1649–60 (see Chapter 8.)

James's great goal was to unite the two kingdoms of Scotland and England, and he was prepared to be patient to achieve success. The idea of fusing the kingdoms of England and Scotland into a 'Great Britain' had appeal. If the names that divided his kingdoms were replaced by an ancient name that united the island, James was convinced that neither England nor Scotland would appear to be losing out to the other.

Regal union – the union of the crowns of Scotland and England in the person of King James – took place on the death of Elizabeth. James's accession to the English throne made him the ruler of England, Wales and Ireland, in addition to his Scottish territories; in effect, a triple monarchy of England and Wales, Scotland and Ireland. He could have been content with the mere addition of titles – multiple kingdoms with absentee kings were not unusual in late medieval and early modern Europe. James, however, was an idealist who wanted complete and harmonious union of the two ancient and formerly hostile kingdoms: England and Scotland.

6.1.1 How strong was the claim of James VI of Scotland to the English throne in 1603?

Elizabeth I died, without producing an heir, in 1603. She had been very careful not to nominate her successor until the last moment. She feared diminished loyalty from ministers who would be keen to ingratiate themselves with a successor, as well as plots against an ageing sovereign. On her deathbed, Elizabeth I signified that her successor was to be James VI, King of Scotland.

The succession of James offered the English stable government under an experienced king with a fertile queen who had already produced two surviving sons and a daughter by 1603. (The couple went on to produce seven children, although only three survived to maturity.)

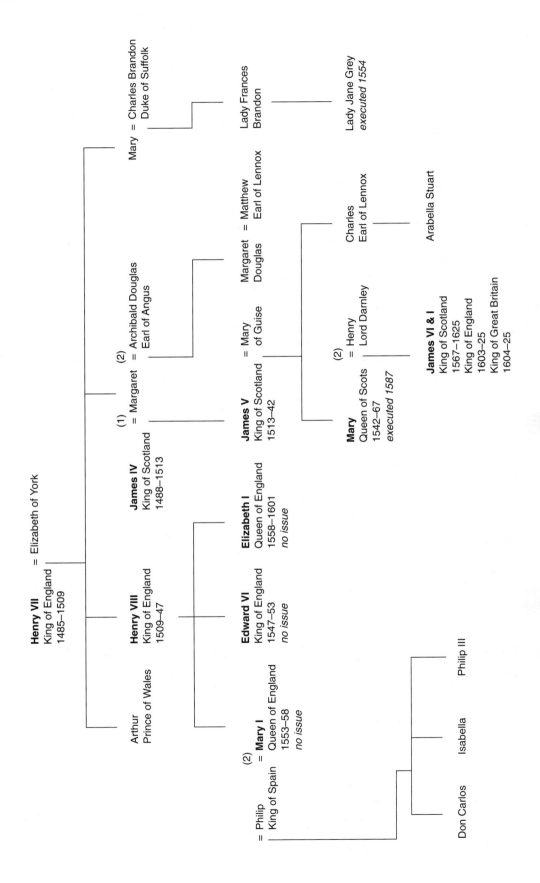

The British succession, 1603

The Scottish succession had not only been anticipated, but also carefully planned by Elizabeth's leading minister, Robert Cecil. He had been in communication with James for several years before the death of Elizabeth.

Both Cecil and James were keen that the new Stuart dynasty in England should get off to a peaceful start. James himself had anticipated his rightful inheritance in the event of Elizabeth dying childless. He had been careful not to anger Queen Elizabeth, even when she was responsible for the execution of his mother, Mary Queen of Scots, in 1587. His first two children after his marriage to Anne of Denmark (1590) were given the English names of Henry (born 1594) and Elizabeth (born 1596). This was a clear indication of what he considered to be their destiny: the English throne. Queen Elizabeth was the last of the Tudors to rule England, and the godmother to the Stuart Princess Elizabeth.

Historical destiny was also apparent. James saw the working out of the theme of union on an even grander scale, that of the whole isle. The union of England and Wales would be crowned by the addition of Scotland, thus uniting a Britain divided since Saxon times, nearly a thousand years before.

The idea of Divine Right of Kings underpinned all the other claims. Like most monarchs of that period, James claimed to rule by **divine right**. He believed that God appointed rulers; they were accountable for their government to God alone. As God had chosen James to rule Scotland, it was the choice of God that James should rule a united kingdom of Great Britain.

James would probably have put the above reasons in the following order:

- Divine right as expressed in his succession by God's will.

- Legitimate succession by linear descent from Henry VII.

- Historical right, fulfilling the union of England and Scotland.

- The wish of Elizabeth I.

His only possible rival was his cousin, Arabella Stuart. She had been brought up in England and was the subject of a number of marriage schemes. James was cautious towards her. Only when she married William Seymour, also with a claim to the English throne, did James show real concern. Arabella was imprisoned in the Tower of London in 1610, and died there in 1615.

Divine right: The political view that claims that royal authority derived directly from God. As a consequence, a particular family or individual is designated by the will of God as ruler of a particular state.

1. Using the family tree on page 132, explain the relationship between Elizabeth I and Mary Queen of Scots.

2. Explain the relationship between Mary Queen of Scots and Lord Darnley.

3. On what grounds would you justify the claim of James VI of Scotland to the English throne in 1603?

4. What was the claim of Arabella Stuart to the English throne?

6.1.2 What was the character of James VI and I as depicted by his contemporaries?

King James ruled Scotland from 1567 until 1603. He ruled England from 1603 until 1625, taking the title King of Great Britain by Royal Proclamation in 1604, signifying the Union of the kingdoms of Scotland and England in his person.

His character was complex. At times, vulgar and impatient; at other times, subtle and cunning, he was the product of a highly dysfunctional family in turbulent times. His mother was Mary Queen of Scots. Mary succeeded her father James V as ruler of Scotland in 1542 at the age of one week. Within a year, she was promised in marriage to the Dauphin of France. Between 1548 and 1561 she lived mostly in France, leaving her mother, Mary of Guise, to govern Scotland during a period of great change in Scotland. The period was known as the Scottish Reformation, in which Scotland broke away from the Catholic Church. Mary was a Catholic and was out of sympathy with the Scottish religious reformers. Her husband died in 1559. Mary made an eminently suitable second marriage to her first cousin, Henry Stewart, Lord Darnley, in 1565. Mary gave birth to James in 1566, hoping that he would be the first to unite the two kingdoms of Scotland and England. The marriage to Darnley was very unhappy. He was involved in the murder of Mary's Italian secretary, David Riccio, in 1566 and was assassinated shortly afterwards.

Mary then married James Hepburn, 4th Earl of Bothwell. Meanwhile an army was raised against Bothwell and Mary. Mary was captured and sent to Loch Leven where she was forced to abdicate. Here she miscarried of twins by Bothwell. She escaped and raised an army. The defeat of her troops at Langside forced her to flee to England for help from Elizabeth. Elizabeth kept her under house arrest for almost 20 years, eventually agreeing to her execution as a plotter against her, in 1587.

With the flight of Mary to England, James was crowned King of Scotland in Stirling Castle at the age of 13 months. An early portrait of James by Arnold Bronkhorst shows a child king dressed as a man with the sparrow hawk, symbolising the manly pursuit of hunting.

Scotland was governed by regents until 1580. In a troubled Scotland, the regencies were unstable and short-lived: the Earl of Moray was assassinated in 1570, the Earl of Lennox was killed in 1571, the Earl of Mar died in 1572. The Earl of Morton exercised control until James made a bid to assert authority in 1580. This was not entirely successful as a group of Protestants organised the Ruthven Raid, which captured James and held him prisoner for a few months until he was able to escape and order the arrest of the Earl of Gowrie, the leader of the raiders. By his early twenties, James was gaining control and applying firm government in Scotland.

He married Anne of Denmark in 1589.

Mary Queen of Scots (1542–1587) by unkown artist

James VI and I, an oil painting by Arnold Bronckorst

Silver medal commemorating the marriage of James VI to Anne of Denmark, 1590

George Buchanan (1506–1582)

A Scottish humanist and scholar. He was forced to flee to France in 1539, because of his satirical verses on the Franciscans. He returned to Scotland in 1652 as tutor to Mary Queen of Scots. Later, he was tutor to James VI, before becoming principal of a college at St Andrew's University, Scotland. He wrote *Rerum Scoticarum Historia* ('A History of Scotland') in 1582, which was biased against Mary Queen of Scots.

Caricaturist: A person who portrays other people in drawings or writing and exaggerates their features and personalities so that they seem ridiculous.

Tract: A short article expressing an opinion on religious, moral or political subjects in order to try to influence people's attitudes.

There is a story that indicates James's strength of character. When Anne of Denmark's voyage to Scotland was delayed by storms in the North Sea – said by some to have been raised by the North Berwick coven of witches – James bravely set sail and spent the winter months with her in Scandinavia, before returning to Scotland.

James's education was a hard one, both in the school of life and in the classroom. His tutors made sure that he was brought up as a good Protestant and a good scholar. George Buchanan, one of the most distinguished scholars of the age, stretched James's mind to the full, turning him into an effective writer of verse, prose and political theory.

James's writing makes impressive reading. Within two years he produced *Demonology* (1597), a treatise on witchcraft, *The Trew Law of Free Monarchies* (1598), a work of political theory, and *The Basilikon Doron* (1599), a work on kingship dedicated to his son. It is no wonder, that when he inherited the English throne in 1603, he described himself as 'an old King needing no lessons'.

There is, however, no doubt that this educated and book-learned king was sometimes too clever by half. He also had a number of personal characteristics that made him an easy victim for the **caricaturist**.

A **tract**, dated 1652, was entitled 'A Cat May Look Upon a King'. It was one of many produced during the Interregnum. It shows a humble tabby alley cat looking at a portrait of James (see below). The portrait is set in an oval frame surrounded by his personal motto *Beati Pacifici* ('Blessed are the Peacemakers'). Underneath is an inscription which reads 'Mars, Puer, Alecto, Virgo, VULPES, Leo, Nullus.' This refers to a prophecy of succession of kings and queens in England from Henry VIII (Mars, the God of war), Edward VI (*Puer*, boy), Mary I (seen as the Fury, Alecto, on account of her persecution of Protestants), Elizabeth I (Virgo, the Virgin Queen), James (Vulpes, the fox), Charles I (Leo, the lion), and the Commonwealth (*Nullus*, no one). James is called 'VULPES' (fox) to indicate his craftiness, or shifty nature.

Title page of the tract 'A Cat May Look Upon a King'

Contemporary views of the character of King James

The key evidence for the character of James is a pen portrait written in 1584 by Monsieur de Fontenay, a relative of the French Secretary of Mary Queen of Scots. De Fontenay visited Edinburgh in 1584 and wrote an account of his impressions of James. It was published 75 years later in Sir Anthony Weldon's *Court and Character of King James*. Weldon himself was dead by then, and according to some was not personally responsible for the publication of the manuscript. By the 1650s, the monarchy had been abolished in England, and verbal abuse of kings was in fashion. During the years of James's reign in England, useful opinions were offered by the Venetian Ambassador and by the King's personal physician, Dr Theodore Mayerne.

Source-based questions: James I as seen by contemporaries

The following exercise places four primary sources in chronological order. The questions invite you to compare, contrast and explain characteristics of James.

SOURCE A

He is learned in many languages, sciences, and affairs of state. He has a marvellous spirit … Having been nourished in fear he still has this fault, that he often dare not contradict the great lords, and nevertheless he likes very much to be considered brave and to be feared … He hates dancing and music in general … He is very rude and uncivil in speaking and eating … and entertainment in the company of women. His gait is bad, composed of erratic steps, and he tramps about even in his room. He likes hunting above all the pleasures of the world, remaining there at least six hours together chasing all over the place with loosened rein. I have only noticed in him three things very bad for the preservation of his state and the government of the same. The first is his ignorance and lack of knowledge of his poverty … The second that he loves indiscreetly … The third is that he is too lazy and too thoughtless and devoted to pleasure, especially hunting … I know that this is excusable in the young but I fear it will continue. However he told me that nothing happened without his knowledge, and that although he spent much time in hunting, he could do as much business in one hour as others could in a day.

Monsieur de Fontenay reports on James as King of Scotland to the French Secretary of Mary Queen of Scots, 1584

SOURCE B

He is sufficiently tall, of a noble presence, his physical constitution robust, and he is at pains to preserve it by taking much exercise at the chase, which he passionately loves, and uses not only as recreation but as a medicine. For this he throws off all business, which he leaves to his Council and to his Ministers. And so one may truly say that he is Sovereign in name and appearance rather than in effect … This is the result of his deliberate choice, for he is capable of governing, being a Prince of intelligence and culture above the common, thanks to his application and pleasure in study when he was young, though now he has abandoned that pursuit altogether.

Report on England presented by Nicolo Molin, Venetian Ambassador, to the Government of Venice in 1607.

SOURCE C

His skin is thin and delicate, so that it itches easily … As regards food he does not much amiss except that he eats no bread … He generally takes no roast meats. Owing to want of teeth he does not chew his food but bolts it. Fruit he eats at all hours of the day and night. In drink he errs as to quality, quantity, frequency, time and order … He has the strongest antipathy to water and all watery drinks. The King used to be given up to most violent exercise in hunting. Now he is quieter and lies or sits more, but that is due to the weakness of his knee joints … His mind is easily moved suddenly. He is very wrathful, but the fit soon passes off … He suffered an attack of melancholy after the death of his son in 1612 … In 1619, after the Queen's death he suffered … fainting, sighing, dread, incredible sadness, intermittent pulse … In 1613 he produced bloody urine, with red sand … frequent vomiting and other nephritic symptoms … The same in 1615 … Arthritis invaded first the right foot, which had an odd twist when walking … The King laughs at medicine … and declares physicians to be of very little use and hardly necessary.

Dr Theodore Mayerne's memoir on the king's health, drawn up in December 1623. Dr Mayerne was an eminent doctor of European status in the first half of the 17th century. After a distinguished early career in Switzerland and France, he became court physician to James I and Charles I.

Source-based questions: James I as seen by contemporaries

SOURCE D

He was of middle stature, more corpulent through his clothes than in his body, yet fat enough, his clothes ever being made large and easy, the doublets quilted for stiletto proof … He was naturally of a timorous (fearful) disposition, which was the reason of his quilted doublets; his eye large, ever rolling after any stranger that came into his presence …; his beard was very thin; his tongue too large for his mouth, and made him drink very uncomely, as if eating his drink … his skin was as soft as taffeta …, which felt so because he never washed his hands, only rubbed his finger ends slightly with the wet end of a napkin, his legs were very weak, … his walk ever circular, his fingers … fiddling about his codpiece. He was very constant in all things (his favourites excepted) … He was ever best when furthest from the Queen … He naturally loved not the sight of a soldier …

He was very witty, and had as many witty jests as any man living, at which he would not smile himself, but deliver them in a grave and serious manner: he was very liberal (generous, free), of what he had not in his own grip, and would rather part with £100 he never had in his keeping; than one twenty shillings piece within his own custody …

He was so crafty and cunning in petty things … as a very wise man was wont to say he believed him the wisest fool in Christendom, meaning him wise in small things, but a fool in weighty matters …

He was infinitely inclined to peace, but more out of fear than conscience, and this was the greatest blemish this king had through all his reign, otherwise he might have been ranked with the very best of our kings.

> *From Sir Anthony Weldon's* The Court and Character of King James, *published 1650. Sir Anthony Weldon had held Court office under James VI and I. After a visit to Scotland in 1617, he produced a satire on the Scots that offended James and all sensible people. Weldon clearly got carried away by his own acidic prose. As a result of this he was dismissed from his post at Court. His* Court and Character *was written some time after his dismissal from court, but not published until after Weldon's own death. It was published one year after the removal of the Stuart monarchy in England with the execution of King Charles I in 1649.*

1. Read Source A.

a) How useful is this source as evidence of the character and appearance of James VI?

b) What aspects of his personality are unfavourable in a king?

c) What are the favourable characteristics of King James?

d) What impression do you get of James's physical appearance and health?

2. Read Source B.

a) How reliable is this extract to the historian studying the character of King James?

b) How far does Source B support Source A as evidence of James's character and appearance?

3. Look carefully at Source C.

How useful is this source to the historian studying the personality of James VI and I?

4. Look at Sources A–D.

a) How reliable are these pen portraits of King James as evidence of James's character?

b) What common characteristics are to be found in Source A and Source D?

c) What are the unfavourable aspects of the king highlighted by Weldon?

d) To what extent might the unfavourable aspects be explained by the evidence from the King's doctor in Source C?

e) In what ways is Weldon not totally critical of King James?

Why do historians differ about the character and personality of King James VI and I?

Plantation of Ulster: Settlement of Scottish and English settlers into Ulster during the reign of King James.

Historical hindsight: Looking back at history, knowing what happened afterwards, e.g. reading events before 1642 as leading to the Civil War.

Whig historians: Those in the tradition of famous 19th-century historians such as Lord Macaulay. They see English history as culminating in the triumph of parliamentary government and the 17th century as a period of constitutional struggle between Crown and Parliament.

1066 and All That: A witty satire on English history written by W.C. Sellers and R.J. Yeatman; originally published in *Punch* magazine in 1930.

1. What are the advantages and disadvantages of 'historical hindsight'?

2. Why might historians differ in their views of James VI and I?

It is true to say that King James VI of Scotland had a much better press than King James I of Great Britain. For too long the wit of Weldon conditioned English attitudes to King James. Weldon's prose style suited the English sense of humour. It probes the qualities that James himself most valued – wisdom and peace – and demolishes them. In addition to this, the most shattering events in the British Isles – civil wars – began in 1637, only 12 years after his death. The wars began in Scotland. Union between England and Scotland was his dearest project; regal union was achieved in his person. Ireland rebelled in 1641 and the **Plantation of Ulster**, with many Scottish settlers from 1610, had been a project of James. When the English Civil War broke out in 1642, problems in religion and Crown–Parliament relations were seen to be key factors. These were areas in which the problems of James were exaggerated by his successor, Charles I. In this sense, James VI and I is the victim of **historical hindsight**. Those who see the English Civil War as the highlight of the 17th century, tend to see the beginning of the road to civil war in the reign of James. **Whig historians** – from Lord Macaulay through to Wallace Notestein and David Harris Willson – regard James's reign as one in which Parliament gained the initiative over the Crown. Finally, his Court, his character and his apparently lack-lustre foreign policy made him appear the pale shadow of his English predecessor, Elizabeth I, around whom the legend of 'Gloriana' developed after her death. Elizabeth was a hard act to follow; James ruled in difficult times and worse times were to follow.

The *1066 and All That* view of James as a king 'who slobbered at the mouth and had favourites' was not shattered until the second half of the 20th century when some scholarly studies – notably by Conrad Russell and Roger Lockyer – inspired research into James's dealings with Parliament, the Church, foreign policy, and the Stuart Court. Revision of many areas of the work of James has inevitably, at some times unwittingly, called for a revision of his personality. He appears less lazy, less inept and less cowardly than previously painted. It is, of course, possible that he has been over-revised, although no one has as yet made him out to be a financial genius! Perhaps Maurice Lee's conclusion is the safest: that while James slobbered at the mouth and had favourites, he was 'not such a bad king after all'.

6.1.3 What was the attitude of James VI and I towards Union?

The question of Union was to James the most important issue at the beginning of his reign. His son, Charles, viewed the achievement of Union as his father's greatest gift to the nation. This is witnessed by the fact that the Banqueting House ceiling, painted for Charles I by the Flemish artist, Rubens, celebrates the theme of Union. James presides over the two figures of England and Scotland united by the Infant Great Britain (see page 196).

Union was, however, more effective in artistic representation than it was in political reality. James's vision exceeded political possibilities. Complete union floundered on the rocks of suspicion, narrow vision and

Vested interest: A strong reason that someone has for acting in a particular way, for example to protect his/her own money, power or reputation.

Blind prejudice: Irrational prejudice/hatred.

Post-nati: Those born after the succession of James I to the English throne in 1603.

vested interest. Ingrained conservatism in church and state blocked real union of key institutions such as Parliament, Law and the Church.

The sort of Union that James had in mind was obviously well ahead of his time. Neither England nor Scotland was ready for such a noble vision. His failure cannot simply be ascribed to English 'racism' – the Scots were equally 'racist' when it came to the idea of complete union with England. In any case, the word 'racist' is inappropriately used about the early 17th century. There are examples on both sides of **blind prejudice** against each other, but the whole notion of a sense of national identity at that time needs further research. It should be remembered that in the early 17th century communications were very poor in England and Scotland, making it difficult to estimate how strong the idea of nationality was outside institutions of Government, Law and Church in both England and Scotland.

The influence of the institutions of the Privy Council and the Court (royal household) was important. The Scottish Privy Council remained in Edinburgh after 1603. James ruled Scotland from London through the Privy Council in Edinburgh. As he put it, in an address adjourning the English Parliament in 1607: 'Here I sit, and govern it with my Pen; I write and it is done; and by a Clerk of the Council I govern Scotland now, which others could not do by the Sword.'

The removal of the Court to Whitehall was probably the most significant change. The fact that James kept a number of Scots in his London Court can be explained not merely in terms of 'Scottish favourites' that annoyed English courtiers, but also as a means of creating a 'British' court.

Traditions of parliaments, law and religion were strongly defended in two ancient kingdoms. These, rather than language in kingdoms, were the 'vehicles' of nationality where varieties of English were the common tongue in all except remote areas. In the Border regions, lack of control and a spirit of independence were apparent. Borderers often regarded themselves as owing little allegiance to either England or Scotland.

By the end of James's reign, there was no union of parliaments, of law or of churches. In some ways, James's achievements were modest:

● repeal of laws hostile to Scotland on the English statute book

● repeal of laws hostile to England on the Scottish statute book

● acceptance of subjects born after 1603 in Scotland (the *post-nati*) as naturalised subjects of the King of England (achieved by verdicts of judges, rather than by Parliament)

● the taking of the title 'King of Great Britain' by Royal Proclamation in 1604.

Yet, in a sense, James's achievements were great in that he successfully governed both kingdoms by retaining the essential institutions of each. By 1610, it had become obvious that institutional union was not an option other than in the institution of monarchy.

Attempts to find common ground in religion led to the Five Articles of Perth in 1618, but there was far from being a national church for Britain (the Kingdoms of England and Scotland).

James was no fool. He would have realised only too well the impossibly high cost of full Union to both England and Scotland. Historian Jenny Wormald suggests that James may have been taking an extreme stance in order to get more out of any compromise.

Was James a visionary?

James's attitude towards Union was apparently visionary. He claimed that he wanted a 'perfect union' of his two kingdoms. He compared their union to a marriage in which he was the husband. James wanted not only a union of the crowns, but also a union of parliaments, law and religion. He wanted a common flag, common currency, and free trade. His subjects perceived that Union was important to him. There are many pageants and entertainments celebrating Union. One – an entertainment on the triumphs of reunited Britannia by A. Mundy, citizen and draper of London, performed for the inauguration of the Lord Mayor of London in 1605 – showed James as a second Brutus. It was a mixture of myth and history that integrates the biblical Noah's Flood with both the Classical Greek Fall of Troy and some early Anglo-Saxon history.

James spoke at length to his First Parliament, justifying Union as:

- fulfilling historical destiny by returning to the ancient kingdom of Britain

- strengthening the economy of the united nations

- carrying out the will of God: 'What God hath conjoined then, let no man separate. I am the husband, and the whole isle is my lawful wife: I am the head, and it is my body: I am the shepherd, and it is my flock … (James to the Commons, 19 March 1604).

Those in Parliament who failed to share his vision were seen as 'blinded with ignorance … and only delighting to fish in troubled waters.' (House of Commons' Journal Vol. 1 p. 43).

'Perfect union' required the Parliaments to accept a number of things:

- James's change in title to King of Great Britain

- naturalisation of the Scottish subjects of the King of England and the English subjects of the King of Scotland

- a union of legal systems

- abolition of laws hostile to Scotland on the English statute book and the abolition of laws hostile to England on the Scottish statute book

- a common religious system

- free trade

- a common currency and system of weights and measurements.

James hoped that his First Parliament would treat Union as the most important matter for discussion.

His initial vision of 'perfect union' became modified out of necessity. A Committee for Union, set up by both Houses of the English Parliament, treated the enthusiasm and idealism of James for Union with extreme caution. The issue of the new style, or title 'King of Great Britain', and its implications, was a serious stumbling block. To short circuit this, James took the title by Royal Proclamation on 20 October 1604, the very first day of the meeting of the group of 39 English and 28 Scottish Commissioners to discuss Union. The historian Roger Lockyer suggests that James was influenced by Sir Francis Bacon in this.

Bacon would have advised that, if James was determined to take the

Royal Proclamation: An edict issued by the king.

Statute: A law passed by Parliament and signed by the sovereign.

new title, a **Royal Proclamation** would be less offensive than insistence on taking the title by **statute**. This would be on the grounds that the former did not change any existing statutes and would still leave the traditional English form valid for future statutes and legal forms.

Royal Proclamation on Style, 20 October 1604

Wherefore we have thought good to discontinue the divided names of England and Scotland out of our regal Style, and do intend and resolve to take … the name and Style of King of Great Britain …

We do … by force of our Kingly Power and prerogative, assume to Our self by the clearness of our right, the name and Style of KING OF GREAT BRITAIN, FRANCE AND IRELAND, DEFENDER OF THE FAITH etc.

---

1. How realistic was James's 'perfect union'?

2. Why was James obliged to change his Style (title) by Royal Proclamation?

Given the problems over the Style (title), James found himself having to struggle to achieve partial union with the naturalisation of Scottish subjects born after 1603, and the repeal of the hostile laws. By 1610, his great scheme of Union was in low profile and the pursuit of 'perfect union' had given way to the idea of gradual union through evolution.

6.1.4 What were the problems facing James in achieving Union?

State and Church

The ideal view of Union, held by James, could only be achieved through the common institutions of State and Church. This created opposition in the Parliaments of England and Scotland, within the Churches and within the Law.

From the Scottish point of view, it appeared that James preferred English versions of the Church and Law, and that a united Parliament would meet in London rather than Edinburgh. The English ruling classes felt threatened by the Crown's increased authority.

Francis Bacon, a supporter of the project and the closest thing that James had to a 'spin-doctor' at the time (April 1604), collected a list of objections to the change of name as expressed by English MPs. They can be summarised as:

● Change of name to Great Britain was not necessary.

● There was no precedent for it.

● Change of name implied dissolution of the old state and setting up of a new one – that was full of dangers and uncertainties.

● There would be confusion over summoning of Parliaments, laws, customs, officers of state, oaths of allegiance etc.

● Problems would be caused in foreign policy, obscuring the high status of England by loss of its name.

- The loss of name would not only be politically and legally difficult, but also unpopular:

> 'There is no worldly thing more dear to men than their name ... The contracted name of Britain will bring into oblivion the names of England and Scotland ... Whereas now England, in the Style, is placed before Scotland, in the name of Britain that degree of priority will be lost ... The change of name will be harsh in the popular opinion, and unpleasing to the country.'

The objections are fairly comprehensive and indicate a range of feelings in the English Parliament, which were also felt in Scotland.

The Venetian Ambassador made the Scottish position clear, in October 1603. He wrote of a meeting of Scottish nobles and their feelings:

> It was to draw up a petition, and send it to the King by the hands of four leading nobles; they are to inform his Majesty that unless he grants the demands contained therein it will be impossible to effect the union of the two kingdoms and will endanger peace. The chief points are that, as England fell by inheritance to the King of Scotland, England is to be considered accessory to Scotland; if that be impossible, then in case only one Council is to govern both kingdom, the Scottish and English are to be equally represented in that Council, while each kingdom shall keep its own name and its own laws.

In short, if England was not to be integrated into Scotland, there must be complete equality between the two and no loss of name or laws.

Vested interest

Naked vested interest is not highlighted by Bacon or by the Venetian Ambassador. It can, however, be seen in contemporary writers such as the Norfolk MP, Sir Henry Spelman. He believed there were many dangers in allowing naturalisation of the Scots. He saw them gaining influence at Court, buying houses, land and offices in England – both in the city and in the country. Spelman believed that naturalisation and support of the King would allow the Scots to dominate offices of state and government, to the detriment of the native English.

Grass-root hostility

Xenophobic: Showing a fear or extremely strong dislike of people from other countries.

There was grass-root suspicion and hostility to the project. The extent of this is difficult to assess. Many writers against Union refer to it. The most **xenophobic** writings come from those within Parliament and the Court. Sir Christopher Piggott, MP for Buckinghamshire, referred to the Scots as 'murderers, thieves and rogues ... who have not suffered above two kings to die in their beds these 200 years'. This did little to promote the Union debates in 1607, although he does seem to have been a **maverick**. Sir Anthony Weldon wrote his so-called 'witty' *Description of Scotland* in 1617, describing the country as 'too good for those that possess it, and too bad for others to be at the charge to conquer it. The air might be wholesome but for the stinking people that inhabit it, the ground might be fruitful had they the will to manure it.' He was not only seriously politically incorrect, but was also frequently carried away by his own prose style.

Maverick: Someone who thinks and acts independently, and does not always do the same as the group that he/she belongs to.

The thinking behind the project

The project had not been clearly thought out. It was difficult to understand what was meant by 'perfect union', what the extent of 'partial union' would be, and what would constitute a 'federal union'.

James, inevitably, blamed his advisers for not warning him how contentious the issue was. The Venetian Ambassador suggested that the bitter debates on Union were not only reviving old hostilities between England and Scotland but were in danger of undermining the King's authority in Parliament.

The ideal of religious Union was just as fraught with difficulties as that involving legal and constitutional. James hoped that the Archbishop of Canterbury would be the Primate (senior archbishop) of Britain. The fundamental problem was that the essential structure of the Scottish Kirk (Church) was Presbyterian (see page 168), while that of the English Church was Episcopal (see page 171). There were bishops in the Scottish church and James had been working for some time to increase their authority with a view to the evolution of a hierarchy based on bishops and the King. James was opposed by Scottish ministers such as Andrew Melville, and was making only slow progress. Melville believed in the separation of the Church and State, seeing them as two authorities. He saw the English church as polluted with Roman Catholicism.

1. How important were constitutional objections to Union?

2. Why was vested interest an important consideration?

3. With what justification did James blame his ministers for delays in achieving Union?

6.1.5 How far was constitutional union achieved?

In the sense of full Union of Parliaments and institutions of government, little – if anything – was achieved in the reign of James VI and I. James soon learnt that a parliamentary Union was out of the question.

By 1604, the question of the Style was blocked by an English Parliament keen to safeguard the integrity and supremacy of English Law. That James took the title 'King of Great Britain' was due to a Royal Proclamation rather than a statute. The fact that he did so hardened the attitude of the First Parliament against Union. Nothing beyond debates and committees had been achieved by the end of the first session of the First Parliament. Delays in the meeting of Parliament, caused by the plague in London in early 1605, allowed the matter to go off the boil.

When the second session of the First Parliament met, it was inevitably dominated by the aftermath of the Gunpowder Plot.

It was not until the third session of the First Parliament (1607) that Union again became a dominant issue. By then, James was fighting on three fronts: free trade, repeal of the hostile laws and the naturalisation of the *post-nati*. One of the opponents to Union, Sir Edwin Sandys, was pushing the idea of 'perfect union' in an attempt to secure the rejection of the whole package by asking for too much. Because of this, James actually opposed a discussion of 'perfect union' in this session.

Some trade benefits followed, and the repeal of the hostile laws was eventually achieved; the naturalisation of the post-nati was achieved but not in a parliamentary way. James was obliged to use the judges and the English courts to achieve this, in the case known as Calvin's Case, or Colville's Case. When the three-year-old Robert Colville, a Scot born after 1603, inherited lands in England from his grandfather, those lands were seized on the grounds that aliens could not inherit English land.

A case was brought on behalf of Colville. Ultimately, 14 judges from the King's Bench and Common Pleas, together with the Exchequer barons and the Lord Chancellor, heard the case. Twelve judges to two decided in favour of Colville, establishing the precedence that James wanted, and thus naturalising the post-nati.

Attempts at a common currency were somewhat half-hearted. New coins called unite coins were introduced. A union flag was designed but used only on ships, and then rarely.

Unite coins issued by James I, 1604–9

> 1. How had James achieved some measures of Union in spite of his First Parliament?
>
> 2. Was Britain anything more than a geographical expression in 1610?

After the Third Session of the First Parliament, little reference was made to Union. James seemed to have settled for a gradual approach. The only real measures towards integration came in religious matters.

In reality, the only sure and certain aspects of Union were that England and Scotland had the same king, the hostile laws were achieved and the post-nati naturalised.

6.1.6 How far was religious union achieved?

Both the Scottish and English Churches were in the Protestant reformed tradition. James was a sincere Protestant. After 1603, he found that the English Church, with its hierarchic organisation and the King as its Supreme Governor, had more respect for monarchy than its Scottish counterpart.

He was aware of the ideas of Andrew Melville and the influence that Melville had in the Scottish Kirk. James ordered Melville to visit England and to be educated in the ways of the English Church. Melville was not to be won over. He was incensed by the fine linen sleeves of Archbishop Bancroft's gown, referring to them as 'Romish rags'. James ordered him to apologise; Melville refused, was imprisoned in the Tower and then sent into exile.

When Archbishop Bancroft died in 1610, George Abbot became Archbishop of Canterbury. He had more in common with the senior Scottish clergy and got on better with them than Bancroft had done. This allowed James to continue his policy in Scotland of advancing the authority of Scottish bishops. A Scottish Parliament had restored bishops to their previous powers in Scotland in 1609, and the policy was continued by the General Assembly of the Church of Scotland, meeting in Glasgow in 1610.

The main object of James's visit to Scotland, in 1617, was to strengthen the links between the Scottish and English Churches. He ordered English-style services to be said in the royal chapel at Holyrood House, his palace in Edinburgh. His main achievement was The Five Articles of Perth, 1618. These were to bring the two churches more in line. They included:

● Holy Communion was to be taken by the communicant kneeling.

● Confirmation was revived and was to be performed by a bishop.

● Private baptism and private communion were to be available for the sick.

● Easter, Christmas and certain other religious days were to be celebrated (Good Friday, Ascension Day, and Whitsunday).

The General Assembly accepted the Five Articles of Perth. These Articles were unpopular in Scotland. They passed the Scottish Parliament by 86 votes to 59. When the Scottish Parliament ratified the Five Articles in 1621, they insisted that there should be no further changes to the religious situation in Scotland. While the Articles were passed, they were not necessarily enforced.

The differences between the English and Scottish churches, caricatured by Weldon in 1617, continued:

'They (the Scots) christen without the cross, marry without the ring, receive the sacraments without reverence, die without repentance, and bury without divine service … They keep no holy days, nor acknowledge no Saint but St Andrew.'

1. Why was there opposition to religious Union?

2. How effectively did James deal with the problems of religious differences?

6.2 Crown, Parliament and finance

Key Issues

● *What was the attitude of James VI and I towards monarchy?*

● *How far did Parliament assert its authority?*

● *How successfully did James deal with the English Parliament?*

● *How far were the financial problems of James of his own making?*

Framework of Events

The First Parliament, 1604–1611

First session (March 1604)
- Buckinghamshire election dispute involving Goodwin and Fortescue
- Case of Sir Thomas Shirley
- Debates on the Union of England and Scotland
- Grievances of Purveyance and Wardship raised
- The Form of Apology and Satisfaction

Second session (1605–1606)
- Issue of Roman Catholics is raised after the Gunpowder Plot
- Grievance of Purveyance

Third Session (1606–1607)
- Union debates

Fourth Session (1610)
- Financial issues: The Great Contract

**The Second Parliament, 'The Addled Parliament'
(5 April – 7 June 1614)**
- Issue of use of Undertakers in elections
- Issue of Impositions

The Third Parliament (30 January 1621 – 6 January 1622)
- Palatinate Question
- Issue of financing foreign intervention
- Attack on monopolists
- Revival of impeachment
- The Spanish marriage issue
- Issue of the nature of the privileges of Parliament
- Commons' Petition
- Protestation of the Commons

The Fourth Parliament (19 February 1624 – 27 March 1625)
(The Parliament was prorogued on 29 May 1624, and dissolved on the death of King James in March 1625.)
- Issue of war subsidies
- Monopolies Act
- Impeachment and fall of Cranfield
- Defensive alliance with United Provinces
- Marriage negotiations with France
- Mansfeld's expedition raised to relieve the Palatinate.

Overview

Prorogue: To bring a session of Parliament to an end without dissolving it, thus keeping open the possibility of another session.

Royal prerogative: Special powers and authority of the sovereign that were not dependent upon the law or Parliament (e.g. the right to summon, prorogue and dissolve Parliament; and the use of emergency discretionary power. The former are called 'ordinary', and the latter 'absolute', prerogative.)

Subsidies: A parliamentary grant of money to the Crown. It was made up of a tax on the value of land and a tax on the value of goods. Therefore, it was a tax on income of landowners and merchants.

Impeachment: A trial or accusation within Parliament. The Commons prosecute and the Lords judge those accused of corruption or treason. Between 1459 and 1621, no one was impeached. Then, in 1621, it was used to attack monopolists.

THE question of James and his Parliaments has dominated examination papers ever since the advent of the examination system. Apart from religion, all the main issues of James's reign in England, together with his aspirations for a British monarchy, have been traditionally viewed in the parliamentary arena. From the late 1970s, the relations between James and his Parliaments came under close scrutiny, to such an extent that earlier ideas on the topic were 'revised' and new research undertaken.

The historian Maurice Lee has revealed that during the 22 years of James's rule as King of England, the English Parliament was in session for only 36 months. This suggests that we should not assume that relations between James and Parliament dominated the reign or that they were in constant tension. It is also important to remember that during the reign of James, as in the reign of Elizabeth, the sovereign not only reigned but also ruled. The King was the government. He was advised by his Privy Council and by Parliament, when he chose to call it. The King alone could summon, **prorogue** and dissolve Parliament. His power and authority was further consolidated by the fact that he:

- appointed men to his Privy Council
- appointed and dismissed judges at his pleasure
- appointed bishops
- created peers of the realm.

Much of the King's power was derived from the **royal prerogative** and supported by the theory of the divine right of kings.

Parliament, however, was important. It fulfilled three important roles:

- It gave advice when called upon to do so.
- It voted **subsidies** or levies of taxes for the Crown.
- It played the same essential part in the legislative process as it had done in the reign of Elizabeth. There could be no statute law without agreement between King, Lords and Commons.

The English Parliament consisted of King, House of Lords and House of Commons. The House of Lords was a very different institution to that of today. In view of the fact that the Crown appointed bishops, judges and peers of the realm, the King's influence over this body was likely to be great. In the reign of King James, the Lords played its customary role in legislation and advice. It was also involved in the revival of the process of **impeachment** in 1621.

The **House of Lords** consisted of the Lords Spiritual – about 27 bishops, namely the Archbishops of Canterbury and York, the Bishops of London, Durham, Winchester and 22 bishops in order of consecration; the Lords Temporal (81 in 1615 and 126 in 1628); the Attorney General (the Crown's legal adviser), and the Chief Justices. In short, it contained representatives from the Church, the landed aristocracy and the Law. They held seats by virtue of rank or inheritance, and all were male.

The **Jacobean House of Commons** consisted of about 467 members. Each shire (county) sent two representatives; each borough sent representatives elected by wealthy citizens. The principality of Wales sent 10 representatives to Westminster. Most MPs were from the gentry; many were lawyers. All were male.

Grievances: Local matters that needed addressing.

Apart from its part in legislation, the House of Commons presented the **grievances** of the localities. These might be redressed though Bills, Proclamations or Pardons. The Commons also voted subsidies, which were in addition to the King's ordinary sources of revenue, such as Crown lands and customs duties. It follows that the Commons might use subsidies as a bargaining counter for the redress of grievances. As financial incapacity dogged early modern monarchies, the role of Parliament became increasingly important. The Commons also played a part in the process of impeachment. It had the right to expel its own members but, in cases where the accused was not a member of the Commons, it cooperated with the House of Lords. The Commons prosecuted; the Lords judged. In this way, the fall of Bacon in 1621 and Cranfield in 1624 were brought about.

The First Parliament of James's reign was the only one of any length. A number of contentious issues were voiced at a testing time for a new and 'foreign' king. James faced difficulties over **privileges of Parliament** in matters of election disputes:

Privileges of Parliament: Free elections, free speech, and freedom from arrest during a parliamentary session were the special privileges claimed.

- A minority asserted the privileges in the Form of Apology and Satisfaction of 1604, although it was never formally presented to the King.
- James's scheme for full union with Scotland and his change in title were avoided.
- Finance, in the form of attacks on impositions (additional customs duties imposed by the King), and the failure of the Great Contract (Robert Cecil's radical proposal to abolish customs such as Purveyance in return for an annual money grant from Parliament).

These problems had poisoned relations between James and his Parliament by the end of 1610.

The Second, or Addled, Parliament of 1614 lasted only a few weeks. It achieved no legislation and saw much confrontation over alleged abuse of elections and use of impositions, before James used his prerogative to dissolve the Parliament. It acquired the name 'addled' because of its confused, or mixed up, nature.

The Third and Fourth Parliaments were dominated by important issues of finance and foreign policy. The vagueness of parliamentary privilege and the royal prerogative were openly raised and tested. The 1621 Parliament ended in hostility and aggression, but by 1624 events in Europe and a temporary alliance between Prince Charles, Buckingham and the Commons, obliged James to make concessions to the Commons. These took the form of inviting the House to discuss foreign policy, agreeing to a Monopolies Act, and setting up a committee to supervise the supply of funds for impending war. The 1624 Parliament saw cooperation, but at a price.

There were a number of issues raised in the parliaments. All were important; most raised questions, either overtly or indirectly, about the authority of the Crown and the privileges of Parliament. The issue of finance posed the most serious threat to the authority of the Crown in that it was at the root of many of the grievances of the House of Commons. The House was less than generous in meeting the demands from the Crown for subsidies. The extent to which majesty was bruised by an assertive Commons has been the subject of much historical debate in recent years.

6.2.1 Did Parliament gain the initiative over the Crown?
A CASE STUDY IN HISTORICAL INTERPRETATION

The near obsession with Crown–Parliament relations in 17th-century English history is understandable for a number of reasons.

1. The curse of historical hindsight

Historically, the 17th century is dominated by the Civil War that broke out in 1642. This can be seen as a struggle between Crown and Parliament for the constitution of England, in which the power of the monarch was clipped and Parliament emerged as the institution exercising sovereignty on behalf of the people. To the 19th-century Whig historians, this was the working out of historical destiny in which the outbreak of the Civil War assumed a significance as great as the Magna Carta had to the lawyers and parliamentarians of the 17th century.

There is a tendency to see Crown–Parliament relations as steadily deteriorating, from the accession of James to a 'high road to civil war', an approach that was traditional among historians in the 19th century, from Lord Macaulay to S.R. Gardiner.

Why is King James's reign highlighted? If anyone is to be blamed for the circumstances that generated civil war, it is Charles I. The simplistic answer is that James was a 'foreigner', a Scot whose succession to the throne of Elizabeth allowed the exaggeration of her successes and stimulated the myth of 'Gloriana'. Above all, the accession of James brought the 'British dimension' that proved so problematical, politically. It was perceived that under James the unresolved political, religious, social and economic problems throughout the British Isles were aggravated, eventually reaching crisis point in the parliamentary arena in 1642.

2. The Notestein Thesis: winning the initiative of the Commons

In an address to the British Academy in 1924, Wallace Notestein, the distinguished American historian, put forward the view that in the early 17th century, Parliament – especially the Commons – was 'winning the initiative' at the expense of the Crown. Notestein argued that, as a result of poor **parliamentary management**, an **Opposition** to the Crown was

Parliamentary management: The King usually tried to control Parliament through the **Speakers** as well as the Privy Councillors. The Speaker of the Commons presided over all debates; Members had access to the Crown through him. As the Speaker did not preside over committees, sometimes the Commons formed a Committee of the Whole House to escape his control.

Opposition: A group within Parliament opposing Crown policies. The issue is whether the Opposition was organised as a result of specific issues and interests (factions), or merely the legitimate voice of grievances from the localities.

Speaker: The person who presides over the House of Commons. The Speaker controls debates and discussions in the House. In the reign of James I, the Speaker was the servant of the Crown rather than the House.

Speakers of the Jacobean House of Commons:
1603 Sergeant Philips
1614 Sir Randolph Crewe
1621 Sir Thomas Richardson
1624 Sir Thomas Crewe

---

developing in the Commons. This was because the Crown failed to exploit the various devices by which it controlled the House. The Commons developed strategies, such as the committee system and the use of the Committee of the Whole House, to avoid royal control by the **Speaker**. Notestein saw James's choice of Privy Councillors as poor. He also argued that James lacked the necessary personal skills to coax a hostile Commons. Notestein argued that James's lack of presence and demeanour together with his interference to the point of 'hectoring' (wearing down with words) made a great contrast to Elizabeth who knew when to make a point and did not cheapen her authority by too many addresses to Parliament. In this sense, James's personality compounded any structural difficulties he inherited from Elizabeth.

3. The nature of historical research in the first half of the 20th century

Historical research played a part in perpetuating the crucial nature of the role of Parliament in historical developments, particularly in the first half of the 20th century. Much research into parliamentary records went into Notestein's thesis. Notestein himself inspired his fellow American historians in ground-breaking editions of the debates of the Jacobean Parliaments. The accessibility of these editions meant that they placed the focus of much research on what happened in Parliament.

While the Court and Privy Council may have been the institutions of day-to-day government, Parliament was the main arena in which local and national interests and issues were raised.

4. Revisionism

By the last quarter of the 20th century, the received wisdom that Parliament was winning the initiative at the expense of the Crown was coming under serious scrutiny. Conrad Russell was one of a number of historians keen to test assumptions with which students approached the reign of James in England, especially his relations with Parliament. In *Parliaments and English Politics, 1621–1629* (published in 1979), Russell is confident that the so-called clashes between James and his Parliaments were more apparent than real. He believes that there was no evidence of Opposition, with a capital 'o', to the Crown, and that Parliament was an event rather than an institution. This had a great impact on other scholars. It generated a number of so-called 'revisionist' investigations of the period as a whole, especially on the relations between Crown and Parliament. It was followed by extensive research by Kevin Sharpe, highlighting the importance of **faction** rather than opposition in the Jacobean Parliaments.

Faction: A group formed around an individual courtier or MP. The people involved had a similar **vested interest** (see page 138) in a particular issue, rather than a programme of ideas. Each faction was flexible and fluid, changing in composition. Factions are not to be confused with Opposition.

Bearing in mind Maurice Lee's calculation of there having been only 36 months of Jacobean parliaments throughout a 22-year reign, it does seem unreasonable to assume that there was a constant struggle between James and Parliament. Given the fundamental role of Parliament – to bring grievances of the localities, to legislate, to advise and to vote subsidies – it is inevitable that groups with vested interests would form and change from Parliament to Parliament. It was also likely that issues of a serious nature would cause disagreement. The disagreements were over specific issues, rather than a concerted and organised campaign to undermine the Crown.

Sheriffs: People in England and Wales appointed by the monarch to organise elections, so could not be elected to Parliament themselves.

Undertakers: Agents who undertook to return MPs favourable to James.

1. Why do historians reach different conclusions on the relationship between James and Parliament?

2. What do you understand by the term 'Revisionism'?

3. How would you differentiate between 'Opposition' and 'faction'?

The King ruled; any undermining of his authority would imperil the stability of the State, Church and social order.

5. The problem of assessment

This further complicates any study of the relative power of Crown and Parliament in this period. How should the parameters of their power be measured? Can we devise an 'index of initiative'? Possible lines of assessment are:

● the extent to which the Crown retained the royal prerogative

● the extent to which Parliament asserted its privileges

● the capacity of the Crown to manage Parliament in session through Privy Councillors, the Speaker and through the choice of members by the creation of **sheriffs**, the use of **undertakers**, and the use of Royal Proclamations.

6.2.2 What was the attitude of King James towards the monarchy?

James VI and I supported the idea of the Divine Right of Kings. He developed the idea in his books and speeches: the *Trew Law of Free Monarchies* (1598) and the *Basilikon Doron* (1599). The former was the first of his political writings; the latter was a set of instructions to his son, Prince Henry. Both were written before he inherited the English throne. In England, three of James's speeches are particularly important: those of 1603 and 1610 to Parliament, and that of 1616 to the Star Chamber.

The theory held that a King ruled because God had chosen him for office. He was, therefore, God's lieutenant on earth and as such was accountable to God alone for his actions. It followed that to disobey a King was to disobey God; it was a sin.

It was a theory that had many possible applications and implications. If the King had no superior other than God, the King did not need to justify his actions to Parliament. Instead, he could exercise emergency power. He was the fountain of Law. It also justified his position as Supreme Governor of the Church. This resulted in the portrayal of James as an Old Testament-style King, authoritarian yet paternalistic. Above all, the theory strengthened important areas of insecurity: James could use divine right to support his succession to the English throne at a time when it was illegal for aliens to inherit land in England. The Succession Act of 1604 stressed James's 'inherent birthright' under 'the laws of God'. The theory of divine right of kings also bolstered his authority over the Church against any papal attempt at the deposition of a heretical monarch. In other words, it supported the royal prerogative.

The royal prerogative belonged to James by virtue of being King. In the middle of the 20th century, the constitutional historian J.R. Tanner defined the royal prerogative as 'the legal exercise of royal authority'.

However, in 1607, Dr John Cowell had produced *The Interpreter*. This defined the concept as being:

> 'The prerogative of the King is that especial power, pre-eminence, or privilege that the King hath in any kind over and above other persons, and above the ordinary course of the common law, in the right of his crown … The King of England is an absolute king.'

The final statement ensured that the Commons ordered Cowell's book to be burnt, on the grounds that it was supporting 'absolute monarchy'. In fact, while James stressed his paramount authority within the State, he was keen to recognise the importance of Parliament in legislation and in raising subsidies. He wished to avoid being seen as a 'tyrant' and he emphasised the benevolent nature of his kingship. Moreover, the last thing that James wanted was to become engaged in a debate that would set the parameters of the royal prerogative. He felt that this was far too dangerous.

The parameters of the royal prerogative were poorly defined. It was a 'mystery of state' – a matter that could not be touched upon or discussed or debated in Parliament. James indicated his attitude towards it in words to the Star Chamber in 1616:

> 'Encroach not upon the Prerogative of the Crown. If there fall out a question that concerns my Prerogative or mystery of state, deal not with it … The absolute Prerogative – Mystery of State – is no subject for the tongue of the lawyer, nor is lawful to be disputed.'

It is generally accepted that there are two areas of the royal prerogative:

1. The 'ordinary' powers to summon, prorogue and dissolve parliaments; to ratify legislation, to create peers and bestow honours; to preside over the prerogative courts, to be the fountain of Law; to pardon criminals; to be the commander-in-chief of the army; to choose his own ministers; to direct foreign policy; to coin money; to regulate trade; and to be the Supreme Governor of the Church. These were generally accepted.

2. The second area concerned the 'absolute' powers that were the prerogative of the Crown in times of crisis: emergency power.

Because of the lack of clear definition, some conflict between Crown and Parliament was to be expected over issues such as **fiscal feudalism**, the nature of parliamentary privileges, foreign policy, emergency power and religion.

1. How important for monarchy was the idea of divine right of kings?

2. What was the difference between divine right and the royal prerogative?

3. In what ways did James assert that 'the state of monarchy is the supremest thing upon earth'?

Fiscal feudalism: Taxes rooted in the Middle Ages when society was feudal (i.e. based on a system of land holding and duties). Such financial devices were very unpopular in the 17th century.

King James on monarchy, from a speech to Parliament, 21 March 1610

'The State of Monarchy is the supremest thing upon earth: For Kings are not only God's Lieutenants upon earth, and sit upon God's throne, but even by God himself they are called Gods ... In the Scriptures Kings are called Gods, and so their power ... compared to the Divine power. Kings are also compared to the Fathers of families: for a King is truly ... the politic father of his people. And lastly, Kings are compared to the head of this Microcosm of the body of man ...

'Kings are justly called Gods, for that they exercise a manner or resemblance of Divine power upon earth. For if you will consider the Attributes to God, you shall see how they agree in the person of a King. God hath power to create, or destroy, make, or unmake at his pleasure, to give life, or send death, to judge all, [and be] accountable to none. To raise low things, and to make high things low at his pleasure, and to God are both soul and body due. And the like power have Kings: they make and unmake their subjects: they have power of raising and casting down:of life and death: Judges over their subjects, like men at the Chess; a Pawn to take a bishop or a Knight, and to cry up, or down any of their subjects, as they do their money. And to the King is due both the affection of the soul, and the service of the body of his subjects ... '

6.2.3 What were the main issues in the First Parliament, 1604–1611?

What were the privileges of Parliament?

Traditionally, the English Parliament claimed three privileges.

1. Free elections to Parliament
The first was that elections to Parliament should be free, in the sense of not being manipulated by the Crown through agents in the localities. By the use of agents, usually known as undertakers, the King could pack Parliament. This operation was challenged in 1614. A more subtle means of manipulation was to appoint well-known critics as sheriffs. Because sheriffs organised the elections in the counties they could not themselves be candidates. It was also possible for the King to issue a royal proclamation that excluded a certain category of person from being a Member. In 1603, for example, James issued a royal proclamation excluding outlaws and bankrupts. While reasonable in itself, it raised the issue of Sir Francis Goodwin in the First Parliament (see opposite).

2. Free speech for MPs

Free speech: The right to discuss important matters of state freely. This might involve issues of foreign policy and other areas thought to be touching on the royal prerogative.

The second privilege was that MPs should enjoy **free speech** during a parliamentary session. This was considered necessary for the giving of sound advice to the Crown. It became a serious issue on a number of occasions, when the King perceived the debates in Parliament as touching upon the royal prerogative. Financial issues were at stake in the first two parliaments, and those of foreign policy and the nature of the privileges of Parliament – were they derived from the King, or did they belong to Parliament as of right? – in the Third Parliament.

3. Freedom from arrest
The third privilege was that of freedom from arrest during a parliamentary session. This was considered critical, because arrest was the logical

1. Why were the privileges of Parliament so important in the 1604 session of Parliament?

2. What was James's attitude towards the privileges of Parliament?

3. In what ways might the privileges of Parliament affect the theory of divine right and the royal prerogative?

outcome of speaking out in Parliament. This privilege was asserted at the beginning of the reign in the case of Sir Thomas Shirley (see page 154).

On occasions such as the creation of The Form of Apology and Satisfaction in 1604 (a document drawn up by a minority in the Commons and never formally presented to James), the King was reminded that he did not have absolute power in religion and that the voice of the people was the voice of God.

It is fair, however, to say that no Parliament challenged the King's authority to rule. While the assertion of the privileges of Parliament was a key theme during the reign, the Jacobean Parliaments completed a great deal of routine business and passed many bills of an essentially local nature. Even the Addled Parliament saw the introduction of 105 bills in only two months of sitting.

The First Session of the First Parliament (1604)

The First Parliament was extremely important for both the Crown and Parliament. As a 'foreign' king starting a new dynasty, James needed a broad base of support within the Parliament to acknowledge his succession, confirm his hereditary and life revenues, and provide advice and legislation for his policies. He needed to proceed with caution as he had promoted a number of his supporters to the House of Lords as a reward for their services and support. The Commons were just as anxious to maintain their privileges as the King was to assert the royal prerogative.

The opening issues involved obvious questions of prerogative and privilege in disputed election matters; other issues which were rooted in prerogative, such as that of Union with Scotland and financial matters, soon dominated the Parliament.

The First Session of the First Parliament saw two election disputes that arose as a result of the Commons' vigilance over their privileges of free elections and freedom from arrest during a parliamentary session.

- The Buckinghamshire election dispute raised the privilege of free elections. In 1603, James had issued a proclamation to the effect that no one who was bankrupt or an outlaw was to be elected to Parliament. In order to enforce this, election returns were to be scrutinised by the Court of Chancery. It had the power to reject returns of Members who violated the proclamation. The Buckinghamshire electors returned Sir Francis Goodwin, who was technically an outlaw. The Court of Chancery declared his election null and void. In a second election in that county, Sir John Fortescue, a government nominee, was returned. The Commons regarded this as an abuse of the parliamentary privilege of free elections and insisted that Goodwin had been wrongly described as an outlaw. Furthermore, they maintained that the House had the right to scrutinise election returns. Long debates on this issue occupied the Commons in March and April 1604. After the exclusion of both candidates, a new election was held and an important compromise was reached. James acknowledged that the Commons was a court of record and a proper, if not sole, judge of election returns. This is a good indicator of the relations between the two. Parameters of authority and privilege were tested, but neither side pushed too far. In this case, James showed himself to be both patient and essentially reasonable in his judgement. While he asserted that MPs derived their privileges from him, James was prepared to consult the judges on the question of eligibility of outlaws.

- The case of Sir Thomas Shirley was raised at the same time as that of Goodwin and Fortescue. He had been elected MP for Steyning, but imprisoned for debt before the Parliament met. This was a clear issue of privilege, which was energetically taken up by the Commons. They summoned the Warden of the Fleet (the debtors' prison in which Sir Thomas was held) to the Bar of the House, and committed Shirley's creditor to the Tower, as well as the arresting officer. They eventually secured the release of Shirley and an Act that allowed the creditors of MPs, released by their privilege of freedom from arrest, to take out new writs against such MPs at the close of the Parliament.

MPs were also keen to let the new King know that they expected him to redress grievances. Many of the grievances were important issues since they involved money-raising devices of the Crown:

Purveyance: The feudal right by which the monarch had provisions, horses and carriages bought for him at prices fixed by the Purveyor. Sir Francis Bacon described Purveyance as the most serious grievance in the kingdom: 'There is no grievance in your kingdom so general, so continual. So sensible (deeply felt), and so bitter unto the common subject.' (Sir Francis Bacon to King James, 16 June 1604)

- The grievance of **purveyance** was deeply felt. Not only were there objections from merchants, who often received only one quarter of the real value of the goods they supplied, but purveyance was also symptomatic of the general wastefulness and chronic corruption of Court officials. As James had a larger household to maintain than Elizabeth, an increase in purveyance was inevitable. With a Parliament keen to establish the principle that the king should 'live of his own' where possible, such an increase was very unpopular. The real problem, however, was what to put in the place of Purveyance. From the point of view of the King, it offered an inflation-proof source of support. Any substitute was likely to be less flexible and to make the King dependent on a parliamentary grant. From the point of view of Parliament, any substitute would have to be found from taxation. This grievance was unresolved.

Wardship: The feudal right of the King over people who were minors. This often involved taking the land of a minor and profits of an estate until the minor came of age. The king also claimed the right to arrange a marriage for an under-age heiress.

- The grievance of **wardship** was raised. This was a lucrative business run by the Court of Wards. Robert Cecil held the office of Master of the Wards. He was aware of the corruption associated with wardship and was sympathetic to those who felt the grievance, voiced in a petition in 1604. Cecil was prepared to look into schemes to compensate the King for wardships, but was opposed by those whose livelihood depended on the survival of the court. It was also opposed by the King himself, who regarded wardship as non-negotiable.

Monopolies: Where a business has total control and therefore no competition. The Tudors and Stuarts gave monopolies to business partly to fill the royal purse. For instance, by 1601 the Queen had granted monopolies for salt, lead, vinegar and seacoal.

- The grievance of **monopolies** was voiced in spite of the great debate it aroused in the last Parliament of Elizabeth and of the judgement given in 1603 that they were illegal.

Composition: Settlement that would compensate the King for his loss of revenue from purveyance and wardship.

Purveyance and wardship were grievances that were deeply rooted in feudalism. In an ideal world, they would have been abolished by **composition**. In the real world, the fact that revenue from such devices was elastic and offered some kind of inflation-proof revenue to a Court whose finances were obsolete, inadequate and corrupt, meant that composition for these devices was difficult to find and ultimately not forthcoming.

- The question of the Union with Scotland has been discussed in some detail earlier in the chapter. It was seen that James envisaged the Union as a 'perfect union', using the imagery of marriage. He envisaged one king, one faith, one language, one law, one people and one name: Britain. This issue occupied much of not only the first, but also the second and third sessions of the First Parliament. James appointed commissioners to look into a common legal system, free trade, one flag, and making the Archbishop of Canterbury the Primate (senior archbishop) of Great Britain. It should be noted that James did not press for the idea of one Parliament once the debates got under way.

The First Parliament was uncooperative; some Members were also hostile to Union. The implications of full, or even partial, Union were great. Union raised the fear of the monarch having the power to change the name of the State, its laws and key institutions. Union threatened an unprecedented increase in the royal powers of prerogative. It is not surprising that Parliament was cagey.

After three sessions of the First Parliament, James had achieved few of his aims. The Commons refused to let him take the style 'King of Great Britain', fearing that the change in name would invalidate English Law. James took the title by Royal Proclamation in 1604. The hostile laws were repealed, but the naturalisation of the post-nati was achieved by the decision in Colville's case, rather than by statute. The limited achievement shows James's inability to manipulate Parliament and his caution and respect for the sensitivities of both the English and Scottish legislative institutions. Union was his greatest enterprise in 1604; by 1610, it had a low profile.

The testing first session ended with The Form of Apology and Satisfaction, 1604. This was a document drawn up by 72 MPs who feared the increase of prerogative at the expense of the privileges of Parliament. It complained that: 'The prerogatives of princes may easily and do daily grow, the privileges of the subject are for the most part at an everlasting stand.' The background to this document was the election disputes of 1604 together with the realisation that James was prepared to assert his authority over the Church, as demonstrated at the Hampton Court Conference. It reiterated the traditional privileges of Parliament as: free elections, freedom from arrest during a parliamentary session and free speech. It reminded the King that Parliament's consent was necessary for changes in religion. While the Form of Apology and Satisfaction was never formally presented to James, its assertion that the voice of the people was the voice of God was at odds with divine right kingship.

Second and third sessions of the First Parliament (1606 and 1606–1607)

The second and third sessions began more cordially because of the relief felt at the discovery of the Gunpowder Plot, and subsidies being voted to encourage James to take an anti-Catholic stand. The grievances of purveyance and wardship were urged, together with complaints at the increase in customs duties as well as long and unfruitful debates on Union.

Fourth session (1610)

The Fourth Session (1610) saw the culmination of a number of serious issues involving finance. From the early years of his reign, James was aware of his financial vulnerability: 'The only disease and consumption which I can ever apprehend as likeliest to endanger me, is this eating canker of want, which being removed, I could think myself as happy in all other respects as any other king or monarch that ever was since the birth of Christ.' (James to his Council, 1607).

This situation was mainly caused by two factors:

● James's financial inheritance

● excessive expenditure.

1. Financial inheritance

● *An inadequate revenue system*

This was the most obvious aspect of James's inheritance from Elizabeth. The bulk of his revenue came from Crown lands, the prerogative and feudal rights (such as the unpopular Purveyance and Wardship), and from **tunnage and poundage**. The income from the former was his hereditary, or ordinary, revenue; the latter was voted for life by Parliament. Crown lands were losing value for at least three reasons:

● Elizabeth had sold off land to the value of £372,000 in the last five years of her reign, reducing the potential income for James.

● Crown lands were rented out, often on long leases with rents below their real value.

● New surveys and a re-assessment of the value of Crown land were overdue.

In short, James needed to put up rents at a time when the gentry hoped to be paying less under a new king.

James could use his prerogative to supplement his customs revenue by **impositions**. This practice was unpopular in Parliament.

While it expected the King to 'live of his own', Parliament could vote the King subsidies, and fifteenths and tenths (a tax on movable goods). These were neither lucrative nor sufficiently forthcoming, although Elizabeth's last Parliament had voted subsidies amounting to over £1 million for the Spanish and Irish wars. Moreover, the English gentry were skilled in tax evasion. No grant was given to James in 1604, as the subsidies voted to Elizabeth had not been fully collected.

James also inherited the financial drain of two military commitments: a war with Spain and campaigns in Ireland.

In 1603, James began his reign with a debt of £422,000. This was not as bad as it looked as the subsidies from the previous reign had not been collected. James was keen to end the Spanish war, the campaigns in Ireland had drawn to a close with English victory in 1603, and the union with Scotland would reduce the cost of border defences. In reality, the system remained inadequate to finance a king whose court was larger than the previous one and who had greater demands upon it in terms of European diplomacy.

● *Endemic corruption and inefficiency*

Corruption and inefficiency among servants of the Crown compounded the inadequate income. Crown servants were rewarded in a variety of ways other than by payment of a salary for a post held. Some had pensions and annuities, some were given tax farms (see opposite), some were given

---

Tunnage and poundage: Customs duties in the form of 'tunnage' (dues levied on each 'tun' of imported wine) and 'poundage' (dues on all imports and exports).

Impositions: Additional duties on imports levied by the Crown by virtue of its emergency powers to regulate trade. As such, they were over and above the normal customs schedules fixed by Parliament.

wardships. The complicated system of patronage and paying for service encouraged corruption and made it difficult to dismiss corrupt officers. Some offices were held as freehold, and sold. The financial weakness of the Crown made it difficult to retire incompetent officers. Any changes could only come as a result of great effort and goodwill.

● Inflation

Inflation: A general increase in the prices of goods and services in a country.

James began his reign during a cycle of **inflation**, in which rising prices and falling wages made money less valuable and exaggerated the impact of declining revenue from Crown land.

2. Excessive expenditure

There is no doubt that James was extravagant by nature. The Archbishop of York wrote to Lord Cecil, as early as August 1604:

> His majesty's subjects hear and fear that his excellent … nature is too much inclined to giving, which in short will exhaust the treasure of this kingdom … His Majesty in Scotland lived like a noble and worthy king of small revenues in comparison, because he wisely foresaw that [expenditure] should not exceed [income]; which I fear his Highness does not in England … but yields almost to every man's petition.

During the years of the First Parliament, James, as a 'foreign' king, had to be seen to be generous. Annual expenditure on royal servants and courtiers was more than double that of Elizabeth, and household expenses were up by 60%, leaving a shortfall of £334,000 between income and expenditure. The historian Roger Lockyer points out, in *James VI and I* (1998), that the subsidies voted by Parliament in 1606, after the Gunpowder Plot scare, were worth about £400,000. The fact that he gave away £44,000 to three of his Scottish courtiers encouraged complaints in Parliament, rather than further generosity. While the spectacular **masques** showed that the English Court knew how to entertain, the expenditure did not generate confidence from Parliament.

Masques: Entertainment on special occasions that combined music, dancing and theatre. Many court masques were written by Ben Jonson and designed by Inigo Jones.

For many reasons, James could not make ends meet, in spite of ending the war with Spain. In some ways, he was a victim of circumstances, such as rising prices, the fall in value of Crown lands, the necessity of three separate courts (King, Queen and that of the Prince of Wales after 1610), and the need to be generous in giving bounty to courtiers. The bottom line was that James, an extravagant king, simply could not manage financially with an out-of-date revenue system.

Advisers such as Robert Cecil (the Earl of Salisbury) were convinced that James and Parliament must cooperate on finance. This proved difficult as it raised the issues of divine right of kings and the royal prerogative.

Attempts to remedy the financial deficit during the First Parliament failed and, at the same time, alienated Parliament.

Tax farming: A system by which a group of merchants was given the right to collect customs duties on behalf of the King. The King was guaranteed a fixed revenue by the farmers, who had every incentive to make a profit for themselves.

● In 1604, Lord Dorset and Sir Julius Caesar produced a New Book of Rates, hoping to compensate for inflation. They also introduced the Great Farm of the Customs. This leased the customs for seven years to a syndicate, in return for £112,400 a year. While farming the customs brought in an annual revenue for the King, the increase in trade after the Treaty of London with Spain bought the greatest benefit to the **tax farming** syndicates.

Robert Cecil by John De Critz the Elder, 1602

Entail: To settle (land, an estate etc.) on a number of persons in succession in order to keep them in royal ownership.

Robert Cecil, the Earl of Salisbury (1563–1612)
The son of Elizabeth's chief minister, William Cecil (Lord Burghley). He became a Secretary of State in 1596 and, as such, played a great part in smoothing the accession of James in 1603. He was astute, even devious, but above all a great servant of the Crown. He became Viscount Cranbourne in 1604 and Earl of Salisbury in 1605. In 1608 he became Lord Treasurer and wrestled with James's financial problems until his death from cancer in 1612. There is an argument for seeing his hand behind many of the key events and issues in the years up to 1612. He secured a peaceful accession for James, negotiated the Treaty of London with Spain in 1604, and was involved with the 'discovery' of the Gunpowder Plot.

- Impositions proved to be the most profitable and most unpopular of all the money-raising schemes. They were levied, by virtue of the royal prerogative, to regulate trade. The judgement in Bate's Case supported them. John Bate was a merchant who imported currants from the Levant. He had refused to pay impositions on his imports on the grounds that these taxes had not been approved by Parliament. The final judgement, by Chief Baron Fleming in the Court of the Exchequer (a prerogative court) in 1606, gave the verdict firmly in favour of the King:

The King's power is double, ordinary and absolute … All customs, be they old or new, are no other but the effects and issues of trades and commerce with foreign nations; but all commerce and affairs with foreigners, all wars and peace, all acceptance and admitting for current, foreign coin, all parties and treaties whatsoever, are made by the absolute power of the King … No exportation or importation can be but at the King's ports. They are the gates of the King, and he hath absolute power by them to include or exclude whom he shall please …

The potential of impositions is obvious. They played an important part in the work of the Earl of Salisbury when he took over the Treasury in 1608.

The work of the Earl of Salisbury

Robert Cecil was a great builder – his finest monuments being the refurbishment of Hatfield House and Cranbourne. His most important work was designed to ward off the financial impotence of the Crown. This took the form of:

- trying to increase the yield from traditional sources of revenue. He increased the income from Crown lands, instigated surveys and raised rents; he raised the revenue from the Court of Wards by 91%.

- instituting economies. Cecil introduced the Book of Bounty to set limits to royal gifts. He was keen to **entail** land, customs and monopolies to prevent them passing out of royal hands.

- the Revised Book of Rates (1608) raised rates to bring in an additional £70,000 on customs duties;

- continuing the use of impositions.

All of these measures were unpopular. None was sufficiently radical to solve the financial problems of the King. The Earl of Salisbury was sympathetic to the grievances of Parliament and aware that the King had to be both bountiful and, at the same time, had to convince Parliament of his sincerity in wishing to address financial issues.

By the time of the Fourth Session of the First Parliament (1610), the financial 'fudge' was wearing thin and the issue of impositions was urgent. When James defined impositions as a matter of prerogative that was not to be discussed by Parliament, the Commons responded with an assertion of their privilege of free speech.

In a characteristically Jacobean compromise, James did allow impositions to be discussed. The debate argued that impositions were an indirect tax and, as such, were against the spirit of the law. James agreed to

Salisbury's Great Contract: The one radical financial solution to date (1610) that created some sort of partnership between Crown and Parliament by remitting the unpopular feudal financial devices in return for a regular revenue from Parliament.

1. *To what extent was finance an important issue in the First Parliament?*

2. *How successfully did Parliament assert its privileges?*

3. *In what ways was the First Parliament a success for King James?*

remit some of the impositions and surrender others in return for suitable compensation. The Revised Book of Rates (1608) had not helped the situation, as it had increased rates to yield around £70,000 more revenue from duties paid by merchants.

In the 1610 session of Parliament, in **Salisbury's Great Contract**, the Earl of Salisbury suggested the surrender of purveyance, wardship and other feudal rights, in return for an annual revenue of £200,000 from Parliament. After initially favourable signals from both parties, the Contract proved, in Salisbury's words, 'still-born'. To the King, the fear of losing elastic feudal revenues in favour of a fixed income that might prove insufficient and leave him at the mercy of Parliament, demeaned majesty. To Parliament, the possibility that the annual sum might prove sufficient – especially during periods of good trade and buoyant customs – was alarming. It might mean that the King had little reason to call Parliament; he was under no constitutional obligation to do so. Such considerations produced doubts and recriminations on both sides. The Great Contract failed and the Parliament was dissolved in January 1611.

6.2.4 Why was the Second Parliament (1614) a failure?

The Second Parliament of 1614 was short, obstructive and hostile. It is known as the Addled (or confused) Parliament. It was steered towards discord by the activities of factions eager to gain personal advantages, and by the resentment of MPs at the continued use of impositions by the Crown.

After the death of Robert Cecil in 1612, James came under pressure from rival factions to fill the key posts that Cecil had held with their supporters. The most active was the Howard faction. It was led by Henry Howard (Earl of Northampton).

Crypto-Catholics: Secret, or closet, Catholics at Court who were keen to retain political influence. James I was well aware of their existence. Provided they were loyal, they remained at Court.

The Howard faction consisted of important peers, such as Northampton, Suffolk and Arundel. They were **crypto-Catholics** and had possibly been involved in the so-called Main Plot of 1603. As crypto-Catholics they favoured a tough line with Parliament, a softening of the anti-Catholic laws, and a foreign policy that supported Spain. This latter was already being advanced by the new Spanish ambassador, Sarmiento (later Count Gondomar).

The anti-Catholic faction was the Abbot–Pembroke group, dominated by the Archbishop of Canterbury, George Abbot, and the Earl of Pembroke. This group sought to frustrate the aims and policies of the Howard faction and to secure the cooperation of the King and a pro-Protestant, anti-Catholic Parliament.

Favourites: Courtiers who were especially favoured by the King.

Given James's preference for male **favourites**, both factions tried to influence the King through his current favourite, Robert Carr (Viscount Rochester). Initially, Carr had no links with the Howards but his friend, Sir Thomas Overbury, favoured the Abbot–Pembroke group. Overbury was likely to use his influence over Carr to block the Howard faction's attempt to secure their promotion to offices such as Lord Treasurer,

Secretary of State, and Master of the Wards (recently vacant after the death of Cecil).

King James was canny enough to avoid an obvious victory for faction. He prevaricated for a while by acting as his own Secretary of State, placing the Treasury in commission, and appointing a neutral Master of the Court of Wards.

The Howards, however, saw an opportunity when Robert Carr fell in love with Lady Frances Howard, wife of the Earl of Essex.

Sir Thomas Overbury was against a marriage of the favourite into the Howard faction. He was confined to the Tower on trumped-up charges and died under mysterious circumstances. The marriage took place in 1613, after a commission heard the Essex divorce case and decided in favour of Lady Frances after her allegations of the impotence of her husband. Carr was created Earl of Somerset a few days before their wedding so that Lady Frances would not lose status. The Essex divorce case was the great 'sleaze' of the period; it made the Court very unpopular and contributed to the decline of the favourite Carr, especially after the accusation of the poisoning of Overbury by Lady Frances in 1615 which led to the imprisonment of Carr and Lady Frances in 1616. (They were not released until 1623.) Meanwhile, the Abbot–Pembroke faction tried hard to find another favourite and, in 1614, introduced George Villiers (later Duke of Buckingham) into the Court.

The erratic influence of faction before the Addled Parliament affected its short, turbulent course.

The Second Parliament was summoned to help James's deteriorating finances. He faced a debt of £680,000 in 1614. James hoped for a supportive Parliament. He encouraged the return of royal nominees and secured the return of over a third of MPs with Court connections. This failed to guarantee success. Instead it brought hostile accusations that he had used undertakers to manipulate the return of members favourable to the Crown.

James tried to appease Parliament by explaining that he had called it out of concern for the growth of Catholicism – an obvious attempt to appease a Protestant Parliament – and that he wanted to make his grandson his heir should Charles die childless. He also asked for subsidies. James denied the use of undertakers, but the Commons insisted that he had abused their privilege of free elections.

It has been suggested that the Howards paid some MPs to be obstructive. The bitter debates on impositions showed a depth of feeling in the Commons beyond faction. Impositions were the most unpopular financial devices of the First Parliament. They had continued after the failure of the Great Contract and the measures to raise revenue after 1611 – such as Salisbury's creation of the new title 'baronet' to be sold as a revenue raiser.

This Parliament also saw an attack on favourites as 'spaniels to the King and wolves to the people' (Sir Christopher Neville), and assertions by the Commons that the Attorney General (the Crown's legal adviser)

Robert Carr, Earl of Somerset (1587–1645) – a miniature by Nicholas Hilliard, c. 1611
Of Scottish origin, descended from the Kers of Ferniehurst. Carr entered England with James in 1603, then spent some time in France. He became a royal favourite in 1607, when he was knighted. In 1611, he was made Viscount Rochester and became the first Scot to sit in the English House of Lords.

Frances, Countess of Somerset, c. 1615, attributed to William Larkin.

Sir Thomas Overbury (1581–1613)
Writer and friend of Robert Carr. Overbury was sent to the Tower for refusing a foreign posting that would have prevented his opposition to the marriage of Carr. He was poisoned on 15 September 1613 at the instigation of the Somersets.

'Cautionary towns': These were towns, such as Flushing, Brill and Rammekins, given to Elizabeth I as security for Dutch debts.

Cockayne Project: A monopoly over the production and sale of finished cloth given to Alderman Cockayne. As the Dutch refused to import finished cloth, the monopoly contributed to a major slump in the cloth trade.

1. Why was the Addled Parliament so called?

2. Which was the most important issue for the Addled Parliament?

3. Was this Parliament a victory for the Crown or Parliament?

should not sit in the House, while the Privy Councillors should only sit with the approval of the House.

The attack on favourites was caused by the Howard divorce case, the continued presence of Scots at Court, resentment at the use of impositions, and in retaliation to the King's request for subsidies. The idea of an extravagant Court justified tightening the strings of the parliamentary purse.

Given this reception, James used the royal prerogative to dissolve the Parliament after two months.

In the eyes of the King, the Parliament was a failure because it did not pass legislation and it did not vote subsidies. Jams believed that it had acted irresponsibly. He described it to Sarmiento as 'a body without a head'.

While James could silence Parliament with dissolution, his main objective – money – was denied him. He was obliged to raise money after this by an unpopular levy on beer, by selling titles of nobility, by selling the **'cautionary towns'** back to the Dutch, and by the disastrous **Cockayne Project** of 1614.

6.2.6 What were the issues in the Third Parliament (1621–1622)?

In many respects, the Third Parliament was the most interesting of James's parliaments. It drew together a number of issues that were as serious as they were diverse. Financial issues were prominent: the question of subsidies for war abroad and a strong attack on the abuse of patents and monopolies at home.

The origins of this parliament lie in the European crisis caused by the outbreak of the Thirty Years War in 1618 (see section 6.4 on foreign policy). While James intended to avoid military engagement, the involvement of his daughter and son-in-law complicated the issue. As long as the Catholic Habsburg triumph was in distant Bohemia, James could provide excuses for lack of meaningful support and intervention. By 1621, not only had Bohemia been lost to Frederick and Elizabeth, but the Bavarians had invaded the Upper Palatinate and the Spanish had occupied the Lower Palatinate. This loss of the hereditary lands of the Palatinate provoked James into calling the Third Parliament in order to assess the amount of parliamentary support he could rely on, should intervention be necessary.

The war issues heightened religious sensitivities in Parliament at a time when **Arminianism** was seen to be on the increase at Court. Even conversion to Catholicism was seen as quite trendy among courtiers.

Arminianism: A religious doctrine associated with Protestanism. Named after Arminius who, at the 1609 Synod of Dort, put forward a view of Protestantism which was more moderate than the religious views of most English Puritans. Arminians were accused by some Puritans of trying to make Protestantism similar to Catholicism. A leading Arminian in England was William Laud, who was Archbishop of Canterbury from 1633 to his death in 1645.

The Court was also vulnerable to criticism in the wake of the Howard divorce scandal. Although by 1621, Carr and Lady Frances were suffering their due punishment, the current Court favourite, George Villiers, was seen to have just as harmful an influence.

Villiers' involvement in Court financial dealings was particularly sensitive by 1621. Between 1614 and 1621, James had tried to raise money by selling peerages and baronetcies, borrowing money, selling crown lands, selling the cautionary towns back to the Dutch and using monopolies.

George Villiers (1592–1628) – attributed to William Larkin, c. 1616

Youngest son of Sir George Villiers. He entered the Court in 1614, supported by Abbot and Pembroke as an alternative to Carr. After Carr fell from grace, Villiers was knighted, made a viscount, and a Gentleman of the Bedchamber (1616). He became Earl of Buckingham in 1617; and Marquis of Buckingham a year later. In 1620, he married Lady Catherine Manners, a wealthy crypto-Catholic. Made a visit to Madrid in 1623 with Charles, before being made Duke of Buckingham. After the failure of the Spanish marriage project, he helped to negotiate the arrangements for the marriage of Charles and Henrietta Maria of France. Buckingham enjoyed more influence during the reign of Charles than that of James. He became very unpopular but was assassinated in 1628. His rise to power was commonly likened to a comet shooting across the sky.

The trade slump after the Cockayne Project of 1614 had left the King short of revenue from customs. It had also made Parliament bitterly critical towards monopolies. The involvement of the Court and favourite in monopolies came to a head in this Parliament.

The course of this Parliament was also influenced by the fact that Speaker Richardson did not provide effective leadership for the Crown. Also, Sir Edward Coke, Hakewell and Sir Edwin Sandys were lively opponents of certain policies.

Parliament had a fourfold agenda:

- to settle the question of liberties and privileges

- to petition James to enforce recusancy laws

- to pursue the question of supply

- to debate the issue of grievances, especially patents and monopolies.

The first item is central to the events in this Parliament. It also pervades the other three.

The mood of the House was shown when it expelled Sir Robert Floyd, a monopolist. In doing this, the House exercised its privilege of expelling and punishing its own members.

Finance: the question of supply

This became the issue that acted as a catalyst. James had appointed a council to estimate the requirements for intervention in Europe. It recommended a force of 30,000 men and an annual sum of £900,000. James was aware that the Commons were unlikely to support this. To test the waters, he asked for an annual military budget of £500,000. Parliament responded with an offer of £160,000. This offer did not encourage James to explain his foreign policy to the House. His failure to do so, given the sensitivities of the House, prompted an attack on monopolists.

Patents and monopolies

These were long-standing grievances of the Commons. They had been hotly debated in the last Parliament of Elizabeth's reign and declared illegal by the judges in 1603. In spite of James declaring his support for this judgement, the Crown continued to issue monopoly grants for new inventions, new industries and for control of old ones. By 1621, the Court and favourites were heavily implicated in the sleaze surrounding monopolies; opponents of these saw Parliament as the place the grievance could be addressed. The Commons demanded an inquiry, especially into those at Court to whom patents had been referred – the 17th-century equivalent of 'name and shame'. An attack on monopolist Members, such as Mitchell and Mompesson, led to the revival of the process of impeachment for Mompesson, whose monopoly for the licensing of inns had offended many. The revival of the process of impeachment, in 1621, offered a way of attacking a royal minister who had become unpopular and corrupt. Given the royal prerogative over the appointment of ministers of the Crown, it became an important issue.

Lord Chancellor Bacon was among the chief referees of patents in 1621. So was Buckingham, but Bacon became the fallguy. He was bitterly attacked by his old enemy, Sir Edward Coke.

Bacon warned James of the dangers of the revival of impeachment: 'Those who will strike at your Chancellor it is much to be feared will strike at your crown.' Coke, Villiers and Cranfield were keen to procure the removal of Bacon. James, under pressure of events and Court faction, had to let Bacon fall when Parliament accused him of corruption. He did try to get the case against Bacon settled by a commission outside Parliament, but this failed. Bacon fell to impeachment, was fined £40,000 and demoted.

Concern for the Protestant cause

This concern produced a discussion on the direction of foreign policy. Like the previous issue, this involved the question of prerogative and privileges. James insisted that foreign policy was a matter of the royal prerogative and that Parliament should concern itself with discussing subsidies, rather than direction of policy. The Commons demanded an explanation of his policy and that firm action should be taken against Spain abroad and Catholics at home. Above all, the House wanted the King to abandon the Spanish marriage scheme. They were insistent that James had invited their comment on policy at the opening of the session. A small subsidy to help the Palatinate was forthcoming, but only ruptured relations with Spain would encourage a larger subsidy. This attitude on the part of Parliament bolstered James's belief in the necessity of the Spanish marriage as a bargaining counter to help his daughter and son-in-law regain the Palatinate. He could see no alternative to a war that he did not want and could not afford. The outcome was a fine exchange of views on prerogative and privilege at the end of the Parliament. The exchange ended in James ripping the page from the **House of Commons' Journal**, dissolving Parliament and vowing never to call it again. He fell back on the Spanish marriage as the solution to the problem of the Palatinate, a solution that was both cost effective and diplomatically preferable.

Sir Edward Coke (1552–1634) Chief Justice of England. Educated at Cambridge and the Inner Temple. Made Solicitor-General (assistant to the Attorney-General) in 1592, then Speaker of the House a year later. King James knighted Coke in 1603. It was he who prosecuted Sir Walter Raleigh. In 1606, he prosecuted the Gunpowder conspirators, before being made Chief Justice of Common Pleas. In 1613 he was appointed to the King's Bench and made a Privy Councillor. He alienated the royal Court by not giving verdicts favourable to them, and lost office in 1616. Coke regained some favour when he allowed his daughter to be married to Buckingham's brother. In 1621, he was involved in the fall of Bacon. Opposed the policies of Charles I in 1626–27, and drew up the Petition of Right in 1628.

House of Commons' Journal: The record kept of the daily proceedings in the House of Commons.

6.2.7 *How successful was the Fourth Parliament (1624–1625)?*

In terms of voting subsidies and legislation, the Fourth Parliament was extremely successful. The return of Prince Charles and Buckingham from Madrid without the Spanish Infanta had encouraged the Commons to expect that James would take up the sword against Spain. The option of a Spanish marriage to solve the Palatinate question had failed. In view of these developments, the most cooperative Parliament of the reign ensued.

- Cooperation was evident in that James actually invited the Commons to advise him on foreign policy. Considering the bitter exchanges between King and Commons in 1621 on this subject, this was indeed a milestone.

- This had implications for the financing of any intervention. The previous Parliament had shown reluctance to offer sufficient financial support for a policy they were urging on the King. In 1624, in order to get a Subsidy Bill, James agreed to Parliament setting up a committee to supervise the spending of a subsidy, and to that money being appropriated to a war effort.

The King's response to the demand from Parliament to break off the Spanish match shows that James, having long resisted war with Spain, would not fight a battle with the 1624 Parliament he could not win:

'He is an unhappy man, that shall advise a king to war; and it is an unhappy thing to seek by blood [that] which may be had by peace … To enter into war without sufficient means to support it, were to shew my teeth, and do not more … I will deal frankly with you: shew me the means how I may do what you would have of me, and if I take a resolution by your advice to enter into a war, then yourselves by your own deputies shall have the disposing of the money; I will not meddle with it, but you shall appoint your own treasurers. I say this with a purpose to invite you to open your Purses … If upon your offer I shall find the means to make the war honourable and safe, I promise you on the word of a King, that although war and peace be the peculiar prerogatives of Kings, yet, … I will not accept Peace without first acquainting you with it.'

- The Subsidy Bill was facilitated by the Monopolies Act of 1624, which banned the granting of monopolies to individuals.

Porphyria: A hereditary disease affecting the metabolism. Symptoms range from severe stomach pains and red/blue urine to mental confusion. James I experienced the stomach pains; his descendant, George III, suffered periods of mental instability.

Lionel Cranfield, Earl of Middlesex (1575–1645)
The most able of James's finance ministers after the death of Cecil. He entered the world of finance as a customs farmer and merchant. Cranfield gained the favour of Henry Howard (Earl of Northampton), becoming Surveyor-General of the Customs in 1613. He became an adviser to Buckingham about the time of the Cockayne Project. Cranfield saw peace, cutting back on expenditure, and financial reform at Court as the best ways of preventing serious financial embarrassment for the King. He fell from favour in 1624.

From this it is obvious that James was prepared to reverse his foreign policy out of necessity, and that Parliament was invited to accept much of the financial responsibility for the implications of this. Key areas, hotly debated in 1621, were smoothed, if not resolved, after the failure of the Spanish marriage in 1623. How much was due to James's realisation that his policy was worn out, how much to weariness on the part of an old king suffering increasingly from **porphyria**, and how much to awareness that Charles and Buckingham seemed to be the darlings of the war faction in Parliament, is difficult to assess. What is certain is that this change in direction meant the end of the career of the only man, after Salisbury's death in 1612, who wrestled with the problems of royal finances: Lionel Cranfield.

Cranfield was the most able finance minister after Salisbury. He had no original, radical ideas, such as Cecil's Great Contract, but was ruthlessly efficient and methodical. He hoped to improve James's dismal financial state by:

● keeping out of foreign commitments

● cutting back on court expenditure

● reforming the Royal Household.

He organised the first successful survey of James's income and estates as the basis of such reform.

Cranfield's emphasis on household economy made him many enemies at Court. By 1624, his determination to avoid the financial suicide of war put him out of favour with a Parliament, supported by Charles and Buckingham, that was eager to avenge the loss of the Palatinate. This also marked a conflict of interest between Buckingham and Cranfield.

Cranfield's attempt to keep favour by introducing a homosexual relative as a possible rival to Buckingham made him a deadly enemy of the current favourite, who was still able to manipulate faction in Court and Parliament to ensure Cranfield's fall by impeachment in 1624.

The superficial harmony between Crown and Parliament masked danger signs for the King. While James protested the supremacy of his power, he had granted concessions – one of them, the Monopolies Act, in statute form. The use of impeachment against a minister must have reminded James of Bacon's fateful words: 'Those who will strike at your Chancellor, it is much to be feared will strike at your Crown.' The sheet anchor of foreign policy – treaties with Spain – was in the process of being severed. Serious anti-Catholicism, generated by debates on the Spanish marriage and the loss of the Palatinate, was to bring religion – an area of the royal prerogative – into the parliamentary arena. In 1624, Pym introduced a petition against the growth of Arminianism at home (see page 180). In short, there was every indication that the harmony would prove short-lived.

1. How far did the 1624 Parliament mark a victory for the House of Commons rather than the Crown?

2. To what extent was finance an important issue in the Jacobean Parliaments?

3. What was the nature of, and how serious was, opposition to Crown policies in Parliament?

Source-based questions: Crown and Parliament

SOURCE A

We have heard by divers reports, to our great grief, that our distance from the Houses of Parliament caused by our indisposition of health hath emboldened some fiery and popular spirits of some of the House of Commons to argue and debate publicly of matters far above their reach and capacity, tending to our high dishonour and breach of prerogative royal … [We] command you to make known to the House … that none therein shall presume henceforth to meddle with anything concerning our government or deep matters of State, and namely not to deal with our dearest son's match with the daughter of Spain, nor touch the honour of that King or any other our friends and confederates … [We] think ourself very free and able to punish any man's misdemeanours in Parliament, as well during their sitting as after …

The King's Letter to the Commons,
3 December 1621

SOURCE B

… And whereas your Majesty doth seem to abridge us of the ancient liberty of parliament for freedom of speech, jurisdiction, and just censure of the House, and other proceedings there … the same being our ancient and undoubted right, and an inheritance received from our ancestors; without which we cannot freely debate nor clearly discern of things in question before us.

The Commons' Petition, 9 December 1621

SOURCE C

In the body of your petition you usurp upon our prerogative royal, and meddle with things far beyond your reach, and then in the conclusion you protest the contrary; as if a robber would take a man's purse and then protest he meant not to rob him ….

And although we cannot allow of the style, calling it 'your ancient and undoubted right and inheritance', but could rather have wished that ye had said that your privileges were derived from the grace and permission of our ancestors and us … yet we are pleased to give you our royal assurance that as long as you contain yourselves within the limits of your duty, we will be as careful to maintain and preserve your lawful liberties and privileges as ever any of our predecessors were ….

The King's Letter from Newmarket,
11 December 1621

SOURCE D

The Commons now assembled in Parliament … do make this Protestation following, that the liberties, franchises, privileges, and jurisdiction of Parliament are the ancient and undoubted birthright and inheritance of the subjects of England; and that the arduous and urgent affairs concerning the King, State, and defence of the realm and the Church of England, and the maintenance and making of laws, and redress of mischiefs … are proper subjects and matter of counsel and debate in Parliament … and that every member … hath like freedom from all impeachment, imprisonment, and molestation (other than by censure of the House itself) for or concerning any speaking, reasoning, or declaring of any matter or matters touching the Parliament …

The Commons' Protestation, 18 December 1621

---

1. Explain what you understand by the term 'breach of prerogative royal' in Source A.

(3 marks)

2. How useful is Source D in explaining the privileges of parliament in 1621? *(7 marks)*

3. Using the sources and your own knowledge, how far were the differences between James I and his 1621 Parliament settled in the 1624 Parliament? *(15 marks)*

Key Issues

- *What problems faced James VI and I in matters of religion in 1603?*

- *To what extent did the year 1618 mark a turning point in the religious policy of James VI and I?*

- *How successfully did James VI and I deal with religious issues during the years 1603–1625?*

6.3.1 Why was religion an important issue during the reign of King James I?

6.3.2 What was the role of the King in the Church of England?

6.6.3 How far did Catholics pose a problem for James I?

6.3.4 How far did the Puritans pose problems for James I?

6.3.5 Was Arminianism an issue in the reign of James I?

6.3.6 Historical interpretation: What was the 'Jacobean compromise' in religion?

Framework of Events

1603	Millenary Petition for reform of the Church of England
	Two plots against James: Bye Plot and Main Plot (to put Arabella Stuart on throne)
1604	Hampton Court Conference
	Proclamation enjoining conformity to Established Church
	Archbishop Bancroft's Canons
1605	Gunpowder Plot: the most dramatic Catholic plot against King James
1606	Oath of Allegiance is drawn up
1610	Abbot is made Archbishop of Canterbury
1611	King James Bible: the Authorised Version
1617	Visit to Scotland by King James to try to bring Scottish Church more into line with the Church of England
1618	Five Articles of Perth
	Declaration concerning Sports: allowed certain games on Sabbath
	Outbreak of Thirty Years War in Bohemia
	Synod of Dort to debate Arminian issues
1621	Third Parliament
1622	Directions to Preachers to restrict reference to foreign policy in sermons
1623	Charles and Buckingham visit Madrid in an attempt to gain the Spanish marriage
1624	Fourth Parliament.

Overview

THE religious policy of James VI and I was the most important issue of his reign. Religious matters influenced both his relations with Parliament and the direction of his foreign policy. Weekly communication with his subjects was through the institution of the parish church, where compulsory attendance was required.

As a Scot brought up under a Presbyterian system, James was met with demands from English Catholics and Puritans at the beginning of his reign. As he was neither Catholic nor Puritan, both groups hoped that he would listen sympathetically to them. His vision was of a British monarchy. Unity and harmony in religion might be a way of achieving his aim.

His handling of opposition groups in England, at the Hampton Court Conference (1604) and after the Gunpowder Plot (1605), allowed James to stamp his authority on the English Church and to exercise a key area of the royal prerogative. By 1610, James had shown that he took his office as Supreme Governor of the Church very seriously.

The middle years of his reign were, generally, a period of quiet consolidation of the Church of England under sovereign and bishops. James's success in achieving a **Jacobean compromise** has been applauded by modern historians, as well as being appreciated by some contemporaries.

Events in Europe made James's policies difficult to achieve. The Thirty Years War and the Arminian question in Europe sharpened religious opinions in England, making religion an explosive issue at the end of the reign. The Catholic danger at the beginning of the reign gave way to a more dangerous force of anti-Catholicism. The Puritan voice became stronger in parliament and more political in its demands. To a large extent, these developments were beyond the control of James and they should not be allowed to detract from the real achievements during his reign.

Jacobean compromise: Balance in religion achieved by King James.

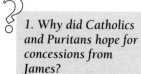

1. Why did Catholics and Puritans hope for concessions from James?

2. Why did James I find the later part of his reign more of a problem in religious matters?

Presbyterian system of church government

1. Consistory of minister and elected elders

↓

2. Presbytery consisting of ministers and elders from a prescribed area

↓

3. Synods consisting of members of several presbyteries

↓

4. General Assembly consisting of ministers and elders.

6.3.1 Why was religion an important issue during the reign of King James I?

Religion was a key issue during the years 1603–1625 for many reasons.

- In the first place, James claimed to rule by divine right. Since he saw himself as answerable to God alone for his actions, it followed that the monarch was superior to all other earthly powers and that to disobey a king was to sin.

'Cuius regio, eius religio': Settlement in 1555 within the Holy Roman Empire after the religious wars. Each prince was to decide whether his territory should be Catholic or Lutheran.

- Since the Peace of Augsburg in 1555, the principle of *'cuius regio, eius religio'* had prevailed. This meant that each state followed the religion of its leader. Therefore religious conformity was equated with loyalty to the head of state; religious deviance or nonconformity was likely to be seen as treason. The King of England wished to consolidate his position as head of Church and State.

- Religious stability was viewed by King James as an essential aim. It was vital for his authority in both Church and State. The fate of his mother, Mary Queen of Scots, had taught him the perils of religious instability in post-Reformation Scotland. He had seen Elizabeth I pursue a *via media* in religion in England in order to secure a broad base of support. His situation in 1603 was a difficult one: educated as a Presbyterian in Scotland, son of a Catholic mother and heir to the Protestant Church of England left by Elizabeth. In some ways James was, as far as religion was concerned, the ideal King of Great Britain and Ireland – the man who might blend together the elements of Anglican, Catholic and Presbyterian. In the real world, the achievement of religious unity throughout his three kingdoms always eluded him, and James fell back on a policy of compromise.

- Religious issues were important because they were often fundamental to developments in foreign policy. James inherited a war with Catholic Spain, which he ended in 1604 by the Treaty of London. To many of his subjects, however, war with Spain was the supreme aim of English foreign policy:
  - Spain was England's 'natural enemy' who aimed to reclaim England for the Catholic faith;
  - Spain had threatened English interests abroad and at home;
  - God and Queen Elizabeth had delivered the nation from the threat of Spanish bondage at the time of the Armada.

James had no such prejudices. He preferred peace and realised that the war with Spain had run its course. After 1604, he sought to safeguard British interests in Europe with a Catholic Spanish marriage for his son and a Protestant marriage for his daughter. This was the basis of his foreign policy – a policy not always appreciated by his subjects. It made religion a very important issue after 1618. When the Thirty Years War broke out in Europe, James faced the greatest dilemma of his reign: how to aid his daughter Elizabeth, married to the Protestant Elector Palatine, and under attack from the Catholic Habsburg forces in first Bohemia and then the Palatinate, while maintaining peace with Catholic powers. His solution was to press for the Catholic Spanish marriage for his son Charles and achieve a diplomatic solution to the problems of his daughter. Religious pressures at home made this policy, ultimately, a failure. By 1624, James was on the verge of reversing his traditional foreign policy.

● Ireland remained an area of religious instability for James. Its predominant Catholicism left it prey to foreign Catholic influence and it proved the launching ground for missions to reconvert England. The weakly-established Anglicanism and the plantation of Scottish Presbyterian settlers in the middle years of the reign further complicated the religious situation in Ireland and made the ideal of a **British Church** elusive.

British Church: A common church for England and Scotland.

Calvinist: Following the extreme Protestant forms used at Geneva by followers of John Calvin.

● In social terms, the parish pulpit was an important means of communication between Crown and people in a society where Sunday religious attendance was compulsory. It was essential for the King to have conforming clergy in order to maintain control over the Church and its congregations.

● The King in England was Supreme Governor of the Church of England. The royal prerogative operated in religious matters at home and abroad. James I was highly sensitive to the royal prerogative and the assertion of divine right.

1. In what ways was religion an area of royal prerogative?

2. What was the importance of religion in foreign policy?

● The very nature of the English Reformation made religion an urgent issue. To some, the Church of England was a reformed Catholic Church; to others, reform was ongoing along **Calvinist** lines, making a complete break from Roman Catholicism.

6.3.2 What was the role of the King in the Church of England?

The King was Supreme Governor of the Church of England 'by Law established'. The Acts of Uniformity and Supremacy of 1559 guaranteed his authority. He inherited the Book of Common Prayer and the 39 Articles of Faith of the Church of England from his predecessor, Elizabeth. James I was at the head of a hierarchic structure inherited from the Catholic Church before the Reformation. Under the King were the two archbishops of Canterbury and York, the bishops, archdeacons, rural deans and parish clergy. The king appointed bishops, and no changes in the church could be made without his approval.

The Church of England was broad-based. James hoped to preserve this by balancing the high-church group against the low-church group. The high-church group retained ceremonies; the low-church group wanted very simple services. This became increasingly difficult in the light of development abroad. By 1625, some polarisation of Puritan (low church) and Arminian (high church) groups was beginning. The former stressed the importance of simplicity of service; the latter stressed the ceremonial aspect of worship, the 'beauty of holiness' and the antiquity of the Church of England.

James took his role as 'Supreme Governor' of this institution very seriously indeed. The Venetian Ambassador wrote to his government in May 1603:

> The King (James) is convinced that the security and peace of the kingdom depend upon the question of religion, and has resolved, in order to put an end to all doubts, to declare himself head and governor

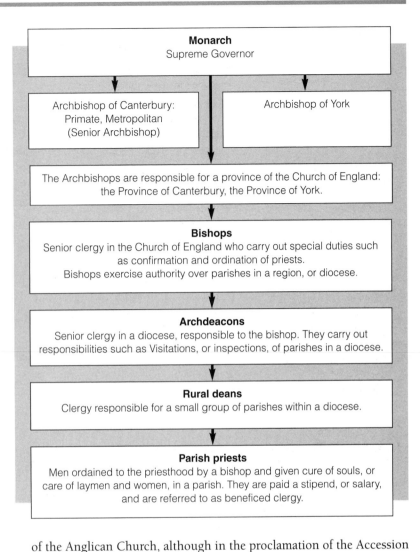

```
                    ┌─────────────────────────────┐
                    │         Monarch             │
                    │     Supreme Governor        │
                    └─────────────────────────────┘
```

Monarch
Supreme Governor

Archbishop of Canterbury:
Primate, Metropolitan
(Senior Archbishop)

Archbishop of York

The Archbishops are responsible for a province of the Church of England:
the Province of Canterbury, the Province of York.

Bishops
Senior clergy in the Church of England who carry out special duties such
as confirmation and ordination of priests.
Bishops exercise authority over parishes in a region, or diocese.

Archdeacons
Senior clergy in a diocese, responsible to the bishop. They carry out
responsibilities such as Visitations, or inspections, of parishes in a diocese.

Rural deans
Clergy responsible for a small group of parishes within a diocese.

Parish priests
Men ordained to the priesthood by a bishop and given cure of souls, or
care of laymen and women, in a parish. They are paid a stipend, or salary,
and are referred to as beneficed clergy.

Sect: A group usually separate from an established group or practice.

Papists: Members of the Roman Catholic Church who believe in the supreme power of the Pope.

1. In what way was the Church of England a hierarchic structure?

2. Why did James refer to the Church of England as 'the true religion, which by me is professed, and by the Law is established'?

of the Anglican Church, although in the proclamation of the Accession he was purposely not called such.

James saw two potential areas of threat, as he indicated in a speech to the Commons in 1604:

'At my first coming, although I found but one religion, and that which by myself is professed, publicly allowed, and by the Law maintained; yet found I another sort of religion besides, a private **sect**, lurking within the bowels of this nation. The first is the true religion, which by me is professed, and by the Law is established: the second is falsely called Catholics, but truly **Papists**: the third (which I would call a sect rather than a religion) is the Puritans and Novelists, who do not so far differ from us in points of religion, as in their confused form of policy and parity.'

The Catholics were the danger from without. James's choice of the word 'Papists' showed that he associated them not with loyalty to the universal church of Christ but to the Pope. As the national religion for centuries, they 'lurked' within the 'bowels of this nation', endangering the well-being of the body of Church and State. The so-called Puritans, as will be seen, posed a different problem.

6.3.3 How far did Catholics pose a problem for James I?

The religious inheritance of James I

Calvinism: A religious faith based on the teachings of John Calvin (1509–1564). Calvin was a French Protestant reformer who wrote 'The Institutes of the Christian Religion' in 1536. The centre of Calvinism was Geneva, Switzerland. The Church had no bishops. Congregations were led by Elders, who chose the minister. Calvinists believed in predestination (see page 51).

James I inherited the Elizabethan Church Settlement (see page 55), which made a compromise between Rome and Geneva as the basis of the Church of England. The Church of England was a *via media* between Roman Catholicism and **Calvinism**. Elizabeth I asserted, 'I will not animate Romanism; neither will I tolerate Newfangledness (Calvinism).' She had followed a cautious policy towards Catholics, aware of the residual strength of Catholicism in remote areas such as Lancashire, Yorkshire, Wales and the Welsh Marches. The Acts of Supremacy and Uniformity imposed a 12d (12 old pennies, one shilling, or 5p) fine on those not attending the Church 'by law established', while refusal of the Oath of Supremacy meant loss of office.

In the 1560s, Elizabeth I took a tougher line against English Catholics. The arrival in England of James's mother, Mary Queen of Scots, in 1568 offered to Catholic extremists in England a Catholic alternative to Elizabeth. Links between Mary Queen of Scots, the Catholic Earl of Northumberland and the Spanish were seen in the Rebellion of the Northern Earls in 1569. Although this rebellion failed, it showed the need for a tougher line was needed against actual and potential dangers from English Catholics. These were in higher profile with the presence of Mary in England and increasing hostility to Catholic powers abroad.

'Regnans in Excelsis': Literally, 'Ruling from on High', the title of the papal bull of excommunication published in 1570 by Pope Pius V. It declared Elizabeth to be a usurper and a heretic, released her subjects from allegiance to her, and told them to disobey her. It placed English Catholics in a difficult position of conflicting loyalties. Elizabeth responded with tough laws against Catholics.

Stronger measures followed the papal bull of Pope Pius V in 1570, *'Regnans in Excelsis'*. This Bull of Excommunication deprived Elizabeth of her 'pretended title' of Supreme Head of the Church, although Elizabeth's title was 'Governor' rather than 'Head'. By virtue of the Pope's authority to depose a heretical monarch, this bull freed Catholic subjects from the obligation of loyalty to Elizabeth. Such an attack on the authority of the English sovereign prompted Parliament to respond with Treason Acts against those who denied the authority of Elizabeth as lawful queen, and against those who brought in bulls from Rome. Harsher measures seemed justified in the light of the Ridolfi Plot in 1571 and of increased seminary priest and Jesuit missionary activities throughout the 1570s, 1580s and 1590s. **Recusancy fines** were increased to £20 per month in 1581 and an Act of 1585 ordered stricter measures against Jesuits and seminary priests.

Recusancy fines: Those who refused to attend the Church of England were obliged to pay these fines.

The Archpriest Controversy of 1594 to 1598 (see page 68) showed the limitations of Catholic unity and the attitude of the Appellants (see page 68) offered a way forward for English Catholics hoping to reconcile secular loyalty with religious loyalty to the Pope. However, the threat of Catholicism after the execution of Mary Queen of Scots was fuelled by events in foreign policy such as the war with Spain, with the Armada as its high point, and English support for the Dutch.

By 1603, English Catholics were regarded as undermining the Church and State. They were restrained by the harsh penal laws of the reign of Elizabeth. Recusancy fines of as much as £20 a month could be imposed on them and recusants were also liable to have two-thirds of their property confiscated for non-attendance at Anglican services. As the collection of such fines was the responsibility of the local Justices of the Peace, these fines were not always strictly enforced, especially if those responsible for collecting them were themselves secret Catholics.

As increase in recusancy fines may mean a change in attitude towards, rather than an increase in the number of, Catholics, it is difficult to estimate the size of the Catholic population. The estimated number of recusants in 1603 was 3,500. Recusancy records were not always accurate; much Catholicism survived in remote areas and there was much secret Catholicism at Court. There were at least three groups of Catholics:

- Recusants who refused to attend the services of the Church of England 'by law established'.

- Conformists who paid occasional lip-service to the Church of England, attending major church festivals in order to escape fines.

- Church Papists who attended the Church of England regularly but maintained their own faith in secret.

While any Catholic made a good scapegoat and was easily linked with plots against Elizabeth, danger from Spain and from Ireland, and the activities of Jesuits, there is no doubt that the majority of English Catholics were loyal to the Crown in 1603. They were keen to avoid the economic hardship of recusancy and the political exclusion suffered by their religion. Their survival was threatened by the advance of Calvinism – in the form of **Presbyterianism** and Puritanism. Such groups saw the Reformation as an ongoing event and were keen to strip the English Church of all vestiges of Rome in **doctrine**, ceremony, liturgy (form of church worship) and structure. The situation was further complicated by the fact that the Church of England had evolved from the Roman Catholic Church. Its structure was based on **dioceses** and parishes. It retained:

- bishops and the priesthood

- **tithes**

- its liturgy which was derived from that of Rome.

Indeed, by 1603, the very nature of the Church of England remained an issue. Was it a reformed Catholic Church – a catholic church with a small 'c'? Was it a reformed church that sought to purge all remnants of Rome? Was it a *via media*? The arrival of a new dynasty, in the form of the son of Mary Queen of Scots, brought new hope to English Catholics.

Presbyterianism: The belief of those who wanted the Church governed by elders rather than by bishops. A form of Calvinism adopted in Scotland.

Doctrine: What is laid down as true concerning a particular religion.

Dioceses: Areas where bishops are in charge of the priests and the spiritual life of all lay people.

Tithes: A tax that had to be paid by lay people to the Church.

James's attitude towards English Catholics

Although James was the son of the Catholic Queen of Scots, his Protestantism was never doubted. He was, however, prepared to take a more tolerant view of Catholics than his predecessor. There are many reasons for this.

- James was, by nature, non-persecuting. His role model of Solomon and his personal motto 'Beati Pacifici' ('Blessed are the Peacemakers') applied equally to domestic as to foreign issues (see section 6.4).

- He was relieved that his accession to the English throne had not degenerated into a war of English succession.

- James strove for loyalty from his subjects that covered as broad a spectrum as possible. Before he obtained the English crown, James was acutely aware of the problem of residual Catholicism in England and crypto-Catholicism at Court. His wife, Anne of Denmark, had converted to Catholicism round about 1600. As a 'foreign king' he not only wanted but needed a broad base of support, including that of conforming Catholics. Before 1603, he had written to the Earl of Northumberland who advised him that 'it were a pity to lose so good a kingdom for not tolerating a mass in a corner'. James replied: 'As for Catholics, I will neither persecute any that will be quiet and give but an outward obedience to the law, neither will I spare to advance any of them that will by good service worthily deserve it.'

- James was keen to assert his sovereignty as King of Great Britain and Ireland. He realised that Catholicism was an issue in all his kingdoms. In Ireland, the majority of his subjects were Catholic – either as the native population or as the Old English. In Scotland, there was a strong Catholic minority in the Highlands. In England and Wales, some Catholicism remained. In all of James's kingdoms, the established, or official, state religion was Protestantism. In that sense, the Catholic problem could assume a British and an Irish dimension.

- James was aware of the divisive nature of extreme anti-Catholicism. The reign of Mary Tudor, plots against Elizabeth and the Spanish Armada had unleashed dangerous forces. Whilst a Protestant country could use such forces to unite people against Catholic Spain's conspiracy for world dominance, those same forces could be dangerous to a new king seeking a policy that was tolerant, although falling short of toleration.

- James feared the Pope's ability to depose a heretical ruler by issuing a papal pull, such as the 1570 Bull against Elizabeth. This can be seen in a proclamation, in 1604, that the Council should 'make it manifest [known] that no state or potentate either hath, or can challenge, power to dispose of earthly kingdoms or monarchies, or to dispense with subjects' obedience to their natural sovereigns'. This same Proclamation urged that all Jesuits and seminary (college-trained) priests should be driven from England. These were the people that James feared as undermining his authority and the loyalty of his subjects.

- James was prepared to acknowledge the Catholic Church as 'our mother church although clogged with many infirmities' (in a letter to Robert Cecil, 1603). This attitude stemmed partly from his wish to avoid confrontation if loyalty was forthcoming, and partly from the hierarchic nature of the Church of England inherited from the Catholic Church, of which the king was now the Supreme Governor.

- James was always prepared to be tolerant towards conformists. Extremists he hated and feared as dangerous to the religious, political and social order.

Early policies towards Catholics, 1603–1606

The early years of James I's reign saw some fluctuation in policy and no serious Catholic attempt on the King's life. James's initially tolerant attitude, however, brought few concessions to Catholics. In May 1603, he ordered the collection of recusancy fines and in doing so stimulated **Watson's plot** against him. The revelation by the Jesuits of this priests' plot revealed the divisions within the Catholic community at the beginning of the reign. Recusancy fines were relaxed (i.e. not collected) in July 1603, partly as a reward for the discovery of the plot. This policy was not appreciated by James's first Parliament. It saw his concessions as producing an increase in recusants and growing boldness among the Catholic community, to the detriment of those of the reformed religion. This Parliament was sensitive to the fact that Puritans had received little or nothing at the Hampton Court Conference (see page 184) and that James had made peace with Spain. They responded with a bill asking that the penal laws against Catholics be 'put in due and exact execution'. The tougher stand on recusancy fines and the implementation of penal laws against Catholics, in 1604, was one of many factors behind the most serious plot of the reign: what has become known as the Gunpowder Plot.

Watson's plot: A plot to capture James and secure the removal of the anti-Catholic laws.

The 1605 Gunpowder Plot

The Gunpowder Plot was like the old-style Elizabethan plots. Some modern historians, such as John Bossy, suggest a possible Spanish connection, with the proposed Spanish support of the Infanta as a successor to Elizabeth. In fact, Guy Fawkes and John Wright (Robert Catesby's agent) were at the Spanish Court in 1603. It is unlikely that the Spanish would have supported such an enterprise – an argument advanced by the historian Alan Dures, in *English Catholicism, 1558–1642* (1983). The main interest of English

An engraving of 'The Gunpowder Plot Conspirators' (Thomas Bates, Robert Winter, Christopher Wright, John Wright, Thomas Percy, Guy Fawkes, Robert Catesby, Thomas Winter), 1605, by an unknown artist

Catholics, at that time, lay in peace with the English government. The attempt by Robert Catesby to blow up the Crown and the English establishment at the Opening of Parliament in 1605, the dramatic revelation of the plot through the Monteagle Letter and the subsequent 'discovery' of gunpowder, treason and plot are the stuff of which conspiracy theories are made. Perhaps the conspirators sensed that time was slipping away for a Catholic takeover, as relations improved between Spain and England. The conspirators themselves were largely from the Midland shires of England, where enforcement of the recusancy fines was being stepped up.

Attempts to see the plot of 1605 as a government plot against Catholics are largely contrived, although Robert Cecil certainly saw the advantage in letting the plot run for a time. By doing this, he achieved the desired effect of making James take a tougher line against Catholics. In fact, Cecil increased the goodwill of Parliament towards James to the extent that they voted him subsidies (grants) and were relieved that he had survived – and they too!

The Gunpowder Plot also raised the issue of the unpopularity of Scots at the English Court. When Guy Fawkes told the King that one of his objectives was to blow the Scots at Court back north of the border, James might have been provoked into addressing that issue.

Results of the Gunpowder Plot

From the King's point of view, the Gunpowder Plot threatened his person and his government. Political capital could be made out of it, with or without justification. James I was more popular than ever before, for his survival as much as for hoped-for anti-Catholic measures. This is shown by the vote of subsidies in the second session of his First Parliament.

Arguably, though, the Plot was a setback to James I's preferred policies. The Act for the Better Discovering and Repressing of Popish Recusants 1606 (see panel) was a way for Parliament to strengthen the existing measures against Catholics.

The Act for the Better Discovering and Repressing of Popish Recusants 1606

- Forbade Catholics to live in or near London

- Forbade Catholics to practise law

- Forbade Catholics to hold public office

- Ordered them to take the Oath of Allegiance (see below)

- Insisted that they have their children baptised as Protestants

- Laid down recusancy fines at the sum of £20.

The Oath of Allegiance, 1606

By the Oath of Allegiance, James hoped to restrain the possible threat from Catholics. He aimed:

'to make a separation between so many of my subjects who, although they were otherwise popishly affected, yet retained in their hearts the print of their natural duty to their sovereign; and those who ... thought diversity of religion a safe pretext for all kinds of treasons and rebellions against their sovereign'.

The Oath required suspected recusants to accept James as the lawful and rightful king of the realm, to reject the Pope's 'pretended' (claimed) authority to depose him and freed his Catholic subjects from allegiance to the Pope. It was strengthened by a clause that required acknowledgement that:

1. the doctrine by which the Pope claimed authority to depose a sovereign was 'impious and heretical'

2. no papal dispensation could free the subject from the Oath of Allegiance.

These two points created a stumbling block for many loyal Catholics.

At first, a number of Catholics took the Oath. After its condemnation by the Pope, applications to take it tailed off. James resorted to a series of pamphlets exchanged between himself and Cardinal Bellarmine to justify the wording of the Oath, but it did not achieve the success that James hoped for.

The effect of the Plot on James

While the Gunpowder Plot forced the abandonment of James's tolerant attitude towards Catholics, because of its possible consequences for himself and his government, he remained more tolerant throughout his reign than many of his subjects. In 1607, he asked judges to show such leniency to captured priests as the law would permit. 'No torrent of blood' was his policy. In a number of speeches to Parliament it is possible to see the pressure James I was under. While he was forced to urge that anti-Catholic laws be upheld, he was keen to distinguish between loyal Catholics, moderates and extremists. James remained opposed to persecution for its own sake; he did, however, use the threat of **popery** to gain parliamentary goodwill at that stage of the reign.

Popery: Term used to refer to the beliefs, practices and teachings of the Roman Catholic Church by people who are opposed to them.

Catholics and Court faction

The important aspect of Catholicism in 1614 came in the form of Court faction and the undermining of the Addled Parliament. With the death of Robert Cecil in 1612, faction had become more prominent as the pro-Catholic Howard faction and pro-Protestant Abbot–Pembroke faction tried to gain control of offices formerly held by Cecil. The Howards were accused of bribing members of the Addled Parliament to create an atmosphere that would ensure a lack of harmony between Crown and Parliament. As the Howards threatened to secure influence over the King's favourite, Robert Carr, the Abbot–Pembroke groups began to groom George Villiers.

At the same time, increasing influence at Court was being enjoyed by the Spanish ambassador, Sarmiento. As James looked to a Spanish marriage to fulfil his dynastic ambitions in Europe, and its dowry to remedy his financial situation at home – especially after the failure of the Addled Parliament – the spectre of Court Catholicism became more of a political issue.

Was 1618 a turning point in James's Catholic policy?

The outbreak of the Thirty Years War in 1618 (see Chapter 6) had a profound impact on James's policies towards Catholics, at home as well as abroad. His daughter, Elizabeth, and his son-in-law, Frederick of the Rhine-

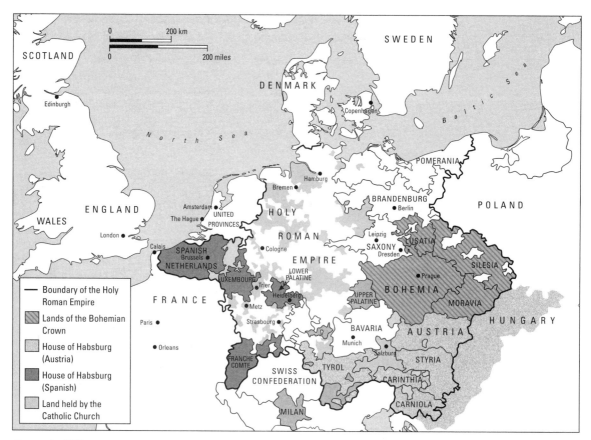

Europe in 1618

Palatinate, fell victim to Catholic powers in first Bohemia and then the Palatinate by 1621, reducing them and their children to almost refugee status in Europe. The war was a catalyst in the sense that it made anti-Catholicism in England a greater threat to James than Catholicism itself.

The increasing involvement of his daughter and son-in-law in the European struggle between Catholic and Protestant interests made it inevitable that James make a stand at some point. He had skilfully avoided commitment in the Bohemian Question in 1618 and, when his son-in-law accepted the Bohemian crown, had flaunted Habsburg authority. The loss of his son-in-law's hereditary lands in the Palatinate in 1621, however, could not be ignored. In the eyes of James, the best way to help his daughter Elizabeth was by achieving the Spanish marriage for his son, Charles. This would have:

- fulfilled his original dynastic aims of a Protestant marriage for his daughter and a Catholic one for his son

- brought a dowry for his empty Treasury

- confirmed his reputation as a peacemaker, restoring the Palatinate to Frederick and Elizabeth through diplomacy, rather than through a war policy that he could not afford.

Counter-Reformation: Attempt by the Pope and Catholic powers to reverse the Reformation of the previous century.

In England, James found that both public and parliamentary opinion was strongly anti-Catholic. The fear was of a **Counter-Reformation** that would eradicate the English Reformation and lead to a Habsburg dominance of Europe. This fear was unleashed in the Third Parliament.

The threat of anti-Catholicism in the Third and Fourth Parliaments

In the last two Parliaments of James's reign (1621–22 and 1624–25), religion – in the form of anti-Catholicism – played a key role. James called the Third Parliament in 1621 to ask for subsidies, anticipating possible help for his daughter and son-in-law after the invasion of the Palatinate by Spanish and Bavarian troops.

In his opening speech, James referred to the fact that some of his subjects believed he was growing cold in religion on account of his treaty with Spain. This he denied. The Commons retaliated with a demand for strict enforcement of anti-Catholic legislation. James replied that there were laws enough against Catholics and that it was not his fault if they were not enforced adequately. This exchange was not, in itself, a new development. What was more serious about this anti-Catholicism was that it spread into two other important areas, namely that of finance and of the royal prerogative.

Monopolists: People who claim the sole right to produce, manufacture, or sell a commodity.

- In the financial sphere, Parliament offered inadequate supplies for a possible intervention in a war that was seen as one heaven-sent to defend Protestantism. They then attacked **monopolists** at home as a means of highlighting a long-standing grievance that was associated with high-church favourites or crypto-Catholics.

- Anti-Catholic feeling encouraged Parliament to claim the right to discuss important matters of state in foreign affairs. The claim to free speech was a feature of all Jacobean Parliaments. In the 1621 Parliament, anti-Catholicism produced an unprecedented attack on the Spanish marriage policy. There were bitter exchanges between the King and Parliament on the nature of the royal prerogative and parliamentary privilege. The Commons' Petition of 1621 and the Protestation of 1621 showed the political strength of anti-Catholicism. Parliament was aware that a Spanish marriage could only be achieved at the expense of concessions to English Roman Catholics. This was considered too high a price to pay. When James dissolved the Parliament – ripping the Protestation out of the Journal of the House of Commons – he hoped never to call it again.

The failure of Charles and Buckingham to secure the Spanish marriage by their mission to Madrid in 1623 ended the hope of a diplomatic solution to the Palatinate question. Their return provoked anti-Catholicism of hysterical proportions. It is not easy to separate the strands of anti-Catholic from anti-Spanish feeling both of which had deep roots in both popular and parliamentary attitudes. Under such circumstances, James saw the wisdom of inviting Parliament to discuss foreign policy. Anti-Catholic and pro-Protestant factors, coupled with the activities of court faction and issues of prerogative and privilege, were the dynamic forces behind some important issues in this Parliament, such as:

- the fall of the Lord Treasurer, Lionel Cranfield, Earl of Middlesex

- the passing of the Monopolies Act

- the Subsidy Bill

- Appropriation of Supplies

Arminians: Followers of the theologian Jacobus Hermans (1560–1609), also known as Jacobus Arminius, who rejected Calvinist ideas of predestination (see page 51) and tended to assume that the authority of the State was superior to that of the Church.

1. What was the attitude of James to Catholics during the years 1603–1606?

2. Was anti-Catholicism more dangerous to the authority of James than Catholicism during the years 1618–1625?

● John Pym's attack on **Arminians**.

So the Catholic question was even more significant at the end of James's reign than at the beginning. The strength of Catholic powers in Europe was a fact that James had the good sense to appreciate. Spain was less of a threat to James personally than to Elizabeth I, yet Elizabeth could use the threat of Spanish Catholic aggression to appeal to, and show solidarity with, her people. Spanish Catholics did not threaten the throne of James, but English anti-Catholicism made it difficult for the King in his relations with Parliament. English Catholics were largely loyal to James. The Gunpowder Plot, a potentially serious blow to his person and his crown, was the work of a disgruntled minority. Catholics – as recusants, Occasional Conformists or Church Papists – could have had as king someone a lot worse than James. The threat from Catholics at home was largely indirect. It often stemmed from a prejudice that was fuelled as much by the tolerant attitude of James to loyal and conforming Catholics as by his desire for a Spanish marriage for his son. While it would be wrong to see James as the founder of the multi-cultural society, he was a tolerant man in an intolerant Europe.

 Exercise on James I's attitude towards Roman Catholics

SOURCE A

I greatly wonder that not only so great flocks of Jesuits and priests dare both resort and remain in England but have so proudly used their functions throughout all parts of England without any control or punishment for the last several years ... And I protest at the daily increase in popery and the proud boasting ... that none shall enter to be king there but by their permission.

James I's letter to Robert Cecil, December? 1602

SOURCE B

I did ever hate alike both extremities in any case, only allowing the middes (middle way) for virtue ... I will never allow in my conscience that the blood of any man shall be shed for diversity of opinions in religion, but I would be so sorry that catholics should so multiply as they might be able to practise their old principles upon us ... I long to see the execution of the last edict against them, not that thereby I wish to have their heads divided from their bodies but that I would be glad to have both their heads and bodies separated from this whole island and safely transported beyond the seas ...

No! I am so far from any intention of

persecution as, I protest to God, I reverence their Church as our mother church although clogged with many infirmities and corruptions, besides that I did ever hold persecution as one of the infallible notes of a false church ...

James I's letter to Robert Cecil, March? 1603

SOURCE C

As for Catholics, I will neither persecute any that will be quiet and give but an outward obedience to the law, neither will I spare to advance any of them that will by good service worthily deserve it ...

A letter to Henry Percy, Earl of Northumberland, 24 March 1603

1. Using Source A and your own knowledge, explain the term 'Jesuits' in the context of the attitude of James towards Catholics.

2. How far do these sources suggest a change in James's attitude towards Catholics?

3. Using the information in the extracts and in this chapter, explain the attitude of James to Catholics during the years 1603–1625.

6.3.4 *How far did the Puritans pose problems for James I?*

The answer to this depends on what is meant by the term 'Puritan'. It also depends on what part of the reign is at issue and whether the 'problems' are seen in a religious, political or foreign policy context.

There is some consensus as to what constituted a Catholic in the reign of James I. 'Puritan' is more difficult to explain. As a term of abuse, it was in use in the middle of the 16th century to indicate those who were killjoys (spoilsports), who frowned on those who enjoyed life. In the last quarter of the 16th century, it was applied to 'the hotter sort' of Protestants, who wanted to remove all traces of Roman Catholicism from the English Church and to continue the process of reform. These people had much in common with Scottish Presbyterians and Dutch Calvinists. They wanted to sweep away popes, priests and bureaucracies that came between man and God, and to get back to the simple authority of the Scriptures.

Vestments: garments worn by priests during ceremonies. Puritans preferred plain black gowns rather than 'Romish rags'.

In establishing her *via media*, Elizabeth had faced opposition from Puritans who opposed strict conformity to the Book of Common Prayer of 1559 and aspects such as clerical dress and the wearing of **vestments**. They were also opposed to altar rails and east-end altars, bowing at the name of Jesus, and elaborate music. All of these were seen as relics of the Roman Church.

'Seditious sectaries': A group outside the established church that stirs up people to undermine it.

Elizabeth had taken a tough line against nonconformists: the 1593 Act Against Puritans referred to such people as **'seditious sectaries'** and 'disloyal persons'.

By 1603, there were two broad groups of so-called Puritans:

1. Those who were moderate reformers within the Church of England, seeking to develop it further as a reformed Church. They wanted a number of changes in liturgy, but were not demanding the removal of bishops.

2. Those who felt that the existing Church of England could not be reformed from within on account of its origins and structure. Such people wanted a complete break with the national church and then the establishment of local, self-governing congregations. They are usually referred to as 'Separatists' or 'Independents'. These were the founders of early communities in Nottingham. Some left England for Holland and then returned, only to leave again as the Pilgrim Fathers at the end of the reign.

Pressure group: An organisation that wishes to influence political decision-making but does not wish to gain political power.

There was no Puritan creed (statement of belief) and the majority of Puritans conformed to the Church of England. They acted as a **pressure group** from within. It was this that made the Puritans, although lacking organisation, more dangerous to James than the Catholics. In a sense, James I knew where he stood with most Catholics. The Puritans, on the other hand, were the enemy to the king's royal prerogative within the Church. They were seeking to dilute the hierarchic nature of the Church of England, of which James was the Supreme Governor.

What did the Puritans want in 1603?

In general, the Puritans wanted:

● the removal of all traces of Catholicism in the ceremonies of the Church of England

- strict emphasis on the Scriptures as the primary authority for Christians

- a preaching ministry with a 'learned' clergy rather than 'dumb dogs'

- strict Sabbath (day of rest) observance

- a godly lifestyle.

The Elect: Those chosen for Salvation after death.

Puritan theology (religious theory) was essentially Calvinist theology with a belief in **the Elect** and predestination. So was much of the theology of the Church of England.

There was no distinct Puritan liturgy, but Puritans were inclined to value sermons and teaching more than ceremonies. They certainly opposed the sacramental symbolism inherited from the Catholic Church, which they regarded as '**the Whore of Babylon**'.

'The Whore of Babylon': Reference to the Catholic Church as corrupt and idolatrous. See the Book of Revelations (xviii.1).

Most Puritans accepted the royal supremacy, the institution of bishops and the hierarchical organisation of the Church of England. Only the Separatists denied these. All so-called Puritans stressed the Scriptures as the ultimate authority for matters of faith and the conscience of the Christian as the final moral and spiritual authority.

As the 'hotter sort' of Protestant, Puritans took their religion very seriously, and this was reflected in their lifestyle. They valued study, meditation and Bible reading. They observed the Sabbath and avoided the ale-house, music and dancing. They aimed to show that they were the Elect by their hard work and self-discipline. They looked for **providences**.

Providences: The will of God revealed in everyday events.

The Millenary Petition, 1603

The moderate Puritans within the Church of England expected much of James I. They were keen for him to show his approval of the need for modification in the established church. The Millenary Petition 'for the reformation of certain ceremonies and abuses of the Church' was presented to the King in 1603. It was signed by 1,000 clergy of the Church of England. The Petition acknowledged the king's authority over the Church. As it made only moderate demands, the Millenary Petition did not constitute a threat to James. Indeed, there had been a tradition, since the Reformation, of each sovereign reviewing the established church. The same was expected of James. The contents of the Petition stress its non-confrontational nature:

> Most gracious and dread sovereign, seeing it hath pleased the Divine Majesty … to advance your Highness according to your just title, to the peaceable government of this church and Commonwealth of England; we the ministers of the gospel in this land, neither as factious men affecting a popular parity in the Church, nor as schismatics aiming at the dissolution of the state ecclesiastical (church); but as the faithful servants of Christ, and loyal subjects to your Majesty, desiring and longing for the redress of divers (several) abuses of the Church, could do no less … than acquaint your princely Majesty with our particular griefs … Now we, to the number of more than a thousand, of your Majesty's subjects and ministers, all groaning as under a common burden of human rites and ceremonies … do humble ourselves at your Majesty's feet to be eased and relieved in this behalf. Our humble suit, then unto your Majesty is, that [of] these offences following, some may be removed, some amended, some qualified.

This has a somewhat heavy, but sincere, tone of reverence, even grovelling. It in no way encroaches upon the royal prerogative; it indicates 'rites and ceremonies' to be the main burden, rather than grievances against the structure of the church. Its four specific requests are politely made:

In the church-service

That the cross in baptism, interrogatories ministered to infants, confirmation, as superfluous, may be taken away: baptism not to be ministered by women, and so explained: the cap and surplice not urged: that examination may go before the communion; that it be ministered with a sermon; that divers terms of priests and absolution, and some others used, with the ring in marriage, and other such like in the Book, may be corrected: the longsomeness (length) of the service abridged: church-songs and and music moderated …: that the Lord's Day be not profaned, the rest upon holy days not so strictly urged: … no ministers charged to teach their people to bow at the name of Jesus: that the canonical scripture only be read in the church.

Concerning church ministers

That none hereafter be admitted into the ministry but able and sufficient men; and those to preach diligently, and especially upon the Lord's day.

For church livings and maintenance

That bishops leave their commendams [benefices which a bishop or other church dignitary held with his bishopric] … that double-beneficed men [clergy who held more than one rectory, vicarage, or curacy] be not [allowed] to hold some two, some three benefices with cure [a clergyman with 'cure of souls' had charge of a parish] …

For church discipline

That the discipline and excommunication may be administered according to Christ's own institution …

These we are able to show to be not agreeable to the scriptures, if it shall please your Highness farther to hear us … or by conference among the learned to be resolved … God, we trust, hath appointed your Highness our physician to heal these diseases …

Your Majesty's most humble subjects, the ministers of the gospel, that desire not a disorderly innovation, but a due and godly reformation.

(from the Millenary Petition)

These requests cannot be seen as a challenge to James's authority. The Petitioners were at great pains to stress their loyalty to the King. Their requests were based on the removal of the vestiges of the Church of Rome from the Anglican Church. There is even an argument for saying that the

Petitioners confirmed and consolidated the prerogative of the King over the Church, since they accepted that the changes they wanted to see could only be authorised by the King.

It is true that the Petition put James under pressure to call a conference and declare his position on the Church. Considering the King's love for debate and the need to assert his authority over religion at the beginning of the reign, he probably welcomed the opportunity offered by the Millenary Petition. He made it clear, however, that what he did not welcome was the spate of petitions that followed the Millenary Petition.

James's decision to call the Hampton Court Conference was a sensible one. It was his response to the Petition. It enabled him to come to grips with the English Church. He was able to assert his supremacy without real confrontation, since the Puritan representatives were essentially moderate men.

The Hampton Court Conference, January 1604

Archbishop Whitgift and eight bishops attended the Hampton Court Conference, which took place during the third week in January 1604. Reynolds, Knewstub, Chaderton and Sparke voiced the view of the reformers. While the bishops were wary of reform, they had little to fear from the Puritans. They were all moderate conformists, none of whom rejected the authority of the bishops.

The most uncompromising of the representatives was from the ranks of the bishops: Richard Bancroft, the Bishop of London and a 'Puritan basher'. He was soon to become Archbishop of Canterbury. James took Bancroft to task for his anti-Puritan stand.

A number of points raised by the Millenary Petition were discussed in a calm manner. These included:

John Whitgift (1530–1604), Archbishop of Canterbury, by unknown artist

- predestination

- aspects of the liturgy of the church

- the requirement that ministers sign that they agree to the Prayer Book

- Sabbath observance

- the recruitment of a learned ministry

- the desire for a new translation of the Bible to be authorised by the King.

James appeared to listen to Puritan requests. He even showed sympathy to them – after all he too favoured a learned ministry. Yet he remained firm that any changes would be made by the bishops. He rejected proposed changes such as the removal of the sign of the cross made on the infant's head during baptism, seeing it as a harmless piece of tradition rather than a remnant of Roman superstition.

Richard Bancroft (1564–1610)

Archbishop of London (1597–1604); Archbishop of Canterbury (1604–10). Bancroft took a strong anti-Puritan line at the beginning of James I's reign. His Canons (see page 227) drove out extreme Puritans from the Church of England after the Hampton Court Conference and undermined any real change. He was successful in the short term, but reaction to the Canons encouraged a pro-Puritan voice in the Commons.

Only when Reynolds raised the issue of more involvement of the lower clergy in the discipline of the church did the conference become more heated.

None of the surviving accounts is clear as to what exactly was wanted by the Puritans. Some hint at changes that might have led the way to a compromise between the Anglican and Presbyterian systems by setting up a number of synods (councils), meeting at levels from the **ruridecanal**, **diocesan** and **provincial**, to the national (whole of the country). This threatened to raise a more serious issue for James as it touched the structure of church government. However, the Puritans had insisted that they were not for some kind of democracy, rather than the ordered hierarchy of the Church of England.

A number of sources agree that the King's temper was raised when Reynolds used the term 'presbytery', referring to a synod 'where the bishop and his presbytery should determine all such points as could not be decided'. His outburst did not end the Conference immediately, but the final day showed that James was not prepared to give much to the Puritans. He urged them to obey their bishops and that, if they were not satisfied with the way their bishops handled matters, to raise such matters with the King personally.

On the last day of the Conference, James promised a number of concessions. The most important were:

- the new translation of the bible that appeared as the Authorised Version in 1611 (see picture)

- attempts to reduce **pluralism** and to secure a learned ministry.

Ruridecanal: A number of parishes grouped together, under a rural dean.

Diocesan: The area of administration of a bishop.

Provincial: The English Church was divided into two provinces: Canterbury and York – each under the administration of an archbishop.

Pluralism: The practice of holding more than one church office or benefice at the same time.

Title page of Authorised Version of the Bible, 1611

James insisted that any reforms were to be carried out by the bishops. Puritan requests for the removal of the cross in baptism, the use of the surplice and cap, and confirmation and 'interrogatories ministered unto infants' remained.

Ambivalent: Having contradictory aims and values.

This somewhat **ambivalent** approach was characteristic of James. He wished to preside over events at Hampton Court and yet was reluctant to make real changes. He was easily bored and yet acutely sensitive to potential erosions of the authority of the bishops and ultimately that of the King within the Church. The unfortunate choice of the word 'presbytery' clearly triggered a reference to the Scottish system in which the King enjoyed less authority than in the English Church. James aimed to consolidate, rather than to concede, his authority over religion in Britain. His action in ending the Conference stifled a debate that might have expanded into the arena of church government and politics; his concessions aimed to emphasise conciliation.

Source-based questions: The Hampton Court Conference

SOURCE A

First Day, 14 January
The King assured us that he called not this Assembly for any innovation, acknowledging the government [of the church] as it now is to have been approved by the manifold blessings from God himself … and in that he had received many complaints … through dissensions in the Church … and much disobedience to the laws … with a great falling away to Popery; his purpose was, like a good physician, to examine and try the complaints.

Second Day (16 January)
Dr Reynolds reduced all matters disliked … into four heads:

1. That the doctrine of the Church might be preserved in purity, according to God's word.
2. That good pastors might be planted in all Churches to preach the same.
3. That the Church government might be seriously ministered, according to God's Word.
4. That the Book of Common Prayer might be fitted to more increase of piety.

Dr Reynolds … desired that … they of the Clergy might have meetings once every three weeks; first in Rural Deaneries … and that things, as could not be resolved upon there might be referred to the Archdeacon's Visitation; and from thence to the Episcopal Synod, where the Bishop with his Presbytery should determine all such points as before could not be decided …

At which speech his Majesty was somewhat stirred … thinking, that they aimed at a Scottish Presbytery, 'which', said he, 'as well agreeth with a Monarchy as God with the Devil. Then Jack and Tom, and Will and Dick, shall meet, and at their pleasure censure me and my Council …

And then putting his … his Majesty said, 'My Lords the Bishops. I may thank you, that these men [Dr Reynolds etc] do thus plead for my Supremacy … But if once you were out, and they in place, I know what would become of my Supremacy. No Bishop, no King, as I said before …'. 'If this be all … that they have to say, I shall make them conform themselves, or I will harry them out of the land, or else do worse.'

Third Day (18 January)
His Majesty shut up all with a most pithy exhortation to both sides for unity. To which they all gave their unanimous assent …

from William Barlow, Dean of Chester, 1604

Source-based questions: The Hampton Court Conference

SOURCE B

His Majesty utterly distasting [Reynolds' Scheme] said that this was rightly the presbytery of Scotland, wherein John and William and Richard and such like must have their censure … and so all the matter is ordered by simple ignorant men. Mr Knewstubbs [said that Reynolds meant] a presbytery only of ministers and not of lay men. To whom said his Majesty I ken [understand] him well enough. And when I mean to live under a presbytery, I will go into Scotland again. But while I am in England, I will have bishops for I had not been so quietly settled in my seat but for them, adding that he had sufficiently tasted of the mischiefs of a presbytery in Scotland.

An anonymous account of the Conference

1. Read Source A. Explain the main demands of the Puritans at Hampton Court as indicated in Barlow's account.

2. Compare the reaction of James to the mention of a 'presbytery' given in Source A with that given in Source B.

3. What evidence is there in Source A that the Conference, in spite of the outburst of the King, ended amicably?

4. Using the sources and your own knowledge, how successfully did James I deal with the problem of Puritans before 1610?

How important was the Hampton Court Conference?

While historians such as David Willson believe that James mishandled the Conference and alienated the Puritans, the King was elated by his success. He wrote to the Earl of Northampton that he had soundly 'peppered' the Puritans. The extracts above show that James I was now aware of the fact that his future lay with the bishops, and that any British Church would have to be along Episcopalian (government by bishops) lines.

The importance of the Hampton Court Conference lies more in what followed the discussions than in the meeting itself. It is also significant that Bancroft succeeded Whitgift as Archbishop of Canterbury in 1604. Both he and James showed an urgent drive to conformity after the Conference. This is seen in three sources dating from 1604:

- In a speech to the House of Commons, James referred to the Puritans as a 'sect rather than a religion … who do not so far differ from us in points of religion, as in their confused form of policy and parity; being ever so discontented with the present government, and impatient to suffer any superiority; which maketh their sect unable to be suffered in any well governed Commonwealth'.

- James issued a proclamation in 1604 'enjoining conformity to the established form of the service of God'.

- The King approved Bancroft's Canons (church laws or rules) in 1604. Convocation drew up these Canons in an attempt to define the laws of the Church so that the Puritans could see whether they were either 'joined with them or severed from them'. Of over 100 Canons, number 36 was the key one. It required the clergy to sign their agreement to three articles:

1. That the King's Majesty, under God, is the only supreme governor of this realm, and of all other his Highness's dominions and countries, as well in all spiritual or ecclesiastical things or causes temporal …

2. That the Book of Common Prayer, and of ordering of bishops, priests and deacons, containeth in it nothing contrary to the Word of God … and that he himself will use the form in the said Book prescribed in public prayer and administration of the sacraments, and none other.

3. That he acknowledgeth all and every the articles … being in number thirty and nine, to be agreeable to the Word of God.

In some respects these Canons were the most important outcome of the Hampton Court Conference. In requiring conformity or loss of benefice, the Canons urged the moderates to conform.

Few Puritans challenged royal supremacy, but some refused to subscribe to the Prayer Book and the Thirty-Nine Articles. A number of petitions followed either against subscription to the Canons or asking for a longer period of grace. James was determined to take a tough line with nonconformists as potential trouble-makers, but was prepared to be lenient to those who conformed. Contemporaries estimated that there were about 300 **Silenced Brethren**. Recent research suggests that about 90 out of over 9,000 ministers were deprived of their living. It would appear that James had learned lessons from the Millenary Petition and the Hampton Court Conference. In his own way he put his stamp upon the Church of England with the Canons. The statement of the Venetian Ambassador, in a letter home in 1605 shows his success:

> Articles have been drawn up, and the Puritan ministers are called upon to sign them or to lose their benefices … Many ministers and many justices refused to subscribe, in the hope that the King would mitigate [soften] his orders, but seeing that he stands firm they have finally yielded and obeyed.

The supporters of the 'Silenced Brethren' caused problems for the King in the form of petitions for their reinstatement. In marginal notes to one such request for toleration, which had included a request for the removal of bishops, James showed his anger. He referred to the Puritans, in 1609, as 'prickles in our side'. 'There can be no unity in the Church if there be no orders [hierarchy] nor obedience to superiors.' It is also possible that ministers who lost their benefices became 'lecturers' or freelance preachers, with the ability to spread radical ideas.

Moderate Puritans remained an issue throughout the reign. Separatists were more serious in that they would not accept the royal authority over the Church, yet they were much less dangerous as their numbers were small during the reign of James I. Also, they were not seeking a reform from within the Church that James did not favour.

James and the Puritans after 1610

The end of the First Parliament in January 1611 and the death of the hard-line Richard Bancroft a year earlier promised better relations between James and Puritans. With no Parliament in session, demands for the

Silenced Brethren: Those who were deprived of their livings, or benefices, for not subscribing to Bancroft's Canons. They were the subject of a number of petitions in Parliament to restore them.

George Abbot (1562–1633)
Archbishop of Canterbury
(1610–33) – a man of moderate
Puritan views. He aimed to
promote the anti-Catholic and
anti-Spanish faction at Court.
Abbot advanced George
Villiers to counter the influence
of Robert Carr and the Howard
faction. Although his religious
ideas were favoured by James,
Abbot struggled towards the
end of the reign because of the
growth of Arminianism at Court.
His enemies also used the fact
that he shot a gamekeeper in a
hunting accident in 1621
against him.

return of the Silenced Brethren were stifled and the moderate George Abbot was made Archbishop of Canterbury. He was keen to prevent a polarisation in the English Church and wished to play down differences between high-church and low-church groups without alienating either. Until the last few years of his reign, James I encouraged a broad spectrum of opinion among the English bishops. He was known to choose men of ability and compassion to the ranks of bishops in the Church of England.

The great glory of the Jacobean Church – the Authorised Version of the Bible – appeared in 1611. This was the product of 54 translators, eager to produce a bible that was a work of great scholarship in a language that the people could understand. This work was widely seen as consolidating the Church of England under James.

Historians who favour seeing the reign of James I as the beginning of the road to civil war in 1642, tend to see his inability to remove what might be called Puritanism as a dangerous weakness. Instead, they equate the growth of a Puritan voice in Parliament with the origins of the Civil War. The historian David Willson wrote:

> [After Hampton Court] the discontent of the Puritans found only too much to feed upon as the reign wore on. A deep fissure was appearing in the Church; and while the bishops turned to the King, Puritans tended to turn to Parliament.

Recent opinions, expressed by specialist scholars such as Kenneth Fincham and Peter Lake, see James I as a shrewd judge of both Puritan and Catholic, as a man able to see beyond the current stereotypes created by their enemies. Unfortunately, his aim of 'the defusing of "radical" Puritanism and rabid anti-popery' ultimately floundered on the rocks of a foreign policy based on peace with Spain at a time of strong anti-Spanish feeling.

In the later part of the reign, there was some Puritan reaction provoked by four issues:

● the Declaration of Sports, 1618

● the Synod of Dort, 1618

● developments in foreign policy

● the rise of Arminianism.

In a number of instances, it is difficult to see a line between Protestant and Puritan reaction.

The Declaration of Sports, 1618
The Declaration of Sports was issued by James after his visit to Scotland in 1617. He had travelled back through Lancashire – a county with many recusants. His motives in introducing the Declaration were mixed:

> The report [of the increase of recusants in Lancashire] made us the more sorry when … we heard the general complaint of our people that they were barred from all lawful recreation and exercise upon the Sunday's afternoon after the ending of all Divine Service, which cannot but produce two evils: the one, the hindering of the conversion of many whom their priests will take occasion hereby to vex, persuading them that no honest mirth or recreation is lawful in our religion, which cannot but breed a great discontentment in our people's hearts, especially of

such … on the point of [converting]; the other inconvenience is, that this prohibition barreth the common and meaner sort of people from using such exercises as may make their bodies more able for war …, and in place thereof sets up filthy tipplings and drunkenness, and breeds a number of idle and discontented speeches in their ale-houses.

Tradition has it that James was moved by the people of Lancashire to allow Sunday sports. While such concessions might have encouraged some Catholics to see the Church of England as less of a killjoy, Puritans saw the Declaration as an attack on Sabbath observance. They caused such resentment to it that James did not press the observation of the Declaration.

Those who championed strict Sabbath observance rose to attack the King from the pulpit. This can be seen in a sermon preached in 1619 by the Rev. William Clough of Bramham in Yorkshire:

William Clough did preach within the parish Church of Bramham … upon the text 'Thou shalt keep my Sabbath'. And in his preaching did utter these words following … Now indeed the king of Heaven doth bid you keep his Sabbath … Now the king of England is a mortal man and he bids you break it. Choose whether of them you will follow.

The Declaration of Sports was clearly an irritant, but James avoided real confrontation – another example of Jacobean compromise.

The Synod of Dort, 1618–1619

This conference was held in the Netherlands. The debate between the traditional Calvinists and the supporters of Arminius, who placed emphasis on the importance of **free will** rather than predestination, had reached crisis point. In matters of theology, James most probably took a Calvinist stand but was fairly tolerant towards English Arminians who seemed more interested in matters of liturgy and ceremony than issues of doctrine. By 1618, he was aware of the potential of this continental debate to have serious repercussions for the religious balance and compromise he had achieved in England. As a committed Protestant, James instructed the English delegates to support the anti-Arminian stand. He realised both where the majority of his subjects stood and where the line of least resistance was drawn.

What was the impact of foreign affairs on the Puritans?

The year 1618 was significant for James's relations with the Puritans. The Book of Sports and the Synod of Dort were contentious issues in themselves. The outbreak of the Thirty Years War had the effect of making English Protestants more radical and of increasing the Puritan faction within Parliament (see Chapter 7). They were fired by anti-Catholicism. They were the dynamic behind a strong Protestant voice in the 1621 and 1624 Parliaments that demanded the abandonment of James's Spanish marriage scheme and favoured intervention in Europe on behalf of Protestants.

In 1622, James issued the Directions to Preachers. These forbade anyone under the rank of bishop or dean to give sermons on contentious theological points. This was a clear indication of the ability of religion to invade the prerogatives of the King and to disturb the compromise in religion. It supported the importance of anti-Catholicism and political Puritanism as forces generated partly by the outbreak of war in Europe.

Free will: The ability of the individual to choose the path of salvation or damnation.

1. What did the Puritans want in 1603?

2. Were they a greater threat to James after 1618 than before?

3. Why did Puritanism become politicised?

6.3.5 Was Arminianism an issue in the reign of James I?

Generally speaking, English Arminians were Protestants who stressed 'the beauty of holiness' and the derivation of the Church of England from the Catholic Church. Learned men discussed Arminian theology. However, to most people, Arminianism meant high-church ritual and ceremonies. It offered a focal point for Puritan anger. By the end of James I's reign, William Laud – an active high-church man – had been brought into the Court by Buckingham.

Laud had accompanied the King on the visit to Scotland in 1617 but James had sent Laud back, fearing his 'restless spirit' and his inability to leave well alone. Buckingham hoped that Laud's introduction to Court would dissuade his mother from converting to Catholicism. Laud did not create the fashion for high-church practices in the Court but his growing influence, together with the writing of high-church men such as Richard Montagu, illustrate the trend that alienated Puritans. They saw Arminianism as a step towards Catholicism.

The issue was complicated by the growing political importance of so-called Arminianism at the Court. James himself remained firmly Calvinist in outlook. He had supported the Calvinist stand at the Synod of Dort. However, he found greater support for his foreign policy and his overall authority and prerogative in church and lay matters from the so-called Arminians.

Richard Montagu's example made a parliamentary issue out of the divide between the high- and low-church elements within the Church of England. Montagu had been alarmed by the success of catholic missions in the Essex area, which claimed that the Church of England was not a true catholic church but a Calvinist one. Montagu wrote a tract called 'A New Gag for an Old Goose'. His aim was to highlight the Catholic origins of the English Church and to deny that it was essentially a Calvinist church. The tract produced an enormous Puritan backlash which echoed in debates in the Commons in 1624. Abbot was urged to discipline Montagu and make him write another tract which would cause less offence to Calvinists/Puritans.

James, irritated by this extreme reaction and potential invasion into areas pertaining to the authority of the sovereign, felt that such a response was not justified. He is said to have exclaimed at the attack on Montagu's orthodoxy: 'If thou be a papist, I am a papist.' The atmosphere was not defused by Montagu's second pamphlet, '*Appello Caesarem*'. The title translates as 'I appeal to Caesar' (i.e. the king). As such, it appealed to the royal authority for support and directly brought the King into the debate. James asked for the opinion of the Dean of Carlisle as to the orthodoxy of Montagu's second pamphlet and subsequently allowed its publication, in spite of the efforts of John Eliot and John Pym to the contrary in the Commons.

The concept of Arminianism is about as useful as that of Puritanism. For most of the reign, it stood for those at the high-church end of the spectrum of ritual and ceremonies – those who stressed the Catholic origins of the Church of England. The doctrinal dispute of free will rather than predestination may, or may not, have been a consideration. After 1618, the more extreme Protestants felt increasingly uneasy as Catholic forces were victorious abroad and high-church men gained influence at home.

Richard Montagu (1577–1641)
An able Cambridge scholar and Canon of Windsor. Ardent champion of the Church of England against both Catholics and Puritans. His views were Arminian and were bitterly attacked in Parliament. Charles I made him Bishop of Chichester in 1628, and Bishop of Norwich in 1638.

---

1. What were the main ideas of English Arminians?

2. Why were Arminians important at the end of the reign of King James?

3. How successfully did James deal with the problem of English Arminians?

6.3.6 *What was the 'Jacobean compromise' in religion?*
A CASE STUDY IN HISTORICAL INTERPRETATION

There is no doubt that James attempted a compromise in religion through-out his reign. Provided that loyalty and outward conformity was guaranteed, James did not wish to persecute. As long as a measure of balance was achieved within the Church of England, James was happy for it to be a broad-based church. Most historians writing on his government credit him with such an achievement. J.P. Kenyon, Maurice Lee, Jenny Wormald and Christopher Durston give credit where it is deserved in his religious policy. Kenneth Fincham and Peter Lake demonstrate James's ability in assessing the significance of both Catholics and Puritans. Dures and Bossy show that his policy towards Catholics was, in the historical circumstances, sound. Roger Lockyer suggests that while James was, in general, a 'more appealing figure than many' in religious policy, by the end of the reign it was becoming difficult to sustain this.

There is an argument for seeing cracks in the Jacobean compromise after 1618. After this date, it became increasingly difficult to hold the Puritans, Catholics and Arminians in an acceptable state of counter-tension due to events abroad, which sharpened religious differences at home and provoked confrontation rather than compromise. In a speech to Parliament in 1624, James showed that he was just as aware of the divisive forces of Catholicism and Puritanism as he was at the beginning of his reign: 'I think it all one to lay down my crown to the Pope as to a popular party of Puritans.'

The historian David Willson sees a division along the lines of bishops and king against Puritans and Parliament beginning after Hampton Court as rather a harsh interpretation. Historical hindsight and the high road to civil war approaches find little favour today.

While James's compromise in England was generally successful, the British Church that he had hoped to create always eluded him. The Church of England enjoyed only nominal supremacy in Ireland; attempts to merge the Scottish and English Churches met with open hostility early on in the reign. Andrew Melville, the Scottish reformer, had made it clear to James that only Christ was 'King and Head of the Church'. He opposed any attempts by James to increase the authority and number of the few bishops remaining in the Scottish Church.

James's last attempt to build a bridge between the English and Scottish churches came with his visit to Scotland in 1617 and the issuing of the Five Articles of Perth. These urged certain procedures characteristic of the English Church, such as kneeling to take communion, at confirmation, and at the celebration of Christmas and Easter. They also contained a request for the Scottish Parliament to accept that the King, advised by senior church officials, could determine the external government of the Church. This met with spirited opposition on the part of some Scottish clergy. When James showed an equally stubborn determination to retain the Five Articles, he secured their formal acceptance but found that they met with a degree of passive resistance in Scotland. He had, however, made his position clear – that he believed that a united kingdom should have a united church.

His religious legacy to his son was generally creditable, but the inherent problems given the deteriorating European situation were such that his son was not capable of dealing with them.

1. In what ways was James's religious policy in England successful?

2. To what extent did James succeed in bringing together the Scottish and English churches?

6.4 The foreign policy of James I

Key Issues

- What were the aims of James VI and I in foreign policy?

- To what extent did 1618 mark a turning point in the foreign policy of James VI and I?

- How successfully did James VI and I deal with foreign affairs, 1603–1625?

Framework of Events

1603	Succession of James VI of Scotland to English throne as James I – no opposition from Spain
1604	War between England and Spain ended by Treaty of London
1609	Truce of Antwerp between Spain and the Dutch
	James plays a part in securing 'Twelve Years Truce'
	Anglo–Dutch fishing disputes
1610	Crisis in the Duchies of Cleves-Julich
	Assassination of King Henri IV of France
1613	Marriage of Princess Elizabeth to Frederick Elector Palatine
	Fishing disputes with the Dutch
1614	Treaty of Xanten is negotiated by England and France to resolve Cleves-Julich crisis
	Unfavourable Dutch reaction to Cockayne Project
1618	May: Defenestration of Prague
	Bohemian Protestants reject authority of Habsburgs
	Outbreak of Thirty Years War
1619	Frederick Elector Palatine accepts the throne of Bohemia
1620	Invasion of Upper Palatinate by Maximilian of Bavaria
	Defeat of Frederick V at battle of the White Mountain
	Spain agrees to help the Austrian Habsburgs by invading the Lower Palatinate
1621	End of Truce of Antwerp
	Petitions and Protestation from Third Parliament against the Spanish marriage
1623	March–September: Buckingham and Charles in Spain
1624	Relations with Spain broken after the return of Charles and Buckingham
	Fourth Parliament urges war preparations
	French marriage treaty is ratified
1625	Mansfeld's expedition to relieve the Palatinate
	27 March: death of James VI and I.

Overview

FOREIGN policy is, without doubt, the area in which James followed his ideals. The most important of these was the pursuit of peace. As King of Scotland he had no particular hatred of Spain, the English arch-enemy of the late 16th and early 17th centuries. By the beginning of the 17th century, the glory of Spain was diminishing. No hostile reaction followed James's accession to the English throne in 1603. His succession to the English throne and the Union of England and Scotland gave him ambition on a grand scale: to balance Europe in peace and harmony; to be the architect of European peace through the marriage of his children. James was not entirely in 'cloud-cuckoo land'. Necessity, as well as idealism, determined the lines of his foreign policy. He realised the cost of war both in terms of money and in obligation to Parliament for war supplies.

James appreciated that peace with Spain would stamp his authority on foreign policy as a key area of the royal prerogative. The Treaty of London with Spain, 1604, remained the dominant treaty of the reign. It was followed by James's help in securing a truce between the Dutch and the Spanish in 1609, and other negotiations to bring harmony to a Europe divided into hostile factions on religious lines.

His policy of marriage with a Catholic and a Protestant state was partially achieved with the marriage of his daughter Elizabeth. James was not to know that the Protestant Palatinate marriage of his daughter in 1613 would cause problems over five years later. With the outbreak of the Thirty Years War in 1618, his policies appeared contradictory to many of his subjects. The idea of supporting Protestantism in Europe through a Catholic marriage for his son Charles was unbearable to ardent Protestants. James's attempts to avoid whole-hearted commitment to Protestant factions after 1618, while they are to be commended for avoiding war until 1625, produced hostile reactions at home. He was seen to follow his Spanish marriage policy to the detriment of Protestantism at home and abroad.

Relations with Spain dominate his foreign policy.

- The Treaty of London of 1604 ended war between them.
- The Truce of Antwerp of 1609 ended hostilities between the Spanish and the Dutch.
- The Palatinate Crisis that clouded foreign policy after 1621 was triggered by the Spanish invasion of the Lower Palatinate.
- The failure of the Duke of Buckingham and Prince Charles to secure the Spanish marriage in 1623 meant that the reign ended with a likely return to an anti-Spanish and pro-Dutch foreign policy.

War was not the preferred policy of James, however.

6.4.1 What was the Elizabethan legacy in foreign policy?

James inherited a foreign policy that was anti-Catholic and anti-Spanish. The lines of Elizabeth's foreign policy had been drawn according to events at home. Catholic plots against the Queen and the Spanish reaction to the execution of Mary Queen of Scots eventually linked the survival of Elizabeth's monarchy to an anti-Spanish policy.

While Elizabeth would have preferred peace, the economic advantages of war with Spain and support for the Dutch in their rebellion against their Spanish overlords offered some reward to merchant adventurers. War with Spain justified attempts to encroach upon Spanish territories in the New World. It made legitimate acts of privateers (essentially licensed pirates) in attacking Spanish treasure ships crossing the Atlantic. It also acted, to the advantage of England, as a thorn in the flesh of trade in and out of the Spanish Netherlands, a trading rival.

In truth, however, English foreign policy was living off its reputation by the end of the 16th century. The days of the exploits of Drake and the Armada were long gone. The legacy of anti-Catholicism was strong, but stalemate in war was the reality for both Spain and England.

1. What was the traditional English foreign policy by 1603?

2. Why was that policy becoming outdated by 1603?

6.4.2 *What was the attitude of James to foreign policy?*

At the beginning of his reign as King of Great Britain, James's attitude to foreign policy was quite clear.

Role model: Someone on whom others model their behaviour or actions.

Solomon: King of Israel from c. 970–c. 933 BC. He succeeded his father, David. Solomon was famous for: bringing peace and prosperity to Israel; building the Temple at Jerusalem as part of a scheme for making Jerusalem a glorious capital city; making peace with neighbouring states through marriage negotiations and through personal diplomacy. James was first compared with Solomon in 1579 on his entry into Edinburgh. His funeral oration in 1625 was a lengthy comparison of James and Solomon. Cynics point out that James might have been a 'son of David' – David Riccio, the possible lover of his mother.

1. His personal motto was '*Beati Pacifici*' ('Blessed are the Peacemakers') and he wished to go down in history as *Rex Pacificus* (the Peaceful King, King of Peace, or Peacemaker). His **role model** throughout the reign was King Solomon. Solomon settled squabbles by diplomacy and reason rather than by confrontation. The theme of James as **Solomon** and peacemaker figures prominently in the Banqueting House ceiling, in London. This was commissioned from the Flemish painter, Rubens, by Charles I to commemorate his father, James. King James is shown in the first panel as bringing peace between England and Scotland through Union (see page 196). Rubens draws on the story of Solomon in the Second Book of Kings. In the Old Testament account, Solomon is asked to judge between two women who each claim the same child. Solomon orders that if the women cannot agree, the child should be divided between them. He realises that the real mother would give her child away rather than see it killed; by such means he establishes the identity of the true mother. In the ceiling panel, James (as Solomon) presides over two female figures (representing England and Scotland), who stand behind an infant. James's judgement is that the child is neither that of England nor Scotland, but 'Great Britain', the offspring of both women. In this sense, Union between England and Scotland is the first act of peaceful foreign policy in the two kingdoms. In the panel above the state chair, and in the side panels, the benefits of good and peaceful government are made clear: peace brings prosperity and plenty.

   Contemporary sources on the character of James support his personal hatred of violence.

2. His Scottish experience had not included war with Spain. He felt no hostility towards the Spanish provided they did not challenge his succession to the English throne.

3. James was a new and 'foreign' king in England who needed a broad base of support. He saw distinct advantages to a peaceful foreign

James as Solomon: the Union of England and Scotland in the Banqueting House ceiling, Whitehall, London – detail from painting by Sir Peter Paul Rubens, commissioned in 1629.

policy. Peace with Spain might guarantee that Spain would not support Catholic plots against him in England and Ireland.

4. Peace would avoid the financial drain of war – an absolute essential at the beginning of the reign.

5. Peace would mean that he did not have to go 'cap-in-hand' to Parliament for war subsidies. Even James, with his lack of financial skill, realised that war would leave Parliament with an advantage as he was dependent upon them for financing any fighting.

6. Peace would encourage an atmosphere in which trade could develop. As tunnage and poundage played such an important part in the royal revenue, this was much to be desired. It would be even better if peace could win trading concessions in Spanish overseas territories.

7. As a peacemaker, James could secure a European role for himself. As he had united Britain and Ireland, he hoped to secure harmony throughout Europe. This role is to be seen in his religious policy and in his policy of **dynastic marriages**. To the cynical, this might seem to be masterly inactivity on a grand scale. James lived and reigned at a very dangerous time in which he tried to find his way through a political minefield.

Dynastic marriages: Marriage of the children of the Stuart dynasty (rulers who belong to the same family) into the leading houses, or dynasties, of Europe in order to secure peace and to balance religious differences.

Source-based question

SOURCE

As [King James] is by nature of a mild disposition, and has never really been happy in Scotland ... so he desires to have no bother with other people's affairs and little with his own; he would like to dedicate himself to his books and to the chase, and to encourage the opinion that he is the real arbiter of peace. He has the suspicion in his mind [that] ... the Pope had occasionally discussed the possibility of uniting France and Spain against England as well as the Turks, and for this reason he is resolved, if possible to stand well with all the Catholic Princes .... He will draw close to the strongest of them, the King of Spain, and will seek to gratify the Emperor, while he is bound to the Protestant Princes by his religion .... From these calculations made in Scotland, the English find it difficult to move his Majesty.

From a letter from the Venetian Ambassador to the Government of Venice, June 1610

a) How useful do you find the Ambassador's explanation of the aims of James's foreign policy?

b) Using the extract and your own knowledge, what were the aims of James's foreign policy before 1610?

c) Why might the Ambassador have difficulty convincing some of James's English subjects of the benefits of peace with Spain?

Why was foreign policy an issue in Crown–Parliament relations?

Thirty Years War: A series of religious and political wars between Catholic and Protestant European states during the years 1618 to 1648. Origins lie in the internal instability of the Holy Roman Empire. The first phase of the war was fought in Bohemia and the Palatinate.

1. In what ways was foreign policy linked to religious issues?

2. In what ways did foreign policy raise issues of finance and royal authority?

Matters of foreign policy were important in relations between Crown and Parliament throughout James I's reign. Parliament was invariably committed to the Protestant cause in Europe; James's attempt to balance Europe, with a Protestant marriage for his daughter and a Catholic one for his son, was not appreciated. It aroused fears of the subjection of England to the ambitions of Spain. There was also fear of a return to Catholicism, or at least unwelcome concessions to English Catholics.

Any foreign commitment required extraordinary finance that could only be supplied by Parliament. Additional financial burdens were not welcomed, even in a generally under-taxed England. Parliament was not likely to vote supplies without some concessions from the Crown. This could produce debates in Parliament that challenged the royal prerogative – especially in the Parliament of 1621, after the outbreak of the **Thirty Years War** in 1618.

Foreign policy, therefore, had the capacity to link key issues such as religion, finance and royal authority.

6.4.3 What was James's policy towards Spain?

'**Natural enemy**': one designed by nature to be fundamentally and eternally hostile; like a poison in the system.

While James was keen to establish and maintain good relations with Spain, his subjects did not share this enthusiasm. Spain was, in the eyes of Parliament, a '**natural enemy**' of England who sought to establish 'universal monarchy' (world domination) at the expense of English religion, trade and nationality. Spain frustrated England in the Americas and Europe. To James, such attitudes were backward looking. He believed that the death of Philip II in 1598 and of Elizabeth in 1603 paved the way for a reconciliation and harmony that would be encapsulated in a treaty. This would be the foundation of his foreign policy and dynastic marriage schemes.

The Treaty of London, 1604

This Treaty was the outcome of negotiation between a Spanish and an English delegation, sitting at Somerset House in London. A picture hanging in the National Portrait Gallery celebrates the event and names the delegates.

Inquisition: A special Church Court set up in 1479 to root out heresy in Spain. It was first directed against lapsed converts from Judaism and Islam, later against Protestants. Punishments ranged from penance, confiscation of goods, imprisonment and finally being handed over to the state to be burnt at the stake.

Robert Cecil is seen at the right-hand side of the picture, leading the English delegation. James was delighted with the overall outcome of peace, telling Parliament that he had delivered the blessing of peace abroad to his subjects. While hostilities ceased and good trade concessions were gained in Spain and the Netherlands, including the exemption of English merchants from the **Inquisition**, James gained no concession on Spanish colonial trade.

The Somerset House Conference, 1604, by unknown artist

The lack of trading concessions with the Spanish colonies generated some opposition to the Treaty at home. Some MPs believed that James should be the leader of a Protestant union against Catholics, and disliked the peace. They saw Protestant England abandoning the Dutch by making peace with Spain. They feared that Catholic faction at Court and possible leniency towards English Catholics would be the outcome of peace with Spain.

Such criticism was somewhat harsh. Peace with Spain was an economic and political necessity. Elizabeth's policy was no longer tenable. The Treaty of London brought many advantages:

- the expansion of trade with Spain produced a favourable balance of trade;

- the pacification of Ireland could proceed more easily in a climate of peace;

- English merchants got a better deal both with increased trading opportunities and freedom from the Inquisition.

The Treaty of London was the sheet anchor of James's foreign policy. It was only abandoned, reluctantly, at the end of his reign.

How important were dynastic marriages in James's foreign policy?

As Solomon had used marriage as a tool to make peace and establish the authority of his monarchy in ancient Israel, James proposed to use his children to maintain the balance of power in Europe. He intended to stabilise Europe and to safeguard his dynasty through a Protestant marriage for his daughter Elizabeth, and a Spanish Catholic marriage for his heir, Prince Henry. After the death of Henry in 1612, Prince Charles became the heir to his throne and his policy.

Infanta: Daughter of the King of Spain. The Infanta Isabella was a possible claimant to the throne of England.

After the visit of the Lord High Admiral (the Earl of Nottingham) to Spain in 1605, to confirm the Treaty of London, it was suggested that Prince Henry should marry the **Infanta** Anne, the elder daughter of Philip III of Spain. Negotiations were attempted in 1605, 1607 and 1611. The main obstacle was the determination of Prince Henry not to marry a Catholic.

Prince Henry, circa 1610, by unknown artist

Prince Charles, circa 1612, studio of Isaac Oliver

Elector Frederick of the Rhine Palatinate
– painting by Gerrit van Honthorst, 1635

Elizabeth Queen of Bohemia – studio of
Michiel van Miereveld

Elector Frederick of the Rhine Palatinate (1596–1632)
Frederick was the Elector (governor) of the Rhine Palatinate and a leading German Protestant in the **Evangelical Union**. His ambition was greater than his political and military strength. Five years after an expensive marriage ceremony to the Princess Elizabeth, he defied the Habsburgs by accepting the Bohemian crown from the Protestant rebels. By 1621, he had lost both Bohemia and the Palatinate, and his family were refugees in the United Provinces. Elizabeth bore him 13 children. Frederick died in exile in 1632. His son regained half his lands at the end of the Thirty Years War in 1648. Elizabeth returned to England in 1661 and died the following year.

Evangelical Union: A league of German Protestant Princes of which the Elector Palatine was the most important.

Heir apparent: Direct heir to the throne; next in line of succession.

The Protestant marriage was achieved in 1613 when Princess Elizabeth married the Elector Frederick V of the Palatinate, the leading light of a group of German Protestant states known as the Evangelical Union. His lands included the Lower Palatinate, an area of strategic importance on the river Rhine around Heidelberg, and the Upper Palatinate, an area lying between the Danube and Bohemia (see map on page 178). As a keen and committed Calvinist, Frederick aimed to champion Protestantism by forming good relations with England, the United Provinces and Bohemian Protestants.

While this marriage showed James's commitment to European Protestantism, he did not mean there to be only one-sided commitment to the Evangelical Union.

When Prince Charles became **heir apparent** in 1612, hopes for a Spanish marriage were revived. The failure of the Addled Parliament of 1614 left James very short of money and therefore very receptive to the suggestion of Sarmiento (later Count Gondomar) that there should be a marriage between Prince Charles and the Infanta Maria. (The Infanta Anne was no longer on offer as she had been betrothed to Louis XIII of France.) A good dowry (marriage portion) would, of course, accompany this.

In 1615, the Spanish sent a number of articles as the basis for discussion of marriage terms. This came to nothing, as Spain wanted any children of the marriage to be brought up as Catholics and the penal laws against English Catholics to be removed. James neither would nor could agree to this. No English Parliament would relax the anti-Catholic legislation. Thus stalemate became the main feature of negotiation until 1617, when Sir John Digby brought back more terms from Spain. This time, the Spanish wanted the repeal of the penal laws against Catholics, the establishment of a Catholic chapel in London, and the appearance of Prince Charles in Spain. Such terms would not receive parliamentary approval. No Protestant English Parliament would remove anti-Catholic legislation.

It might be said that, by this time, the idea rather than the reality of the second dynastic marriage was in the interests of both Spain and England.

Continuing negotiations would ensure that neither side was hostile to the other in Europe.

With the outbreak of the Thirty Years War in 1618 and the involvement of his son-in-law in Bohemia, the Spanish marriage became the main objective of James's foreign policy.

By 1621, Frederick had lost both Bohemia and the Palatinate to Catholic Habsburg forces. James hoped that such a marriage would induce Spain to withdraw from the Palatinate and help to restore the Elector. His persistence with this policy produced a hostile Third Parliament, and the visit of Charles and Buckingham to Madrid before the policy was finally abandoned, under pressure from his Fourth Parliament.

In spite of the ultimate failure of his dynastic marriage policy, it proved a means by which James avoided military engagement in Europe throughout his reign.

In what ways did foreign policy towards Spain change after 1618?

Policy towards Spain after 1618 was closely interlinked with James's policy towards the Holy Roman Empire. It reflected the growing tension in Europe between the Evangelical Union and the **Catholic League**, the impending expiry of the Twelve Years Truce, and the outbreak of the Thirty Years War.

When his son-in-law accepted the throne of Bohemia in 1619, James was expected to support him in a war against the Habsburgs. James did not wish to become involved in hostilities in Europe, even when his son-in-law was driven from Bohemia after the battle of the White Mountain.

In 1620, Spain agreed to help the Austrian Habsburgs in their fight against Frederick by invading the Lower Palatinate. This was a disaster for Frederick and Elizabeth: the loss of their hereditary lands left them as refugees in Europe. Its significance was even greater: it gave Spain control of a key route to the Spanish Netherlands, at a time of impending hostilities against the Dutch with the expiry of the Truce of Antwerp.

The implications of this Spanish support for the Austrian Habsburgs were very significant. James had few realistic options. He lacked:

- a standing army
- sufficient financial backing for military intervention
- sufficient funds to support mercenary troops.

Above all, he was ideologically and emotionally opposed to intervention.

He hoped for a diplomatic solution to the situation. In 1620, Gondomar, the Spanish Ambassador, returned to England after nearly two years' leave. Relations between James and Gondomar had always been good. The historian Charles Carter has shown that they had a mutual respect for each other as well as determination to avoid war, discrediting older views that Gondomar was dominating James's policy. It was certainly in the interests of both countries to avoid war with each other. The idea of the Spanish marriage offered the diplomatic solution that James wanted, and the way to keep England from engaging in war against Spain.

Catholic League: A union of Catholic powers in Germany that was opposed to the Evangelical Union of Protestant states.

A print of Gondomar shown in Thomas Scott's hostile pamphlet, *Vox Populi* ('The Voice of the People'). Gondomar is depicted as the wily Italian political philosopher, Machiavelli. The Latin captions translate loosely as 'A finger in every pie' and 'Worthy of the Spanish people'.

What do the commode and asses show about feelings towards the Spanish?

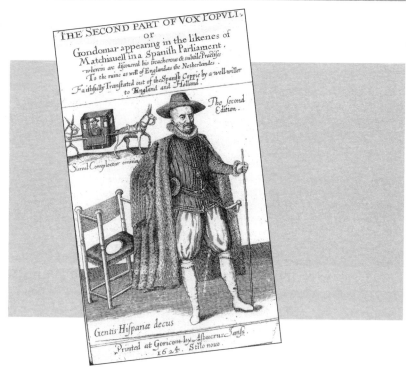

James had sent 2,500 troops to the continent as a presence to indicate concern over the Palatinate, but forbade them to fight. He believed that it was morally right to defend the Palatinate, but not Bohemia. The fall of Bohemia and invasions of the Palatinate forced James to call the Third Parliament, in 1621.

How important was the Third Parliament in James's foreign policy?

Events abroad and James's foreign policy towards Spain produced a very vocal Parliament in 1621.

● It offered James inadequate subsidies for an active foreign policy (see page 197).

● It showed its strength by reviving the process of impeachment to attack monopolists and bring about the fall of Bacon (see page 163).

● Some MPs asserted that James had invited them to debate foreign policy. This meant that foreign policy led to debates on matters of the royal prerogative and parliamentary privilege. MPs made it clear that they were against the Spanish marriage and that this had led to the 'insolvency of the papists'.

● The Commons' Petition of 3 December urged the King to 'take your sword into your hand', to 'aid those of our religion in foreign parts', to 'direct the point of your sword' against Spain, to take a tough line against Catholic recusants, and to marry Prince Charles to a Protestant. This shows the importance of foreign policy as stimulating key issues in the Third Parliament: finance, religion, prerogative and privilege, such as direction of foreign policy and free speech.

● The King responded by forbidding the Commons to discuss matters 'tending to our prerogative royal' and censured them for daring 'to meddle with our dearest son's match with the daughter of Spain'.

Commons' Protestation of 1621:
Asserted the right of the House of Commons to discuss 'affairs concerning the King, State, and defence of the realm and of the Church of England, and the maintenance and making of laws, and redress of mischiefs and grievances which daily happen within this realm'.

His attitude produced the **Commons' Protestation of 1621**. In this, the Commons asserted its right to discuss the 'urgent affairs concerning the King, State, and defence of the realm and of the Church of England …' as 'the ancient and undoubted birthright and inheritance of the subjects of England' (i.e. not dependent upon the grace of the sovereign).

The King's anger and frustration was shown when he ripped the page containing the Protestation out of the House of Commons' Journal and dissolved the Parliament.

The Spanish policy had not eroded the powers of the Crown as such; James had used the royal prerogative to dissolve a troublesome Parliament. It had, however, produced serious issues that obstructed cooperation between the King and Parliament at a critical time.

After the dissolution of the Third Parliament, James persisted in seeking a diplomatic solution. He was adamant that no Spanish marriage would take place before the Spanish withdrew from the Palatinate and before they helped to negotiate its return to Frederick.

'I like not to marry my son with a portion of my daughter's tears.'

How did the visit to Madrid of Charles and Buckingham affect foreign policy?

The visit to Madrid by Charles and the Duke of Buckingham in 1623 was the last attempt to achieve the Spanish marriage and find a peaceful solution to the problem of the Palatinate. When this failed, Buckingham began to favour a French marriage for Charles. Both Charles and Buckingham then looked to secure the recovery of the Palatinate without Spanish help. Their activities did much to undermine the traditional policy of James that was based on the Treaty of London and balance between Catholic and Protestant powers in Europe to be achieved through marriages.

What impact did the Fourth Parliament have on foreign policy?

The Fourth Parliament of James's reign was keen for war with Spain. In contrast to his attitude in the previous Parliament, James invited the advice of the Fourth Parliament on foreign policy. The Duke of Buckingham and Charles supported action against Spain. Opposition from Lionel Cranfield was removed by his impeachment (see page 165). The Venetian ambassador noted not only Cranfield's corruption, but also the fact that he had Spanish sympathies as a cause of his own removal. Cranfield had also opposed war on financial grounds. He tried to bring about the fall of Buckingham, as the King's favourite, by introducing his homosexual cousin into the Court. Cranfield was thus expendable on a number of grounds. Financial support for war was gained by the King agreeing to the impeachment of Cranfield and the signing of a monopolies bill – reviving a big issue from the previous Parliament. This secured a subsidy bill. It by no means gave the King a free hand; the subsidies voted for war were to be appropriated and administered by a committee nominated by the Commons.

By the end of the reign, the sheet anchor of James's foreign policy – peace with Spain – was about to be severed. The Commons dissolved all

Protestantism: A movement formed by branches of the Christian Church which broke away from the Catholic Church in the 16th century.

Puritanism: A movement, largely within the Church of England, to 'purify' the Church by removing all traces of Catholicism from its structure, organisation and form of worship. A 'hotter sort' of Protestantism.

1. How successful was James's policy towards Spain before 1618?

2. In what ways was 1618 a turning point in foreign policy?

3. How far do you accept the view that the success of the marriage policy for James's daughter caused the failure of that for his son?

> **Count Mansfeld, Peter Ernst von Mansfeld (?1580–1626)**
> A mercenary general who was prepared to sell his services to Protestant rulers, such as James I, in the war against Catholics in Europe. As there was no standing army in England at the time, mercenaries played an important role in foreign expeditions.

treaties with Spain and voted £300,000 for a naval war. Approaches were made to France for a marriage between Charles and Henrietta Maria. Buckingham and Charles were keen to get James to accept a treaty with the Dutch, a treaty with Denmark, and to equip an expedition under Count Mansfeld to relieve the Palatinate. Hostile **Protestantism**, political **Puritanism** and anti-Catholicism played an important role in the final years of James's Spanish policy.

It cannot, however, be argued that foreign policy gave the initiative to Parliament at the end of the reign. The 1621 Parliament had created problems for the King that were aggravated by foreign policy – lack of sufficient subsidies; attack on monopolists; revival of impeachment; fall of Bacon; assertion of free speech on key issues; the Petition; the Protestation. These issues were important, but did not make James dependent upon Parliament. He ended the session by using the prerogative of dissolution of Parliament. To some extent, the 1624 Parliament saw an unprecedented cooperation between Crown and Parliament: invitation to discuss foreign policy; subsidies voted; treaties with Spain dissolved. The cost was the fall of Cranfield, the Monopolies Act, the attack on Arminians (see page 191) and appropriation of supply. The potential of these matters to make the King dependent on Parliament was, however, great.

6.4.4 *What was James's policy towards the Holy Roman Empire?*

1. *The Cleves-Julich dispute*

Holy Roman Empire: First established in 800 by the coronation of Charlemagne. It became the preserve of the Austrian Habsburgs from the 15th century onwards. Its attempt to indicate unity of government in central European states and its devotion to Catholicism was at odds with the fragmented Empire after the Reformation and religious wars. Since 1555, the rulers of the various states had decided for Catholicism or Protestantism. The Evangelical Union and Catholic League reflected these divisions.

In 1609, James intervened in the **Holy Roman Empire** on the vacancy in the duchies of Cleves, Julich and Berg. The area was strategically important on the Lower Rhine Valley and offered easy access to the United Provinces (the Netherlands). Duke William of Cleves, whose death produced a disputed succession that threatened to divide Europe, had ruled it. France and England were determined to keep the duchies in Protestant hands, while Spain and the Empire favoured a Catholic candidate. The assassination of Henri IV of France, in 1610, ensured that no major war broke out. James emerged as a leading champion of Protestantism when peace was finally secured in 1614.

2. *The Protestant marriage, 1613*

The sympathy of James for the German Protestant Union was shown in the marriage of his daughter Elizabeth to the Elector Frederick of the Palatinate. James hoped to balance this with a Catholic marriage for his son, keeping the peace of Europe through a foreign policy based on dynastic marriages. This was a popular marriage in the eyes of Protestant England.

The Spanish European empire and the Palatinate region in 1640

James's work in the Cleves-Julich crises and the Protestant marriage met with the approval of the Puritans. In reality, he had insufficient funds to intervene if pushed to implement the treaty ending the Cleves-Julich dispute. The historian Roger Lockyer, in *James VI and I* (1998), points out that neither the Emperor nor the Governor of the Spanish Netherlands had signed the agreement, and that they refused to hand over their strongholds. Pressure from James resulted in no more than assurances of goodwill. This disappointed the German princes, the Dutch and concerned Protestants in England. It appeared that, after the death of Henri IV of France in 1610, James was not likely to wield the Protestant sword.

In the long run, the popular Palatinate marriage caused James a great many problems as it raised the hopes of the Puritans – and many Protestants. They expected a firm commitment to the Protestant powers abroad. James, however, intended his marriage policies to avoid war between Catholic and Protestant powers. When Frederick became involved in the Thirty Years War, this produced the greatest crisis of James's reign.

3. Bohemia and the Palatinate Question

Defenestration of Prague: The event that started the Thirty Years War in 1618. Bohemian Protestants broke up a meeting of the Imperial Commissioners in the Hradshin Palace at Prague by throwing two Catholic councillors and their secretaries out of the window (defenestration). This signalled rebellion against the authority of the Emperor in Bohemia.

In May 1618, the **Defenestration of Prague** began the Thirty Years War in Europe. In 1619, the Bohemians rejected Archduke Ferdinand as King and elected Frederick of the Palatinate. The Bohemian Protestant minority feared the Catholic extremism of Ferdinand, the heir apparent to the Holy Roman Empire. As a Protestant and father-in-law, James was expected to support Frederick when the Habsburgs went to war against him. Frederick asked for his advice, expecting him to rally to the idea of defending Protestantism.

In fact, James did not approve of Frederick accepting the Bohemian throne. His sensitivities to his financial problems, his love of peace, quest for stability in Europe through a Spanish marriage, and genuine hatred of rebellion – all made him cautious of intervention.

Before James could reply, Frederick had accepted the throne. This placed James in a difficult position because he had accepted the Spanish suggestion, in 1618, that he should act as mediator in the Bohemian question. This role suited James – especially as he wished to marry his son Charles to the Spanish Infanta.

It is a tribute to James that he managed to avoid calling a parliament until 1621. His apparent, though not real, 'coldness' towards his son-in-law's loss of Bohemia in 1620, and the Spanish invasion of the Palatinate, had unleashed:

● strong anti-Catholic feelings

● hostility to the power of the Habsburgs

● hatred of Spain and the perceived influence of Gondomar (Spanish Ambassador in England).

These events produced a series of Puritan tracts and made that voice much stronger and more political in Parliament. The height of this was in the 1621 Parliament.

Pulpit: Place in a church from where the priest preached.

While James could dissolve a disobedient parliament, he found control of the **pulpit** more of a problem. In 1622, he used the Directions on Preaching to muzzle the 'hot' Protestant voice. All clergy below the rank

Book of Homilies: A set of prescribed sermons to secure the orthodoxy of the clergy and aid those of little education.

of bishop and dean had to avoid all mention of predestination, 'bitter … speeches' against the Church of Rome, and all 'matters of State' in their morning sermons. Afternoon sermons were restricted to ones from the **Book of Homilies**. Buckingham boasted to Gondomar: 'No man can now mutter a word in the pulpit but he is presently catched and set in straight prison.' Ardent Protestants linked the idea of the recovery of the Palatinate with the scrapping of the Spanish marriage and war; James hoped that he could restore the Palatinate and avoid war through the Spanish marriage. Meanwhile, Frederick and Elizabeth were in exile at the Dutch court and Puritans urged action.

The attempt by Buckingham and Charles to achieve the Spanish marriage and restore the Palatinate through the intercession of Spain, failed. Public rejoicing in England produced a great anti-Catholic and anti-Spanish backlash. This speaking out against foreign policy created a counter-group that was hostile towards Parliament, Puritanism and the Dutch Republic. It fostered the idea of a Puritan plot against the monarchy that James had always feared. The historian Tom Cogswell points out that the measures James took tended to inflame fears about his religious and political reliability.

The ill-health of the King dominated the last Parliament. By then, James was reluctantly aware of the need for positive action to restore the Palatinate – so he let Parliament discuss foreign policy, pass the Monopolies Act to secure the Subsidy Act, and allowed the fall of Cranfield.

1. In what ways did James I get involved in matters affecting the Holy Roman Empire before 1618?

2. Why was he reluctant to intervene in the Holy Roman Empire after 1618?

6.4.5 *What was James's policy towards the United Provinces?*

Until the 1604 Treaty of London with Spain, England and the United Provinces had anti-Spanish interests in common. They had religious and cultural bonds, but they were great commercial rivals for the carrying trade.

The historian Joel Benson maintains that James's policy towards the Dutch was broadly in line with English popular feeling. It was a policy that was, essentially, ambivalent. James's overriding aims were to achieve and maintain peace in Europe, and to generate wealth for England through trade and industries.

The Dutch felt betrayed by England making peace with Spain. They were reluctant to make peace with Spain. James was keen to gain European peace. After much negotiation, English, French and Dutch diplomats achieved the **Twelve Years Truce** between Spain and the Dutch in 1609. This was seen as an achievement for the allies and a humiliation for Spain as it implied recognition of Dutch independence. As this Truce ran out, much apprehension was created in Europe.

During James's reign, disputes between England and the United Provinces over fishing rights, the cloth trade (the Cockayne Project of 1614) and the East India trade were common. James did, however, sell the 'cautionary towns' back to the Dutch for the sum of £215,000, in 1616.

Poor relations with the Dutch over the East India trade culminated in the Massacre of Amboyna in 1623 in the Spice Islands. This might have produced war had James not needed Dutch support as relations with Spain deteriorated.

Twelve Years Truce: The Truce of Antwerp was partly negotiated by James to bring about a break in hostilities between the Dutch and the Spanish. It was negotiated in 1609.

1. In what ways did James pursue an ambivalent policy towards the Dutch?

2. Did the Dutch pose a greater threat than the Spanish to the interests of Great Britain during James's reign? Explain your answer.

6.4.6 *Not such a fool after all in foreign policy?*
A CASE STUDY IN HISTORICAL INTERPRETATION

1. To what extent was James's foreign policy a success?

2. How far were its failures beyond his control?

For over 20 years James successfully pursued the peace of Europe. His many reasons for doing so were sincere, and what happened when his son pursued an active policy against Spain for the relief of the Palatinate shows the wisdom of James's policy of peace.

The Bohemian and Palatinate issues created forces that he could not control. These heightened the sensitivity of religious feelings in England to a far greater extent than at the beginning of the reign.

The Palatinate marriage led to his involvement in affairs that he would have preferred to avoid; the pursuit of the Spanish marriage produced popular opposition to his policy and undermined his attempted solutions.

James realised that his country's economy was not geared for war. Members of Parliament lived to be proved wrong in their dreams of championing Protestantism abroad and of re-living the victories against Spain during the reign of Elizabeth.

The views of historians

Modern pacifists, rather than his contemporaries or many historians, have generally applauded James's actions. Influenced by some splendidly hostile anti-Spanish material, such as Thomas Scott's *Vox Populi* and Thomas Middleton's *A Game at Chess* (1624), earlier views have depicted James as the weak, cowardly king who failed to stand up against the bullying Habsburgs in Spain and the Empire. He was seen by his 1621 Parliament as failing to take up the Protestant sword. A number of Puritan pamphlets labelled him an unnatural father who would not go to the aid of his daughter and son-in-law in Bohemia and the Palatinate. James has been attacked as the willing victim to the schemes of the Spanish ambassador, Count Gondomar, and as a bystander when Buckingham swept Charles off on an impossible mission to achieve the Spanish marriage in Madrid in 1623.

Recent historians have offered much-needed reappraisals, cutting through the propaganda of the 17th-century writers. Charles Carter has shown that relations between James and Gondomar were far from one-sided. He points out that James understood the Spanish ambassador. They had mutual respect for each other's diplomatic cunning and abilities. Ultimately, both wished to avoid a war between England and Spain and they used the Spanish marriage as a means of preventing this for as long as possible. Roger Lockyer has defended Buckingham's role in Madrid, showing that the Duke exercised a restraining hand on the impetuous Charles. The most academic study of foreign policy is by Tom Cogswell, who gives a detailed study of the interaction of foreign and domestic policies in the later Parliaments of James, and shows the increasing role of Parliament in influencing policy of the period.

Increasingly, it is being appreciated that the foreign policy of James had a number of flaws and faults – especially in the lack of clarity and explanation of policies to the Elector Palatine, and to Parliament. In the long run, James could not avert war at the end of the reign; he did, however, avoid it for as long as possible.

Source-based questions: James I, Parliament and foreign policy in the 1620s

SOURCE A

The next cause of my calling this Parliament is one particular urgent necessity, which is the miserable spectacle that no man can look upon without a weeping eye ... The Palatinate invaded, which I so laboured to prevent ... and now I am to provide for wars that my son-in-law may be restored to those his ancient possessions which are yet lost; and nothing can be expected from you without begging as a man would beg an alms ... For I declare unto you that if I cannot get it with peace, my crown and my blood and the blood of my son shall not be spared for it. But I can do nothing without sustenance from my people; and never King of England had less supply than I have had, considering these extraordinary occasions previously mentioned ...

The King's Speech in Parliament, 30 January 1621

SOURCE B

His Majesty now perceives that the whole weight of the recovery of the Palatinate will rest upon his shoulders alone;

That he has as yet no preparations nor money or anything necessary for taking an adequate army so far into the continent among the most vigorous forces of the Austrians; that he could receive no help; he has always had such an aversion for this ... that if he was cold before he now seems ice, and if ever he inclined to negotiations he now thinks of nothing else ...

A report from the Venetian Ambassador, 7 May 1621

SOURCE C

He is an unhappy man, that shall advise a King to war; and it is an unhappy thing to seek by blood, which may be had by peace ... To enter into war without sufficient means to support it, were to shew my teeth, and do not more ...

I will deal frankly with you: shew me the means how I may do what you would have of me, and if I take a resolution by your advice to enter into a war, then yourselves by your own deputies shall have the disposing of the money; I will not meddle with it, but you shall appoint your own treasurers. I say this with a purpose to invite you to open your Purses ... If upon your offer I shall find the means to make the war honourable and safe, I promise you on the word of a King, that although war and peace be the peculiar prerogatives of kings, yet, ... I will not accept Peace without first acquainting you with it.

The response of King James to the demand from the 1624 Parliament to break off the Spanish match.

---

1. Read Source C.

Explain what is meant by the term 'peculiar prerogatives of kings' with reference to foreign policy.

2. How useful is Source B in explaining the foreign policy of King James in 1621?

3. Use the sources and your own knowledge. How important was foreign policy in Crown–Parliament relations from 1621 to 1625?

7 Charles I and the origins of the English Civil War, 1625–1642

7.1 Why did Charles I call three Parliaments, 1625–1629?

7.2 Why did Charles I rule for 11 years without Parliament, 1629–1640?

7.3 Why did Charles I have problems with Parliament, 1640–January 1642?

7.4 Historical interpretation: The 'high road' to Civil War?

Key Issues

● *How important was the personality of Charles I in determining events, 1625–1642?*

● *Was finance the key issue in Crown–Parliament relations?*

● *How important was religion in creating opposition to the policies of Charles I?*

● *How important were events in Ireland and Scotland in weakening the monarchy of Charles I?*

● *Why did the reforming legislation of the Long Parliament fail to prevent a breakdown in relations between King and Parliament?*

Framework of Events

1625	March: accession of Charles I
	May: marriage of Charles I to Henrietta Maria
	June–August: First Parliament
	September: Cadiz Expedition
1626	February–May: Second Parliament
	Conference on religion at York House
	Laud is made Bishop of Bath and Wells
	September: Forced Loan
1627	October: expedition to La Rochelle
	November: The Five Knights' Case
1628	March 1628 – March 1629: The Third Parliament
	June: The Petition of Right
	August: assassination of Buckingham
1629	March: The Three Resolutions of the Commons
1630–31	Books of Orders issued to sheriffs
1632	Wentworth is made Lord Deputy of Ireland
1633	Laud is made Archbishop of Canterbury
1634	Ship money is levied on maritime districts
1635–9	Ship money is levied on inland areas
1636	Scottish Canons introduced.

1637	Case of Prynne, Burton and Bastwick in Star Chamber
	Ship Money case
	Laud's Liturgy in Scotland
1638	National Covenant is signed in Scotland
1639	First Bishops' War
1640	13 April: opening of the Short Parliament
	5 May: dissolution of the Short Parliament
	August: Scottish invasion and victory at Newburn
	3 November: opening of the Long Parliament
	11 December: Root and Branch Petition
1641	March: attempted impeachment of Strafford
	April: attainder of Strafford
	10 May: Charles signs the Bill of Attainder
	12 May: execution of Strafford
	October: outbreak of Irish Rebellion
	22 November: The Grand Remonstrance passed in the Commons
1642	4 January: attempted arrest of the five MPs.

Overview

King Charles I
(1600–1649), portrait by
Daniel Mytens, 1631

THE reign of Charles I, until the attempted arrest of the five MPs in January 1642, divides clearly into three phases:

● 1625–1629
● the years of the Personal Rule, 1629–1640
● 1640–January 1642, the reforming phase of the Long Parliament.

Throughout all three periods, historians agree that the character of the King is a factor crucial to the evolution of events.

Charles was born on 19 November 1600, at Dunfermline Castle. He was the youngest surviving child of James VI and I and Anne of Denmark (see family tree on page 13). He was less robust than his brothers and sisters, and remained in Scotland for a while after his family moved south. A recent biographer, Charles Carlton, stresses Charles's emotional insecurity in the shadow of his energetic brother Prince Henry, and as a result of inadequate parenting on the part of James and Anne. Charles's sister, to whom he was devoted, left Britain in 1613 on her marriage to the Elector Palatine. Charles was sensitive, shy and reserved. His stammer gave him poor communication skills and compounded a tendency to create an impression of personal inaccessibility. He was single-minded to the point of intransigence. This was seen in his loyalty to the Duke of Buckingham, and in his firm determination to safeguard the principles of divine right monarchy and of the Episcopal Church of England. He sought order and harmony, believing these this could be achieved through rigid, hierarchic structures in Church and State of which he was undisputed head. This was expressed in all aspects of his rule, especially in the ordered Court presided over by Charles and Henrietta Maria (the unpopular, spirited, French princess whom he married in 1625 when she was only 15). The Court was aloof and exclusive, aesthetically outstanding (Charles I was one of the greatest art collectors of the century), but much less of a point of contact between Crown and subject than in the previous reign. The King's sense of his own authority was so great that he was inclined to see all dissent in terms of a conspiracy against him. While these aspects of his character did not in themselves create his problems, they made it difficult for him to solve them.

It is true to say that the legacy of King James was not a particularly good one. However, Charles I had neither his father's ability to turn a blind eye to problems nor the opportunity to do so.

Charles inherited several problems. Sir Philip Warwick, one of Charles's courtiers, wrote about 'this sour humour in the stomach of the nation', in 1625. While the last Parliament of the reign of James had been very supportive of Charles and the Duke of Buckingham, the harmony was more apparent than real. It was soon shattered by failures in foreign policy and resentment at the influence of Buckingham. Below the surface, the issue of religion remained. This was sharpened by the growth of Arminianism at home, the dangers to Protestantism abroad, and the increase of Catholicism at Court with the entourage of Henrietta Maria. Finance, the most serious aspect of Charles's legacy, became more severely stretched by foreign intervention against both Spain and France – as his father and Cranfield had foreseen. All historians support the catastrophic impact of wars on an outmoded financial system. Crisis point was reached here in 1627. The parameters of prerogative and privilege were tested in areas of finance, the impeachment of Buckingham, and were beginning to be seen in matters of religion. After a period of four years, described by the historian Lawrence Stone as 'the first tremors' leading to the earthquake of civil wars, Charles embarked on a period of **Personal Rule** in 1629.

Personal Rule: Rule by the King without Parliament. The King relied on his prerogative powers for the exercise of his authority.

The Personal Rule demonstrated both the strengths and weaknesses of Charles's government and character. Whig historians saw this period as a 'tyranny'; those less hostile as a period of benevolent rule. Charles's reliance on prerogative was matched by a genuine desire to streamline and centralise authority in the interest of efficient government. His success in bringing in revenue, by both legal and dubious measures, was evident until about 1637. During that year, John Hampden voiced opposition to Charles's financial measures in the Ship Money case. In the Court of the Star Chamber, Prynne, Burton and Bastwick raised opposition to Archbishop Laud's strict measures for religious uniformity. Also in 1637, Charles's attempt to impose a new Prayer Book on the Scots met with such distaste that the Scots were inspired to rebel. The first Bishops War of 1639 returned Charles to the unhappy situation of the first period of his reign: chronic financial incapacity. Inability to subdue the Scottish rebellion without financial support from Parliament ended the Personal Rule in 1640.

The recall of Parliament failed to produce a settlement. The Short Parliament was dissolved when it refused subsidies without redress of some of the grievances of the Personal Rule. A second Bishops War convinced Charles of the need to call the Long Parliament in November 1640. Under the leadership of John Pym, the Long Parliament exacted harsh revenge on Charles in the form of:

● the removal of Strafford and Laud
● the passing of legislation that reversed many of the financial expedients of the Personal Rule

- the introduction of legislation curbing the royal prerogative over the summoning, prorogation and dissolution of Parliament
- the call for a reduction in the power of bishops.

The outbreak of rebellion in Ireland at the end of October 1641 brought many issues to a head: anti-Catholicism; finance; the authority of the King as well as the fundamental fear of some that Charles could not be trusted to command an army for Ireland. Increasing frustration at the erosion of his prerogative led Charles I to attempt to arrest the leaders of the opposition in Parliament, as traitors, in January 1642. After the failure of this display of authority, London was no safe place for the royal family. By the end of January, Charles and his family had left for Hampton Court. Once he had left London, a return was only possible after successful negotiation with Parliament, or military victory.

An English Civil War was not a possibility in 1625. Neither was it a possibility in 1640. Volumes have been written on its 'origins' and 'causes'. The historian Geoffrey Elton was keen to assert that there was no high road to civil war. It is appropriate, therefore, to examine events and discuss historical interpretation at the end of the chapter.

7.1 Why did Charles I call three Parliaments, 1625–1629?

The contemporary courtier, Sir Philip Warwick, wrote in his *Memoirs*, 'It was a clear prophecy of a downfall unto this land, when a King and his two houses of parliament thus dissatisfactorily and often part from one another.' Many issues provoked the calling of three Parliaments in four years. Instability generated frustrations that were both symptoms and causes of problems. Disaster abroad, in the form of the failure of Count Mansfeld's expedition to relieve the Palatinate, soon ended the euphoria of the 1624 Parliament of King James.

The First Parliament (June–August 1625)

The First Parliament was quick to use the power of the purse against Charles when he failed to explain his foreign policy and persisted in a continental strategy against Spain instead of waging a traditional Elizabethan-style war on the high seas that would have brought spoils and bounty. Aware of the necessity of subsidies for a monarchy already financially embarrassed, Parliament voted Charles tunnage and poundage for one year only, instead of for life. In view of Charles's determination to restore the Palatinate and honour commitments to subsidise his ally the King of Denmark, as well as to maintain troops in the Low Countries, this was a serious blow. Tunnage and poundage made up the bulk of the customs duties. This action by Parliament was a clear protest at the accelerated use of impositions during James's reign. The King would have to collect tunnage and poundage with or without the consent of Parliament. This action was, in many ways, a challenge to the King. Likewise, when two subsidies were voted in June 1625, it was less than a quarter of what Charles needed. The financial screw was further tightened when the Commons ordered an inquiry into the spending of the 1624 subsidy.

Lack of harmony was also evident in the attack on the growth of Arminianism. This issue had been raised in 1624. Pym persisted in attacking Richard Montagu, whose anti-Calvinist stand and advocacy of the Catholic origins of the Church of England he found offensive. The attack on Arminians and crypto-Catholics was very important. It was generated by factors such as:

- the Catholic successes in the Thirty Years War that seemed to threaten the English Reformation;

- the presence of French Catholics attending a Catholic Queen;

- the influence at Court of high-church men who were staunch supporters of royal absolutism and who stressed the Catholic origins of the English Church;

- the fact that the favourite, Buckingham, was taking advice from William Laud, the Bishop of Bath and Wells, who had been brought into the Court to try to prevent the conversion of Buckingham's mother to Catholicism. This same Laud had alarmed James I, in 1617, by his excessive zeal and inability to leave well alone on the Scottish visit.

MPs could see the influence of Buckingham in so many areas of concern. The hostility of Parliament culminated in an attempt to withhold supplies until Buckingham was removed. This was serious as it raised the issue of the right of Parliament to influence the King's choice of advisers, as well as representing a personal attack on the favourite by Pym, Eliot and Wentworth.

While Charles could use the royal prerogative to dissolve this hostile session, he remained financially weak. The failure of the **Cadiz Expedition** compounded Charles's problems in 1625.

Cadiz Expedition, 1625: Badly organised, badly trained and badly equipped, this expedition aimed to destroy the Spanish Fleet at Cadiz harbour. Ill-fed troops raided the wine stores with disastrous results. Its return showed the extent of incompetence in high places.

The Second Parliament (February–May 1626)

The Second Parliament proved unsatisfactory both to the King and to Parliament. In spite of an attempt to influence Parliament by making vocal MPs such as Sir Edward Coke and Sir Thomas Wentworth sheriffs, the Commons was determined to remove the Duke of Buckingham. The strategy was to vote for subsidies but leave them in committee stage until Buckingham had been successfully impeached. The 'name and shame' attack on Buckingham was pressed by Sir John Eliot. He accused him of corruption in the Articles of Impeachment: 'Our honour is ruined, our ships are sunk, our men are perished; not by the sword, not by the enemy, not by chance, but … by those we trust.'

This attack on the favourite produced a predictable response from the King: 'I would not have the House to question my servants, much less one that is so near me.'

In spite of imprisoning Eliot and Sir Dudley Digges for insolence in the Commons, and the Earl of Arundel for leading the opposition in the Lords, Charles had to dissolve Parliament in order to save Buckingham from impeachment and himself from a nasty debate on abuse of parliamentary privilege.

Interval between the Second and Third Parliaments (1627)

The interval between the Second and Third Parliaments produced important developments. When war broke out with France, it was popularly regarded as Buckingham's War – an ego trip for the favourite, attempting to redeem himself with Protestants after the French marriage treaty that

Cardinal Richelieu (1585–1642)
The able and astute chief minister of Louis XIII. He hoped to bring French Protestants (Huguenots) under tighter control by restricting their privileges granted by Henri IV in the Edict of Nantes. It was feared that Buckingham aspired to similar power.

Forced Loan (1626): It was customary for the Crown to demand a forced loan from the wealthy. This one was controversial. It was demanded of all who would normally pay parliamentary subsidies and intended to bring in the equivalent of five subsidies. It was seen as a blatant attempt to raise 'taxation' without Parliament's consent.

Habeas corpus ('You may have the body'): A legal writ that protects a person from arbitrary arrest by requiring that he (the body) be brought before a judge or a court to determine the legality of the arrest. If it is deemed valid, he must submit to trial; if invalid, he must be released. It safeguards the subject against arbitrary and indefinite imprisonment.

Attorney General: A country's chief law officer who advises the monarch or government.

had loaned ships to France. In the deteriorating relations between Cardinal Richelieu and the French Protestant Huguenots, it was feared that the English Protestant mariners might be involved in hostilities against Huguenots. Buckingham, smarting under the perceived affront to England when France made a separate peace with Spain in 1626, tried to relieve the Huguenots at La Rochelle. He thus involved England in two wars, simultaneously and unsuccessfully. It was a serious drain on finances. It further reduced the credibility of Buckingham and made the French Catholic Queen of England even more unpopular.

Finances were stretched. Lack of effective financial support from two Parliaments led Charles to go beyond the ordinary expedients of selling Crown land, borrowing, and increasing income from fines. He began to collect tunnage and poundage without the consent of Parliament and called for a **Forced Loan** in 1626. This was intended to bring in five subsidies. Charles expected that all loyal subjects contribute and that the clergy would preach the duty of the subject support the King. Charles stressed in his Proclamation that the 'aid' was needed 'for the necessary defence of our Honour, our religion, and kingdoms'. While Richard Sibthorp and the Arminian clergy were prepared to preach that a person sinned if he/she did not obey the sovereign, some contemporaries saw non-parliamentary ways of raising revenue as illegal, and a dangerous precedent.

Much of the Forced Loan was collected in 1627, but 76 people refused to pay. A number of these were either arrested or conscripted into the army. Forced Loans had precedents; arresting those who refused to pay was challenged in the Five Knights' Case. These knights claimed the right of *habeas corpus*. They did not challenge the Forced Loan as such, but complained that the King had imprisoned by 'special command' those who had refused to pay. They argued that Charles could only imprison by the law of the land and that 'special command' was a dangerous power for the King to assume. Charles believed he was justified by his prerogative of emergency power. The judges found for Charles, on the grounds that he was the fountain of law and 'all justice is derived from him'. This was not surprising as the King appointed and dismissed judges at his pleasure. It should be noted, however, that no absolute right for the King to imprison without cause stated was asserted as a result of this judgement. The **Attorney General**, Robert Heath, recorded that the King had a 'general' right to imprison without trial rather than an absolute one.

This case shows the implications of Charles's financial expedients, supported as they were by high-church clergy, and necessitated by the disasters of war, the maladministration of Charles and Buckingham and the lack of parliamentary cooperation. Fears of the inordinate extension of prerogative were raised. This ensured that the Third Parliament met in tense circumstances, in March 1628.

The choice of Laud to preach the opening sermon was not popular. Archbishop Abbot had been suspended for not supporting the Forced Loan. Laud, a client of Buckingham, represented not only unpopular religious ideas, but all that was odious about the corrupt system of patronage controlled by Buckingham.

The Third Parliament (March 1628 – March 1629)

In the first session of the Third Parliament, Charles's release of those who had refused to pay the Forced Loan did little to assuage hostility.

Sir John Eliot (1592–1632)
Member of the Cornish gentry. MP for St Germans and Newport. At first, a client of Buckingham but as Vice-Admiral for Devon he saw the disasters of foreign policy. Led the attack on Buckingham in 1626. He refused to pay the Forced Loan. Drew up the Petition of Right in 1628. A year later, Eliot was imprisoned after the Three Resolutions.

A Committee of Grievances was formed to consider 'the liberty of the subject in his person and in his goods'. Sir John Eliot and Sir Edward Coke were vocal in their opposition to recent developments of forced loans and alleged arbitrary arrest. This came to a head in the Five Knights' Case: 'Upon this dispute not only our lands and goods are engaged, but all that we call ours. These rights, these privileges, which made our fathers freemen, are in question.'

The agenda of the Committee of Grievances covered not only the issues of the Five Knights' Case, but also those made necessary by war: the billeting of soldiers in private houses, and punishment by martial law as a result of which ordinary law was suspended. These were grievances that were hitting especially hard at the maritime constituencies of MPs like Sir John Eliot.

The outcome of the Committee was a list of resolutions against the grievances that became the Petition of Right, 1628:

> That no freeman ought to be detained or kept in prison or otherwise restrained by the command of the King or the privy Council … unless some cause of his commitment … be expressed.
>
> That no tax … loan, or benevolence, or other like charge, ought to be commanded or levied by the King or any of his ministers, without common consent by Act of Parliament.
>
> That your Majesty will be pleased to remove the said soldiers and mariners [billeted in private houses].
>
> That commissions for proceeding by martial law may be revoked and annulled.

Coke was determined that Parliament should present the Petition for signature as a statute. 'Let us put up a Petition of Right; not that I distrust the King, but that we cannot take his trust but in a parliamentary way.' To sweeten this bitter pill for Charles, five subsidies were voted pending the signing of the Petition. To hasten his decision, Parliament mounted another attack on Buckingham as 'the grievance of grievances' (Coke). Reluctantly, Charles agreed and made the Petition law.

The Petition was a clever device and its form of acceptance was crucial. It took the Five Knights' Case to the national arena and, if Charles agreed to it as a statute, he would be acting illegally if he subsequently went against it.

Charles's desire to gain the subsidies and to protect Buckingham secured the Petition.

The assassination of Buckingham

The assassination of the Duke of Buckingham, in the interval between the first and second sessions of the Third Parliament, offered a way forward to Charles. The Duke was in his house in Portsmouth, taking stock after a second failure at La Rochelle and planning a third expedition, when he was assassinated by a disgruntled patriot, John Felton. A cannier king than Charles would have used Buckingham as a 'fall guy'. Instead, Charles was appalled by the assassination. He saw it as a conspiracy – which it was not – and took an even more entrenched attitude towards Parliament.

The role of Buckingham in the Crisis of the 1620s

Historian Roger Lockyer has challenged the traditional view that Buckingham was a *valido* (a minister who exercised real power). He

The Duke of Buckingham and his family, 1628, unknown artist after Gerrit van Honthorst

believes that the nature of Buckingham's influence, especially in the reign of James, has been exaggerated. He has revised old views of Buckingham as the Sejanus (the evil and corrupt councillor of the Roman Emperor Tiberius) of James and Charles. The historian Donald Wilkinson points out that, in an age when a direct attack on the Crown was undesirable, a scapegoat was needed – and Buckingham provided this.

The Duke of Buckingham was, however, involved in all areas of grievance:

Foreign policy

- He had been involved in the Spanish marriage negotiations.

- He had advocated war in 1624 with Spain and in 1627 with France.

- His treaties had failed to secure an effective anti-Habsburg bloc and committed Charles to subsidies for the United Provinces and Denmark.

- The Cadiz Expedition which he had led was a dismal failure at the beginning of the new reign.

- His expeditions to La Rochelle, in 1627 and 1628, failed.

While Buckingham protested his lack of sufficient financial support for these enterprises, and the King had overall responsibility for them, the impact of the failure on morale was deep.

Religion

- Buckingham promoted Laud and championed Montagu.

- His support for Arminians was shown at the York House Conference in 1626.

- He was, however, following the religious policy of the King.

Patronage

Buckingham has been accused of closing the patronage system and promoting his cronies, such as Sir John Eliot, Lionel Cranfield and William Laud. Faction was, however, built on shifting sands: Cranfield was dropped, Eliot became an opponent, and Laud tried to distance himself when Buckingham came under attack. Buckingham's apparent, if not real, control of patronage made enemies for himself and problems for Charles.

Evil councillor with a direct impact on Crown–Parliament relations

There is mounting evidence that Charles took decisions for himself, but Buckingham did have influence in the Privy Council. This was behind calls for Parliament to be involved in the royal choice of ministers. His attempted impeachment was a factor in the dissolution of the first two parliaments and the lever to secure the Petition of Right. Even his removal fostered bad blood between Charles and Parliament.

French marriage

The Duke of Buckingham encouraged bad relations between Charles and Henrietta Maria on a 'divide and rule' principle. He played a key role in events leading to the outbreak of war with France in 1627.

In some respects, Buckingham was the author of the grievances; in others, he was a scapegoat as 'the grievance of grievances'. Perhaps the last words should lie with the Royalist courtier, Sir Philip Warwick:

> '[Buckingham's] want of experience, as having never seen the reverse of fortune, made him too great an enterpriser to succeed in what he unadvisedly undertook; for besides moulding the court to the advantage principally of his own family … he unadvisedly runs the King into a war with [Spain] … which he knew the present King's treasures could not discharge … It was soon perceived how numerous and considerable the ill-willers to Buckingham's greatness were at court, so as the popular lords in the Upper House … and the great orators in the Commons … made this session more unfortunate than the former Parliament.'

The second session of the Third Parliament

This session was very hostile. The Commons accused Charles of breaching the Petition of Right and complained about a breach of parliamentary privilege in Rolle's case. Rolle was an MP and a merchant who had had his goods confiscated for not paying tunnage and poundage. MPs protested that the privilege of freedom from arrest extended to goods as well as to the person. John Pym wanted this issue raised in the House. The real development, in 1629, was the open attack on Arminians. This was started by Charles's promotion of Richard Montagu to Bishop of Chester and William Laud as Bishop of London. This two-pronged attack on finance and religion made Charles call for an adjournment of Parliament. This provoked a disturbance in Parliament, on 2 March. Members refused to adjourn and Denzil Holles and Benjamin Valentine held the Speaker, Sir John Finch, in the chair: 'God's wounds, you shall sit till we please to rise!' Sir Miles Hobart locked in any MPs who preferred to leave while the Three Resolutions were passed. These condemned as traitors anyone who brought about changes in religion, introducing Arminianism and popery, and anyone who advised the levying and collection of tunnage and poundage, as well as anyone who collected it.

This shows the extent of deterioration in relations, with the focus firmly on issues of finance and taxation, both involving the parameters of

1. What part was played by the Duke of Buckingham in the problems between Crown and Parliament?

2. To what extent was war responsible for the breakdown between Crown and Parliament in 1629?

3. Why were finance and religion important issues at this time?

the royal prerogative. These grievances were too deep to be removed by the assassination of Buckingham. The personality of Charles was also relevant; he saw a conspiracy at work, calling his Commons 'seditious' and Eliot's supporters 'vipers'. Regardless of the Parliamentary sensitivity to privilege, he ordered the arrest of the ringleaders for detention 'during his pleasure'. Charles dissolved Parliament on 10 March, after nine MPs had been arrested. (Eliot died in the Tower in 1632; Strode and Valentine remained in prison until 1640.)

The drama of the occasion exaggerates its importance. The fact that MPs had to be locked in to pass the Three Resolutions indicates that there was no unilateral opposition to the King. While this was supposedly to safeguard members against royal troops, a number of MPs would have preferred to slip out before the Three Resolutions were pushed through. There was no intention to reduce the King's capacity to rule, rather to make him respect the Petition of Right and to purge his Court of Arminians and crypto-Catholics. In 1629, the victory went to the King who had the capacity to dissolve a troublesome Parliament.

7.2 Why did Charles I rule for 11 years without Parliament, 1629–1640?

Charles had no intention of ruling for a definite, or an indefinite, period without Parliament. In his Declaration of 10 March, he maintained that he had been driven 'unwillingly out of that course', and that he intended to recall Parliament 'when such as have bred this interruption shall have received their punishment'. He was convinced of a conspiracy 'that all things may be overwhelmed with anarchy and confusion'. Charles stressed his determination to maintain the divinely ordained order in Church and State and his belief in divine right: 'Princes are not bound to give an account of their actions, but to God alone.'

Rule without Parliament was not illegal, provided the King remained within the framework of the law. Apart from Parliament, all the normal institutions of government operated. There is no evidence of an attempt to change the framework of the constitution, or to set up a **tyranny**. Indeed, Charles lacked the financial, military and administrative capacity to have an effective tyranny. He wanted efficient and effective government. This policy is given the name of '**Thorough**'. Charles intended to rule by benevolent prerogative power, but the absence of the contact point of Parliament and the apparent inaccessibility of the Privy Council and Court were threats to many areas of law, finance, and religion. In the minds of some parliamentarians, the experiences of the 1620s made prerogative rule synonymous with arbitrary rule. Later Whig historians, such as Lord Macaulay and G.M. Trevelyan, see the years without Parliament as years which justify the description of the 'Eleven Years Tyranny'.

To sustain a personal rule and to anticipate a cooperative Parliament at the end of it, Charles needed to avoid confrontation in the following areas:

● financing his rule without Parliament

● asserting his authority in matters of law, religion, choice of Councillors throughout the monarchy.

His subjects wanted rule that was firm and fair. Recent research by the historian Kevin Sharpe stresses the success of the Personal Rule in a

Tyranny: Cruel or unjust rule by someone who has absolute power over everyone else in the country or state.

'Thorough': Used by William Laud, in correpondence with Wentworth, to describe the policy of government used by Charles I.

number of areas, until the crisis in Scotland. By 1637, Charles I's policies were being openly challenged. By 1640, the Personal Rule ended as a result of the accumulated tensions in key areas. Until then, aspects of Charles's rule were benevolent in intention.

How successfully did Charles finance his Rule without Parliament?

Finance was the key issue

The ambitious foreign policy of the 1620s was at the bottom of many of the problems facing Charles. He made peace with France in 1629, and with Spain a year later. This was important in enabling a Personal Rule. War in Britain – the First Bishops War of 1639 – wiped out most of the successes between the years 1630 and 1637.

Between 1630 and 1634, ministers such as Richard Weston (Earl of Portland) at the Treasury and Francis Cottington at the Exchequer were able to increase the revenue without causing major excessive opposition. They used devices such as:

- impositions (worth about £200,000 a year)

- collecting tunnage and poundage without the consent of Parliament

- improving the efficiency of revenue collection.

These resulted in a three-fold increase in revenue from the Court of Wards and a five-fold increase in the amount raised from recusancy fines. A loophole in the 1624 Monopolies Act, which had banned the granting of monopolies to individuals, saw them granted to companies instead – the most famous of these was the so-called 'Popish Soap Monopoly' that was bringing in £29,000 a year.

Old statutes were revived to bolster feudal revenue

The Distraint of Knighthood (1278) allowed the King to fine anyone holding land to the value of £40 a year and above who had not taken up a knighthood. This had rarely been used since the mid 16th century. Charles sent out teams of commissioners, in 1630, to enforce it. A range of fines might be imposed according to the value of land. There was opposition, but it was not dangerous. Wentworth used the Council of the North very effectively against repeat offenders in Yorkshire. Estimates suggest that it brought in £100,000 for the first few years.

Forest laws were enforced. Traditionally, forests belonged to the King and any encroachment or attempt to develop industries there was illegal. This was doubly unpopular in that forest boundaries were defined in favour of the King. Since those who had undertaken enterprises there were not forced to dismantle them and move out, it was obvious that forest fines could generate a regular income.

A similar action was taken with enclosure fines and fines on the City of London (for contravening bans on new buildings near the capital). Pym argued that if a building was a nuisance, it should be removed after a fine; if not, there should be no fine.

Ship money was the most exciting device. Charles argued its necessity on account of the activities of pirates and dangers abroad. In 1634, the first levy was made on London and other ports; in 1635, it was extended to the whole country. It was seen as a violation of the Petition of Right,

Ship money: A levy on maritime counties to provide ships, or the money equivalent, to defend the nation in times of crisis.

John Hampden (1594–1643)
Was educated at Oxford and the Inner Temple. He was a friend of Eliot and was imprisoned in 1626 for refusing to pay the Forced Loan. Hampden made his great stand when he refused to pay ship money in 1635. He refused to pay the £1 assessment on his Buckinghamshire estates. Attorney General Bankes argued the case for ship money on the grounds of precedent, authority and necesssity. Oliver St John cleverly argued that while the King could decide on a state of emergency, in the case of ship money the 'emergency' could not have lasted from 1634 until 1637. Ultimately, the 12 Common Law judges found for the King by seven votes to five. Three of the five said it was an illegal tax, two found against the King on a technicality of wording. In some ways, this was a moral victory for Hampden but, by 1638 and 1639, events in Scotland were in high profile. By 1640, about one-third of ship money was coming in and Charles risked alienating local sheriffs by asking them to make good the deficit.

and as an illegal extension of ship money. The King sought the advice of his judges, in December 1635. They agreed that he had the right to levy ship money in times of danger, and that he could decide what constituted a 'time of danger'. Levies on the whole country followed in 1636 and 1637, yielding as much as impositions, so much so that many feared that the King would soon have the financial capacity to rule without Parliament indefinitely. Most people paid, or shifted the burden to someone else, because they feared a breakdown in government more that they feared the levy. Even when John Hampden made it a national issue in the Court of the Exchequer, ship money continued to be paid until 1639.

While these financial devices were not popular, and a number were of doubtful legality, opposition was contained until at least 1635 (arguably 1638). Historian Kevin Sharpe sees ship money as one of the most successful measures of the Personal Rule, collapsing only in the wake of the crisis of the First Bishops' War. While this is an important corrective to the Whig interpretation of financial exactions of a tyrannical nature, there is no doubt that there was opposition, and that it was organised. Another historian, Derek Hirst, argues that men such as Hampden, Lord Saye and Sele, and the Earl of Bedford unified their efforts against Charles's exactions. They met in the Providence Island Company, of which Pym was a member. Seen in the light of the Petition of Right and the Three Resolutions, the implications of Charles's measures were serious and wide ranging. Their cumulative impact, in the absence of Parliament, was dangerous. Charles's measures were not only seen as arbitrary, they were also regarded as undermining the propertied classes. Charles's inability to finance campaigns against the Scots in 1639 provided the catalyst to a revolt of the taxpayers in 1639 and 1640.

How successfully did Charles assert his authority in England and Wales?

Charles I relied on the prerogative courts and councils during this period. The Court of Star Chamber was used to gag and discipline opponents of his policies. It could mete out harsh fines and mutilations. The Council of the North, based in York, was very active under Sir Thomas Wentworth in imposing royal decrees. Through courts such as these, Charles exercised unpopular coercive power independent of common law. Research by J.P. Kenyon and Kevin Sharpe counsels caution when estimating the extent of abuse of prerogative. The image of arbitrary rule through prerogative courts is powerfully created by contemporary victims and legally educated former MPs. Whig historians perpetuate it. Perhaps what is really important is the extent of the perception of abuse of the prerogative courts rather than the statistical reality.

The royal Court was also important in supporting the King. The death of Buckingham had left a vacuum that was never really filled. The overall tone of the Court appeared crypto-Catholic, although the fact that Charles had hammered Catholics with recusancy fines should discredit accusations that he was pro-Catholic. Also, Laud and Wentworth were not of Catholic sympathies.

Books of Orders

One of the main problems for Charles was how to maintain tight links with the localities. In 1630 and 1631, Books of Orders were sent to sheriffs of the counties for distribution to local magistrates. Charles designed them as a means of dealing with an economic crisis, and they largely concerned the operation of poor relief. A hierarchy of administrative authority, from the Privy Council, the assize judge and the sheriff, down to local parish officers was envisaged. It is easy to see this as threatening bureaucracy. In actual fact, their purpose was specific and the Books of Orders soon fell into disuse. Similarly, Charles's scheme of the 'exact militia' to reform the operation of the local militia by giving them some professional training, did not survive long enough to provide the King with an effective military capacity.

Religion

This offered Charles the strongest link with the localities, outside the judicial and administrative systems. He was Supreme Governor of the Church of England, a hierarchic structure reaching from the King and Archbishops into the parishes. As attendance at church on Sunday was obligatory, control of the pulpit was a political, as well as a religious, issue.

Religious sensitivity was heightened by the Catholic successes in the Thirty Years War, the increase in Court Catholicism and the growth of Arminianism. This contributed to the development of Puritanism in a political form, accelerating the polarisation of the Protestant Church of England into the pro-Calvinist Puritans and the anti-Calvinist Arminians. According to historian Conrad Russell, in *The Causes of the English Civil War* (1990), the Commons' Resolutions of 1629 marked the most important religious statement in Parliament since the early years of Elizabeth I. Archbishop Abbot remained out of favour until his death in 1633; the so-called Arminians consolidated influence. Laud became Archbishop of Canterbury in 1633, and Richard Neile became Archbishop of York in 1632.

Arminians, Laudians, high-church men and anti-Calvinists: a fudge?

The term 'Arminian' is loosely used when referring to the reign of Charles I. The Dutch theologian, Arminius, took an anti-Calvinist stand against predestination. He stressed the importance of free will and good works in achieving salvation. While the theological point is a characteristic of English Arminians, their importance lies in the prominence they gave to ritual and ceremony: 'the beauty of holiness', and the sanctity of the authority of bishops derived from Christ's calling of Peter. This meant that they were stressing the Catholic origins of the English Church at a time when Calvinist Puritans wanted the removal of all vestiges of the Roman Church, 'the Whore of Babylon'. In this sense, English Arminians were both anti-Calvinist and anti-high-church men. In the late 1620s and 1630s, they were

William Laud (1573–1645)
Son of a Reading clothier. A scholar, fellow and President of St John's College, Oxford. Laud was an opponent of George Abbot. He was given slow promotion under James I. As a client of Buckingham, he entered the Royal Court. Rapid promotion followed, under Charles. His work as Bishop of London and Archbishop of Canterbury made him unpopular. Laud was imprisoned by the Long Parliament, and executed in 1645.

Laudians in that they followed the ecclesiastical programme of William Laud. Its political implications were the tightening of royal control of the Church through rigorous discipline of dissidents, as well as attempts to improve the economic foundations of the Church.

How important was the work of William Laud: Thorough, Church and State?

Laud was personally unpopular. Sir Simond D'Ewes described him as 'a little, low red-faced man of mean parentage'. Lambert Osbaldeston, a master at Westminster School, called him a 'little, meddling, hocus-pocus'. Apart from using Buckingham to get into the Court, and associating with Wentworth in the pursuit of centralisation, William Laud was a loner. The policies he pursued were insensitive. The bureaucratic efficiency with which he pursued them realised the fears expressed by James as early as 1617: 'He hath a restless spirit, and cannot see when matters are well, but loves to toss and change and bring things to a pitch of reformation floating in his own brain.' Coming from the master of masterly activity, this should be looked at cautiously. There is no doubt that Laud's single-mindedness and sincerity, commendable in themselves, were very risky in the religious climate of the 1620s and 1630s. Kevin Sharpe has rightly stressed that Laud was following the policies of the King. He plays down Laud's so-called Arminianism. Laud was made a scapegoat for the religious ills of the country but, without Laud, the policies of Charles I would not have been carried out with such efficiency.

Laud was feared for the conservatism of his ideas. Calvinists hated:

- Laud's belief that the Church of England was part of the universal catholic church and that he was trying to reverse the Reformation

- his rejection of predestination

- his stand that the institution of bishops was *jure divino* (by divine right): '… that from the apostles' time, in all ages, in all places, the Church of Christ is governed by bishops, and lay elders never heard of till Calvin's new-fangled device at Geneva'

- his stress on the close relationship between King and clergy – seen clearly in his opening sermons to the 1625 and 1626 Parliaments, urging obedience to the sovereign as being necessary for the maintenance of the divine order

- his association with Buckingham until 1628 and with the Arminians who preached in favour of the Forced Loan.

The thorough pursuit of religious policies was even more provocative.

Bishop of London (1628–1633)

Visitations: Inspections conducted by the Bishop into matters of discipline and the running of the parish churches in his diocese.

- As Bishop of London, Laud enforced **visitations**, in order to crack down on clerical nonconformity. He ordered:
  - the clergy to wear vestments
  - the altar to be positioned at the east end of the church
  - that the congregation should bow at the name of Jesus
  - conformity to the Book of Common Prayer.
- Laud's necessary improvements to the fabric of St Paul's Cathedral were attacked by John Bastwick as 'making a seat for a priest's arse to

sit in'. Its west front was based on designs by Inigo Jones, for the Church of Il Jesu, the headquarters of the Jesuits at Rome.

Impropriated tithes: The right of a lay person to collect tithes and appoint a minister. Laud was opposed to this practice as it gave influence to laity at the expense of the Church.

- Laud supported Attorney General Noy in an attack on **impropriated tithes** that culminated in their dissolution in 1633.

Archbishop of Canterbury (1633–1645)
As Archbishop, Laud pursued and extended his policies at London.

Metropolitan visitations: The Archbishop of Canterbury is the Metropolitan of England. During a visitation from his commissioners, the authority of the local bishop was suspended. Laud's visitations were the first for a hundred years.

- He instituted **metropolitan visitations** to discipline not only Puritan clergy, but also lenient bishops. Surplices and vestments had to be worn, altars were moved and railed off, and lecturers (preachers) were regulated. The altar controversy was a bitter one. To Laud, the altar was 'the greatest place of God's residence upon earth'. To the Puritans, the altar was a table upon which to celebrate the Last Supper. It should be part of the body of the Church and not moved to the East, elevated and railed off. This 'zero tolerance' of nonconformity was seen as 'meddling'. Laud's emphasis on ceremony was 'hocus-pocus', whereas to Laud 'ceremonies are the hedge that fence the substance of religion from all the indignities which profaneness and sacrilege too commonly put upon it'.

- Laud tried to regain impropriated tithes and adjust tithes in order to improve the economic position of the Church. The historian Christopher Hill argues that Laud did little to improve the economic basis of the Church, but alienated many in attempting it. Since the Reformation, a number of gentry had held impropriated tithes, and feared losing them.

William Prynne (1600–1669)
Puritan pamphleteer and lawyer. Educated at Oxford and Lincoln's Inn. His 'Histriomastix' in 1632 attacked actors, especially female, for immorality. He was brought before the Star Chamber in 1634 and 1637 for his attack on bishops in 'News from Ipswich'. He was fined, mutilated and imprisoned. Prynne was released by the Long Parliament.

- Laud's membership of the Privy Council involved him in politics and the Star Chamber judgements. The case of Prynne, Burton and Bastwick in 1637 did little to win him friends, although those three gentlemen were far from courteous in their criticism of the establishment, especially the bishops. Bastwick hurled abuse at the bishops, in his *Letany:*

> Great and mighty are their privileges, and yet they are neither thankful to God nor the King … but would have more. They have the keys of heaven to shut out whom they will. They have the keys of hell, to thrust in whom they please. They have the keys also of our purses to pick them at their pleasure … They have the keys likewise of all the prisons in the kingdom …

Sedition: Speech, writing or behaviour intended to encourage rebellion or resistance against the King or government.

Earlier, in 1637, the Court of the Star Chamber had 'fined the three … £5,000 apiece to the king … to stand in the pillory … Bastwick and Burton to lose their ears, and Prynne the remainder of his ears; Prynne to be stigmatised on both cheeks with the letters S.L. signifying a seditious libeller: all of them to suffer perpetual imprisonment.' They were indeed guilty of **sedition** but, to the Puritans, the letters S.L. signified 'Stigmata Laudi'.

- Laud was seen as an enemy of Parliament who hoped to become the Richelieu of England.

- Laud's actions in England, on behalf of the King, inflamed religious issues within the Church of England that dated back to the Elizabethan Settlement. He stimulated anti-Catholic feeling that had existed in

England since the Armada and had been compounded by the Gunpowder Plot, the Thirty Years War and Court Catholicism. His actions did not directly provoke either the collapse of the Personal Rule or the outbreak of war. However, seen in the broader perspective of religion throughout Britain and of Laud's influence extending beyond 1640, some historians see religion as the key factor (see section 7.4).

● Laud's work in Ireland and Scotland aggravated the opponents of Charles in the three kingdoms. In Ireland, he supported the centralising policies of Wentworth. These alienated both Catholics, by trying to regain church lands in Ireland, and Calvinists, who resented the imposition of Laud's brand of Protestantism on the Church of Ireland. In Scotland, Laud drew up 'that fatal Book', as Henrietta Maria called the new Scottish liturgy. In *The Personal Rule of Charles I* (1992), Kevin Sharpe argues that the responsibility for the dramatic events in Scotland in 1637 belongs rightly with Charles rather than Laud. Charles Carlton records, in *Charles I, the Personal Monarch* (1995), the nervous tension of Laud and his anxiety dreams during the period before 1640. Carlton argues that Laud saw the dangers of military intervention in Scotland. In a sense, Laud became the scapegoat while the offensive liturgy known as 'Laud's Liturgy', and the resulting wars, 'The Bishops Wars', were seen as being fought to prevent the imposition of an English system on Scotland. In this sense, Laud played a key part in precipitating the crisis of 1640. By the time the war broke out in 1642, Laud had been a 'guest of His Majesty' in the Tower for over a year, and many of the 'innovations' he was accused of had been removed. As with Buckingham, Laud was so inextricably involved in issues that were both religious and political that his removal did no more than remove a limb after the poison had spread.

How successfully did Charles assert his authority in Ireland and Scotland?

Recent research by Conrad Russell (1990, 1991), Martyn Bennett (1995) and Peter Gaunt (1997) has focused on the British and Irish dimension as a key factor of the Personal Rule which contributed both to its collapse and to the ensuing crises that produced war in 1642.

James VI and I achieved much in Ireland and Scotland by not pushing too far too soon. During the Personal Rule, Charles I needed to assert his authority in all his kingdoms. As in England, that meant centralisation, the increase of revenue and pushing religious conformity.

Ireland

In Ireland, Wentworth (known as 'Black Tom Tyrant') ruled as Lord Deputy with apparent success as far as the English were concerned. His **mandate** from the King was to make his control over Ireland effective by extending law and order and promoting the Church of Ireland (the Church of England in Ireland). He was to reverse the situation by which expenditure on Ireland had outstripped income from it by £20,000 a year, by bringing in money from customs and the development of industry and trade. Wentworth was the right man for the job. He carried out his work with what the historian Terence Ranger calls 'the combination of cunning, idealism and self-interest'.

Mandate: Authority given to someone to govern a particular territory.

Poyning's Law (1494): This said that all existing English laws should be applied to Ireland, and that no parliament could be held there without the permission of the King who could approve the agenda of the Irish Parliament and annul its statutes. It left the Irish legislature dependent upon the Crown.

By 1635, Wentworth seemed to be having great success in Ireland. He had defeated his political opposition by playing off the 'New English' (those who had settled in Ireland after the English Reformation; that is to say, Protestant settlers) against the 'Old English' (those who had settled in Ireland before the Reformation; Catholic settlers). He avoided corruption by concentrating power in himself and his cronies, having removed political opponents on grounds of corruption. The four Courts – High Commission, Wards and Livery, Castle Chamber and the Commission for Defective Titles – pursued Laud's church policies, exacted feudal revenue, hounded political opponents and pressed the royal claim to lands. The Dublin Parliament in 1634–1635, operating under **Poyning's Law**, set up the hated Commission for Defective Titles and the Court of High Commission, and voted six subsidies.

Wentworth had success in encouraging industries such as glass, linen and horse breeding. He invested his own money in unsuccessful attempts to start an iron industry and genuinely supported the interests of Irish exports, so increasing revenue. It should be pointed out that Wentworth and his friend Radcliffe were the biggest tax farmers in Ireland! He was also successful in trebling the size of the Irish army and giving it better training and equipment, and developing the navy as a means of protecting maritime trade.

This looked, and was, a considerable achievement. In other areas, Wentworth was less successful. In the long run, his successes were turned, in the hands of opposition, into failures. The religious problem in Ireland was too deep-seated to be solved. The existing native Catholics, Old English, New English and Ulster Presbyterians resisted Laud's brand of Anglicanism. The Primate of Ireland, the Archbishop of Armagh, was of Calvinist outlook. He resented the activities of the Court of High Commission and Wentworth's promotion of his own supporters to senior positions. Wentworth's religious policies closely involved the land problem in Ireland. He tried to regain impropriated tithes and church lands at the expense of the powerful enemies such as the Earl of Cork. The historian Terence Ranger maintains that, in many of these cases, Wentworth was both prosecutor and judge, defying existing situations and Irish common law and showing a lack of political judgement overall. His policy for increasing Crown lands was ruthless, but of limited success. He rode roughshod over Lord Falkland's **Graces**, but failed to secure a plantation of Connacht. The Earl of Clanricarde challenged his policies in Galway in the English Privy Council.

Graces: These were issued by Lord Falkland to secure Irish loyalty in the late 1620s. They remitted some recusancy fines, granted titles of land for 60 years occupancy, and imposed an Oath of Allegiance rather than Supremacy.

Until the crisis in Scotland, Wentworth had certainly ruled ruthlessly in the interests of the King. To that extent, he was the efficient administrator. His policies were those of confrontation rather than compromise. Both Hugh Kearney (1959) and Terence Ranger show how Wentworth alienated the two groups upon which he might have built a power base: the Protestant New English and the Catholic Old English. This was partly due to his nature, but largely because of his church policies. These may have originated in his need to keep Laud as an ally in England.

Historians Lawrence Stone and Terence Ranger see Wentworth as part of a conspiracy to use Ireland as a blueprint for an absolutism that could be extended to England. Kearney does not accept this. He argues that Wentworth had, in some ways, a Tudor attitude towards Ireland and was prepared to follow a 'conquest' and 'plantations' policy. As such, he was bound to alienate the Old English. His advocacy of Laud's policies secured the enmity of the New English, bolstered by the Scottish Presbyterian settlers of King James's Plantation of Ulster. This had the undesirable effect of strengthening links between the New English and the Protestant opposition to Charles at home.

In a sense, it was the removal of Wentworth to deal with the Scottish Rebellion that created the most instability in Ireland. It removed his firm hand and unleashed the longer-term problems of the Ulster Plantation. To make sure that the Ulstermen did not help the Scots, he had imposed the Black Oath on Ulstermen in 1639. This made them swear not to join a **covenant** against Charles, or take up arms against him. Wentworth's failure against the Scots and his subsequent trial and execution were more responsible for the Irish Rebellion than his work in Ireland. His removal caused alarm in Ireland at the 'hot' Protestantism of the English Parliament and at its sympathy for, and possible collusion with, the Scots.

Covenant: A solemn and binding agreement – in this case to defend their religion.

Scotland

In Scotland, religion proved to be the catalyst to challenge the authority of Charles and ultimately to end the Personal Rule. The imposition of the **Canons** in 1636 and of the **Liturgy** in 1637 brought to a head the issues of nationality, religion and property in Scotland. The high-church coronation of Charles at Edinburgh in 1633 had alarmed the Presbyterians. Charles's attempts to regain alienated Scottish Crown lands were menacing to landowners. The Liturgy was the signal for rebellion. Its reading in St Giles Cathedral, Edinburgh, turned into riot as Jenny Geddes threw her stool at the Dean of St Giles, shouting 'Wilt tha say Mass in ma lug [ear]?'

Canons: Laws of the Church regulating discipline.

Liturgy: Rules defining the way that religious services are carried out in the Christian Church.

Laud became the scapegoat. When the Scots drew up The National Covenant (1638), they protested their loyalty to the King but refused to accept the 'innovations' of the Liturgy. This challenged the authority of a King jealous of his prerogative. He saw a conspiracy between Scottish Presbyterians and English parliamentarians and realised that force might be necessary against the Covenanters. Attempts to reach agreement with the Scots through the Edinburgh Parliament and the General Assembly, failed. It appeared to the Scots that Charles intended to enforce the Canons and Liturgy by force.

The First Bishops War, 1639

The Bishops War in 1639 was ultimately provoked by Charles's determination to assert his authority over 'rebels'. The agenda of the 'rebels' was complicated, varied and deep-seated, although its catalyst was religion. The King's army of 20,000 men mounted a half-hearted invasion that was ended by the Pacification of Berwick. Further dealings with the General Assembly and the Scottish Parliament reached a deadlock which provoked Charles into proroguing the Scottish Parliament and putting the government of Scotland into the hands of a committee led by Wentworth and Laud. Charles's inability to subdue the Scots was revealed by the lacklustre campaign. The feudal method of raising troops and money for such an undertaking was found wanting. Wentworth advised the King to call Parliament for support against the Scots. Laud was wary of creating a national arena for the airing of grievances against the Personal Rule.

Without doubt, the Scottish crisis ended the Personal Rule and started a crisis, in 1640, which had implications throughout the Three Kingdoms. It did not necessarily cause the war in 1642.

1. How important was the religious issue during the Personal Rule?

2. How far was Charles successful in raising revenue?

3. To what extent was 1637 a turning point in the Personal Rule?

4. How important were developments in Ireland and Scotland at this time?

7.3 Why did Charles I have problems with Parliament, 1640 – January 1642?

As Laud anticipated, far from rallying round the King, Parliament began an attack on illegal taxation, abuse of prerogative courts, church 'innovations' and the advance of popery. It was bitter and focused. The attack was ably led by John Pym.

The Short Parliament

The attitude of the Short Parliament forced Charles to dissolve it within weeks, on 5 May. While Laud was attacked as the author of many of the grievances, he did not help himself by keeping Convocation in session after the dissolution of the Short Parliament. This issued 'The Seventeen Canons of 1640', which confirmed policies such as:

● the placing of the altar at the east end of the church

● asserting the divine right of regal authority

● making teachers and clergy take an oath saying that they would never agree to 'alter the government of this Church by archbishops, bishops, deans and archdeacons etc.'.

Laud's enemies named this the 'Etcetera Oath', saying that people could be made to swear support for anything. The Convocation further angered Parliament by voting Charles £20,000. Hatred for Laud was at its greatest. He was perceived as an 'evil councillor', driving a wedge between the King and his subjects.

At this point, Charles had the capacity to dissolve a troublesome Parliament. Within a year, he had lost that prerogative.

The Long Parliament

The Long Parliament posed problems that could only be settled by compromise and good will. Both sides were ultimately found to be lacking in these attributes in the unstable years 1640–1642. Once again, the catalyst to the calling of Parliament was trouble from Scots who were unhappy at Charles I's actions in 1639 and encouraged by his military incapacity. In August 1640, the Scots occupied Newcastle with little opposition from the ailing Earl of Northumberland. Wentworth (created Earl of Strafford in 1640) suggested a solution that to the King was alarming: 'You have an army in Ireland. You may employ them here to reduce this kingdom.' It raised the real fear that a largely Catholic Irish

---

John Pym (1583–1643)
West-country lawyer by training. Pym was a vocal opponent of the maladministration of the wars by Buckingham, and was against Arminians. He first entered Parliament in 1614, and sat as MP for Calne in 1621–24. From 1625 onwards, he represented Tavistock. His family was associated with the Earl of Bedford. As Treasurer of the Providence Island Company, he actively opposed the policies of Charles in the 1630s. He emerged as leader of the Short and Long Parliaments. Pym secured the removal of Strafford and Laud, maintained the initial unity of the Parliament, securing reforming legislation. By the end of 1641, he envisaged a Catholic conspiracy in England. He drafted the Grand Remonstrance. Pym's opposition meant that he was one of the MPs that Charles tried to arrest in 1642. When war broke out, he became the leader of the war effort by raising revenue for the fight. His final achievement was the alliance with the Scots in December 1643. His influence was so important in Parliament that he was known as 'King Pym'.

army could be used to support arbitrary rule. Meanwhile, the Earl of Strafford was sent north to supervise the campaign.

If confidence is a key to success, Strafford's words are prophetic: 'Pity me for no man ever came to so lost a cause.' As the Scots advanced towards Ripon, Charles failed to secure sufficient military help and called a Council of Peers at York. That insisted on an armistice with the Scots. The Treaty of Ripon guaranteed the calling of another Parliament, as it was agreed that the Scots should occupy the north of England until the English Parliament had been consulted on a final settlement. Until then, the Scots should be given £850 a day to maintain their army until a treaty was signed. Given the financial crisis of 1639–40, the Long Parliament met on 3 November, confident that Charles could easily prorogue or dissolve it and thereby shirk the need to redress the grievances of the Personal Rule. It created serious problems for Charles. These involved a gradual weakening of his authority during 1640 and 1641. War was neither possible nor desirable in those years. By the end of 1641, Charles I, never one for compromise, was beginning to fear that capitulation rather than compromise was demanded of him.

An attack on 'evil councillors', who epitomised the success of the Personal Rule until 1639, robbed Charles of Strafford and Laud. It also undermined his prerogative of choosing his own ministers. Laud was impeached and imprisoned in December 1640, and a number of the Privy Council were either arrested or fled. No specific Articles of Impeachment were laid against Laud until 1643. Then he was accused of subverting religion, the fundamental laws of the realm, and the rights of Parliament. The attack on Strafford was more vehement. He had many enemies in the north of England and in Ireland. He was a man of ability whose removal would signify a victory for those wishing to eradicate 'thorough'. It also marked a personal victory for Pym who denounced Strafford as an apostate (someone who had betrayed the principles he had supported in the early 1620s):

> 'a man who in the memory of many present, had sat in that House an earnest vindicator of the laws, and a most zealous ... asserter and champion for the liberties of the people; but that it was long since he turned apostate from those good affections, and according to the custom and nature of apostates, was to become the greatest enemy to the liberties of his country, and the greatest promoter of tyranny that any age had produced.'

Twenty-nine general and 28 specific Articles of Impeachment failed on grounds of procedure. Much hung on Sir Henry Vane's account that he had heard Strafford's intention to use the Irish army 'to reduce this kingdom'. As Vane was deaf, and the statement was made in the context of the Scottish crisis, it was doubtful evidence. As the 1352 Statute of Treason required two witnesses, the impeachment, and the attempt to establish a principle of cumulative treason by virtue of general conduct of office, failed. In April, the House fell back on removing Strafford by **Act of Attainder**. Pym felt that this was going too far, but 204 MPs voted for attainder and 59 against. (A number did not attend the debate.) Even fewer turned up in the Lords, where the Act of Attainder passed by 26 votes to 19 on 7 May.

Charles was deeply moved by Strafford's fate. Having promised that not

Act of Attainder: An Act of Parliament declaring a subject guilty without a formal trial.

Own Consent Act: An Act passed in May 1641 stating that the Long Parliament could not be dissolved without its own consent.

a hair on his head should be harmed, the weakness of his own position and his fear for the safety of his country and family made him sign the Act of Attainder and agree to the **Own Consent Act**. Rumours of an attempted army plot to save Strafford came to nothing. The offer to save him by giving Pym the post of Chancellor (proposed by the Earl of Bedford) failed with Bedford's death. Strafford was executed on 12 May after attempts to commute his sentence to imprisonment failed. Charles I is said to have commented: 'My lord of Strafford's condition is better than mine.'

How successful was the Long Parliament in reversing the grievances of the Personal Rule?

1   The attempt to reverse 'arbitrary' actions of the Personal Rule made real progress, especially after the Earl of Strafford's removal. The Triennial Act, of February 1641, prevented a Personal Rule of more than three years' duration. It set up the mechanism by which a parliament could be called without the authority of the King after a period of three years. The possible loopholes of prorogation or summary dissolution were closed by the Own Consent Act in May.

2   Determination to ensure that the King ruled within the framework of the Law was seen in the Acts that announced collection of tunnage and poundage without the consent of Parliament (June 1641) and the abolition of ship money (August 1641) illegal. Monopolies were suppressed, the boundaries of forests were restored, and no one could be compelled to accept a knighthood against their will or be fined for refusal. Such measures cut from under the King the capacity to support a Personal Rule, now limited in duration by the Triennial Act. Very important was the removal of the prerogative courts that had given Charles coercive power. The Star Chamber and such courts went, and the power of the Privy Council to commit was subject to *habeas corpus*. On paper at least, the grievances of the 1620s and 1630s were being remedied. The unity of the attack on prerogative, together with the removal of many of his ministers, made Charles powerless to resist. His basis of support had been eroded by the actions of Parliament and by the meekness of his supporters in the light of the reforming zeal of 1640–41. Charles simply could not have fought a war in 1640 or 1641. He did not have sufficient support or military capacity. There was, however, no intention of reducing the King to the extent that it would provoke war. What was wanted was reform and harmonious relations.

3   The determination to eradicate Laudism destroyed the unity of the Long Parliament. Pym had always sensed the danger of raising the religious issue. Laud was imprisoned rather than brought to trial. Unity was maintained in negative actions: Laud's altar rails were removed, altars were moved from the east end, and aspects of ceremony were scrapped. Unity was maintained when the judgements against the popular heroes Prynne, Burton and Bastwick were reversed. While reform of religion was an issue that united subjects, just what the nature of that reform was to be polarised opinion, and was politically dangerous. As early as December 1640, the Root and Branch Petition was introduced into the Commons, demanding '… that the said government (of the Church by bishops) with all its dependencies, root and branches, may be

Iconoclasm: Attacks on images and statues in churches.

abolished'. A number of radical proposals was published and moderates feared anarchy. **Iconoclasm** produced a fear of lawlessness and of attacks on property in general. The fear of extremism helped to increase the support for the King in an unstable situation. Traditional authorities were being challenged in the two areas from which the hierarchic nature of authority emanated: King and Church. This marked the end of the honeymoon period for the Long Parliament. It coincided with the fear that Charles might use an army against Parliament, with suspicion created by his visit to Scotland in 1641 to sound out support and, above all, with the outbreak of The Irish Rebellion at the end of October 1641.

4   The Irish Rebellion was, according to the historian S.R. Gardiner, 'the event which precipitated the division of parties'. The Rebellion can be seen as a revolt of Irish Catholics who feared that the zeal of the Long Parliament would favour Scottish Presbyterians in Ulster, who already held Irish land, and would dispel the years of religious fudge in Ireland by attempting to eliminate Catholicism. The fact that it was staged in the King's name did him no favours. Its implications were far reaching. Exaggerated reports from Ireland made out that 40,000 Protestants were brutally killed. Given the inherent anti-Catholicism in England, it was rumoured that the London Catholics would soon revolt. By November 1641, two issues had been raised upon which Charles I could never compromise:
* the right to choose his own advisers
* his right to raise and command armies to serve outside their own counties.

Grand Remonstrance: A document drawn up, printed and circulated at the end of 1641, designed by John Pym.

5   The **Grand Remonstrance** of November 1641 shows the extent to which relations between Charles and the Long Parliament had worsened. It was designed by Pym to flush out Charles I's supporters. Ultimately, it consolidated his 'party'. The Grand Remonstrance was in three parts:
* The first analysed the root of the problem in terms of a conspiracy: 'a malignant and pernicious design of subverting the fundamental laws and principles of government upon which religion and justice of this kingdom are firmly based'. Catholics, evil councillors and courtiers had cut off the King from his people.
* The second part summarised the achievements of the Parliament to date; namely, its reforming legislation. However, it stressed how far reform had been hampered by the remaining bishops and papists.
* The third section resolved to reduce the power of the bishops and 'unburden the consciences of men of needless and superstitious ceremonies, suppress innovations, and take away the monuments of idolatry'. It urged the King 'to employ such counsellors, ambassadors and other ministers, in managing his business at home and abroad as the Parliament may have cause to confide in'.

The Remonstrance shows the pervasive nature of religious grievances and the extent to which the royal prerogative was being eroded. The printing and publishing of the Grand Remonstrance was especially inflammatory. Pym did this without, as was customary, seeking the consent of the Lords. Moderates saw and feared it as an appeal to the people. The increasing support for the King was shown by the fact that the Remonstrance passed the Commons on 22 November by 159 votes to 148, a narrow victory of only 11 votes. Charles responded to the petition, promising to look into allegations of abuse but asserting his right to choose his own ministers. His intention to call for volunteers to quell the Irish Rebellion polarised opinions yet further.

The attempted arrest of the five members, in January 1642, was provoked by the Commons impeaching 12 bishops as well as by the rumour that the Queen was about to be impeached. It was a foolish action, possibly inspired by the Queen. The attempted arrest of Pym, Hampden, Haselrig, Holles, and Strode not only breached parliamentary privilege, but caused acute embarrassment. The Speaker, William Lenthall, when asked to hand over the five MPs, replied, 'Sire, I have neither eyes to see nor tongue to speak in this place but as the House is pleased to direct me.' In 1629, the Speaker had been assaulted for obeying the King; in 1642, he was clearly the servant of the House. This drama gave great political capital to Charles I's opponents. Its closeness to the Irish Rebellion encouraged anti-Catholic hysteria on a scale similar to 1605. The situation was too dangerous for the Queen and Charles. It was rumoured that the King intended to regain London by force. As the situation in Ireland worsened and control of the militia became imperative, the chances of compromise with Parliament evaporated. By February, the Lords voted to exclude bishops from the House. In March, the Militia Bill – not signed by the King – was issued as the Militia Ordinance. It placed the militia under the control of Parliament. The use of ordinances gave Parliament the mechanism to govern without the King's consent. By April, the King had been denied entry into Hull and went on to make York the centre for recruiting. His rejection of the Nineteen Propositions at York showed his determination to prevent the loss of further authority. Both sides were recruiting before Charles raised his standard at Nottingham on 22 August 1642. In some ways the more interesting question is when did the civil war begin, rather than why. Certainly, after leaving London in January, Charles I had left the initiative with those who were pushing for further reform.

1. How important was the work of Pym during the Long Parliament?

2. What was the significance of the Irish Rebellion?

3. How far was Charles responsible for the breakdown with Parliament?

7.4 The 'high road' to Civil War?
A CASE STUDY IN HISTORICAL INTERPRETATION

Historiography: The different ways in which historians of all periods have looked at a problem.

The 'causes of the English Civil War' provide the most investigated topic in English **historiography**. It has gained a new lease of life in the wake of historical research, which promotes the role played by affairs in Scotland and Ireland in resisting English government. The debate has been engaged ever since the 17th century. Excellent surveys of the historiography of this are given by H. Tomlinson and by R.C. Richardson. Contemporaries such as Edward Hyde (later Earl of Clarendon), Richard Baxter and Lucy Hutchinson are astute, informative and involved.

The Whig interpretation of the causes of the Civil War held sway in the late 19th and early 20th centuries. The leading exponents of this have one thing in common – they could all write brilliant prose. Lord Macaulay, S.R. Gardiner and G.M. Trevelyan are worth reading for their fluent, persuasive writing. They tell a good story well. The theme is of monarchy frustrating the evolution of parliamentary government. In this sense, the Civil War is part of an evolutionary political process – there is a 'high road' to civil war. Religion emerges as important in that the Puritans were not only religious enemies of arbitrary rule, but political enemies, too.

Another long-term view is that of the Marxist interpreters. Here the social and economic motives are the dynamics of history, the sub-structure that determines politics, while religion is the superstructure. Marxists see the progress of history as the result of class struggle. In 17th-century England, the major fault-lines were the result of the decline of feudal economy and society (represented by Charles I) and the emergence of a bourgeois, capitalist society (represented by the opponents of Charles in the Providence Island Company). The War was part of this process which, in turn, was part of the overall progression to a classless society. This approach places great emphasis on opposition to Crown policies coming from rising gentry and emergent commercial interests. The historian Christopher Hill was influenced by this theory, linking religion to its social and economic substructure. R.H. Tawney links religion to the rise of capitalism. Lawrence Stone (1972) is also influenced by the ideas of the Marxists. He sees the causes in terms of 'preconditions', 'precipitants' and 'triggers'.

In recent years, research has produced great developments, moving away from long-term causes.

Revisionism

This is a term that has long outgrown its strength. It has come to mean anyone challenging Whig or Marxist ideas. One of the first to do so was Alan Everitt. In 1968, he challenged the idea that the members of the Long Parliament met as a 'body of revolutionaries' to attack the King. The leading exponent of radical new ideas is Conrad Russell who, in writings in 1979, 1990 and 1991, offers the most exciting and challenging work of the period. He places less emphasis on long-term 'causes' than on events from the time of the Scottish rebellion. Russell argues that the inter-related opposition to Charles, in his three kingdoms, was generated by the problem of multiple religions and a king bent on uniformity. This produced a crisis that Charles I could not handle. The War was thus a British event. Russell analyses Charles's decision to fight as the product of 'diminished majesty' brought about by seven factors:

- the Bishops Wars
- Charles's defeat in the British Wars
- the failure of Charles and Parliament to reach a settlement
- the failure of Charles to dissolve or prorogue the Long Parliament
- the choice of sides after the Irish Rebellion and the Grand Remonstrance
- the failure to negotiate after January 1642
- 'diminished majesty'.

Charles was central to all those events and non-events – an inept King ruling multiple kingdoms.

The historian Kevin Sharpe, in a massive study of the Personal Rule (1992), has revised old views. He sees the 1630s as a period of domestic reform shattered by the decision to fight the Scots, which caused financial and administrative collapse. Religious revisionism was encouraged by Nicholas Tyacke (1983) who sees the rise of Arminianism, rather than

Puritanism, as an issue in the crisis. John Morrill (1984) argues that of the main 'perceptions of misgovernment', 'It was the force of religion that drove minorities to fight'; 'I believe it is almost impossible to overestimate the damage done by Laudians …'.

While there are different emphases among the Revisionists, they all agree with Derek Hirst (1985) that Charles was out of his depth and an inept king. Anthony Fletcher (1981), in a detailed analysis of 1640–42, argues for the importance of events and issues of those years rather than long-term ideological issues.

Post-Revisionism

Richard Cust and Ann Hughes (1989) stress the broader cultural, social and economic aspects raised by religious and political issues. In *The Causes of the English Civil War* (1991), Ann Hughes writes: 'Hence the opposition to Charles was not particularist, … but general, concerned with the nature and direction of one central government.' Johann Sommerville (1989) argues that the deep-rooted causes of the War go beyond the 'functional breakdown' after 1639.

So, where do we go from here? You should read contemporary sources and draw your own conclusions. There was a functional breakdown in 1639–40. Religion was a highly emotive and contentious issue. Charles was an inept king. His monarchy was overstretched in three kingdoms. The Long Parliament was like no other Parliament of Charles's reign. The problems specific to his reign had long-term, wide-ranging origins. Ultimately, Charles I made a personal decision to fight for his prerogative.

1. Why do historians differ in explaining the origins of the English Civil War?

2. What do you understand by the term 'Revisionism'?

3. Were there any 'long-term' causes of the English Civil War?

Source-based questions: The origins of the English Civil War

SOURCE A

The great taxations … of ship money and the great sums laid upon us by the Lord Lieutenant and his Deputy Lieutenants, some of them being Recusants. They impose what they please upon whom they please when it comes to charges and arms, sparing some with great ability to pay and forcing those charged to train and muster men at their own expense … We feel that we do not own our estates, and are wholly at their will and pleasure.

A Petition to Parliament by the inhabitants of Lancashire, ?1640 (adapted from a document in the Lancashire County Record Office)

SOURCE B

It may be worth observing, that all the historians, who lived near that age, still represent the civil disorder and convulsions as proceeding from religious controversy, and consider the political disputes about power and liberty as entirely subordinate to the other … Disuse of Parliaments, imprisonment, … ship money, and arbitrary administration; those were loudly … complained of. But the grievances which tended chiefly to enflame the Parliament and nation were the surplice, the rails placed about the altar, the bows on approaching it, the liturgy, the breach of the Sabbath … the use of the ring in marriage, and of the Cross in baptism … The disorders in Scotland entirely, and those in England mostly, proceeded from so mean and contemptible an origin.

From The History of Great Britain *by David Hume (1754)*

Source-based questions: The origins of the English Civil War

SOURCE C

The English Civil War was not an isolated event. Charles ruled over three kingdoms, and within three years he faced armed resistance in all three of them, Scotland in 1639, Ireland in 1641, and England in 1642 … The study of the resistance in the three kingdoms overwhelmingly suggests the possibility that all three were connected, and therefore that we should be looking for causes in the things all three had in common: that they were members of a union of multiple kingdoms, and they were all ruled by Charles I. It may be that the main reason why the causes of the English Civil War have created so much difficulty is our insular error in looking for them only in the study of English history: we have been trying to discover the whole of the solution by studying part of the problem.

From The Causes of the English Civil War *by Conrad Russell (1990)*

1. Using the Sources and your own knowledge, explain the meaning of the terms:

a) 'Recusants' (Source A)

b) 'ship money' (Sources A and B)

2. Use Sources B and C.

How far do their authors express differing views of the origins of the English Civil War?

3. Use all the Sources and your own knowledge.

How far were the policies of Charles I during the years 1637–1642 responsible for the outbreak of War in 1642?

8 · Civil Wars, the Interregnum and Oliver Cromwell

8.1 The Civil Wars, 1642–1649

8.1.1 How was England governed during the Civil Wars?

8.1.2 What were the Royalists' advantages and what problems did they face?

8.1.3 What were the Parliamentarians' advantages and what problems did they face?

8.1.4 Who won the battles and why?

8.1.5 Why did Parliament win the First Civil War?

8.1.6 Historical interpretation: How and why did radical ideas and groups develop?

8.1.7 Why was the search for a settlement unsuccessful?

8.1.8 Why was the King executed?

Key Issues

- Why did Parliament win the First Civil War?

- Why, despite attempts at a negotiated settlement, was the King executed?

- Did the events of December 1648 – January 1649 constitute a revolution?

Framework of Events

1642	10 January: King leaves London after failing to arrest the 5 MPs
	February: Bishops are excluded from House of Lords by Clerical Disabilities Bill
	5 March: Militia Ordinance
	23 April: King is denied entry to Hull
	June: Nineteen Propositions presented to Charles; Commissions of Array are issued; King's reply to Nineteen Propositions
	4 July: Parliament establishes Committee of Safety
	12 July: Parliament votes to raise an army; fleet declares in favour of Parliament
	22 August: King raises his standard at Nottingham
	23 October: battle of Edgehill
	13 November: Royal forces are turned back at Turnham Green
1643	1 February: Oxford Propositions
	May: peace negotiations fail
	June: Solemn League and Covenant is drawn up; ratified by both Houses of Parliament (September); Assembly of Divines set up to plan reform of Church
	September: King signs Cessation treaty with Irish rebels
	December: death of John Pym
1644	January: Independents in Assembly of Divines publish 'An Apologeticall Narration'
	2 July: battle of Marston Moor
	24 November: Uxbridge Propositions
1645	February: Ordinance creating the New Model Army
	April: Self-Denying Ordinance; Clubman risings in the west
	14 June: battle of Naseby
	September/October: Clubman risings in south-west and Wales
1646	5 May: King surrenders to Scots
	June: surrender of Oxford
	13 July: Newcastle Propositions

1647	February: Scots hand King to Parliament for £400,000; Parliament votes to disband the army
	April/May: army petitions and election of Agitators
	June: seizure of King by Cornet Joyce; General Council of Army set up; 'Representation of the Army' is published
	23 July: Heads of the Proposals presented to King (formally presented 2 August)
	October: 'Agreement of the People' is published
	28 October – 1 November: Putney Debates
	11 November: King escapes from Army custody at Hampton Court
	13 November: King is recaptured on Isle of Wight
	14 December: Four Bills put to King
	26 December: King signs Engagement with Scots
	28 December: King rejects the Four Bills
1648	January: Parliament votes No Further Addresses to King
	April: Windsor Prayer Meeting; Second Civil War breaks out
	July: Scottish invasion on behalf of King
	September: Second Civil War ends in Parliamentary victory
	November: Army demands King be put on trial
	5 December: Commons vote King's reply to their commissioners constitutes a basis for negotiation
	6 December: Pride's Purge
1649	4 January: Parliament's 'Three Resolutions'
	20–27 January: trial of Charles I
	30 January: execution of Charles I
	15 March: abolition of monarchy
	17 March: abolition of House of Lords.

Overview

Nineteen Propositions: Peace proposals put to the King in June 1642. For the main terms see page 239.

Standard: The King's personal coat of arms on a flag.

Sieges: Military operations in which an army tries to capture a town by surrounding it and preventing food or help from reaching the people inside.

Solemn League and Covenant: An alliance negotiated by John Pym between Parliament and the Scottish Covenanters. The English Parliament was to pay the Scots £30,000 a month for the upkeep of the Scottish Army to fight for them against the King. The English agreed to introduce a presbyterian system into England and Ireland.

Royalist: Supporter of the King.

AFTER the King's abortive attempt to arrest those whom he regarded as the parliamentary ringleaders, England slid into civil war. Although there was no declaration of war for seven months, the preparations for war, the continued provocative actions of Parliament and the intransigence of Charles I make it difficult to see how war could have been avoided. The **Nineteen Propositions** put to the King in June 1642 can hardly be interpreted as a realistic basis for negotiation. Charles rejected them in no uncertain terms. When the King raised his **standard** at Nottingham, in August of that year, it was clear that a state of war existed. The main issue for historians lies in explaining the victory of Parliament in this First Civil War. Initially, Charles held the advantage, with more experienced generals and more supporters from the higher social classes. However, he was not decisive enough to take advantage of this. Parliament's forces quickly learned military lessons and benefited in the long term from controlling the navy and the wealthier areas of the country.

The war continued for four years. It consisted largely of **sieges**, with nine major battles. In late 1643, an agreement known as the **Solemn League and Covenant** brought the Scots into the war on Parliament's side. However, after the battle of Marston Moor, they were largely preoccupied with events north of the border where the **Royalist** Scots had seized the initiative. Meanwhile, the King engaged with the Irish, to the embarrassment of many of his Protestant English supporters, and with little military advantage. By late 1644, Parliament's main problem lay in the reluctance of its generals to show commitment to beating the

Self-Denying Ordinance: Parliamentary law that demanded the resignation within 40 days by members of both Houses of all the military and civil offices (positions) held since November 1640.

Cavalry: The group of soldiers in an army who fight on horses.

Leveller: Member of a radical political and religious group which became influential in the New Model Army (see page 241) in the aftermath of the First Civil War. The Levellers proposed widening the franchise (right to vote), religious toleration and reform of the legal system to make it fair to all.

Providence: Widely-held belief that all events were ordained by God; nothing happened by chance.

Rump: A term referring to those who sat in Parliament from 6 December 1648 until its forcible dissolution by Oliver Cromwell in April 1653. Initially, 71 MPs sat in the Rump but after the execution of the King, another 83 decided to resume their seats. The Rump was recalled by the Army in 1659, but failed to establish stable government

Military coup: An event in which government is taken over by the army, using force.

King. The early months of 1645 saw lengthy and sometimes bitter debate in Parliament. This led to the **Self-Denying Ordinance**, and the appointment of Sir Thomas Fairfax as Lord General of the Parliamentary forces, with Oliver Cromwell commanding the **cavalry**. This series of events is the first of many where historians disagree about Cromwell's motivation. The training of a New Model Army followed. By late 1645, Parliament was clearly winning and the King finally surrendered to the Scots in April 1646. The fall of Oxford the following June marked the end of hostilities.

Historical debate about the period 1646–48 has centred on the reasons why a settlement with the King proved elusive. Charles recognised the lack of unity among his opponents and hoped to use it to his advantage. This highlights the importance of his beliefs and actions in causing his downfall. The politicisation of the army also needs to be taken into account. Wary of the motives of the MPs and angered by the failure to address their material needs, the soldiers refused to disband. Instead, they elected representatives to a Council and drew up a document, the 'Representation', stating their position.

The extent to which the soldiers' actions were influenced by **Leveller** ideas has also been the subject of disagreement among historians. Many of the documents of the period suggest that members of the Army held more radical views than the population as a whole. Matters came to a head following the King's engagement with the Scots and the Second Civil War. The Army now saw itself as God's instrument in dealing with a king who had deliberately ignored God's **providence**. When Parliament voted to continue negotiating with the King, Colonel Pride's regiment purged Parliament. This led directly to the trial and execution of Charles I. Subsequently, the **Rump** debated the form that England's government should take. Six weeks later, both the monarchy and the House of Lords were abolished.

The historian Barry Coward claims, in *The Stuart Age* (2000), that the events of December 1648 to January 1649 constituted a revolution. Certainly, the act of executing a king in public was in itself revolutionary. Other historians, such as Derek Hirst in *England in Conflict* (1999), contest this label for the events as a whole. They suggest instead that what happened amounted to a **military coup**. However, most historians agree that, at least in relation to long-term political developments, the Glorious Revolution of 1688–89 and its aftermath were more significant.

8.1.1 How was England governed during the Civil Wars?

Magazine: Collection of military guns and ammunition. In 1642, the magazine at Hull consisted of army equipment returned to it after the Second Bishops' War. There was enough arms and ammunition for 16,000 men.

Although it would be wrong to regard the Civil War as inevitable after Charles's failed attempt to arrest the five members of Parliament, there was little sign of a serious bid to avoid war. When Charles left London, on 10 January, it soon became clear that both he and Parliament were exploring military options, with control of the **magazine** at Hull being the main objective. The next day, Charles appointed the Earl of Newcastle as governor of Hull while Parliament nominated Sir John Hotham to the same position. Although the Mayor and Corporation initially rejected both nominees, they were finally persuaded to accept Hotham. Charles travelled north and in April sent his son, the Duke of York, and the Elector Palatine in a bid to secure Hull. In a serious blow to the King, from both a strategic and a military point of view, Sir John Hotham refused Charles entry to the town. He made it clear that the stronghold and port of Hull would be Parliamentarian.

From the spring of 1642, the two sides were establishing the means to raise armies. The use by Parliament of an **Ordinance** to do so was a further provocation to the King. Equally, in using the **Commissions of Array** to raise his army, Charles was emphasising his willingness to use any means to retain control, just as he had done during the Personal Rule. A great blow to Parliament was the loss of the **Great Seal**. In May, Lord Keeper Littleton sent the Seal to the King in Oxford. This threw Parliament's administration of justice into disarray and prevented it from fulfilling the legal functions of government. It was not until mid-1643 that Parliament issued its own Great Seal, which was immediately condemned by the King.

In June 1642, Parliament offered Charles, now in residence in York, the Nineteen Propositions. Supposedly a set of proposals to avoid war, there is little to suggest compromise in this document.

Ordinance: Legislation passed by the two Houses of Parliament but lacking royal assent. Over 500 were passed by Parliament between 1642 and 1647.

Commissions of Array: Orders sent to a county-based committee to raise troops. Introduced by Edward I, it had fallen into disuse in the 16th century when **Lords Lieutenant** became responsible for the militia.

Lords Lieutenant: Appointed by the monarch. There was one appointed for each county by the end of Elizabeth I's reign. A Lord Lieutenant's main task was to organise the militia.

Great Seal: The state seal used to make official all documents and instructions issued by the government.

Nineteen Propositions

Including:

- Parliament was to approve the King's choice of advisers and important government decisions.

- The King was to take Parliament's advice in reforming the Church.

- Parliament was to control the militia and the education of the King's children.

Not surprisingly, given this attack on his rights, Charles's response was negative. If this were passed, he said, 'we should remain but the outside, but the picture, but the sign of a King'.

An allegory (in which the characters and events are symbols of something else) of the Civil War, published in 1642.

Sporadic fighting occurred during the summer of 1642, but the war did not officially start until the King raised his standard at Nottingham on 22 August. Clarendon relates that the same night a 'very strong and unruly wind' blew down the flag and it proved impossible to erect it again for several days. In any case, few had as yet responded to Charles's call to arms.

How did each side raise its army?

Parliament had to raise men without reference to the King. It therefore passed the Militia Ordinance. It gave control of the Army, allowing Parliament to appoint Lords Lieutenant and their Deputies in the counties. These were the men who would be responsible for raising the county militias.

The King had to use an alternative means for raising his army. He chose to use the Commissions of Array to do so. They did succeed in persuading some areas to declare for the King, but this was rarely translated into action. It was the issuing of military commissions to individuals that produced a series of regiments which were eventually brought together to form an army.

By October 1642, 24 of the 42 counties had accepted Parliament's Ordinance, while only 11 accepted the King's Commission. The remaining seven had so far avoided making a choice. However, the taking of sides was more complex than this suggests. While in some counties the gentry genuinely believed in one cause or the other, in others, such as Leicestershire, the final decision depended on the balance between rival gentry groupings within the county. Northamptonshire declared for Parliament because the Royalist gentry had left to join the King and the remaining gentry rallied around John Pym. The historian John Morrill, in *The Revolt of the Provinces* (1976), identifies 22 counties and numerous towns where neutrality pacts were drawn up.

Parliament, governing largely through committees drawn from the membership of both Houses, provided for its army through the Committee of Safety (set up in July 1642). The Committee of Both Kingdoms replaced this in February 1644, after the Covenant with the Scots was agreed. County committees were set up by Parliament in the winter of 1642–43, initially to organise the army. Their powers grew to include tax collection, enforcing religious laws and the administration of justice. The King, meanwhile, coordinated his military efforts around Oxford by means of the royal Council of War. In the other areas under Royalist control, the services of local magnates as lieutenant-generals were sought, despite their military inexperience. By using influential local men, Charles hoped to gain the maximum level of cooperation possible. In the early months of the war, this strategy proved unsuccessful from a military

A woodcut of the King raising his standard in a high wind in Nottingham in August 1642.

Prince Rupert (1619–1682) – unknown artist, after Sir Peter Lely, c. 1665–70

Nephew of Charles I, with some military experience on the continent. He joined Charles at Nottingham in August 1642 and fought in numerous engagements during the First Civil War, starting as General of the Horse and being promoted by degrees to Commander-in-Chief of the King's forces. Rupert was temporarily banished by Charles I after the fall of Bristol (1645). He took part in naval action, 1648–52. After the Restoration, he occupied various offices in Charles II's government, particularly in the Navy.

Sir Thomas Fairfax (1612–1671)
With his father, he led Parliament's forces in Yorkshire at the outset of the Civil War with varied fortune. He commanded the cavalry at Marston Moor (1644) and was appointed Commander-in-Chief of the New Model Army (1645), winning numerous victories in both the First and Second Civil Wars. He supported the Army in its quarrel with Parliament and favoured the execution of the King, although he refused to sit as a judge in the trial. He resigned his commission in 1650 and took no further active part in politics, except in 1659–60.

Robert Devereux, third Earl of Essex (1591–1646)
Commanded Parliament's army at Edgehill and Turnham Green (1642), captured Reading, relieved Gloucester and won the first battle of Newbury (1643), failed to take Oxford and defeated at Lostwithiel (1644). He defended the Earl of Manchester in his quarrel with Oliver Cromwell and resigned his commission in anticipation of the Self-Denying Ordinance.

Impressment: Means of raising a conscript army. All men aged 18–50 were liable for military service but orders were carefully administered to avoid provoking opposition.

Localism: Interest in one's own area rather than in the fortunes of the country as a whole.

Eastern Association: A group of East Anglian counties responsible for the Parliamentarian army in their area.

New Model Army: Parliament's professional army, established on the suggestion of Waller and Cromwell.

Infantry: Soldiers in an army who fight on foot rather than on horses.

Dragoons: Mounted infantry.

1. **Which side had the more effective means of raising an army, Parliament or the King?**

2. **Which side had the more effective generals?**

---

standpoint. So Charles appointed men of proven military experience to command each area, including his nephews Princes Maurice and Rupert.

Impressment was introduced by Parliament in August 1643. The Royalists also did so in November 1643, following Parliament's lead, in order to avoid initiating opposition. The number of men at arms at any one time varied. Armies in the field ranged between 15,000 and 20,000, but the numbers fluctuated significantly, with armies 'melting away' between major engagements.

Nevertheless, the war was one of the bloodiest in English history. It has been estimated, using records from the time, that 84,000 soldiers died – 34,000 Parliamentarians and 50,000 Royalists. Of these, only 17% of Parliamentarians and 12% of Royalists died in one of the nine major battles. Siege warfare, with its exposed attacks, was particularly bloody; if the siege was successful, the victors were merciless towards the defenders. Contemporary estimates of the numbers who died as a result of the war range from 100,000 to 300,000. Modern estimates suggest that 180,000 may have died directly or indirectly, representing 3.6% of the population.

One of the problems faced by King and Parliament was **localism**. When Parliament encountered resistance among the militias to serving outside their own county, Regional Associations were set up. Of these only the **Eastern Association** was really effective, with Oliver Cromwell a prominent and successful officer.

In February 1645, after experiencing various problems including a lack of commitment from its generals, Parliament created the **New Model Army** by Ordinance. This provided for a single national army, although the armies of the associations and the county militias continued to function. It was to have 22,000 men. The 14,400 **infantry** were to be paid 8d (pence) a day and the 6,600 cavalry and 1,000 **dragoons** were to receive 2 shillings (10p) a day. In addition, there would be over 2,300 officers. The commander-in-chief was Sir Thomas Fairfax. The Earl of Manchester had been forced to resign his command, although he and the Earl of Essex continued to sit on the Committee of Both Kingdoms, which controlled the army. The Self-Denying Ordinance of April 1645 aimed to separate the political leadership from the military. However, Oliver Cromwell was exempted from it and was appointed Lieutenant-General of the Horse, Fairfax's second-in-command. Cromwell's temporary exemption was periodically renewed throughout the remainder of the war.

How did the Scots and Irish become involved in England's War?

In 1643, John Pym recognised the benefits to be gained by an alliance with the Scots. From a military point of view, they would provide experienced soldiers. From a political point of view, their involvement would force Parliament to adopt a more radical church settlement than the moderate MPs wanted. Despite the reservations of the moderates, Pym was able to conclude the Solemn League and Covenant with Parliament on 25 September 1643. The Scots were to provide 21,500 troops in exchange for £30,000 a month. Plans for religious reform were to be drawn up by an **Assembly of Learned and Godly Divines**. The moderates were placated by terms that avoided outright commitment to a presbyterian church.

Irish involvement was assured when Charles signed a truce with the Irish rebels in September 1643. He did so in order to free his army in Ireland so that it could come to his aid. Consisting of 6,000 experienced foot soldiers and 700 cavalry, it could have played an important part in Charles's campaign. However, although the Irish who made their way to England, Scotland and Wales were successfully deployed at various locations, they were largely ineffective because parliamentary control of the navy meant they arrived in small groups. For example, in January 1644 at the Battle of Nantwich, Fairfax easily overcame 2,500 Irish.

The loyalty of the troops was also in doubt; some were captured and some changed sides. Besides this, Parliament was able to make propaganda from the King's agreement with Catholics who had promised him £30,000 but no troops. Attempts to negotiate a second peace treaty, in 1645, were even more unpopular. Charles's own supporters, for the most part solidly Protestant, were horrified and the ardour of many was reduced.

How did each side finance the war?

Providing for large armies was a major consideration, as any examination of 17th-century government finance will reveal. It required both sides to apply themselves immediately to the task of raising revenue. Parliament introduced the Committee for the Advance of Money on 26 November 1642. It raised loans and imposed assessments on those who did not pay voluntarily. The Sequestration Committee of 27 March 1643 confiscated and administered the lands of Royalists – classified as those who had voluntarily contributed to the Royalist cause, and Catholics. The Committee for Compounding of August 1645 returned their lands to Royalists and Catholics on payment of a fine. By 1649, Parliament had raised about £1.8 million by punishing these 'delinquents'.

Two taxes were introduced: the weekly (later, monthly) assessment was collected from 22 February 1643. This was a **land tax** raising revenue equivalent to a parliamentary subsidy every two weeks. Kent paid more each month in assessment than in a whole year of ship money. On 22 July 1643, **excise tax** was introduced. It was applied to many consumables, including meat, salt and beer. As a result, it was very unpopular. However, since it meant better-paid soldiers there was a benefit.

At first, the King relied on gifts from his supporters, including **plate** donated by the Oxford Colleges. Besides this, in the areas controlled by the King, every householder had to pay a local tax as well as irregular levies for fortifications and convoys. The King appointed civilian county committees which, like those of Parliament, acted mainly as tax collectors. From July

Assembly of Learned and Godly Divines: A group of 120 clergy and 30 laymen, and later 8 Scottish commissioners, appointed by Parliament in 1643. They were to determine the form to be taken by a national church on the basis of the Solemn League and Covenant. The Assembly issued the Directory of Worship to replace the Book of Common Prayer, as well as a plan for the presbyterian system of church government.

1. To what extent was Scottish involvement in the war a benefit to Parliament?

2. To what extent was the King disadvantaged by Irish involvement in the war?

Land tax: Taxes levied on the basis of how much land a person owned.

Excise tax: A tax on home-produced beer, cider and perry, and a range of imported luxury items. It was new and unpopular.

Plate: Household utensils made of gold or silver.

1643, they exploited the lands of local Parliamentarians. Following Parliament's example, excise duty was introduced in May 1644. It was ordered by the King's parliament at Oxford, which could claim greater validity than that sitting at Westminster.

During the war, the English were taxed far more heavily than previously. Ultimately, this led to serious discontent. The advantages of Parliament over the King were that Parliament controlled wealthier areas which could better afford to pay and that consequently their more regularly paid soldiers were less inclined to arouse hostility by seizing what they needed without compensating the owners.

What changes were made to the Church?

Changes in the Church were made by Parliament not the King. During the war, these changes affected only those areas Parliament controlled, and then not fully. In February 1642, Parliament had finally voted to exclude the bishops from the House of Lords in the Clerical Disabilities Bill, thus ending their political role and decreasing the King's influence in Parliament. The more moderate of Parliament's supporters remained wedded to the **episcopalian** structure of the Church of England. However, as the war widened to include the Scots, Parliament was obliged by the terms of the Solemn League and Covenant to draw up plans for the reform of the Church. The Covenant with the Scots, signed in 1643, committed Parliament to introduce a presbyterian system into England. For this purpose, an Assembly of Learned and Godly Divines was appointed. The Assembly issued the Directory of Worship in 1644, and a year later its use was authorised by Ordinance.

The Assembly also drew up the Calvinist Confession of Faith and the promised plans for changing the structure of the Church. The decisions of the Assembly were not, however, unanimous. A minority of members was more independently minded and, in January 1644, five of them issued alternative proposals in 'An Apologeticall Narration'. Much has been made of the so-called toleration this put forward, although in fact its proposals were similar to those of the mainstream members. Nevertheless, it was a significant development in view of the political clashes between the Presbyterians and Independents later in the 1640s.

Besides these changes, Parliament turned its attention to the clergy. The Committee for Scandalous Ministers ejected Royalist clergy, while the Committee for Plundered Ministers provided support for godly ministers expelled from Royalist areas.

Due to the circumstances of the war, these reforms were implemented patchily, often initiated by local communities. Local studies have revealed widespread and active resistance to Parliament's Ordinances concerning religion.

- Feasts continued to be observed.

- The Directory of Worship was not used.

- Those who failed to comply were not prosecuted.

Neither the King nor Parliament provided a clear lead. The historian John Morrill suggests, in *The Impact of the English Civil War* (1991), that the main reason for the conservatism was that the majority preferred the Episcopalian Church.

Which side was better able to finance its war effort, Parliament or the King? Explain your answer.

Episcopalian: Based on the structure of the Episcopalian Church, i.e. with bishops.

8.1.2 What were the Royalists' advantages and what problems did they face?

The Royalists had the obvious advantage of having the rightful ruler of the country as their leader. Obedience was imprinted on the minds of the populace, and the King could expect his orders to be followed. However, there was no swift response to the Commissions of Array. It is noticeable that Charles's organisation of the war effort was less coherent than that of Parliament. Also, he introduced potentially unpopular measures, such as impressment and excise duty, only after Parliament had taken the lead.

The traditional view is that those of higher rank among the élite tended to support the King. This gave him an initial financial and, perhaps, military advantage. More of the Lords supported the King than supported Parliament and there is plenty of evidence of generous donations to the royalist efforts from members of the higher gentry. It would, however, be difficult for individuals to sustain this level of financial support. This class also traditionally provided the officers within the army and many had experience in the wars then raging on the continent. It could be interpreted as a sign of the King's indecisiveness that he made himself commander-in-chief. He certainly did not always listen to the best advice. Examples include fighting at Naseby rather than withdrawing to regroup, and aiming to defeat Parliament outright as advocated by Queen Henrietta Maria rather than suing for peace as Edward Hyde suggested.

As King, Charles could also call upon foreign help. He benefited particularly from the military experience of his nephew Prince Rupert who, with his younger brother Prince Maurice, volunteered to fight for his uncle. The Royalist generals were noted for their use of new methods.

Woodcut of Prince Rupert hiding in a bean field after the battle of Marston Moor.

Rupert brought in continental-style earthworks around towns, modified the cavalry charge and introduced converging columns of infantry. However, these methods could only bring short-term advantage since the Parliamentarians quickly copied them. It is noticeable that Rupert never maintained such control over his troops on the battlefield as Oliver Cromwell did. This was an important factor in losing key battles. While it was acceptable for the King to call on his Dutch relations – Rupert and Maurice had fled to the United Provinces with their parents in 1621 – calls for French help organised by the Queen were less popular because of Catholic associations. Even so, Rupert's involvement was also open to adverse propaganda. Although he was not particularly religious he would have classed himself as a Lutheran (see page 50). Yet when his personal baggage was captured at Marston Moor, a Parliamentarian woodcut (see left) showed it to be full of Catholic objects such as a crucifix. When the King's writing cabinet was captured at Naseby and he was found to have been corresponding not only with the Queen's French relations for assistance but also with the Pope, the Parliamentarian propagandists made the most of it. This was in addition to the anti-Catholic propaganda generated by the Irish agreements.

At the outset of the war, the King controlled the north and west of England, along with Wales. Although control of Newcastle meant that

Clubman risings: Armed action by groups mainly comprising yeomen farmers, formed in many western and southern counties in 1645. They objected to the atrocities committed by the armies, particularly the King's (which was less well paid). These groups were neutral but as they wanted peace they tended to be more sympathetic to the New Model Army because it was likely to win the war sooner.

coal supplies were secure and that London was cut off from its main source of fuel, the Royalist areas were generally poorer than those occupied by Parliament. Nevertheless, the inhabitants had to pay local taxes, contribute to irregular levies for fortifications and convoys, and supply field armies when they were in the area. The military authorities could conscript horses, carts and tools when needed. Plundering by underpaid soldiers added to the problems. From the start, tax collection was in arrears and the Royalists had to employ soldiers to force people to contribute.

It should come as no surprise, then, that the **Clubman risings** of late 1644 and 1645 were concentrated in Royalist-held areas. While there was variety in the timings and intent of these risings, that they occurred deep within Royalist areas is significant. The risings were initially suppressed, but recurred after the battle of Naseby. Although the Parliamentarians experienced some problems from them, by mid-1645 those who wanted the fighting to end tended to regard Parliament's army in a better light than the King's army. This was probably because Parliament's army was in a stronger position and more likely to bring the war to a swift conclusion. It has been suggested that it was the failure of local communities to cooperate, rather than the Parliamentary army, which finally defeated the King.

Perhaps the most significant factor in the King's defeat was his loss of control of the Navy. Despite the money spent on it in the 1630s, the Stuarts were not seen as great supporters of the Navy. In particular, his failure to respond to demands for better conditions for sailors counted against Charles. In March 1642 he ordered the Lord High Admiral, the Earl of Northumberland, to appoint Sir John Pennington as Commander of the Fleet. The Lord High Admiral ignored the King and gave the post to Parliament's nominee, the Earl of Warwick. Warwick, who was an experienced sailor, immediately moved to secure Hull for Parliament, preventing supplies reaching the King in York. He then removed much of the magazine to London. When the King was in a winning position in 1643, he constantly had to watch his rear because Parliament still controlled Hull and Plymouth, as well as Bristol for some of the time. This prevented Charles from marching on London.

The Navy was also used to blockade ports, preventing Charles from importing supplies or reinforcements and from capitalising on trade in tin from Cornwall or coal from Newcastle. Warwick resigned his command as a result of the Self-Denying Ordinance in April 1645 having raised sailors' pay, introduced careful costing of ventures and made good appointments as captains. His Vice-Admiral, the equally popular William Batten, took over.

1. What were the strengths and weaknesses of the King's position in the First Civil War?

2. Was the King's defeat in the First Civil War inevitable?

8.1.3 *What were the Parliamentarians' advantages and what problems did they face?*

Despite its weak military showing at the beginning of the war, Parliament had two significant advantages over the Royalists:

● the areas of the country it controlled

● the support of the Navy.

Parliamentary control of London was critical, and it was the King's main objective to regain his capital city. London – the centre of commerce and credit – gave Parliament an enormous financial advantage. Not only were the merchants very wealthy, with the Livery Companies paying for London's defences but, as much of England's trade went through the port of London, Parliament could collect large sums in customs duties. London provided up to 80% of the Parliamentary assessment. The capital also provided a constant pool of manpower. As the seat of government, it contained the central law courts, the machinery of government and the printing presses. During the war, there were three Parliamentary newspapers to every Royalist one. Propaganda was also an important tool in discrediting the enemy, highlighting the enemy's atrocities as well as his dubious religious and foreign associations.

Besides London, the south and east also contained England's most important industrial area – the Weald, with its iron industry producing cannons. This advantage was later offset; by 1645, the Royalists were fully exploiting the iron industry in the Forest of Dean. Parliament also controlled the main ports and **arsenals**, largely by good luck. Hull's decision to become and remain Parliamentarian was very close. The advantages of controlling the Navy will be clear from a consideration of the King's problems.

Arsenals: Buildings where weapons and pieces of military equipment are stored and made.

Parliament's organisation was superior from the beginning. Government had to be improvised since there were no legal means at Parliament's disposal, but the methods introduced were applied across all lands under its control. Before he died, John Pym negotiated a crucial agreement. In June 1643, the Solemn League and Covenant between Parliament and the Scots was drawn up. This increased the forces available to Parliament and enabled them to take control of the north. The religious terms of the Solemn League meant that the Westminster Assembly was set up. While the need to introduce a presbyterian church system into England made agreement with the King harder, the benefit of this new Assembly was that religious debate no longer took place in Parliament. Given the widening division among the Westminster MPs over the religious question, this was opportune.

Disagreements over the conduct of the war reached a climax in late 1644. Had religion entered the equation at this point it is likely that the more conservative members would have prevailed, there would have been no New Model Army and no change in Parliamentary military leadership. The basic division was between:

● those who wanted to avoid defeat at all cost

● the more radical group who were determined to win the war.

The former, such as the Earl of Manchester, preferred to negotiate a peace and wanted a presbyterian church settlement. The latter, including Oliver Cromwell, favoured a more tolerant, independent approach to religion. The Earl of Manchester stated his case by declaring that, 'If we beat the King ninety and nine times yet he is the King still, and so will his posterity be after him, but if the King beat us once we shall all be hanged, and our posterity made slaves.' The Scots backed Essex in his attack on Cromwell's view, but the **Independents** countered with the suggestion of a Self-Denying Ordinance which would remove the command from Essex and Manchester. The appointment of Sir Thomas Fairfax as commander-in-chief represented a victory for the Independents, but the Lords were uncooperative in approving his list of officers. Equally, the vote on Cromwell's exemption from the Ordinance was very close in the Lords.

Independents: In religious terms, this refers to those who believed in freedom of conscience. Here it is used in its political sense. The Independents were usually identified as the 'war party', which stood for vigorous prosecution of the civil war and the outright defeat of the King.

Following these developments, the Parliamentary bid for victory was pursued with greater determination.

The New Model Army has gained a reputation as the most successful army of the war. It was financed more generously than any other. Between April 1645 and June 1647, its infantry was paid 76% of the time and the cavalry 58% of the time, both at comparatively high rates. It had free access to London for its supplies of clothing, gunpowder, arms, and so on. For its other needs it was able to pay its way, buying food locally from its wages. All this was to Parliament's advantage, as a comparison with the Clubman reaction to Royalist armies demonstrates.

The Army was noted for its religious zeal. This is probably a result of the high proportion of generals and junior officers who were devout Puritans and of the harsh discipline imposed by Fairfax for such norms as swearing, fornication and drunkenness. Godliness fostered high morale and standards of personal conduct. The chaplains, who encouraged Bible study, prayers and the observation of fast days and days of humiliation, encouraged religious enthusiasm. Mottoes on the standards reinforced the messages. Above all, the Army came to see itself as an instrument of God's providence. This was a development that was to have significant consequences during the subsequent search for a settlement with the King. From a military point of view, the New Model Army came into its own from June 1645 with its victory at Naseby.

1. What strengths did Parliament's side possess at the beginning of the First Civil War?

2. How did Parliament strengthen its position during the First Civil War?

3. What problems did Parliament face in fighting the First Civil War?

8.1.4 Who won the battles and why?

It is debatable whether it was the advantages and disadvantages of the two sides or their ability to win battles that decided the war. Certainly, the war could not have been won by Parliament without victories in the field. Mid 17th-century armies comprised artillery, infantry (including dragoons) and cavalry. Warfare consisted largely of sieges, sackings and skirmishes, with set-piece battles a rarity. Although England had largely avoided involvement in the Thirty Years War, and had concentrated on building up the navy rather than modernising military tactics, it was clear from the start that the lessons of modern warfare had to be learned. In particular, neither side could win a battle without instilling some discipline into its army.

The idea was that the infantry would occupy the centre of the line, protected from behind by the artillery and on the flanks by the cavalry. Artillery had developed greatly, and was used particularly in sieges. It was also probably the most frightening of weapons on the battlefield, inflicting horrible injuries. Eye-witnesses reported seeing limbs flying in all directions, an entire file of men six-deep with their heads struck off, bowels and brains splattered in men's faces. The acrid smoke from the guns was a serious handicap to those downwind.

Developments in the early stages of the Thirty Years War had emphasised the importance of infantry drilling as a means of creating an efficient fighting force, able to respond quickly to the needs of the battle. Since the natural reaction of inexperienced soldiers was to flee the battlefield, there was a need to programme them to override their instincts. The infantry – a mixture of **musketeers** and **pikemen** – was trained to form up in a line. Apart from the battle of Edgehill, when the Royalist army used the Swedish

Musketeers: Infantry (foot) soldiers who were armed with hand guns. These guns (muskets) were slow to load and their effective use in battle depended on drilling. In hand-to-hand combat, the muskets were used as clubs.

Pikemen: Foot soldiers who operated in formation, carrying long pikes with which they defended their musketeers by pointing them towards the advancing cavalry.

formation, Civil War armies drew up in the more straightforward Dutch arrangement that required less skill and drilling. The infantry advanced on the enemy, firing their muskets when they were two pikes' length (10 metres) away. Then they engaged the enemy in 'push of pike'.

In reality, this manoeuvre was seldom carried out. A contemporary stated that not one pikeman in 20 was sufficiently skilled, resolute or strong enough to damage the enemy in a 'push of pike'. The main benefit of drilling was to discourage the men from breaking rank, especially when facing a cavalry charge. They should also re-establish their formations quickly if they fell into confusion. This was difficult to achieve, although in practice a cavalry charge would not be successful unless the infantry broke ranks. Horses would pull up when faced with an unbroken line of men or pikes. It is noticeable that the panic that led men to abandon the battlefield usually began at the rear of the infantry, when awareness of the horror ahead of them overcame any sense of loyalty or discipline.

As with the infantry, so with the cavalry; theory and practice did not always match up. Armed with wheel-lock pistols, or carbines and sabres, the cavalry were supposed to charge with the knee of one soldier virtually interlocked with that of his neighbour. However, horses could not be persuaded to break lines of infantry if they stood their ground. It is clear from the accounts of the battles that the cavalry was successful in dispersing the infantry only when it came upon men already engaging the enemy either from the rear or on the flank. This is true of Oliver Cromwell's successful moves at both Marston Moor and Naseby.

The battle of Edgehill

The first major battle of the war and the only one of 1642 took place at Edgehill in Warwickshire on 23 October. The King's aim was to open up the route to London by defeating the Earl of Essex's army. Essex's aim was to prevent this from happening. By mid-October, the Parliamentarians had gathered an army of about 15,000 men, while 13,500 had rallied to the King's cause. Charles I was his own Commander-in-Chief, and his general

Engraving showing officers directing fighting at Edgehill, 23 October 1642 – from a stylised representation by Van der Gucht.

was the Earl of Lindsey. His most experienced officer was his 23-year-old nephew, Prince Rupert.

The two sides drew up their forces in the normal way, with infantry in the centre flanked by cavalry regiments. Since neither side had uniforms, the Parliamentarians wore orange scarves to distinguish themselves from their opponents. After the initial engagements, the Royalists held a winning position; some of the Parliamentarian cavalry had deserted to the King and the rest had fled. A body of the Parliamentarian infantry also ran away. However, after their charge, Prince Rupert's cavalry failed to regroup. Instead, they pursued fleeing Parliamentarians to the village of Kineton, some 4 kilometres behind the lines, where they proceeded to loot Parliament's baggage train. Only when 5,000 Parliamentarian reinforcements came upon them did they return to the battlefield. The timing was opportune since the Parliamentary infantry, aided by two small groups of cavalry, had forced back their Royalist counterparts who were in danger of losing the day.

The battle ended inconclusively, with both sides too exhausted to continue fighting. Many of those involved were horrified by the experience of fighting their fellow countrymen and, in some cases, members of their own families. The Earl of Lindsey was killed, and a young Royalist reported that the Earl of Essex only escaped because he was in an alehouse.

What is now clear is that had the King acted quickly he could have taken London. The Earl of Essex withdrew towards Warwick, leaving the road to London open. However, Charles hesitated, moving to Oxford to garrison the town and set up a base. This allowed Essex to reach London before Charles and to mobilise the London-trained bands. Charles declined to engage with the 20,000-strong Parliamentarian force, which he faced at Turnham Green on 13 November. The opportunity for a speedy victory was lost. Charles retreated to Oxford for the winter and entered into peace negotiations on the basis of the Oxford Propositions between February and April 1643. Their failure rested mainly on the presbyterian church settlement demanded by Parliament, together with the King's belief that he could win the war.

> *There was not a clear victory for either side at Edgehill. What, then, was the significance of the battle of Edgehill?*

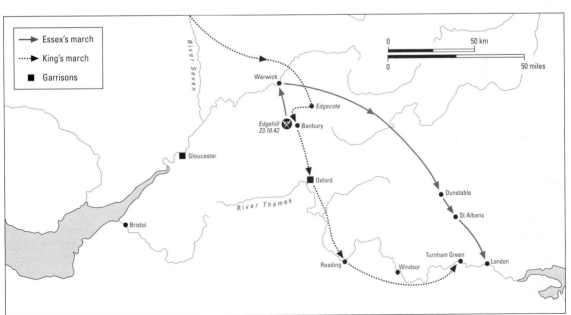

Movements of the armies after the battle of Edgehill, 1642

The battle of Marston Moor

Fought to the west of York, on 2 July 1644, the battle of Marston Moor turned out to be of great strategic importance. It had a major impact on the conduct and outcome of the Civil War. On it depended control of the north of England. The King had certainly held the advantage in the early months of the war. His armies took much of the north of England, although Hull remained Parliamentarian. However, the way south was blocked as a result of Oliver Cromwell's success in organising the army of the Eastern Association.

Equally, the Royalists made gains in the south-west, most notably capturing the port of Bristol on 26 July 1643. The Earl of Essex successfully raised the siege of Gloucester in September 1643 and was able to continue back to London after drawing the battle of Newbury. The King had also made a political mistake in making a treaty with the Irish.

In the autumn of 1643, the Scots had entered into the Solemn League and Covenant with Parliament and Scottish forces crossed the border in January 1644. They advanced to York, a Royalist city, to which Parliament's armies then laid siege. The battle of Marston Moor took place with the arrival of a relieving force led by Prince Rupert. Rupert's force grouped to the west of York, but it took Parliament's leaders some time to appreciate what the Prince was planning. By this time, Parliament's armies were strung out along the road to Tadcaster where it was assumed Rupert would try to cross the river Wharfe. The Scots were hastily recalled as Parliament's army was temporarily outnumbered at Marston Moor, although their forces in the area outnumbered the King's by three to two. Fortunately for Parliament, the Marquis of Newcastle's men were slow to leave York and did not begin arriving at the battlefield until 2 p.m., at which point some sporadic firing began. Newcastle's men were not finally in position until 4 p.m., by which time Parliament had regained the

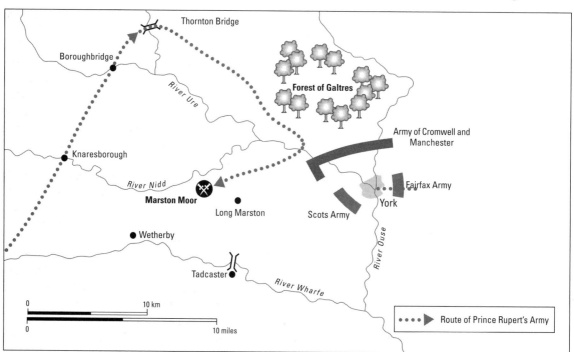

The battle of Marston Moor, 2 July 1644

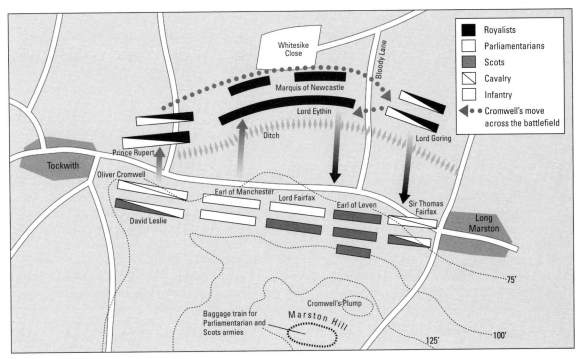

The battle of Marston Moor in detail

numerical advantage. With perhaps as many as 46,000 men in total on the two sides, this was the largest battle of the war. Fighting proper began at 7.30 p.m., in the middle of a thunder and hail storm, with the whole Parliamentarian army advancing. Neither of the Royalist leaders were ready, having assumed it was too late for a battle that day.

The Royalists, on the Moor, had the advantage of open ground. The Parliamentarians were on a slight ridge but were operating in knee-high wet and slippery rye. Between the two sides was a ditch that was so deep as to present a formidable obstacle to advancing cavalry. On the Parliamentarian left, Cromwell's forces met those of Prince Rupert. After some fighting at close quarters, the Royalists fled to the north. On the Parliamentarian right, Fairfax's men fared less well, partly as a result of having to cross the ditch. However, Fairfax's opponent, Sir George Goring, was unable to regroup his cavalry after the initial charge, so their success was not decisive. With the infantry fighting in the centre being inconclusive and all five of the main commanders missing from the battlefield for prolonged periods, it was action by Oliver Cromwell that led to Parliament's victory. He wheeled his men, who had remained in his control after the initial charge, to the position originally held by the Royalist left. They first drove the remaining Royalist cavalry from the field, then attacked their infantry. Superior discipline among Cromwell's men seems to have been the key to victory.

The battle ended at about 10 p.m. Around 4,000 Royalists, but only 300 Parliamentarians, died. Even Prince Rupert's dog, Boy, was killed. Both sides had their baggage trains plundered; Parliament had captured Prince Rupert's packhorse carrying his personal papers and private possessions.

Despite the decisive victory, Parliament did not take full advantage of the situation. The siege of York was resumed, and the city was captured on 16 July, giving Parliament control of the north. Meanwhile, the Earl of

Essex was having less success in the south-west, where over 10,000 Parliamentary troops surrendered at the battle of Lostwithiel. In Scotland, the Royalists were so successful that the Parliamentarian Scots spent most of the rest of the war regaining ground north of the border. The second battle of Newbury, on 27 October, was indecisive despite the King being heavily outnumbered. This was largely because of uncertainty about the precise aims of the war on the part of the Parliamentary commanders. The earls of Essex and Manchester, along with a significant group of MPs, were unhappy about the implications of the Scottish alliance for a religious settlement.

The proposals put to Charles in the Uxbridge Propositions included the suggestion that he take the Covenant and introduce Presbyterianism into England. Charles quickly rejected the proposals. The conflict between Parliament's military leaders, particularly the Earl of Manchester and Oliver Cromwell, over the objectives of the war, reached a climax. This led to the Ordinance to set up the New Model Army and the Self-Denying Ordinance. The reforming zeal of Cromwell and his associates had won the day, just. From this point, there was no doubt that the war could only end when one side conceded defeat.

> **1. Why did Parliament win the battle of Marston Moor?**
>
> **2. What was the significance of the victory?**

The battle of Naseby

The battle of Naseby on 14 June 1645 was the last major engagement of the First Civil War, and at last provided a vindication of Parliament's decision to raise the New Model Army. Nevertheless, in the months before the battle, the King still had room for hope. His forces were doing well in the west around Bristol, although further north Chester lay under siege. There were also good signs in Yorkshire where Prince Rupert had taken Pontefract castle after defeating the Parliamentarians at Melton Mowbray. The Scottish Royalists were also successful at this time, with a string of victories. Nevertheless, there were also signs of war-weariness. In particular, the development of the Clubmen revolts – in protest at the tax-collecting methods as much as the level of taxation – suggested that it would be difficult to extend the war much longer.

The battle of Naseby followed a series of sieges. Oxford was besieged by Parliament. Then Leicester quickly fell to the Royalists, leading Fairfax to abandon Oxford. However, the King did not retain the initiative. Goring and his cavalry left for the south-west. They failed to appear at Naseby. The northern cavalry also set off for home, although they responded to the call to battle. The King was persuaded by his more reckless advisers to engage the New Model Army, which he rudely referred to as the 'New Noddle', although he could have withdrawn westwards. It was military suicide to attack uphill against a force nearly double the size of his own.

At dawn on 14 June, the two armies were drawn up against one another about 1,200 metres apart. The King had some 8,000 men, while Parliament fielded 14,000. Each side was on a ridge with an area of marshy ground between. Parliament faced into a strong wind. The deployment of troops followed the usual pattern. On this occasion, the Royalists attacked first. While the infantry engaged in the centre of the field, Prince Rupert battered the Parliamentary left wing under Henry Ireton. Rupert's men prevailed, chasing Ireton's men to Naseby village but then became bogged down in rifling the Parliamentary baggage.

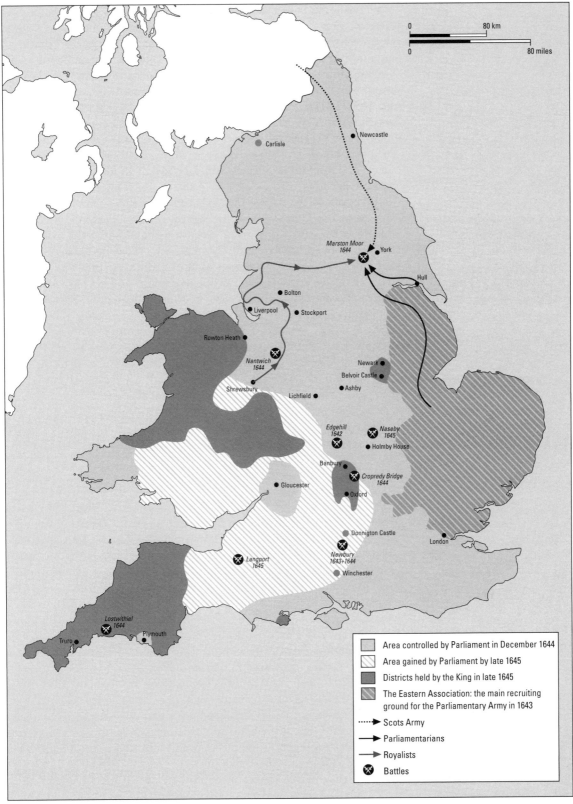

The course of the Civil War, 1644–1646

Yet again the failure of the Royalist cavalry to regroup proved critical. Prince Rupert was absent from the field for about an hour. By the time he returned the battle was lost. On the Parliamentary right, Oliver Cromwell had forced the Royalist northern cavalry from the field then turned on the King's infantry. Ireton's remaining cavalry had by now also attacked the Royalist infantry. Thousands of Royalists were captured and later paraded through London. More importantly, their baggage was seized. The King lost all his artillery, much of his arms and ammunition, many of his best infantry and his baggage carriers. From a propaganda point of view, it was the loss of his writing cabinet that proved most damaging. In it was found incriminating correspondence with the Irish Catholics, the French and even the Pope.

However, as the Earl of Manchester remarked, despite being beaten, Charles was still king and much of his cavalry remained intact. The New Model Army pursued Goring westwards, and although they were hampered by Clubman activity this was more anti-Royalist than Parliament. Ultimately, Clubmen supported the army they thought most likely to bring the war to a swift conclusion, and that was the New Model Army. In July, Goring was defeated at Langton. Bristol, under Prince Rupert, fell in September and Charles angrily relieved his nephew of his command. The Scots Royalists' success finally ended with their defeat at Philiphaugh. The last battle was at Stow-in-the-Wold in March 1646. In April, Charles left Oxford and surrendered to the Scots at Newark. The war was over, but negotiations for peace would not prove any easier just because the hostilities had ceased.

1. Why did Parliament win the battle of Naseby?

2. What was the significance of the Parliamentary victory at Naseby?

3. Why did the war not end immediately after the battle of Naseby?

8.1.5 Why did Parliament win the First Civil War?

There is no simple answer to this question based on a single cause. All the factors mentioned above had a role to play. The challenge is to devise a convincing explanation taking all of the causes into account. The weight given to factors may depend on the precise question asked. For example, an explanation of Parliament's victory requires different emphases from a consideration of the King's defeat. Historians used to concentrate on the battles themselves, regarding military victory as the key. The revision of this view was to place the stress on underlying factors, particularly what was happening in the localities. More recently, the trend has been to take a balanced approach. Yet the historian Ronald Hutton still concludes, in *Reactions to the English Civil War* (1982), that in the end it was the failure of the localities to cooperate with the King and his consequent inability to supply his armies that forced him to surrender.

Good historical explanation depends on analysis and evaluation. Establishing a range of explanatory factors is the first step. The ability to collect revenue, muster and equip an army and provide effective military leadership are obvious prerequisites of victory. Besides this, in a prolonged war maintaining support, enthusiasm and momentum by practical and propaganda means are also important.

Historians analyse causes in different ways. In the Civil War, there were some underlying factors that created the conditions in which Parliamentary victory was possible. Into this category might fall Parliament's control of the wealthy south-east of England, especially

London, along with control of the navy and the widespread fear of Roman Catholicism. The comparative weakness of the King in these respects needs to be considered. In addition, there are factors that came into play later and increased the probability of Parliamentary victory. Pym's actions during 1643 in relation to the Scots and the Westminster Assembly were significant. That the more radical party in Parliament prevailed in 1644–45 was also important in focusing Parliament on victory. Chance factors, such as the unanticipated qualities of Oliver Cromwell as a cavalry leader, are also relevant. In addition to the conditional factors, which would become significant only in the event of a protracted war, was the King's hesitation after Edgehill and his treaty with the Irish rebels. The former meant that he lost the benefit of having more experienced commanders and faced the problem of supplying his armies over a long period. The latter was significant in the context of anti-Catholicism as it antagonised not only his enemies but also many of his allies.

Having analysed the role of factors in an explanation, the next step is to evaluate their role by establishing their relative importance. Again, there are a variety of possible approaches. Some causes may seem pivotal because many other factors depended on them. Parliamentary control of the navy was significant for a number of reasons:

- preventing the King receiving supplies of arms and reinforcements

- preventing a march on London

- supplying besieged Parliamentary coastal garrisons.

It is also worth asking if a factor is necessary to the explanation. One way of determining this is to speculate about what would have happened if a particular event or action had *not* taken place. Useful examples to consider would be whether Parliament could have won without the Scots – thus testing the importance of Pym's contribution – or without Oliver Cromwell as Lieutenant General of the Horse in the New Model Army at Naseby.

It is also worth considering how contemporaries viewed the situation. After all, the King did not surrender until well after the battle of Naseby, and historians can understand or at least explain his optimism until late on in the war. This makes it difficult to disagree with the conclusion that war-weariness, as manifested in the Clubman revolts, was critical in the King's defeat. However, this factor depended on the King's inability to raise adequate revenue to finance his war efforts. Equally, Parliament's access to the greater wealth of the south-east of England is not sufficient to explain their victory since it was irrelevant at the beginning of the war. Thus the King's decision to fall back on Oxford after Edgehill, rather than proceed immediately to London, is also necessary if the outcome is to be explained satisfactorily.

1. What reasons have been suggested for Parliament's victory in the First Civil War?

2. What do you consider to be the most important reason for Parliament's victory? Explain your answer.

8.1.6 *How and why did radical ideas and groups develop?*
A CASE STUDY IN HISTORICAL INTERPRETATION

One of the most interesting developments during the Civil War period was the emergence of a number of radical sects and groups of both religious and political persuasion. The leaders were often educated and from the lower gentry but most of those involved came from the lower classes, although not the very bottom rungs of society. Relatively little is known about them and this has given rise to much debate and even speculation among historians in their efforts to explain how these radical groups developed.

Historians such as H. Shaw, in *The Levellers* (1973), emphasise the social and economic conditions of the period as factors causing this development. They feel these conditions blocked upward mobility for those at the level of copyholder in rural areas and craftsmen in the towns. The dislocation of the economy caused by war, along with a series of poor harvests beginning in 1646, increased the frustration felt by these groups. This caused them to come up with radical solutions.

What is certain is that the Reformation had encouraged some people to interpret the Bible for themselves. The particular pattern followed by the English Reformation led to impatience with the slow pace of reform, especially regarding the organisation of the Church. Nevertheless, **Separatism** was not widespread in pre-Civil-War England. The Laudian reforms of the 1630s forced many who had previously accepted the Church of England into open defiance. According to F.D. Dow, in *Radicalism in the English Revolution* (1989), the subsequent abolition of the Court of High Commission in 1641 opened the floodgates. Although Parliament attempted to re-impose censorship from 1643, the circumstances of the war impeded progress. The existence of a wide range of ideas encouraged demands for toleration, if only in self-interest. This, in itself, amounted to a radical political solution at variance with the disciplined national church advocated by the Assembly of Divines.

In the years following the outbreak of civil war, **Congregationalism** and the Baptist sect both developed. As a natural development of Puritanism, it is difficult to differentiate the followers of Congregationalism from those of the mainstream national church. Some of its ministers, for example, continued as parish clergy until the Restoration. **Baptists** were more easily distinguished from the norm. A distinction should be made between General Baptists, who believed in a universal salvation, and Particular Baptists, who believed that salvation was only available to the true believer. The former were in danger of being associated with the Anabaptists of the 1530s. The Confession of 1644, issued by the seven London churches, indicated the need felt by Particular Baptists to establish a form of organisation and discipline within a movement which grew significantly during the civil war years. Separatism was centred in London where, by 1646, there were perhaps three dozen separate Churches with several thousand followers.

The situation during the Civil War also encouraged those who advocated lay participation in Church decision making. Indeed, the Assembly of Divines included 30 laymen, as well as 120 clergy. Later in the period, some radical religious sects went one step further, giving equal say and status to women.

Separatism: Complete separation from the Church of England. Separatist groups emerged in the reign of Elizabeth I, but had largely disappeared by 1640.

Congregationalism: Like Presbyterianism but advocated greater independence for individual churches.

Baptists: They believed in the baptism of believers – the ceremony taking place when a person was old enough to make a conscious decision to accept Christ's grace – rather than in indiscriminate infant baptism.

Millenarianism: The belief, based on the Book of Revelation in the Bible, that the second coming of Christ would be a prelude to his 1,000-year rule on Earth. Some millenarians interpreted the events of the 1640s to indicate that this event was imminent and would occur in England.

Fifth Monarchists: A radical religious group who believed that the second coming of Christ was about to occur.

They based their ideas on the prophesy of Nebuchadnezzar's dream that 'the fifth monarchy' of Christ's Kingdom on earth would come about after the collapse of four other kingdoms. Thomas Venner was the leader of the militant Fifth Monarchists. In their rising in 1661, he and about 50 others held off the London-trained bands for 4 days before their defeat. Venner and 10 others were executed in 1661.

Seekers: A broad term referring to those who were seeking the truth about religion. They had often rejected the established Church, seeking the truth through revelation from the Holy Spirit as well as, or instead of, through study of the Bible. They were, consequently, receptive to Quaker ideas.

Quaker movement: A group of religious radicals who taught that the voice of

the Holy Spirit, speaking to individuals, represented the ultimate religious authority. Quakers believed all were equal before God and, consequently, refused to behave deferentially to their social betters. They objected to the established Church and so refused to pay tithes. They were persecuted, particularly after the Restoration, because of these subversive ideas. (See section 8.2.)

Of all the radical religious ideas, **millenarianism** (see panel) flourished most widely. Millenarianism had been strong for some time, particularly since the Reformation, but again the insecurity engendered by civil war meant that it made a greater impact at this time. Many people held millenarian ideas; some took the idea so seriously that, after the execution of Charles I, they rejected earthly monarchy altogether, looking only for signs of the reign of King Jesus. These were the **Fifth Monarchists** (see panel). Uncertainty is also important in explaining why so many religious radicals could be described as '**Seekers** of the Truth'. Their as yet unfulfilled quest was to be a significant factor in the spread of the **Quaker** movement in the next decade.

The background of the Reformation and developments before and during the First Civil War make it unsurprising that religious radicalism should flourish. However, political radicalism also began to take hold during the Civil War. The historian Glenn Burgess, in *The Impact of the English Civil War* (1991), traces its origins to the 'Calvinist theory of resistance'. This justified the resistance of lesser magistrates (in England, the MPs) to a tyrannical ruler (Charles I). The tactics used by the Long Parliament had widened political debate to the lower orders. Radical thinkers developed the resistance idea and made demands for individual rights.

The study of classical civilisations and their political ideas also influenced the better educated to question accepted forms of government. It is apparent that the Parliamentarian approach to the constitution encouraged the concept of **natural rights**. Lawyers such as John Selden, seeking to establish a legal basis for the 'ancient constitution', argued that it rested largely on customary rights including 'the ancient law of freedom'. Although it has proved impossible to trace direct links from 14th-century **Lollard** heresy, the idea of equating equality before God with social and economic equality is evident in mid-17th-century **radicalism**.

The New Model Army, with its emphasis on promotion for the able regardless of social origin and its high level of physical mobility, soon gained a reputation for spreading radical ideas. Many officers were supportive of soldiers who were accused of unlicensed preaching. Uncertainty among local magistrates added to the possibility that this would go unchecked. The historian Mark Kishlansky, in *Reactions to the*

Natural rights: Rights possessed by all men regardless of, and having priority over, any man-made laws.

Lollard: A follower of John Wycliffe (1320–1384), a heretic. As well as criticising the Roman Catholic Church, Lollards showed that they regarded the social hierarchy as unbiblical – most famously in their rhyme 'When Adam delved and Eve span, who was then the gentleman?'

Radicalism: The principle of thorough reform of religious or political institutions.

Agitators: Representatives of the ordinary soldiers who were elected, in April 1647, to a council to discuss political grievances with their officers.

'Representation of the Army': Written by Henry Ireton (1611–1651), this document put forward the ideas of the Army about how England should be ruled. It included suggestions for reform of Parliament and the Church and justification for the Army's political response: 'We are not a mere mercenary army.'

Putney Debates: Discussion among members of the Army Council including the grandees and agitators. It was held in Putney Church in October–November 1647. The debates centred round Leveller ideas as expressed in the first '**Agreement of the People**'.

'Agreement of the People': A set of constitutional ideas drawn up by the Agitators and Levellers in October 1647 and debated at Putney.

English Civil War (1982), challenges the idea that the New Model Army had a political programme before Parliament's attempt to disband it in February 1647. However, the speed with which the Army responded and the way in which it did so, electing **agitators** to a council and producing the '**Representation of the Army**', suggests that the Army was ripe for radical ideas. During the search for a settlement with the King, the **Putney Debates** show that some members of the Army Council were willing to contemplate very radical solutions indeed.

How have historians explained the development of radicalism?

Until the second half of the 20th century these radical groups were not the subject of historical research. Constitutional historians of the 19th century, such as T.B. Macaulay in *History*, sought mainly to explain the development of Britain's parliamentary system. To them, the Levellers were of some significance, promoting and justifying the extension of the franchise. However, Levellers were not studied for their own sake.

By the early 20th century some historians, including R.H. Tawney in *Religion and the Rise of Capitalism* (1926), were investigating the socio-intellectual background of the English Revolution, establishing links between Protestantism and major economic developments. However, this and the debate that followed, concerning the 'rise of the gentry', were still concerned with the upper echelons of society. It was, rather, the work of economic historians such as Joan Thirsk in *Agrarian History of England and Wales* (vol. IV, 1967) that provided evidence on which to base theories about the development of radicalism.

In the 1950s, A.G. Dickens investigated the origins of the English Reformation, at first in the York Diocese (*Lollards and Protestants in the Diocese of York, 1509–1559*, published in 1959) then extending to the country as a whole (*The English Reformation*, 1964). He traced challenges to the Roman Catholic Church, of the sort later manifest in Protestantism, to the Lollard heresy of the 14th century. It was such challenges to established religion that some historians claimed to be the forerunners of mid-17th-century radicalism. The work of Keith Thomas, starting with *Religion and the Decline of Magic* published in 1971, established the existence of a tradition of superstition and of disrespect towards the established church. These studies, like those of Tawney, provided an insight into the origins of radicalism.

In the 1930s, Christopher Hill had begun investigating the 17th century from a Marxist perspective. Initially, he too was concerned with the constitutional revolution, but recognition of the origins of more modern ideas and ideals in the other, unsuccessful English Revolution of the mid-17th century, led to a study of this phenomenon in its own right. In 1972, Hill published *The World Turned Upside Down*. Thereafter, debate has centred on the strengths and weaknesses of his central thesis. Hill argues that long-term social and economic trends encouraged the breakdown of the feudal ties of obligation and obedience and the existence of a greater proportion of wage-earners. This led to an increase in the numbers of masterless men. This, he claims, created the conditions in which radicalism became a possibility. Hill even identifies class antagonism as a characteristic of pre-Civil War disputes. He demonstrates that the particular circumstances of the 1640s built on the pre-existing conditions to make the development of radicalism more likely. Besides the use of the

The Leveller leaders: a case study

The most well-known political radicals of the period were the Levellers. It was this group which apparently influenced the Army and produced the 'Agreement of the People' that was debated by the Army Council at Putney in October 1647. A consideration of the backgrounds of leaders such as John Lilburne, William Walwyn and Richard Overton can be used to throw light on the origins of radicalism in general.

John Lilburne (1614–1657)

A native of county Durham who moved to London in about 1630 as an apprentice to a cloth merchant. There he attended Sunday morning prayer and Bible study meetings and was associated with the Baptists, among the most numerous of the nonconformist sects. He was clearly affected by the case of Burton, Prynne and Bastwick, because in 1638 Lilburne appeared before the Court of Star Chamber, accused of having illegally helped to publish and import a pamphlet written by Bastwick. What is more significant is Lilburne's attitude towards the Court. When placed in the **pillory**, as part of his punishment, he had to be gagged to stop him holding forth on his rights as a freeborn Englishman, which in his opinion gave him freedom of both speech and religion. He followed this up with at least four pamphlets on the subject while imprisoned in the Fleet. In 1642, he enlisted in the regiment of Lord Brooke, a known champion of religious toleration. In 1644, he refused to swear to the Solemn League and Covenant because it committed Parliament to a presbyterian church settlement. He then retired from the army.

In the interim, he was captured after the battle of Edgehill and brought before a royal court on a charge of treason. Again, he challenged the right of the court to try him, this time using language that brought his sanity into doubt and thereby possibly saving his life. He then returned to London where he came into contact with Walwyn and Overton. He was in conflict with Parliament when he was accused of slandering the Speaker and was brought before a parliamentary committee to answer charges. Again he challenged their right to try him, basing his arguments on infringement of his rights as stated in the Magna Carta. His troubles continued when he was summoned before the Lords for making remarks about the Earl of Manchester. Again he stood up for his rights, for which he was imprisoned in the Tower. These events provided the opportunity for Lilburne to promote his ideas in the pamphlet 'England's Birthright Justified'. His wife and associates publicised his cause and formulated the Leveller programme of **popular sovereignty** and individual rights.

William Walwyn (1600–1680)

A man of very different origins. His main role in Levellerism was to contribute ideas. He came from a prosperous family and after a classical and humanist education he was apprenticed in London and became a Merchant Adventurer. From his background in humanist reason he developed a range of ideas. He rejected predestination and believed in the right of laymen to preach and in religious toleration. He concentrated on the concept of God's love, reaching the conclusion that human compassion should extend to care of the poor and unemployed. He took his ideas on social responsibility even further, suggesting that the aims should be to remove poverty and eliminate economic inequality.

Richard Overton (active 1642–1663)

Less is known of Richard Overton, although it is clear that he had sufficient education to enable him to argue in a disciplined way. His main role in the Leveller movement was as a propagandist. He is first heard of in 1641, publishing pamphlets attacking Archbishop Laud and the bishops. In fact, he held dangerous religious ideas, denying the immortality of the soul and coming close to atheism. Certainly, he attacked the clergy in general and the payment of tithes to them, favouring complete religious toleration. In 1646, together with Walwyn, he published the 'Remonstrance of Many Thousand Citizens' demanding the abolition of the monarchy and a representative parliament based on a wide franchise as well as individual rights.

> What does an examination of the early careers of the Leveller leaders suggest about the origins of political radicalism?

Pillory: A wooden frame with holes through which head and hands were placed as a punishment.

Popular sovereignty: Power lying with the people.

London mob by Pym and the opportunities offered by the collapse of censorship in 1641, Hill focuses on the New Model Army as a group of wandering, masterless men. The Army, he suggests, provided the catalyst for the Levellers to gain influence. The economic hardship generated by disruption of trade during the war, and added to by the poor harvests of 1647–49, ensured a pool of discontented disciples for the extremists.

Hill offers a plausible explanation for the appearance of a range of radical groups, both religious and political, but does it reflect reality? Much research on individual groups of radicals has been undertaken since 1972. To some extent the existence of long-term causes has been challenged. Gerald Aylmer's *The Levellers in the English Revolution* (1974), while acknowledging their intellectual origins in the Renaissance and Puritanism, stresses that the particular circumstances of 1644–46 enabled the Levellers to come to the fore. In *The Impact of the English Civil War* (1991), Glenn Burgess traces the radical style of rhetoric back as far as Parliamentarian propaganda of the early 1640s. Derek Hirst's *England in Conflict, 1603–1660* (1999) claims that Leveller prominence was down to Lilburne's egocentric genius.

There have also been studies that demonstrate that participation in politics extended below the traditional ruling élite well before the 1640s. In *The Representation of the People? Voters and Voting in England under the Early Stuarts* (1975), Hirst showed this in relation to the franchise, calculating that between 27% and 40% of adult males were eligible to vote in early Stuart England. Between 1985 and 1995, research has shown an overlap between popular and élite culture. In the early 1980s, on the basis of regional studies, Buchanan Sharp (*In Contempt of All Authority: Rural Artisans and Riots in the West of England 1586–1660*, 1980) and Keith Lindley (*Fenland Riots and the English Revolution*, 1982) traced the origins of popular unrest to local rather than national issues.

Some historians, such as Mark Kishlansky, are still engaged on a study of the English Revolution from the point of view of what happened at Westminster. Many others look at the past from what Hill has called 'the worm's eye view', investigating the response of ordinary people to the extraordinary times in which they lived. The scope is great. As Hill points out in *The World Turned Upside Down* (1972), 'Each generation rescues a new area from what its predecessors arrogantly and snobbishly dismissed as "the lunatic fringe".' He and his followers are undaunted by attacks from historians such as Mark Kishlansky on the grounds that 'nothing has done more to diminish the centrality of the English Revolution that did occur'.

Kishlansky, writing about the New Model Army in *Reactions to the English Revolution* (1982), refutes Hill's thesis that the New Model Army comprised masterless and therefore radical individuals. Firstly, the social origins of the New Model Army's officers had already been shown to be more diverse and higher than was previously suggested. Secondly, Kishlansky rejects the idea of social determinism, the assumption that masterless forest dwellers and fenlanders would necessarily react against authority and discipline when they encountered it and that those who possessed little would automatically subscribe to egalitarian theories.

Like many other areas of historical debate about the English Revolution, historians of opposing political persuasions generate the differing theses. At present there is no sign of any synthesis of the two schools of thought on the origins or indeed the significance of radicalism.

1. How can the different views of historians concerning the origins and place of radicalism be explained?

2. Which theory do you find most convincing?

3. What do you consider to be the most important cause of the growth of radicalism at this time? Explain your answer.

8.1.7 Why was the search for a settlement unsuccessful?

Over the years, many sets of peace proposals were put to Charles I by Parliament. He rejected them all. This makes it tempting to blame the King for the failure to reach a settlement. His character meant it was hard for him to negotiate. His belief in the divine right of kings made it impossible for him to accept either the implicit admission of his guilt or limitations on his power, such as the restriction on his right to bestow mercy denoted by the lists of war criminals. This, however, over-simplifies matters. After all, Charles made significant concessions to Parliament in 1640–41 and surely his position was even weaker now. Assuming that he was not aiming to become a martyr, this is not how Charles perceived the situation. Firstly, he failed to recognise that his position was weaker than it had been before the civil war commenced. Secondly, it was apparent to the King that his opponents were not united in their quest for a settlement. During the war, there had been clear signs of division, manifested in the debates of the winter of 1644–45. It must have seemed to Charles that the longer he prevaricated, the more likely it would be that his opponents would break rank, thus enabling him to reach a more advantageous settlement.

If Charles was counting on disunity among his opponents, then it is important to identify the reasons for these divisions. Parliament had made Charles a number of propositions (see table on page 263) before and during the war. After his surrender, they were adapted to become the Newcastle Propositions. The only substantial difference between June 1642 and July 1646 lies in the religious settlement proposed. This can be attributed to the signing of the Solemn League and Covenant. The problem now lay in the process of negotiation, carrying with it the implication of compromise. The majority in Parliament might be willing to step down from the harsh terms dictated in the proposals, but its soldiers had fought the war and had taken seriously the cause for which they risked their lives. Nine months after the Newcastle Propositions were put to him, Charles's third reply, in May 1647, indicated a willingness to compromise on matters relating to church and the military. By then, it was too late. The Army's suspicions about Parliament's intentions had been roused and a new dimension added to the equation.

Why did the Army become politicised?

In August 1647, the Army put forward to Charles peace terms known as the 'Heads of the Proposals'. They were in many respects more lenient than those offered by Parliament. The radical clauses lay in the religious settlement, which demanded toleration for all Protestants by denying the right of church authorities to compel and in the demands for a reformed Parliament. Religious differences lay at the root of the political division between Parliament and Army. However, they do not explain why the Army – the servant of Parliament – took it upon itself to seize the King and devise its own peace proposals. In the spring of 1647, Parliament proposed to disband the Army. It was expensive to maintain and surplus to requirements other than in Ireland. Unfortunately, Parliament failed to take account of the material concerns of the soldiers. Their pay was in arrears, in the case of the cavalry regiments by 43 weeks. Besides this, the soldiers wanted guarantees of indemnity from prosecution for actions carried out during the war. Some of the soldiers were to be sent to Ireland. How were they to be supplied and paid? At this stage, the only political element lay in the impression of some of the soldiers that they had fought for religious toleration, an element clearly missing from Parliament's peace proposals.

Faced with Parliament's failure to respond to their concerns, the Army took action. Months of military inactivity allowed Leveller ideas to prevail in some regiments. Agitators started to reveal the radical concepts now current in the Army. They referred to their liberties and freedoms, and to their rights as freeborn citizens which they claimed were denied them. Fairfax was told to bring the Army under control, while Henry Ireton formulated the Army's position. The Army Council, set up in June, balanced Agitators with officers. The 'Solemn Engagement' was agreed. Cornet Joyce's seizure of the King made it clear that a settlement involving the monarch was envisaged at this stage. It also gave the Army the initiative. A complex sequence of events ensued, in which the Army intimidated Presbyterian MPs. Independent MPs then fled Westminster while the Presbyterians returned, and finally the Army restored the Independents. The King, emboldened by his apparent indispensability, showed preference for the Army proposals as they would allow a separate settlement with each of his three kingdoms. However, by this time, Colonel Rainsborough had already concluded that further negotiation with the King was useless.

'Solemn Engagement': Adopted unanimously by the Army at the mutinous meeting at Newmarket on 29 May 1647, in response to Parliament's threat to disband them. It stated that the army would resist disbandment until the Army Council had negotiated satisfactory terms.

The General Council of the Army, presided over by Fairfax, 1647.

What does the difference in size between Fairfax (centre) and the other members of the Council suggest?

The terms of the peace proposals put to the King

	Nineteen Propositions (June 1642)	Oxford Propositions (February 1643)	Uxbridge Propositions (January 1645)	Newcastle Propositions (July 1646)	Heads of the Proposals (presented to King, 28 July; approved by Army, 1 August 1647)	Four Bills (December 1647)
Parliament	Triennial Act stands	Triennial Act stands	Triennial Act stands	Triennial Act stands; King's legislative veto limited	Biennial Parliaments: apart from its guarantees, the Triennial Act to be repealed. Greater equality in distribution of seats.	Triennial Act stands; King's legislative veto limited
Privy Council	Parliament to approve 15–25 members					
Officers of State	Parliament to approve 16 specified officers	Parliament to nominate 13 officers	Parliament to nominate 13 officers	Parliament to nominate 13 officers	Parliament to nominate for 10 years	
Militia	King to accept Militia Ordinance	King to settle, with Parliament's advice	To be settled by Commissioners named by Parliament	Parliament to control for 20 years	Parliament to control for 10 years	Parliament to control for 20 years
Church government	Reformed with Parliament's advice	Bishops abolished; Assembly of Divines to reform church	Bishops abolished; King to accept Solemn League and Covenant; reforms advised by Westminster Assembly	Bishops abolished; Presbyterian Church for 3 years	Bishops could not force; Covenant (i.e. Presbyterian Church) could not be forced on anyone	Bishops abolished; Presbyterian Church for 3 years, but freedom of worship for Protestants
Catholics	Existing laws to be enforced strictly	Existing laws to be enforced strictly	Existing laws to be enforced strictly, especially at Court	Existing laws to be enforced	Existing laws to be repealed and new ones passed	Existing laws to be enforced and extended to Ireland
Royalists not to be pardoned		2	Over 100: 58 named along with various rebels	38 named; list open-ended	5	7 named, along with various categories of rebels and traitors
Dismissals from office		2 for life	48 for life	48 for life	Parliament's enemies for 5 years	48 for life

Grandee: A senior officer in the New Model Army.

'Engagement': A secret agreement drawn up between Charles I and the Scots. The Scots would help Charles regain his status as king in return for a union of the two kingdoms and assurance that Charles would introduce Presbyterianism for a trial period of 3 years.

1. **Explain how and why the Army became a political force.**

2. **What was the significance of the politicisation of the Army in the search for a settlement with the King?**

The most radical stage of the proceedings then occurred. Leveller influence was at its height. The Army held the King, who preferred its proposals, and it had occupied Westminster. But the Army was not united in its aims. Suspicion of Oliver Cromwell's negotiations as both **Grandee** and MP, as well as the arrival of Scottish Commissioners to speak with the King, brought matters to a head. At Putney Church, the Army Council debated new and radical proposals contained in the 'Agreement of the People'. Records of the debates provide historians with a fascinating insight into the extent to which radical thinking had developed. But the discussion was relevant to the course of events only in as much as it convinced the Grandees of the need to regain the initiative.

The Army Council was dispersed and the rendezvous at Ware provided the Grandees with the excuse to re-impose discipline. Interpreting the actions of some soldiers who arrived without their officers as mutiny, they court-martialled the ringleaders. The unfortunate Richard Arnold was chosen by lot to undergo his sentence on the spot. The remaining two meetings occurred without incident. The civilian Leveller leaders petitioned Parliament but were arrested. The Grandees used the opportunity provided by the decision to reduce the army by 50% in January–February 1648 to undertake a political purge of the most radical regiments.

However, by this time the King had shown his complete disregard for the process of negotiation. His escape to the Isle of Wight, the offer of peace proposals and his protracted consideration of the Four Bills based on them, all revealed him to be playing for time while he negotiated the 'Engagement' with the Scots. Reacting to his negative response to the Four Bills, as well as to news of the 'Engagement', Parliament voted that no further addresses be made to Charles. This was a less radical solution than impeachment and the imposition of a settlement without reference to the King, as proposed by Oliver Cromwell.

8.1.8 Why was the King executed?

The Second Civil War, deliberately instigated by the King, marked the point of no return for the Army. At the Windsor Prayer Meeting of April 1648, first mention is made of Charles Stuart 'that man of blood'. The Army increasingly regarded itself as the instrument of God's providence in dealing with Charles, whom they interpreted to be the Antichrist ignoring God's will. From a military point of view, the war was relatively insignificant. Uprisings in England were poorly coordinated in relation to the Scottish invasion, although Royalist support was stronger than Fairfax had anticipated. However, by September when the war was over, a political solution had still to be found. Despite the Vote of No Addresses, Parliament could not envisage a settlement without the King and sent commissioners to negotiate with him on the Isle of Wight. The Army leaders were, by now, clear that Charles had abdicated his right to rule and demanded that he be put on trial.

When Parliament voted, on 5 December, that indications given to its commissioners suggested that there was scope to re-open negotiations, the Army acted. The following day, Colonel Pride's regiment stood outside the House with a list of MPs who were to be arrested. Many others were to be prevented from entering the House. When MPs got

Pride's Purge: On 6 December 1648, following Parliament's vote that there were grounds for continuing negotiations with the King, Colonel Pride's regiment excluded from Parliament all those whom they regarded as sympathetic to the King. This left a 'rump' of those who, subsequently, voted to place the King on trial for treason.

1. How important were Charles I's actions in bringing about his trial and execution?

2. How important was the Second Civil War in causing the trial and execution of Charles I?

3. 'Without the politicisation of the Army there would have been no trial and execution.' How far do you agree?

wind of the events, many stayed away or fled. Those admitted, either on 6 December or in the few days after the event, became known as the Rump. This small group of 71 MPs could certainly not claim to represent the people of England. It simply reflected the view of the Army, a minority opinion. Hence it is legitimate to regard **Pride's Purge** as a military coup.

Oliver Cromwell was admitted to the Rump, but his initial attitude to the King has been the subject of debate. On 23 December 1648, he allegedly made a final attempt to compromise with Charles without any strings attached. However, by late December he had set aside any misgivings and was encouraging the House of Commons to put Charles on trial. Once the decision had been made to do so, in early January 1649, the outcome was manipulated to such an extent as to be a foregone conclusion. When the Lords rejected the Ordinance to set up a High Court of Justice to try the King, the Commons assumed sole legislative authority. The Commons appointed judges whom they supposed would be against the King and during the trial Charles was sent away when he challenged the right of the court to try him. After the court found him guilty, it is alleged that Cromwell forced several of the judges to sign the death warrant. However, other sources, such as Lucy Hutchinson in her *Memoirs of the Life of Colonel Hutchinson* (1671), deny that this happened. The execution on 30 January was public but was carefully stage-managed to avoid trouble. Having taken such a dangerous step, those who were now in charge had to remain so if they were to avoid being condemned as traitors.

Did the trial and execution of Charles I amount to a revolution?

In order to answer this question some consideration must be given to the meaning of the term 'revolution'. To scientists, and indeed to people in the 17th century, its meaning lies in turning a full circle and hence returning to the starting point. For historians, the definition is more complex. The term denotes some far-reaching change that has long-lasting implications, but how far reaching and how long lasting would be open to debate. For **Marxist historians**, the term has a more specific meaning: revolution being the means by which society is transformed suddenly and violently from one form of organisation or government to another, marking the transition from the dominance of one class to that of another.

Marxist historians: Historians who interpret the past on the basis of the writings of Karl Marx (1818–1883). He regarded all history as the story of class struggle through which each country follows an inevitable series of stages, leading to Communism.

As the only occasion in English history when a monarch was publicly tried and executed, the events of December 1648–January 1649 are of great interest. The contemporary significance is also undeniable. Besides the King, many of the traditional ruling élite were excluded from government either by choice or forcibly. Subsequently, for the only time in its history, England was ruled as a **republican commonwealth**. Yet the historical significance, the basis on which the claim to revolution should be judged, is far from clear. The monarchy was restored 11 years later with many of its powers intact. This is not to say that monarchs after that time could afford to forget the lessons of 1648–49. Contractual theories of government being explored in the mid-century were more fully formed by 1689 and were used by Parliament to justify the so-called 'Glorious Revolution'. Above all, the experience of civil war seems to have influenced the behaviour of those in the ruling élite deeply, causing them to close ranks so that cooperation rather than conflict

Republican commonwealth: A government by the people, without a king, for the benefit of the people.

'Military coup' or 'revolution'? Which is the better description of the events of December 1648–January 1649?

became the means for constitutional development in England. However, beyond the upper level of society the impact of mid-century events was far less profound. Religious diversification was to be a permanent feature of society, soon to be accepted in law, but social and political relationships changed gradually and indirectly as a result of the political upheaval of the 1640s and 1650s.

Source-based questions: Why was King Charles I executed?

SOURCE A

The King being at the Isle of Wight, the Parliament sent him some propositions to be consented to in order for his restoration. The King granted many of them and some he granted not. The chiefest thing which the King stuck at was the utter abolishing of Episcopacy. Archbishop Usher there took the rightest course, who offered the King his reduction of Episcopacy to the form of the Presbytery. And he told me himself that before the King had refused it, but at the Isle of Wight he accepted it.

From The Autobiography of Richard Baxter, *published in 1696, edited by N.H. Keeble*

SOURCE B

The question in dispute between the King's party and us was 'Whether the King should govern as a god by his will, and the nation be governed by force like beasts: or whether the people should be governed by laws made by themselves, and live under a government derived from their own consent.' Some of the commissioners who had been with the King pleaded in the House for an agreement with him, as if they had been employed by him; the others with more ingenuity acknowledged that they would not advise an agreement upon those terms, were it to prevent a greater evil that was like to ensue upon the refusal of them.

From The Memoirs of Edmund Ludlow *(1698) Vol.1 edited by C.H. Firth*

SOURCE C

That the said Charles Stuart, being admitted King of England, and therein trusted with a limited power to govern by and according to the laws of the land; yet, out of a wicked design to erect and uphold in himself an unlimited and tyrannical power to rule according to his will, and to overthrow the rights and liberties of the people, hath traitorously and maliciously levied war against the present Parliament and the people therein represented. And for the further prosecution of his said evil designs he doth still continue his commissions to the Earl of Ormond and the Irish rebels and revolters associated with him. By all which appeareth that the said Charles Stuart hath been, and is guilty of all the treasons, murders, rapines, burnings and mischiefs to this nation, acted and committed in the said wars, or occasioned thereby.

From the charge of treason against the King, 20 January 1649

---

1. With reference to Sources B and C, and to information contained within this chapter, explain the meaning of the two phrases highlighted in the sources:

a) 'the King should govern as a god' (Source B)

b) 'his commissions to the Earl of Ormond and the Irish rebels and revolters' (Source C).

2. Study Sources A and B.

Compare the opinions in these sources about the main problems faced in negotiating an agreement between King and Parliament.

3. Using all three sources and your knowledge of the period, explain why Charles I was executed.

8.2 The Interregnum, 1649–1660

Key Issues

- Why was there no stable political settlement in the years 1649–1660?

- What were the successes and achievements of Republican government?

- What is the historical significance of the Interregnum?

Framework of Events

1649	February: Council of State
	March: abolition of Monarchy and House of Lords
	May: Commonwealth, Burford
	September: Commonwealth, Drogheda
	October: Commonwealth, Wexford
1650	Adultery Act; Blasphemy Act; Dunbar
1651	Worcester; Navigation Act
1652	Dutch War begins
1653	April: dissolution of Rump
	July: Nominated Assembly
	December: Instrument of Government
1654	End of Dutch war; Act of Union with Scotland; First Protectorate Parliament
1655	Penruddock's Rising; capture of Jamaica; Rule of the Major Generals begins
1656	Second Protectorate Parliament; debate on James Nayler's case
1657	Sindercombe's plot; end of rule of Major-Generals; Humble Petition and Advice
1658	3 September: death of Oliver Cromwell; Richard becomes Lord Protector
1659	Third Protectorate Parliament meets
	May: Army recalls Rump, Richard Cromwell retires into private life
	August: Booth's rising
	October: Army stops Rump meeting; Committee of Safety
	December: Fleetwood recalls Rump
1660	February: Monck's army crosses Scottish border and arrives in London
	March: secluded members readmitted to Rump; Long Parliament dissolves itself
	April: Convention Parliament opens; Declaration of Breda
	May: Restoration of monarchy; landing of Charles II at Dover.

Overview

Interregnum: Literally, 'between reigns' – the period in English history when England was a republic, 1649–60.

As the only period of republican government in England's history, the **Interregnum** has been the subject of extensive study and great debate among historians. The King had been executed and the monarchy abolished but those who had carried out these actions had no clear plan of what was to replace monarchic government. After a period of turmoil and uncertainty, the ruling élite looked for security and settlement. The radical groups that had emerged during the Civil War period sought fundamental changes in the political and religious rights of the people, while firm supporters of monarchy never accepted the new government. In addition, members of the ruling élite were not united in their ideas about how to achieve their goals. The role of the Army and the extent of its influence on government was hotly contended at the time and has been argued over by historians. Equally controversial have been questions regarding the nature and style of Oliver Cromwell's rule as **Lord Protector** from December 1653 until his death in September 1658. While many historians recognise paradoxes in Cromwell's behaviour, which they seek to explain, others – most recently J.C. Davis, in *Oliver Cromwell* (2001) – claim that when Cromwell's motives are properly understood, his actions are perfectly consistent with them.

Lord Protector: The title used for a non-royal head of state. The name was originally used for the person ruling in place of a monarch who was a minor.

The fact that the Interregnum lasted only 11 years and ended with the restoration of the Stuart monarchy in the person of Charles II (son of the executed King Charles I), might lead to the conclusion that the Interregnum had little impact on the development of the English constitution. However, examination of the Restoration Settlement shows that, in both political and religious terms, the events of the previous 20 years could not be ignored. In concentrating on the failure of the Interregnum there is the danger of regarding restoration of the monarchy as inevitable. Yet government functioned reasonably effectively until the final months of the Interregnum; so there is no simple explanation for the failure of republican government.

8.2.1 What did the Rump achieve?

When Charles I was executed, all that remained of the Long Parliament was its Rump, that is, those 71 MPs who had survived Pride's Purge on 6 December 1648 and had chosen to remain in the House of Commons during the revolutionary events of December 1648–January 1649. Forty-three of them had signed the king's death warrant. In addition, a further 83 MPs resumed their seats in the following few months of constitutional debate. Altogether, 211 members sat at various times between January 1649 and April 1653, when Oliver Cromwell and the Army forcibly dissolved the Rump.

The Rump's first task was to establish who was to rule the country and under what conditions. The framework of government was debated in February and legally established between March and May of 1649. Despite the misgivings of some, including Oliver Cromwell, no alternative was found but to abolish the monarchy and the House of Lords. The new government, declared to be a **commonwealth**, consisted of an executive, the Council of State and a parliament. The Council was composed of 41

Commonwealth: A nation or state composed of people who have similar political interests.

members, of whom 34 were MPs and 5 were peers. The Rump excluded the most radical army officers from the Council. The Council began to meet in February 1649. It was elected for one year only and was subject to scrutiny by the Rump, which did not stop meeting as it had yet to vote for its dissolution. In effect, Parliament was the executive, as well as the legislative, power within the country because of the overlap of personnel.

The type of government that was established was conservative, despite the abolition of monarchy. The **franchise** was not extended and the Council of State was appointed not elected. The Levellers had hoped that the new constitution might be influenced by the 'Agreement of the People' (see page 259). It was not, and when Lilburne and three other Leveller leaders attacked Parliament in the pamphlets 'England's New Chains Discovered', they were imprisoned in the Tower of London despite their valid claim that this was in breach of their rights. The subsequent mutinies in the Army, to some extent Leveller-inspired, presented Cromwell with the opportunity to eliminate Leveller influence in that institution by having the mutineer leaders shot.

Having established itself, the new government could begin to deal with other pressing issues. These included the need to suppress the continuing rebellions in Ireland and Scotland, and to defend England from the attempt by Charles Stuart, eldest son of Charles I, to invade and seize his crown. These concerns, as well as the Dutch War that began in 1652, had implications for the role of the army and navy. They required an unacceptably high level of taxation. The need for a religious settlement was clear, although the solution was not. Many radicals hoped that the new government would take the opportunity to reform the legal system and end fiscal and economic policies that benefited the rich at the expense of the poor. While the Rump was successful in defending England and subduing the Irish, other policies met with less approval, especially in the eyes of Oliver Cromwell and the Army.

What did the Rump achieve in Ireland and Scotland?

Ireland had been in rebellion since October 1641. As a mainly Catholic country whose men had fought for the King during the first Civil War, it posed an important challenge to the Rump and all it stood for. The response was to appoint Oliver Cromwell Lord Lieutenant of Ireland and to hope that the Army could be as successful against the Irish as it had proved to be against the King. In May 1650, Cromwell returned to England, his work mostly accomplished as a result of the superior training and more secure supply system of the English army. In the course of this campaign, that consisted largely of sieges, occurred the controversial **massacres** at Drogheda and Wexford. As a result of the English victory, land was redistributed in Ireland, with the Catholic share being reduced from 60% in 1641 to 20% by 1660. The Catholic peasantry was impoverished and the government was also able to write off some of its debts by encouraging soldiers and creditors to accept land in Ireland in lieu of what was owed them.

The Rump was then in a position to send Cromwell, now Commander-in-Chief of the Army, to deal with Scotland where Charles Stuart had been declared King and had landed in June 1650. Despite divisions among the Scots along the lines of religion, Charles hoped to use their support in order to defeat England. Although Cromwell made some minor tactical errors in

Franchise: The right to vote in an election, especially one in which people elect a parliament.

Massacres: Indiscriminate killings, with violence and cruelty.

The Government of England during the Interregnum

	Commonwealth February 1649–April 1653	Nominated Assembly April–December 1653	Instrument of Government – a constitution for the British Isles 1653–1657	Humble Petition and Advice 1657–1659
Executive	Council of State: 41 members, appointed by Rump. Fairfax and Cromwell the only army officers.	Council of State with 10 members. Expanded to 13 in May. At first 7, then 9, were army officers. Appointed by the Army.	Oliver Cromwell was Lord Protector for life. He had to take the advice of a Council of State (maximum 21 members), whose members he could not appoint or dismiss. When Parliament was not in session Cromwell could issue Ordinances. He could only veto legislation that attempted to alter the constitution.	Kingship offered to Oliver Cromwell, but rejected by him. He remained Lord Protector. Cromwell to name his successor. Council with a maximum of 21. Cromwell to take the advice of the Council. Cromwell to control the Army with the consent of Parliament.
Legislative	Parliament. The franchise was to be decided and the Rump to dissolve itself and call elections for a new Parliament. (This did not happen.)	A Nominated Assembly of 140 men (nicknamed Barebone's Parliament) was chosen by the Council of Officers. The Assembly declared itself to be a parliament.	A uni-cameral parliament of 460 members, including 30 from Scotland and 30 from Ireland. Seats distributed on basis of taxation. Men with personal property worth £200 could vote. Royalists were to be excluded from the first four parliaments by the Council of State. Parliament to approve all appointments to high office. Parliament to meet for at least 5 months every 3 years.	A bi-cameral parliament. The 'Other House' to have 40–70 members, nominated by Cromwell. He could not choose those barred from the Lower House. Parliament to meet at least every 3 years.
Religion	To be decided by the Rump. Apart from the Blasphemy and Adultery Acts, which gave the secular powers authority over areas previously controlled by the Church, no progress was made.	The Nominated Assembly was intended to bring about Godly reform. Changes to the Church were debated, and the vote taken to continue with tithes. The Assembly handed power back to Cromwell when discussion on religion reached stalemate.	State Church, but no coercion. Freedom of worship for all, except Catholics and Episcopalians. Jews were officially re-admitted to England.	Freedom of worship for all, except Catholics and Episcopalians.

the early stages of the campaign, the Scots were resoundingly defeated at Dunbar in September. The campaign continued for a further year, with the Scots invading England, not being beaten until the battle of Worcester a year to the day after Dunbar. Thereafter, an English army of occupation financed by the Scots was able to ensure there was no further rebellion.

What religious, social and financial policies did the Rump follow?

By 1649, there had been years of debate about the religious settlement to be adopted by Parliament. The abolition of the Court of High Commission, the signing of the Solemn League and Covenant with the Scots and the Directory of Worship published by the Westminster Assembly of Divines in 1645–46 had certainly not led to religious unity. Indeed, radicalism continued to flourish. Some sects and individuals challenged the foundations of society, as well as religion, and now it was time for the Rump to restore order. But what was that order to be?

Just as ideas had proliferated among the population as a whole, so with the MPs. Firstly, the issue of religious uniformity or toleration had to be decided. The idea of a national church appealed both to Presbyterians and to the more conservative MPs who favoured the control and discipline that this would provide. Parliamentarians such as Cromwell and outspoken radicals outside parliament considered that toleration within broad limits should form the basis of any legislation. Cromwell and many in the Army also regarded part of their mission as the introduction of a godly reformation, a reformation of manners. Apart from passing laws against blasphemy (swearing) and adultery, which meant that measures could be taken against extremists such as **Ranters**, and repealing the Elizabethan legislation making weekly attendance at the Church of England compulsory, the Rump achieved little. Tithes – the subject of attack from those who did not subscribe to the national church – remained. A Committee for the Propagation of the Gospel was appointed in 1652, but the lack of unity in Parliament prevented any decisions being reached. The Rump had failed to satisfy the people who had put it in power.

The members of the Rump were clearer about their views on society and the law. All of them were from the traditional ruling élite and many were lawyers or merchants. They appreciated the minefield that legal reform presented and confined themselves to a few minor alterations, the most significant of which was probably the introduction of English rather than Latin and French as the language of the courts. This was a disappointment to those hoping for improved access to the protection of the law through a less exclusive, cheaper and faster process. Again the Army, which saw itself as God's instrument in overthrowing the old regime, was among those groups hoping for reform. It was therefore disappointed by the Rump's performance. Another source of discontent for those seeking reform was that current trading practices such as monopolies were protected to the benefit of merchants, not the public.

The Rump was relatively successful in its financial policies, in the sense that the government raised vast sums of money. Crown and Church lands were sold and the property of Royalists was confiscated and the income appropriated. However, although income was high it did not meet expenditure. Royalists were unlikely to be reconciled to **sequestration**, despite their having been absolved of their actions in the wars by the Act of Pardon and Oblivion.

Ranters: An alleged sect that appeared in 1650–51. Those associated with it behaved in socially unacceptable ways (see pages 288–290).

Sequestration: The confiscation of Royalist lands to finance the Civil Wars. Later, Royalists were allowed to pay a fine for the return of their lands.

What were the Rump's most important achievements?

8.2.2 Why did Oliver Cromwell become Lord Protector?

A contemporary engraving of Praise-God Barebone, a member of one of Cromwell's Parliaments, which was called 'Barebone's Parliament' after him.

Power vacuum: A situation in which there is no ruler or government system in place.

In 1653, significant changes were made to the constitution. In April, Oliver Cromwell, who had been Commander-in-Chief of the Army since the resignation of Fairfax in 1650, led a group of troopers into the House of Commons. They forcibly ejected the members. A notice reading 'This House is to be let, now unfurnished' was placed on the door. Cromwell handed authority to the Council of Officers. While General Lambert presided over a Council of State, Major-General Harrison made a more radical, biblically based proposal that a high-court assembly be nominated to rule. Some Independent churches made suggestions about who might be included, but the Council of Officers made the choices.

This Nominated Assembly, representing Scotland and Ireland as well as England and Wales, met from July to December. It declared itself to be a parliament, although Harrison's original intention had probably been to dispense with such discredited earthly institutions. The members began to debate a legislative programme, but gradually divisions emerged among them. However unjustified, the assembly had too low-class and radical a reputation to be successful. Its nickname, the 'Barebone's Parliament', is a reflection of this since the name was that of a radical religious member, Praise-God Barebone. The more moderate members handed power back to Cromwell and a **power vacuum** existed again.

Lambert had clearly anticipated this move. Having withdrawn from politics when the assembly declared itself a parliament, he put new plans to Cromwell and the Council in November. Within a few days, he produced a constitutional document called the 'Instrument of Government'. Initially, the crown was offered to Oliver Cromwell, but in December he accepted instead the title Lord Protector. This was an acceptable title for a head of state. He was to take the advice of his Council of State and call Parliament to meet for at least five months every three years.

Why did Cromwell forcibly dissolve the Rump?

By late 1651, when Oliver Cromwell had succeeded in defeating the Rump's immediate enemies, the Rump had done little that equated with his or the Army's ideals. Besides the failure to satisfy them regarding religion and the legal system, no progress had been made in securing the regime. The Rump was still sitting and had not made arrangements for electing a successor. This was a necessary precursor to the Rump dissolving itself and calling a general election. This made for a serious situation; if the Commonwealth was to survive, the franchise had to be adapted in order to ensure that a pro-monarchic parliament would not result.

In April 1653, Cromwell brought about the dissolution of the Rump. The Army entered the House and expelled the members. As with so many of Cromwell's actions, this controversial intervention has been the subject of heated debate among contemporaries and historians. Cromwell himself gave different justifications of his motives, but the irony of the event is clear. As Dorothy Osborne wrote three days later, comparing Cromwell's actions with those of Charles I in 1642: 'If Mr Pym were alive again I wonder what he would think of these proceedings, and whether this would appear as great a breach of the privilege of Parliament as the demanding of the five members.'

The nature of Cromwell's dissatisfaction with the Rump, from a

Bulstrode Whitelocke (1605–1675)
Refused to take any part in the King's trial. He was appointed Ambassador to Queen Christina of Sweden in 1653. Also served as Keeper of the Great Seal and Lord President of the Council. When Charles II was restored to the throne, Whitelocke was frequently consulted on both legal and religious matters.

Edmund Ludlow (1617–1692)
Served in the army until his election as MP for Wiltshire in 1646. Having signed the King's death warrant, he was placed in charge of the army in Ireland after the unexpected death of Ireton in 1651. A Republican, he refused to accept the Protectorate regime and went into exile in France.

Lucy Hutchinson (1620–unknown after 1675)
Daughter of the Lieutenant of the Tower. She was a skilled linguist and very well-read. Married John Hutchinson in 1638. John took a leading part in promoting the Parliamentarian cause. He and Lucy were committed Congregationalists and republicans, opposing the Protectorate. Following her husband's death in 1664, Lucy composed the *Memoirs of the Life of Colonel Hutchinson*, which were completed by 1671.

constitutional point of view, is far from clear. On his return to London, he is reported to have expressed the opinion, 'If it may be done with safety and preservation of our rights, both as Englishmen and as Christians, that a settlement of somewhat with monarchic power in it would be very effectual.' A year later, the same writer reported that Cromwell asked, 'What if a man should take upon him to be King?' The historian Ronald Hutton points out, in *The British Republic 1649–1660* (2000), that these reported conversations were written down 10 years later when Bulstrode Whitelocke, who recorded the remarks, would have been eager to associate himself with Royalist sympathies. However, the memoirs have been accepted by many historians.

There is ample evidence of Cromwell's political conservatism elsewhere, yet the reason he gave publicly was that the Rump was trying to maintain itself in power. Doubtless referring indirectly to the dissolution of the Rump, he told the first Protectorate Parliament, 'That Parliaments should not make themselves perpetual is fundamental.' This equates with the version of events he gave to the Nominated Assembly, in a speech in July 1653, when he criticised the Rump for its plan to fill the House by means of by-elections rather than calling a general election.

Edmund Ludlow's memoirs, however, tell a different story. They relate how a power-hungry Cromwell, who had already ensured his support in the Army, acted to take control when he realised that the Rump was about to dissolve itself. Another contemporary, Lucy Hutchinson, in her *Memoirs of the Life of Colonel Hutchinson* written in 1671, goes so far as to suggest that it was the very success of the Rump, together with its need to reduce taxation by disbanding the Army, that led to Cromwell's coup. However, like Whitelocke's, these are by no means objective accounts. The commitment of Ludlow and Hutchinson to the Commonwealth colours their memories.

Historians have been similarly divided on the matter. In *The Rump Parliament, 1648–1653* (1974), Blair Worden puts Cromwell's actions down to 'a kind of ideological schizophrenia'. In *Oliver Cromwell* (2001), J.C. Davis seeks to explain away the apparent ambiguities. He treats contemporary sources with caution and relies on evidence that is not in dispute. For example, Davis interprets Cromwell's failure to seize power for himself and the similarities between the Instrument of Government and the 'Heads of the Proposals' as evidence of Cromwell's consistency.

This range of interpretations of events seems to rest on differences of opinion about the Rump's position and intentions. The Rump was clearly aware from the start that it was unrepresentative and should consider fresh elections. In March 1649, the Rump expressed the intention of dissolving itself as soon as was safe; in May, there was army pressure for this. However, the Rump's alternative suggestion was for carefully managed elections in the constituencies whose MPs no longer sat. This proposal was raised several times and was used by Cromwell as evidence that the Rump was trying to perpetuate itself. The Rump knew that its position was sticky, for despite the abolition of the unpopular county committees it had proved impossible to restore local government to local control. Even those JPs who had supported Parliament in the war were reluctant to take the Engagement (see page 264). Hence, local government remained in the hands of outsiders. Securing the regime and calling fresh elections must have seemed mutually exclusive.

Equally, the Army's charge that the Rumpers were self-seeking had some truth in it. After initial moves towards reform, the MPs reverted to policies in the interests of their class or groups within it. Attempts at law reform foundered on the self-interest of lawyers. The Navigation Act of 1651 and the Dutch War begun in 1652, both intended to benefit merchants, could also be criticised for this reason. The personal fortunes amassed by some members reinforced the impression.

Eventually, pressure from the Army began to force the issue. When Cromwell pressed for the Rump's dissolution on his return to London in 1651, the members tried to revive their earlier plan. Then they agreed to dissolve no later than November 1654. By 1652, war plans were distracting them, but it was the methods by which they financed the war with the confiscation of Royalist lands that had been guaranteed to them by the Army that tested the Army's patience too far. Nevertheless, Cromwell managed to avoid direct Army involvement at this point.

By early 1653, the Rump was certainly discussing its dissolution and it appears that it was the content of the bill to do so that pushed Cromwell to take action. Clearly, given the level of unpopularity of the regime, the elections would need careful management to avoid the restoration of the Stuart monarchy. Apparently, Cromwell was not satisfied that the bill for new elections would guarantee the Commonwealth's survival. In March and April, the Rump debated the bill, with the Army growing increasingly restless. But when reports emerged that MPs appeared to be pushing it through over-hastily, Cromwell returned to the House. He saw what was happening and began chiding the members. 'You have sat here too long

A contemporary Dutch print showing Cromwell dissolving the Rump Parliament. The owl (far right front) represents the stupidity of the members.

1. On what grounds could the Army justify the dissolution of the Rump, which it had created four years earlier?

2. Why did the Rump fail to bring stability to England's government?

for the good you do,' he told them. 'In the name of God, go!' and he called the musketeers to his aid. The bill they were discussing did not survive; Cromwell removed and destroyed it. He gave varied accounts of its contents, but even after his death Rump MPs were not prepared to defend it. Historians have tried to establish its terms but with no firm evidence they can only guess.

What did the Nominated Assembly achieve?

It used to be claimed that the Nominated Assembly was designed by Harrison to introduce the rule of the saints. It is true that Harrison was a Fifth Monarchist and that he viewed the assembly as a prelude to the Second Coming of Christ. Equally, Cromwell was committed to a reformation of manners and may have believed that the best way to achieve the stability that the Rump had failed to establish was to allow the godly to rule. General Lambert, too, was influential as the President of the Council of State, set up in late April. His main concern was that England should have a republican form of government.

In his opening speech to the Assembly, Cromwell made its aims clear. The Assembly was not intended to be permanent. It was to meet until 4 November 1654 when another body, to be nominated by this one, would oversee the succession in government. The Assembly was told that 'this may be the door to usher in things that God hath promised and prophesied of'. The moral reform that was envisaged is partly responsible for the radical religious reputation of the Nominated Assembly, but this was surely undeserved. Although between 40 and 50 members were Independents and sectaries, the majority had administrative experience as members of the traditional ruling élite and most were of more moderate persuasion.

The Assembly's main achievements lay in reform of the law – an issue at the heart of Leveller and Army demands, but which had proved beyond the Rump. The members were divided into 15 committees, which discussed various matters and drafted significant reforms. Thirty Acts were passed during the Assembly's short life and several major bills were in preparation when it dissolved itself. In considering the legal system, the Assembly drew on the work of the Hale Commission (a body established by the Rump in 1651 to advise on reform but whose recommendations had been largely ignored):

● Improvements were made to the laws regarding debtors.

● Civil marriages were introduced (though patchily observed).

● Most importantly, the Court of Chancery was abolished.

Based on the legal profession's concept of equity, which was considered too arbitrary, too slow and therefore expensive, this was a significant move in making the legal system more accessible. However, the Assembly did not go so far as to reduce the laws to the size of a pocket book, in line with popular demand. Other progressive aspects included the consideration of more humane treatment of the insane and the provision of greater protection for travellers on the highway.

The Assembly also made further moves to unite the countries of the British Isles, to revise the excise and rationalise the treasuries. Of these, the last was necessary for the wellbeing of the Commonwealth. The revision of the excise was more problematic. Anti-militarist feeling surfaced again and with the excise blocked and monthly assessments under attack, unpaid sailors began rioting.

Why did the Nominated Assembly fail?

The Nominated Assembly's reputation rests on the radicalism of some of its members. However, it is probably the popular response to its reforms that provoked the divisions within it and caused the more moderate members to hand power back to Cromwell. Reforms of the legal system gave rise to demands to go beyond rationalisation, to sweep away the existing laws and to introduce **Mosaic law** as part of the Fifth Monarchist programme of preparing for the rule of King Jesus. Such demands from the radical pulpits of London must have unsettled the moderate and conservative majority of members.

Mosaic law: Law based on the Ten Commandments given by God to Moses on Mount Sinai, according to the Old Testament Book of Exodus.

The most radical demands were heard in relation to religious reform. Whatever Cromwell's intention, the sizeable minority of radicals in the Assembly – consisting mainly of Fifth Monarchists and sectaries – seriously believed their mission was to prepare for the Second Coming. There were popular demands that all forms of organised religion be removed, but as usual the sticking point among the members was more mundane. Although the Assembly had voted to maintain tithes, the bill outlawing patronage in church livings would have reduced gentry control. It is significant that it was introduced in November, at a time when the attendance of the more moderate members was ebbing, and hence their majorities were shrinking.

Although the moderates showed their dominance in early November, when a second and more conservative Council of State was chosen, the debate on the clergy seems to have precipitated action. After the first clause of the bill was narrowly defeated, the moderate members handed power to Cromwell while soldiers ejected those who continued to meet from the Commons. Cromwell's amazement suggests that he was not party to this plan, so it is difficult to lay a charge of ambition on him in relation to what followed. Others, clearly, had been appraised of what was to occur. Within a few days a new constitution, prepared by John Lambert, who had withdrawn to his estates in Yorkshire when the Nominated Assembly was appointed, was under discussion.

1. **On what basis should the success of the Nominated Assembly be judged?**

2. **How successful was the Nominated Assembly?**

3. **Why did the Nominated Assembly fail to bring stability to England's government?**

How was England to be governed under the Instrument of Government?

The government of Britain was to be headed by a Lord Protector. That Oliver Cromwell was chosen for this position and appointed for life owes much to his dual role as MP and Commander-in-Chief of the Army. In both positions, he had gained respect. Given that the Army, which was now in control, was committed to parliamentary government but that it wanted to retain enough influence to ensure its political point of view was taken into account, Oliver Cromwell was the only person for the job. Although contemporaries, such as Major-General Harrison, accused Cromwell of ambition and were of the opinion that he had betrayed the revolution, it is difficult to back up the former claim. If Cromwell had wanted to be head of state, surely he would have seized power in April rather than waiting until December. Cromwell himself

Dutch caricature of Oliver Cromwell

WITHAL

Ik wist het blinde graauw van 'Hol-ziek Engeland.
Door Loosheid tegens 'Huis van Stuart op te ruven:
Nu buigt den Breedenraad voor myn gestrengen hand
Des zal my Londen haast op 's Konings Zeetel kruyen.

later remarked, 'I saw we were running into confusion and disorder and would necessarily run into blood.' This suggests that rather than being ambitious, Cromwell reluctantly took on the role of Lord Protector to preserve the cause.

A further criticism was that Cromwell behaved like, and perhaps regarded himself as, a king. He was granted £200,000 a year as well as

Crown lands. However, as the poet Andrew Marvell (see page 332) observes in 'The First Anniversary':

> 'Abroad a king he seems, and something more,
> At home a subject on the equal floor.'

The trappings of royalty were needed to convince foreigners of the legitimacy of the regime.

The **Instrument of Government** represented an attempt to learn from England's recent constitutional upheavals. The executive comprised a single-person restrained by a Council and also by Parliament. The arrangements incorporated electoral reforms and restrictions on the legislative veto of the Protector. Recognising that Parliament, as well as the Head of State, could be tyrannical the executive and legislative were separated. No legislation was allowed which would alter the fundamentals of the Instrument. This prevented Parliament from undermining the religious toleration that was introduced. The historian Barry Coward, in *The Stuart Age* (2nd edition, 1994), contrasts the Nominated Assembly and the Instrument, describing the latter as 'a victory for the conservative wing of the army'.

Instrument of Government: A constitution drawn up by General Lambert in 1653.

1. Why was the Protectorate established?

2. Why was Oliver Cromwell chosen as Lord Protector?

8.2.3 What did the Protectorate achieve?

Cromwell's rule achieved a good deal that can easily be overshadowed by concentrating on an analysis of the weaknesses, which led to the downfall of the Protectorate. There was success in:

● maintaining law and order and defending the country from overseas invasion

● reconciling some of the traditional ruling élite to the regime

● the encouragement of economic development and raising England's international prestige.

Commonwealthsmen: Those who supported the idea of government by Parliament and Council, without a Head of State such as a Lord Protector.

The lack of trouble from Royalists and **Commonwealthsmen** was achieved through a combination of luck and skill. Charles II gave no clear lead to his followers, John Lilburne died in prison after his return from exile and opponents in the army who did not resign were either cashiered or dispersed across the British Isles. That the regime remained relatively tolerant of a range of religious views and practices could also be regarded as a mark of success in that it fulfilled Cromwell's aim and anticipated later developments.

How did Cromwell approach 'healing and settling'?

In many ways, Cromwell's actions can be regarded as paradoxical. In religious terms, he was remarkably tolerant for the period. In political terms, he was undoubtedly conservative. Cromwell was also pragmatic, appreciating that the regime could not survive without a wide range of support particularly from London merchants and civilian office-holders. He was, perhaps, too optimistic in supposing that this could be achieved so soon after the divisive events of the 1640s and early 1650s, and in the context of a constitution introduced by the Army.

Cromwell tried to reconcile the traditional ruling élite to the regime.

His Council contained civilians and military men in a ratio of 2 : 1. Apart from four officers, the military men were no longer active soldiers. He aimed to relax central government pressure on the localities, placing greater trust in the county gentry. In his opening speech to the First Protectorate Parliament, he criticised religious and political extremists including Levellers, Ranters and Fifth Monarchists.

There was, undoubtedly, some success. Since they derived their privileges from central government, merchants were not obstructive, and many civil servants and local officials were too concerned with their careers to allow their consciences the upper hand. The Engagement requiring those associated with the regime to take an oath of loyalty was repealed, thus widening the number who would serve. The bench of judges became less harsh towards Royalists. The quality of civil servants during the Protectorate was an improvement on those of the early Stuarts and the service was less corrupt. Corruption, though, was still present. Several officials were prosecuted for the trade in **promissory notes** given to soldiers in lieu of pay. John Thurloe is credited with the Civil Service's functioning, particularly the network of foreign and domestic intelligence agents and the efficiency achieved by making limited-term appointments whose renewal was subject to satisfactory performance.

Early measures appealed to the moderates. For example, access to the Court of Chancery became easier and cheaper. After the first Parliament, too, there were concessions. Action was taken against dissenters who disturbed church services and the assessment and size of the army were reduced. General Monck was dispatched to Scotland where there was considerable unrest. In Ireland, English soldiers and investors were encouraged to settle confiscated lands. The latter represented a less drastic step than dismissing the Commander-in-Chief and Civil Governor, Fleetwood, as advocated by Henry Cromwell.

What did the Protectorate's religious policies achieve?

The Instrument of Government enshrined toleration of most Protestants in the Constitution. Parliament's attempts to alter this were blocked. Under the Humble Petition and Advice – the new constitution introduced in 1657 – Cromwell had to accept some intolerant measures, such as harsh treatment of Catholics. These were not enforced. Interpreting the Protectorate's religious toleration as an achievement may, however, be taking too modern an attitude.

The Protectorate did succeed, where preceding governments had failed, in creating a more organised Church while keeping state control to a minimum. From March 1654, a **Committee of Triers** representing a broad range of religious views approved the appointment of ministers. From August 1654, **Ejectors** expelled unfit ministers. This was carried out on the basis of ministers' level of morality, knowledge of the Christian faith and capacity to preach, rather than on rigid tests. Landowners who could present nominees to livings were not, therefore, deprived of this right. A wide range of religious practices was tolerated, with many using the old forms of worship while **gathered churches**, such as Baptists, established a national organisation. There were also **ecumenical** groups, the most famous being the Worcestershire Association of Richard Baxter. In an effort to improve the quality of the ministry the income of poorly endowed clergy was supplemented.

John Thurloe (1616–1668)
Served Parliament and the Interregnum governments in various capacities, 1645–60. Arrested by the Royalists on a charge of high treason in 1660, but released on condition he made his services available to the new Secretaries of State.

Promissory notes: Notes promising future payment of cash.

Committee of Triers: A committee that approved the appointment of church ministers.

Ejectors: Commissioners who sacked clergymen considered unsuitable for their posts.

Ecumenical: Belonging to a range of religious views.

Gathered churches: A 17th-century term for independent congregations.

Richard Baxter (1615–1691)
A Puritan minister, of conservative political views. He was horrified by the radical religious views of the New Model Army. Although he opposed the execution of the King, he served successive regimes, but was excluded from the Church in 1662. His account of his life was published in 1696.

Cromwell was committed to introducing a godly reformation of manners. Measures were introduced suppressing alehouses and Sunday sports. Although these often form the basis of criticism of Cromwell on the grounds of his intolerance, his aspirations were shared by many of the gentry.

What successes were there in the Protectorate's foreign policy?

Oliver Cromwell's foreign policy has been the subject of debate. It was certainly successful in raising England's profile among its neighbours and ensuring that Charles II had no continental base from which to launch an attack. However, it was expensive and founded on the outdated principle that foreign relations should be governed by religious considerations.

When Cromwell took office, England was at war with the Dutch. The war reflected the commercial rivalry between the two countries, which had flared after the Rump's Navigation Act of 1651 restricted the carrying trade to and from English ports. The war went against Cromwell's principle of a Protestant union, while the United Provinces was eager to end an economically damaging conflict. Peace was concluded in April 1654. The merchants in whose interests the war was fought accused Cromwell of not having secured sufficiently advantageous terms. The Dutch agreed to abide by the terms of the Navigation Act and undertook not to provide Charles II with a base, but they declined to enter Cromwell's projected Protestant alliance against Spain. The prestige of having beaten the Dutch led to trade agreements with Sweden, Denmark and Portugal.

War with Spain fulfilled Cromwell's ambition of attacking the great anti-Christ of Europe, although it is not certain who was responsible for the decision. Some historians have accused Cromwell of failing to appreciate that Spain was a declining power, and that France would emerge as the great threat to the European balance of power. However, few recognised this in the 1650s. It is fairer to criticise Cromwell's failure to acknowledge the changing priorities in forming alliances; commercial considerations were beginning to take precedence over religious ones. Nevertheless, since Cromwell came to office with no diplomatic experience and had such a pronounced sense of religious mission his priorities were unsurprising. There are arguments to suggest that the war was in the interests of some English merchants, and that mercantile considerations explain the decision to limit the war to attacks on Spanish colonies in the West Indies.

Whatever the reasons for the war, it was not a success. A poorly planned and executed attack on Hispaniola (Haiti) failed to meet any of its objectives. Having withdrawn from Hispaniola, the Navy was diverted and Jamaica was captured. At the time, this seemed a poor prize for so great an expense. While some have interpreted this project as evidence of Cromwell's bourgeois tendencies, promoting overseas empire building – he did encourage English settlement of Jamaica – most accept that religious, rather than imperialist, considerations were behind Cromwell's foreign policy.

Relations with France do not, however, fit this pattern, while conflicting religious and commercial interests meant that policy towards the Baltic states would remain uncertain. Cromwell's alliance with France against Spain lasted until 1659 and committed England to military support for French incursions into the Spanish Netherlands. England gained Dunkirk. Policy towards the Protestant states of the Baltic fluctuated during the

?

1. *What do you consider was the most important achievement of the Protectorate?*

2. *To what extent did Oliver Cromwell fulfil his aims as Lord Protector?*

Protectorate; Oliver Cromwell allied England with Sweden but his son and successor, Richard, was less tolerant of Swedish control of the Sound between Sweden and Denmark.

Overall, Cromwellian foreign policy was viewed by contemporaries as a success, particularly in comparison with that of James I and Charles I, and later in comparison with Charles II's.

8.2.4 Why did the Protectorate collapse?

Richard Cromwell (1626–1712)
Son of Oliver Cromwell. Proclaimed Lord Protector on 3 September 1658, he was a reluctant leader. He fled to Paris in 1660, moved to Italy in 1666, returning to England in 1680.

'Rule of the Major-Generals': Name given to the system whereby England was divided into areas each under the rule of a Major-General. Their role was to keep law and order, collect the decimation tax, search out plots, suppress vice and encourage virtue.

The Protectorate collapsed in the spring of 1659 within seven months of the death of Oliver Cromwell. Apparently, the regime had relied too heavily on his dual role of bridging the divide between Army and civilians. His son Richard, who succeeded him, lacked political experience. This version of events is based on the developments of the Protectorate's final months, when it appeared to collapse from within. Richard Cromwell did not retire into private life as a result of external pressure from either royalists or republicans; it was his own army that precipitated his renunciation of power.

However, this interpretation ignores fundamental weaknesses and unresolved problems. The regime was too closely associated with army involvement in government, hardly a sound basis for legitimacy. The **'Rule of the Major-Generals'** had confirmed that army influence was unacceptable. Even when Lambert's Instrument of Government was replaced by the civilian Humble Petition and Advice, the traditional ruling élite had at best tolerated it, not wishing to risk further civil unrest. Most of the gentry continued to regard monarchy as the most appropriate form of government for England. Particularly serious was the financial predicament of the Protectorate. Taxes had been reduced, but expenditure, especially on foreign enterprises, had not been cut sufficiently.

What were the political weaknesses of the Protectorate?

In offering policies designed to appeal to a range of people the Protectorate pleased no one. The extremists on both sides would never be satisfied with it, nor would the gentry show it much enthusiasm. As Austin Woolrych remarks, in *England without a King, 1649–1660* (1983), 'In a nation torn by so many recent divisions government by consensus was scarcely possible.'

From the outset, commonwealthsmen were opposed to the Protectorate. Sir Arthur Haselrig and Thomas Wood made this clear in the first Protectorate Parliament, which met in September 1654. They and others attacked the extent to which, under the Instrument of Government, the Lord Protector could act independently of Parliament. Cromwell's response was to remind members that it was a condition of them taking their seats that they should accept the fundamentals of the constitution. As a result, Commonwealth sympathisers were excluded from the Parliament. Even then the Parliament failed to cooperate with Cromwell, rewriting the constitution with unacceptable terms, passing no legislation and granting no tax.

Consequently, it was dissolved at the earliest possible opportunity – that is, after five lunar (rather than the longer calendar) months had passed.

The second Protectorate Parliament was also uncooperative, even though significant measures had been introduced to assure its compliance, including the issuing of conciliatory proclamations and the reduction of both the assessment and the size of the Army. When the second Parliament met, about a hundred MPs were excluded and others withdrew in sympathy, reducing the membership by around a third. Nevertheless, this Parliament also challenged the policies of the Lord Protector. MPs debated the case of James Nayler at length before punishing him harshly. They refused to finance a continuation of the Rule of the Major-Generals, and then presented Cromwell with suggestions for changes in the constitution which were later embodied in the Humble Petition and Advice. Cromwell found it as difficult as Charles I had to work with Parliament. In his frustration, he possibly adopted more dictatorial methods with it than had his royal predecessor.

The disaffected outside the regime also threatened the Protectorate. John Lilburne had returned to England in 1653 but was acquitted of treason by the Nominated Assembly. However, Cromwell had him imprisoned in the Channel Islands where he died.

It was the Royalist rising of 8 March 1655, known as Penruddock's Rising, that started the experiment of the Rule of the Major-Generals. The rising itself was feeble because Charles II failed to give a clear lead to his supporters, and government spies had warned that a rising was planned. Royalist sympathisers were dealt with harshly, not to say illegally. The innocent and untried were transported alongside the guilty to the West Indies. A **decimation tax** on Royalists financed the new layer of regional government.

The attempt to assassinate Cromwell by the Leveller Miles Sindercombe in 1657 focused attention on the weakness of the Instrument of Government in not providing a clear line of succession. It was one of the contributory reasons for the offer of the crown to Cromwell. Thomas Venner's Fifth Monarchist rising of April 1657 aimed to remove Cromwell in order to introduce the rule of the saints.

This opposition may not have presented a significant challenge to the regime, but it did encourage reactions of dubious legality. In the case of the Rule of the Major-Generals, the response was destabilising. Cromwell has been charged with having no clear policies, but merely reacting to circumstances. In his answer to these challenges it is clear how this charge could be supported.

Decimation tax: A fine of 10% levied on those Royalists who had not demonstrated a change of heart and who had an annual income over £100 or over £1,500 in goods.

1. Summarise and explain the political weaknesses of the Protectorate.

2. How significant were the political weaknesses of the Protectorate?

What was the impact of continued military influence in government?

The Rule of the Major-Generals highlighted the fundamental weakness of Oliver Cromwell's Protectorate. By dividing England into 10 (later 11) districts, with an army officer in charge of each, Cromwell alienated many of the gentry. Cromwell's stated aim was to heal and settle, yet when he could not persuade his fellow rulers that his policies were right, he resorted to illegal methods, including compulsion by the army. He submitted to the second Protectorate Parliament in that he made no attempt to preserve the experiment when Parliament voted not to continue funding it. Indeed, since many Cromwellian civilians including his own relations voted against the decimation tax, Cromwell must have been behind the attack on the system. Nevertheless he failed to conciliate parliament or bring about lasting settlement.

Civilian Cromwellians responded with a new constitutional suggestion. What eventually became the Humble Petition and Advice was preferable to many, not simply because it reduced Cromwell's powers by offering him the crown, added an Upper House to Parliament and made firmer arrangements for the succession when Cromwell died. It was also preferable because it was a civilian rather than a military-inspired document. Cromwell's motivation in his protracted agonising over acceptance of the crown and his eventual refusal of the title of king will be discussed in the next chapter. The new constitution was implemented, except that Cromwell remained Lord Protector.

The Rule of the Major-Generals has been characterised as the imposition of strict Puritan values on an unwilling nation. This view relies partly on contemporary reactions to some of the more draconian measures regarding Sabbath observance and the banning of various entertainments. However, not all Major-Generals were equally vigorous in enforcing such measures. Once in place, their requests for advice and encouragement from Lord Protector and Council were largely ignored.

Of more significance was the general hostility of local government officials. The new scheme did not aim to replace them. Indeed, many Major-Generals leaned heavily on the existing officials, and it was this that was resented. Given that these were the very men who sat, or were represented, in Parliament, the whole experiment appears a costly mistake in terms of Cromwell's aims. The system was not a military dictatorship in that the Major-Generals were not given exclusive powers, yet it provided further evidence that Cromwell relied too heavily on the Army.

Why was the influence of the Army so important in undermining the Protectorate?

What financial problems did the Protectorate have?

Throughout the Interregnum, financial problems dogged the government; expenditure consistently outstripped income. The Rump had spent £1 million more each year than it collected and the Dutch war increased this deficit. In 1654, expenditure exceeded income by £350,000. After the First Protectorate Parliament, Cromwell cut the assessment to £60,000 per month, compensating with a reduction in the size of the army and a decrease in soldiers' pay. However, this did not solve the problem.

Equally, decimation tax was insufficient to finance the Rule of the Major-Generals. Once the Rule of the Major-Generals had been abandoned, Richard Cromwell's second parliament granted £400,000 for the war against Spain, as well as £1.9 million a year. However, no methods for raising this money were established. The assessment was reduced to £35,000 per month. Government income still failed to meet the annual military costs of £250,000. In the end, difficulties in financing the military played a key role in Richard Cromwell's failure.

The extraordinary expenses of war should be set in the context of the need to maintain armies in Scotland and Ireland, where finances were equally problematic. This was an expensive regime. The English were more heavily taxed than under the first two Stuarts. But while Cromwell recognised the need to reduce taxation it was difficult to see how expenditure could be cut back. The only way in which the Cromwellian regime's financial arrangements could be seen as an improvement on Charles I's

1. Why were the financial problems of the Protectorate so difficult to solve?

2. How important were its financial problems in ending the Protectorate?

was that taxes were not imposed arbitrarily. Nevertheless, Richard Cromwell did face challenges. The London merchant, George Cony, refused to pay customs duties on the grounds that the regime was illegal. Since Cony had to lose the court case if the regime were to survive, the legal process was severely undermined. Three lawyers who undertook to defend him were imprisoned, while four judges who objected were dismissed from office, and a fifth resigned.

What effect did the death of Oliver Cromwell have on the Protectorate?

Oliver Cromwell's health deteriorated during 1658. On 3 September, he died of a fever. He had named his son, Richard, as his successor. The transfer of power took place smoothly and with many positive signs, such as army acceptance of the new Protector despite Richard's civilian credentials. The death of Oliver Cromwell had been feared by republicans as an opportunity for Royalists to seize power, but Charles II's supporters failed to respond to his calls for an uprising. It gradually became clear that Richard Cromwell was ill-equipped to reconcile the conflicting interests of civilians and army, and that the Protectorate's days were numbered.

Richard Cromwell had had no useful apprenticeship for the role of Head of State. He had spent the early years of the Interregnum as a country landowner in Hampshire, among like-minded Presbyterian squires. Although he had sat in both Protectorate Parliaments, being promoted to the Upper House under the Humble Petition and Advice, he held no political office until he became a member of the Council of State in 1657. Other than serving in the Parliamentarian army in the Civil War, he lacked military experience.

Nevertheless, the Army was not hostile to Richard's accession, perhaps believing that so inexperienced a leader would easily be controlled. Early indications were of amicable relations between him and the Grandees. Richard recognised the need to pay the soldiers more effectively and made proposals for improving the situation to the leading officers. The Grandees were also concerned about Richard having command of the armed forces in view of his lack of experience. This issue was addressed satisfactorily.

Civilians were also encouraged. Richard's accession appeared to promise the dominance of civilian over military. Richard was moderate in his religious views and sympathetic to the traditional ruling élite. When the third Protectorate Parliament met, in January 1658, it seemed that it would cooperate over the need to address the dire financial situation. It accepted the new constitutional arrangements and approved the sending of the Navy to watch developments in the Baltic, where the United Provinces was attempting to gain ground while Sweden and Denmark engaged in war. It then turned to the issue of finance.

Parliament received a report indicating that government deficit was running at £330,000 a year. There was also £2.5 million of debts, including £890,000 in army arrears. Parliament decided to question the figures rather than address the situation. Richard's tactless response to the concerned army officers – persuading Parliament to vote that the Council of Officers

1. Did Richard
Cromwell inherit an
impossible task?

2. 'The main problem
for Richard Cromwell
was that he was not
the man his father
was.'

To what extent do you
agree with this
statement?

could only sit with Parliament's permission and that officers must agree not to compel parliaments – was followed by an order to dissolve the Council of Officers. When Parliament began to debate the formation of a militia controlled by themselves, Charles Fleetwood and John Desborough, who had always hoped to retain their influence over the Protector, reacted by demanding the dissolution of Parliament. Colonels, who had previously been loyal, left London to join the mutiny.

The failure to meet the material demands of the soldiers swayed them against the new Lord Protector. Richard Cromwell responded by agreeing to the officers' demand that he dissolve Parliament. Despite considerable support for the Protectorate among the Grandees on the Army Council, the view of the junior officers and rank-and-file prevailed. On 5 May 1659, the Army Council voted to recall the surviving members of the Rump Parliament. Since he could gain no support from either the army in Scotland or that in Ireland, Richard reluctantly retired. The Protectorate had ended.

How can the collapse of the Protectorate be explained?

The inadequacies of Richard Cromwell may have prompted the end of the Protectorate, but he had inherited a political and financial situation that would have proved challenging to anyone. The regime was fundamentally unstable. Civilian support was essential, as Oliver Cromwell had recognised. The existence of both radical and Royalist opponents, who frequently united against the Protectorate, for example in producing anti-government propaganda, created the dilemma that the regime could not survive without army backing. This, together with an expensive if successful foreign policy, meant that the government was permanently in financial difficulties and had to rely on cooperation from Parliament. This, too, presented difficulties. The Civil War had been fought to defend the rights of Parliament from a tyrannical king, but the membership of all Interregnum parliaments was restricted to those who might be relied upon to support the regime. Relations between Army and Parliament were never harmonious. On occasions, the Army interfered more than Charles I had. There were many underlying conditions rendering the long-term survival of the Protectorate unlikely.

In addition, developments during the Interregnum had polarised radicals and conservatives. In particular, civilian Cromwellians viewed the growth of religious radicalism with increasing unease. Some of the sects threatened to undermine the social and moral fabric on which the gentry depended for their authority. The ruling élite was, therefore, inclined to close ranks and push for a less tolerant religious position. This ran counter to the continued religious radicalism of the rank-and-file of the Army whose support was still necessary.

1. Explain how
underlying problems
weakened the
Protectorate.

2. To what extent can
the collapse of the
Protectorate be
explained by events
after the death of
Oliver Cromwell?

While Oliver Cromwell was able to maintain an uneasy balance between the two sides, he failed to reconcile the conflict. In retrospect, it is not surprising that his death triggered the sequence of events that led to the collapse of the Protectorate. However, with hindsight this raises other questions, chief among them being why the collapse of the Protectorate did not lead more swiftly to the restoration of monarchy.

Source-based questions: Why did the Protectorate collapse?

SOURCE A

In spite of the expressions of the army through Lieutenant-General Fleetwood and the address presented by a number of officers, promising complete submission to His Highness and a determination to defend him against all comers, for some days past ill feeling and disputes seem to have arisen between the Protector and some of his troops, out of which evil consequences might easily arise, capable of upsetting the current state of affairs and of bringing about changes prejudicial to the government. On some colonelcy falling vacant the Protector, who claims also to have succeeded his father as generalissimo of all the forces, without which his other office is worth little or nothing, granted it to Montagu, who commands the Channel squadron. The officers of the army took exception to this. Some of them went to the Protector and expressed their views in a manner not altogether seemly, intimating their intention to have Fleetwood as their generalissimo, and that his highness ought not to make any sort of military appointment without a council of war. The Protector tried to answer soberly, but he could not refrain from making his answer very sharp.

From a letter written by the Venetian ambassador in London, 25 October 1658

SOURCE B

The army set up Richard Cromwell, it seemeth, upon trial, resolved to use him as he behaved himself; and though they swore fidelity to him, they meant to keep it no longer than it pleased them. And when they saw that he began to favour the sober people of the land, to honour parliaments, and to respect the ministers whom they called Presbyterians, they presently resolved to make him know his masters, and that it was they, and not he, that were called by God to be the chief protectors of the interest of the nation. He was not so formidable to them as his father was, and therefore everyone boldly spurned at him.

From The Autobiography of Richard Baxter, 1692, edited by N.H. Keeble

SOURCE C

The key problem is to analyse the reactions of the traditional rulers of the counties and boroughs to Cromwellian government. The weakness of the Stuart cause in the 1650s suggests that there were aspects of Cromwellian government that they found attractive. Government during the 1650s did not break down. In some respects it was very efficient and went some way towards satisfying the craving of the political nation for a return to stable, ordered government. At the same time it did not lose touch entirely with the revolutionary ideals of the 'godly reformation', of the Good Old Cause. Despite its achievements, Cromwellian government secured the loyalty of only a minority and Oliver's legacy to his son was, if not hopeless, very insecure.

From The Stuart Age by Barry Coward, 1980

SOURCE D

[Oliver Cromwell's] regime had won acquiescence, if not popularity. But it harboured one weakness, which was both dangerous and increasing. Cromwell's bickering with his first Parliament had left him with a revenue falling short of expenditure by £400,000 per annum. Upon this had been hurled the weight of his Spanish war. At his death, Cromwell's government was two million pounds in debt and had no opportunity to borrow further. The shortfall of the regular account ensured that each month the pay of the armed forces would slide further into arrears. Indeed, as the grants made by Parliament were due to expire in the following year [1659], there would come a time when almost no money would be available at all, and the government would collapse.

From The Restoration by Ronald Hutton, 1985

Source-based questions: Why did the Protectorate collapse?

SOURCE E

For all his moderation, Cromwell was a formidable symbol of the Good Old Cause, and thus himself a major obstacle to settlement. His death and the peaceful accession of Richard gave the Protectorate one more chance of gaining the loyalty of the counties. Through the parliamentary debates of the early months of 1659 can be sensed the gentry's hopes that Richard might succeed where his father had failed, might break the grip of the army and the 'godly party', and return to normal methods of government. But the fatal internal contradictions of the Protectorate – its attempt to pursue settlement while depending for its survival on an army dedicated to the Good Old Cause – led instead to Richard's own downfall.

From 'Settlement in the Counties 1653–1658', in The Interregnum, *edited by G.E. Aylmer, 1972*

1. With reference to Sources A and B and information contained in this chapter, explain the meaning of the two phrases highlighted in the sources.

a) 'his highness ought not to make any sort of military appointment without a council of war' (Source A)

b) 'it was they, and not he, that were called by God to be the chief protectors of the interest of the nation' (Source B).

2. Study Sources A and B.

3. Compare the explanations in these Sources of the problems faced by Richard Cromwell in his relations with the army.

4. Using all the Sources and the information contained in this chapter, explain why the Protectorate collapsed.

8.2.5 What developments were there in political and religious radicalism during the Interregnum?

The Interregnum period seems to have been one in which radicalism reached a wider audience than ever before. Censorship existed, but it was not as strict between 1641 and 1660 as it had been before or was to be afterwards. Printing presses were cheap and there was a larger literate audience than previously. In *The World Turned Upside Down* (1972), Christopher Hill suggests that the proliferation of pamphlets may have contributed to their extremism in order to give sales advantage. The sources are, therefore, numerous. Their interpretation, however, is problematic.

By 1649, the influence of the Levellers was waning. The Grandees had regained the initiative in the Army by late 1647, although this was not apparent until the spring of 1649. In May allegedly Leveller mutinies were suppressed, most famously at Burford. The attack on the Rump by John Lilburne in his two pamphlets 'England's New Chains Discovered' was too close to the truth to tolerate. The **Digger**, or True Leveller, commune on St George's Hill in Surrey, led by Gerrard Winstanley, was the longest surviving and largest of nearly a dozen such squats on common land. However, local conservative hostility to the group ensured its eviction in April 1650 – a year after it had come into existence.

Some gathered churches, such as Baptist and Congregationalist, were already well established. Because of their moderate views and behaviour they were able to take advantage of the relative tolerance of the

Digger: A member of a group of primitive communists who put Leveller ideals of economic equality, common ownership and cooperation into practice. Gerrard Winstanley, the Digger leader, wrote about a social revolution that would give the land back to the people.

Interregnum regimes to consolidate their positions. By 1649, questioning of accepted Puritan doctrines, particularly predestination (see page 51), had placed many in a position of 'seeking the truth'. From this position developed a wide range of more or less radical sects. According to historian David Underdown, in *Pride's Purge* (1971), 'Zionism, vegetarianism, a dozen other "isms" were in the air. All things were possible, the world was to be made new, the reign of King Jesus was just around the corner.' Of most concern to the authorities were those who exceeded the bounds of decency. The Rump Parliament clamped down, passing the Adultery and Blasphemy Acts in 1650. They singled out Ranters as a sect whose outrageous behaviour had to be stopped, but whether or not there was ever such a sect is open to debate. Meanwhile, a group of 'Publishers of Truth', later known as Quakers, had begun their work. In 1647, George Fox had left his Leicestershire home and begun his travels. By 1660, there were probably about 35,000–40,000 Quakers, and Fox was emerging as their most influential leader. Fear of the radicalism of this group, which extended to challenging social and economic conventions as well as attacking established religious practices and organisation, was a contributory factor in causing the restoration of monarchy.

Why did political radicalism fail to make a significant impact during the Interregnum?

Leveller ideas were very radical for the time. While the leaders may have blamed the Grandees for the demise of the movement, it is difficult to avoid the conclusion that their beliefs were too radical and too remote from the concerns of ordinary people to have significant appeal. Besides this, the leaders were imprisoned at crucial moments. In any case, most of their support was drawn from groups whose interests only partly coincided with those of the Levellers, for example the New Model Army and the gathered churches of London.

The Levellers believed that the people of England should be represented in a House of Commons in which they vested power and that the Commons should not act against the fundamental constitutions and customs of the land. A more far-reaching position was voiced by Richard Overton in 1646, in *An Arrow against all Tyrants*. He stated, 'by natural birth all men are equal ... born to like propriety, liberty and freedom'. Other Leveller leaders also went beyond the more famous demand for an extension of the franchise, suggesting:

● reform of the economy to eliminate privileges

● an overhaul of the legal system, particularly as it discriminated against the poor through harsh punishments for minor offences and costly legal fees.

Religious toleration was also a Leveller cause on the grounds that the state should not legislate on matters of conscience.

While many of these issues did affect ordinary people, the language of the Levellers and the methods by which they wanted to achieve their ends were too remote from their potential supporters. Ordinary people usually expressed their grievances through minor riots and disturbances, for example the destruction of enclosures or fen drainage systems. These incidents were localised and restricted to single issues, because ordinary people reacted to circumstances rather than visualising alternative political structures. They were not accustomed to attacking the foundations of government, rather the individuals or local institutions which they blamed for their current predicament. Hence, they would be unlikely to support Levellerism. Where the Leveller programme did coincide with that of organised groups, such as the gathered churches, support for Levellers was limited. Once the Commonwealth had been established with a commitment to some degree of religious toleration, the gathered churches had no further interest in the Leveller programme.

Considerable rank-and-file Army support for the Leveller programme was apparent at the Putney Debates of October–November 1647. Agitator Petty said, 'We judge that all inhabitants that have not lost their birthright should have an equal voice in elections.' Colonel Rainsborough justified this view: 'For really I think that the poorest he that is in England hath a life to live as the greatest he. And therefore truly, sir, I think it's clear that every man that is to live under a government ought first by his own consent to put himself under that government.' However, the rendezvous at Ware illustrated that the soldiers were subject to army discipline and that when this clashed with their Leveller interests it was army discipline that prevailed. The Grandees, having regained the initiative, were able to maintain it. At Burford and other mutinies in April and May 1649, the authorities took decisive action to eliminate radicals. Thereafter, the Army was regularly purged of individuals who challenged the political leadership, even though it was used by the Grandees on several occasions to change the government.

The Leveller leaders were enthusiastic and energetic, but so committed was Lilburne to the cause that he acted from principle rather than pragmatism. Other Leveller leaders could be equally blunt. Numerous attacks on individuals and institutions brought Leveller leaders before the courts, providing them with a platform from which to challenge the legitimacy of the government. Clearly, all Interregnum regimes fell far short of the Leveller ideal of representative government, but no regime could allow those who publicly voiced such criticisms to remain at liberty. The Leveller campaign became increasingly personal, in the sense that general principles of inequality and denial of liberty were illustrated by the authorities' treatment of Lilburne in particular. Inevitably, this marginalised their cause and imprisonment took its toll on Lilburne himself. He appears to have found comfort in Quakerism before his death, in prison, in 1657.

What was the most important cause of the Levellers' failure to make an impact during the Interregnum?

What was Ranterism and why was it suppressed?

Ranterism has provoked a major disagreement among historians. A.L. Morton first drew attention to the term in *The World of the Ranters* (1970), classifying Ranters as a loose-knit group with considerable influence. In *Blasphemy, Immorality and Anarchy: The Ranters and the English Revolution* (1987), Jerome Friedman claims that, 'There can be no doubt that the Ranters were the most radical and the most peculiar sect of the Cromwellian Interregnum.' At the other extreme, J.C. Davis states in *Fear, Myth and History* (1986), 'There can be little doubt that there was a fictional or mythical image of Ranterism created in the early 1650s.' Responding to Davis, Christopher Hill writes, in an article entitled 'The Lost Ranters' (1987): 'I prefer the phrase "Ranter milieu" to "sect" or

Pantheism: The belief that God is present in everything. Based on the biblical version of creation, but perverted by radicals to the idea that as God created sin, sin was a part of God and therefore should be acted out.

Antinomianism: Based on predestination. If someone was 'saved', everything he or she does is good, even if conventional morality holds it to be a sin. Sin is in the mind, and to be free of it a person should act out the 'sin'.

Muggletonians: A millenarian sect whose leaders were Lodowick Muggleton and John Reeve.

1. Why were Ranter ideas and behaviour intolerable in the 17th century?

2. Why might the government have been responsible for the anti-Ranter pamphlets?

"movement".' Hill argues that in the heady days after the execution of the King a range of extreme religious ideas existed but without the discipline of organised sects. Millenarianism, **pantheism** and **antinomianism** were all current, and some may even have put the last of these into practice. Sects emerged from this that we can recognise either because they evolved a more formal organisation shortly afterwards or because they still exist today. However, to attempt to identify anything as formal as a sect in 1650 is to anticipate developments.

There were a number of individuals who were accused of Ranterism at the time. They include Laurence Clarkson, Jacob Bauthumley and Abiezer Coppe. All published works challenging accepted beliefs and behaviour, although it is impossible to infer a coherent Ranter doctrine from their writing. There are also 15 anti-Ranter pamphlets, published to shock, using imagery that would immediately bring to mind deviance and atheism in the mind of the 17th-century reader. Links between the authors and printers of these pamphlets, as well as with Royalist writers, also suggest deliberate sensationalism designed to undermine the government by criticising its tolerant religious policies. Reliable evidence to back up the claims of these pamphlets does not exist. Many people were accused of Ranterism, but this might happen as sects such as Quakers and **Muggletonians** struggled to establish internal disciplinary procedures and to dissociate themselves from over-enthusiastic brethren. Ranter confessions, such as 'Copp's Return to the Wayes of Truth' and Clarkson's spiritual autobiography *The Lost Sheep Found* are also problematic since their purpose was not necessarily to record the activities in which they had allegedly been involved.

The Ranters illustrate the problems encountered in studying the beliefs and activities of those below the ruling élite. The evidence is limited and interpretation problematic. Assumptions and prejudices have to be removed from the documents. A knowledge of contemporary writing styles and forms is needed for effective reading of the sources. The anti-Ranter pamphlets probably reveal more about the fears of those who wrote them than about the Ranters themselves, but this does not mean that they are of no use. Indeed, in terms of explaining developments in government, an understanding of how deep-seated the fear of radicalism could be is essential in accounting for the conservatism of the Restoration settlement.

An engraving of Ebenezer Elliot, 'The Ranter', at a field meeting in Yorkshire

Why did Quakerism spread so widely and so rapidly during the Interregnum?

A number of factors explain the rapid spread of Quakerism. Unlike Levellerism, the Quaker message had widespread appeal, building on the quest for salvation pursued by many who had rejected the established and gathered churches. Effective leadership also distinguishes Quakerism from the Leveller movement. However, like the Levellers, the Quakers seemed to pose a direct threat to the ruling élite, since they challenged many of the assumptions on which social order depended. By 1660, such was the fear of Quakerism and such was the extent of its spread that it was possible to believe that Quakers would soon come to dominate the country.

Central to the Quaker religious message was the belief that everyone was equal before God and could attain salvation. It was a message of hope for all, which contrasted with predestination. Many Quakers had experienced periods of self-doubt as they sought to establish whether they were among the elect. From their beliefs they concluded that a direct relationship with God through the Holy Spirit was more important than rigid reliance on the Bible. After all, this had produced the churches of the **Second Age**, which had fallen into error, preventing ordinary people from voicing their revelations, and insisting that the clergy were supported by the laity through tithes. They rejected conventional theological disputation in which texts were quoted to prove a point, relying on plain speaking of what God revealed to them.

George Fox seems to have reached his conclusions via a different route, being profoundly aware of sin and hypocrisy rather than over-troubled by fears about his salvation. He rejected the idea that only men with a university education were capable of preaching God's word, breaking convention further by recognising that males did not have a monopoly on access to God's revelations. Fox recognised in Christ the sole source of comfort and salvation. He also developed a strong sense of social justice. The Quakers were notorious for rejecting the social conventions of speech and gesture that reinforced the obedience and deference, which those lower in the social hierarchy were supposed to show to their betters. Besides this, Fox condemned the oppression of the poor, through both excessive taxation and punishment for crimes against property. He also had high moral standards, objecting to drunkenness, cheating and all swearing, including bidding people 'Good morrow' and taking oaths in court.

Fox began his missions in 1647, spreading the word first in the Midlands, then in the north. In 1654, when the movement was firmly established in the north, he decided to convert the south of the country to Quakerism (or 'the Truth'). Groups of two or three Quakers travelled widely, often converting existing groups of Seekers (see page 257), just as they had further north. Unlike the Levellers, the Quakers found a ready audience because they gave practical organisation and support to pre-existing groups. This is important in explaining the speed with which the organisation grew. However, it was through the skills of leadership that first regional, then national, meetings were established. As early as 1652, regional meetings were held every three weeks in East Yorkshire. This practice also built on existing foundations; Westmoreland Seekers held monthly meetings before the arrival of Fox. The first national annual meeting was held at Skipton, Yorkshire, in 1657.

Second Age: Many radicals referred to the First Age as that of God and the Old Testament; the Second Age as that of Christ and the New Testament; and the Third Age, which they believed was just beginning, as that of the Holy Spirit with knowledge of God achieved through divine revelation.

George Fox (1624–1691)
Founder of the Society of Friends (Quakers). He became a travelling preacher in 1647. In 1650 he was imprisoned for blasphemy at Derby. This was where the name 'Quakers' was first applied rudely to Fox and his followers, supposedly because he suggested that Judge Bennet should 'quake at the word of the Lord'. He made a missionary journey to America in 1671–72.

James Nayler (?1617–1660)
A yeoman farmer from West Yorkshire. He became a wandering preacher before meeting Fox. Led a successful Quaker mission to London before succumbing to the hysteria of his followers in Bristol.

Blasphemy: The saying or doing of something that shows disrespect for God.

1. Why did the Quaker message have such widespread appeal?

2. What was the most important reason for the conversion of so many to Quakerism by 1660?

3. Compare the strengths and weaknesses of the Leveller and Quaker movements.

Of all the Interregnum's radical groups, the Quakers were unusual in becoming established in rural areas away from the capital. Their initial success was largely in sparsely populated areas, where parish organisation and influence were weaker than in urban or densely populated rural areas. Systems of poor relief, for example, which were supposed to be organised by the parish, had already been set up by some groups of Seekers. It had always proved more difficult to recruit well-educated clergy to the remote and poor northern parishes.

From the time of their mission to the south, the Quaker leaders began to experience persecution. They might be arrested as vagrants, for non-payment of tithes or for their eccentric behaviour. This strengthened them in their resolve to spread the message. It encouraged greater internal discipline and hence a stronger, more resilient organisation. Most important was the James Nayler case. In 1656, James Nayler rode into Bristol on a donkey, re-enacting Christ's entry into Jerusalem. He was arrested for **blasphemy**. Tension already existed within the leadership. The Parliamentary debate and consequent bad publicity enabled Fox to disown Nayler, insist on greater discipline of the more enthusiastic members, and confirm his own position within the movement. Nayler's subsequent flogging, branding and imprisonment broke his health.

The strength of Quaker numbers on the eve of the Restoration frightened the authorities. Although they were becoming more disciplined, many Quaker practices were integral to their theology and posed serious threats to the social fabric. Quakers were, therefore, viewed as anarchic. They clearly had widespread appeal, with anywhere from 35,000–60,000 followers. The ruling élite no doubt accepted the upper estimate in their increasing anxiety at the instability of the last year of the Interregnum.

How widespread was religious radicalism during the Interregnum?

It is difficult to estimate how widespread religious radicalism was in terms of numbers. Estimates vary widely, as can be seen from the possible numbers of Quakers by 1660. There were probably never more than 10,000 Fifth Monarchists. Baptists, whether Particular or General, were relatively numerous, with the Particular Baptists establishing a national organisation by 1660. Both kinds of Baptists had adherents spread over a wide area of the country.

This should be set in the context of a religiously conservative nation. Despite attempts to establish a godly nation of puritanical believers, central government had a limited impact on religious practices. Although there was increasing persecution of episcopalian clergy after Penruddock's rising, use of the old prayer book continued even in some London churches.

The national Presbyterian Church was stronger in terms of effective preachers than the Church of England had been, even though there was a shortfall in clergy in some areas. There was a good deal of toleration of a range of beliefs, with many parish clergy expressing no strong doctrinal views. Cooperation was apparent in the voluntary regional associations of clergy, which existed in 14 counties by the time of Cromwell's death. Had it not been for the near anarchy of 1659–60, concerns over the extent of religious radicalism might not have arisen.

Why, when such a small proportion of the population adopted radical beliefs, was radicalism of such concern to the ruling élite?

What was the long-term impact of the spread of religious radicalism?

Political radicalism had little immediate effect except in the negative sense. From 1649, the ruling élite acted to ensure that those who spoke of the rights of freeborn Englishmen were silenced. Fear of popular involvement in politics extended at least until the Glorious Revolution (see Chapter 10), which was carefully managed by members of the élite. By the 19th century, however, groups such as Chartists who campaigned for one man, one vote, made reference to their 17th-century predecessors. However, it is impossible to trace a direct link between popular political ideas of the 17th and 19th centuries if only because of the nature of the activity and of the evidence.

Religious radicalism had more obvious and immediate consequences. By 1660, many **nonconformist** groups were so well established that persecution could not eliminate them. The Cavalier Parliament decided on a narrow, rather than a comprehensive, Church of England. This ensured the survival of these gathered churches whose ministers would not conform to the established Church and whose members chose to meet in secret even if they occasionally attended the parish church.

The debate between those who favoured a comprehensive state church and those who preferred a narrower definition of the Church of England continued until 1689, when the Toleration Act allowed most Protestant nonconformists to worship freely, with certain provisos. Intolerance of nonconformist participation in politics remained until 1828.

The exclusion of nonconformists from the universities also had an impact. After the Glorious Revolution, **Dissenting Academies** were established. Many of those who challenged the increasingly unrepresentative and corrupt nature of Parliament in the later 18th and early 19th centuries were taught in these institutions.

Nonconformist: Someone who refuses to follow the practices of the Church of England.

Dissenting Academies: Educational institutions set up by non-Church of England Protestants who were permitted to become teachers by the Toleration Act of 1689.

8.2.6 Why was monarchy restored?

The restoration of the Rump of the Long Parliament in May 1659 emphasises what had long been apparent and what distinguishes the mid-17th century English Revolution from later ones. The revolutionaries lacked a constitutional programme to replace what had been discarded. The Army had again seized power, but had to fall back on a previously rejected institution to rule. From the start, there was tension between Army and Rump, just as there had been in the earlier Commonwealth period. Thereafter, the frequent transfers of power reveal the political bankruptcy of the Interregnum:

- the expulsion of the Rump in October 1659
- rule by the Committee of Safety (October–December)
- followed by the re-assembly of the Rump
- finally, the restoration of the Long Parliament in March 1660, after the intervention of General George Monck.

This should be set in the context of increasing fears that religious radicals, particularly Quakers, were about to seize power and increasing anarchy as, for the first time since the execution of the King, there was wide scale refusal to cooperate with the government.

The Stuart monarchy was restored after the Long Parliament had dissolved itself in March 1660 to be replaced by the Convention Parliament in April. This institution negotiated with Charles II on the basis of the Declaration of Breda to restore the monarchy, proclaiming him King on 8 May 1660. Ironically, few of the limitations on monarchy, which had made agreement between Charles I and Parliament so difficult to achieve, were implemented.

What evidence is there that monarchy was still considered to be the best form of government for England?

When Charles I was executed, the Rump Parliament began to consider the most suitable form of government for England. That they settled on a Commonwealth and abolished the monarchy had more to do with the fact that none of Charles's sons was considered to be suitable for the post than because monarchy was thought to be redundant. Historians such as Barry Coward, in *The Stuart Age* (1994), interpret the Protectorate period as a retreat from revolution. The fact that not only was Cromwell offered the crown in 1657, but also that John Lambert considered including the institution of monarchy in the Instrument of Government, provides further evidence that monarchy was regarded as the natural form of government for England.

Enthusiasm for a Stuart monarchy was, however, notable for its absence. Charles II had been in exile since the defeat of the Scottish invasion of England in 1651. He had failed to organise effective rebellion in his own favour despite attempts by his followers in England to seize power. What is most surprising is the failure of Sir George Booth to gain significant support for his rising in August 1659. He took control of Cheshire and parts of Lancashire and North Wales, but Charles II was unable to organise foreign help (mainly because Spain and France had just signed the Treaty of the Pyrenees). The uprising was quickly suppressed when the Commonwealth army arrived.

Nevertheless, the efforts of successive Interregnum regimes to ensure that parliamentary membership was denied to Royalists is a further demonstration of the strength of Royalist feeling. It is generally accepted that free elections at any time during the Interregnum would have resulted in a Parliament that would have restored monarchy. That the majority of the ruling élite continued to favour monarchic government and was never really reconciled to republicanism, even after 10 years of fairly effective government, helped to create the conditions in which restoration of monarchy was possible if not likely.

Using your knowledge of the 17th century and the information in this section, explain why monarchy continued to be the favoured form of government for England.

Why did the Interregnum fail to provide a stable form of government?

It is difficult to avoid the conclusion that continued army influence on government was the main factor causing instability in government during the Interregnum. While each change of constitutional arrangement may have had a range of causes, including particular policies or actions by the rulers, army involvement is a common factor.

The events after the First Civil War are unique in English history in creating an army that acted as a political force. That the Army should be paid by the government but not be controlled by it was unacceptable to most of the ruling élite. Lacking the ability to counter the Army's force, civilians could not prevent its interference. Although it was Army pressure that prevented Cromwell from accepting the crown in 1657, the new constitution was resented by the Army because it was not their suggestion. Curtailing the Protector's powers and introducing a second chamber into Parliament reduced Army influence. The continued dominance of the Army prevented many civilians from supporting the government wholeheartedly. Both Oliver and Richard Cromwell recognised the need for civilian support, and both tried to gain it. Oliver knew, however, that he relied more on the Army than on civilians, while Richard worked to achieve civilian support but lost power because the ordinary soldiers lost faith in him and he gave no clear lead to those in the Army who did support him.

In 1653 the Army had produced two alternative means of ruling the country, but by 1659 there were stronger internal divisions. Many of the Grandees still favoured the Protectorate, but they were over-ruled by the junior officers and rank-and-file who demanded the return of the Rump Parliament. This underlines the political bankruptcy of the Interregnum. No new suggestions were forthcoming at this juncture. Further problems created by divisions within the Army will become apparent when the role of General Monck is examined.

Why did it prove so difficult to establish a lasting form of government during the Interregnum?

George Monck (1608–1670)
A career soldier who fought for the King in the First Civil War, and Parliament thereafter, mainly in Ireland and Scotland. After the Restoration, he served Charles II.

What role did Monck play in the restoration of monarchy?

General Monck was one of the less politically involved army Grandees. At each change of regime or leader, he declared his loyalty. When the Rump was dismissed in October 1659, Sir Arthur Haselrig, one of its leaders, had appealed for help. Monck responded, moving his army to the English border. This action, along with the Navy declaring for the Rump, caused the Committee of Safety to restore the Rump. Monck then moved south, declaring that he was acting to defend Parliaments. Whether he meant the Rump or the whole Long Parliament is uncertain. Nevertheless, when he arrived in London, which was in almost open rebellion, he readmitted the secluded members. The republicans were in a minority. Monck's agreement with the secluded members was that they would dissolve the Parliament and call fresh elections. This they did. This agreement meant that restoration of monarchy was a certainty. Monck's actions had been decisive in securing this event.

Monck then conducted secret negotiations with the court of Charles II. This led to Charles's Declaration of Breda, drawn up with advice from Edward Hyde who was in turn influenced by Monck's suggestions. Monck presented it to the new Convention Parliament. Its terms were so reasonable and the situation in England so chaotic that the Restoration was secured unconditionally. Again, Monck's actions served to speed events and affect their course. When Charles II triumphantly entered London, Monck was at his side. The historian Barry Williams, in *The Elusive Settlement* (1984), regards him as the crucial figure in the events leading to the Restoration.

How important were the actions of Charles II in bringing about the Restoration?

The actions of Charles II were also important. Inevitably, his political and religious leanings were a major concern and possible barrier to restoration of the monarchy. Having accepted the advice to base his court in the Protestant Netherlands rather than a Catholic country, Charles gave enough hints about his approach to politics and religion to satisfy the Convention Parliament.

In the Declaration of Breda he demonstrated many of the characteristics apparent after he became King. He was prepared to compromise his principles in order to achieve his ends. The Declaration was a clever statement of terms. Charles would allow Parliament to deal with several difficult issues, which would inevitably prove divisive. All were to be pardoned for their part in the revolution unless Parliament decided otherwise. Charles expressed a preference for religious toleration, but would allow Parliament to settle the issue of religion. Much Crown and Royalist land had changed hands; again, Parliament would decide how to resolve this matter.

In issuing this document, Charles certainly eased his accession to the throne. He also ensured that, at least initially, many of the tensions of Restoration England were deflected from him. However, by the time the Declaration was read to Parliament it was a case of when, rather than if, the Restoration would occur. Charles's actions are important in explaining the timing of the Restoration and its terms, rather than whether or not it would happen.

1. How important was the role of Charles II in bringing about the restoration of monarchy?

2. Explain what you think was the most important reason for the restoration of the monarchy.

8.2.7 What was the significance of the Interregnum?
A CASE STUDY IN HISTORICAL INTERPRETATION

In 1660, when the republican experiment was over, those involved probably reflected on how the period had affected their lives. They were also in a position to judge its wider contemporary significance, just as people nowadays comment on events reported in the news. What they could not do was what historians can, which is to assess the historical significance of the Interregnum. Knowledge of the Restoration period, as well as the ability to analyse the course of events and hence evaluate their importance, play a part in this.

As the historian Ronald Hutton, in *The British Republic* (2000), comments, 'A superficially good case could be made that the Interregnum was one of the least significant periods of English history.' The circle seemed to have gone full turn, with monarchy and Church of England restored and Parliament resuming its former role and format. Writing in the early 18th century, Bishop Gilbert Burnet concluded the section on the Interregnum in his *History of My Own Time* (published after his death): 'Thus we have passed through the times of public ruin and confusion, and are now entering upon a more regular history, and a scene of action more delightful.' Burnet was keen that his readers should learn the lessons of history; his opinion of the Interregnum is, therefore, abundantly clear.

As time went on, however, the Interregnum took on a different significance for historians. The classic Whig interpretation of historians such as T.B. Macaulay in his *History of England* was of a false dawn of parliamentary supremacy, prefiguring the 19th-century triumph of parliamentary democracy. This view prevailed until the mid-20th century when alternative interpretations provoked debate.

Marxist historians such as Christopher Hill identify the English Revolution as the first 'bourgeois revolution', with the rising merchant and commercial classes ousting the feudal aristocracy from power. The revolution created the necessary conditions for their economic advance. Historians such as R.B. Merriman, in *Six Contemporaneous Revolutions* (1938), set the English Revolution in the context of a wider European crisis in which revolutionary events in France, Portugal, Catalonia, Naples, Sicily and Ukraine were deemed to have similar causes. This interpretation also has its weaknesses, not least of which is the difficulty in establishing a class basis for the revolutionary actions in England. Studies of each of the areas of Europe that experienced unrest have tended to highlight the differences rather than the similarities.

Historian Derek Hirst, in *England in Conflict, 1603–1660* (1999), has more recently challenged the Whig interpretation on other grounds. The classic Whig view tended to ignore the Restoration period, 1660–88, as a discontinuity in the inevitable rise of Parliament. The next step was the Glorious Revolution of 1688–89. That interpretation has serious flaws. The restored monarchy was potentially very powerful, lacking significant restrictions. As Hirst points out, 'parliamentary ways only survived by a narrow margin'. In many ways, continuity with the Tudor and early Stuart constitution is apparent. Relations between Crown and Parliament were often tense and at times hostile. Charles II attempted to dispense groups from the law and he ruled without Parliament for four years at the end of his reign. James II dispensed Catholics from the laws that prevented them from holding office and continued Charles II's policy of recalling and reissuing borough charters in order to influence elections. The path to parliamentary democracy was insecure and uncertain.

Nevertheless, this places the emphasis on conflict between Crown and Parliament, just as used to be the case with Elizabethan and early Stuart history. More recent revisions – for example, John Miller's *After the Civil Wars* (2000) – recognise cooperation between the two institutions as the dominant theme in post-Restoration England, even if at times relations were strained. The ruling élite, including the monarch, had learned many lessons. Although Charles II clashed with Parliament, he was prepared to compromise at least some of his principles. James II dispensed with some parliamentary laws, but would not engage in battle to defend his position. Monarchs exercised greater caution in their dealings with Parliament, unable to forget the fate of Charles I. Most importantly, the threat that the gentry had experienced to their traditional role in government meant that they would never again challenge the monarch as relentlessly as they had in the Long Parliament.

The English Revolution has also been considered by Ronald Hutton, in *The British Republic* (2000), in the context of the British Isles. Just as no assessment of its causes would be complete without reference to events in Ireland and Scotland, so its significance has also been judged in this wider sense. During the Interregnum, the British Isles had been united under one government for the first time, albeit enforced by English military presence. England was clearly the dominant partner, and when the Act of Union reunited Scotland with England in 1707 it was again carried out in the interests of England.

To what extent does your study of the 17th century to 1660 suggest that the Interregnum marked a break with the past?

What if the English Revolution had not occurred? Ronald Hutton concludes *The British Republic* by suggesting that without the revolution the Crown's power would have been weaker and the ruling élite less intent on creating a stable settlement. The Restoration could be interpreted as a period when the ruling élite began to identify its interests with those of monarchy and to close ranks to ensure that the lower orders were excluded from power and influence.

8.3 Oliver Cromwell

Key Issues

● *What motivated Oliver Cromwell?*

● *What were Oliver Cromwell's aims in government?*

● *Why has Oliver Cromwell provoked so much controversy among contemporaries and historians?*

8.3.1 To what extent was Cromwell a self-made man?

8.3.2 Historical interpretation: Cromwell in Ireland

8.3.3 Religious beliefs or personal ambition: what motivated Oliver Cromwell?

8.3.4 How consistent was Cromwell the politician?

8.3.5 Why did Cromwell refuse to become King Oliver?

8.3.6 Why is Oliver Cromwell such a controversial figure in English history?

Framework of Events

1599	Birth of Oliver Cromwell
1628	Cromwell is elected MP for Huntingdon
1640	Elected MP for Cambridge in the Short and Long Parliaments
1642	Raises a troop of soldiers and ambushes a Royalist convoy outside Cambridge; fights at battle of Edgehill
1643	Joins army of the Eastern Association
1644	Made Lieutenant-General of the army of the Eastern Association under the Earl of Manchester; takes part in battle of Marston Moor
	Supports liberty of conscience in the national church
	Quarrel with Earl of Manchester about prosecution of the war
	Supports Self-Denying Ordinance and creation of New Model Army
1645	Exempted from Self-Denying Ordinance; victory at Naseby
1647	Negotiates with King on The Heads of the Proposals; takes part in Putney Debates; suppresses army mutiny at Ware
1648	Takes part in Second Civil War; arrives in London after Pride's Purge; commits to trial of Charles I
1649	Signs death warrant of Charles I; puts down army mutiny at Burford; leads expedition to Ireland; sieges of Drogheda and Wexford
1650	Commander of force against Scotland; battle of Dunbar
1651	Battle of Worcester
1653	Dissolves Rump Parliament; is installed as Lord Protector
1654	Triers and Ejectors Ordinances
	Ends Anglo-Dutch war
	Union with Scotland; first Protectorate Parliament; Western Design expeditionary force sets off
1655	Defeat of Western Design; appointment of Major-Generals; readmission of Jews into England is discussed
1656	Second Protectorate Parliament; Nayler's case
1657	Humble Petition and Advice is presented; Cromwell refuses the crown; resignation of Lambert as a Major-General
1658	Second session of Second Protectorate Parliament; death of Oliver Cromwell.

Overview

THE aim of this chapter is to examine some of the controversies surrounding the role of Oliver Cromwell in the English Revolution, rather than to provide an exhaustive account of his life and actions. From the preceding two chapters, it appears that Cromwell played a central part in many events between 1642 and 1658, yet his importance should not be exaggerated. The impact of his rule on the lives of ordinary people in England was limited. He never instigated constitutional reform and he bequeathed an impossible inheritance to his son Richard. Nevertheless, no study of the English Revolution can ignore a figure who, for both contemporaries and historians, has been the subject of so much debate.

8.3.1 To what extent was Cromwell a self-made man?

The wheels of 17th-century politics were oiled by patronage. Men achieved their position because of who they knew, more than by their abilities. Family ties, friendship with prominent local figures and the sharing of common political causes all contributed to the status a man achieved. Initially, Oliver Cromwell depended on all these networks. Yet he was unable to make an impact in the Long Parliament, remaining in relative obscurity until he achieved military prestige during the First Civil War. The Self-Denying Ordinance would have prevented him from continuing in this role had he not been exempted from it.

Oliver Cromwell, portrait by Robert Walker, 1649

A contemporary, Edward Hyde, proposed the idea that Oliver Cromwell was a 'self-made man, risen from obscurity'. As Earl of Clarendon, Hyde published a history of the period. He was remarkably fair to Cromwell considering that he sided with the King in the Civil Wars. However, this does not mean that everything Hyde wrote was accurate. The Earl of Manchester had levelled the same accusation of humble origin at Cromwell earlier, in 1644, in their public quarrel about the aims of the First Civil War. However, the Earl of Manchester's remarks are hardly likely to be objective.

Historians have sometimes chosen to repeat Manchester's and Clarendon's assessment of Cromwell's origins. It fitted well with the values of 19th-century historians who themselves advocated the idea that men could rise to greatness from lowly birth. Modern historians such as Antonia Fraser (*Cromwell, Our Chief of Men*, 1973) and Peter Gaunt (*Oliver Cromwell*, 1996) have also taken the view that Cromwell was a self-made man. John Morrill, who has researched Cromwell's origins thoroughly, concurs with the part of the interpretation that places him fairly low within the ruling élite. In *Oliver Cromwell and the English Revolution* (1990), he describes Cromwell's position in 1640 as 'an estate manager only recently recovered from a spell as a yeoman'. Cromwell's material circumstances had declined as he reached adulthood. His social status had suffered as a consequence of this and of his disagreement, in the 1630s, with the ruling **oligarchy** of his home town of Huntingdon.

Oligarchy: A small group ruling a town or city.

In Morrill's opinion, Cromwell's election as Member of Parliament for Cambridge in 1640 can only be explained by his connections with influential magnates such as the Earl of Warwick. While the evidence for these connections may be thin, Morrill argues, there is no other reason why a man who only became a **freeman** of Cambridge in January 1640, after the elections for the Short Parliament were called, should be elected. This suggests that Cromwell was not wholly 'self-made'. However, the question remains as to whether or not Cromwell rose to prominence through his own virtues, through ambition, or as a result of his contacts.

Freeman: A citizen with political rights.

Cromwell and the Long Parliament

In the Long Parliament, before the outbreak of Civil War, Cromwell was not a prominent figure. He was noted for his plain speaking, but this was hardly an asset. Clarendon said that little notice was taken of Cromwell at first. He failed in his attempt to plea for John Lilburne's release from prison. When he attacked an MP who was defending the bishops, his language was so extreme that many members interrupted him. He was nearly called to the bar, meaning that he would be suspended from the House. However, Cromwell also promoted the idea of regular meetings of parliament, calling for annual parliaments. This was eventually adopted as the Triennial Act. He was not always ignored, nor was he a parliamentary leader. Connections alone were not sufficient to raise his profile.

By late 1641, the members of the Long Parliament were more divided but also more susceptible to suggestions of the King's treachery. When news of the Irish Rebellion broke, it was Cromwell who suggested that a militia should be formed under the Earl of Essex, another of his natural parliamentary allies. After the King's attempt to arrest the five members in January 1642, it was Cromwell who moved for defence measures to be brought in. At this stage, Cromwell was no longer regarded as a liability. His direct approach was more appropriate in these changing circumstances and MPs were more willing to listen to him.

Cromwell the soldier

Cromwell's enthusiasm for the Parliamentary cause was apparent from the outset. Even before the King raised his standard at Nottingham, Cromwell had been engaged in action. He was sent by Parliament to organise a force in his local area around Ely and Cambridge. Cromwell seized Cambridge Castle and prevented the colleges from sending their plate to the King at York.

Cromwell rose fast through the ranks of the army. The records are unclear about his role in the battle of Edgehill, although he was present. After this, he took an increasingly prominent part in Parliament's war effort. Convinced that Parliament needed better-trained cavalry, Cromwell raised a regiment in his local area early in 1643. By autumn, he was speaking of the honest, godly men of his troop. He berated the Suffolk committee who criticised his choice of captain: 'I had rather have a plain russet-coated captain that knows what he fights for than that which you call a gentleman and is nothing else.' He was notable for his indifference to social rank and religious persuasion; provided men had enthusiasm and ability they could serve under him.

By this time, Cromwell was a captain in the army of the Eastern Association. It was his determination to provide for the material needs of his **Ironsides**, as well as his growing list of military successes, that added to his reputation as an officer. As the war progressed, it became clear that Parliament would need more reliable forces. To organise this, the Earl of Manchester became the Major-General of the Eastern Association in August 1643.

Ironsides: The nickname given to Cromwell's cavalry in the army of the Eastern Association.

At first, the Earl of Manchester and Cromwell seemed to share a common purpose. Both were determined on a godly reformation and both were clear that their army should not be under the direct orders of the Earl of Essex, as this could be to the detriment of the war effort in the eastern counties. This coincided with Cromwell's promotion to second-in-command under Manchester and with his appointment to the Committee of Both Kingdoms. Viscount Saye and Sele nominated him to the latter position. Within a year, however, a difference over goals had divided Manchester and Cromwell.

Cromwell's quarrel with the Earl of Manchester

The issue of war aims arose after the battle of Marston Moor. Had Parliament's Army acted decisively, the King could have been defeated in months. Instead, both Essex and Manchester hesitated because they were reluctant to beat the King outright. The opportunity was lost. When called to account by the Committee of Both Kingdoms, Cromwell launched his attack on the Earl of Manchester, accusing him of being 'backward to all engagement'. This was backed up by Sir William Waller and Sir Arthur Haselrig. After narrowly avoiding being impeached, Cromwell, together with his allies in the Lords such as Viscount Saye and Sele, abandoned personal confrontation. Instead, they introduced what became the Self-Denying Ordinance. A struggle between the Lords and the Commons ensued. The controversy lies in whether or not Cromwell was prepared to sacrifice his own military career for the sake of defeating the king.

1. How did Cromwell's social contacts help his rise to power?

2. How did Cromwell's success as a soldier contribute to his rise to power?

3. What evidence is there that Cromwell was motivated by ambition between 1640 and 1646?

One view suggests that Cromwell had little to lose. In the event of the Ordinance not being passed, Cromwell would not need to resign. If it were to be passed, Cromwell's allies in Parliament would prevail, and he might expect to be exempted from it. Thus Cromwell was taking a calculated risk in proposing the Ordinance.

The counter-argument is that Cromwell could certainly not have guaranteed that he would be exempted from the Ordinance. In the debate about the Ordinance, an unsuccessful attempt was made to exempt Essex. Trying to exempt Cromwell at this point would have invited charges of self-interest. Although Cromwell was later exempted from the Ordinance, this was only on a temporary basis: it had to be renewed periodically. This left Cromwell politically vulnerable and unable to press Parliament for the cause of religious toleration. As a result, he had no influence on political developments until at least the end of the First Civil War. By this time, his military reputation had also contributed to his influential position.

8.3.2 *Cromwell in Ireland*
A CASE STUDY IN HISTORICAL INTERPRETATION

Royalist papacy: Catholic support for the King.

In 1649 Cromwell, along with most Englishmen, would have regarded Ireland as a stronghold of **Royalist papacy**, which had to be re-conquered. This is clear from as early as 1647, when Cromwell offered his arrears of pay plus an additional £5,000 to invest in an Irish campaign. By 1649, many Catholics had joined with the Protestant Royalists of the Marquis of Ormonde. There was a further, independent, group of rebel Catholics as well as other Royalist Protestants. Few Irish were allied to the Commonwealth cause. This was in contrast to the situation in Scotland where the new English government could ally with one of the factions. Ireland had to be conquered. This is what Cromwell set out to achieve in August 1649.

By the 19th century, in the legends of Irish nationalists, Cromwell had become the personification of English violence in Ireland. His reputation rested mainly on events following the breaking of the sieges at Drogheda and Wexford. An historian who proposed this view of Oliver Cromwell was the Rev. Denis Murphy, in *Cromwell in Ireland, A History of Cromwell's Irish Campaigns* (1883). Not only had Cromwell massacred soldiers, but his men had murdered civilians as they rampaged through the towns after the sieges were broken. However, as the historian Jason McElligott points out, in *Cromwell, Our Chief of Enemies* (1994), 'changing perceptions of Cromwell in 19th-century Ireland seem to have been based largely upon the folk memory of the illiterate classes'.

The task of modern historians has been to distinguish history from legend, to trace the origins of the stories of atrocities and to ascertain whether or not they have any basis in fact. Nevertheless, too many modern historians have accepted the assumptions of the 19th century. Derek Hirst, writing in *England in Conflict, 1603–1660* (1999), takes a traditional view. He states that Cromwell killed not only soldiers who refused to surrender at Drogheda, but also civilians. He also lost control of his men at Wexford, leading to the slaughter of about 2,000. Hirst explains this uncharacteristically barbarous act as exacting revenge for the massacre of Protestants by the Catholic Irish in 1641. He concludes that, 'The strenuousness of his justifications to Parliament betrays his awareness that it was not a pretty moment in his career.' Describing events at Wexford as God bringing a just judgement, though, was Cromwell's normal response after a victory. In any case, Hirst's interpretation depends on accepting the figures for those killed that have been handed down over the years.

Barry Coward, in *Oliver Cromwell* (1991), also accepts the received interpretation: 'The brutal behaviour of his troops towards soldiers and civilians alike – for which he [Cromwell] was personally responsible – at the first engagement of the war, the siege of Drogheda (3–10 September 1649), and that he sanctioned at the siege of Wexford (2–10 October 1649) ...'.

Other recent historians, such as David Stevenson in *Oliver Cromwell and the English Revolution* (1991), concentrate on establishing the conventions of 17th-century warfare. They rest their case on a comparison of events in Ireland with those in sieges in the Thirty Years War. They would argue that Cromwell must be judged on the basis of the protocols of the

17th century. The Geneva Convention did not govern Cromwell and nor should we expect him to subscribe to its values.

On this basis, some historians have been more sympathetic to Cromwell. David Stevenson, for example, says that what happened at Drogheda and Wexford was typical behaviour after a siege, in the context of European warfare of the period. At Drogheda, the governor refused to surrender after a breach had been made in the walls. He thereby forfeited the **right to quarter** in the accepted conventions of 17th-century warfare. Stevenson's account of events is based, however, on the early 20th-century interpretation by W.C. Abbott, in *The Writings and Speeches of Oliver Cromwell* (1937–1947). Of Abbott's edition of Cromwell's speeches and letters, it has been written, in *Oliver Cromwell and the English Revolution* (1990): 'Abbott has an appearance of scholarly solidity which disguises hundreds of factual errors, some very poor and uncritical editing and some unreliable texts.'

Right to quarter: Soldiers who surrendered were spared slaughter.

An alternative interpretation, supplied by P. Gaunt in *Oliver Cromwell* (1996), is that, 'Cromwell felt that by letting loose such terror at Drogheda, the Irish would be in fear and less inclined to resist, strongholds would be more inclined to surrender at the first summons and overall, therefore, English and Irish lives would be saved...'.

Some modern English and Irish historians have taken a different approach. They have assumed the far harder task of trying to discover the truth of what happened in Ireland. Writing in the 1990s, they have come to the conclusion that the Irish nationalist version of Cromwell was largely mythical and created for corrupt political purposes. Tom Reilly concludes, in *Cromwell: An Honourable Enemy* (1999), that 'it remains a sad fact that the perception of the battles of Drogheda and Wexford in modern Ireland is riddled with historical inaccuracies. This is the result of the plethora of 19th century misconstructions of the

Cromwell's siege of Drogheda, September 1649

events from the pens of bigoted writers and from the subsequently unbalanced Irish educational system of the twentieth century.' He believes that although 3,000 were killed at Drogheda, this does not represent a full-scale massacre of the town's inhabitants. Besides this, and contrary to popular myth, 'What is manifestly clear is that Cromwell is nowhere on record as having ordered an indiscriminate slaughter of non-combatants during any battle in his life.'

James Scott Wheeler claims, in *Cromwell in Ireland* (1999), that not only did Cromwell not create anti-Irish or anti-Catholic feeling, but that also he was conciliatory towards the Irish. He appreciated that, in the absence of a sympathetic section of the population, the people had to be won over if the conquest were to succeed. These historians would also point out that Henry Ireton and others, who carried out the redistribution of land in Ireland after Cromwell left, were responsible for far greater suffering.

No doubt the argument will continue. Inevitably, it is difficult to detach interpretations of Cromwell from events in modern Ireland.

Why have Cromwell's actions in Ireland been the subject of so much debate among historians?

8.3.3 Religious beliefs or personal ambition: what motivated Oliver Cromwell?

What were Cromwell's religious beliefs and aims?

This is a question that has only been discussed by historians relatively recently. Cromwell's contemporaries, who published numerous attacks accusing him of personal ambition, rarely questioned his religious sincerity. Nineteenth-century historians made assumptions about Cromwell's beliefs that fitted their religious concerns and their image of the Lord Protector. However, Cromwell was neither the champion of Presbyterianism nor of the sects. Nor did he want religious toleration.

Recently, historians such as Blair Worden (in *Toleration and the Cromwellian Protectorate*, 1984) and J.C. Davis (in *Oliver Cromwell and the English Revolution*, 1990) have reached the conclusion that although Cromwell wanted to create Christian unity, he believed there was no fixed route to godliness. Cromwell's aim of liberty of conscience was not the same as toleration. It represented the first move towards unity. Although he had dealings with men of a range of religious persuasions, this did not mean that he accepted all their views. He was intolerant of those who wanted to prescribe particular religious forms. Cromwell regarded godliness, not uniformity, as the measure of acceptability. He was not prepared to coerce. This explains the priorities of the Committee of Triers in admitting men to the ministry and Cromwell's reluctance to impose Presbyterianism or any other form on the nation. There were no church courts, leaving ministers with the dual problem of the sects and apathy. The Ejectors were only active in a few areas and local committees were apt to be taken over by extremists

How did Cromwell explain events?

Cromwell relied on providence to explain events. He did so consistently, and therefore appeared sincere. As the Civil War progressed, he spoke with increasing confidence of God's cause. He attributed his success to providence. Cromwell was convinced of the need to execute the King on these grounds. Had the execution been carried out because men wanted it, regicide (killing the King) would not have been acceptable. Such was Cromwell's conviction that God was behind the action that he was adamant in his arguments for execution. The defeat of the Irish and of the Scots was also providential, confirmed by the coincidence of the victories at Dunbar and Worcester on his 'lucky day', 3 September.

Frequent references to necessity and providence might have provoked the criticism that Cromwell was trying to justify actions that were to his benefit. But if Cromwell attributed his successes to God's intervention, then surely this detracted from the praise that could have been heaped on him. The victor of Drogheda, Wexford, Dunbar and Worcester saw himself as God's instrument, rather than as a military hero.

Cromwell was also willing to use providence to explain failures. When the godly reformation seemed to be faltering, early in 1654, he ordered national days of fasting and humiliation. When the expedition to Hispaniola ended disastrously, he attributed it to God's displeasure at the failure of God's chosen people (the English) to do God's will.

He questioned constantly whether or not he was carrying out God's will. When he was offered the crown in 1657, Cromwell consulted the Bible for evidence of God's direction. As J.C. Davis observes, in *Oliver Cromwell* (2001), 'In the case of his decision about Kingship, as in many other decisions, there is good evidence that these were the twin authorities to which he turned.'

The consistency with which Cromwell cited the Bible provides further evidence of his sincerity. In expelling the Rump Parliament, Cromwell likened himself to Moses leading the Israelites towards the Promised Land. This analogy had already been used by contemporaries. Unfortunately, like the Israelites, the members of the Nominated Assembly fell out among themselves. Cromwell felt that he was experiencing the frustration that Moses had. He allowed the Nominated Assembly to collapse. That this led to his promotion to the position of Lord Protector confirmed that he was to be God's instrument. On this occasion, providence benefited him, but he was a reluctant leader.

> *How can Cromwell's frequent references to providence be used to illustrate his sincerity?*

Cromwell's reliance on seeking God's providence can also be used to explain his apparent lack of long-term policies. Cromwell addressed each circumstance as it arose, consulting the Bible and his own conscience to discern God's will. He was reactive, but with a purpose: the introduction of Godly reform.

Was Cromwell driven by personal ambition?

Contemporary criticism of Cromwell was levelled at him at particular times during the late 1640s and 1650s. The main charge was that he put personal ambition above loyalty to his friends and allies, that he used people for personal gain.

The first time Cromwell was the subject of an attack was from the Levellers. The events leading to the King's illegal trial and execution demonstrated a disregard of the rights of freeborn Englishmen that was shocking to his former associates. While debating the 'Agreement of the People' at Putney, Cromwell was also negotiating with the King on the 'Heads of the Proposals'. Conveniently for Cromwell, and somewhat suspiciously, the

? What is the
significance of this
interpretation of Oliver
Cromwell?

An engraving showing Cromwell
standing in state at Somerset
House, 1659. He is shown as
having shed his armour
(representing the military origins
of his power) and put on the
trappings of royalty.

Tyrant: A ruler who has absolute
power over other people, and who
uses this power cruelly and unjustly.

? How convincing is the
charge that Cromwell
was driven by
ambition?

King escaped from the custody of one of Cromwell's relations (presenting the opportunity to end the Putney debates and call the rendezvous of the Army) to the custody of another on the Isle of Wight. Although he was absent from London, Cromwell has been accused of masterminding Pride's Purge. He certainly argued strongly for the trial and execution of the King, which clearly denied Charles his rights. Cromwell was a member of the unconstitutional Rump Parliament that overrode John Lilburne's right to justice.

Surprisingly, contemporaries thereafter failed to make negative comment on Cromwell's actions until he became Lord Protector. It would have been hard for the English to criticise his military successes, but even the military coup of April 1653 was ignored, by and large. However, in assuming the role of Head of State Cromwell invited criticism, which reached a torrent with the offer of the crown in 1657. Former allies of all persuasions denounced him as a power-hungry **tyrant**. Immediately after his death, both praise and criticism were surprisingly muted.

It was during the Restoration period that many of his contemporaries began to make their criticisms of Cromwell. As the historian John Morrill notes, in *Oliver Cromwell and the English Revolution* (1990), the negative view of Cromwell as personally ambitious 'derives rather too much from the reflections of contemporaries written down much later, through the distorting glass of the Restoration, when both experience and prudence prevented accurate recollection'.

Some historians, such as J.P. Kenyon in *Stuart England* (1985), have accepted the charges levelled at Cromwell by his contemporaries, as well as those regarding his treatment of the Irish. Although there is clear evidence that Cromwell did not seek financial gain, evidence of his precise involvement in events such as the Army's kidnapping of the King in June 1647 and the introduction of the Instrument of Government (see page 278) has been more difficult to find.

Above all, debate has centred on Cromwell's desire to be King. Whatever the conclusions regarding his reasons for refusing the crown in 1657, it is clear that there were other times when he could have seized the throne, yet he did not. After his triumph against the Scots in 1651 he was given an income of £4,000 a year and the use of Hampton Court Palace. Such was his status that he could have become King, but he made no bid to do so.

In 1653, he could have taken power immediately on the dissolution of the Rump. He had the opportunity, but there was no suggestion that he would take on such a role. When kingship was discussed at the time the Instrument of Government was drawn up, Cromwell made it clear that he was not interested. Whatever his motives and however long he took to reach a decision, Cromwell refused the crown in 1657. No doubt the commonwealthsmen and republicans were shocked by his lengthy deliberations, but in the context of the religious aims stated above, Cromwell's hesitation appears in a more favourable light.

8.3.4 How consistent was Cromwell the politician?

Cromwell's consistency of aims was questioned by contemporaries and has been queried by historians since, such as by Blair Worden in *The Rump Parliament, 1648–1653* (1974). As he often seemed to benefit from developments that disadvantaged their causes, Cromwell's contemporaries accused him of being manipulative. However, it must be noted that neither Levellers nor Fifth Monarchists recognised, as Cromwell came to do, that politics is the art of the possible and that aims had to be achieved by practical means. Adjustments had to be made to take account of changing circumstances: the Civil Wars and the various constitutional arrangements of the Interregnum. Yet there is also an argument holding that Cromwell was consistent in his aim to promote civil and religious liberties.

The arguments for and against consistency depend on an understanding of what Cromwell's political aims were. He was not the author of any of the constitutional documents of the period. His utterances on the subject generally show him to have been conservative in outlook, favouring a settlement with many of the features of monarchic rule. Cromwell was a reluctant regicide. The only time he was involved with negotiations for a settlement with the King was on the basis of the Heads of the Proposals. These were the most conservative peace proposals put to the King; even the religious terms allowed for the continued existence of bishops.

The Levellers felt deceived because Cromwell engaged with them in the Putney Debates at the same time that he was trying to achieve a settlement with the King. However, his aim was not to allow the Levellers to influence him into more democratic views, but to maintain relations between the Army and Parliament. The Levellers misunderstood his aims. Hence, when they were sidelined and eliminated as a political force, they accused Cromwell and the other Grandees of betraying them.

The precepts of the Heads of the Proposals – a single head of state, parliamentary government and relative religious toleration – can be seen to recur as Cromwell's ideal constitutional form. Above all, he seems to have aimed for stability, for 'healing and settling'. Cromwell was never a Fifth Monarchist, accepting the need to execute the King in order to make way for the rule of King Jesus. So accepting the role of Lord Protector was not a sign of his inconsistency. Cromwell claimed that he dissolved the Rump because it aimed to perpetuate itself by calling by-elections rather than a general election, thus denying the right of the people of England to representative government. He accepted the Instrument of Government, which provided for a single head of state, regular representative parliaments, religious toleration and joint control of the militia as its fundamentals.

However, the counter-argument holds that Cromwell was a reluctant partner of Parliament. Given the impulsive way in which he dissolved the Rump, marching in with more force than Charles I had used in his attempt to arrest the five members, it seems fair to suggest that Cromwell was prepared to disregard parliamentary privileges. Cromwell gave as his excuse the Rump's plans to perpetuate itself, but it is far from clear that this is what was happening and Cromwell himself destroyed the evidence. Cromwell railed at each of his Protectorate Parliaments, making it clear that he had little patience with their concerns and debates. This all suggests that Cromwell was indeed inconsistent, only favouring representative government when its members' views coincided with his own. In 1654, when some MPs refused to accept the religious fundamentals of the Instrument of Government, they were excluded from the House. When Parliament seemed to have lost its sense of proportion over James Nayler, Cromwell favoured the introduction of a second chamber.

Cromwell undoubtedly benefited from the discrediting of the more extreme political and religious groups, but their fate was probably inevitable in the context of 17th-century society. He also benefited from the demise of the Rump in the sense that, ultimately, he became Head of State. However, this does not seem to have been his aim. He never had absolute power, except perhaps in the first few months of the Protectorate. Nor was he a military dictator. He did not enrich himself or his family, although he did raise many of them to important positions. Under the stress of his position he became increasingly ill and died a disappointed man who had made only limited progress towards achieving his aims.

> *Using the information in this section of the book, discuss the claim that Cromwell was consistent in his political aims.*

8.3.5 Why did Cromwell refuse to become King Oliver?

Alderman: A member of the governing body/city council.

Oliver Cromwell grappling with his chief opponents. His right foot is on a Scotsman, a pleading Frenchman is carried under his left arm, his legs are clasped around the neck of an Irishman and his right hand holds the guts of a Hollander. A griffin with a sword is placing a crown on his head and he is surrounded by scenes of his various exploits.

In January 1657, a plot by the Leveller Miles Sindercombe to assassinate Oliver Cromwell was discovered. This highlighted a problem with the Instrument of Government: the means of appointing a new Lord Protector on the death of Cromwell was unclear. This led to speculation about what might happen. The three armies in each of the kingdoms – England, Scotland and Ireland – might all favour a different candidate. Renewed civil war could be the result. In this case, might not the Royalists seize the opportunity to place Charles Stuart on the throne? It was clear to Cromwellians that action was needed.

On 23 February, the London **Alderman** Sir Christopher Packe introduced a document into Parliament proposing that the crown be offered to Cromwell. In March, after prolonged discussion in Parliament, the proposal was offered to Cromwell as the Humble Petition and Advice.

Cromwell himself had already become frustrated with some aspects of the Instrument of Government. The prolonged debate on the case of James Nayler, and the harsh punishment handed out to him suggested to Cromwell that a second chamber in Parliament was needed. It would temper the excesses of the Commons. The Humble Petition and Advice included this addition to Parliament.

However, the Humble Petition and Advice was unpopular with the Army. A petition against monarchy, signed by 100 army officers, was drawn up. Cromwell hesitated before making a decision. In April, he met with the parliamentary commissioners to explain why he hesitated (see Sources D and E on page 311). In May he rejected the Crown, accepting a revised version of the Humble Petition and Advice. He gained the right to nominate his successor, but in other ways his powers were limited. In June, Cromwell was crowned as Lord Protector.

The reasons for Cromwell's hesitation in reaching a decision were commented on by those involved at the time, and Cromwell himself offered an explanation. This began a debate that has continued since. It centres round Cromwell's motivation. Was he politically ambitious, aspiring to the royal title or did he regard the crown as 'but a feather in a man's cap'? Did he hesitate in order to ascertain God's providential will through prayer and by consulting the scriptures?

 ## Source-based questions: Why did Oliver Cromwell refuse the crown?

SOURCE A

I have paid my respects to the house of Cromwell's ambassador, when we exchanged compliments. Afterwards he spoke of the Parliament of England. He said they wanted his master to take the title of King, but he seemed reluctant to do this since he wields more authority in his present position than he would as King, because he would be obliged to concede and renew many privileges and jurisdictions to Parliament such as were granted by Henry VIII.

From Francesco Giustiniani, Venetian ambassador in France, to the Doge and Senate of Venice, 27 March 1657, in Calendar of State Papers Venetian, *ed. A.B. Hinds, vol. XXXI (1657–59)*

SOURCE B

I suppose you have heard of the address made by one hundred Officers, to his Highness yesterday sevennight, that his Highness would not hearken to the title King because it was not pleasing to his army, and was a matter of scandal to the people of God, of great rejoicing to the enemy; that it was hazardous to his own person, and of great danger to the three nations; such an assumption making way for Charles Stuart to come in again.

His Highness said, the time was, when they boggled not at the word King, for the Instrument by which the Government now stands, was presented to his Highness with the title in it and

he refused to accept of the title. But how it comes to pass that they now startle at that title, they best knew. That, for his part, he loved the title, a feather in the hat, as little as they did.

That it is time to come to a settlement, and lay aside arbitrary proceedings, so unacceptable to the nation. And by the proceedings of this Parliament, you see they stand in need of a check, or balancing power, (meaning the House of Lords, or a House so constituted) for the case of James Nayler might happen to be your own case. By their judicial power they fall upon life and member, and doth the Instrument allow me to control it?

From The Diary of Thomas Burton vol. I, *ed. J.T. Rutt. Burton is reporting on a discussion that took place on 7 March 1657, between Cromwell and the Officers who presented a petition to him urging against acceptance of the crown.*

SOURCE C

The Kingship is not (I should say) so interwoven in the laws but that the laws may still be executed to equal justice, and with equal satisfaction of the people, and equally to answer all objections as well without it as with it. Truly though the kingship be not a mere title but a name of office that runs through the whole of the law, yet it is not, from the reason of the name, but from what is signified. It is a name of office plainly implying the supreme authority. As such a title hath been fixed, so it may be unfixed. And certainly they, the primary legislative authority, had the disposal of it, and might have had it, and might have detracted from it, and so may you. And if it be so that you may, why then I say there is nothing of necessity in your argument, but all turns on consideration of the expedience of it. I have somewhat of conscience to answer as to the matter, why I cannot undertake this Name. Truly the Providence of God hath laid aside this Title of King providentially: and that not by sudden humour or passion. It hath been by issue of Ten or Twelve Years Civil War, wherein much blood hath been shed. And God hath seemed Providential, seemed to appear as a Providence, not only in striking at the Family, but at the Name. I will not seek to set up that which Providence hath destroyed, and laid in the dust; I would not build Jericho again! And this is somewhat to me, and to my judgment and my conscience. This, in truth, it is this that hath an awe upon my spirit.

From Oliver Cromwell's Letters and Speeches vol. II and III, *ed. T. Carlyle. Cromwell to representatives of the second Protectorate Parliament, 13 April 1657.*

SOURCE D

A committee was appointed for a free conference with his Highness to satisfy him of the reason and necessity of their [Parliament's] demands. And yesterday his Highness gave answer to them. That for his part he values not one name more than another. But in respect many godly men that have hazarded their lives in this cause are dissatisfied with it, and Providence having with the old family eradicated the old title, he thinks it his duty to beg of the Parliament not to put that upon those good men which they cannot swallow, though it may be their weakness. I believe his Highness is jealous there may be some distemper in the army.

From: a letter dated 13 April 1657, written by John Bridge, an Irish MP in the Second Protectorate Parliament, to Henry Cromwell, Lord Deputy in Ireland

SOURCE E

May 1657
Cromwell endeavoured by all possible means to prevail with the officers of the army to approve his design, and knowing that Lieutenant-General Fleetwood and Col. Desborough were particularly averse to it, he invited himself to dine personally with the Colonel, and carried the Lieutenant-General with him, where he began to droll with them about monarchy, and speaking slightly of it, said it was but a feather in a man's cap, and therefore wondered that men would not please the children, and permit them to enjoy their rattle. But they assured him, that there was more in this matter than he perceived; that those who put him upon it were no enemies to Charles Stuart; and that if he accepted of it, he would infallibly draw ruin on himself and friends. Desborough went home, and there found Col. Pride and having imparted to him the design of Cromwell to accept the crown, Pride answered, 'he shall not'. 'Why', said the Colonel, 'how wilt thou hinder it?' To which Pride replied, 'Get me a petition drawn, and I will prevent it.' This petition was subscribed by a majority of those officers relating to that part of the army which was then quartered about the town. As soon as the notice of it was brought to Cromwell, he sent for Lieutenant-General Fleetwood and told him that he wondered he would allow such a petition to proceed so far, which he might have hindered since he knew it to be his resolution not to accept the crown without the consent of the army. The House received a message from Cromwell, that they would meet him in the Banqueting House: so the members came to Whitehall, and Cromwell with great ostentation of his self-denial refused the title of King.

From The Memoirs of Edmund Ludlow, *1698, C.H. Firth (ed.)*

---

1. *Summarise the reasons given in each Source for Cromwell's refusal of the Crown.*

2. *Use Source D. Explain how sincere you think Cromwell is in his explanation of his actions.*

3. *Explain which of the Sources you think provides the most reliable explanation of Cromwell's refusal of the crown.*

4. *Using all the Sources and the information contained in this chapter, examine the claim that Cromwell's refusal of the crown was consistent with his religious and political views.*

8.3.6 Why is Oliver Cromwell such a controversial figure in English history?

Cromwell is the only major non-royal Head of State the English people have had. His is the name associated with the one experiment in republican government in England. This alone makes him a figure of immense interest. He was the leader at a time of unprecedented discussion about how the country should be ruled, and when there was political turmoil and uncertainty. Debate about constitutional matters took place among people of a social rank far below that of the traditional ruling élite. All had their own ideas, and most felt that these were a reflection of God's will for England. Inevitably, Cromwell could not please everyone, and in disappointing many he offended not only their political ideals but also their religious convictions. There was not constant criticism during his lifetime, but when it surfaced it was damning.

After the restoration of the monarchy, the bodies of Cromwell and two others of the regicides were dug up and mutilated. Inevitably, those who wrote their reflections on the events of the previous 20 years were influenced by the prevailing hostility to Cromwell and his associates. The myths created thereby have proved hard to dispel.

Historians have often praised or condemned Cromwell on the basis of their own values. The most recent trends in historical thinking, however, have encouraged interpretation of the past in its own terms, rather than distorting actions and events by making assumptions about the developments that were occurring. This is thought to produce a more honest version of the past. No doubt the debate will continue, as historians continue to re-think the past.

What does this picture show about attitudes to Cromwell immediately after the Restoration?

How do you explain these attitudes?

The corpses of Cromwell, Bradshaw and Ireton are drawn and quartered and their heads stuck on spikes.

The reign of Charles II, 1660–1685

Key Issues

● To what extent did relations between Crown and Parliament deteriorate?

● To what extent did religious toleration develop?

● To what extent did relations between England and Continental Europe change?

Framework of Events

1660	April: Taxes raised to pay arrears to troops; financial settlement agreed
	May: Hyde is appointed chief minister; Church of England and bishops are restored
	August: Act of Indemnity and Oblivion
	September: Navigation Act
	October: Worcester House Declaration
	December: Dissolution of Convention Parliament
1661	January: Fifth Monarchist uprising
	April: Hyde becomes Earl of Clarendon; Savoy Conference
	May: Cavalier Parliament
	June: Annulment of all legislation without royal assent
	December: Corporation Act
1662	Militia Act; Uniformity Act; Quaker Act; Licensing Act; first Declaration of Indulgence
1663	Withdrawal of Declaration of Indulgence
1664	Triennial Act; Conventicle Act
1665	February: Second Dutch War begins
	October: Five Mile Act
	Major outbreak of plague
1666	Great Fire of London
1667	June: Dutch burn English ships in Medway
	Louis XIV invades Spanish Netherlands
	July: Treaty of Breda ends Second Dutch War
1668	Triple Alliance (England, United Provinces, Sweden)
1669	Negotiations begin for Secret Treaty of Dover
1670	Second Conventicle Act; Secret Treaty of Dover
1672	March: Third Dutch war begins; Second Declaration of Indulgence
1673	March: Withdrawal of second Declaration of Indulgence; Test Act
1674	February: Treaty of Westminster ends third Dutch War
	Danby becomes Charles's chief minister
1676	Compton Census

1677	Marriage of Mary to William of Orange
1678	July: Treaty of Nijmegen
	August: Oates reveals Popish Plot
	December: Danby falls from power; Second Test Act
1679	Cavalier Parliament is dissolved; Danby impeached; first Exclusion Bill
1680	October: Second 'Exclusion' Parliament meets
	November: Exclusion bill passes Commons but is rejected by Lords
1681	January: Second 'Exclusion' Parliament is dissolved
	March: Third 'Exclusion' Parliament is dissolved after one week
	Persecution of Dissenters intensifies
1682	November: Shaftesbury goes into exile
	First new borough charters issued
1683	Rye House Plot
1684	First steps to ease persecution of Catholics
1685	Death of Charles II.

Overview

I N May 1660, the monarchy was restored. Such was the speed with which this was done that little consideration was given to the precise terms for restoration. The settlement was enacted by Parliament over the following five years. However, as subsequent events showed, the powers of Crown and Parliament were still open to interpretation. Charles's Declarations of Indulgence, both withdrawn as a result of parliamentary pressure, are examples of this. The closing of ranks among the ruling élite in an effort to avoid further destabilisation meant that the religious laws known as the Clarendon Code created a narrow definition of the Church of England. This closing of ranks is also apparent in the increasing control

The coronation of Charles II at Westminster Abbey, 23 April 1661

over the poor, as shown in the Act of Settlement of 1662. The position of Protestant nonconformists may have been clear in law, but attitudes to the need for uniformity in religion were changing. This led to debate on the character of the Church of England. Although the authorities persecuted dissenters relentlessly at certain times in the reign, the general trend was towards greater toleration.

New legislation did not resolve the issues over which Crown and Parliament had disagreed in the early 17th century. Besides this, the Settlement left a legacy of discontent among the many Royalists who felt they had not been compensated for the sacrifices they had made during the 1640s and 1650s. However, during Charles II's reign, the economic climate improved. Greater stability in the second half of the 17th century – following a century of population growth, inflation and periodic disruption caused by wars – allowed trade to flourish. Among other effects, the resulting increase in customs duties held significant benefits for Crown finances.

The workings of politics during Charles's reign were complicated by rivalries between government ministers within the Court. At first these centred round Edward Hyde, who was created Earl of Clarendon in 1661 but fell from power in 1667. The **Cabal**, which came after him, was by no means united and collapsed as a result of parliamentary opposition to the French alliance of 1670 and the Declaration of Indulgence of 1672. The Earl of Danby followed, and he struggled to maintain good relations between Crown and Parliament in the context of Charles's pro-French foreign policy. This was despite concerted efforts to manage Parliament. Danby remained in power until 1678. The consequent split between 'Court' and 'Country' in the 1670s can be interpreted as marking the origin of political parties. It can also be argued that these did not emerge until the appearance of **'Whigs'** and **'Tories'** during the Exclusion Crisis in 1679. It is possible to trace these divisions as far back as the disagreements over the Restoration Settlement itself.

The most contentious political conflict of the reign arose in 1679. The heir to the throne, James Duke of York, probably converted to Catholicism in 1669. This was made public by his refusal to receive Easter communion in 1673. Parliament

---

Cabal: The nickname of Charles II's chief ministers, 1667–1673. The name arises from the initial letters of their surnames: Clifford, Arlington, Buckingham, Ashley Cooper and Lauderdale. Although they were grouped together, they did not hold identical political aims.

'Whigs': Supported exclusion. The nickname derived from the Scottish Covenanters' rebellion.

'Tories': Supporters of the legitimate succession. The nickname was a reference to Catholic Irish bandits.

Edward Hyde, first Earl of Clarendon (1609–1674)
First became an MP in 1640. In Long and Short Parliaments, he attacked Charles I's actions and supported the impeachment of the King's minister Stafford. When the Civil War began, he followed Charles to Oxford, was knighted and made Chancellor of the Exchequer. On the King's defeat in 1646, Hyde followed Prince Charles to Jersey, where he began his *History of the Rebellion* (published in 1702–04). In 1651 he became chief adviser to the exiled Charles II. Created Earl of Clarendon at the Restoration. His influence was further increased by the marriage of his daughter Anne to James Duke of York. Extremists hated his moderation, however, and he lost Charles's support by openly expressing disapproval of the King's private life. Went into exile after the Dutch wars (1667). The Clarendon Code was named after him (see page 321).

Sir Thomas Osborne, first Earl of Danby (1632–1712)
Born in Yorkshire; first entered Parliament in 1665 as a member for York. In 1668, he was appointed Treasurer of the Navy, and became a Privy Councillor and Lord High Treasurer in 1673. That year he was made Viscount, then Baron, Osborne. In 1674, he was granted the title of Earl of Danby. He served as Charles II's chief minister (1673–8), following Anglican and pro-Dutch policies. He was also party to Charles's secret negotiations with Louis XIV in 1677 and 1678. In 1679, he was impeached and imprisoned until 1685. He objected to James II's Catholic and arbitrary actions. Danby was one of the seven signatories to the letter inviting William of Orange to invade in 1688. By 1690, he had almost total control of government. He was impeached again in 1695 for receiving bribes from the East India Company; by 1699 had resigned all his offices.

passed two Test Acts, in 1673 and 1678. Catholics were excluded from public office and from sitting in Parliament. Parliament also began to discuss limitations to crown control over the Church of England in the event of the Governor of the Church of England being a Catholic. In 1679, following Titus Oates's revelation of the Popish Plot (1678), the Exclusion Crisis began. 'Whig' MPs, led by Shaftesbury, attempted unsuccessfully to exclude the Duke of York from the succession, while 'Tories' supported the hereditary succession. In 1681, Charles dissolved Parliament for the third time in quick succession. He ruled for the last four years of his reign without calling Parliament. During this period, the recalling and remodelling of **borough charters** to allow a greater degree of crown control over elections suggests that for a second time **absolutism** may have been the intention of a Stuart monarch.

Borough charters: Documents issued by the Crown to towns setting out the terms on which they were allowed to govern themselves, including their right to elect MPs.

Absolutism: A form of government in which the ruler is unrestricted by the law or any other means.

The motives governing Charles II's foreign policy are also hotly debated. The late 17th century saw a significant adjustment in the balance of power in Europe. Commercial and even colonial considerations played some part in international relations. During Charles's reign, foreign policy was clearly the preserve of the monarch but such was his level of secrecy that disagreements about whether his policy was governed by principle or expediency are difficult to resolve. What is clearer is that compared with its standing in Europe during the Interregnum, England lost ground. Although its navy was relatively strong by 1685, the size of the Army was constrained by Charles's finances. The humiliating events of the second Dutch War and the poor showing of the military in Europe during the reign added to this impression.

9.1 *What form did the Restoration Settlement take?*

At the end of Charles I's reign, negotiations were under way to ensure that Parliament met regularly and had control over a number of roles previously regarded as the monarch's prerogative, such as the appointment of ministers and control of the militia. However, it was clear that many of

What does this source suggest about the popularity of the Restoration?

Charles II's triumphal entry into London, 1660

these restrictions were regarded as necessary purely because of Charles I's style of government rather than because there was hostility to the institution of monarchy itself. This is reinforced by the fact that the Rump Parliament initially undertook to place the king on trial for his life, only later discussing and carrying out the abolition of monarchy. Hence, a simple explanation of the lack of restrictions on Charles II lies in the fact that he was a different person from his father.

When he became King, Charles II was a relative unknown. He had lived most of his adult life abroad. From 1651 until his expulsion from France in 1655, he lived at the court of his cousin Louis XIV. He then moved to Brussels in the Spanish Netherlands and finally, on the eve of the Restoration, to Breda in the United Provinces of the Netherlands. Thus, on the advice of his English supporters, he dissociated himself from Catholic Spain, identifying with a Protestant state. Besides this, he had issued the Declaration of Breda – a most reasonable statement of the terms on which he was prepared to be King of England. The presentation of the Declaration to Parliament by General Monck, and the suggestion by him that it be accepted as providing sufficient guarantees, had hastened the restoration of monarchy.

The Declaration of Breda stated that Charles would issue a general pardon to all except those exempted by Parliament. Charles suggested 'liberty for tender consciences', but would allow Parliament to decide the church settlement. Parliament was also to resolve disputes over land ownership that arose where Crown, Church and Royalist lands had been confiscated or sold to pay fines or the decimation tax. The soldiers were to receive their back pay and Monck's forces were to be accepted into the King's Army. This satisfied both Parliament and the Army. It implied that the new King, unlike his father, was prepared to work with Parliament. It showed that he was not vengeful. Non-Anglicans apparently had nothing to fear from him and taxation would be reduced since much of the Army would be disbanded.

These and other issues were decided by the Convention and Cavalier Parliaments. The Convention Parliament met on 25 April 1660, its election being the result of the Long Parliament finally dissolving itself. The Convention did not split into clear groupings, making it difficult to categorise MPs. About half its members were Parliamentarians, many of them Presbyterian but some more radical. The remainder were Royalist, despite the Long Parliament having excluded them. This did not, necessarily, make them cooperative with the King, particularly since he seemed to side with the Presbyterians.

When the Cavalier Parliament was elected early in 1661, the membership reflected a Royalist backlash in response to plots and rumours of plots in late 1660 and early 1661 – including Venner's Fifth Monarchist uprising (see page 257). Besides this, intrigues and rivalries within the royal court meant that Parliament was less manageable and that legislation focused more on repression than conciliation. This is particularly apparent in the legislation concerning the Church of England.

What powers did the restored monarchy possess?

Despite the conflicts of 1640–1648, when monarchy was restored it was clear that sovereignty lay unconditionally with the King. With the exception of the Presbyterians and Puritans in the restored Long

Charles II displaying his prowess, despite his military defeats of the 1650s. Dressed in full armour, he holds the baton of command and wears the imperial crown upon his head.

'Touching for the King's Evil': A medieval practice in which the King supposedly cured sufferers from the skin disease scrofula by touching them. It was symbolic of the derivation of royal power from God.

Power to dispense: A prerogative right that allowed the King to exempt a person from the effects of a law.

1. Which Crown powers were (a) restored at the Restoration? (b) not restored at the Restoration?

2. Was Charles II in a stronger or weaker position than Charles I had been in (a) 1625, (b) 1641?

Parliament of 1660, contemporaries accepted that this should be the case. Indeed, some of them wanted the monarchy to be stronger, regaining the powers it had exercised in the 1630s. In the end, the restored monarchy's powers were fundamentally those of 1641. Legislation assented to by Charles I remained on the statute book. Groups within the ruling élite clearly had different ideas about exactly what royal power amounted to. The Ancient Constitution had emphasised cooperation and consensus, using the image of the 'body politic' to illustrate the concept. Parliamentarians regarded Parliament as the custodian of the common good. Royalists and the Church preferred the divine right theory of monarchy. Charles himself emphasised his God-given powers by reviving the practice of **'touching for the King's Evil'**.

By 1660, however, the ruling élite regarded revolution from below as a greater threat to the stability of the realm than misuse of royal power. Events since 1642 had demonstrated that attempts to alter the balance of power could lead to chaos and confusion. The Licensing Act of 1662 aimed to censor the press in order to reduce criticism of the government. Even during the Exclusion Crisis, the Whigs rejected the idea that the monarch might be effectively bound by conditions.

Monarchy remained personal, with the King's prerogative powers still fundamental to the workings of politics. The King retained many of these powers, but some, which had been curtailed or removed during the Long Parliament, were gone for ever.

- Charles II retained the right to choose his ministers and to control matters of war and peace.

- The bishops were restored to the House of Lords, reversing an Act to which Charles I had assented in February 1642.

- The King's power to appoint judges was maintained. In 1668, Charles II changed the terms himself from 'during [their] good behaviour' to 'during my pleasure'.

In 1661, his power was augmented when control of the militia was restored to the Crown, reversing the Militia Ordinance of 1642. The Triennial Act of 1664 stated that the calling of Parliament every three years was desirable, but failed to establish sanctions to be carried out in the event of the King not complying. Consequently, it marked a retreat from the 1641 Act. The King's feudal rights were not returned to him. Nor were the prerogative courts, abolished in 1641, re-established. The King's **power to dispense** with a law for the benefit of an individual had not seemed an important issue. However, Charles's two attempts to dispense groups from the religious laws – his Declarations of Indulgence – resulted in him being forced into retreat. On both occasions, the declarations were withdrawn on Parliament's insistence.

What action was taken against Parliamentarians?

The King had indicated that he would not seek revenge towards those who had sided with Parliament against his father. Indeed, since some of those who had made his return possible were ex-parliamentarians he could hardly condemn them en masse. Although legally all who had fought against his father were traitors, a general pardon was promised. This made it clear that the new regime was learning from the mistakes of the past. The concern was that the Army of 1660, like that of 1646, would refuse to disband without a general pardon. The 'Act of free and general pardon, indemnity and oblivion' received the royal assent in August 1660. It remained unchanged despite the efforts of the Cavalier Parliament the following year.

The Act was complex. It pardoned all crimes committed during the wars and the Interregnum, except murder unconnected with the wars, rape and witchcraft. Those **regicides** who were dead or had run away were also excluded. Regicides who had surrendered when summoned, were to be tried. If they were convicted of treason, they could only be executed by Act of Parliament. Equally, others not directly connected with the King's death but excluded from office, were only to be tried at Parliament's request.

In the event, only 30 were exempted from the general pardon and of these 15 were executed. The last sentence to be carried out was on Sir Henry Vane. In a grisly revenge, the bodies of Oliver Cromwell, Henry Ireton and John Bradshaw were exhumed, symbolically hanged, and then reburied in unmarked graves.

Regicides: Those involved in the death of the King (Charles I).

Why were so few parliamentarians punished for their role in the Civil Wars and Interregnum?

How was the land issue settled?

The transfer of lands that had taken place during the Civil Wars and Interregnum left a legacy of ill-feeling even after the settlement was completed. Much Crown and Church land had been sold. The lands of some Royalists had been confiscated. Both Royalists and Catholics had had to sell land in order to pay fines or debts incurred. Those who had purchased such land feared that it would be seized without compensation and returned to its former owners. The King told Parliament that it could resolve the issue, but the concern must still have remained.

The land issue was extremely complex. Consequently, the Commons felt unable to deal with the matter and instead allowed the King to sort it out. As a result, there was no Act of Parliament on the issue. Each case was dealt with separately by a commission set up by the King. However, this issue left less of a legacy than might have been expected. Some of the biggest purchasers of confiscated lands were excepted from the Act of Oblivion. Hence, in their turn, they had their land confiscated and returned to its previous owners. Others were former tenants of the lands who now re-negotiated their leases, often on favourable terms. In other cases, the commissioners awarded compensation to purchasers on an individual basis. Many Royalists and Catholics had previously managed to regain their lands with help from intermediaries and friends. Even John Lambert had helped his Catholic relatives to recover their lands. The only landowners who were permanently disadvantaged were those who had been forced to sell their lands to pay debts or fines. They numbered far fewer than has sometimes been supposed, although they may be included among the disgruntled Royalists.

How was government to be financed?

Under the early Stuarts, the financing of government had proved a problem. While the monarch was expected to 'live of his own', Parliament took no account of the erosion of the Crown's ordinary revenues as a result of inflation. Nevertheless, parliamentary grants of extra taxation accounted for a decreasing proportion of Crown income, leading to fears that the monarch could manage without this revenue. This would have had the effect of rendering Parliament redundant or at least powerless. After Charles I's Personal Rule, the Long Parliament had limited the Crown's ability to raise extra-parliamentary taxation by outlawing the collection of ship money in 1641 and **feudal tenures**, such as wardship, in 1645.

During the Civil War period and the Interregnum, Parliament had succeeded in raising revenue at an unprecedented level over a sustained period. It had done so by means of a land tax – the assessment – whose collection was made more efficient than that of the parliamentary subsidy because each county was required to provide a set sum of money. This guarded against the under-assessment that had increasingly eroded the value of parliamentary subsidies in the late 16th and early 17th centuries. In addition, excise duty had been introduced on certain goods. By 1660, initial problems had been eliminated, leaving a lucrative source of income. Charles II inherited a more sophisticated and efficient fiscal system than existed in his father's reign. However, the extensive sales of Crown lands during the Interregnum meant that government would be financed from tax rather than the monarch's personal wealth.

Against this background, the Convention Parliament considered the financial position of the newly restored monarchy. At first, MPs appeared to favour retention of control of government finances. The Restoration seemed to offer the ideal opportunity to prevent absolutist monarchy by such means. Customs and excise were granted for short periods and then renewed. A Commons committee investigated arrears of excise. The money being raised to pay army arrears was kept in the City rather than the Exchequer, and was administered by another parliamentary committee. Much of the legislation passed by the Long Parliament, along with some Parliamentary Ordinances, was retained. The abolition of feudal tenures was confirmed in May 1660. The monarch was compensated for the loss of this revenue by £100,000 a year raised from land tax. This was later altered to half the value of the excise, which proved to be worth more than £100,000 a year.

However, by mid-1660 the tone of the Convention seemed to change. In July, the King was granted tunnage and poundage for life. He was later granted £229,000 for his immediate needs, although this sum by no means met these. The concept of the monarch 'living of his own' re-emerged and a committee was established to investigate Charles II's revenues. A decision was reached that the King needed an annual income of £1,200,000. Means were sought to maximise the King's income from existing sources in an attempt to ensure that he would receive this. Much Crown land was restored to the monarch, and measures were introduced to prevent this being rented out on low or excessively long leases. Income from the Post Office and the sale of wine licences was also investigated.

The Cavalier Parliament added to the measures introduced by the Convention. In 1661, it granted an assessment of £1,200,000 to be collected over 18 months. A **hearth tax** was introduced in 1662. This proved

Feudal tenures: Conditions under which property of the King was held. These dated from the Middle Ages.

Hearth tax: a tax levied on each fireplace in a building. It was in effect a wealth tax as the rich had fireplaces in more rooms than the poor. Some hearths, such as those used for industry, were exempt.

extremely unpopular. Collection was difficult. The degree of cooperation by Justices of the Peace (JPs) was variable and officials were often attacked. The Excise Act of 1663 granted JPs jurisdiction over excise. Consequently, its collection became less arbitrary and more efficient. Also, in 1663, a bid to allow Parliament to scrutinise government accounts was not sustained.

The financial settlement was unsatisfactory, but neither Charles nor Parliament was aware of this at the time. As historian Tim Harris observes, in *Politics under the later Stuarts* (1993), 'the inadequacies of the financial settlement … were the result of miscalculation rather than a deliberate attempt to limit the Crown through the power of the purse'. The sum of £1,200,000 estimated by the Parliamentary committee as being the cost of government was no more than an informed guess. At the time the estimate was made, a range of parliamentary committees was still administering much government finance, making it difficult to assess the level of expenditure. Nevertheless, Charles did not object to the sum suggested. Government expenditure consistently exceeded £1,200,000 a year during the reign of Charles II, and this was only partly a result of his personal extravagance.

The MPs were consistently optimistic regarding the level of income that could be expected from various sources. For example, customs yielded less than was estimated during the years immediately following the Restoration because trade was temporarily depressed by war. As a result, Crown income did not reach £1,200,000 until about 1680. So, for the first two decades of his reign, Charles relied heavily on Parliament for extra grants.

In what form was the Church of England restored?

The Church of England was restored and enforced through a series of Acts passed by the Cavalier Parliament. The settlement did not comply with the King's request from Breda for 'liberty for tender consciences', but it acknowledged the existence of nonconformists and dissenters. Initial signs were promising for moderate Puritans and dissenters alike. During 1660, the King indicated to the Quaker Richard Hubberthorne that he had no intention of persecuting loyal subjects for their religious views. Initial ejections of ministers from their livings were limited. The Worcester House Declaration of October 1660 implied that doctrine would not be rigid and that the power of the bishops would be balanced by advice from Presbyterian representatives. Apparently, the settlement would create a **comprehensive church** of England. The suggestion of a comprehensive church did not, however, please all Presbyterians, since some were still intolerant. Although some historians, such as R. Bosher in *The Making of the Restoration Settlement: the Influence of the Laudians, 1649–1662* (1951), have suggested that Hyde wanted a narrow church, comprehension is probably what he wanted at this time. So it is ironic that the laws enforcing a narrow church came to be known as the **Clarendon Code**.

Gradually, the King recognised that his wishes would not be granted. The proposals made at Worcester House were rejected by the Cavalier Parliament, by 183 votes to 157. Although the margin was not great, this defeat occurred unusually on the bill's first reading. When the **Savoy Conference** met, the King seemed to be more reconciled to a narrower church settlement. He instructed that the conference, set up to consider

1. What evidence is there that Parliament expected the King to 'live of his own'?

2. Why did Parliament not take the opportunity to ensure the King was reliant on Parliament for an income?

Comprehensive church: When referring to the Church of England, this means a broad church that aims to be inclusive of a wide range of Protestant practices.

Clarendon Code: A series of Acts passed by Parliament, in 1661–65, directed at nonconformists and designed to secure the supremacy of the Church of England.

Savoy Conference: A meeting of 12 bishops and 12 Presbyterians to consider Charles II's proposals on religion.

Royal assent: The final stage of a parliamentary bill becoming law, when the monarch signed it.

Thirty-Nine Articles and Prayer Book: The doctrine and practices of the Church of England as established by the Elizabethan Church Settlement (see Chapter 4).

What does the publication of this pamphlet indicate about the public reaction to the resignations of these ministers?

alterations to the Prayer Book, should only make changes if they were really necessary, as people were used to the old Prayer Book.

The first of the Acts to receive **royal assent**, the Corporation Act (see chart opposite), marked an attempt by Royalist Anglicans to dominate municipal government. Having seen many Parliamentarians retain their offices in the shires, they were determined on revenge. Strict enforcement of the law meant that many lost their positions in the corporations as a result of the Act. However, as it lapsed in 1663 they were able thereafter to regain their posts with a minimum of conformity.

It soon became clear that the mood of the Cavalier Parliament did not match that of 1660. Anglicans, who wanted a return to the church of the **Thirty-Nine Articles and Prayer Book**, dominated Parliament. The Act of Uniformity went further than the Elizabethan demands on the clergy, by insisting on subscription to all the articles. Articles 34–36, concerning the Church's right to impose ceremonies not ordained by scripture, were not excepted. Anglicans were not interested in comprehension or toleration. In the latter, they reflected the general mood of intolerance towards the sects, especially the more radical ones such as Quakers, which had permeated the Interregnum period as well.

The number deprived of their livings by the Act of Uniformity suggests that, despite the willingness of some to serve the regime, there were significant numbers of educated men whose consciences would not allow them to do so. The extent to which the Book of Common Prayer continued to be used throughout the Interregnum in many parishes has been recognised recently. While the restoration of the Church can be interpreted as a victory for the landed gentry, it was also popular far below their social level.

Farewell sermons preached by Dr Calamy etc., 1663.

The Restored Church of England

1660	Church of England and bishops restored	Allowed the bishops to take their places in the House of Lords.
1661	Corporation Act	Barred from municipal office those who would not swear allegiance to the crown, renounce the Solemn League and Covenant and worship according to the rites of the Church of England.
1662	Act of Uniformity	Required clergymen and teachers to be practising Anglicans and to testify to their consent to the Book of Common Prayer. Over 2,000 ministers and teachers were deprived of their posts during 1660–62 and a further 1,000 were deprived by this Act.
1662	Quaker Act	Decreed harsh punishments of fines and transportation for membership of the Quaker sect.
1664	Conventicle Act (Elizabethan Acts against separatists and recusants still on statute book.)	Rendered it illegal to hold nonconformist meetings attended by more than five adults who were not members of the household in which the meeting was held. Penalties for non-compliance: first offence £5 fine or 3 months in prison; second offence £10 fine or 6 months in prison; third offence £100 fine or transportation. Lapsed in 1668; replaced 1670. New Act focused penalties on nonconformist preachers and hosts of meetings.
1665	Five Mile Act	Prohibited ministers and teachers expelled under the Act of Uniformity from residing within five miles of their former parishes, or of any corporate town or city.

1. What aspects of the pre-civil war Church of England were

(a) restored,

(b) not restored?

2. Why was so much hostility to the sects shown in the church settlement?

Five members: The five MPs regarded by Charles I as his leading opponents, and whom he attempted to arrest by entering the House of Commons with 300 troops on 4 January 1642.

Nevertheless, since support for it was far from universal, with close votes in the Commons on a number of points, religious issues continued to divide the ruling élite. Equally, enforcement of the laws against nonconformists and dissenters, while severe, was often carried out by a small number of the county JPs.

What was the legacy of the Restoration settlement?

The general leniency towards the King's enemies and those of his father created resentment among loyal Royalists. Charles II was judged to be too ready to forgive his enemies and forget his friends. However, Charles was aware that the restoration of monarchy was not universally popular, and probably regarded Presbyterians and former Parliamentarians as potentially more dangerous than convinced Royalists. He was also mindful of the debt he owed to Monck who, according to Clarendon, used his position to further the careers of his friends and relations. Besides Monck, the King appointed Ashley Cooper and others who had served during the Interregnum to his Privy Council. Even Denzil Holles, one of the **five members**, was included. Perhaps Charles also thought it wise to use men with recent experience of government.

Anthony Ashley Cooper, first Earl of Shaftesbury (1621–1683)
Born in Dorset; educated at Oxford and Lincoln's Inn. He first entered Parliament in 1640 as MP for Tewkesbury. He fought for the King in the first Civil War, but changed sides in 1644. He served Cromwell's government during the Interregnum. Ashley Cooper served Charles II as Chancellor of the Exchequer from 1661 and supported the policy of toleration. He was a member of the Cabal (see page 315) from 1672, after which he emerged as an opposition leader. Until the Exclusion Crisis, he had no base of support in Parliament. As Whig leader, he used unscrupulous methods in pursuit of his policy of exclusion. He was acquitted of treason by a grand jury but was forced into exile in November 1682 after his planned uprising failed to materialise. He was a frail man, often in pain from an internal ulcer, which was drained through a silver tap in his side.

While Royalists were able to redress the balance when it came to the Church settlement, overall the Restoration left a bitter legacy. Constitutional issues remained unclear, especially the extent to which the King should use or be independent of Parliament, and be constrained by the law. Divisions in religious opinions were even more serious and led to repeated clashes in Parliament, and between Parliament and King. These were concerned with the issue of what to do about the relatively large numbers outside the Church of England. Should the Church become more comprehensive to accommodate them, or should the law become more tolerant of Protestant dissenters? The issue was further complicated by the failure to make a clear distinction between Catholic and Protestant dissenters. Continued anti-Catholicism, with the strong association of popery (Catholicism) with **arbitrary government**, was a recurring theme in Restoration England.

Arbitrary government: Government not bound by rules.

9.2 What developments took place in relations between Crown and Parliament?

The Restoration settlement may have left many important issues unresolved, but relations between King and Parliament usually focused on cooperation. There were few general elections during the reign of Charles II. The Cavalier Parliament, elected in 1661, was not dissolved until January 1679. There were then three elections in quick succession for the three 'Exclusion' parliaments, after which no parliament was called for the final four years of Charles II's reign.

The **Whig interpretation**, with its **teleological** approach, was strongly stated by the 19th-century historian T. Macaulay. In his *History of England*, he characterised the Cavalier House of Commons as aggressively using the power of the purse to interfere with the King's prerogative powers. 'The great revolution of the 17th century, that is to say, the transfer of the supreme control of the executive administration from the Crown to the House of Commons, was, through the whole existence of this [Cavalier] Parliament, proceeding noiselessly, but rapidly and steadily.'

Whig interpretation: The tendency of historians to write on the side of Protestants, to praise successful revolutions and to interpret as progress those events that seem to lead to the present political system.

Teleological: Interpreting events as though they inevitably led to the eventual outcome. In the case of the Whig interpretation of history, this outcome was the development of parliamentary democracy in England.

Other more recent historians also have the opinion that Restoration Parliaments played a part in long-term developments. For example, Joseph Tanner suggested in *English Constitutional Conflicts of the Seventeenth Century* (1928) that the Crown had been irretrievably weakened by the events of 1640–60. Christopher Hill argues, in *The Century of Revolution, 1603–1714* (1961), that the intellectual consequences of the English Revolution were more important, with the ideological foundations of the old order being undermined by new ideas. The theory of divine right had been discredited and replaced with a contractual theory of monarchy.

Revisionist interpretation: A version of history that rejects the Whig approach, regarding history as being an account of events as they were experienced and interpreted by contemporaries.

The **revisionist interpretation** of Restoration Parliaments took the opposite approach. Instead of considering the place of each parliament in the overall development of parliamentary democracy or of changing constitutional values, individual parliaments were analysed in the context of events at the time. Since contemporaries could not know where events were leading it was assumed there was no pattern of development to be traced.

In *After the Civil Wars* (2000), the historian John Miller proposes a third way. He takes a thematic approach. It is of a conservative ruling élite struggling to make the old constitution work rather than pursuing a vision of parliamentary sovereignty. Parliament's major concern was defence from the twin evils of popery and arbitrary government. Contemporaries were not aware of their role within far-ranging constitutional developments. Like their Tudor and early Stuart predecessors, the Commons and especially the Whigs were not particularly aggressive. Whig MPs, in strong opposition to the Crown in 1679–81, avoided association with the ideas of mid-17th-century republicanism. However, they were discredited during the Exclusion Crisis when they engaged popular support for their cause, as this was reminiscent of the revolutionary methods of Pym during the Long Parliament, and of Civil War.

Besides the intentions and actions of Parliament, it is important to consider those of Charles II. Was the regime viable or fatally flawed? The King's attitude to his subjects, especially in Parliament, was distrustful.

- He interpreted their advice as disaffection, perhaps because he could not hear the Commons' debates for himself.

- He allowed faction within his Privy Council, playing ministers off against each other because he distrusted them.

- He abandoned unpopular ministers when they were attacked by Parliament.

- His policies were provocative.

Although the French alliance made political sense at least in the early years of the reign, it led to suspicions that Charles had absolutist tendencies. His conciliatory stance towards dissenters did nothing to endear him to his natural allies in Parliament, the Cavaliers. With regard to his foreign policy, the historian Geoffrey Holmes, in *The Making of a Great Power* (1993), has observed that 'one must be careful not to confuse political agility with patriotism or genuine statesmanship'. In domestic policies, while Charles usually operated on the basis of what was practical rather than on principle, his success in the long term was the result of good fortune as much as good judgement.

Did Parliament exercise the 'power of the purse'?

In reverting to the idea that the King should live of his own, the Cavalier Parliament deprived itself of an obvious method of controlling royal policy. That it could do so, if to a limited extent, depended on miscalculation of the cost of government and over-optimism about the income that could be expected from various sources. Thus, for much of his reign, Charles was dependent on Parliament for extra funds for ordinary expenses, and he certainly could not pursue an active foreign policy without parliamentary backing.

During the reign, government receipts increased greatly, to the point where income could have been sufficient to meet expenditure in the 1680s. This was achieved by three main methods:

- Tax revenue, particularly customs and excise payments, increased as trade flourished towards the end of the reign.

- Collection of revenue was made more efficient.

- From 1670, Charles received pensions and lump sum payments from Louis XIV.

In short, by the 1680s, Charles was the client of Louis XIV rather than subject to the control of Parliament. However, this does not mean that Parliament was never able to exercise the 'power of the purse' and Charles was subordinate to Louis XIV more in foreign than domestic policy.

Annual government income gradually increased between 1660 and 1685. In the 1660s, the average was about £700,000; in the 1670s about £1,000,000; and it only reached the projected £1,200,000 in 1681–82. The worst financial crisis of the reign was in 1671–72. The third Dutch War began before Charles had the opportunity to request funds from Parliament. Such was the pressure from his creditors that, on 20 January 1672, Charles issued an Order in Council known as the Stop of the Exchequer. He simply ceased paying most of his debts. This measure was not repeated; a better solution was to raise more tax. This was necessary because, despite the increase in his income, Charles's debts also grew. This was the case even under Danby's regime in the 1670s.

Another tactic that addressed Parliament's concern that revenue was incompetently managed, and which was favoured by Treasury ministers of the period, was administrative reform. Parliamentary measures such as the 1662 Fraud Act, the 1663 Staple Act and the 1673 Plantations Act focused on the collection of customs, with attention being given to the way colonial trade was funnelled through the ports. By 1676, the government earned £100,000 from tobacco imports – more than the Virginia planters did.

Farmed revenue: Taxes collected by men who had bought the right to do so from the Exchequer.

The greatest drive for reform came from within the government, starting with the Treasury. In 1667, a committee of five was given oversight of the Treasury and it gradually took control. When new officers were appointed, their commissions could be withdrawn, rather than being patents which were regarded as the 'property' of the post-holder. From 1671, **farmed revenue** was gradually placed in the hands of commissioned officers. In 1683, even the collection of excise was brought under this system. Although it is impossible to measure the extent to which increased revenue was a result of these measures, it was certainly a contributory factor. That these reforms also reinforced the idea of sovereignty – the government no longer delegated this power – was probably only a secondary consideration.

Notwithstanding some improvements in the Crown's finances, Parliament was able, in practice, to exercise the power of the purse. As a result of the Restoration settlement, it was only in time of war that this was really effective. The consequences of extraordinary government expenditure, while trade was being adversely affected, made the monarchy vulnerable to pressure. In the crisis of the late 1670s, Parliament was not in such a strong bargaining position as it had been earlier. As hostility between Crown and Parliament increased, so too did the Commons' reluctance to grant financial aid – at least not without conditions attached.

There are many examples of Parliament attempting, often successfully, to exercise the power of the purse. However, by the 1680s the demands of Parliament were too extreme and the financial position of Charles too strong for further concessions. The ability of Parliament to use finance to pressurise the King diminished during the reign as a whole.

In 1673–74, Charles was forced to withdraw his second Declaration of Indulgence. At this time, he also had to accept the first Test Act and end the war against the Dutch. This reversal of policies held wider implications. It left the Cabal isolated and disintegrating. Clifford was removed as Lord Treasurer under the terms of the Test Act because he was Catholic.

In 1677, the Commons granted both a subsidy of £584,978, specifying that it was for the Navy, and three years' additional excise revenue. However, further supply was conditional on an alliance against France. They voted that 30,000 troops should be raised to fight France and granted, in principle, £1,000,000 for six months. In the event, only £300,000 was actually raised. This may have been intentional. Again there were wider implications. Charles made further secret treaties with Louis XIV, in August 1677 and May 1678. The shorter the King was kept of money, the more likely he was to seek other sources of revenue. This was reminiscent of the behaviour of Charles I in the 1630s. However, from Charles II's point of view, French subsidies also carried a price. While he gained £75,000 from Louis XIV in the 1670s and £325,000 in the 1680s, he had made promises regarding both religion and the calling of parliaments. Had these terms been revealed, he would have been in deep trouble. If he antagonised Louis, Louis might publicise the terms to which Charles had agreed.

In the 'Exclusion' Parliaments, one concern was precautions to be taken in event of a Catholic monarch succeeding. To ensure that such a monarch was relatively harmless, the Commons offered Charles £200,000 to disband the Army. This was finally achieved only in the summer of 1679. In January 1681, Parliament offered Charles £600,000 in exchange for excluding his brother from the succession. Charles refused and **prorogued** Parliament, never to call it again. As with Charles I in 1629, the monarch might conclude that the trouble involved in meetings of Parliament did not bring sufficient financial reward to merit calling it. In any case, part of the agreement with Louis XIV was not to call Parliament. Though Charles might suggest compromises, such as limiting the power of a Catholic monarch, he had no intention of undermining the royal prerogative so far as to alter the succession at Parliament's request.

Did Parliament successfully challenge the King's prerogative rights?

The Restoration settlement left the monarch with a surprising number of his prerogative rights intact, considering the restrictions proposed to Charles I in the 1640s. In retrospect, Parliament might have regretted this, but in the elation of 1660 the terms seemed appropriate. During the course of his reign, Charles II had to guard his prerogatives jealously. Many were challenged, but it is difficult to find evidence that Charles lost ground. The more outrageous suggestions, such as Shaftesbury's proposal in the 1670s that Charles divorce Catherine of Braganza and remarry in order to produce a Protestant heir, met with failure. Shaftesbury was dismissed as Lord Chancellor.

The King's right to choose his ministers

Following the medieval practice revived earlier in the century, the Commons attempted to impeach Charles's ministers on several occasions. Both Clarendon and Danby were the subject of such moves. In Danby's case it was even suggested that he be **attainted**, as Strafford had been in 1641. However, in attacking the King's ministers, Parliament avoided criticising the monarch himself. On occasion, it appeared that Charles was

Prorogued: Brought a session of Parliament to an end without dissolving it, thus keeping open the possibility of another session.

1. To what extent could Parliament limit the King by keeping him short of money?

2. To what extent could Charles II act independently of Parliament?

Attainted: Accused of treason through an Act of Attainder.

happy to let his ministers go. He certainly made little, if any, attempt to save them. In Clarendon's case, he completely abandoned him.

By 1667, Charles regarded Clarendon as a liability. He had never really appreciated that Charles was lazy and found the business of government tedious. Unlike Danby, he was not prepared to work through Charles's mistresses. Charles had been angered in 1660 by the marriage of Clarendon's daughter, Anne, to his brother James on the grounds of her pregnancy. By 1667, Clarendon was unpopular and Charles was prepared to sacrifice him. The combination of an unsuccessful war against the Dutch, the Plague of 1665 and the Great Fire of London of 1666 meant many were disillusioned with the new regime. The King was persuaded to dismiss Clarendon, then urge the Lords to find him guilty when the Commons impeached him. Realising that his fate was sealed, Clarendon fled abroad – where he completed writing his prejudiced history of his life before dying in Montpellier in 1674. The King had certainly abandoned his chief minister, but his fall was more the result of political rivalries at Court than of action by Parliament. Clarendon went because his rival, the Duke of Buckingham, and his allies made him the focus of attack. Charles II was content that this should be so.

The group of ministers known as the Cabal fell in 1673–74. While they did not constitute a cabinet in the modern sense, and there were other influential ministers at the time, they were all associated with alliance with France in foreign policy and relative toleration in religious matters at home. When these two policies were discredited, the Cabal ministers lost their positions. The Anglo–French failure in the third Dutch War (1673–74), together with the reaction to James Duke of York's public avowal of Catholicism, meant their policies were in ruins. Charles was forced by Parliament to withdraw his second Declaration of Indulgence and to accept the Test Act, which would deprive both his brother and Lord Clifford of their offices. Clifford later committed suicide. Shaftesbury was dismissed as Lord Chancellor on the pretext of his suggestion that Charles divorce his wife. Relations between Arlington and Buckingham, which had never been good, deteriorated into bitter recrimination. 'As with Clarendon,' David Smith writes in *The Stuart Parliaments 1603–1689* (1999), 'Charles allowed parliamentary hostility towards unpopular ministers to run its course.'

Danby fell from power in 1678–79. He had increasingly upset the 'Country' party by his methods of parliamentary management. These led some to believe his aim was to dispense with Parliaments. Charles's persistent pro-French stance and the association of popery with arbitrary government also undermined him. In May 1675, there was an attempt to impeach Danby because of the belief that he was trying to dispense with Parliament. He survived. However, in the late 1670s, Charles undermined Danby by secretly negotiating with Louis XIV. Danby reluctantly agreed to the 1677 and 1678 treaties.

Danby fell as a result of the anti-Catholic hysteria generated by the Popish Plot. Besides the close association of popery, arbitrary government and Danby's methods of controlling Parliament, he was reluctant to disband the standing army on the grounds that it might be needed to counter Catholics. In December 1678, the former ambassador to Paris revealed Danby's part in the secret treaty negotiations. This sealed his fate. The Commons introduced impeachment articles against Danby. This time,

Charles seemed more supportive of his minister. He prorogued, then dissolved, Parliament on 24 January 1679. Attacking Danby was the main concern of the first 'Exclusion' Parliament, which met on 6 March 1679. Danby resigned as Lord Treasurer on condition that he received a royal pardon. The MPs considered a Bill of Attainder, arguing that although the King had the right to pardon individuals, he should not have used it on this occasion. Danby then negotiated a five-year imprisonment in the Tower of London as an alternative. Charles had saved his minister's life, although Parliament had succeeded in bringing about his removal from office.

The King's right to control the militia

In 1678, Charles used his power of veto on a public bill for the only time in his reign. It concerned his control of the militia. Parliament wanted to extend the period of service of the militia because of the papist threat, but Charles thought this impinged on his right to dismiss the militia at will. Charles countered Parliament's attempt to remove the Duke of York's supporters from military and naval office on the grounds that he alone had the right to appoint officers.

The King's right to call, prorogue and dissolve Parliament

The Triennial Act of 1664 demonstrated that Parliament had not thought it was necessary to make provision for the eventuality that they would not meet within the specified three years. Charles had seemed so amenable to the idea of working with Parliament and so dependent on the goodwill of the gentry, that sanctions were unnecessary. By the late 1670s, the situation was not as favourable to Parliament. In 1675, Shaftesbury tried to have Parliament dissolved on a legal technicality. The purpose was to force Danby's **placemen** to seek re-election, but he was not supported by the majority of MPs who had no wish to face the electorate. In 1677, Parliament re-assembled after a break of 15 months. Shaftesbury and others argued, on the basis of a medieval statute, that since Parliament had been prorogued for over 12 months it had, effectively, been dissolved. They were sent to the Tower by their fellow peers and the Commons too were unsympathetic.

Placemen: MPs who had gained their seats through government influence on the voters.

During the Exclusion Crisis, Charles made skilful use of his powers to prorogue and dissolve Parliament. In the case of the third 'Exclusion' Parliament he also invoked his right to call Parliament to meet at a venue other than Westminster. When Charles did not call Parliament for the last four years of his reign, there were few voices raised in complaint. Not only this, the Duke of York was restored to the Privy Council and Danby released from the Tower with no accompanying outcry. Ultimately, the majority of MPs believed that Charles would call Parliament when it was necessary.

The King's right to decide his foreign policy

Since 1621, the issue of how far the King could control his foreign policy, given his dependence on Parliament for money, had been in the open. This situation continued during Charles II's reign. On occasion, as shown above, financial grants were tied to particular causes or policies. However, Charles made it clear that Parliament had no brief to determine foreign policy. As was the case with the militia, he guarded his prerogative rights firmly.

1. To what extent was Charles II able to exercise his prerogative rights?

2. Did Charles II try to extend his prerogative rights?

3. Did Parliament try to restrict the King's prerogative rights?

4. Was the exercise of prerogative rights an important source of conflict between King and Parliament?

Lords temporal and spiritual: The members of the House of Lords. The Lords temporal were members of the nobility, while the Lords spiritual were the two archbishops and the bishops who also sat in the Lords.

The King's right to dispense from the law

Application of the law was at the King's pleasure, but it was generally accepted that individuals would be dispensed from particular laws to avoid injustice. When Charles suggested that the laws in relation to Catholic recusants and Protestant nonconformists be relaxed, he was extending the scope of this right. On both occasions that Charles made his intentions clear, Parliament was adamant that the law should stand. Charles had misread the situation. Neither Catholics nor dissenters were as numerous as Charles supposed. He had thought that the two together constituted over half the population. His political position was also too weak. Regardless of the mood of the country as a whole, the grip of the Anglicans in Parliament was strong. Dissenters were dubious of accepting the King's offers at face value because these included toleration of Catholics. Anglicans and dissenters both feared papists.

To what extent was Charles II able to manage Parliament?

Besides Charles II's exercise of the right to appoint **Lords temporal and spiritual**, there were two ways in which his government might influence the composition of Parliament. In both the 1660s and the 1680s, a substantial number of borough charters were reissued and during Danby's ascendancy he made significant efforts to generate 'Court' support in Parliament.

Representatives of boroughs held four-fifths of the seats in the House of Commons. Where these were small, or where the electorate was confined, there was the danger that the Crown might try to influence the election. If the monarch controlled admission to municipal office, and the right to vote was confined to the corporation, then royal control was assured. Since James II issued new borough charters (see page 316) with a view to influencing parliamentary elections, it was assumed that Charles II had the same motive. However, this view has been challenged. In the 1680s, Charles's aims cannot have been to influence the composition of the Commons since he had no intention of calling Parliament. Instead, the historian R. Pickavance, in *The English Boroughs and the King's Government: a Study of the Tory Reaction, 1681–85* (1976), argues that Charles wanted to control local magistrates whose job it was to enforce the law. This provides an acceptable explanation for new charters in the 1680s but cannot apply to the 1660s. In *The Crown and Borough Charters in the Reign of Charles II* (1985), John Miller provides a different explanation. He claims that, in the 1660s, new charters were issued mainly at the instigation of local Royalists eager to ensure the election of like-minded men. The passing of the Corporation Act reduced the number of new charters because it achieved the same end by a different means.

There is less doubt about the motives behind Danby's actions. He had experience of using patronage at the Treasury, from 1673. What had been relatively informal methods of producing a loyal group in the Commons became more deliberate by 1675. The Anglican Royalists and bishops in the Lords comprised just over half the members. Systematic use was made of **proxy voting**. By 1675, the government controlled three-quarters of these, with just over half in the hands of Privy Councillors. On Danby's prompting, an average of 13 of the 27 bishops attended the House. Danby further secured their support through conferences with them and clear support for the Anglican cause.

Proxy voting: The practice in the House of Lords of nominating another Lord to vote for an absent peer.

Danby needed to create a 'Court' party in the Commons. He attempted this partly by using bribes. The 'Country' party nicknamed him 'Bribe-Master General', such was the extent to which he gave offices and **sinecures** to former Royalists. However, in the 17th century, the receipt of bribes did not necessarily influence people's behaviour and Danby had access to neither the money nor the range of offices that Walpole enjoyed in the 18th century. Danby also encouraged 'Court' supporters to attend the House promptly at the beginning of each parliamentary session by sending out letters.

Overall, the results of Danby's actions were unsuccessful. Although he did encourage a 'Court' grouping, the extent of this is unclear and it was at the expense of strengthening opposition. His methods alienated those MPs who were more fearful of arbitrary government than of conflict in Parliament. Danby's efforts to convince Parliament that Charles was thoroughly Anglican and that England would thenceforth follow a Protestant foreign policy were undermined by Charles. Hence, he was increasingly unpopular in Parliament.

Sinecures: Paid offices, which had few or no duties to be performed.

?
How effective were Danby's efforts to gain support for the Crown in Parliament?

How and why was Charles II able to survive the Exclusion Crisis?

The anti-Catholic mood of Restoration England has only been hinted at so far. The Exclusion Crisis, which dominated Charles II's last years, saw the sentiment reach a peak of hysteria. Although Charles survived the attempt to exclude his brother from the succession, the fear of Catholicism did not disappear. In 1660, anti-Catholicism was the legacy of over a century of Protestant propaganda, linking popery firstly with disloyalty to the state and later with the arbitrary form of government that was soon to be labelled absolutism.

Fear of popery manifested itself at various times during the reign of Charles II. To historians writing in the 1970s, such as John Miller in *Popery*

?
How does this picture help to explain the events of the Exclusion Crisis?

A Pope-burning procession, 1679

'Universal monarchy': The idea of one monarchy in control of the world. In the 16th century it was feared that Spain aspired to this position, while by the reign of Charles II France seemed to be aiming for this.

Waldensians: An austere Christian group. They were followers of the 12th-century merchant Peter Waldo. Their chief centre was in the Alps in south-east France.

Andrew Marvell (1621–1678)
Marvell was first a poet, then a politician. After leaving Cambridge University and travelling on the continent, he was tutor first to Lord Fairfax's daughter then to Oliver Cromwell's ward, William Dutton. From 1657, he assisted the poet John Milton, who was losing his sight. He entered Parliament in 1659 as MP for Hull and was re-elected in 1660 and 1661. He opposed both arbitrary government and religious intolerance. Although he accepted the Restoration, he became increasingly disillusioned with monarchy. His last poetry was circulated only in manuscript form, but its anti-monarchic message was so strong that it was believed his life was in danger. When he died there were rumours that he had been poisoned, although he was actually killed by his incompetent doctor.

and Politics in England 1660–1688 (1973), the hysteria generated seemed irrational, amounting to paranoia. In the European context, it seems more realistic. Since the beginning of the Thirty Years War, the proportion of Europe under Catholic government had grown significantly. Even the Protestant United Provinces was 40% Catholic and was threatened by Louis XIV. There is debate over whether Louis XIV was viewed as more sinister because he was deemed to be trying to remove Protestantism or because he aimed to establish **'universal monarchy'**. Certainly the fate of the **Waldensians** at his hands, in the 1650s, was taken to be symbolic of his intentions. Rumours that the Great Fire of London of 1666 was started deliberately by a French Catholic typify what seemed possible.

Under Danby, the recusancy laws were strictly enforced in the aftermath of the Declaration of Indulgence debacle. However, neither this nor Danby's strong support for Anglicanism could mask the harsh reality that the heir to the throne was a Catholic and the suspicion that Charles's sympathies lay in that direction. James Duke of York probably converted to Catholicism in 1669. This became a matter of public knowledge in 1673 when he failed to receive communion at Easter. Later that year, James married the Catholic Mary of Modena. This prompted Parliament to voice fears of what would happen when James succeeded to the throne. He was excluded from his office as Lord High Admiral by the first Test Act of 1673 and almost lost his seat in the Lords by the second in 1678. The Lords wanted him to retain his seat; the Commons voted by 158 to 156 that he should be exempted from the Act. Suggestions were made about the amount of influence a Catholic Governor of the Church might have, including the idea that the bishops should have more control over church appointments.

Andrew Marvell published a tract in 1677 entitled 'Account of the Growth of Popery and Arbitrary Government'. This voiced the concerns. These were also stated by the contemporary Sir Henry Capel, MP: 'From popery came the notion of a standing army and arbitrary power … Formerly the crown of Spain, and now France, supports this root of popery amongst us; but lay popery flat, and there's an end of arbitrary government and power. It is a mere … notion, without popery.'

In November 1678, William Staley was put to a gruesome death in London, having been found guilty of treason probably because he was a Catholic. Within weeks, four more Catholics had been tried and convicted and others were in prison awaiting trial. Apart from Staley, they had all been implicated in the Popish Plot revealed by Titus Oates and Israel Tonge. The evidence was implausible, but such was the atmosphere of distrust that the revelations seemed credible. Perhaps it suited some politicians to believe them. Oates and Tonge alleged that there was a conspiracy to murder the King, place James Duke of York on the throne and remove Protestantism in England, possibly in conjunction with a French invasion. Fears were heightened when the lawyer to whom Oates had made his deposition was found murdered.

This was the context in which the King was forced to accept the Test Act of 1678. The former ambassador to Paris made his revelations implicating Danby in the secret negotiations with Louis XIV, and Danby fell from power. Finally, the Cavalier Parliament was dissolved and fresh elections were called.

The first so-called 'Exclusion' Parliament did not proceed immediately

What does this picture tell an historian about the attitude of the English towards the Pope?

Titus Oates and the Pope, 1679. The Pope is being warned by an imp of Satan that retribution is near. He turns so suddenly that his hat falls off.

1. Which ideas helped to determine the outcome of the Exclusion Crisis?

2. Which actions of the two sides helped to determine the outcome of the Exclusion Crisis?

3. Which events and circumstances helped to determine the outcome of the Exclusion Crisis?

In each case, explain your answer.

with plans to alter the succession. Impeachment of Danby and the need for fair trials were addressed. However, it was then revealed to the Commons that James's former secretary had been in correspondence with both France and the Pope. Charles tried to diffuse the situation by making suggestions on how a Catholic monarch might be restrained, but the Commons debate showed that many, following Shaftesbury's lead, were uncompromising in their attitude. An exclusion bill was introduced in May and passed its second reading by 207 votes to 128. A furious Charles prorogued, then dissolved Parliament.

A newly elected Parliament was prorogued until January 1680 and, meanwhile, Shaftesbury was dismissed from the Privy Council. He orchestrated a petitioning campaign in favour of exclusion. The Parliament finally met in October 1680 amid signs of a loyalist backlash. This was brought about partly because Shaftesbury's involvement of the populace in the petitioning campaign was reminiscent of the way Pym had manipulated public support for the Parliamentarian cause during the Long Parliament. It was also partly because of the involvement of ordinary people in politics that permeated the Civil War and its aftermath. Nevertheless, many MPs still supported exclusion. A bill that passed its three readings in the Commons was defeated by 63 votes to 30 in the Lords, with Charles himself attending most of the debate. The Commons offered instead £600,000 if Charles would agree to exclusion. Charles responded by proroguing Parliament.

The third 'Exclusion' Parliament was called to meet at Oxford. Charles hoped that away from the capital, in a traditionally loyal city, Parliament would be more conciliatory. His hopes were misplaced. He made his final offer. On his death, his Protestant niece Mary and her husband William of Orange would act as regents for Mary's father, James. James would be King in name only. The Commons rejected his proposal and introduced a third exclusion bill. Parliament was dissolved after just one week.

In the aftermath, those who opposed exclusion – the Tories – tightened their grip on local government and implemented a renewed campaign against dissenters. Charles began the process of recalling and reissuing borough charters, enabling his supporters to carry out a purge of the Whigs. The Whigs' cause was further weakened when, in desperation, Shaftesbury courted Charles's illegitimate son, the Duke of Monmouth, as a possible alternative successor. Monmouth toured Cheshire, seeking support for his cause. However, Shaftesbury's flight to the United Provinces in November 1682 was an acknowledgement that his campaign had failed. He died two months later.

Explaining the failure of the Exclusionists

The events of the Exclusion Crisis occurred within a relatively short timespan. Explaining the success of Charles and the failure of the exclusionists using an analysis based on the role of underlying conditions and triggers would, therefore, be inappropriate. A more effective analysis would be one based on the respective roles of attitudes and ideas, actions and intentions, and of causes, including both circumstances and events. An assessment of what each kind of explanation can, and cannot, explain would lead to an evaluation of the relative importance of the different factors.

The Exclusion Crisis occurred within the context of hysterical anti-Catholicism. This can explain the initial concerns of the MPs, as well as the reasons that the Whigs were able to orchestrate their petitioning campaign in the provinces. However, there were other influential attitudes involved. The Tories were able to play on the fear of the ruling élite that England would again be plunged into civil war, with all that meant for their control and influence. They were able to convince their supporters of the similarity between Whigs and the extremists in the Long Parliament because of the actions of the Whigs. It was also apparent in the parliamentary debates that, following Scotland's support for Charles II in 1649–51, MPs were worried that if James were excluded from the English throne he might find support in Scotland. This could lead to war as James tried to establish his claim to the throne of England. The likelihood that the Scots would support the legitimate Stuart successor, rather than one imposed by the English Parliament, would later be the reasoning behind the Act of Union with Scotland in 1707.

Another set of ideas concerned the basis for the legitimacy of monarchy. While some argue that Charles I had discredited divine right monarchy, as yet no definitive justification of contractual monarchy had been established. Thus, an explanation centring on ideas and attitudes indicates that the Tories probably had more hope of success than the Whigs.

This is also the case with regard to an explanation focusing on actions and the intentions behind them. Charles skilfully used his prerogative powers to dissolve Parliament when he faced defeat. He was even smarter in proroguing the second 'Exclusion' Parliament before it had met. The substantial interval between the first and second Parliaments allowed the Whigs to discredit themselves, creating the fear of popular involvement in politics and a consequent loyalist backlash. Thus, the actions of both sides contributed to the eventual outcome. After the last 'Exclusion' Parliament, Tory actions in the localities further enhanced Charles's position, while Whig courting of Monmouth and recourse to violence further undermined their cause.

Besides exercising his prerogative rights, Charles continued to negotiate with Louis XIV. In March 1681, he gained a lump sum of £40,000 as well as annual grants of £115,000 for the next three years provided he did not call another Parliament. Coupled with his substantial income from customs, actions and events conspired to place Charles in a strong position.

The **Rye House Plot** demonstrates how fears aroused by Whig actions influenced events. This alleged Whig plot to murder the King and the Duke of York on their return from the races at Newmarket was about as

Rye House Plot: A plot devised by Richard Rumbold. The King and his brother left the races at Newmarket early, so the plot was unsuccessful. The conspirators were betrayed and six leading Whig exclusionists were unfairly implicated.

convincing as the Popish Plot in terms of hard evidence. Nevertheless, it formed the basis for the prosecution of the Whig leaders who were tried and executed, while the Earl of Essex committed suicide in the Tower before he could be brought to trial.

Set against Charles's strengths were the radicalism and the tense atmosphere generated by the frequent elections of the years 1679–81, which tended to favour the Whig cause. Nevertheless, on balance, it is clear that those favouring the legitimate succession were destined to prevail. This is because the Whigs were potential revolutionaries, but the underlying tendency in the 17th century was towards conservatism. Given time, which the Tories were given by Charles's prorogation of Parliament, their cause was far more likely to succeed.

The reasons for Charles II's victory may be clear, but which, if any, is more important? Anti-Catholicism and the association of popery and arbitrary government had been such strong themes since at least 1670 that it could be argued that the factor that countered that fear must have been critical. The only prospect more frightening to the ruling élite than losing their rights and freedoms to the King was losing them to the people. The legacy of the Civil Wars was, arguably, the strongest influence on the eventual outcome. This suggests that the actions of Charles and the Tories on the one hand and of the Whigs on the other were only significant in as far as they aroused these fears. Hence ideas played a more important part in explaining Charles's success than the actions of either side.

It would be possible to argue an alternative case. Since the ideas were present throughout, it might be argued that it was the actions of both Charles and the Whigs that determined which set of ideas would prevail. The question might then be raised as to whose actions were more important, Charles's or the Whigs'? It could, for example, be argued that Charles's actions in proroguing Parliament provided the Whigs with the opportunity to discredit themselves, that their actions would not have been likely without his, and that therefore Charles's actions are of greater importance in the explanation.

> *Construct an argument justifying the view that Charles II's improved financial position was the most important cause of his survival in the Exclusion Crisis.*

Was Stuart absolutism either planned or possible?

In the light of his failure to call Parliament after 1681, some historians such as Barry Coward in *The Stuart Age* (2nd edition, 1994) have referred to the last four years of Charles's reign as the beginning of the second Stuart absolutism. When considered in the context of the reign of James II, the claim seems more justifiable. However, Charles did not know, and could not predict, what his brother would do. The historian John Miller argues, in *The Restoration and the Reign of Charles II* (2nd edition, 1997), that while Charles was impressed by Louis XIV's regime, this regime was developed in response to a specifically French system and was therefore not applicable to England. He also suggests that Louis XIV was more interested in practicalities than ideology. This may imply that Charles was unlikely to attempt to recreate the French system in England. If he had, then he would have encountered significant difficulties. Charles would not have had the support of ministers and officials that Louis XIV had. Also, he relied on the support of a large proportion of the ruling élite to enforce the law in the localities. MPs who were drawn from this gentry class would have opposed absolutism. The English Parliament recognised that it was in a stronger position than the equivalent institutions in France

1. *What factors made the introduction of absolutism possible in the reign of Charles II?*

2. *What factors made the introduction of absolutism unlikely in the reign of Charles II?*

3. *To what extent were contemporary fears that Charles II inclined towards absolutism justified?*

since the King was still dependent on it for the introduction of new laws. Even if the King was becoming more financially independent in ordinary circumstances, he was incapable of pursuing an active foreign policy without the backing of Parliament.

However, Charles did agree not to call Parliament again in his 1680s treaty with Louis. Given his distrust of Parliament and recent experience of it, this is not surprising. Nevertheless, the English were right in supposing that Charles would call Parliament again if it proved necessary.

Source-based questions: The Exclusion Crisis

SOURCE A

The Lord Chancellor's Speech was as followeth: ... I am commanded to tell you that His Majesty is willing that provision may be made first to distinguish a popish [Catholic] from a protestant successor; then to limit and circumscribe the authority of a popish successor in these cases following; that he may be disabled to do any harm.

First in reference to the Church: His Majesty is content that care be taken that all ecclesiastical and spiritual benefices and promotions in the gift of the crown may be conferred in such a manner that the incumbents shall always be of the most pious and learned protestants ...

In reference to the state and the civil part of government: as it is already provided that no papist [Catholic] can sit in either House of Parliament so the King is pleased that there may never want a parliament when the King shall happen to die but that the parliament then in being may continue indissoluble for a competent time ... as no papists can by law hold any place of trust so the King is content that no Lords or others of the Privy Council, no judges of the common law, or in Chancery shall at any time during the reign of any popish successor be put in or displaced but by the authority of Parliament ...

In reference to the military part: the King is willing that no Lord Lieutenant nor no officer of the navy during the reign of any popish successor be put in or removed but either by the authority of parliament or of such persons as the parliament shall entrust with such authority. It is hard to

invent another restraint to be put upon a popish successor considering how much the revenue of the successor will depend upon the consent of Parliament ...

From the Journal of the House of Commons,
30 April 1679

SOURCE B

The Commons' debate on the Exclusion Crisis, 11 May 1679.

SIR JOHN KNIGHT: It is impossible that the Protestant Religion should be preserved under a popish prince; it is as inconsistent as light and darkness. ...How impatient are the Papists till the King is out of the way, that the Protestants may be destroyed!

MR DUBOIS: The King offered us many gracious things in his speech. The King's life will be so much the more in danger by how much the Papists think their case desperate. There is no way to defeat their execution of their plot like taking away their hopes and, unless by some vote you determine the succession, you will never put the Papists out of hopes of accomplishing their design.

SIR THOMAS PLAYER: I join with the motion that has been made for an eternal banishment of the Duke of York out of England. But this bill will not let the King safe, therefore besides the Duke's banishment I desire that he may be excluded from the throne and all papists whatsoever by law. It is most visible ... what danger the King's person is exposed to and from where all the dangers that the King has been in do come. It is from the prospect of a popish successor ... The offers made to you by

Source-based questions: The Exclusion Crisis

the King are fine things but they will not do this great work.

SIR EDMUND JENNINGS: … banishing the Duke will not do your business. If you have any papists in England you will never be secure. Therefore I propose a Bill, 'that all papists that will not conform to the Church of England may have liberty to sell their estates, to be gone and never return more'.

MR HAYDEN: For us to tie a popish successor with laws for the preservation of the Protestant Religion is binding Samson with willows. He will break them when he is awake. … I think a prince is made for the good of the people and where there is a popish prince that may succeed, I think we ought to secure ourselves against the succession. There is great inconvenience that may be assigned in every proposal I have heard today but there is least inconvenience in a Bill to exclude the Duke of York by name from the crown of England.

MAJOR BEAKE: In this great point our very souls are concerned. Many motions have been made but I will inform you of a fact before you. If we have no better security for our religion than paper laws I doubt not but a popish successor will ignore them. We know that royal authority put in the scale of parliamentary authority has ever overbalanced it …

MR POWLE: How little security have we that this exclusion of the Duke of York shall not end in civil war? Many princes have extended their power by prerogative, yet by your laws you have preserved your liberties to this day; I hope you will transmit them to posterity. If an Act of Parliament be made for securing a parliament sitting at the death of the King and for officers of state, bishops and judges to be left in office, I would trust to that. If the successor should be a papist, sufficient unto the day is the evil thereof. If a prince would secure himself, he must do it by ways and means acceptable to the people, if he consults his own tranquility.

MR SWYNFIN: We have a kind of prospect and representation of what the laws can do already. One would have thought that our own laws would have been strong enough against all things relating to popery. … We have laws that make it treason to make a reconciliation with the Church of Rome; treason for a priest or Jesuit to be here … The Papists have dioceses and general councils and correspond with Rome … And all this under a

Protestant King. Now what has furthered this? Nothing but the hopes of the papists of a popish king.

We are looked upon here by foreigners as more popish than protestant. Our alliances and counsels are all that way.

SIR FRANCIS WINNINGTON: As this Bill will be hard for the Duke so it is hard for us to be deprived of our civil liberties which will be at the power of a prince that governs as the Pope shall give his determination …

MR VAUGHAN: It is proposed that the Parliament shall have the choice of civil and ecclesiastical officers … If you provide thus against the Duke you take away all royal power and make the government a commonwealth. The King must give consent to the laws you make and this is trying to bell the cat's neck by mice, and that will signify nothing when the crown, in effect, is upon the Pope's head. …

From Debates of the House of Commons, 1667–1694 by Anchitel Grey MP, published 1769

---

1. With reference to Sources A and B and information contained in this chapter, explain the meaning of the two phrases highlighted in the sources.

a) 'no papist [Catholic] can sit in either House of Parliament' (Source A)

b) 'We know that royal authority put in the scale of parliamentary authority has ever overbalanced it.' (Source B)

2. Study Sources A and B.

Summarise the arguments given by the MPs both for and against Charles II's proposals in Source A.

3. Using the Sources and information contained in this chapter, explain why the Whigs proposed excluding James, Duke of York, from the succession.

9.3 *When and why did political parties emerge?*
A CASE STUDY IN HISTORICAL INTERPRETATION

Whig historians – such as David Ogg in *England in the Reign of Charles II* (1955) – interpreted the reign of Charles II as one in which the struggle to establish the relative powers of monarch, Lords and Commons continued. More recent historians acknowledge that this gives greater purpose to the 'workings of politics' than existed. It would be more accurate to describe this process as crisis management, with the various institutions reacting to circumstances rather than actively seeking to win power at each other's expense. In view of Charles II's apparent lack of positive aims – his only stated one being to avoid going on his travels again – the latter interpretation seems more convincing. Equally, for the first decade of the reign there were no identifiable groups of MPs working for consistent goals. However, T. Harris argues, in *Politics under the Later Stuarts* (1993), that the origins of the groups that emerged later in the reign can be traced back to the early 1660s and the legacy of the Restoration settlement.

A case can be made for the existence of parties in the aftermath of the Restoration. During the 1660s, contemporaries referred to groups or 'parties' within Parliament. However, references to 'the courtiers' or 'the court party', and to 'country gentlemen' or 'the patriots', can also be found in the 1620s. John Miller argues, in *After the Civil Wars* (2000), that these terms do not signify the existence of political parties as they are now understood.

Other historians concentrate their arguments on developments in the 1670s, when Danby's attempt to create a core of sympathetic MPs led to the emergence of groupings known as 'Court' and 'Country'. Danby had lists of MPs who supported the government drawn up. John Plumb argues, in *The Growth of Political Stability in England 1675–1725* (1967), that 'greater control of Parliament by the executive or greater independence from it became the crux of politics'. In *Subjects and Sovereigns: the Grand Controversy over Legal Sovereignty in Stuart England* (1981), historians Corinne Weston and Janelle Greenberg take a similar approach. They identify theory of government as being the factor that determined an MP's views. The main conflict in politics, they say, was between those who believed that the King was the only supreme governor and those who thought he shared sovereignty with Parliament.

In *The Restored Monarchy 1660–1688* (1979), J.R. Jones argues that although the 'Country' grouping of the 1670s evolved into the Whigs of the Exclusion Crisis, there is no parallel relationship between Court and Tory. In *The Stuart Parliaments 1603–1689* (1999), David Smith disagrees. He claims that there was continuity between the two pairings in terms of both personnel and ideas. In *Politics under the Later Stuarts* (1993), Tim Harris also expresses scepticism about the existence of parties before 1679, arguing that politics before that date was confined to Whitehall and Westminster, with no effort to raise support for the groups in the localities. He also raises the issue that there was a range of disagreements between those in Parliament. At national level, these concerned both constitutional and religious issues. An understanding of how they interacted is necessary before groupings can be explained.

During the Exclusion Crisis, the terms 'Whig' and 'Tory' began to be applied to the two opposing factions within Parliament. There is little argument that these did constitute political parties, albeit embryonic. The Whigs took a contractual view of royal authority, arguing that resistance was justifiable in the case of monarchs who betrayed their coronation oaths. They were sympathetic to nonconformists, believing that the best defence against Catholicism was a united Protestant front. They regarded Parliament as the guardian of Protestantism, popular liberty and property. The Tories championed divine right monarchy and the idea that civil authority is derived from God. They upheld the established Church, rejecting both toleration and comprehension. The Tories believed that the greatest danger of arbitrary government came from republicans and nonconformists who would undermine royal power.

Despite agreement that two groupings did exist by 1679, there is still debate as to how far these constituted parties. Although both Whigs and Tories courted support in the localities, there was little in the way of modern party organisation. Even the basic Whig concept of contractual monarchy was not stated clearly until John Locke published his two 'Treatises on Civil Government' in 1689. The identification of political parties during the reign of Charles II also depends on the period being set in the wider context of the following three reigns. The two groups resurfaced during the Glorious Revolution. By the time of Queen Anne and the 'Rage of Party', there is no doubt about what they each stood for. Identifying the 'origin of party', like tracing the development of parliamentary democracy, can sometimes benefit from hindsight.

1. Define the term 'political party' as it is used now and as it was used in the 17th century.

2. To what extent were there groups identifiable as parties

a) in the 1660s?

b) in the mid-1670s?

c) at the time of the Exclusion Crisis?

3. Why have historians disagreed about the appearance and development of political parties during the reign of Charles II?

9.4 What developments took place in attitudes to Protestant nonconformists?

As is the case with Whig historians regarding relations between Crown and Parliament in the Restoration period, there is a danger in any examination of religious policy and views that we are influenced by the knowledge that a Toleration Act was passed in 1689. It is also important to be aware of the limitations of that Act. Catholics were not tolerated. It was not until 1778 that the Catholic Relief Act allowed them to worship freely. Not all Protestants were given the right to follow their beliefs. Non-Anglicans were excluded from politics by the Corporation and Test Acts – until 1828 for Protestants and 1829 for Catholics. Nor could nonconformists enter the universities. These terms and exceptions reflect the prejudices that were a hallmark of Restoration, later Stuart and Hanoverian England.

The Restoration settlement represented an Anglican backlash in reaction to the events of the previous 20 years. In 1662, the Act of Uniformity legally defined nonconformists. Any minister or teacher who would not testify to their 'unfeigned assent and consent to all and everything contained and prescribed in and by the book entitled the Book of Common Prayer' would be deprived of his living. The renewed Elizabethan Act against seditious sectaries meant that those who refused to receive communion in the Church of England were punished for their dissent unless they conformed within three months. Nonconformity could result in the confiscation of goods or even death. The Quaker Act (see page 323) of the same year targeted a sect that had been singled out for persecution during the Interregnum and which had seemed particularly frightening at the time of the Restoration.

Who were dissenters and nonconformists?

Those who refused to attend Church of England services were technically classed as dissenters. Some of them held different beliefs from those of the established church. They included members of a variety of sects such as Quakers and Baptists. They were totally separate from the Church of England and did not wish to be included in it. These were the true dissenters.

Nonconformists were also persecuted for their failure to attend Anglican services. They differed from dissenters in holding basically the same beliefs as Anglicans, but rejecting aspects of the Act of Uniformity. For clergy, this might involve:

● refusal to submit to ordination by a bishop

● not wanting to give 'unfeigned assent and consent' to the Book of Common Prayer, for example on the grounds that they rejected a service with no scope for extempore prayer

● refusal to swear to accept church government by bishops or a renunciation of the Solemn League and Covenant.

Laity: The body of people who were *not* clergymen.

On the other hand, many clergy attended Anglican services despite their misgivings, but also presided over nonconformist meetings. Equally, many of the **laity** overcame their misgivings by attending Church of England services occasionally or for only part of the service. The nonconformist meetings might be attended by a range of people, some of whom had separated themselves entirely from the established church, while others attended both Anglican and nonconformist meetings. Other meetings might consist almost exclusively of people who also attended Church of England services. Only rarely was communion celebrated at these meetings.

In order for these nonconformists to be won back to the Church of England, some changes would be necessary. For deprived clergy, alterations were needed to the Act of Uniformity. For the laity, less drastic modifications to ceremony and liturgy might be sufficient. However, as the reign progressed, a new generation of Puritan nonconformists developed. Unlike the older generation, they had no wish to be incorporated into the Church of England. The case for remaining separate was strengthened after the experiment with licensing following the King's Declaration of Indulgence of 1672.

Estimates of the number of dissenters are usually based on Bishop Compton's census of 1676. This survey suggested that less than 5% of the population were full nonconformists. Given that the purpose of the census was to convince the King that nonconformists posed no threat to the country and that vigorous enforcement of the church laws would not result in rebellion, the figure of 5% may be an underestimate. Deliberate distortion of the figures should not be assumed as the clergy who carried out the census did not necessarily know its purpose. However, as the comments below the figures for the census show, it is unclear as to which people were nonconformists. This might mean that the figures are unreliable since different criteria were applied.

An additional problem is one of definition. Although there were some who held definite and extreme views, all dissent had emerged from within a broadly Protestant framework. Just as during the Interregnum many individuals defied categorisation, so too in the reign of Charles II. Many

The Compton Census, 1676

The census covered the province of Canterbury; figures for the province of York were assumed to be one-sixth of those for Canterbury.

	Conformists	Nonconformists	Papists
Province of Canterbury	2,123,362	93,151	11,878
Province of York	353,892	15,525	1,978
Totals	2,477,254	108,676	13,856

In taking these accounts we find these things observable:
1 That many left the Church upon the late [Declaration of] indulgence who did before frequent it.
2 Sending for the present enquiries has caused many to frequent the Church ...
3 That the Presbyterians are divided. Some of them come sometimes to church; therefore such are not wholly Dissenters ...
4 A considerable part of Dissenters are not of any sect whatsoever.
5 Of those who come to church, very many do not receive the sacrament [communion] ...

(Source: *Calendar of State Papers Domestic*, [4] 1693)

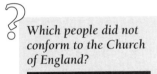

Which people did not conform to the Church of England?

who attended the Church of England shared the general puritan outlook of dissenters. Often they were inconsistent; for example, the contemporary Bulstrode Whitelocke sometimes celebrated Christmas and sometimes did not. Some Quakers were married or buried in Church and had their children baptised there. Even the names of the denominations on licenses issued under Charles II's 1672 Declaration of Indulgence are unreliable. What is certain is that there was debate in Parliament over what should be done.

The debates over comprehension and toleration

In the England of Charles II it was still generally accepted, as it had been in the reign of Elizabeth I, that conformity in religion was necessary for the unity and loyalty of the country. Nevertheless, in the intolerant climate of the Restoration a church settlement was enacted which inevitably excluded a proportion of the population. In doing so, the authorities moved away from the inclusive principles of the Elizabethan settlement, creating a church more reminiscent of Charles I's and Laud's in the 1630s.

The church settlement remained an area of debate in Parliament. This was partly because it did not meet with the King's approval, but also because the Anglican backlash that produced it was not in line with the wishes of many of the gentry. In practice, they found themselves, in their role as Justices of the Peace, prosecuting and punishing their neighbours. Although this was carried out vigorously by some, it is also clear from the uneven numbers of convictions across the country and at different times during Charles's reign, that not all magistrates were equally committed.

Those who sought to alter the settlement wanted two different kinds of change.

● Some wanted to broaden the Church to make it more comprehensive. However, it would be a mistake to regard this as representing a more tolerant attitude. One of the main arguments for making the Church of England more comprehensive was that it would thereby isolate dissenters, making it easier to eliminate dissent. For this reason, dissenters themselves objected to such a move.

● The second approach was to introduce a measure of toleration. This was also intolerant in that by allowing some dissenters to worship freely, it would be possible to distinguish the harmless ones from those who were still considered to be a threat to the political or social order. However, a case for toleration was sometimes made on economic grounds. If England wanted to compete with the successful Dutch then it could not afford **emigration** or to hinder immigration, especially when skilled workers were involved. Persecution of dissenters was likely to give rise to depopulation.

Emigration: When people leave their native country to go and live in another country.

The argument for retaining the settlement as it stood was based on experience. The broad church of the early 17th century was considered to be weak because it was internally divided. Internal splits were seen as more damaging than the existence of large numbers outside the church.

The issue was raised in Parliament on numerous occasions during Charles II's reign. The first was in 1663 after the King had expressed his wish, in December 1662, for a Declaration of Indulgence. In doing so, the King offended Parliament in two ways:

● By attempting to use the royal prerogative to dispense groups from the law.

● By craving indulgence for both Catholics and Protestant dissenters.

Comprehension: The inclusion of nonconformists within the Church of England.

In 1667 and 1668, **comprehension** bills were drafted by MPs but were not presented to the House of Commons. The King was urging Parliament to be more liberal but there is little evidence that any in the church hierarchy were sympathetic to the idea of comprehension.

Toleration: Liberty for non-Anglican Protestants to worship freely.

The issue of **toleration** arose in 1667 over a bill to naturalise immigrants. Dutch and French settlers in England were allowed their own churches which were exempt from the Act of Uniformity. Naturalising the members would mean that they were subject to English law and could not, therefore, worship freely. This was seen as inappropriate since these foreign 'stranger' churches had caused no problems and the economy benefited from the skills and expertise of the immigrants.

In 1670, the new Conventicle Act gave Charles the impression that he would be allowed to dispense individuals from the law. However, the effective persecution in London that followed the passing of the Act showed the power of the authorities. With the outbreak of war against the Dutch, Charles issued his second Declaration of Indulgence in March 1672. Again, it applied to Catholics as well as dissenters, although the terms for Catholics were less liberal. The King would control dissenters as they could only meet in approved places under licence. Although licences were granted to Presbyterians and Baptists, none were granted to Quakers. Some dissenters hesitated to apply for licences, concerned that Catholics were included in the measure. The tone of the Declaration was bold, but Charles was privately concerned that Parliament would oppose it.

In 1673, Parliament did force the King to withdraw the Declaration. The MPs objected more to the manner in which it was issued than to the matter it concerned. The idea that the King could use his dispensing powers and his claim to rule over the Church in this way was worrying.

He was going beyond dispensing individuals from the law to dispensing groups. Churchmen left the arguments to Parliament but were dismayed by the King's action. The King failed to gain the support of the dissenters and lost Anglican support. This was serious in the context of other contemporary developments in the succession and foreign policy. The impression that Charles favoured both popery and arbitrary government was reinforced. His new chief minister, Danby, urged Charles to adopt a more supportive stance towards the established church.

When the Commons asked the King to withdraw his Indulgence, they also introduced a bill to ease the position of Protestant dissenters, though not the feared Baptist and Quaker sects. Ministers need only renounce the Covenant and subscribe to the 36 doctrinal Articles. The King was sympathetic to this move towards a more comprehensive Church, but the bill foundered on disagreements between the Lords and the Commons and never became law.

A further comprehension bill was introduced into the Lords in 1674, but when Parliament was prorogued it had made little progress. In both Houses, there were strong feelings for and against comprehension. Meanwhile, the situation regarding the licences issued under the Declaration of Indulgence remained unclear. They were finally revoked only in 1674.

By the later 1670s, the situation had changed again. During the second 'Exclusion' Parliament, both a comprehension and a toleration bill failed to pass the Commons. Although no previous moves to do so had succeeded, the real prospect of a Catholic monarch led Parliament to urge for a distinction between the treatment given to Protestant nonconformists and Catholics by preventing the former from being prosecuted under Catholic penal laws. The intense anti-Catholicism aroused by the revelation of the Popish Plot fuelled the debate. The idea behind the relaxation of persecution was that Protestants should unite against the Catholic threat, but a vicar who stated this in the pulpit was forced to withdraw the suggestion. Again no bill was passed, although the main concern was that the existing legislation should not be applied inappropriately.

In 1682, the obligation in the Act of Uniformity to renounce the Solemn League and Covenant expired. This cannot have been much compensation in the light of the fiercest persecution of dissenters in the reign. The Tory reaction to the 'Exclusion' Parliaments meant that once again narrow and intolerant policies were enforced. However, in Parliament as a whole an increasing number of voices had been raised for some changes to the laws.

Overall, the cause of comprehension lost momentum and that of indulgence acquired greater attraction. If nothing else it entered the realm of the politically possible. In Charles's final years, the Anglican Tories were on the rise and they favoured a narrow church. Comprehension was no longer the aim of either the politicians or the Presbyterians who might earlier have been reconciled to the established church. Given that many persisted in remaining outside the Church, indulgence provided the best solution.

1. Give examples to show that the debate on the Church was based on (a) religious principles; (b) political expediency.

2. To what extent was religion a political issue in the reign of Charles II?

How far was there conformity within the Church?

If the law had been followed to the letter, the restored Church of England would have been uniform throughout the country. Since the Act of Uniformity concentrated on making the clergy subscribe to a clear set of beliefs and practices, there should have been little scope for variation. The Church courts were restored in 1661 to enforce Church law. However, compared with their position before 1641 they had little authority since prerogative courts such as **High Commission** were no longer there to support them. In addition, the bishops were fairly lax in imposing uniformity on the clergy. For example, the wearing of surplices was not universal. Nevertheless, since the Anglican Church controlled the universities, as those ministers of dubious conformist principles died out, the clergy came more in line with the law. Even so, many bishops seemed to be more concerned with the lifestyle and morals of the clergy than with the way they conducted services. As dissenters gained support because of their sober living and honesty, so pressure was brought on the clergy to avoid drunkenness, tobacco smoking, cock-fighting and other undesirable pastimes.

High Commission: A prerogative court. It was the senior church court and was abolished in 1641.

Bishops were also concerned with the physical neglect of churches. Many were in a ruinous state after the Interregnum. Coupled with the poverty of many parishes, this meant the Church needed the support of the local squire. This could be a mixed blessing as the squire might have other priorities. The rescheduling of the times of services to accommodate visits to horse-races was not unknown.

Gentry support was also needed to enforce the laws against dissenters, especially since the King was not enthusiastic about wiping out dissent. In many places, this was accomplished successfully. By 1685, most dissenting meetings had been suppressed and many people attended Church, if infrequently and without taking communion. They regarded it as a social duty. Even dissenters might attend marriages or burials.

In the Restoration period, there was an increasing emphasis on taking communion; it was regarded as a sign of being an Anglican for the purposes of the Corporation Act, for example. By 1660, the laity were out of the habit of taking communion. Communion had never been administered frequently in the Church of England and the Puritan emphasis on sermons meant that the practice of taking communion had become even rarer. Often parishioners simply said they did not want to receive communion, rather than making excuses such as having fallen out with their neighbours or not having suitable clothes to wear. After the Restoration, less weight was placed on preaching. **Catechising** was regarded as a more effective way of teaching people the basics of their faith, which included the need for obedience to lawful authority and sober living. If sermons were preached, the emphasis was on the application of the faith to everyday life. Although many attended Church, practice in services varied from parish to parish. The involvement and commitment of the laity varied considerably.

Catechising: Instructing on the faith through question and answer.

To what extent and why was Church practice dependent on the gentry?

To what extent were dissenters persecuted?

Application of the law was different in different places and at different times during the reign of Charles II. Why were there peaks and troughs in the degree to which the laws against dissenters and recusants were enforced?

Yorkshire Plot, 1663: A rebellion of dissenters in Yorkshire and other northern counties that was too poorly coordinated to amount to a serious threat. It did, however, lead the Earl of Clarendon to accept the need for stern measures against dissenters.

The first real onslaught against dissenters came in early 1661, fuelled by Venner's Fifth Monarchist rising (see page 257). The authorities were made doubly anxious because the transition from the old to the new militia system left them vulnerable in the event of rebellion. The authorities also clamped down on those who were not meeting their militia-raising obligations. Similarly, in 1663, rumours of the **Yorkshire Plot** were fuelled by fears that the militia was inadequate. What was, in fact, a non-event was soon dealt with. Although some suspects languished in jail for years – Francis Howgill, imprisoned in Appleby after the Yorkshire Plot, died there in 1669 – this was the exception. Most were released on bonds of security.

The historian John Miller, in *After the Civil Wars* (2000), argues that Parliament became more intolerant to dissenters during the 1660s. He points out that the 1670 Conventicle Act was more arbitrary than that of 1664. It was also permanent. The 1670 Act rewarded informers and penalised officers who did not prosecute on the evidence.

The Declaration of Indulgence of 1672, which allowed the licensing of dissenting places of worship and preachers, caused renewed persecution. The Declaration was withdrawn in 1673 and although the licences were not revoked until later, magistrates lost no time in attempting to close the meeting places. In any case, there had been a reluctance to grant licences for public buildings as opposed to private houses.

In contrast, at the time of the Popish Plot and Exclusion Crisis, the Whigs courted nonconformists. The Rye House Plot and the Tory reaction of the last four years of Charles II's reign brought the temporary relaxation of attitudes to an end. This period constituted the most severe bout of persecution. Such was the extent of their dominance that the Tories succeeded in breaking down resistance to the persecution of dissenters, which had been evident previously.

In conclusion, John Miller argues that 'there is only limited evidence of sustained persecution or extensive sectarian bigotry for much of the reign and that when religious divisions began to bite deeply, from the mid-1670s, they did so in conjunction with a growing political polarisation'.

There is plenty of evidence that magistrates and parish officials were reluctant to prosecute their neighbours. This might be a result of marriage or kinship ties with the offenders or because of considerations of simple humanity. To avoid acting against nonconformists, Thomas Pepys refused to serve as a JP, Sir John Busby made sure he was not at home when informants called and a London sheriff told the bishops that he could not trade with his neighbours one day and send them to jail the next. In 1682 in Bridlington, Yorkshire, local constables allowed themselves to be imprisoned rather than arrest Quakers. They then proceeded to pay over £700 worth of fines incurred by Quakers. When they were forced to seize the Quakers' goods, they encouraged the inhabitants of Bridlington to buy the confiscated goods cheaply and return them to their owners.

There was, nevertheless, considerable persecution. This ranged from minor harassment to mass imprisonments of whole congregations. The figures for those released from prison on the occasion of various amnesties bears witness to the extent of Quaker imprisonment. At the King's coronation in 1661, over 500 Quakers were released in York and more than 4,000 in England as a whole. Similar numbers were freed in

Indulgence: A grant of religious liberty.

honour of the King's marriage in 1662, and later in the year when the King first attempted to introduce **indulgence**.

The conditions in prison were harsh. The Quaker Richard Hubberthorne died in 1662 as a result of his many imprisonments. Edward Burrough died in Newgate jail. There were many others. About 450 Quakers, as well as seven of the 215 clergy who were imprisoned after being ejected from their livings, died in jail.

However, the example of the Welsh Quaker Richard Davies shows that imprisonment was not always restricting. In theory, he spent most of the 1660s in jail but in fact his 'prison' consisted of a house separate from the main jail in Welshpool. He could come and go as he pleased. John Bunyan's imprisonment, between 1660 and 1672, was also relatively lax.

At the time of the onslaught on dissenters of the early 1680s many were jailed. By 1682, there were over 700 Quaker prisoners in England and many more impoverished or bankrupted by fines. However, by then the Quakers, as well as the Baptists, were better organised than at the Restoration. The Quakers had annual meetings and strict internal discipline as well as support networks. As a result, they survived. The example of the Bridlington officials also shows the extent to which toleration was growing largely as a result of the sober living and reputation for honesty, which the dissenters had earned.

Besides imprisonment, dissenters might be fined which could ruin whole families. Punishments also included seizing all of the offender's belongings. Further relatively minor problems were created by excommunication from the Church of England. This meant, for example, that dissenters could not receive parish poor relief. However, measures such as this were applied inconsistently; some received poor relief, while others did not.

Another means of prosecuting Quakers was on the grounds that they were vagrants. Itinerant preaching was a hallmark of Quakerism, with individuals travelling the country to encourage congregations and instil internal discipline. If arrested with no apparent means of support, this could lead to imprisonment. A further ploy was to arrest Quakers on the basis of an accusation, not necessarily backed up by evidence, then ask the accused to take an oath. Since Quakers refused to do so, they were imprisoned.

1. List and explain the reasons for persecution of dissenters.

2. To what extent does the evidence suggest that the persecution of dissenters was motivated by political rather than religious factors?

9.5 How successful was Charles II's foreign policy?

An assessment of Charles II's foreign policy must take into consideration the changing fortunes of England's European neighbours, as well as the methods employed and actions taken. The extent to which Charles's policies were in his own or in England's best interests has been debated at length. In *Restoration England and Europe* (1979), J.L. Price believes they were in England's because the gains made by France in 1660–88 were relatively minor and therefore not damaging to England. G. Holmes, in *The Making of a Great Power* (1993), considers that there was no guarantee that royal policy would serve England's interests. However, Charles was not an entirely free agent since an active foreign policy depended on parliamentary subsidies. While the extent of English prejudice and knowledge of European affairs are debatable, all government ministers recognised the impossibility of persuading Parliament that a pro-French foreign policy was in England's interests.

What developments were taking place in Europe in 1660?

For a century, Protestant England had followed a foreign policy that acknowledged the dominance of Spain in Europe and the world. This depended on a balance of power between Catholics and Protestants in Europe. However, the end of the Thirty Years War with the Treaty of Westphalia in 1648 placed France in a strong position and reduced the lands held by Protestant powers greatly. In addition, the unrest of Louis XIV's minority known as the Frondes had ended. In 1661, Louis personally took over the reins of power on the death of his chief minister, Cardinal Mazarin. Meanwhile, chance had decreed that Spain had a weak monarch who produced a sickly heir. Coupled with years of continuous warfare, this placed Spain in terminal decline. This was highlighted by the Treaty of the Pyrenees between France and Spain in 1659 and Spain's subsequent inability to meet the terms of the treaty by paying the dowry of its infanta (princess) who married Louis XIV. This led to French attacks on the Spanish Netherlands in 1667–78 in compensation. England's involvement in Europe should have taken all this into account.

Equally, as was suggested in the chapter on the Interregnum, there had been a swing away from religion as the determinant of international relations to a situation where commercial and colonial considerations held sway. Charles II should, therefore, have taken note of the growing strength of the United Provinces. However, since war often damaged trade, it did not necessarily provide a solution for merchants. Besides this, Jean-Baptiste Colbert, Louis XIV's finance minister, was making hostile moves, for example by imposing tariffs on imports in 1667. The extent to which Charles II took these changing circumstances into account is debatable since his management of foreign policy seemed to be more concerned with securing his domestic position than England's in Europe.

Destinations of domestic exports from and sources of imports to London, average 1663–69 (%)

	Ireland/ Scotland	NW Europe	Baltic, Scandinavia, Russia	Spain, Portugal, Mediterranean	Far East	America
Exports						
Woollens	0.4	31.7	5.5	56.55	1.3	4.6
All goods	1.8	36.6	4.4	47.8	1.4	8.0
Imports						
All goods	0.8	36.7	7.8	31.0	11.7	12.0

The figures in the table suggest that, because of the heavy weighting of English trade towards Spain and the Mediterranean, if Charles were interested primarily in trade his priority should be peace in the Mediterranean and good relations with Spain. However, this does not take into account Spain's reluctance to open up its colonial trade to England. This had resulted in war in 1655 in an attempt by England to open trade to the American colonies by force.

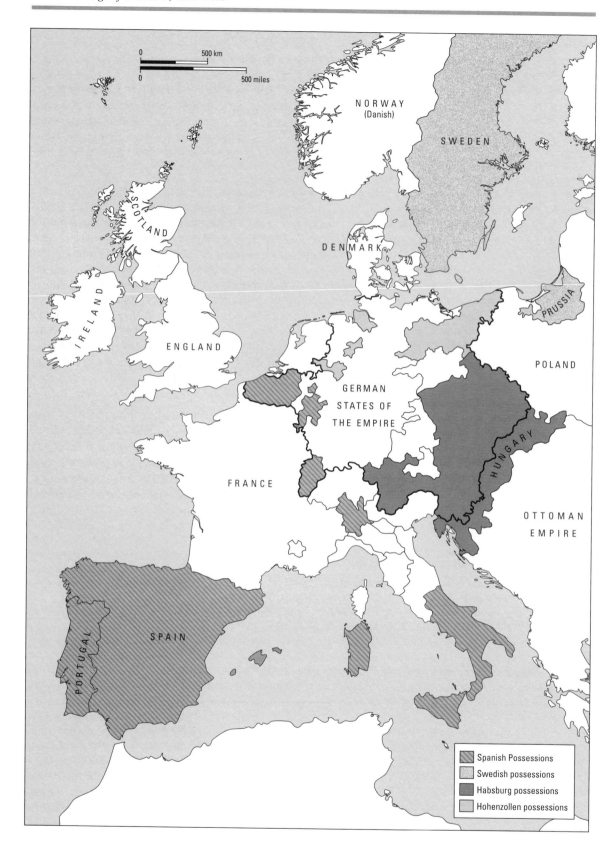

Europe in 1660

How did Charles II manage foreign policy?

The Restoration never questioned that foreign policy was the prerogative of the monarch and any suggestion that MPs should dictate its course met with a hostile reception from Charles II. The English administrative system provided the King with two secretaries for the conduct of foreign relations. Their job was to manage the diplomatic service and to advise the monarch. One secretary dealt with northern Europe and the other with southern Europe. During Charles II's reign, the advice of the most able of his secretaries was in line with royal policy. In any case, Charles took a personal interest in foreign affairs. In doing so, he was aided by the lack of unity among his Privy Councillors. Frequently, their conflicting advice reflected their political rivalries rather than the best interests of Britain. Foreign policy was indeed British in the sense that Charles was king of all the countries in the British Isles and the Scots concurred with his decisions regarding foreign policy.

Making use of the expertise he believed he had gained on his 'travels' during the 1650s, Charles followed his own inclinations. He certainly had experience, contacts and knowledge of foreign languages. Most notably, he engaged the services of his sister Henrietta Anne, Louis XIV's sister-in-law. She married Louis's brother in 1661 and was instrumental in negotiating the secret Treaty of Dover in 1670, shortly before her death.

Charles used his knowledge of languages to talk directly with foreign ambassadors. As a result, even Charles's closest advisers often had no idea of the actions he was taking – as with the peace initiatives of 1678 leading to the Treaty of Nijmegen between France and the United Provinces, as well as the aforementioned secret Treaty of Dover. The French and Venetian governments may have been more aware of his intentions than his own ministers. Between 1672 and 1674, the Dutch built up a bloc of MPs hostile to the Anglo–French alliance.

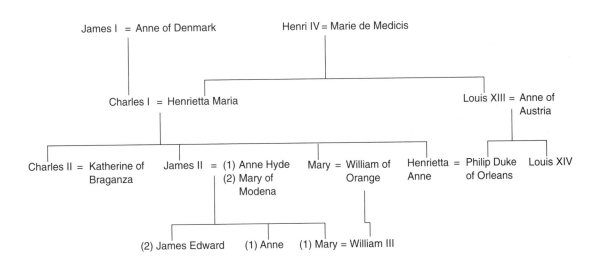

Family tree of the Stuarts, showing the relationship to the French and Dutch royal families

What were the aims and motives of Charles II's foreign policy?

The historian J.D. Davis points out, in 'International Relations, War and the Armed Forces' (1997), that it was difficult for any monarch in this period to have a long-term foreign policy based on principles because overall trends in European development were unclear. Nevertheless, both Charles II and James II paid lip-service to following a policy which showed concern for trade. Instructions to British diplomats and naval commanders bear this out.

Charles II's true intentions are unclear, largely because of his methods. He lied, or was at best economical with the truth. He was also secretive, even untrustworthy. On the surface, his policies appeared inconsistent and unpredictable. Foreign observers, however, were aware that the influence of faction and Parliament on English foreign policy meant that consistency was not to be expected.

Nor can historians agree on the motives of Parliament in pressing for particular policies. This is especially the case with the second Dutch War of 1665–67. In *Profit and Power: A Study of England and the Anglo-Dutch Wars* (1957), C. Wilson wrote that it was the result of pressure from the London merchants who wanted to seize trade from its competitor. Paul Seaward, in *The Restoration 1660–1688* (1991), holds the opinion that economic complaints masked a desire for honour and prestige. In *Britain and the World 1649–1815* (1980), J.R. Jones is of the opinion that the war had little to do with the Dutch, but rather resulted from the outgrowth of factional struggles at Court. S. Pincus, in *Popery, trade and universal monarchy: the ideological context of the outbreak of the second Anglo-Dutch War* (1992), considers the pressures for war in relation to a campaign against 'universal monarchy' and in opposition to the Calvinist, pluralist, republican Dutch. Thus the United Provinces represented the opposite of English religious, political and commercial interests. Whatever its reasons, Parliament showed its enthusiasm by granting £2,500,000 for the war in November 1664.

For much of his reign, Charles effectively followed two foreign policies. Publicly, he agreed to demands for hostility towards France. The reverse should have been alliance with Protestant powers, but this was more problematic since the Dutch were commercial rivals. Relations with the Dutch were further complicated by dynastic considerations. In 1650, Charles's nephew, William of Orange, had been deprived of his traditional role as governor by a republican coup, and this was not restored until 1672. Charles's policy centred around alliance with France through a series of secret treaties and agreements, in which he was granted one-off payments and pensions in exchange for a variety of domestic and foreign policy measures.

Contemporaries were largely unaware of the secret treaties, although political rivalries meant that some came to light; for example, the discrediting of Danby in December 1678. As J.D. Davies observes, in *International Relations, War and the Armed Forces* (1997), historians may have more knowledge of the agreements, but they find it equally difficult to discern Charles's aims.

● Did Charles genuinely admire Louis XIV?

● How devoted was he, if at all, to the promotion of Catholicism?

- Was he totally governed by the desire to become financially independent of Parliament?

- Did he aspire to absolutism?

All these questions are debated, but unresolved. They are likely to remain so, since discussion of Charles's motives can only be based on what is known of his actions and the circumstances in which they were carried out. An examination of Charles's foreign policy must centre round these questions, identifying arguments for and against each claim.

What were England's foreign relations in Charles II's reign?

Charles II's reign can be divided into four main sections with regard to foreign policy. The first three coincide with the periods of ascendancy of his leading ministers, while the last spans the Exclusion Crisis and the final years when fears of political instability meant continental powers hesitated to involve England in their affairs.

Charles II's reign began unspectacularly. The Commonwealth's Spanish War ended, although no formal peace was signed. In 1661, a treaty with Portugal arranged the marriage of Charles to Catherine of Braganza. England gained Tangier and Bombay, but the large **dowry** seemed more important. Dunkirk was sold to France in 1662 without a formal alliance being negotiated.

Dowry: The money and goods that are gifts from a woman's father to the man that she marries.

More significantly, relations between England and the United Provinces became increasingly strained. The Navigation Act of 1651 was renewed and the Royal Africa Company challenged the **Dutch Guinea trade**. Prominent members of the Royal Africa Company, including the Duke of York, pressed for war against the Dutch. Their motives may have been to scare the Dutch or to undermine Clarendon who was reluctant to engage in war. Charles himself was probably more influenced by antipathy to what the United Provinces stood for, in political and religious terms. Although a case can be made for Charles championing England's commercial interests, modern scholars, such as Geoffrey Holmes in *The Making of a Great Power* (1993), are more inclined to the view that he was uneasy about England's involvement in the war.

Dutch Guinea trade: Trade between the United Provinces and the west African coastal area known as Guinea.

War broke out in 1665. It was made possible by the enthusiasm of Parliament in granting the necessary taxation. At first, the war went well for England, but its fortunes deteriorated when France and Denmark–Norway joined the war on the side of the Dutch in 1666. The Dutch defeated the English Navy in June and the English naval victory off North Foreland in Kent failed to redress the balance. Parliament was reluctant to grant further tax for the war, suspicious that what had already been supplied had been misspent. Despite peace overtures, the Dutch attacked the English fleet at its moorings in the River Medway, inflicting a humiliating blow by towing away the 'Royal Charles', England's largest ship. Clarendon was made a scapegoat for a war he had not favoured. England's poor showing was a contributory factor in his downfall. The Treaty of Breda, which ended the war, only restored the pre-war situation.

Charles II's foreign policy of 1667–74 was more complex and more controversial. This was largely because by this time there were two policies, the public and the secret. The former began in 1668 with the Triple Alliance of England, the United Provinces and Sweden to pressurise Louis XIV into a moderate settlement of the 'War of Devolution'. In this war, Louis XIV was engaged in laying claim to the Spanish Netherlands in lieu of the dowry that was promised him in the Treaty of the Pyrenees. The alliance placated Charles's ministers. Parliament was also sufficiently confident to grant funds. Although there were doubts over Charles's sincerity in entering into the alliance, it was clear that he was mindful that French domination of the Spanish Netherlands would threaten English trading links with the United Provinces. Also, tariffs on imports recently established by Colbert suggested that France was a potential rival. However, this did not prevent Charles from making his next move.

The secret Treaty of Dover in 1670 marked the triumph of Charles's secret policy. The negotiations were carried out with Charles's sister, Henrietta Anne, as **proxy** for Louis XIV. The Duke of York and Lord Clifford represented Charles. Later, Arlington was also made aware of the terms when he signed the treaty, but everyone else was duped by the public treaty of the same name. The only evidence of Charles pursuing commercial interests here lies in the fact that England gained two small but strategically important islands in the Scheldt from France. Bearing in mind the other terms, neither this nor the anticipated capture of Dutch naval vessels can have been the primary motive for the treaty. A joint Anglo–French venture against the United Provinces was planned. If it were successful, England would gain several small towns and William of Orange would become **puppet ruler** of a small state. The clause that was never made public during Charles II's reign contained Charles's commitment to convert to Catholicism and to begin the re-Catholicisation of Britain. In return, he gained a subsidy of 2,000,000 livres (French currency) and 6,000 troops to quell any consequent rebellion.

Proxy: A person who is given the authority to act or make decisions for someone else.

Puppet ruler: A ruler under the control of a higher power.

What damage was done to the English ships, according to this source?

Engraving showing the Dutch in the Medway, June 1667

It is possible to explain Charles's alliance with Louis XIV. Blood and marriage closely related the two. Charles might be in a better position to influence his cousin from within an alliance. By preventing a Franco–Dutch alliance, Charles was avoiding a more serious challenge to England's interests. Charles might also gain revenge for the humiliations of the Second Dutch War and the re-instatement of his nephew William of Orange. The problem with this explanation lies in that it fails to account for the Catholicising clause. Historians have debated whether Charles genuinely held Catholic sentiments, if the Catholic sympathies were real but short-lived, or if financial considerations lay behind the commitments he made.

In 1671, despite the lack of popular support for the French alliance, Charles engineered an excuse for a third Dutch war. This directly flouted the 1668 Triple Alliance. Again, the war did not go according to plan, either on land or at sea. French armies overran Utrecht but not Holland. The Dutch reinstated the House of Orange in its traditional roles and set about organising resistance to the French. The Dutch fleet attacked, pre-empting a joint Anglo–French attack. In 1673, the Dutch began to regain lost ground and the French withdrew as both the Spanish Netherlands and Germans threatened. At home, defeats had the effect of discrediting Arlington and Buckingham who had supported the war. In February 1674, Charles reneged on (ignored the terms of) the Treaty of Dover. Instead, he made a separate peace, the Treaty of Westminster, with the Dutch. Thus he proved himself totally untrustworthy by flouting the terms of both his alliances within three years.

Between 1674 and 1679, France, Spain and the United Provinces continued to wage war. English trade benefited since British ships were the only secure carriers in the Mediterranean, but this was fortuitous rather than planned. Meanwhile, Charles maintained his separate public and secret foreign policies. He acted as mediator in the European war, while continuing to receive subsidies from Louis XIV. His new chief minister, Danby, urged an anti-French policy in order to gain the support of Parliament. This bore fruit in 1677 when a marriage was arranged between William of Orange and Charles's Protestant niece, Mary, the elder daughter of James Duke of York. Perhaps Parliament's grant of money for the navy in recognition of this change of policy helped to persuade Charles.

By 1678, preparations were being made to enter the European war on the side of the Dutch but the Peace of Nijmegen ended the war before England could join in. In any case, Charles had secretly been taking the initiative in negotiating the peace, although his secretaries knew nothing about this.

After the revelations of the Popish Plot and the events of the Exclusion Crisis that followed, England was largely inactive in continental affairs. The only positive public initiative was an alliance with Spain, entered into in 1680. In 1683, England officially recognised what had long been reality and abandoned Tangier to the Moors. Foreign powers were wary of England's instability and the possibility of renewed civil war. Although continued subsidies and pensions from Louis XIV enabled Charles to avoid calling Parliament between 1681 and 1685, they were insufficient to finance an active foreign policy. Not calling Parliament was one of the conditions on which Charles was given French money, suggesting that he was planning to rule without Parliament.

1. What evidence is there to support the view that:

(a) Charles II was a client of Louis XIV?

(b) trade was Charles II's primary concern in foreign policy?

(c) domestic factional disputes determined England's foreign policy in the reign of Charles II?

2. To what extent was Parliament able to influence Charles II's foreign policy?

How far did England's relations with continental Europe change during the reign of Charles II?

In comparison with the Interregnum period, England's position in Europe was generally weaker during Charles II's reign. The main reason for this was financial. Whereas the Interregnum governments had levied high levels of revenue, Charles II's ability to tax his people was constrained by Parliament. This had a significant impact on the King's ability to maintain and build up his armed forces.

Nevertheless, Charles was in a strong position in 1660. He benefited from the reputation England had acquired under the Interregnum governments, yet he had no obligations to other states and they did not know where his ambitions lay.

During peace-time, the English navy normally had between 30 and 40 vessels, used to defend trade. Although it was the most expensive department of government, and Charles II and his brother took personal interest in it, the Navy soon lost the pre-eminence it held in 1660. Both the French and the Dutch outbuilt the English in the 1660s. Between 1660 and 1675, the English built only 50 warships while the Dutch built 98 and the French 150. However, in the 1670s, a construction programme put England's navy on a more equal footing with those of its rivals. The Army was another matter. As mentioned, no English monarch could afford a standing army. During the Interregnum, internal security measures had necessitated the maintenance of three armies, but with the restoration of monarchy the danger of rebellion receded. Since the Navy was England's means of defence, a standing army was not only unnecessary but also provocative to Parliament. Europeans may have regarded post-Restoration England as being in a different league, but England was not significantly weaker in 1685 than in 1660. Its performance in the European wars of the 1690s demonstrated that, when Parliament wished to finance its involvement, England was a considerable force.

Most importantly during this period, England's position in continental Europe must be viewed in the context of the changing European balance of power, of changing trading patterns and of increasing colonial interests. Overall, change cannot be judged in relation to one reign alone.

The figures in the table show the relative importance of the main English ports. They reveal the expansion of English trade in the later 17th century and that those ports which expanded fastest were those benefiting from Anglo–American trade, especially Bristol.

Customs revenues at the chief English Ports in the Restoration period (£s)

PORT	1672	1676	1687*
London	502,312	569,531	586,905
Hull	22,527	20,213	18,649
Exeter	15,729	17,038	20,761
Bristol	56,922	65,908	46,820
Newcastle	8,889	9,419	10,583
Plymouth	14,102	16,564	19,139
Lyme Regis	6,518	4,438	5,269
Southampton	3,220	6,632	4,310
Dartmouth	3,516	1,263	745

* New customs duties first levied in 1685 are included in these figures, which are not, therefore directly comparable with those for 1672 and 1676.

(Source: W.B. Stephens, *Seventeenth Century Exeter*, University of Exeter, 1958)

How successful was Charles II's foreign policy?

9.6   *The reign of Charles II: an assessment*

Studying the reign of Charles II in isolation from those of his forebears and successors creates problems of interpretation. Just as local historians struggle to ascertain what is significant and what is not in a locality, without contextual knowledge of national trends, so the examination of a limited period can distort the grasp of the significance of events within it.

Awareness of the important issues of the 17th century is a good starting point, although a century is equally as arbitrary a period as a single reign in relation to historical developments. The main themes of the reign of Charles II for the political historian must be:

● the development of monarchic powers, including the relationship between Crown and Parliament

● the development of political parties

● the extent to which politics and religion were interrelated

● England's place in the changing relationships and balance of the European powers, especially in western Europe.

There are hints of relationships between the countries of the British Isles, but since these were unusually settled during Charles II's reign they figure little here.

Certainly, it is impossible to understand the course of politics in the reign of Charles II without appreciating the political and religious impact of the reign of Charles I and the Interregnum on the whole population, but more especially on the ruling élite. Equally, interpretations of relations between Crown and Parliament and of the development of political parties are coloured by what happened next.

In addition, the reign of Charles II marked significant change in longer-term economic and social development. Population growth slowed and so, consequently, did inflation. This change would have been imperceptible for contemporaries since there were still problems with the food supply in years of bad harvest. They would not have been aware either that Europe was just emerging from the '**little ice age**' of the 17th century. The extent to which overseas trade expanded would also have been difficult to gauge at the time. Although the Treasury was now engaged in collecting accurate data on customs from each of the ports, there would have been few figures with which to compare.

From a social point of view, it has been argued that Britain was becoming more secularised. The new **Latitudinarian** approach in religion, the founding of the Royal Society and growing religious toleration can all be cited as evidence of this. The idea that all Englishmen could share a single religious outlook was all but defunct. Nevertheless, religion remained a source of political conflict for years to come, particularly in the reign of Queen Anne with cries of 'the Church in danger'. In the reign of George III, the Gordon Rioters of 1780 caused more damage to London than the French revolutionaries did to Paris in 1789.

Society may have been becoming more polarised, with the gentry jealously guarding their privileges and authority. The suspicion with which they viewed lower-class radicalism and the danger of revolt and rebellion is apparent in their suppression of the sects and in the Tory reaction to Whig tactics during the Exclusion Crisis. The paternalist

'**Little ice age**': Between about 1550 and 1700 the English winters were colder than average to an extent which had a considerable effect on an agriculture-based economy.

Latitudinarian: The belief that reason and personal judgement were of greater value than church doctrine.

1. How far were political and religious developments during the reign of Charles II influenced by the Interregnum?

2. To what extent did James Duke of York's conversion to Catholicism mark a turning point in relations between Charles II and Parliament?

3. To what extent was religion a political issue during Charles II's reign?

4. Was the strength of Charles II by 1685 more the result of good fortune or of good judgement?

5. How important was the reign of Charles II in the development of limited monarchy in England?

attitude evident in the Elizabethan Poor Laws was giving way to a more authoritarian approach. However, although the 1662 Settlement Act made life more difficult for the poor, and the 1671 Game Law restricted the social background of those who could hunt, harsh legislation such as the Waltham Black Acts of 1724 was still some way off.

The England of Charles II was one of transition. There was still much unsettled business following the political upheavals of the mid-17th century. England was moving slowly from being a minor state on the fringe of Europe to being a colonial power. The political events of the next reign were critical in determining the final course of events.

James II, William III and the Glorious Revolution

10.1 The reign of James II, 1685–1688

10.1.1 Historical interpretation: The reign of James II
10.1.2 How important was James II's character in shaping the events of his reign?
10.1.3 How secure was James's position when he became King of England in 1685?
10.1.4 In what ways did James II alienate his supporters, 1685–1688?
10.1.5 Why was Exclusion achieved in 1688?

Key Issues

- *How strong was James II's position when he became King of England in 1685?*

- *Did James II want to turn England into a Catholic country?*

- *How seriously did James's policies threaten stability in Church and State?*

Framework of events

1685	February: accession of James VII and II; Parliament not aggressive towards him
	May: Duke of Argyll's Rebellion in Scotland
	June–July: Monmouth's Rebellion is defeated; execution of Monmouth
	October: Revocation of the Edict of Nantes by Louis XIV of France
1686	Directions to Preacher forbid anti-Catholic sermons
	Godden v Hales Case is used to secure dispensing power
	'Closeting' begins in order to promote Roman Catholics to office
1687	James suspends the penal laws against Catholics and Dissenters
	April: Declaration of Indulgence
	Expulsion of Fellows of Magdalen College, Oxford
1688	April: Second Declaration of Indulgence
	10 June: birth of Prince James Edward
	30 June: letter from the 'Immortal Seven' to William of Orange.

Overview

WITHIN a short period of three years (1685–1688), James VII of Scotland/James II of England managed to turn a favourable political situation, engineered by Charles II and the Anglican Tories, into a situation that was beyond his control. It was not necessarily a situation in which a revolution was inevitable, but it was one in which he pressed the panic button, in December 1688 – not once but twice. As a result of what appears to have been a nervous breakdown, James's first attempt to flee across the English Channel to France not only demonstrated the fact that he could not cope with the presence in England of William of Orange, but destroyed his personal credibility and confidence, making a second flight the necessary outcome.

His smooth accession in 1685 was remarkable amid the hysteria of the Popish Plot and the Exclusion Crisis from the previous reign, and the growing power of Louis XIV, threatening French hegemony in Europe. However, James's hold on power was fragile and, in some ways, it was a triumph of idealism that a Catholic king could rule a Protestant country by a combination of goodwill and respect for the law. When James was supported in the suppression of two rebellions in 1685, Anglican Tories hoped that legitimacy and stability would survive long enough for James to be succeeded by his Protestant daughter, Mary, and her husband, William of Orange. With considerable reluctance, support fell away as it was perceived that James was undermining the three pillars of the English State – Parliament, Law and the Church – and pursuing French-style absolutism.

Reluctance to break the ties of loyalty and obedience was overcome by the birth of a son to James and his Catholic wife, Mary of Modena, on 10 June 1688. Given his wife's record of stillbirths and infant mortalities, it was unlikely that this Catholic heir would survive to found a Catholic dynasty. (Mary had already produced 10 children between 1674–88, 5 of whom were stillborn, and only one of whom lived beyond the age of one year.) Given the political climate in which James had prorogued Parliament since the end of 1685, and showed every indication of trying to pack it to achieve the repeal of the Test and Corporation Acts, Parliament, Law and Church were hardly in safe hands by June 1688. Catholic conspiracy plots resurfaced in the form of the ridiculous idea that the infant was not the child of James and Mary, but a healthy baby smuggled into her bed in a warming pan. What made James unable to sustain his government was not the reaction of William of Orange to events in England, but James's own reaction to William's actions. This reaction helped James to create the conditions that led to his own downfall and to the Glorious Revolution of 1688–1689.

10.1.1 *The reign of James II*
A CASE STUDY IN HISTORICAL INTERPRETATION

Whig historians, especially Lord Macaulay in the mid-19th century and G.M. Trevelyan, writing in 1904 and 1938, see the reign of James as a great landmark in history. In their opinion, the problems of balance of power in the state, unresolved by civil war and the Restoration, were tackled after the removal of James. Thereafter, England was on the road to a Protestant constitutional monarchy and parliamentary government. James II's reign was characterised by the pursuit of absolutism and popery.

As with conspiracy theories earlier in the century, events in Europe were important. Louis XIV's effective centralisation of power and his drive for **hegemony** in Europe encouraged Whig historians to assume that James was a vassal of France at a time when Louis was taking drastic measures against Huguenots (French Huguenots) with the Revocation of the Edict of Nantes in 1685. This had been issued by Henri IV in 1598 and guaranteed religious freedom to Huguenots. It alarmed Protestants throughout Europe.

Central to the Whig interpretation is the image of a 'glorious and bloodless revolution against a tyrant', in 1688. Research on the Revolution (see section 10.2), and on the nature of the British state in

Hegemony: The domination or control by one country over a group of others, especially if it is a member of that group.

1685–88, has to some extent 'revised' old views. Most arguments revolve around the intentions of James. These are very difficult to determine. J.R. Western argues, in *The English State in the 1680s* (1971), that England under James II seemed to be moving inexorably towards absolutism: 'James II … needed judges who would not only enforce the law but sanction its being bent.' In 1978, John Miller wrote more sympathetically of James: 'If James stretched his powers beyond conventional limits, he did so because he could not achieve his objectives without doing so. In accusing him of trying to establish absolutism, his contemporaries and later historians confused means with ends.' Another historian, W.A. Speck (1989), does not accept the idea that absolute methods were the means of achieving religious toleration: 'The French model of absolute kingship appealed to him. The notion that all he really sought was religious toleration for Catholics, and that he only resorted to the increase of royal authority as a means to that end, and not as an end in itself is ultimately unconvincing.'

The outcome of James's policies was loss of support; the scale of this is arguable. J.R. Jones, in *Country and Court* (1978), maintains that 'James's policies affected a wide spectrum of opinion, and the opposition that they provoked was something far more than an upper-class conspiracy or "aristocratic revolution". The Revolution of 1688 was no mere **palace coup**.' Barry Coward suggests, in *Stuart England 1603–1714* (1997), that:

- James II's policies on their own did not lose him his throne

- the 'Immortal Seven' men who wrote the Letter to William did not ask him to 'invade'

- William's intentions were not crystal clear

- James retained the support of a number of Tories.

The character of James is central to the position he found himself in by the end of 1688. It is the key to his actions and policies. The birth of his son accelerated events and conspiracies against him.

Palace coup: Revolution from within the Court or government.

1. Why do historians reach different conclusions about the reign of James?

2. In what ways is 'historical hindsight' important in their judgements?

3. Why do historians find difficulties in analysing James's aims?

10.1.2 How important was James's character in shaping the events of his reign?

While Charles II had much in common with his grandfather (James I), James II was in many ways much more like his father (Charles I). He was the third son of his father, born in the early years of the Personal Rule. The insecurities of the 1640s took place at the same time as his adolescence. In 1644, James was given the title 'Duke of York'. Four years later, he fled from the Parliamentary forces and spent the next 12 years in exile in France and the Low Countries. He was given the post of Lord High Admiral in 1660 and gave good service during the Dutch Wars. His conversion to Catholicism made him a victim of the Test Act (1673), while the Exclusion movement was aimed at removing him from succession when it looked as though Charles II would die without a legitimate heir. Like his father, James had a total devotion to the principle of divine right of kings and to his religious faith. They differed in that Charles I died a martyr for the Church of England, whereas James was 'martyred' politically for the Church of

King James II (1633–1701) by
Sir Godfrey Kneller, 1684

Penal laws: Laws in a country that
are concerned with crime and
punishment.

*1. Which
characteristics did
James II and his father,
Charles I, share?*

*2. Why did Charles II
hold such a poor
opinion of his brother
James?*

*3. Did James II's
character suggest that
he was an unsuitable
successor to Charles II?*

Rome. They shared the same tunnel vision in matters
political and personal.

James persisted in marrying Anne Hyde, daughter
of the Earl of Clarendon (1659/1660), in spite of his
brother's disapproval. They had 8 children, of
whom 2 daughters – Mary (1662–1694) and Anne
(1665–1714) – survived to become queens. These
daughters were Protestant.

Two years after Anne Hyde's death, James married
the Catholic Mary of Modena in 1673. This was after
the revelation of his own conversion. They had 12
children, of whom only two survived: James Edward
(1688–1766) and Louisa (1692–1712). Unlike
Charles I, James had a number of mistresses.
Charles II used to say that they were so ugly they
must have been sent as a penance. In fact, his lack of
wit and sparkle made James the butt of a number of
quips in his brother's Court. In the heat of some
alleged Catholic plots and conspiracies to replace
him with the Catholic James, Charles felt confident:
'I am sure that no man in England will take away my
life to make you King.' His devotion to principle was
both a strength and a weakness. Gilbert Burnet, a
contemporary Protestant bishop, was relatively kind
to him as a person. The superficial and gratuitous wit
of the Duke of Buckingham shows how the Court
saw him, in spite of his obvious bravery and courage
as an officer: 'Charles (II) could understand if he
would, James would understand if he could.'

James II lacked the subtlety and ability of Charles
II to let sleeping dogs lie. The historian Paul Seward wrote, in 1986, that
while the Marquis of Halifax referred to the 'immoderate love of ease' of
Charles II, 'James, by contrast, had an immoderate sense of mission'. Like
many inflexible people, he was prone to panic under pressure and there
was no Plan B. Plan A was always to free English Catholics from the **penal
laws** as a stage in winning back England to the Catholic faith. James
believed that the Restoration and his accession made that plan providential. His attempts to regain his throne show a lack of political realism in
the face of 'abdication' declared on his behalf by the Convention of Lords
and Commons, in February 1689. He continued to be recognised as King
during his exile in St Germain, in France, until 1697.

10.1.3 *How secure was James's position when he became King of England in 1685?*

While there may not have been great enthusiasm in 1685, James II's accession went so smoothly that James was confident to attend a public mass two days later. He also took possession of the life revenues voted to Charles before Parliament met to sanction them.

A number of factors accounted for this apparent reversal of entrenched anti-Catholicism:

● Charles II had defeated Exclusion by:
 – his skill in proroguing the Exclusion Parliaments
 – his ability to keep cool and not be panicked by Shaftesbury and the Whigs
 – the mistaken policies of the Whigs that caused fears of another civil war
 – the fact that supporters of Exclusion were divided as to who should replace Charles: Monmouth, or William and Mary.

● Charles had consolidated his Parliamentary victory over the Whigs, weakened by the death of Shaftesbury, by his use of **Quo Warranto** proceedings against Whig boroughs. This meant that, when Parliament met in 1685, it was staunchly Tory and keen to stress its loyalty.

Quo Warranto: Writs asking towns by what authority they exercised local government. It was a device by which charters could be withdrawn from towns and then reissued to make sure that the municipal personnel was loyal to the Crown. Charles II issued Quo Warranto writs against the influence of the Whigs.

● Charles had been able to rule from 1681 until 1685 – technically breaching the Triennial Act – with the support of the Anglican Tories, keen to consolidate their position against the Whigs. To them, James represented legitimate succession. Provided he did not destabilise the balance between Church and State, and ruled within the framework of the Law, James would be accepted. After all, he was in his fifties and not expected to live for a very long time. As things stood in 1685, a Protestant daughter, Mary, would succeed him.

● James II showed his desire for stability in a speech to the Parliament and Privy Council:

 'I have been reported to be a man for arbitrary power, but that is not the only story to be made of me; I shall make it my endeavour to preserve this government both in Church and State as it is now by law established. I know the principles of the Church of England are for Monarchy, and the members of it have showed themselves good and loyal subjects; therefore I shall always take care to defend and support it.'

This was clearly what the Anglican Tories wanted to hear.

● James was in a good position financially as revenue was increasing. This would allow him to avoid unpopular financial support from France. It would also make him less financially dependent upon Parliament.

Covenanters: Originally those who supported the National Covenant (1638) to defend the Scottish Presbyterian Church. In 1685, the Covenanters opposed the Catholic James VII and II.

How did the rebellions in 1685 work in the new King's favour?

The first rebellion was in the Highlands where the Duke of Argyll led the **Covenanters** in rebellion, in May 1685. Lack of effective planning made this easy to crush. Argyll was executed in June, as an example to other possible rebels. This strengthened James's position. He was seen to have suppressed a rebellion. Also, many of those alive in 1685 were aware that the Civil War in 1642 had its origins in a Scottish revolt.

Monmouth's Rebellion, in June 1685, was more dangerous. James Scott (Duke of Monmouth and Buccleuch; son of Charles II) had originally hoped for a joint invasion with Argyll, with help from William of Orange. The latter did nothing to encourage the Duke of Monmouth. Monmouth hoped that his Protestantism would overcome the stigma of his illegitimacy and that he would gain the support of the old Whig exclusionists. After landing at Lyme Regis, Dorset, with 80 men, the Duke of Monmouth marched inland. By the time he entered Taunton, on 18 June, he had about 6,000 followers. Here, he declared himself King. He promised parliamentary government and religious toleration.

The Duke of Monmouth went on to take Bridgwater, but was unable to take Bristol. Meanwhile, James II had acted promptly. He offered a reward for Monmouth's capture, raised the local militia and sent John Churchill to organise a campaign against the Duke. The outcome was the battle of Sedgemoor. The Duke of Monmouth was defeated and captured. He was then taken to London and executed, in July 1685.

Why did Monmouth's Rebellion fail?

There were a number of factors:

- His supporters were enthusiastic but badly equipped and militarily inexperienced.

- Monmouth lacked sufficient support from the gentry. Those who were prominent in 1688 were still loyal to James II. John Churchill, James's best soldier, remained loyal. Even William of Orange sent troops to help James.

- Monmouth represented illegitimacy and instability. James II had given no grounds to suggest that he would break the promise he made in 1685.

How important was Monmouth's Rebellion?

It both strengthened and weakened the position of James.

- James II showed that he could be tough. After the rebellion, about 100 people were executed within the space of a week. The infamous Judge Jeffreys dealt efficiently with rebels and those who had aided them, at the Bloody Assizes. He had about 2,500 prisoners to deal with. Around 300 were executed and 800 transported to far-off lands. In view of the innate conservatism in 1685, the maintenance of order and stability was seen to be essential. It appeared that James could do this better than Monmouth.

- The rebellion gave James II the excuse to ask for a standing army.

- It encouraged the promotion of Roman Catholics to important offices and the conversion of those who wanted personal gain.

- It weakened James in that it raised issues of law. He was accused of abusing *habeas corpus* (the writ that protects the individual from arbitrary imprisonment by requiring that any person arrested be brought before a court for formal charge and, if no legal cause for arrest is shown, that he be released).

1. Why did Parliament support James in 1685?

2. How serious was the threat from rebellions in 1685?

3. In what ways did Monmouth's Rebellion strengthen James's position and in what ways did it weaken it?

- It revived the Whigs. The execution of Monmouth removed the dilemma of whether to put forward a case for William or Monmouth. Exclusionists now focused on William and Mary.

When Parliament reassembled, in November 1685, James II had strengthened his support by making Jeffreys Lord Chancellor, and the convert Sunderland President of the Council and Secretary of State. Tension in the country was increased, but more by Louis's Revocation of the Edict of Nantes than by the actions of James. When James insisted that his militia was inadequate and asked to retain Catholic officers in spite of the Test Act, he found Parliament reluctant. He prorogued it to avoid an attack on the power he claimed as King to exclude individuals from the operation of a statute. His period of cooperation with the Anglican Tories in Parliament finished in November 1685. Prorogations of Parliament continued until July 1687, when James dissolved it by Proclamation.

10.1.4 In what ways did James II alienate his supporters, 1685–1688?

While James II avoided dissolution until 1687, he became increasingly reliant on the Duke of Sunderland, who was in the pay of Louis XIV, and the Jesuit Father Petre. Two measures, in 1686, further pressured the Anglican Tories:

- The Case of Godden v Hales (June 1686) was heard by a packed Bench. It was a case deliberately brought to achieve the verdict that the King wanted. Sir Edward Hales, a Catholic, had been given an Army commission in contravention of the Test Act. The judgement that 'the King of England is a sovereign prince, and the laws are his laws, whence it follows that it is part of his prerogative to dispense with penal law as he sees fit and necessary' was a clear threat to Parliament and statute. It opened the way for promotion of more Catholics to office.

- The establishment of the Court of High Commission set up a court with the powers to conduct visitations and to discipline the church and the universities. It was clearly aimed at curbing anti-Catholic sermons and opposition to the King's propaganda. James admitted to the French ambassador, Barrillon, that he intended it to undermine the Church. One of its first acts was to suspend the Bishop of London, Compton, for refusing to suspend Dr Sharp of St Giles for speaking against Catholics. This Court was seen by some as illegal after the acts abolishing the prerogative courts in 1641.

These measures allowed the further promotion of Catholics and subservient Anglicans into Army, university and civil posts. When riots broke out after the opening of a Catholic Church in London, in July 1686, James stationed an army of 13,000 men with Catholic officers on Hounslow Heath.

By the end of 1686, his attempts to show the power of prerogative in order to intimidate the Anglican Tories had not worked; nor had it provoked the conditions that would generate revolution. In 1687, James began to increase pressure on the Tories to cooperate over the issues of repeal of the Test and Corporation Acts by trying to build up an alliance with the Dissenters, or Nonconformists.

Dispensing power: The power the King claimed to dispense individuals from the operation of a statute.

Suspending power: By this the King claimed the power to suspend the operation of a statute, rather than merely suspending individuals from it.

In January 1687, he dismissed his Tory ministers, Rochester and Clarendon, and relied on a Catholic inner council to support his plan to free both Catholics and Dissenters from the Test Act. So far he had used **dispensing power**. In April, he used **suspending power**. This was seen as a back-door way of repealing a statute without Parliament.

The First Declaration of Indulgence (April 1687) suspended the penal laws against Catholics and Dissenters. James's hopes of securing the support of the latter were misplaced. John Bunyan and Richard Baxter simply did not trust any scheme to introduce toleration at the expense of undermining the laws. Bishop Burnet commented on the Declaration and the reaction to it:

> 'In April the King set out a declaration of toleration and liberty of conscience for England ... He expressed his aversion to persecution on the account of religion, and the necessity that he found of allowing his subjects liberty of conscience, in which he did not doubt of the concurrence of his parliament: he renewed his promise of maintaining the church of England, as it was by law established: but with this he suspended all penal laws in matters of religion ... This gave great offence to all true patriots, as well as the whole church party. The King did now assume a power of repealing laws by his own authority.'

This Declaration openly undermined the King's promise in 1685.

Attacks on the universities were mounted through the Court of Ecclesiastical Commission. When the fellows of Magdalen College, Oxford, refused to accept a Catholic President, they were replaced with Catholics.

Why did the Protestant nonconformists not support him?

If James had been able to find a power base of Catholics and Dissenters (nonconformists), he might have been able to pressure the Anglican Tories into repealing the Test and Corporation Acts.

● Ultimately, the Dissenters associated Catholicism with absolutism and had more in common with the Anglicans than the Catholics.

● They were divided among themselves, making united policy difficult.

● They did not trust James.

● They had reason to hope that the Anglicans would compromise with them. The Marquis of Halifax, in his *Letter to a Dissenter*, urged them to wait until 'the next probable Revolution'.

● Archbishop Sancroft set up a committee to investigate changes in the Prayer Book, to give it more appeal to Dissenters.

● They were alarmed by James's policy of trying to influence MPs and to remodel corporations in order to to get a pliable parliament.

By the end of 1687, James had failed to secure an alliance with the Dissenters. He was not prepared to modify his policy.

What happened next?

The Second Declaration of Indulgence (April 1688) ordered the Declaration to be read from the pulpit on two consecutive Sundays. This

The Seven Bishops committed to the Tower in 1688, unknown artist.

Petition of the Seven Bishops: Archbishop Sancroft of Canterbury, Bishops Ken of Bath and Wells, Lake of Chichester, Lloyd of St Asaphs, Trelawney of Bristol, Turner of Ely, and White of Peterborough asked to be excused from reading the Declaration on the grounds that doing so would mean obedience to the law and that suspension of the law was illegal.

Seditious libel: Stirring up the people through inflammatory writing.

1. What evidence is there of the political sympathies of the author of the cards?

2. What is the importance of showing Catholic churches being burnt?

3. How useful are these cards as evidence of opposition to James II?

put the Anglican clergy in a difficult position. Reading it aloud meant that they agreed with it; refusing to read meant that they offended the Dissenters. This provoked the **Petition of the Seven Bishops**.

The fact that the Petition was printed and circulated made James refer to it as 'a standard of rebellion'. James arrested the bishops for **seditious libel**. To get maximum attention, the bishops refused to pay bail and were sent to the Tower. Their case was argued on the basis that a subject has the right to petition the Crown. Their acquittal, on 30 June, met with great public rejoicing. James II's policies had proved confrontational and his single-minded pursuit of the repeal of the penal laws against Catholics had led to him breaking his promise of 1685. They had produced a defiant

Playing card of Monmouth's entry into Taunton

Playing card of the hanging of Protestants in the West Country

Playing card of Catholic church burnings

reaction from the bishops. They had not produced a revolution. Between the arrest of the bishops and their acquittal, one event acted as a catalyst: the birth of James, Prince of Wales, on 10 June 1688.

Before this event, a Protestant succession seemed assured. Mary of Modena, aged 30, had already given birth to 10 children, mostly stillborn. The heir presumptive was James's Protestant daughter, Mary. James was 54 – old by 17th-century standards. It was obvious that, in the fullness of time, the death of James would 'exclude' him peacefully and bring about a Protestant succession. On 10 June, Mary of Modena gave birth to a son. Anti-Catholic hysteria made the most of the fact that the birth was one month premature and not attended by the usual number of Protestant dignitaries. It was seen as a Catholic plot. James was accused of substituting a baby, hidden in a warming pan, to achieve a Catholic dynasty. The birth was certainly providential.

The Letter of the Immortal Seven, 30 June 1688

The birth of James Edward, together with the actions of the 7 bishops inspired 7 men (Shrewsbury, Compton, Devonshire, Russell, Danby, Sidney and Lumley) to write to William of Orange, on 30 June, expressing their fears. They asked William to come to England to restore liberty and to protect the Protestant Church. They explained that:

'the people are so generally dissatisfied with the present conduct of the government in relation to their religion, liberties and properties (all of which have been greatly invaded) and they are in such expectation of their prospects being daily worse, that your Highness may be assured there are nineteen parts of twenty throughout the kingdom who are desirous of change, and who, we believe, would willingly contribute to it, if they had such a protection to countenance their rising as would secure them from being destroyed before they could get to be in a posture able to defend themselves.'

This letter did not, in itself, guarantee an invasion. Six months elapsed between the letter and the flight of the King of England. James's character and policies had put him in a dangerous position. If he could have achieved a packed Parliament he would have been in a far stronger position than his father or brother had ever been. The implication of this for Parliament, Law and Church were far reaching. What is obvious from the Letter of the Immortal Seven is that its authors believed that only William could bring about the desired change.

1. What part was played by religion in the loss of support for James?

2. Why was James able to rule without Parliament after November 1685?

3. How seriously did James threaten the ideal of rule by law?

4. How important was the birth of Prince James Edward in encouraging opposition to James?

10.2 The Glorious Revolution and the Revolution Settlement of 1688–1689

Key Issues

● Why was James II overthrown?

● What impact did the Glorious Revolution have on Ireland and Scotland?

● How 'revolutionary' was the Revolution Settlement of 1689?

10.2.1 In what ways did James II hasten his own downfall?

10.2.2 How important was William of Orange in bringing about the downfall of James II?

10.2.3 How did the Glorious Revolution affect Ireland in 1688–1691?

10.2.4 What impact did the Revolution of 1688 have on Scotland?

10.2.5 Historical interpretation: How 'revolutionary' was the Revolution Settlement of 1688–1689?

Framework of Events

1687	4 April: Declaration of Indulgence
1688	27 April: Second Declaration of Indulgence
	10 June: birth of Prince James Edward, Prince of Wales
	July: invitation is made to William of Orange
	20 September: William of Orange's Declaration from The Hague
	5 November: William lands at Torbay
	12 November: Declarations from the gentry for William
	16 November: beginning of desertions from James II's Army
	23 November: James abandons plan to confront William militarily
	8 December: James II sends his family to France
	22–23 December: James II flees England for France
	December – February 1689: Interregnum
1689	1–23 February: Convention 'Parliament'
	12 February: Bill of Rights
	13 February: William and Mary are offered joint monarchy
	12 March: James II lands in Kinsale, Ireland
1690	12 July: battle of the Boyne
1691	13 October: Treaty of Limerick ends War in Ireland.

Overview

THE political events of 1688–1689 have resulted in much controversy among historians. In *The English Revolution* (1938), the historian G.M. Trevelyan stated that 'The ultimate view that we take of the Revolution of 1688 must be determined by our preference either for royal absolutism or for parliamentary government. James II forced England to choose once for all between these two.'

According to Trevelyan and other Whig historians, England was faced by a stark choice in 1688. It had a Catholic King, James II, who was planning to establish a system of royal government in England similar to that in France and other European monarchies. Together with his attempt to create an absolute monarchy,

James II was also intending to convert England back to Catholicism. These twin objectives created such animosity in England that the aristocracy reacted by inviting William of Orange to replace James II on the throne. Their aim was to preserve the Protestant religion and to prevent absolute monarchy.

The role of James II in creating the conditions for his own downfall is central to any understanding of the political revolution of 1688–1689. What must also be considered are the motives of William of Orange and those aristocrats who invited him to Britain to replace James – by itself, a revolutionary act.

Although regarded as a near bloodless overthrow of James II in England, the events of 1688 sparked considerable change in Ireland and Scotland. In both kingdoms, the conflict between **Jacobite** and **Williamite** led to armed conflict. In Ireland, in particular, the conflict created the conditions for protracted warfare, which did not end until the Treaty of Limerick in 1691. The 'Revolution of 1688' also led to political change within the British Empire, most noticeably in the American colonies.

Finally, the general political changes of 1689 have also caused debate among historians. Did these changes really constitute a political revolution?

Jacobite: Supporter of James II of England after his abdication; a partisan of the Stuarts after the revolution of 1688–89.

Williamite: Supporter of William of Orange (King William III of England).

10.2.1 In what ways did James II hasten his own downfall?

According to G.M. Trevelyan, James II was the prime suspect for causing the Revolution of 1688. He noted, in *The English Revolution* (1938), that 'James had tried to put the King above Parliament and above the law.'

In contrast, the historian Barry Coward, in *The Stuart Age* (1980), states that 'historians have now established that James II was not the villain described by Whig historians. His aim was not to establish Catholicism as the sole religion of the country, nor to eradicate Protestantism by force. Nor did he intend to rule without parliament or to govern unconstitutionally.'

So why was James II overthrown? The historian Sir George Clark noted, in *The Later Stuarts* (1955), that 'kings are symbols, and James's history is the history of that which he symbolised'. By 1685–88, England was a country with strong anti-Catholic feeling. The Popish Plot and Exclusion Crisis had shown this in Charles II's reign. Foxe's 'Book of Martyrs' had fuelled Anti-Catholicism since the Reformation, where Mary I was portrayed as returning England to Catholicism by force and repression between 1553 and 1558. It was believed that a Catholic monarch, like James II, might use similar tactics. Fears were compounded by events. The bloody and repressive handling of the Monmouth rebels, in 1685, was an example. Also, the revocation of the Edict of Nantes, in the same year, saw around 400,000 French Protestants (Huguenots) expelled by Louis XIV of France.

James II's aim of giving full religious freedom and political rights to Catholics had all but been achieved within the first two years of his reign. In the elections to Parliament in May 1685, James was able to use royal control and influence to ensure a clear Tory majority. The Whigs, who had opposed his accession to the throne during the Exclusion crisis, were reduced to 40 seats. Even though Parliament was generally sympathetic to James, it was not submissive. This was shown in the second session of Parliament (9–20 November 1685), when James II made clear his aim not to disband the army raised to suppress the Monmouth Rebellion.

Instead, he used the monarch's prerogative powers and influence to win concessions for Catholics. He used the Godden v Hales Case of June 1686 to exclude individual Catholics from the Test Act. By 1688, James II had ensured that approximately 25% of JPs were Catholic. In April 1687, James began a campaign to pressure Magdalen College, Oxford, to accept Catholics. James II was also able to offer commissions to Catholics to become officers in the armed forces.

To win support for toleration from Protestant Nonconformists (Dissenters), James issued two Declarations of Indulgence, on 4 April 1687 and 27 April 1688. In both, James promised a policy of general religious toleration, which he hoped would be passed by Parliament by the end of 1688. James II used his royal prerogative to suspend the Test Acts, Corporation Act and penal laws against Catholics and Protestant Nonconformists. These declarations caused considerable unease, not only among Anglicans, but also among Dissenters, because the House of Commons had already declared illegal the use of the royal prerogative in religious matters on two previous occasions: 1663 and 1673. James's opponents feared he might be trying to increase royal power at the expense of Parliament.

To achieve permanent change James needed Parliament to repeal the Corporation Act of 1661 and the Test Acts of 1673 and 1678. From the autumn of 1687, James attempted to pack Parliament with his supporters. To do this, he used royal influence in borough seats. Although James II's 'packed' parliament never met, J.R. Jones suggests (in *The Revolution of 1688 in England*, 1972) that James could have succeeded in his plan to achieve a permanent settlement.

The event that completely changed the political situation was the birth, on 10 June 1688, of James Edward, heir to the throne. Until then, if James had remained childless Mary, his Protestant daughter, would have succeeded him. Faced with the possibility of a Catholic dynasty and the growth in influence of Catholics since 1685, the fear of a Catholic takeover became only too apparent to James II's opponents. James's actions, together with the birth of his son, helped to unite Anglican and nonconformist against him.

Even so, James II could have survived. His actions, following William of Orange's arrival at Torbay on 5 November, made a bad situation worse. It would seem that James lost his nerve. The 'protestant wind' that brought William to Torbay also prevented James's fleet from intercepting him. James was also unnerved by risings against him in Cheshire, Yorkshire and Nottinghamshire. The Yorkshire rising was particularly worrying as it was led by a prominent Tory, the Earl of Danby. The situation was compounded by the defection to William of John Churchill, the Army's second-in-command.

James did not confront William with armed force even though his army was larger. To make matters worse, James had allowed the county militias to fall into decay because he hoped to rely on his standing army. This position was clear on 23 November, at Salisbury, when James II retreated to London rather than face William on the battlefield.

Secondly, even when trying to negotiate with William, James again created problems for himself. On 8 December, he sent his wife and child to France. Then he suffered the embarrassment of capture by Protestant fishermen, at Faversham, Kent, between 11 and 16 December before he

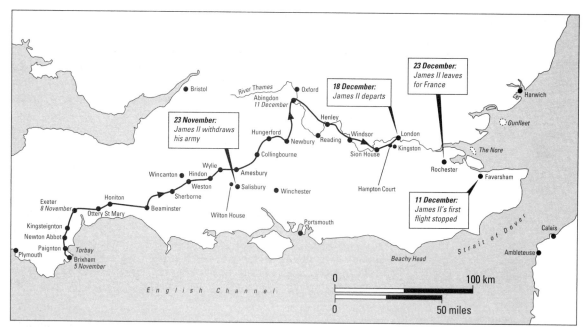

William's route to London, 1688

1. What actions did James II take which caused so much disquiet among his subjects in England?

2. To what extent was James II responsible for his own downfall?

was released and returned to London. James's absence had resulted in a breakdown of law and order in London and in political chaos amongst the political élite. Following William's entry into London on 18 December, James succeeded in fleeing to France by 23 December.

As the historian Barry Coward notes, 'James's collapse of nerve ensured that when William reached London he had the support of all leading Whigs and Tories. His decision not to stay in England removed the final obstacle to the "Glorious Revolution" and a change in monarch.' However, when James fled he did not hand over authority to anyone. His decision to disband the Army and to throw the Great Seal of Office into the river Thames might suggest that he planned to create political chaos in which he might eventually regain control. James's escape to France merely provided the final sign of weakness.

1. In the first paragraph, what reasons does James II put forward for issuing the Declaration of Indulgence?

2. In the first paragraph, what powers does James II claim for the monarch?

3. Is the Declaration of Indulgence anti-Anglican? Give reasons for your answer.

The Declaration of Indulgence, 4 April 1687

We, therefore, out of our princely care and affection unto all our loving subjects, that may live at ease and quiet, and for the increase of trade and encouragements of strangers, have thought fit by virtue of our royal prerogative to issue forth this our Declaration of Indulgence, making no doubt of the concurrence of our two Houses of Parliament when we shall think it convenient for them to meet.

In the first place we do declare that we will protect and maintain our archbishops, bishops and clergy, and all our subjects of the Church of England in the free exercise of their religion as by law established.

We do likewise declare that it is our royal will and pleasure that all manner of penal laws in matters ecclesiastical, for not coming to church, or nor receiving the sacrament, or for any nonconformity to the religion established be immediately suspended.

10.2.2 How important was William of Orange in bringing about James II's downfall?

Stadtholder: Hereditary office held by members of the Orange family within the Dutch Republic.

William of Orange, **Stadtholder** of the Dutch Republic, was the grandson of Charles I and the great-grandson of William the Silent, one of the defenders of Dutch Protestantism against Spain in the late 16th century. Since 1672, he had faced the might of Catholic France under Louis XIV in a protracted war to save the Dutch Republic from French domination. He was also married into the Stuart royal family. He had married James II's eldest daughter, Mary. He had impeccable credentials for the defence of English Protestantism against the threatened takeover of the country by Catholics.

Therefore, William seemed an obvious choice to answer the call, in 1688, when James's opponents feared the King's supposed plans for England. In July 1688, an invitation to intervene in England was brought to William by Arthur Herbert, former vice-admiral of England. Signatories to the invitation were Danby (a leading Tory), Russell (a cousin of Lord Russell) and Henry Sidney (a former minister to the Dutch Republic and the Bishop of London who had been suspended by James). They also included three peers: Lord Lumley, Lord Shrewsbury and Lord Devonshire. According to the historian Bill Speck, in *Reluctant Revolutionaries* (1987), 'the bulk of those whom James had alienated were not converted to theories of resistance. Only a minority of radical Whigs took seriously the notion that it was legitimate to resist a tyrant. Even those who invited William to come over did not hold out the offer of the Crown. They merely asked him to intervene to put pressure on the king to summon a free parliament.'

But why did William accept this offer? According to J.R. Jones, in *Country and Court, England 1658–1714* (1978):

> William has been depicted as scheming to seize possession of the English throne in order to satisfy a life's ambition, but, in reality, he never regarded influence in, or control over, England as an end in itself but rather as the necessary means of strengthening forces available to him, in his self-imposed task of checking and defeating French aggression.

Electorate: A state within the Holy Roman Empire that had the right to vote for a new Holy Roman Emperor on the death of his predecessor.

By the summer of 1688, a European war seemed likely because of a disputed election in the western German **electorate** of Cologne. This was likely to involve another war between France and the Dutch Republic. If war had taken place in the summer of 1688, William would not have been able to intervene in England. However, Louis XIV delayed military incursions into the Palatinate, in the Rhineland, until late September. This provided William with the military opportunity for intervention.

Supporters had also kept William informed of developments in England. William of Orange had become aware, as early as April 1688, that to prevent James implementing his pro-Catholic policies he would have to intervene. Intervention was given a boost by the rise of anti-Catholic feeling during the trial of the Seven Bishops and the birth of James Edward, Prince of Wales.

Finally, William was informed that James planned to increase the size of his Army over the winter of 1688–69. This would also involve an increase in the number of Catholic officers.

Even so, William took considerable risks. By intervening in England, in November 1688, he left the Dutch Republic exposed to possible French attack. On landing, he faced a well-equipped army much larger than his own force. Until he landed, William was unaware of precisely how much support he would receive.

William benefited from much good fortune. The 'protestant wind' that kept James's navy in port allowed William to sail down the Channel to land at Torbay, in Devon. Opposition to James had been increased following his bloody repression of the Monmouth rebellion. In addition, Sir Edward Seymour and the Marquis of Bath, leading landowners in the West Country, openly sided with William. The Dutchman was also aided by risings in the North and Midlands. On 15 November, Lord Delamere was able to take over Cheshire and, 6 days later, the Earl of Devonshire captured Nottingham. The following day, the Earl of Danby captured York. These developments helped to turn the tide in William's favour.

Anti-Catholic feeling within James's Army increased when he brought over Irish Catholic regiments to strengthen his force. Also, the Rose Tavern group of Army officers, who opposed James, helped to organise defections that undermined the Army's morale during late November.

William of Orange was also aided by James II's loss of nerve at the critical moment, on 23 November, when he retreated from Salisbury to London. Nevertheless, William's decision to enter London on 18 December helped force James to seek a second attempt to escape to France (22–23 December). Without James's decision to leave the country, William would not have been in the position to be offered the throne. From 5 November to 23 December, William was able to win over Whig and Tory alike either by his moderate statements about his actions or, more importantly, by his silence. He was also aided by the widespread anti-Catholic feeling in London, which had forced James's hand in seeking refuge in France by early December.

From the end of December 1688 to the offer of the throne to William and Mary in February 1689, Britain faced a political vacuum. James had not abdicated and was still, technically, King. The overthrow of James had taken place with minimal bloodshed in England. However, these events had a profound effect on both Ireland and Scotland.

1. Why did William believe he could force James II from the throne?

2. To what extent was William's success due to good luck?

10.2.3 How did the Glorious Revolution affect Ireland in 1688–1691?

Unlike the kingdoms of England and Scotland, the kingdom of Ireland contained a sizeable and influential Catholic population. Prior to 1688, the 17th century had seen conflict between the Catholic Irish and Protestant settlers from England and Scotland over the control of land. In the Cromwellian Settlement, and confirmed by the Restoration Settlement, the Protestant settlers had acquired over half of Ireland's agricultural land. Catholic hopes of recovering lost lands were dashed by William's success in England, in November–December 1688.

James and William were primarily concerned with who should rule over the kingdom of Ireland, rather than who should own the land. Following his departure from England in late December 1688, James II arrived at Kinsale, County Cork, on 12 March 1689. His arrival resulted in major warfare, which finally confirmed the land settlements of the 17th century and the subservient position of Catholics within Ireland.

For James to succeed, he needed the support of the Catholic Irish. Under the leadership of Richard Talbot (Earl of Tyrconnel), an army of

40,000 was available to support James's cause. However, the Catholic Irish took matters into their own hands, on 7 May, by calling their own parliament in Dublin. In what was, technically, an illegal assembly, the Irish Parliament abolished Poyning's Law (see Chapter 7). This had made the Irish Parliament subordinate to England's Parliament and ended all judicial appeals from Ireland to England. This 'patriot parliament' virtually declared Irish independence from England.

In military terms, James's Irish allies began 1689 with military success. They had moved into Protestant-dominated Ulster and besieged the town of Londonderry. However, a turning point in the military campaign occurred on 10 August 1689, when Colonel Kirke broke the siege by sending in a naval frigate and three merchant ships up the river Foyle to the besieged town. On 23 August, General Schomberg, at the head of a Williamite army of 20,000, landed at Carrickfergus, near Belfast. By the winter of 1688–89, Schomberg was able to capture most of Ulster.

On 24 June 1690, William landed at Carrickfergus. With a multinational force of over 40,000 (including Dutch, Danish and French Protestant troops), he marched south towards Dublin. On 12 July, William's forces narrowly defeated James's Army in the battle of the Boyne. This battle, long hailed as a Protestant victory in northern Ireland, led to James's flight from Ireland. Yet it did not end the war. The military campaign continued through 1690, with the capture of Waterford and Cork from Jacobite forces. In 1691, Jacobite forces in the west of Ireland were subdued with the final major battle occurring at Aughrim, County Galway, in July 1691. The final Irish city to fall to William's Army was Limerick which fell after a long siege at the end of September 1691.

The Treaty of Limerick (13 October 1691) brought the armed conflict in Ireland to an end. There has been much controversy over the terms of treaty. Its military articles allowed the Catholic Irish army to withdraw to France.

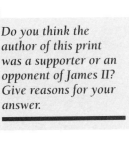

Do you think the author of this print was a supporter or an opponent of James II? Give reasons for your answer.

A contemporary print of James II at the battle of the Boyne, 1690

Penal code: All the laws that are concerned with crime and punishment.

1. In what ways were the political and religious issues in Ireland different from those in England?

2. To what extent were the events of 1688–1691 a turning point in Irish History in the 17th century?

The Irish also hoped to receive public recognition of Catholicism and the restoration of all their estates, which had been taken by the Williamite Army during the war. In fact, the treaty stated that Catholics should 'enjoy such privileges in the exercise of their religion as are consistent with the Laws of Ireland; or as they did enjoy in the reign of King Charles II.'

However, the Treaty had to be ratified by an Irish parliament dominated by Protestants. An English Act of 1691 had banned Catholics from that parliament. It was finally ratified, in an amended form, by the 1697 parliament. By that time, the Irish Parliament had introduced a **penal code** against Catholics. The Cromwellian and Restoration land settlements were confirmed and extended. Catholics were barred from public office and the professions. In addition, Catholic priests and high clergy were banned from Ireland. Although never fully put into effect across the whole country, the penal code turned Irish Catholics into a subservient class.

In the late 18th century, Henry Grattan, an Irish Protestant parliamentarian in favour of greater parliamentary freedom for Ireland, stated:

> The revolution of King William has been called by the gentlemen on the other side of the House, a glorious revolution – glorious it certainly was for England – for Ireland it was disastrous in the extreme.

Ireland in the late 18th century

10.2.4 *What impact did the Revolution of 1688 have on Scotland?*

Scotland, although a predominantly Protestant country, was Presbyterian rather than Anglican in persuasion. Like in England, there was strong opposition to Catholicism across all strata of society. Nevertheless, James II's policy of religious toleration did receive some support in Scotland. His 'Letters of Indulgence' granted Scottish Protestant religious freedom in the manner which his Declarations of Indulgence had in England. However, the political revolution in England did have the effect of splitting the Scottish nobility and rekindling support for the Stuart royal family in the Highlands.

Even when William called a meeting of the Scottish estates, Edinburgh Castle was still held for James by the Duke of Gordon. It only surrendered to William's forces in July 1689.

The key Jacobite supporter in Scotland was John Graham of Claverhouse (Viscount Dundee). Dundee had support in the Highlands, where Catholicism survived as an influential force. His decision to raise an army in defence of the Jacobite interest had all the makings of the civil war which had affected Scotland under Montrose in 1644–45. Even though Dundee won the battle of Killiecrankie against a Williamite army under Mackay, in the summer of 1689, Dundee's death at that battle helped to save the Lowlands from invasion.

However, the Scottish nobles were sufficiently cautious in the Convention of Estates not to create a split in their ranks between Jacobites and Williamites. At the opening of the Convention, Bishop Alexander Rose

1. What events do you think the songsheet celebrates?

2. How reliable is the songsheet as evidence of support for William and Mary in London in 1690?

Songsheet produced in London in 1690

1. In what ways was Scotland affected by the Revolution of 1688 in England?

2. Why was Scotland not threatened by civil war in 1689?

of Edinburgh was allowed to offer a prayer to restore King James, but went on to declare the need to 'settle and secure the Protestant Religion, the Government, Laws and Liberties of the Kingdom'. As the historian Bruce Lenman noted, in a lecture in the early 1990s, this moderate tone 'goes far to explain why only half a dozen members of the Convention left it with Dundee. The Scottish nobility handled the Revolution rather well. They choked the dreadful threat of widespread civil war. Once James lost his grip on England, they made it clear that there was no way he was to return … in Scotland.'

10.2.5 How 'revolutionary' was the Revolution Settlement of 1688–1689?
A CASE STUDY IN HISTORICAL INTERPRETATION

The Revolution Settlement, 1688–1689

- When James II fled England for France, in December 1688, he left the country in political limbo. He had not abdicated, nor had William made any public declaration that he had deposed James. In January 1689, on the advice of members of the aristocracy, William summoned a convention (a parliament in all but name). It met from 1–23 February. Some Whigs advocated exclusion of James, as they had done between 1678 and 1681. Others supported the idea of a **regency**. William complicated matters by making it known that he would not accept the post of regent or **prince consort** to Mary. As a result, William and Mary were offered the posts of joint monarchs. William was to exercise governmental powers.
- Anne Stuart (the future Queen Anne) allowed William to take precedence over her. In addition, monarchs had to declare their support for, and defence of, the Protestant religion by law established (the Church of England). The revolution not only marked the triumph of William II over James II, and of Protestantism over Catholicism, it

overthrew the principle of primogeniture by which the Crown had passed from one monarch to another since 1509. The establishment of the Protestant Succession set aside not only James II, but also his son and grandsons – James III, Charles III and Henry IX.
- However, the new joint monarchs were to be subject to a Bill of Rights, agreed on 12 February, which became law on 16 December 1689. It declared that the Glorious Revolution had occurred because of mismanagement by James II. The Bill of Rights was a restatement of ancient rights held by Parliament, such as the need for parliamentary authority before taxes could be collected.
- The Revolution Settlement also included the Mutiny Act, passed for a year at a time, which gave the King authority to impose military discipline on the armed forces.
- The Toleration Act of 1689 freed Protestant nonconformists from the penal laws, as long as they took an oath of loyalty to the monarch. They were, nevertheless, barred from public office like Catholics.
- Finally, the Triennial Act, passed in 1694, allowed for elections to Parliament at least every three years.

Regency: Ruling on behalf of a rightful and lawful ruler. It usually applies when the monarch is a minor (under age).

Prince consort: Husband of the ruling monarch.

How revolutionary was this settlement?

The historian Sir George Clark, writing in 1955, stated that 'The Revolution was a great event. It established the British type of constitutional monarchy.'

G.M. Trevelyan, writing in 1935, stated that 'The Revolution gave England an ordered and legal freedom, and through that it gave her power.' The Bills of Rights was 'an agreed contract freely made between Crown and people which prevented, for all time, a repetition of the tragedies of the Stuart kings. The Revolution, while leaving the King the source of executive power, subjected him to the Law, which was to be interpreted by independent Judges, and could only be altered by Act of Parliament.'

By their accounts, the Revolution of 1688–89 seems quite radical. According to Whig historians, the events of 1688–89 were merely the culmination of a century of struggle for political power between Crown and Parliament. As a result of the English Revolution of 1642–60, Parliament triumphed. From 1660 to 1688, the monarchy re-asserted itself. The Glorious Revolution was merely the last part of this process, which created a constitutional monarchy. The historian Sir Herbert Butterfield, in *The Whig Interpretation of History* (1931), accused Whig historians of writing with historical hindsight. He felt they created a sequence of events that suggested a natural progression from absolute, or unlimited, monarchy to limited, or constitutional, monarchy. Therefore, the radical and inevitable nature of 1688–89 no longer seems certain. The historian Sir Lewis Namier, in his studies of politics in the reign of George III (1760–1821), highlighted the re-assertion of royal power and questioned the Whig view that monarchy progressively became more limited.

Also, the term 'revolution' must be used with caution. The meaning of the term in the 17th century is different from its use today. In 17th-century England, revolution means returning to the norms of the past. The Whigs of 1688–89 believed that they were bringing the constitution and monarchy back into balance after the reign of James II. James, and to a lesser extent Charles II, had been accused of acting unconstitutionally. They, the Whigs, were merely restoring the mixed or limited monarchy of the past.

Marxist historians, such as Christopher Hill, also view the events of 1688–89 as being the result of long-term factors and developments. However, they see the roots of the Revolution in economic terms. The rise of a commercial middle class and the early stages of capitalism in England acted as the agents of political change.

In many ways, the political changes brought about by 1688–89 were not particularly great. The historian J.R. Jones, in *Country and Court, England 1658–1714* (1978), states that:

> The Revolution Settlement was unspectacular and pragmatic, but it provided a basis for stable and generally acceptable government. Only James's own right, and that of his immediate family were infringed and overthrown. The actual legislation of 1689 was incomplete, leaving many issues unresolved. It was only with the Act of Settlement of 1701 that the legislative work [started] by the Convention Parliament was at last completed.

1. **What changes were made as a result of the Revolution Settlement of 1688–89?**

2. **Why have historians disagreed over the significance of the changes made in 1688–89?**

3. **In what sense were the changes of 1688–89 revolutionary?**

The Settlement was aimed to win support from the majority of Whigs and Tories. After the Settlement, support for Jacobitism (the return of the Stuarts to the throne) was very limited in England, but survived in more rigorous form in Scotland.

Geoffrey Holmes is more strident in his views. Writing in *Britain after the Glorious Revolution, 1689–1714* (1969), he describes the Revolution Settlement of 1688–89 as 'one of the most misapplied and misleading terms which historians have ever had the misfortune to coin'. As the historian Roger Lockyer notes, 'It did not establish parliamentary government. The King was left free to choose and dismiss ministers as well as his judges, and he could summon, dissolve, prorogue and adjourn Parliament as he saw fit (as long as it fitted in with the Triennial Act). The "glory" of the Revolution consisted in its conservatism: it kept the traditional constitution and made only minor adjustments to bring it back into balance.'

It is true that many of the features of government seemed to remain unchanged: monarch, Privy Council, Parliament. However, the Bill of Rights of 1689 did change monarchic power quite radically. In future, to use the royal prerogative in suspending laws, raising money and creating a standing army in peacetime, the monarch needed the consent of Parliament.

To ensure that Parliament was available to offer its consent, the Triennial Act was passed. Finally, the Toleration Act of 1689 at last acknowledged in law that England was no longer an exclusively Anglican country even though the Church of England remained, and still remains, the established or State church.

 Source-based questions: The English Revolution of 1688–1689

SOURCE A

The fundamental question at issue in 1688 had been this: Is the law above the King or is the King above the law?

James II attempted to make the law alterable wholesale by the King. This, if it had been permitted, must have made the King supreme over Parliament and, in fact, a despot [dictator]. The events of the winter of 1688–89 gave the victory to the opposite idea, which Chief Justice Coke had enunciated earlier in the century, that the King was the chief servant of the law, but not its master; the laws should only be alterable by Parliament – King, Lords and Commons together. It is this that makes the Revolution the decisive event in the history of the English Constitution. It was decisive because it was never undone as most of the work of the Cromwellian Revolution was undone.

From The English Revolution 1688–1689 *by G.M. Trevelyan (1935). G.M. Trevelyan was a leading Whig historian.*

SOURCE B

The key question about 1689 is whether it established a new king on the throne, or a new type of monarchy? From the late 18th century, Burke looked back over a hundred years and saw the Revolution as but 'a small and a temporary deviation from the strict order of a regular hereditary succession.' It is true that some contemporaries thought they were changing the constitution, not just the monarch. Yet the revolutionary content of 1689 is to be found less in direct limitations on the monarch's power, and the banning of Roman Catholicism as the royal religion, than in the fact that the normal order of succession was overridden when the crown was offered to William and Mary. Debates in the English Convention show how reluctantly Parliament interfered with the divine right succession.

From The Revolution and the Constitution *by Jennifer Carter (1969)*

SOURCE C

England did experience a political revolution in 1688 and 1689. Absolutism gave way to limited monarchy. While this might seem to be nothing more than a re-assertion of the Whig case, there are several major qualifications to be made to the interpretation. There was nothing unconstitutional about the bid for absolutism under the later Stuarts. Nor was it doomed to failure.

Both Charles II and James II worked for the most part within the letter of the law. The notion that there were legal limitations on their authority imposed by an ancient constitution, requiring them to account for their action to Parliament, is a Whig myth. Moreover, they were backed by powerful sections of the political nation who regarded the Crown as an essential ally of the Church of England. It was James II's Catholicism which severed the link between Crown and Church. When, in pursuit of his aim of achieving toleration for Catholics, he was prepared to jettison the Anglican Tories and turn for support to Dissenters [Protestant nonconformists] then the alliance broke down.

From The Reluctant Revolutionaries *by W.A. Speck (1988)*

---

1. Using Sources A and C and information from this chapter, explain the meaning of the following terms in the context of the Glorious Revolution of 1688–1689.

a) 'hereditary succession' (Source A)

b) 'limited monarchy' (Source C)

2. Use Sources A and C.

How far do these two sources agree on what took place in the Revolution of 1688–1689?

3. Use Sources A–C and information from this chapter.

How significant were the political changes made in the Revolution of 1688 to 1689 for England?

Further Reading

CHAPTER 2   *English government under Elizabeth I, 1558–1603*

Texts designed for AS and Advanced level study

Elizabethan Parliaments, 1559–1601 by M.A.R. Graves (Longman, 2nd edition, 1996)
Elizabeth I by Christopher Haigh (Longman, 1988)
The Government of Elizabethan England by A.G.R. Smith (Arnold, 1967)

Texts suitable for more advanced reading or personal investigations

The Emergence of a Nation State: the Commonwealth of England, 1529–1660 by A.G.R. Smith (Longman, 1984)
Tudor England by John Guy (OUP, 1988)
The Later Tudors: England, 1547–1603 by Penry Williams (OUP, 1995)
The Tudor Regime by Penry Williams (OUP, 1979)
The Reign of Elizabeth I edited by Christopher Haigh (Macmillan, 1984)

CHAPTER 3   *Religion in Elizabethan England*

Texts designed for AS and Advanced level study

Elizabeth I: Religion and Foreign Affairs by J. Warren (Hodder and Stoughton, 1993)
The English Reformation 1530–1570 by W.J. Shiels (Longman, 1989)
The Elizabethan Parliaments 1559–1603 by Michael Graves (Longman, 1987)
English Catholicism 1558–1642 by A. Dures (Longman, 1983)
Elizabeth I and Religion 1558–1603 by Susan Doran (Routledge, 1994)
Elizabeth I by Wallace MacCaffrey (Edward Arnold, 1994)
The Later Reformation in England, 1547–1603 by Diarmaid MacCulloch (Macmillan, 1996)

Texts suitable for more advanced reading or personal investigations

Elizabeth I by Christopher Haigh (Longman, 1988)
The Royal Supremacy in the Elizabethan Church by Claire Cross (Allen and Unwin, 1969)
The Stripping of the Altars by Eamon Duffy (Yale University Press, 1992)
The Elizabethan Puritan Movement by Patrick Collinson (Cape, 1967)
The Later Reformation in England by Diarmaid MacCulloch (Macmillan, 1990)

CHAPTER 4   *Elizabethan foreign policy*

Texts designed for AS and Advanced level study

England and Europe 1485 to 1603 by Susan Doran (Longman, 1986)
Elizabeth I: Religion and Foreign Affairs by J. Warren (Hodder and Stoughton, 1993)
The Tudor Years edited by John Letherington (Hodder and Stoughton, 1994)

Texts suitable for more advanced reading or personal investigations

Tudor England by John Guy (OUP, 1988)
The Emergence of a Nation State by A.G.R. Smith (Longman, 1984)
The Making of Elizabethan Foreign Policy 1558–1603 by Richard Wernham (University of California Press, 1980)
Reformation and Revolution by R. Ashton (Paladin, 1984)
Tudor Ireland by Steven Ellis (Longman, 1985)

CHAPTER 5   *Social, economic and cultural history in the reign of Elizabeth I*

Texts designed for AS and Advanced level study

Poverty and Vagrancy in Tudor England by John Pound (Longman, 1971)

Texts suitable for more advanced reading or personal investigations

The Age of Elizabeth: England under the Later Tudors 1547–1603 by D.M. Palliser (Longman, 2nd edition, 1992)
The Later Tudors: England 1547–1603 by Penry Williams (Clarendon Press, 1995)
England's Agricultural Regions and Agrarian History, 1500–1750 by Joan Thirsk (Macmillan, 1987)
The English Woollen Industry, 1500–1750 by G.D. Ramsay (Macmillan, 1982)
English Overseas Trade 1500–1700 by Ralph Davies (Macmillan, 1973)
Inflation in Tudor and Early Stuart England by R.B. Outhwaite (Macmillan, 1968)
Industry in Tudor and early Stuart England by D. Coleman (Macmillan, 1975)

CHAPTER 6   *James VI and I, 1603–1625*

Texts suitable for AS study

Years of Turmoil, Britain 1603–1714 R. Wilkinson (ed.) (Hodder and Stoughton, 1998)
James I by Christopher Durston (Routledge, 1993)
The Early Stuarts by Katherine Brice (Hodder and Stoughton, 1994)
Regicide and Republic, England 1603–1660 by Graham Seel (CUPress, 2001)

Texts designed for AS and Advanced level study

James VI and I by Irene Carrier (CUP, 1998)
Stuart England by Barry Coward (Longman, 1997)
James I by S.J. Houston (Longman, 2nd edition 1995)
James VI and I by Roger Lockyer (Longman, 1998)
The Early Stuarts, A Political History of England, 1603–1642 by Roger Lockyer (Longman, 2nd edition 1999)
The Early Stuart Kings, 1603–1642 by Graham Seel and David Smith (CUP, 2001)

Texts suitable for more advanced reading or personal investigations

James VI by his Contemporaries by R. Ashton
  (Hutchinson, 1969)
Scotland James V – James VII by Gordon Donaldson
  (Edinburgh, 1990)
The Union of England and Scotland, 1603–1608 by Bruce
  Galloway (CUP, 1986)

CHAPTER 7   *Charles I and the origins of the English Civil War, 1625–1642*

Texts suitable for AS study

Charles I by Angela Anderson (Longman, 1998)
The Early Stuarts by Katharine Brice (Hodder and
  Stoughton, 1994)
The Coming of the Civil War, 1603–49 by David Sharp
  (Heinemann, 2000)

Texts designed for AS and Advanced level study

The English Civil War by Martyn Bennett (Longman,
  1995)
The Civil Wars in Britain and Ireland by Martyn Bennett
  (Blackwell, 1997)
*Kingdom or Province? Scotland and the Regal Union
  1603–1715* by Keith M. Brown (Macmillan, 1992)
The Causes of the English Civil War by Norah Carlin
  (Blackwell, 1999)
Charles I, The Personal Monarch by Charles Carlton
  (Routledge, 1995)
The English Revolution by Barry Coward and Christopher
  Durston (Murray, 1997)
Charles I by Christopher Durston (Routledge, 1998)
Charles I by C. Daniels and John Morrill (CUP, 1988)
The Causes of the English Civil War by Ann Hughes
  (Macmillan, 2nd edition, 1991)
Charles I by Brian Quintrell (Longman, 1993)
The Debate on the English Revolution Revisited by R.C.
  Richardson (Routledge, 1991)
The English Wars and Republic by Graham Seel
  (Routledge, 1999)
The Causes of the English Civil War by Conrad Russell
  (Oxford University Press, 1990)
The Personal Rule of Charles I by Kevin Sharpe (Yale
  University Press, 1992)

CHAPTER 8   *Civil Wars, the Interregnum and Oliver Cromwell*

Texts designed for AS and Advanced Level study

The Civil Wars 1640–1649 by Angela Anderson (Hodder,
  1995)
The English Civil War by Martyn Bennett (Longman,
  1995)
England in Crisis 1640–1660 by David Sharp
  (Heinemann, 2000)
The English Wars and Republic, 1637–1660 by Graham
  Seel (Routledge 1999)
The Interregnum by Michael Lynch (Hodder, 2nd edition,
  2002)
The English Republic by Toby Barnard (Longman, 1982)
Oliver Cromwell by James Mason and Angela Leonard
  (Longman, 1998)

Texts suitable for more advanced reading or personal investigations

The English Revolution 1642–1649 by D.E. Kennedy
  (Macmillan, 2000)
The British Republic 1649–1660 by R. Hutton
  (Macmillan, 2nd edition, 2000)
Oliver Cromwell by Barry Coward (Longman, 1991)
Oliver Cromwell by J.C. Davis (Arnold, 2001)

CHAPTER 9   *The reign of Charles II, 1660–1685*

Texts designed for AS and Advanced Level study

The Restoration and the England of Charles II by John
  Miller (Longman, 2nd edition, 1997)
Restoration England 1660–1688 by Robert Bliss
  (Routledge, Lancaster pamphlets, 1985)

Texts suitable for more advanced reading or personal investigations

The Reigns of Charles II and James VII and II edited by
  L.K.J. Glassey (Macmillan, 1997)
English Puritanism 1603–1689 by J. Spurr (Macmillan,
  1998)
The Making of a Great Power by Geoffrey Holmes
  (Longman, 1993)
Country and Court: England 1658–1714 by J.R. Jones
  (Arnold, 1978)

CHAPTER 10   *James II, William III and the Glorious Revolution*

Texts designed for AS and Advanced level study

An Introduction to Stuart Britain by Angela Anderson
  (Hodder and Stoughton, 1999)
*Stuart England, 1603–1714: the Formation of the British
  State* by Barry Coward (Longman, 1997)
Stuart England by Angus Stroud (Routledge, 1999)
Charles II and James II by Nicholas Fellows (Hodder,
  1995)

Texts suitable for more advanced reading or personal investigations

The Stuart Age by Barry Coward (Longman, 1980)
Tudor and Stuart Britain by Roger Lockyer (Longman,
  1964)
Country and Court: England 1658–1714 by J.R. Jones
  (Arnold, 1978)
*Politics under the Later Stuarts: Party Conflict in a Divided
  Society, 1660–1714* by Tim Harris (Addison-Wesley,
  1995)
The Glorious Revolution by John Miller (Longman, 1997)
James II by John Miller (Yale University Press, 2000)
James II and English Politics by Michael Mullett
  (Routledge, 1993)
James II by Bill Speck (Longman, 2002)
The English State in the 1680s by J.R. Western (Blandford,
  1972)
The Revolution of 1688 in England by J.R. Jones
  (Weidenfeld and Nicholson, 1972)
James II, A Study in Kingship by John Miller (Wayland,
  1977)
*Reluctant Revolutionaries, Englishmen and the Revolution
  of 1688* by Bill Speck (OUP, 1988

Index

MAIN INDEX